Rules and Practices of International Investment Law and Arbitration

International investment law and arbitration is its own 'galaxy', made up of thousands of treaties to be read in relation to hundreds of awards. It is also diverse, as treaty and arbitration practices display nuances and differences on a number of issues. While it has been expanding over the past few decades in quantitative terms, this galaxy is now developing new traits as a reaction to the criticisms formulated across civil society in relation to the protection of public interests.

This textbook enables readers to master and make sense of this galaxy in motion. It offers an up-to-date, comprehensive and detailed analysis of the rules and practices which form international investment law and arbitration, covering its substantive, institutional and procedural aspects. Using analytical and practice-oriented approaches, it provides analyses accessible to readers discovering this field anew, while it offers a wealth of in-depth studies to those who are already familiar with it.

Yannick Radi is Professor of International Law at the Faculty of Law of UCLouvain and a guest professor at Sciences Po Law School in Paris where he lectures on international investment law and arbitration. He is also a consultant on international arbitration matters.

T0391448

The Law in Context Series

Editors: Kenneth Armstrong (University of Cambridge)
Maksymilian Del Mar (Queen Mary, University of London) and
Sally Sheldon (University of Kent).

Since 1970 the Law in Context series has been at the forefront of the movement to broaden the study of law. The series is a vehicle for the publication of innovative monographs and texts that treat law and legal phenomena critically in their cultural, social, political, technological, environmental and economic contexts. A contextual approach involves treating legal subjects broadly, using materials from other humanities and social sciences, and from any other discipline that helps to explain the operation in practice of the particular legal field or legal phenomena under investigation. It is intended that this orientation is at once more stimulating and more realistic than the bare exposition of legal rules. The series includes original research monographs, coursebooks and textbooks that foreground contextual approaches and methods. The series includes and welcomes books on the study of law in all its contexts, including domestic legal systems, European and international law, transnational and global legal processes, and comparative law.

Books in the Series
Acosta: *The National versus the Foreigner in South America: 200 Years of Migration and Citizenship Law*
Ali: *Modern Challenges to Islamic Law*
Alyagon Darr: *Plausible Crime Stories: The Legal History of Sexual Offences in Mandate Palestine*
Anderson, Schum & Twining: *Analysis of Evidence, 2nd Edition*
Ashworth: *Sentencing and Criminal Justice, 6th Edition*
Barton & Douglas: *Law and Parenthood*
Baxi, McCrudden & Paliwala: *Law's Ethical, Global and Theoretical Contexts: Essays in Honour of William Twining*
Beecher-Monas: *Evaluating Scientific Evidence: An Interdisciplinary Framework for Intellectual Due Process*
Bell: *French Legal Cultures*
Bercusson: *European Labour Law, 2nd Edition*
Birkinshaw: *European Public Law*
Birkinshaw: *Freedom of Information: The Law, the Practice and the Ideal, 4th Edition*
Broderick & Ferri: *International and European Disability Law and Policy: Text, Cases and Materials*
Brownsword & Goodwin: *Law and the Technologies of the Twenty-First Century: Text and Materials*
Cane & Goudkamp: *Atiyah's Accidents, Compensation and the Law, 9th Edition*
Clarke: *Principles of Property Law*
Clarke & Kohler: *Property Law: Commentary and Materials*

Zander: *Cases and Materials on the English Legal System, 10th Edition*
Zander: *The Law-Making Process, 6th Edition*

International Journal of Law in Context: A Global Forum for Interdisciplinary Legal Studies

The *International Journal of Law in Context* is the companion journal to the Law in Context book series and provides a forum for interdisciplinary legal studies and offers intellectual space for ground-breaking critical research. It publishes contextual work about law and its relationship with other disciplines including but not limited to science, literature, humanities, philosophy, sociology, psychology, ethics, history and geography. More information about the journal and how to submit an article can be found at http://journals.cambridge.org/ijc.

Rules and Practices of International Investment Law and Arbitration

YANNICK RADI

UCLouvain – Faculty of Law, Belgium

CAMBRIDGE
UNIVERSITY PRESS

University Printing House, Cambridge CB2 8BS, United Kingdom

One Liberty Plaza, 20th Floor, New York, NY 10006, USA

477 Williamstown Road, Port Melbourne, VIC 3207, Australia

314–321, 3rd Floor, Plot 3, Splendor Forum, Jasola District Centre,
New Delhi – 110025, India

79 Anson Road, #06–04/06, Singapore 079906

Cambridge University Press is part of the University of Cambridge.

It furthers the University's mission by disseminating knowledge in the pursuit of
education, learning, and research at the highest international levels of excellence.

www.cambridge.org
Information on this title: www.cambridge.org/9781107102101
DOI: 10.1017/9781316182383

© Yannick Radi 2020

First published 2020

A catalogue record for this publication is available from the British Library.

ISBN 978-1-107-10210-1 Hardback
ISBN 978-1-107-49957-7 Paperback

Preface

International investment law and arbitration is its own 'galaxy'. This field is vast, made up in particular of thousands of treaties to be read in relation to hundreds of arbitration awards. Added to this is the diversity of this field of law, as both State treaty practice and the practice of arbitration tribunals display nuances and differences on a number of issues. While it has been expanding dramatically over the past few decades in quantitative terms, this galaxy is now evolving and developing new traits as a reaction to the criticisms formulated across civil society in relation to the protection of public interests.

I have designed this textbook to enable readers to master and to make sense of this galaxy in motion. It offers comparative studies of the rules and practices that form international investment law and arbitration, as well as analyses of the legal issues that arise from them. All aspects are covered – substantive, institutional and procedural – that pertain to the protection of foreign investors and public interests, as well as to the settlement of investor–State disputes. I have paid specific attention to the most recent developments in the field with regard to both treaty and arbitration practices as well as arbitration rules. This is not only intended to ensure that this study of positive law is up-to-date, but also to take stock of the impact of the societal context and concerns on the contemporary features and content of international investment law and arbitration. In addition to the rules and practices of which this field is composed, the book also focuses on the numerous rules of public international law that are relevant thereto.

In writing this textbook, I have combined an analytical approach setting out the framework and guiding the analysis with a practice-oriented approach that places treaties and arbitration awards at the core of the analysis. This practice-oriented approach is further served by the online digest available to readers which goes hand-in-hand with this book. This methodology makes the analyses offered accessible for those readers who are discovering this field anew, while providing in-depth material for readers who are already familiar with this field and who will find in the very detailed analyses of practices and in the focus on contemporary developments a wealth of information and food for thought. This will not only be of interest for readers looking for practice-oriented analyses of international investment law and arbitration, but also for those interested in the societal and policy drivers of the field as well as in the theoretical dimension of the discipline. Beyond this readership, the book will be useful for all those interested in public international law and international litigation who will find within the analyses insights into a number of issues that arise also in other fields of international law and in general international law more broadly.

International investment law and arbitration is a fascinating galaxy. I hope you will be as interested in exploring this galaxy within the pages of this book as I have been in writing it.

Prof Dr Yannick Radi
Professor of International Law
October 2019, Paris

Contents

Acknowledgements

Writing a textbook is a long journey. I am grateful to the editorial staff of Cambridge University Press for their continuous support on this journey. My gratitude also goes to Gwen Lehane and Aurélie Debuisson for their thorough editorial assistance in finalising this textbook. Finally, I am thankful to UCLouvain for providing the institutional setting that has enabled me to work on this textbook.

Abbreviations

States

UAE   United Arab Emirates
USA   United States of America
USSR Union of Soviet Socialist Republics

Institutions

ASEAN   Association of Southeast Asian Nations
BLEU   Belgium–Luxembourg Economic Union
COMESA   Common Market for Eastern and Southern Africa
EU   European Union
IBRD   International Bank for Reconstruction and Development
ICC   International Chamber of Commerce
ICJ   International Court of Justice
ICSID   International Centre for Settlement of Investment Disputes
ICTY   International Criminal Tribunal for the Former Yugoslavia
ILC   International Law Commission
ILO   International Labour Organization
IMF   International Monetary Fund
ITO   International Trade Organization
IVSC   International Valuation Standards Council
LCIA   London Court of International Arbitration
MIGA   Multilateral Investment Guarantee Agency
OECD   Organisation for Economic Co-operation and Development
OPIC   Overseas Private Investment Corporation
PCA   Permanent Court of Arbitration
PCIJ   Permanent Court of International Justice
SADC   Southern African Development Community
SCC   Stockholm Chamber of Commerce
UN   United Nations
UNCITRAL United Nations Commission on International Trade Law
UNCTAD United Nations Conference on Trade and Development
UNGA   United Nations General Assembly

| WHO | World Health Organization |
| WTO | World Trade Organization |

Instruments

ARSIWA	Articles on Responsibility of States for Internationally Wrongful Acts
CAFTA–DR	Dominican Republic–Central America Free Trade Agreement
CETA	Comprehensive Economic and Trade Agreement
CPTPP	Comprehensive and Progressive Agreement for Trans-Pacific Partnership
ECT	Energy Charter Treaty
FCTC	Framework Convention on Tobacco Control
GATT	General Agreement on Tariffs and Trade
ICCPR	International Covenant on Civil and Political Rights
NAFTA	North American Free Trade Agreement
PACER Plus	Pacific Agreement on Closer Economic Relations Plus
TTIP	Transatlantic Trade and Investment Partnership
USMCA	United States–Mexico–Canada Agreement
VCLT	Vienna Convention on the Law of Treaties

Standard Terms

BIT	bilateral investment treaty
CIL	customary international law
DCF	discounted cash flow
FDI	foreign direct investment
FCN treaties	Friendship, Commerce and Navigation treaties
FET	fair and equitable treatment
FPS	full protection and security
FTA	free trade agreement
GPLRCN	general principle of law recognised by civilised nations
ICS	investment court system
ICTs	international courts and tribunals
IIA	international investment agreement
LIBOR	London InterBank Offered Rate
MFNT	most-favoured-nation treatment
NGO	non-governmental organisation
WWII	Second World War

Table of Treaties

1 International Investment Agreements

Note: As explained in Chapter 2, the notion of international investment agreement is used across the book as a generic expression to cover two types of treaties: bilateral investment treaties and free trade agreements containing an investment chapter. No mention is made of this generic expression in this table, but instead each treaty is listed in reference to the type of treaties of which it consists or using its 'official' title. The treaties are listed in alphabetical order, the ordering taking as a point of reference for most of them the first State mentioned in their 'official' title.

These treaties are available on the website of the UNCTAD Investment Policy Hub.

2 International Investment Agreement Models and Drafts

Note: The models are available on the website of the UNCTAD Investment Policy Hub.

Table of Arbitration Rules

Table of Awards, Decisions, Orders and Judgments

1 Investor–State Arbitration Awards, Decisions and Orders

Note: This table provides the 'full' title of all the awards, decisions and orders that are referred to across this textbook, noting that use is made in the book of an abbreviated title for some of them.

These awards, decisions and orders are available on the website of ICSID, the PCA and italaw.

2 Judgments and Advisory Opinions of the Permanent Court of International Justice and of the International Court of Justice

3 Other Awards and Judgments

Part I

The History and Sources of International Investment Law and Arbitration

1

The History of International Investment Law and Arbitration

Introduction

International investment law and arbitration has a long history dating back to the nineteenth century. As explained below and detailed throughout this book, it has since then developed and adapted following the political and societal forces at work both domestically and internationally. The balance between the interests of developing States and developed States and, more fundamentally, between public and private interests has played a key role in this process. It can be seen that the balance struck between these interests over different periods of time explains to a large extent the evolutive features of this field of law. This holds true with regard to the set of rules governing both the relations of foreign investors with the States in which they invest, i.e. the 'host States', as well as the settlement of the disputes between them, i.e. 'investor–State disputes'.[1]

To make sense of this evolution and for the purpose of this historical contextualisation of the study of international investment law and arbitration, it is useful to distinguish between three key stages in its history and to examine the respective societal context and legal features pertaining to each.

1.1 The Origin of International Investment Law and Arbitration

Preliminary Remarks

In terms of the origin, it is worth noting at the outset that it would be improper to refer to 'international investment law'. Indeed, the international law rules in question were originally not limited to regulating the relations of host States with foreign investors, but more broadly their relations with foreign private persons, often referred to as 'aliens' in the literature. Likewise, these rules did not operate exclusively in relation to investment operations, as international investment agreements (IIAs) do today. For these reasons, it is more

---

[1] The term 'host States' is used throughout the book to designate the States in the territory of which foreign investors invest. The term 'investor–State disputes' designates the disputes between foreign investors and the host States in which they invest.

appropriate to refer to the 'law of the protection of aliens abroad', which constitutes the origin of international investment law.

1.1.1 Societal Context

The development of the law of the protection of aliens abroad derives from the expansionist and imperialist ambitions formulated and put into practice by European States from the nineteenth century. Many justifications were given for these ambitions – among them and of specific interest with regard to the history of international law is the declared will of European States to spread civilisation to all nations.

The distinction that this entails between alleged 'civilised States' and 'uncivilised States' was well accepted in European societies and beyond at that time. The incorporation of general principles of law said to be 'recognised by civilised nations' in the Statute of the Permanent Court of International Justice (PCIJ), as well as the preparatory works to this Statute conducted by the Advisory Committee of Jurists, are particularly telling in this regard. In that sense, Gong explains in his seminal study of the standard of civilisation in international law: 'Nowhere in the debates did anyone question the distinction between "civilized" and "uncivilized". It was an assumption ever made manifest, though ever articulated per se. Each of the jurists on the committee, representing ten different countries, accepted the standard of "civilization" as a given.'[2]

Of course, those States unilaterally designed that standard of civilisation to be spread around the world; it was nothing other than a 'self-made' mirror of their own societies. This appears clearly in the key components of that standard, as summarised by Gong:

1. A 'civilized' State guarantees basic rights, *i.e.* life, dignity, and property; freedom of travel, commerce and religion, especially that of foreign nationals;
2. a 'civilized' State exists as an organized political bureaucracy with some efficiency in running the state machinery, and with some capacity to organise for self defence;
3. a 'civilized' State adheres to generally accepted international law, including the laws of war; it also maintains a domestic system of courts, codes, and published laws which guarantee legal justice for all within its jurisdiction, foreigners and native citizens alike;
4. a 'civilized' State fulfils the obligations of the international system by maintaining adequate and permanent avenues for diplomatic interchange and communication;

---

[2] G W Gong, *The Standard of 'Civilization' in International Society* (Oxford University Press 1984), at 75.

5. a 'civilized' State by and large conforms to the accepted norms and practices of the 'civilized' international society.[3]

In fact, this standard and this self-assigned mission of civilisation were used as a tool to reinforce the hegemony of European States and the dissemination of their model. As noted by Abi-Saab, 'to be recognised as a sovereign, as a subject of international law and as a member of the international community, it was needed to be "civilised", meaning to internalise and comply with European values, standards and models'.[4]

1.1.2 The Treatment of Foreign Private Persons by Host States

As a result of the expansionist and imperialist ambitions of their States of nationality, i.e. their 'home States',[5] Europeans spread across the world to settle and develop a vast array of activities; over time, they were joined by persons originating from other developed States. Those persons often found the treatment granted by the domestic law of their host States to be insufficiently protective of their interests, as compared to the treatment they received under the domestic law in force in their home States or in other developed States. To mitigate this difference, European private persons and States started to argue that in such situations the former should benefit from a specific treatment more protective than that enjoyed by the nationals of their host States under domestic law.

The treaties of friendship, commerce and navigation that had been concluded since the late eighteenth century were largely unhelpful for achieving this objective, having been developed mainly to regulate the relations between States in equivalent economic and political situations. In the context of the asymmetric relations that characterised their expansionism, European States relied on different legal strategies. For instance, they concluded 'unequal treaties' with China pursuant to which China conceded notably restrictions on the exercise of its sovereignty over European private persons. More systemically, they also claimed that properties abroad were protected by the doctrine of *droits acquis* and, later, by the requirement to provide full, adequate and effective compensation in the case of expropriation, a requirement known as the 'Hull formula'. Finally, and most importantly, they argued that a minimum standard of treatment existed under international law.

As examined in Chapter 5, this standard entails that if the treatment granted by the domestic law of the host State to private persons falls below a minimum standard set out in international law, foreign private persons shall be provided

---

[3] Ibid., at 14.

[4] G Abi-Saab, 'General Course of Public International Law' (1987) 201 *Recueil des Cours de l'Académie de Droit International* 9, at 54 (translation by the author).

[5] The term 'home States' is used in this book to designate the States from which investors investing abroad originate.

a standard of treatment corresponding (at least) to that minimum, meaning to the basic rights established under international law. This assertion was fiercely denied, in particular by the Argentinian lawyer Calvo, who supported the application of the national treatment. In his view, foreign private persons could not pretend to be granted a treatment more favourable and protective than the treatment enjoyed by the nationals of host States under their domestic law, in the same way as they could not be subject to a treatment less favourable and protective. This doctrine, which was developed by Calvo as early as 1868, spread over South America, becoming enshrined in statutes, constitutions and regional treaties. Article 9 of the 1933 Montevideo Convention on Rights and Duties of States provides, for instance: 'The jurisdiction of states within the limits of national territory applies to all the inhabitants. Nationals and foreigners are under the same protection of the law and the national authorities and the foreigners may not claim rights other or more extensive than those of the nationals.'

Irrespective of this legal recognition of the national treatment at the domestic and regional levels, the controversy as to the treatment to be granted to foreign private persons in host States was ultimately settled on the international plane in favour of the minimum standard of treatment. This standard was supported by a general practice and an *opinio juris* which led to its recognition as a customary international law rule. Beyond the traditional conception of *opinio juris* as a sense of legal obligation to carry out a certain practice, power politics played no doubt a significant role in this process. To understand this, the conception of *opinio juris* proposed by Stern is enlightening:

> The content of the *opinio juris* of each State depends on its situation in the international order. The will of a State, even if it is not a will of power, entails an element of power. Thus, some States have the feeling to be bound because they wish so, because they consent freely to this; on the contrary, some States have the feeling to be bound because it is impossible for them not to have such a will, because the rule is imposed on them. A customary rule is a rule that is conceived of as such by the will of States which can impose their point of view.[6]

It is also worth noting the key role played by international judicial bodies in the development of this customary international law rule. For instance, the decision of the Mexico–United States Claims Commission in *Neer (USA)* v. *Mexico* is often considered as having played a major role in consolidating the customary status of the minimum standard of treatment (1926, Award, para. 4). In that sense, the arbitration Tribunal in *Windstream Energy LLC* v. *Canada* noted that the Commission did not rely on any direct evidence of State practice in that case (2016, Award, para. 352).

---

[6] B Stern, 'La coutume au coeur du droit international: quelques réflexions' in *Mélanges offerts à Paul Reuter : Le droit international, unité et diversité* (Pedone 1981) 479, at 498 (translation by the author).

More generally, international judicial bodies contributed greatly to promoting the views and standards of European States as to the treatment of foreign private persons by their host States. An archetypal illustration of this trend can be found in the award rendered by Lord Asquith of Bishopstone in *Petroleum Development Ltd (Trucial Coast)* v. *Sheikh of Abu Dhabi* (1939, Award, at 144). To settle the dispute, the Sole Arbitrator applied 'principles rooted in the good sense and common practice of the generality of civilized nations'. With regard to a set of English law rules, he insisted that they were 'so firmly grounded in reason, as to form part of this broad body of jurisprudence – this "modern law of nature"'. This is to be compared with this opinion that he gave as regards the domestic law in force in Abu Dhabi, noting that it would be 'fanciful to suggest that in this very primitive region there is any settled body of legal principles applicable to the construction of modern commercial instruments'.

1.1.3 The Settlement of Disputes between Host States and Foreign Private Persons

The domestic tribunals of host States were the 'natural' judicial fora to settle the disputes arising between host States and foreign private persons. Yet, the politicisation of these tribunals, stemming from their tendency – whether real or perceived – to favour the other branches and organs of the State apparatus made domestic legal orders largely unsuitable for the settlement of such disputes in the eyes of those persons and their home States. It is for this reason that at that time they already internationalised the settlement of such disputes. Two main approaches developed in this respect.

The first of these involved the home State. Originally, this involvement consisted in particular of a practice known as 'gunboat diplomacy', meaning the threat or the actual use of force by that State, especially to recover contractual debts owed to their nationals by host States. This practice came to a head when Germany, Italy and Great Britain sent warships to block and shell Venezuelan ports in 1902. This event led ultimately to the adoption in 1907 of the Hague Convention Respecting the Limitation of the Employment of Force for the Recovery of Contract Debts – known as the 'Drago–Porter Convention' – which prohibits that practice. Article 1 provides:

> The Contracting Powers agree not to have recourse to armed force for the recovery of contract debts claimed from the Government of one country by the Government of another country as being due to its nationals. This undertaking is, however, not applicable when the debtor State refuses or neglects to reply to an offer of arbitration, or, after accepting the offer, prevents any *compromis* from being agreed on, or, after the arbitration, fails to submit to the award.

As set out by Article 2 of that Convention, such arbitration is governed by the 1907 Hague Convention for the Pacific Settlement of International Disputes whose Article 53.2 refers to those disputes arising from contract debts claimed from one Power by another Power as due to its nationals.

More generally, diplomatic protection constitutes another mechanism that facilitated the internationalisation of the settlement of the disputes between host States and foreign private persons through the endorsement of the claims of the latter by their State of nationality. As explained in Chapter 10, this mechanism elevates the dispute, with the original dispute between the host State and the foreign private person under the domestic legal order becoming an inter-State dispute between this host State and his State of nationality, to be settled in the international legal order. No doubt, diplomatic protection was of interest for foreign private persons who could thereby get the support of their State of nationality. It nonetheless had major drawbacks, in particular the politicisation of the process. States have no obligation under public international law to endorse the claims of their nationals; to put it differently, the exercise of diplomatic protection is purely discretionary. This leaves the door open for other State interests, aside from those of the national concerned, to come into play in deciding whether or not to exercise diplomatic protection. Another major drawback comes from the lack of any obligation for States to transfer to their nationals any compensation that they may have ultimately received from host States.

It is worth noting that another mechanism, lump-sum agreements negotiated between host States and the States of nationality in relation to a multitude of claims emanating from their nationals, does not display such a drawback. Indeed, and as explained in Chapter 10, the total amount paid by the host State is then allocated to the nationals concerned.

The drawbacks of diplomatic protection help to explain the development of a second approach from the late nineteenth century to internationalise the settlement of disputes between host States and foreign private companies. This approach consisted of introducing into contracts (usually concession contracts) concluded between host States and foreign private companies a compromissory clause granting jurisdiction to arbitration tribunals to settle any dispute arising from the application and interpretation of those contracts. It should be emphasised that this mechanism does not confer any role for the home States in the settlement of those disputes which directly place foreign private companies in opposition to their host States. In fact, these contracts – often called 'State contracts' in the French-speaking literature – were the first type of instruments to establish arbitration as the dispute settlement method to settle such disputes, long before the conclusion of international investment agreements.

1.2 The Emergence of International Investment Law and Arbitration

1.2.1 Societal Context

The period following the Second World War (WWII) marked the beginning of a new era on the international plane characterised by the enlargement of international society and by the ambivalence of the relationships between its members, marked by both cooperation and conflict.

This enlargement resulted from decolonisation and the wave of newly independent States that followed. These States acquired a political sovereignty that granted them 'membership' in the international society and the right to become members of international organisations.

Those organisations existed in the pre-war period, as illustrated by the League of Nations, but their numbers increased significantly after WWII. This trend evidenced the growing will of States to transcend their individual interests and to cooperate to reach common objectives, as did the recognition by the International Court of Justice (ICJ) of the functional legal personality of the United Nations (UN) in its 1949 Advisory Opinion in *Reparation for Injuries Suffered in the Service of the United Nations*. In addition to the UN, which has a very broad scope of competence, this will of States to cooperate materialised in particular into economic matters, notably with the creation in 1944 of the International Monetary Fund (IMF) and the International Bank for Reconstruction and Development (IBRD).

Even though international organisations were focused on cooperation and the realisation of common objectives, it remains that their functioning, and the international society more broadly, was still influenced by the will of States, or of group of States, to protect and promote their own interests. This became quickly apparent in investment matters and, more generally, in the views and policies that they formulated about multinational corporations.

The main fault line emerged between developing States and developed States. The latter were eager to promote economic globalisation and to facilitate the operations of their corporations worldwide, in particular investment operations. On the other hand, the former, including newly independent States, sought to reinforce their economic sovereignty and to ensure their control over the operations of multinational corporations across their territories.

In order to understand the societal context in which international investment law and arbitration emerged, it is crucial not to oversimplify the conflicts of interests that existed at the time as well as to stress that fault lines existed also within these two groups of States. None of these were completely homogeneous: the interests and strategies of their members differed in many respects.

In this regard, it is noteworthy that, depending on the circumstances, even the individual policies and practices of each State yielded to different interests and strategies, which made them at times quite inconsistent. This appears in particular when comparing the strategies adopted by these States at the multilateral and bilateral levels.

1.2.2 The Treatment of Foreign Investors by Host States

In the post-war period, the multilateral attempts to regulate the conduct of host States *vis-à-vis* foreign investors and their investments through legally binding instruments failed at different stages. The Havana Charter, which aimed at the establishment of the International Trade Organization (ITO) and which contained an Article on investment matters (Article 12), was adopted in 1948; but because of the refusal of the Congress of the United States of America (USA) to ratify the Charter, it never entered into force as other States parties then declined to ratify it. The project put forward at the Organisation for Economic Cooperation and Development (OECD) to conclude a multilateral treaty focusing specifically on the protection of foreign property also failed. The interruption of the negotiations in 1967 left the text under discussion, which was based on the 1959 Abs-Shawcross Draft Convention on Investments Abroad, as a draft. Yet, as explained below, this draft played an important role in shaping the bilateral treaty practice of European States. It is to be emphasised that this failure cannot be attributed to the opposition between developing States and developed States, as only developed States were involved in the negotiation of that treaty.

It was at the United Nations General Assembly (UNGA) that the interests of developing States and those of developed States collided on the occasion of the adoption of a series of resolutions put forward by the former. Of course, those resolutions were non-binding, but it remains that they constituted the main multilateral instruments adopted at that time addressing the treatment of foreign investors and their investments by host States.

It is worth noting at the outset that there was no such opposition between those two groups in the first years and decades following the creation of the UN. This is well evidenced by the 1962 UNGA Resolution 1803 (XVII) on the Permanent Sovereignty over Natural Resources, which was agreed by both developing and developed States. Content-wise, this Resolution was in line with customary international law and gave a role to international law in the treatment and protection to be granted to foreign investors and their investments by host States. For instance, Paragraph 4 provides that in the case of nationalisation, expropriation or requisitioning pursuant to a public purpose, 'the owner shall be paid appropriate compensation, in accordance with the rules in force in the State taking such measures in the exercise of its sovereignty and in accordance with international law'.

This initial consensus is to be contrasted with the claim of developing States to a New International Economic Order declared in the 1974 UNGA Resolution 3201 (S-VI) and detailed in the 1974 UNGA Resolution 3281 (XXIX) establishing the Charter of Economic Rights and Duties of States.

With regard to nationalisations and expropriations, for instance, the latter Resolution does not link compensation to international law, but provides that in those cases an 'appropriate compensation should be paid by the State adopting such measures, taking into account its relevant laws and regulations and all circumstances that [it] considers pertinent' (Article 2.2.c). Hence, no mention is made of international law anymore. Likewise, Resolution 3281 (XXIX) grants this right to each State: 'To regulate and exercise authority over foreign investment within its national jurisdiction in accordance with its laws and regulations and in conformity with its national objectives and priorities. No State shall be compelled to grant preferential treatment to foreign investment' (Article 2.2.a). In other words, that Article brings back into play the national treatment once promoted by Calvo and rejects the minimum standard of treatment. Unsurprisingly, those Resolutions were opposed by developed States.

In addition to the fact that those Resolutions did not as such enter the corpus of positive international law due to their lack of bindingness, this opposition prevents us from considering them as embodying a general practice and an *opinio juris* evidencing new customary international law rules. In that sense, the Sole Arbitrator appointed in *Texaco Overseas Petroleum Company (TOPCO)* v. *Libya* noted:

> The conditions of the adoption of Resolution 3281 (XXIX) proclaiming the Charter of the economic rights and duties of States evidence ... without any ambiguity the lack of any consensus of the generality of States concerning [its] most important provisions ... Article 2 of this Charter must be viewed as a political declaration rather than as a legal declaration, which forms part of the ideological strategy about development and, as such, supported only by non-industrialised States. (1977, Award, paras. 85–86; translation by the author)

Those Resolutions have yet been considered as having undermined existing customary international law rules on the treatment and protection of foreign private persons. Whatever the exact impact they had, there is no doubt that they contributed greatly to creating a legal insecurity which was detrimental for all stakeholders interested in foreign direct investment (FDI) operations. This holds true for foreign investors and their home States, but also – and primarily – for developing States themselves, which needed FDI operations to foster their economic development. As noted by Broches, 'private foreign investment is of great quantitative importance as a supplement to a necessarily limited volume of public development finance, and in many periods has accounted for between one-third and one-half of total capital flows'.[7]

Without trying to second-guess the motives that drove the policies of developing States, this certainly helps to explain why they accepted as of 1959 to

---

[7] A Broches, 'The Convention for Settlement of Investment Disputes' (1987) 136 *Recueil des Cours de l'Académie de Droit International* 331, at 343.

conclude treaties at the bilateral level which were in stark contrast to the rules that they were promoting at the multilateral level: the well-known bilateral investment treaties (BITs), which have traditionally conferred protection to the investors of either State party and their investments when they invest in the territory of the other State party. The first of those treaties was adopted by Germany and Pakistan in 1959, which initiated an impressive treaty practice promoted by European States. Three remarks can be formulated in this respect.

First, it is noteworthy that the USA did not embrace this treaty practice at that time, their first BIT being adopted in 1982 with Panama.

Second, the role played by the above-mentioned 1967 OECD Draft Convention on the Protection of Foreign Property in shaping this practice must be noted. Indeed, European States used it as a template when drafting their respective models that they then used to conclude their BITs with developing States. By doing so, they followed the recommendation formulated by the OECD Council in its 1967 Resolution on the Draft Convention that this Draft be used 'as a basis for further extending and rendering more effective the application of the principles of international law that it contains'.

A third point concerns the oft-formulated criticism as regards the unbalanced features of this BIT practice. This criticism is founded upon three main reasons that pertain respectively to the conclusion, content and effect of BITs.

As to their conclusion, those treaties were often hardly negotiated; their text was in fact often very close to the BIT model brought by the latter.

Content-wise, those BITs only impose obligations upon States and none upon foreign investors. This comes from the fact that those two issues were decoupled at the time: on the one hand, the issue of foreign investors' rights promoted by developed States and, on the other hand, the issue of foreign investors' obligations put forward by developing States. Only the first of these is being dealt with in those BITs. At the multilateral level, the issue of foreign investors' obligations and more generally multinational corporations' obligations was mainly discussed at the OECD; this led to the adoption in 1976 of the first version of the Guidelines for Multinational Enterprises.

Concerning their effect, those BITs – although they are de jure reciprocal – only benefited de facto the nationals and corporations of developed States as it was only these who were investing abroad.

Beyond these features of BIT practice at the time and the lack of balance that they display, it is important to keep in mind the context outlined above and not to detach this practice from the other components of international investment law and arbitration in order to have a correct understanding of the field as it emerged.

Faced with political risks in developing States and with uncertainties as to the treatment they could expect in this regard, foreign investors had become cautious in planning FDI operations. It is in light of this context that the policy connection between BIT practice and the insurance against political risks examined in Chapter 9 appears, as it can also be seen in the subrogation provision contained in BITs. To reassure their investors and encourage them to invest in developing States that were in real need of FDI operations, developed States decided to grant insurance against political risks for their investors operating abroad. But only investments made in developing States that had consented to protecting foreign investors, either in their domestic law or by means of a BIT, could be granted such an insurance. In other words, developed States consented to granting insurances and thereby encouraging FDI operations which ultimately contributed to the economic development of developing States, provided that those latter States granted a protection to their investors that was in line with their standards and expectations. In situations in which political risks did materialise, developed States compensated their investors and were then subrogated in their right to seek reparation from the developing States concerned.

To understand the emergence of international investment law and arbitration, one cannot focus only on BITs; they must be considered in relation to the entire field, and in particular in relation to insurance policies and contracts. The importance of insurance against political risks is further evidenced by an idea that had been discussed since the 1950s: to create an international insurance agency. This idea eventually led to the adoption in 1985 of the Seoul Convention that established the Multilateral Investment Guarantee Agency.

1.2.3 The Settlement of Disputes between Host States and Foreign Investors

As explained above, investor–State arbitration had emerged as of the late nineteenth century in State contracts as a substitute for domestic courts and diplomatic protection to settle disputes arising from the interpretation and application of those instruments.

It is worth mentioning that the first BITs concluded provided only for an inter-State dispute settlement mechanism. In this regard, Arbitrator Söderlund in *Blue Bank International & Trust (Barbados) Ltd* v. *Venezuela* noted, in reference to Newcombe and Paradell,[8] that the 1969 Italy–Chad BIT was the first to incorporate investor–State arbitration with an unqualified State consent (2017, Award, Separate Opinion, para. 21).

That approach initiated in State contracts was confirmed by the adoption in 1965 of the Convention on the Settlement of Investment Disputes between States and Nationals of Other States which established the International Centre for Settlement of Investment Disputes (ICSID Convention). In fact – although the activity of ICSID remained limited until the 1990s – that Convention has greatly contributed to putting

---

[8] A Newcombe, L Paradell, *Law and Practice of Investment Treaties: Standards of Treatment* (Kluwer 2009).

investor–State arbitration at the forefront of the settlement of investor–State disputes.

This is apparent in the ICSID Convention and in the Report of the Executive Directors of the IBRD on that Convention. Concerning diplomatic protection, Article 27 and the Report (para. 33) provide that the home State of the foreign investor cannot exercise its diplomatic protection once the host State and that investor have consented to submit, or have actually submitted, their dispute to arbitration under the Convention. This becomes possible only if the host State fails to comply with the arbitration award. As regards domestic courts, States retain the right to require the exhaustion of local remedies as a condition of giving their consent to arbitration under Article 26 of the ICSID Convention; but, as is explained in the Report, this Article contains a presumption that, in the case of silence of the parties in this regard, their intention is that they agree to have recourse to arbitration to the exclusion of any other remedy or the exhaustion of other remedies (para. 32).

In addition to offering a venue to internationalise and depoliticise the settlement of investor–State disputes, it is noteworthy that ICSID was created with the view to fostering the economic development of developing States, in particular newly independent States. This appears clearly in the first paragraph of the Preamble of the ICSID Convention in which the Contracting States consider 'the need for international cooperation for economic development, and the role of private international investment therein' as well as in the Report of the IBRD Executive Directors where they state that '[i]n submitting the attached Convention to governments, [they] are prompted by the desire to strengthen the partnership between countries in the cause of economic development' (para. 9). This specific purpose is visible also in the preparatory works of the Convention; this is reflected in the Documents concerning the origin and formulation of the ICSID Convention, whose Part A begins as follows:

> Early in the first Development Decade, which spanned the 1960s, it became increasingly clear that if the plans established for the growth in the economies of the developing countries were to be realized, it would be necessary to supplement the resources flowing to these countries from bilateral and multilateral governmental sources by additional investments originating in the private sector. To encourage such investments, the competent international organizations considered several schemes designed to remove some of the uncertainties and obstacles that faced investors in any foreign country and in particular in many of the States that had only recently attained independence and self-government and whose need for outside capital was greatest. (1970, Vol. 1, at 1)

In other words, the rationale underlying the Convention is to offer a procedural protection to foreign investors as a tool to encourage them to invest in order to stimulate the economic development of developing States. In this respect, it can be noted that a similar rationale has been found by some arbitration tribunals when interpreting the preamble of international investment agreements (IIAs). For instance, the Tribunal in *Joseph Charles Lemire v. Ukraine* stated in relation to the 1994 USA–Ukraine Agreement:

> The main purpose of the BIT is thus the stimulation of foreign investment and of the accompanying flow of capital. But this main purpose is not sought in the abstract; it is inserted in a wider context, the economic development for both signatory countries. Economic development is an objective which must benefit all, primarily national citizens and national companies, and secondarily foreign investors. Thus, the object and purpose of the Treaty is not to protect foreign investments *per se*, but as an aid to the development of the domestic economy. (2010, Decision on Jurisdiction and Liability, paras. 272–273)

The primacy of State economic development among the objectives assigned to the ICSID Convention as well as the consensual nature of its negotiation helps to explain why both developing States and developed States agreed on the establishment of ICSID.

As explained in Chapter 11, ICSID is not an arbitration tribunal that settles disputes. Instead, and as suggested by its name, it can be equated to a 'dispute settlement centre' which assists in particular arbitration tribunals operating under the ICSID Convention and Arbitration Rules. In fact, ICSID is the first institutional setting ever created that is dedicated to the settlement of investor–State disputes.

As such, it can be contrasted to other dispute settlement centres that do not deal only with such disputes. For instance, the Permanent Court of Arbitration, which was created by the 1899 Convention for the Pacific Settlement of International Disputes, also assists in particular in the settlement of inter-State disputes relating to a broad range of public international law matters. The International Chamber of Commerce International Court of Arbitration, created in 1923, provides another example, assisting primarily in the resolution of commercial disputes. By the same token, the ICSID Convention can be contrasted to other instruments that do not only play a role with regard to investor–State arbitration, but also to commercial arbitration. Mention can be made here of the 1958 New York Convention on the Recognition and Enforcement of Foreign Arbitral Awards, or of the Arbitration Rules of the United Nations Commission on International Trade Law (UNCITRAL), whose first version was adopted in 1976.

With such a focus, the ICSID Convention was a pioneer in the sense that it highlighted the opportunity to develop rules and mechanisms adapted to the specificities of investor–State disputes. Further evolutions have taken place since then, in particular in response to the criticisms – discussed below – which have been formulated against international investment law and arbitration in the 2010s.

1.3 The Rise and Crisis of International Investment Law and Arbitration

Preliminary Remarks

To make sense of the contemporary evolution of international investment law and arbitration, it is necessary to join the discussions of two overlapping stages that at first glance may seem at odds with each other. The first of these is characterised by the compelling rise of treaty and arbitration practice, while the second is marked by the legitimacy crisis faced by this field of law. This 'joinder' is required insofar as the legitimacy crisis is to a large extent rooted in the considerable increase in the conclusion of IIAs and initiation of arbitration proceedings. That being said, and as explained below, it is noteworthy that this crisis is also due to other factors that are alien to the inner features of international investment law and arbitration.

1.3.1 Societal Context

Specific events and deep-rooted trends at the international level have greatly contributed to the evolution of international investment law and arbitration as of the 1980s.

From a geopolitical perspective, one can refer for instance to the fall of the Union of Soviet Socialist Republics (USSR) in 1991 and to the series of BITs that were concluded in its aftermath. European integration offers another significant example: the competence granted to the European Union (EU) on investment matters has led it as of the 2010s to engage in and promote significant reforms of international investment law and arbitration. This engagement can be contrasted with the contemporaneous mistrust of the US administration with the regime and its consequent retrenchment from international initiatives and negotiations. This is well illustrated by the withdrawal of the USA from the Trans-Pacific Partnership Agreement in 2017.

From an economic perspective, the growing globalisation of the economy and the multilateralisation of FDI operations in particular have also significantly impacted international investment law and arbitration. This is notably so inasmuch as this trend has contributed to blurring the traditional association between 'developed States' and 'home States of investors' on the one hand, and 'developing States' and 'host States of investors' on the other. Developing States have become home States, just as developed States have become host States. This has led to a diversification of the interests that each State seeks to protect and promote through international investment law. In particular, developed States have started to pay more attention to the limits that international investment agreements place on the normative prerogatives of States parties.

In addition to State interests and policies, it is interesting to note that the views and interests promoted by non-governmental organisations (NGOs) operating worldwide have also gained over that period an increasing importance in the public debate and in international settings. This has also influenced the evolution of the regime.

Closely related to the above, international investment law and arbitration has also been deeply impacted by evolutions and events occurring at the domestic level. One major such evolution consists of the realisation across domestic societies of the very existence of this field and the subsequent criticisms formulated against it, in particular by local NGOs. This has been the case with regard to some high-profile cases, such as *Philip Morris* v. *Uruguay*, and with regard to the negotiation of mega-regional free trade agreements (FTAs) containing an investment chapter – for instance, the negotiation of the Comprehensive Economic and Trade Agreement (CETA).

In relation to the above-mentioned dismantlement of the traditional association between 'developed States' and 'home States of investors' and 'developing States' and 'host States of investors', it should be borne in mind that these criticisms have spread over each continent. This includes countries, in particular in Europe, that had historically been friendly to international investment law and arbitration. As a result, pleas for reform have been made with the view to making it more protective of public interests and to bringing greater transparency and publicness into dispute settlement.

Additionally, it can be noted that these criticisms and calls for reform have been formulated in relation to more systemic criticism expressed by domestic societies against global trends. This is well illustrated by the increasing mistrust displayed across those societies as of the eve of the twenty-first century *vis-à-vis* international law and institutions, as they have been seen as unduly interfering with domestic affairs. This holds true also with regard to the globalisation of the economy and the growing impact of multinational corporations on domestic societies.

1.3.2 The Treatment of Foreign Investors by Host States and the Protection of Public Interests

Since the adoption of the first BIT between Germany and Pakistan in 1959, treaty practice in international investment law and arbitration has been on the rise. More specifically, the bilateral practice of States has exploded; according to the figures made available by the United Nations Conference on Trade and Development (UNCTAD) in August 2019, 2911 treaties had been adopted by that time.[9]

To this figure one can add 388 treaties, notably FTAs containing an investment chapter, which have also been adopted over these decades. The number

---

[9] UNCTAD 'Investment Policy Hub', available at https://investmentpolicy.unctad.org/interna tional-investment-agreements.

of those FTAs, among which many have a regional or mega-regional reach, has grown significantly in the 2010s, partly as a result of the difficulties encountered at the World Trade Organization (WTO). This FTA practice was notably initiated by the North American Free Trade Agreement (NAFTA) adopted by Canada, the USA and Mexico in 1992; it is worth noting that this Agreement was renegotiated, leading to the adoption in 2018 of the United States–Mexico–Canada Agreement.

As illustrated by those FTAs containing an investment chapter, regional or mega-regional initiatives have become powerful in investment treaty-making as of the 1990s; this can be contrasted with the fact that no international convention with a global reach has been adopted over that period. More precisely, regionalism has proven to be a successful way to adopt treaties or to guide treaty practice, as has been the case in particular on the African continent. With regard to treaties, reference can be made to the Common Market for Eastern and Southern Africa (COMESA), whose Member States adopted in 2007 the Investment Agreement for the COMESA Common Investment Area. The Pan-African Investment Code adopted in 2015 by the Member States of the African Union offers a good example of an initiative intended to guide treaty practice. Beyond these successful initiatives, mention must also be made of the failure of regionalism, in particular of the interruption of the negotiation of the Multilateral Agreement on Investment initiated at the OECD in the 1990s.

Those African initiatives also illustrate that developing States have been increasingly concluding IIAs between themselves. In the context of those treaty relations between developing States, the traditional association between 'developing States' and 'host States of investors' is of course meaningless. But more generally, this association has become less and less relevant even in their relations with developed States; indeed, because of the multilateralisation of FDI operations, the BITs concluded between those States have started to acquire a de facto reciprocal dimension. This means that the traditional association between 'developed States' and 'home States' has also become moot. This is further evidenced by the IIAs concluded between developed States and by those cases in which these States have acted as defendants in arbitration proceedings, such as the USA in the NAFTA context.

Content-wise, all of this has had an impact on States' investment policies and IIA rules. On the side of developed States, significant changes were put in place in the 2010s with a view to protecting public interests. This objective has been achieved mainly by limiting foreign investors' rights, but also – as examined in Chapter 8 – by placing new obligations upon States and on those investors. It is noteworthy that this evolution has resulted not only from the increased risk for developed States in facing arbitration proceedings, but also more generally from the growing importance given to human rights and sustainable development in international law and policies.

The same approach has been adopted by developing States in their treaty practice over the same period, as illustrated by the 2016 Morocco–Nigeria IIA. On the other hand, other treaties concluded between developing States appear to be quite similar to the treaties that they had concluded with developed States in the early years of international investment law and arbitration, and whose object focuses on the protection of foreign investors and investments. The IIA adopted by Kenya and Kuwait in 2013 exemplifies this trend.

1.3.3 The Settlement of Disputes between Host States and Foreign Investors

As explained above, investor–State arbitration emerged and developed very early as a convenient tool to settle investor–State disputes.

In spite of this, other mechanisms and methods have been used at times alongside investor–State arbitration. The exercise of diplomatic protection has led landmark cases to be settled by the International Court of Justice – for instance, the *Elettronica Sicula S.p.A.* case between the USA and Italy decided in 1989. Reference can also be made to the establishment of the Iran–United States Claims Tribunal by the 1981 Algiers Declarations in the aftermath of the 1979 hostage crisis at the US Embassy in Tehran and the subsequent freezing of Iranian assets by the USA. This Tribunal has been endorsed in particular with the task of resolving the claims of US nationals against Iran and of Iranian nationals against the USA arising from debts, contracts, expropriations or other measures affecting property rights.

More fundamentally, it was only in the 1990s that investor–State arbitration practice expanded. This can be seen from the ICSID statistics issued in August 2019.[10] Between 1972 and 1996, a maximum of four ICSID arbitration cases were registered each year by the Centre; since 1996, this figure has been growing regularly, to reach a maximum of fifty-five cases registered in 2018. This is due in particular to the combined effect of the incorporation in treaty practice of investor–State arbitration with unqualified consent as of 1969 – something explained in Section 1.2.3 – and of the award rendered in 1990 in *Asian Agricultural Products Ltd (AAPL)* v. *Sri Lanka*. As discussed in Chapter 11, foreign investors have since then mainly initiated arbitration proceedings against host States – regardless of the existence of any contract concluded between them – by simply resorting to the offer to arbitrate contained in IIAs. Put in relation to the above-mentioned explosion of IIA practice, this practice, often referred to as 'arbitration without privity' following Paulsson's seminal piece,[11] has greatly contributed to increasing the number of claims filed against host States.

---

[10] ICSID, 'The ICSID Caseload: Statistics', Issue 2019-2 (August 2019), available at https://icsid .worldbank.org/en.

[11] J Paulsson, 'Arbitration without Privity' (1995) 10 *ICSID Review* 232.

This increase also explains to a large extent the above-mentioned criticism formulated against investor–State arbitration and the subsequent initiatives undertaken to reform the settlement of investor–State disputes.

Of course, public interest considerations have always been at stake in such disputes. However, the increase in the number of proceedings has made investor–State arbitration more visible for domestic societies, which has raised the issue of its impact on public interests and of the adequacy of investor–State arbitration to settle those disputes.

As a result, two strategies have been adopted to reform dispute settlement in this field. The first of these consists in the reform of investor–State arbitration, in particular in order to make it more transparent and open to the public. This is evidenced by the 2006 revision of the ICSID Arbitration Rules and also by the new revision process of those Rules launched in 2016. This is further illustrated by the United Nations Convention on Transparency in Treaty-Based Investor–State Arbitration adopted in 2014. More radically, the second approach has been intended to downplay the role of investor–State arbitration or even to replace it with other methods of dispute settlement. This is exemplified by the 2016 CETA, which provides for the establishment of a permanent court, as do the discussions initiated in 2018 at UNCITRAL, where the opportunity to create a multilateral permanent court has been under consideration.

2

The Sources of International Investment Law and Arbitration

Introduction

The rules governing the conduct of host States with regard to foreign investors – and, in some instances, which govern the conduct of foreign investors themselves and that of home States – as well as those which govern investor–State dispute settlement, are largely to be found in international law sources. This is evidenced by the 'treatification' of the field explained in Chapter 1 and by the predominance of international investment agreements (IIAs) since then. For that reason, this chapter focuses on sources of international law as they relate to international investment law and arbitration. In line with the classical dichotomy adopted in public international law as reflected in Article 38 of the Statute of the International Court of Justice (ICJ), the chapter provides an analysis of the primary and subsidiary sources of international investment law and arbitration. It also examines the role of equity and of soft law instruments in this regard.

At this preliminary stage, it is worth mentioning that domestic law sources also have some relevance here, both direct and indirect. They can directly govern the conduct of host States and that of foreign investors. But, they can also have an indirect impact in that they can be used as a material source of international investment law. This is evidenced, for example, by the incorporation of the notion of distinct investment-backed expectation – discussed in Chapter 6 – in a number of IIAs in the aftermath of the bilateral investment treaty (BIT) Model adopted by the United States of America (USA) in 2004. Indeed, this notion was developed by the US Supreme Court in its 1978 Decision in *Penn Central* v. *New York City* with respect to the right to property.

2.1 Primary Sources

Following the classification of primary sources in public international law, this section examines in turn the relevance of treaties, customary international law (CIL) and general principles of law recognised by civilised nations (GPLRCN) as sources of international investment law and arbitration.

2.1.1 Treaties

Preliminary Remarks

As explained in Chapter 1, treaties have since the 1960s played a predominant role in international investment law and arbitration.

With regard to investor–State arbitration, it is worth highlighting two instruments at the outset: (1) the 1965 Washington Convention, which established the International Centre for Settlement of Investment Disputes (ICSID) and which governs in particular ICSID Convention arbitration proceedings; and (2) the 2014 United Nations Convention on Transparency in Treaty-Based Investor–State Arbitration. The treaty nature of those instruments is notable due to the fact that – as discussed below – most instruments setting out rules governing investor–State arbitration proceedings can be seen as having a soft law nature.

This subsection focuses on international investment agreements. It will also introduce another category of treaties that have some relevance here, albeit indirectly.

2.1.1.1 International Investment Agreements

Preliminary Remarks

International investment agreements are treaties concluded between States which govern their respective conduct in their capacity as host State towards the investors of the other contracting State(s) investing in their territory. In some instances, these treaties also govern the conduct of States in their capacity as home State as well as the conduct of investors themselves.[1] In addition, these treaties govern the settlement of investor–State disputes, which has traditionally consisted mainly of investor–State arbitration.

The increase in the number of IIAs concluded as of the 1960s has placed IIAs at the forefront of international investment law and arbitration. However, this does not mean that those agreements enjoy any legal supremacy; indeed, public international law sets no hierarchy between treaties, CIL and GPLRCN.

This subsection sheds light on IIAs by (1) classifying the main types of treaties falling into this category of agreements; (2) clarifying the purpose of these treaties; (3) mapping their content; and (4) specifying their scope of application.

---

[1] When used in relation to IIAs, the references across the textbook to 'investors'/'foreign investors' and 'investments'/'foreign investments' designate the investors of the States parties to the agreements (their home States) and their investments, respectively. Likewise, the reference to 'host States' designates the States parties to those agreements in the territory of which these 'investors'/'foreign investors' invest. More generally, and unless otherwise specified, the references to 'investors' and 'investments' designate 'foreign investors' and 'foreign investments', respectively.

a Typology of International Investment Agreements

Preliminary Remarks

There is some variety in the expressions used by contracting States to name the instruments at hand in this subsection. These instruments are mainly referred to as 'agreement', such as the 2016 Comprehensive Economic and Trade Agreement, or 'treaty', such as the 1994 Energy Charter Treaty. These terminological differences are of no consequence, as is made clear in Article 2.1.a of the 1969 Vienna Convention on the Law of Treaties, which provides that '"treaty" means an international agreement concluded between States in written form and governed by international law, whether embodied in a single instrument or in two or more related instruments and whatever its particular designation'.

More fundamentally, these instruments are further grouped into various categories of treaties, mainly IIA, BIT and free trade agreement (FTA). The overarching category is IIA, which is used as such throughout this book. Certain differences are visible between BITs and FTAs pertaining to both the number of States parties and the object of the instruments. These differences between these two categories of IIAs are discussed in the following subsections.

i Bilateral Investment Treaties   The main feature of BITs to be mentioned here pertains to the specificity of their object. They focus on the regulation of host States' conduct *vis-à-vis* foreign investors and on investor–State arbitration. Mainly as a reaction to the criticism formulated against international investment law and arbitration in the 2010s, some BITs concluded as of that period have also had as their object the regulation of foreign investors' conduct and, more generally, the protection of public interests. By the same token, some of these treaties have also replaced or limited the role of investor–State arbitration in the settlement of investor–State disputes. In this respect, it is worth recalling that the first BIT to have ever been adopted – the 1959 Germany–Pakistan BIT – did not provide for investor–State arbitration; as explained in Chapter 1, the 1969 Italy–Chad BIT seems to have been the first BIT to incorporate investor–State arbitration with an unqualified State consent.

Additionally, the bilateral nature of BITs and their number can be contrasted with the mixed 'performance' of multilateral treaties in IIA practice. In fact, at the time of writing this book in 2019, there had never been concluded a multilateral investment treaty with a global reach. Multilateralism has only been successful at the regional level, as is illustrated by the Common Market for Eastern and Southern Africa (COMESA), whose Member States adopted in 2007 the Investment Agreement for the COMESA Common Investment Area. But here again, regional multilateralism has also displayed its limits as can be seen from the failure of the negotiations initiated twice at the Organisation for Economic Co-operation and Development (OECD) in the 1960s and 1990s.

Multilateralism proves to have been more successful with regard to the adoption of FTAs containing an investment chapter as opposed to stand-alone multilateral investment agreements.

ii Free Trade Agreements with an Investment Chapter   In its classification of treaties containing investment provisions,[2] the United Nations Conference on Trade and Development (UNCTAD) distinguishes between three main types of conventions: (1) treaties with limited investment-related provisions concerning, for instance, the free transfer of investment-related funds; (2) treaties that contain 'framework' clauses, for example with respect to cooperation in the area of investment; and (3) broader economic treaties that include those obligations typically found in BITs, largely seen in the FTAs containing an investment chapter.

Those FTAs that incorporate an investment chapter, which is content-wise *mutatis mutandis* analogous to BITs, were on the rise in the 2010s partly as a result of the difficulties encountered at the World Trade Organization. As a result, they have become a key instrument in international investment law and arbitration. Similar to BITs, treaty practice displays a trend towards extending the object of the investment chapter contained in FTAs to encompass the regulation of foreign investors' conduct and, more generally, the protection of public interests. Likewise, some of these FTAs have replaced investor–State arbitration with other forms of dispute settlement to settle investor–State disputes.

Some of those FTAs have a bilateral dimension, as exemplified by the Agreement adopted by Brazil and Chile in 2018. However, a number of FTAs are multilateral treaties with a regional or mega-regional reach, such as the 2017 Pacific Agreement on Closer Economic Relations Plus (PACER Plus). Those FTAs exemplify the importance of regional initiatives in investment treaty-making.

b The Purpose of International Investment Agreements

Closely connected to the object of IIAs discussed above is the issue of their purpose. What are IIAs for? Which objectives do States pursue when they conclude such agreements? The answer to those questions is largely to be found in the preamble of these agreements which, as examined in Chapter 12, play an important role in treaty interpretation; in some IIAs, a specific provision lays out their objectives (e.g. 2016 Morocco–Nigeria IIA, Article 2). However, it remains difficult to provide a clear-cut general answer as to what States' objectives are in concluding these agreements. This is due to the nuances and differences found throughout treaty practice, both from a synchronic and diachronic standpoint. This difficulty also results from the fact that preambles often resemble a fuzzy patchwork of various elements – the

---

[2] UNCTAD 'Investment Policy Hub', available at https://investmentpolicy.unctad.org/inter national-investment-agreements.

drafting of these preambles makes it difficult to appraise the 'status' of each of these elements and the interplay between them.

A series of three core elements commonly mentioned throughout the preamble of many IIAs can be observed from treaty practice, namely: (1) 'cooperation between States'; (2) 'investment'; and (3) 'development'. In most treaties, 'cooperation between States' appears as a general element, while the elements relating to investment and development are more concrete. Particular attention is paid in this subsection to the last two elements, about which three preliminary remarks can be made.

First, note should be taken of the different ways in which preambles refer to 'investment' and 'development'. With regard to 'investment', mention is made mainly of the stimulation of foreign investments, their promotion, as well as their protection. Turning to 'development', treaty practice in relation to this element has evolved over time. Originally, preambles referred only to economic development or prosperity, while in IIAs concluded in the 2010s, reference has also been made to sustainable development (e.g. 2017 Rwanda–United Arab Emirates (UAE) IIA). In line with this evolution, which entails that the purpose of those IIAs encompasses the protection of the environment and labour standards in particular, some preambles mention specific public interests, typically health, safety or the environment (e.g. 2017 Israel–Japan IIA), or, more generally, the right of States to regulate (e.g. 2019 Australia–Uruguay IIA).

A second remark as to 'investment' and 'development' is that these elements can be seen either as proper objectives or simply as policy statements, depending on the drafting of the preambles and in particular the verbs chosen to introduce them. At times the drafting and the verbs make it difficult to even appraise precisely which 'status' States parties intended to grant to each element.

Finally, agreements vary in the characterisation of 'investment' and 'development' as being main elements or instead as being subsidiary and instrumental elements. This depends again on the language used in the preambles.

Keeping these preliminary remarks in mind, one can identify two main trends in IIA practice.

A first trend adopted by States is focusing the preamble on 'investment'. This is often the case with the preamble of agreements forming part of a process of economic integration and trade liberalisation. This is exemplified by the Preamble of the 2017 China–Hong Kong SAR China IIA:

> To promote and protect investments by investors of the Mainland [footnote omitted] and the Hong Kong Special Administrative Region (hereinafter referred to as the 'two sides') in the other side, to progressively reduce or eliminate substantially all discriminatory measures on investments between the two sides, to protect the rights of investors and to promote achieving progressive liberalisation and facilitation of investments of the two sides, as

well as to further enhance the level of bilateral economic and trade exchanges and cooperation.

As a variant of the above, the preamble of some IIAs, while focusing on 'investment', link it with public interest considerations. For instance, the Preamble of the 2017 Israel–Japan IIA provides that the Parties recognise that the promotion of investment and the creation of stable, equitable, favourable and transparent conditions for greater investment, 'can be achieved without relaxing health, safety and environmental measures of general application'.

The second trend displayed by IIA practice conceives of the promotion, protection and treatment of foreign investments as stimulating 'tools' or as 'vectors'. In this respect, some preambles refer only to the stimulation of States' economic development, such as the Preamble of the 2017 Colombia–UAE IIA, which provides: 'Recognising the need to promote and protect foreign investments with the aim to foster the economic prosperity and economic development of both Contracting Parties.' Others mention the stimulation of both foreign investments and economic development, as seen in the Preamble of the 1986 USA–Bangladesh IIA: 'Recognizing that agreement upon the treatment to be accorded [to] such investment will stimulate the flow of private capital and the economic development of the Parties.'

Notably, subsequent US treaty practice has evolved to include in the preamble elements relating to or forming part of the notion of sustainable development. For instance, the Preamble of the 2008 USA–Rwanda IIA provides: 'Desiring to achieve these objectives in a manner consistent with the protection of health, safety, and the environment, and the promotion of internationally recognized labor rights.' Other IIA preambles make direct reference to sustainable development, such as the Preamble of the 2016 Argentina–Qatar IIA, which provides:

> Highlighting the need for all foreign investment to be consistent with the promotion of the economic development of both Contracting Parties; Intending to create and maintain favorable conditions for investments by investors of one Contracting Party in the territory of the other Contracting Party; Recognising the need to promote and protect these investments with the aim to foster the economic prosperity of both Contracting Parties ... Encouraging the sustainable development of the Contracting Parties.

c The Content of International Investment Agreements

As evidenced across this book, a comparative analysis of IIA provisions reveals a number of nuances and differences in terms of both structure and content. Yet, IIAs share notable similarities in terms of patterns, features and provisions, which have evolved over time. In analysing this evolution and for the purposes of this discussion, one can distinguish between two successive periods of time: the 1960s–2000s and 2010 onwards.

During the first period, European States were the key actors in initiating treaty practice, which they largely designed using their own BIT models. These models were based on the 1967 Draft Convention on the Protection of Foreign Property prepared at the OECD. It comes as no surprise, then, that the BITs they concluded with developing States – many of which are still in force – display common patterns, features and provisions. They contain a limited number of provisions – often vague – which focus on foreign investors and investments. Those provisions mainly address five sets of issues.

First, these BITs provide for definitions and delineate their scope of application, an issue which is discussed further below.

Second, they regulate the promotion, the admission and the establishment of the investors of either State party and their investments in the territory of the other State party.

A third common feature of these BITs consists of a set of provisions that regulate the conduct of the host State with regard to the treatment of the investors of the other State party and their investments in various situations and at different stages of investment operations. Typically, they incorporate provisions conferring the right to investors (1) to be treated fairly and equitably; (2) to be granted full protection and security; (3) not to be discriminated *vis-à-vis* nationals and other foreign investors; and (4) to make free monetary transfers. Some treaties also contain a provision concerning the respect by host States of their commitments undertaken to the benefit of investors, known as an 'umbrella clause'. In addition, these BITs set out conditions as to the legality of expropriations and nationalisations, in particular requiring compensation, as well as a provision dealing with the compensation due in situations of armed conflict or internal disorder.

A fourth feature is the incorporation of a dispute settlement provision that provides for and governs investor–State arbitration. It should be noted that BITs also deal with the subrogation of home States in the rights of their investors when the latter have received compensation under an insurance contract. This is to be distinguished from the dispute settlement provision which addresses disputes arising directly between BIT States parties.

Finally, these BITs commonly contain a set of provisions relating to their entry into force, duration and termination.

All of these provisions still form part of the treaty practice initiated in the 2010s; however, IIA practice has since then been characterised by three main evolutions largely triggered by the criticisms formulated at that time against international investment law and arbitration. It is interesting to note that, while European States took the lead and shaped treaty practice over the above-mentioned period, the USA has greatly contributed to designing IIA practice over the second reference period, in particular through the dissemination of key provisions of their 2004 BIT Model.

The first evolution – which results in fact from the two mentioned below – concerns the drafting of IIAs. The provisions of these IIAs are much more detailed, those details being provided either in the provisions themselves or in annexes. This holds true with respect to investor–State arbitration as well as to the treatment and protection due to foreign investors and their investments.

The second evolution to be noted consists of the provision of a series of limitations – which were rare in the IIAs concluded over the first period – placed on the protection and treatment conferred to foreign investors and their investments, the aim of this being the protection of States' public interests and of the right of States to regulate. These limitations can apply to the treaty as a whole – for instance by the incorporation of a security exception clause – or can instead concern specific provisions, such as the expropriation provision. In the same vein, there is an evolution towards incorporating provisions that place obligations upon States and foreign investors with a view to protecting and promoting sustainable development and human rights.

With regard to investor–State arbitration, the third evolution displays an increasing trend towards the regulation of different aspects of dispute settlement, the aim being in particular to reinforce the legitimacy of arbitration tribunals in the eyes of civil society members. This trend is also visible in those IIAs that replace investor–State arbitration with other dispute settlement mechanisms, such as referring investor–State disputes to a permanent court.

d The Scope of Application of International Investment Agreements

International investment agreements have traditionally conferred rights upon the investors of States parties which protect them from the host State party in which they invest. To benefit from these rights, private persons and their assets must be covered by the relevant IIAs, which begs the question of the scope of application of these agreements.

In some IIAs, the scope of application is defined in a specific provision. For instance, Article 2 of the IIA adopted by Kazakhstan and Singapore in 2018 provides in its relevant part that 'the provisions in this Agreement shall apply to all investments made by investors of the State of one Party in the territory of the State of the other Party, whether made before or after the entry into force of this Agreement'. Many IIAs do not contain such a provision, but rather the same relevant elements that inform their scope of application can be found elsewhere in the agreements, in particular in the definitions provided for at the start thereof.

Irrespective of their exact 'location', those elements, the compliance with which condition the application of the IIAs, have two dimensions – material and personal. The material element entails that the asset at stake must qualify as a covered investment under the IIA at hand – this includes that it must be acquired in the territory of a State party to that agreement and in accordance with the timing set out therein. In this respect, treaty practice shows that assets acquired both prior to or subsequent to the entry into force of the agreements are usually covered. The personal element requires that this asset be acquired by a private person, whether a natural person or a legal person, who is connected, through a 'link' specified in the IIA, to another State party to the agreement. As evidenced in Chapter 14, the definitions of an investment and of an investor under IIAs are in fact very much intertwined. If the material and personal elements are fulfilled, the asset and the person concerned qualify respectively as a covered investment and a covered investor, and can as such benefit from the protection conferred by the IIA's substantive provisions against the host State's conduct.

It is worth noting that if investments made before the date of entry into force of the IIAs are usually covered by those agreements, investments and investors are protected against conduct occurring only as of that date. That date is usually set at the time when States parties have notified to each other the fulfilment of the domestic procedures relevant for entry into force purposes (e.g. 2001 Italy–Ecuador IIA, Article 13), or a few days or weeks after that date (e.g. 2019 Australia–Uruguay IIA, Article 17.1). In a few IIAs it is set at the date of the signature of the agreements (e.g. 1976 Korea–United Kingdom IIA, Article 12).

This date of entry into force constitutes the critical date for the application of the non-retroactivity principle as notably stated in Article 28 of the 1969 Vienna Convention on the Law of Treaties: 'Unless a different intention appears from the treaty or is otherwise established, its provisions do not bind a party in relation to any act or fact which took place or any situation which ceased to exist before the date of the entry into force of the treaty with respect to that party.' With regard to the law of State responsibility, it also constitutes the critical date for the application of the doctrine of inter-temporal law stated in Article 13 of the 2001 Articles on Responsibility of States for Internationally Wrongful Acts: 'An act of a State does not constitute a breach of an international obligation unless the State is bound by the obligation in question at the time the act occurs.' In relation to the timing of the asset's acquisition mentioned above, one should mention that IIAs do not protect an asset which becomes owned or controlled by a natural or legal person connected to an IIA State party after the occurrence of the State conduct at hand; the fact that the conduct takes place after the entry into force of the agreement changes nothing in this regard.

The protection conferred by IIA substantive provisions to foreign investments and investors against host States' conduct lasts for the period during which agreements are in force. Bilateral investment treaties, for instance, provide that they shall remain in force for a certain period of time (e.g. ten years for the 2004 Egypt–Mongolia BIT, Article 13.1; fifteen years for the 2019 Australia–Uruguay BIT, Article 17.1). They also usually specify that this period is renewed for further periods, be they similar to the initial period of time (e.g. Egypt–Mongolia IIA, Article 13.1) or different (e.g. 2001 Italy–Ecuador IIA, Article 14.1); the Australia–Uruguay BIT provides in that sense that the Treaty can remain in force indefinitely (Article 17.1). This is so unless the BIT is terminated by either party after the end of the initial period. The provision in BITs of such a possibility for unilateral termination is without prejudice of the possibility for States parties to agree on a termination at any time, as provided in Article 54 of the 1969 Vienna Convention on the Law of Treaties. After termination, investments and investors are as a matter of principle no longer protected by the substantive provisions of an IIA against host States' conduct. Yet, agreements usually contain a 'sunset clause' that provides for an exception as regards investments made before the date of termination. In such situations, the treaties remain in force for an additional period equivalent to the initial time period (e.g. Egypt–Mongolia IIA, Article 13.2) or the 'renewal' time period (e.g. Italy–Ecuador IIA, Article 14.2); as a result, those investments and investors are still protected by IIA substantive provisions during that period.

Whether persons and their assets fall within the scope of application of IIAs is not only crucial in determining whether or not they can benefit from the protection granted by their substantive provisions, but – as explained in Chapter 14 – it also plays a pivotal role with regard to the benefit of the procedural protection conferred by the agreements, namely investor–State arbitration and the establishment of the jurisdiction of arbitration tribunals. In practice, those elements attached to the scope of application of IIAs as well as the issues that they raise are discussed in relation to jurisdictional matters. For didactic purposes, then, the analyses of the definition and notion of investment and investor are 'centralised' in Chapter 14 which focuses on jurisdiction and admissibility matters.

2.1.1.2 Other Relevant Treaties

In addition to IIAs, there is a series of treaties that display some relevance as to the conduct of host States and foreign investors as well as the settlement of investor–State disputes. Strictly speaking, they do not constitute sources of international investment law and arbitration as these matters do not constitute the specific object of these treaties. Instead, they contain provisions that confer rights and impose obligations as well as provisions pertaining to dispute settlement that can be relevant in the context of foreign direct investment (FDI) operations. In this respect, one can refer for instance to human rights conventions, which grant rights to private persons and thereby to investors. Of particular relevance in this regard is the right to property. This is illustrated by the *Yukos* case, which led to the initiation of proceedings before both arbitration tribunals and the European Court of Human Rights in relation to the 1994 Energy Charter Treaty and the 1950 European Convention on Human Rights, respectively.

2.1.2 Customary International Law

Preliminary Remarks

Article 38 of the ICJ Statute refers to 'international custom, as evidence of a general practice accepted as law'. Although that formulation can be criticised inasmuch as it is in fact the 'general practice accepted as law' which evidences 'international custom', and not the other way around, this provision draws attention to the two elements that constitute the cornerstone of customary international law from the standpoint of positivism: an objective element, namely States' general practice, and a subjective element, i.e. their *opinio juris sive necessitatis*. According to this 'two elements' theory, which was developed in particular by the ICJ, the general practice consists of a constant, widespread and virtually uniform State practice which, to satisfy the subjective element, shall have been born of a sense of legal obligation.

Although those two elements aim at formalising and rationalising this source of law, the customary process and the ascertainment of customary rules have in fact been characterised by a lack of formalism. This results from the complex interaction between the practices of States on the one hand, and between State practice and the practice of international courts and tribunals (ICTs) on the other hand, which both ground and shape CIL. As seen in this section and examined in particular in Chapter 5, all of this characterises CIL in international investment law and arbitration.

To appraise the role of CIL in this field of law, attention must be paid to its relevance as a source of law in and of itself, and to its interaction with other sources of international law.

2.1.2.1 The Relevance of Customary International Law

As explained in Chapter 1, CIL played a fundamental role with regard to the 'law of the protection of aliens abroad', from which the origin of international investment law and arbitration stems. Indeed, the first international law rules that protected foreign private persons from their host States had a customary nature. This is illustrated by the minimum standard of treatment.

Later on, CIL influenced States and policy-makers more generally when initiating and developing their IIA practice; it constituted a material source from which they drew. In that sense, some IIA provisions can be seen as a codification of CIL rules. The expropriation provision, and in particular the compensation requirement that forms part of the conditions of legality of expropriation, exemplifies this trend.

This 'treatification' process has led to CIL losing its supremacy in this field of law, with myriad treaties taking its place. Since then, foreign investors have sought first and foremost the protection granted by IIAs. In spite of this relegation, however, CIL has not been deprived of all relevance in international investment law and arbitration.

First, despite the impressive network of IIAs concluded over time, foreign investors may still at times need to rely on CIL, typically in those situations in which no IIA was concluded between their home State and the host State in which they invested.

Second, CIL also appears relevant as a material source with regard to those IIA provisions which – in one way or another – link a treaty rule to CIL. As examined in Chapter 5, this method is used particularly by States parties in drafting the fair and equitable treatment provision.

Third, CIL still plays an important role for those issues pertaining not to international investment law, but to wider issues of public international law which are relevant to investor–State arbitration – for instance, with respect to issues of State responsibility.

2.1.2.2 The Interplay between Customary International Law and Other Sources

a The Interplay between Customary International Law and Treaties

As discussed above, CIL has impacted and still impacts on IIAs. But another potential interplay between CIL and IIAs can be contemplated – that is whether IIAs can impact on CIL by leading either to the evolution of existing customary rules or to the creation of new ones. This facet is at times addressed by arbitration tribunals. For instance, in *Mondev International Ltd* v. *USA*, the Tribunal explained:

> [T]he vast number of bilateral and regional investment treaties (more than 2000 [footnote omitted]) almost uniformly provide for fair and equitable treatment of foreign investments, and largely provide for full security and protection of investments. Investment treaties run between North and South, and East and West, and between States in these spheres *inter se*. On a remarkably widespread basis, States have repeatedly obliged themselves to accord foreign investment such treatment. In the Tribunal's view, such a body of concordant practice will necessarily have influenced the content of rules governing the treatment of foreign investment in current international law. (2002, Award, para. 117)

In fact, this interplay raises complex theoretical issues in public international law, in particular whether, and if so, under which conditions, treaties can influence CIL.

Part of the answer to that question was provided by the ICJ in its 1969 Judgment in the *North Sea Continental Shelf* cases with respect to the equidistance principle contained in Article 6 of the 1958 Geneva Convention on the Continental Shelf. The Court stated:

> In so far as this contention is based on the view that Article 6 of the Convention has had the influence, and has produced the effect, described, it clearly involves treating that Article as a norm-creating provision which has constituted the foundation of, or has generated a rule which, while only conventional or contractual in its origin, has since passed into the general *corpus* of international law, and is now accepted as such by the *opinio juris*, so as to have become binding even for countries which have never, and do not, become parties to the Convention. There is no doubt that this process is a perfectly possible one and does from time to time occur: it constitutes indeed one of the recognized methods by which new rules of customary international law may be formed. At the same time this result is not lightly to be regarded as having been attained.
>
> It would in the first place be necessary that the provision concerned should, at all events potentially, be of a fundamentally norm-creating character such as

could be regarded as forming the basis of a general rule of law ... With respect to the other elements usually regarded as necessary before a conventional rule can be considered to have become a general rule of international law, it might be that, even without the passage of any considerable period of time, a very wide-spread and representative participation in the convention might suffice of itself, provided it included that of States whose interests were specially affected ... Although the passage of only a short period of time is not necessarily, or of itself, a bar to the formation of a new rule of customary international law on the basis of what was originally a purely conventional rule, an indispensable requirement would be that within the period in question, short though it might be, State practice, including that of States whose interests are specially affected, should have been both extensive and virtually uniform in the sense of the provision invoked; – and should moreover have occurred in such a way as to show a general recognition that a rule of law or legal obligation is involved. (paras. 71–74)

As it appears, three cumulative conditions must be met for a treaty provision to generate a CIL rule: (1) the provision must have a fundamentally norm-creating character; (2) there must be a very widespread and representative participation in the convention, including that of States whose interests are specially affected; and (3) there must be an extensive and virtually uniform State practice – including that of States whose interests are specially affected – supported by an *opinio juris* in conformity with the provision at hand.

As mentioned, these conditions were set out by the ICJ in relation to the interplay between a multilateral treaty – the Geneva Convention on the Continental Shelf – and CIL. In comparison, there is a key feature which differentiates international investment law from the situation contemplated by the Court in that case, namely the lack of a multilateral treaty with a global reach and, instead, the existence of a network of IIAs among which BITs are preeminent. This begs the question as to whether those conditions can be applied and satisfied in the context of the interplay between CIL and a network of treaties. This is of particular relevance with regard to the third condition laid out by the ICJ. Irrespective of the issue of its uniformity, State practice pertains largely to those BITs, which raises the issue of whether this practice can be seen as qualifying as a relevant State practice and as expressing States' *opinio juris*.

b The Interplay between Customary International Law and Arbitration Awards and Decisions

As mentioned above, the 'two elements' theory law is focused on States, meaning on their practice and their *opinio juris*. However, this focus does not prevent international courts and tribunals from taking judicial practice into consideration to ascertain the existence and content of CIL rules. Some tribunals, in particular in the field of international criminal law, have in fact gone one step further, tending instead in some decisions to confer a primacy to judicial practice.

Mutatis mutandis, this trend is also visible, to some extent, in investor–State arbitration. As discussed in particular in Chapter 5, there exists a diffuse tendency across arbitration practice to determine the content of CIL rules not in relation to the practice and *opinio juris* of States, but instead in relation to past arbitration awards and decisions. This amounts to a 'self-referential' practice adopted by some tribunals that do not focus on State practice, but rather on their own views and those expressed by past arbitration tribunals. From the perspective of the theory of sources of public international law, such a 'self-referential' practice does not merely lead to the replacement of State practice with arbitration practice, but tends more fundamentally to substitute CIL with *jurisprudence constante*, which is discussed in Section 2.2.1.

2.1.3 General Principles of Law Recognised by Civilised Nations

The GPLRCN have been conceived of from the end of the Second World War (WWII) onwards as those principles that are common to domestic legal systems worldwide and which can be transplanted into the international legal order.

This requirement of universality and of representativeness has not always been prevalent. Indeed, as highlighted by the reference to 'civilised' in Article 38 of the ICJ Statute, which derives directly from the Statute of the Permanent Court of International Justice (PCIJ), those principles were viewed in the first part of the twentieth century as those common to the States that considered themselves as being civilised, meaning mainly European States. As explained in Chapter 1, such a conception was due to the expansionist and imperialist mindset that governed the conduct of international affairs and international law at that time.

Since the decolonisation that followed the end of WWII, universality and representativeness have formed part of the essence of the general principles of law recognised by civilised nations. This holds true in public international law and in international investment law and arbitration in particular. On the other hand, they do raise practical and linguistic difficulties. Indeed, it can be seen from arbitration practice – and also the literature – that an enquiry into domestic laws is frequently limited to those materials that can be accessed and understood by States, foreign investors, arbitrators and scholars.

Regardless of these difficulties, it remains the case that this source of international law is hardly relied upon in investor–State arbitration. This does not come as a surprise inasmuch as this source is intended to avoid '*non liquet*', meaning situations in which a dispute cannot be settled because of a gap in the law; in such situations, this source is used to fill this gap by drawing on rules from domestic legal orders. Given the 'treatification' of international investment law and arbitration from the 1960s, those situations have become rare.

2.2 Subsidiary Sources

As evidenced by Article 38 of the ICJ Statute, subsidiary sources are considered in public international law as means that can be used for the determination of rules of law. Subsidiary sources are twofold: (1) the judicial decisions of mainly international courts and tribunals; and (2) in the words of the Statute, the 'teachings of the most highly qualified publicists of the various nations'. Each source is discussed in turn in this section in relation to international investment law and arbitration

2.2.1 Judicial Decisions

In public international law, judicial decisions cannot be resorted to as such, in particular by adjudicators, to settle a dispute. As mentioned above, they can only be used subsidiarily to determine the rules of law. In addition to this is the limited force given to the decisions of ICTs, in that they are only binding upon the parties to the disputes at hand. This means that there is no rule of binding precedent – also known as *stare decisis* – in public international law, and as such ICTs are bound neither by their own past decisions nor by the past decisions of any other ICT.

The role and status of judicial decisions in international investment law and arbitration, in particular arbitration awards, is de jure identical. They constitute a subsidiary source and they are only binding upon the parties to a particular dispute. This is illustrated by Article 53 of the ICSID Convention.

In practice, in particular due to the normative vagueness that has traditionally characterised many IIA provisions, disputing parties and arbitrators have very often referred to past awards and decisions rendered by investor–State arbitration tribunals in their reasoning to give a content and a meaning to those provisions. On the other hand, it is noteworthy that references to the judicial decisions of other ICTs have not been as frequent. When such decisions are alluded to, arbitration tribunals mainly refer to judgments of the PCIJ and of the ICJ, typically in relation to public international law issues such as the law of State responsibility, as well as to awards of the Iran–United States Claims Tribunal and judgments of the European Court of Human Rights, principally in connection with expropriation provisions within IIAs.

At the core of the systematic mention of past awards and decisions rendered by investor–State arbitration tribunals is the question of their concrete role and status, in particular whether they play only a subsidiary role, or whether they actually play a bigger role akin to a primary source. Interestingly, this question is often tackled by arbitrators, revealing many nuances and differences of opinion. This can be seen in the opinions adopted by the members of the Tribunal in *Burlington Resources Inc.* v. *Ecuador*:

> As stated in the Decision on Jurisdiction, the Tribunal considers that it is not
> bound by previous decisions. Nevertheless, the majority considers that it must

pay due regard to earlier decisions of international courts and tribunals. It believes that, subject to compelling contrary grounds, it has a duty to adopt solutions established in a series of consistent cases. It further believes that, subject to the specifics of a given treaty and of the circumstances of the actual case, it has a duty to seek to contribute to the harmonious development of investment law, and thereby to meet the legitimate expectations of the community of States and investors towards the certainty of the rule of law. Arbitrator Stern does not analyze the arbitrator's role in the same manner, as she considers it her duty to decide each case on its own merits, independently of any apparent jurisprudential trend. (2012, Decision on Liability, para. 187)

This statement evidences that some arbitrators do conceive of a series of consistent past arbitration awards or decisions, meaning *jurisprudences constantes*, as a source of law to be followed in the future by arbitration tribunals; this is subject to the specifics of the factual circumstances of each case and of the IIA at hand. It is also evident from this statement in *Burlington Resources Inc.* v. *Ecuador* that other arbitrators adopt the opposite point of view. Of course, this controversy raises legal issues pertaining in particular to the lack of binding precedent in investor–State arbitration as well as to its *ad hoc* nature. However, as evidenced by the words used by the arbitrators in that statement, in particular the reference to 'duty', it can be seen that this controversy also raises a deontological issue. Indeed, the role to be given to past arbitration awards and decisions depends to a large extent on one's own conception of the role and function of arbitrators.

2.2.2 Teaching of Publicists

The expression used in Article 38 of the ICJ Statute, i.e. 'teaching of the most highly qualified publicists of the various nations', may at first glance be confusing.

First of all, the reference made to 'teaching' may give the impression that only purely academic works produced by scholars, such as those published in law journals, are encompassed by this subsidiary source. It has in fact a larger scope than this. It is well accepted that this source also encompasses works that do not qualify as a 'teaching' *sensu stricto*, but which have a more practice-oriented nature, like the work of the International Law Commission of the United Nations.

By the same token, when put in relation to international investment law and arbitration more specifically, the reference to 'publicist' might lead to the conclusion that only the 'teachings' of public international lawyers are relevant with regard to this subsidiary source. This would exclude thereby the 'teaching' of, for instance, international commercial lawyers, which is yet important in this field of law. In this respect, there is of course a need to adjust the scope of this source from what was originally conceived at the time of the drafting of the PCIJ Statute in order to make it compatible with the specifics of international investment law and arbitration.

In reality, this source of law plays a limited role in practice. This is clear from the dearth of references made to scholarly works in arbitration awards. There are of course exceptions – for instance, the work of the International Bar Association with respect to dispute settlement matters.

2.3 Equity

As can be seen from Article 38 of the ICJ Statute, the recourse to equity to settle a dispute in public international law is subject to the agreement of the parties. This also applies to international investment law and arbitration; for instance, Article 42.3 of the ICSID Convention provides that tribunals have the power to decide a dispute '*ex aequo et bono*' only if the parties so agree. This requirement is explained by the fact that the settlement of a dispute *ex aequo et bono* entails that the rules of international law can be set aside, the settlement being based instead on considerations of justice drawn from the specifics of each case and the perceptions of the arbitrators.

Given the broad discretion that equity confers to adjudicators, it comes as no surprise that no party to any investor–State dispute has ever authorised – in the cases known – a tribunal to decide a dispute *ex aequo et bono*.

Equity *ex aequo et bono* cannot be confused with equity '*intra legem*', which has on the contrary been exercised by tribunals in deciding cases; this form of equity does not lead to the setting aside of the law, but rather requires acting within it. The reason for this exercise is the normative indeterminacy that has traditionally characterised some IIA provisions, typically the fair and equitable treatment standard, and the need to give concrete meaning and substance to these otherwise vague and nebulous provisions. This has led arbitration tribunals to strike a balance between investors' interests and public interests into guiding the application of these provisions and to take particularly into consideration the facts of each case.

2.4 Soft Law Instruments

Soft law is a broad category under public international law which encompasses all those instruments that are non-binding. A classic example of such instruments is provided by the non-binding resolutions adopted by international organisations, such as the General Assembly of the United Nations (UNGA). Due to its broad definition, this category can also be seen as encompassing practice-oriented works otherwise characterised as 'teaching of publicists'.

The field of international investment law and arbitration has been marked by the adoption of a number of notable soft law instruments, with regard to the rules pertaining to the treatment and protection of foreign investors as well as to investor–State arbitration.

As to the former, we can refer to the UNGA Resolutions – discussed in Chapter 1 – which were adopted in the context of the New International Economic Order promoted by newly independent States and developing States in the 1960s and 1970s. The 1992 World Bank Guidelines on the Treatment of Foreign Direct Investment also illustrate this category.

With regard to investor–State arbitration, many of the sets of arbitration rules used to govern proceedings can also be characterised as soft law instruments. They constitute sets of best practices that are proposed by institutions. Reference can be made for instance to the Arbitration Rules proposed by the Stockholm Chamber of Commerce, or the Rules of the United Nations Commission on International Trade Law (UNCITRAL). In this respect, it is worth recalling that the Rules governing ICSID Convention arbitration proceedings do not fall within that category, precisely because they are contained in a binding instrument, i.e. the ICSID Convention.

Part II

The Substantive Protection of Foreign Investments and Public Interests

3

Introduction to the Substantive Rules Protecting Foreign Investments and Public Interests

Introduction

Like Part II more generally, this chapter focuses on those rules contained in international investment agreements (IIAs), and in particular on those agreements concluded in the 2010s. This focus allows for not only a contemporary view on the content of IIAs, but also offers a comprehensive overview of the substantive rules that form part of treaty practice. Indeed, the rules contained in the IIAs concluded over the second half of the twentieth century focused on the substantive protection and treatment of foreign investments and investors. Although these rules have evolved in the IIAs concluded since that time, they have not disappeared. In addition, new rules have emerged in recent treaty practice that aim at the protection of public interests. This chapter introduces the rules that pertain to these objects, providing an explanation of the specific rationale for each rule as well as their main features. A more detailed analysis of the most important rules and the issues they raise is provided in the subsequent chapters.

3.1 Rules Pertaining to the Protection and Treatment of Foreign Investors and Investments

Preliminary Remarks

The IIA rules pertaining to the protection and treatment of foreign investors and their investments in host States' territory cover various situations as well as various stages of foreign direct investment (FDI) operations. In this respect, a distinction can be made between these rules on the basis of whether they address *ex ante* the promotion, facilitation, admission and establishment of investments, or *ex post* the protection and treatment of investors and investments. As to the latter, one can also highlight those rules which, in light of arbitration practice, appear to be the most important or at least the most frequently relied upon by foreign investors.

Prior to introducing all these categories, it is worth emphasising the specificity of the rule on subrogation within IIAs. A good example of this rule is found in Article 13 of the 2018 Argentina–Japan IIA:

If a Contracting Party or its designated agency makes a payment to an investor of that Contracting Party under a guarantee, a contract of insurance or another form of indemnity that it has entered into with respect to an investment of such investor in the Area of the other Contracting Party, the latter Contracting Party shall recognise the subrogation or transfer of any rights the investor would have possessed under this Agreement with respect to such investment but for the subrogation, and the investor shall be precluded from pursuing these rights to the extent of the subrogation.

Such a rule is to be understood in connection with the insurances against political risks granted by home States to their investors investing abroad. The overall package 'insurance and subrogation' aims ultimately at protecting foreign investors and their investments; yet, subrogation as such protects home States' interests as it makes it a treaty obligation for host States to recognise the subrogation or transfer of rights from the investors to their home States. All of this is examined in detail in Chapter 9.

3.1.1 Promotion, Facilitation, Admission and Establishment

3.1.1.1 Promotion and Facilitation

As illustrated by the title and the preamble of many IIAs, the promotion of foreign investments is an objective assigned to those agreements. In many treaties, one finds also a specific provision dealing with promotion whereby States parties commit to encouraging investments in their relations *inter se*. As analysed in Chapter 4, agreements differ with regard to the nature of the obligation they place upon States and their exact content. A few IIAs refer in a similar way to the facilitation of investments.

3.1.1.2 Admission and Establishment

Under public international law, States have no obligation to open their borders to foreign persons, goods or capital. As for international investment law, IIA rules pertaining to admission and establishment specify the extent to which and the modalities according to which the investors of each contracting State and their investments are to be accepted in the territory of the other contracting State(s). None of these rules confers an absolute right in this respect; as discussed in Chapter 4, those rules differ in fact as to the degree of discretion that they leave to States parties on those matters.

3.1.2 Protection

3.1.2.1 Main Rules

The main IIA rules and standards protecting the investors of each contracting State and their investments in the territory of the other contracting State(s) are usually subdivided into two categories: the standards of treatment and the prohibition of illegal expropriation and nationalisation.

a Standards of Treatment

The main standards of treatment are fourfold. They consist of (1) fair and equitable treatment (FET); (2) full protection and security (FPS); (3) the prohibition of negative differentiations; and (4) umbrella clauses.

i Fair and Equitable Treatment   Among the standards of treatment, the FET standard has the broadest scope; it is composed of a set of sub-standards that cover various situations harmful to foreign investors and their investments. They consist of, for instance, the prohibition of denial of justice as well as the prohibition of arbitrary and discriminatory treatment. With respect to arbitrary and discriminatory treatment, it is worth noting that a number of IIAs contain a specific treatment standard that overlaps with the FET standard. Regardless of whether or not it is contained in the same Article as the FET standard, those IIAs provide *mutatis mutandis*: 'Neither Contracting Party shall in any way impair the management, maintenance, use, enjoyment, extension, or disposal of such investments by unreasonable or discriminatory measures' (2018 Turkey–Cambodia IIA, Article 2.2).

Many of these sub-standards that form part of the FET standard have initially been largely shaped by arbitration tribunals, which were faced with the task of clarifying the normative content of this standard due to its vague drafting. On the other hand, some agreements concluded in the 2010s provide greater detail as to the content of the FET standard, thereby 'codifying' to a large extent arbitration practice, or part of it. As examined in Chapter 5, many of the IIAs concluded over that period also bring some clarification as to the interplay between the FET standard and the customary law minimum standard of treatment.

ii Full Protection and Security   The FPS standard has formed part of the protection granted to foreign persons for a long time, imposing an obligation of due diligence upon host States with regard to the treatment to be granted to those persons and their properties. The exact scope of the protection conferred by this standard incorporated in IIAs has been the subject of debate among arbitration tribunals, in particular as to whether it covers legal security and protection against the conduct of State organs, in addition to the well-accepted coverage of physical security and protection against private persons' conduct. As analysed in Chapter 5, a number of IIAs concluded in the 2010s provide some clarification on this point with a view towards circumscribing the scope of the protection afforded by that standard.

iii National Treatment and Most-Favoured-Nation Treatment   The standards of national treatment and most-favoured-nation treatment (MFNT) are often said to be 'relative standards'. This means that, rather than providing an absolute standard of protection to foreign investors and their investments, they instead confer on them only the right not to suffer negative differentiations *vis-à-vis* the nationals of host States and other foreign investors, respectively. In other words, they confer the right on foreign investors to receive treatment which is no less favourable than that received by these groups. As such, the treatment received by domestic investors constitutes the benchmark by which the national treatment standard is applied, in the same way as the treatment received by other foreign investors constitutes the benchmark for the application of the MFNT standard.

Another source of relativity consists of the reference made in most IIAs to 'in like circumstances' in relation to the national treatment standard and the MFNT standard. This is well illustrated by the national treatment provision of the 2017 Israel–Japan IIA which reads as follows: 'Each Contracting Party shall in its Territory accord to investors of the other Contracting Party and to their investments treatment no less favorable than the treatment it accords in like circumstances to its own investors and to their investments with respect to investment activities' (Article 2). The result of this reference is that these standards operate only when the investors of a home State party can be said to be in circumstances 'alike' to those in which the nationals of the host State party or other foreign investors are, respectively.

In addition, it can be noted that treaty practice displays an increasing incorporation of limitations into IIAs which have the effect of restricting the scope of application of both standards with regard to specific situations and matters.

iv Umbrella Clauses   From the perspective of public international law, there exists a clear-cut distinction between the international legal order and domestic legal orders. This helps to explain why, for instance, domestic law is considered and treated as a matter of fact by international courts and tribunals. Another consequence of this distinction which is of much interest for foreign investors relates to the fact that the violation by a host State of a commitment undertaken in its domestic legal order – typically a contractual commitment – does not entail, as such, a violation of international law.

To remedy this situation, the parties to some IIAs have built on a proposal formulated in the 1950s by Lauterpacht to the Anglo-Iranian Oil Company with respect to the settlement of the Iranian oil nationalisation disputes. In doing so, these States parties incorporated into their agreements a provision that brings commitments made by host States towards investors under their legal order under the treaty 'umbrella', with the result that a violation of those commitments can entail State responsibility. This explains why those provisions are usually referred to as 'umbrella clauses'.

b   Prohibition of Illegal Expropriation and Nationalisation

Expropriation and nationalisation are sovereign prerogatives of States. For that reason, they have never been prohibited in public international law. Instead, and as explained in Chapter 1, they have been subject to conditions of legality, in particular the payment of prompt, adequate and effective compensation. All IIAs follow the same approach in this regard, in making the legality of nationalisation and expropriation, both direct or indirect, subject to the fulfilment of a set of conditions, mainly a public interest objective, non-discrimination, the respect of due process, and the payment of compensation. As to the latter, each IIA has traditionally set out further details, in particular the applicable standard of compensation.

As explained in Chapter 6, the category of indirect expropriation has traditionally been left unspecified in IIAs, leading to fierce debates in arbitration practice as to the criteria to be used in determining whether a measure constitutes an indirect expropriation. Closely connected to this debate is the distinction between expropriatory and regulatory measures, which has also been the subject of much debate, notably in relation to whether compensation is due in a given factual situation. As examined in Chapter 6, a great number of agreements concluded in the 2010s have addressed these issues by providing criteria for identifying instances of indirect expropriation and by distinguishing between expropriatory and regulatory measures.

3.1.2.2 Other Rules

In addition to the main rules and standards discussed above, IIAs contain other rules that aim at the protection of foreign investors and investments. This subsection introduces those rules that are most frequently, though not always, incorporated into IIAs. More precisely, and in line with the approach explained in the introduction, this subsection sheds light on the specific rationale and the main features of each of them without detailing the nuances and differences displayed by treaty practice.

a   Prohibition of Performance and Managerial Requirements

When investing in the territory of host States, foreign investors contribute to stimulating economic development as well as the job market. In order to take the best advantage of the presence of these investors, host States may be tempted to impose performance requirements, for instance by requiring investors to achieve a given level of domestic content, or a certain transfer of technology. Such conduct can dissuade foreign investors from investing and ultimately impact negatively the host States' economic development.

For these reasons, some States have prohibited such performance requirements in their IIAs. Even though this treaty practice, notably initiated by the USA, was not widespread at the outset, it began to spread in the 2010s, in particular within the investment chapter of free trade agreements (FTAs). This can be seen, for example, in Article 8.5 of the 2016 Comprehensive Economic and Trade Agreement (CETA):

1. A Party shall not impose, or enforce the following requirements, or enforce a commitment or undertaking, in connection with the establishment, acquisition, expansion, conduct, operation, and management of any investments in its territory to:
   (a) export a given level or percentage of a good or service;
   (b) achieve a given level or percentage of domestic content;
   (c) purchase, use or accord a preference to a good produced or service provided in its territory, or to purchase a good or service from natural persons or enterprises in its territory;
   (d) relate the volume or value of imports to the volume or value of exports or to the amount of foreign exchange inflows associated with that investment;
   (e) restrict sales of a good or service in its territory that the investment produces or provides by relating those sales to the volume or value of its exports or foreign exchange earnings;
   (f) transfer technology, a production process or other proprietary knowledge to a natural person or enterprise in its territory; or
   (g) supply exclusively from the territory of the Party a good produced or a service provided by the investment to a specific regional or world market.

2. A Party shall not condition the receipt or continued receipt of an advantage, in connection with the establishment, acquisition, expansion, management, conduct or operation of any investments in its territory, on compliance with any of the following requirements:
   (a) to achieve a given level or percentage of domestic content;
   (b) to purchase, use or accord a preference to a good produced in its territory, or to purchase a good from a producer in its territory;
   (c) to relate the volume or value of imports to the volume or value of exports or to the amount of foreign exchange inflows associated with that investment; or
   (d) to restrict sales of a good or service in its territory that the investment produces or provides by relating those sales to the volume or value of its exports or foreign exchange earnings.

3. Paragraph 2 does not prevent a Party from conditioning the receipt or continued receipt of an advantage, in connection with an investment in its territory, on compliance with a requirement to locate production, provide a service, train or employ workers, construct or expand particular facilities, or carry out research and development in its territory.

4. Subparagraph 1(f) does not apply if the requirement is imposed or the commitment or undertaking is enforced by a court, administrative tribunal or competition authority to remedy a violation of competition laws.

5. The provisions of:
   (a) subparagraphs 1(a), (b) and (c), and 2(a) and (b), do not apply to qualification requirements for a good or service with respect to participation in export promotion and foreign aid programs;

(b) this Article does not apply to procurement by a Party of a good or service purchased for governmental purposes and not with a view to commercial resale or with a view to use in the supply of a good or service for commercial sale, whether or not that procurement is 'covered procurement' within the meaning of Article 19.2 (Scope and coverage).

6. For greater certainty, subparagraphs 2(a) and (b) do not apply to requirements imposed by an importing Party relating to the content of a good necessary to qualify for preferential tariffs or preferential quotas.

7. This Article is without prejudice to World Trade Organization commitments of a Party.

In addition to the prohibition of performance requirements, treaty practice displays an additional prohibition concerning management requirements. The 2017 Israel–Japan IIA exemplifies this prohibition: 'Neither Contracting Party may require that an enterprise of that Contracting Party that is an investment of an investor of the other Contracting Party appoint to senior management positions, or as senior executives, a natural person of any particular nationality' (Article 7.1). Such a prohibition is important for foreign investors as it ensures in particular that host States cannot oblige them to appoint one of their nationals to a certain senior position.

In spite of the incorporation of this prohibition in a number of agreements, it is worth noting that many IIAs adopt a different approach towards the composition of boards of directors. For instance, Article 9.2 of the 2005 USA–Uruguay IIA provides: 'A Party may require that a majority of the board of directors, or any committee thereof, of an enterprise of that Party that is a covered investment, be of a particular nationality, or resident in the territory of the Party, provided that the requirement does not materially impair the ability of the investor to exercise control over its investment.'

b Transparency

Transparency has gained an increasing societal and legal importance over the past few decades. This holds true in public international law and in international investment law and arbitration in particular. In relation to the latter, transparency has impacted many aspects of this field of law as well as many dimensions of the relations between host States and foreign investors. As examined in Chapter 11, this is true in particular in investor–State arbitration. Another illustration of this impact can be seen in relation to the FET standard, which has been conceived of as containing a transparency substandard. More specifically, some IIAs contain a dedicated provision placing obligations of transparency on host States, typically the obligation to make available to interested persons the measures they adopt in relation to matters covered by the agreements. This practice is well illustrated by Article 12 of the 2015 Canada–Burkina Faso IIA:

1. The Parties shall progressively endeavour to improve the transparency of their legislative, regulatory, administrative, and judicial processes in compliance with their respective domestic acts and regulations.
2. Each Party shall ensure that its laws, regulations, procedures, and administrative rulings of general application respecting a matter covered by this Agreement are promptly published or otherwise made available in such a manner as to enable interested persons and the other Party to become acquainted with them.
3. To the extent possible, each Party shall:
    1. publish in advance any measure referred to in paragraph 2 that it proposes to adopt; and
    2. provide interested persons and the other Party a reasonable opportunity to comment on that proposed measure.
4. Upon request by a Party, the other Party shall provide information on a measure that may have an impact on a covered investment.

c Reparation of Losses in Armed Conflict Situations and Internal Disorders

History teaches us that foreign investment operations can be conducted in countries where conflicts break out. This is well exemplified by the events that took place in Libya in the course of the 2010s. This has led States to incorporate into their IIAs a specific provision dealing with reparation for the losses suffered by foreign investors in such situations.

Those provisions do not provide for a general right of reparation. As a common denominator, they generally set a relative standard, granting foreign investors the right to a treatment which is no less favourable than that granted to national investors or to other foreign investors. Some agreements go one step further by setting an absolute standard that applies in certain specific circumstances, typically when the losses result from the requisition of investors' property by the forces of the host State. The 2014 Korea–Kenya IIA illustrates this broader approach:

1. Investors of one Contracting Party, whose investments suffer losses owing to war or other armed conflict, a state of national emergency, revolt, insurrection, riot or other similar situation in the territory of the other Contracting Party, shall be accorded by the latter Contracting Party, as regards restitution, indemnification, compensation or other forms of settlement, treatment no less favourable than that which the latter Contracting Party accords to its own investors or to investors of any third State.
2. Without prejudice to paragraph 1 of this Article, investors of one Contracting Party who, in any situations referred to in that paragraph, suffer losses in the territory of the other Contracting Party resulting from: (a) requisitioning of their property by the latter Contracting Party's forces or authorities; or (b) destruction of their property by the latter Contracting Party's forces or authorities which was not caused in combat action or was not required by the necessity of the situation, shall be accorded by the latter Contracting Party

restitution, compensation or both. Such compensation shall be prompt, effective and full and in accordance with Article 4 from the date of requisitioning or destruction until the date of actual payment. (Article 5)

d   Repatriation and Transfer

As discussed in Chapter 14, the expectation to make a profit is sometimes considered as an inherent characteristic of an investment. Irrespective of this issue, there is no doubt that foreign investors do expect that their investments will generate a profit. Such a profit would be worthless if they could not transfer it freely in their home State or anywhere else. More generally, foreign investors expect to make all sorts of transfers out of the territory of host States, such as transferring the proceeds of the sale or liquidation of their investments.

These economic expectations and necessities have given rise to the provision of a right to repatriation and transfer in IIAs. Aside from the nuances and differences that they display, virtually all of them confer – as a matter of principle – such a right to foreign investors. This principle can be subject to certain limitations, which are examined further in Chapter 7. All of this is exemplified by Article 9.9 of the 2018 Comprehensive and Progressive Agreement for Trans-Pacific Partnership:

1. Each Party shall permit all transfers relating to a covered investment to be made freely and without delay into and out of its territory. Such transfers include:
   (a) contributions to capital;[footnote omitted]
   (b) profits, dividends, interest, capital gains, royalty payments, management fees, technical assistance fees and other fees;
   (c) proceeds from the sale of all or any part of the covered investment or from the partial or complete liquidation of the covered investment;
   (d) payments made under a contract, including a loan agreement;
   (e) payments made pursuant to Article 9.7 (Treatment in Case of Armed Conflict or Civil Strife) and Article 9.8 (Expropriation and Compensation); and
   (f) payments arising out of a dispute.
2. Each Party shall permit transfers relating to a covered investment to be made in a freely usable currency at the market rate of exchange prevailing at the time of transfer.
3. Each Party shall permit returns in kind relating to a covered investment to be made as authorised or specified in a written agreement between the Party and a covered investment or an investor of another Party.
4. Notwithstanding paragraphs 1, 2 and 3, a Party may prevent or delay a transfer through the equitable, non-discriminatory and good faith application of its laws [footnote omitted] relating to:
   (a) bankruptcy, insolvency or the protection of the rights of creditors;

    (b) issuing, trading or dealing in securities, futures, options or derivatives;

    (c) criminal or penal offences;

    (d) financial reporting or record keeping of transfers when necessary to assist law enforcement or financial regulatory authorities; or

    (e) ensuring compliance with orders or judgments in judicial or administrative proceedings.

5. Notwithstanding paragraph 3, a Party may restrict transfers of returns in kind in circumstances where it could otherwise restrict such transfers under this Agreement, including as set out in paragraph 4.

e   Better Treatment Conferred by Another Instrument

A number of IIAs are considered by States parties as a 'floor' and not as a 'ceiling' with regard to the protection and treatment to be granted to their respective investors and their investments. Such agreements envisage the possibility that they may be entitled to receive better treatment under another instrument and provide that, in such a case, this treatment shall apply to them. For instance, Article 10.1 of the 2014 Belarus–Cambodia IIA provides:

> If the provisions of law of either Contracting Party or obligations under international law, existing at present or established hereafter between the Contracting Parties in addition to this Agreement, contain a regulation, whether general or specific, entitling investments made by investors of the other Contracting Party to a treatment more favourable than is provided by this Agreement, such provisions shall, to the extent that they are more favourable to the investor, prevail over this Agreement.

3.2 Rules Pertaining to the Protection of Public Interests

Preliminary Remarks

In particular during the 2010s, local populations, domestic policy-makers and non-governmental organisations (NGOs) have been very critical of international investment law and arbitration, denouncing its negative impact on host States' right to regulate and, more generally, the lack of attention paid in treaty and arbitration practices to public interests. These criticisms have greatly contributed to bringing about significant changes in treaty practice. In addition to the evolution of the rules governing the settlement of investor–State disputes analysed in Part III, as well as the more frequent reference made to public interest considerations in the preamble of many IIAs, this evolution has translated into the incorporation of a series of new rules geared towards the respect and protection of public interests. These rules can be classified into two main categories: (1) the rules limiting the protection afforded to investors and their investments; and (2) those placing obligations upon States and investors to respect and protect public interests. These two categories are analysed in

Chapters 7 and 8, respectively; the present subsection introduces the main rules which form part of these two categories.

3.2.1 Public Interest Limitations on Foreign Investors' Protection

Preliminary Remarks

In early treaty practice, limitations on the protection afforded to foreign investors were rare in IIAs. Such limitations concerned typically the MFNT provision, in relation to more favourable treatment conferred by virtue of custom unions. Since then, limitations have increasingly been incorporated into IIAs, particularly during the 2010s. In addition to the above-mentioned criticism, this evolution has also certainly been triggered by the changing situation and dynamic between developing States and developed States. As explained in Chapter 1, traditionally, developing States were almost exclusively host States while developed States were home States. However, the multi-lateralisation of the flow of FDI – and the consequent de jure bilateralisation of BITs concluded between developing and developed States – as well as the conclusion of IIAs between developing States themselves and developed States themselves, have blurred this clear-cut allocation of roles. Notably, this has resulted in developed States taking on also the role of host States and, as a result, appearing as defendants in arbitration proceedings.

All of this has contributed to the convergence of the interests of developing States and developed States as well as to the alignment of their IIA policies, which are no longer radically driven by their traditional respective statuses as host States and home States. In particular, this evolution has placed all these States in a 'catch-22' situation. In their capacity as home State, they seek the greatest possible protection and treatment for their investors, while also seeking to shield as far as possible their sovereign prerogatives and public interests in their capacity as host State. This situation has played a significant role in the progressive incorporation of limitations into IIAs, restricting the protection granted to foreign investors in order to better protect States' prerogatives and public interests. Interestingly, such limitations may in some agreements apply to just one State party, or to a group thereof; this is telling about how each State deals with this 'catch-22' situation they are all in.

Given the variety of interests driving these limitations, their content varies widely. Some have been included as a reaction to certain issues that have been at stake in arbitration practice, such as public debts, or more generally the right to regulate. Others pertain to interests that are seen as crucial by specific States, such as land.

Those limitations can also be distinguished on the basis of their scope of application in that some apply to the entire IIA while others are confined to specific provisions. The main limitations that form part of these two categories are introduced in this subsection; they are all analysed in Chapter 7.

3.2.1.1 Limitations Applicable to IIAs

There are many examples of limitations on the protection of foreign investors and investments that apply to IIAs as a whole. Some of these have a very specific focus, pertaining to matters such as taxation or public debts. Others encompass a larger set of situations and therefore restrict to a greater extent the protection conferred on investors by IIAs. This is the case, for example, with regard to limitations that aim to protect the right of States to regulate, as well as those limitations known as 'general exceptions' and 'security exceptions'. These three main types of limitations are introduced in the following subsections.

a   Right to Regulate

The right to regulate is a sovereign prerogative of States under public international law. Only States themselves can place limits on this right, typically via treaty obligations. In this respect, the IIAs that have traditionally been concluded and the way they have been applied by arbitration tribunals have been criticised for granting an excessively high standard of protection to investors and their investments, infringing thereby this right to regulate for the benefit of public interests such as the environment or public health. This has led States parties to incorporate limitations into their IIAs in order to safeguard this right, particularly in those IIAs concluded in the 2010s. While these limitations differ somewhat, in particular as regards the conditions attached thereto, they all provide *mutatis mutandis* that measures enacted to protect a public interest shall not be considered as being prohibited by or in breach of the agreements.

b   General Exceptions

While the details of the general exceptions clauses incorporated within IIAs will be analysed in Chapter 7, it is worth noting in this introductory chapter that such clauses all derive directly from Article XX of the 1947 General Agreement on Tariffs and Trade (GATT), which was incorporated into the 1994 GATT at the time of the establishment of the World Trade Organization (WTO). For the purpose of this introduction, it is therefore worth referring to this 'founding provision' in full:

> Subject to the requirement that such measures are not applied in a manner which would constitute a means of arbitrary or unjustifiable discrimination between countries where the same conditions prevail, or a disguised restriction on international trade, nothing in this Agreement shall be construed to prevent the adoption or enforcement by any contracting party of measures:
>
> (a) necessary to protect public morals;
> (b) necessary to protect human, animal or plant life or health;
> (c) relating to the importations or exportations of gold or silver;
> (d) necessary to secure compliance with laws or regulations which are not inconsistent with the provisions of this Agreement, including those relating to customs enforcement, the enforcement of monopolies operated under

paragraph 4 of Article II and Article XVII, the protection of patents, trade marks and copyrights, and the prevention of deceptive practices;

(e) relating to the products of prison labour;

(f) imposed for the protection of national treasures of artistic, historic or archaeological value;

(g) relating to the conservation of exhaustible natural resources if such measures are made effective in conjunction with restrictions on domestic production or consumption;

(h) undertaken in pursuance of obligations under any intergovernmental commodity agreement which conforms to criteria submitted to the CONTRACTING PARTIES and not disapproved by them or which is itself so submitted and not so disapproved;

(i) involving restrictions on exports of domestic materials necessary to ensure essential quantities of such materials to a domestic processing industry during periods when the domestic price of such materials is held below the world price as part of a governmental stabilization plan; Provided that such restrictions shall not operate to increase the exports of or the protection afforded to such domestic industry, and shall not depart from the provisions of this Agreement relating to non-discrimination;

(j) essential to the acquisition or distribution of products in general or local short supply; Provided that any such measures shall be consistent with the principle that all contracting parties are entitled to an equitable share of the international supply of such products, and that any such measures, which are inconsistent with the other provisions of the Agreement shall be discontinued as soon as the conditions giving rise to them have ceased to exist. The CONTRACTING PARTIES shall review the need for this sub-paragraph not later than 30 June 1960.

In a way similar to this Article, the general exceptions clause within IIAs typically provides that the agreements shall not be construed as preventing host States from adopting measures relating in particular to the protection of human, animal or plant life or health, the protection of the environment and the conservation of exhaustible natural resources. In this regard, it can be noted that this clause overlaps with the right to regulate limitation introduced above.

c   Security Exceptions

Similar to the general exceptions clauses, those IIA clauses often labelled 'security exceptions' have their origin in the 1947 GATT. Given this origin, it is worth introducing security exceptions clauses by quoting in full Article XXI GATT:

Nothing in this Agreement shall be construed

(a) to require any contracting party to furnish any information the disclosure of which it considers contrary to its essential security interests; or

(b) to prevent any contracting party from taking any action which it considers necessary for the protection of its essential security interests
   (i) relating to fissionable materials or the materials from which they are derived;
   (ii) relating to the traffic in arms, ammunition and implements of war and to such traffic in other goods and materials as is carried on directly or indirectly for the purpose of supplying a military establishment;
   (iii) taken in time of war or other emergency in international relations; or
(c) to prevent any contracting party from taking any action in pursuance of its obligations under the United Nations Charter for the maintenance of international peace and security.

As with Article XXI GATT, the security exceptions clause found within IIAs generally covers situations in which host States shall not be considered as being prevented from, or required to adopt, specific measures under the agreements. Those situations/measures are usually threefold: (1) no requirement to disclose information contrary to essential security interests; (2) no prevention from taking action necessary for the protection of essential security interests; and (3) no prevention from taking action pursuant to obligations with respect to the maintenance of international peace and security.

3.2.1.2 Limitations Applicable to Specific IIA Provisions

Treaty practice in the 2010s has displayed a proliferation of limitations applicable to the protection granted to foreign investors by specific IIA provisions. Those limitations are very diverse, reflecting the multiplicity of policy interests driving States' treaty practice. In this respect, it is worth noting also that in some IIAs those limitations do not apply to all States parties. This diversity makes it impossible to provide a full picture of those limitations. That being said, main trends emerge from practice, with the most frequent limitations concerning (1) expropriation; (2) the national treatment and the MFNT standards; (3) repatriation and transfer; and (4) performance requirements.

a   Expropriation

We have seen above States incorporating into their IIAs a limitation that aims to protect their right to regulate. Following the same rationale, States have also attached a specific limitation to the protection conferred on foreign investors under the expropriation provision. The incorporation of such a specific limitation can be explained by the fact that the debate surrounding the right of host States to regulate has mainly focused on indirect expropriation and on the difference between expropriatory and regulatory measures. In a way similar to the 2004 US BIT Model that initiated this practice, most of the IIAs that contain this specific limitation provide *mutatis mutandis* that non-discriminatory measures that are designed and applied in such a way as to protect a public interest do not constitute an indirect expropriation. As examined in Chapter 6, most of those IIAs place 'a limitation on this limitation' as regards the severity of the impact of State measures on investments.

b National Treatment and Most-Favoured-Nation Treatment

The limitations applicable to the national treatment and MFNT standards illustrate very well the diversity of the specific limitations that can be found in IIAs. A typical limitation concerning the national treatment standard applies to cross-border capital transactions, where the temporary adoption or maintenance by host States of non-conforming measures is permitted, in particular in the event of serious difficulties with regard to balance of payments and external finance, or a threat thereof. The limitations on the MFNT standard cover a broad range of matters as diverse as taxation, subsidies, aviation, fisheries, or maritime matters.

c Repatriation and Transfer

As mentioned above, IIAs confer a right of repatriation and transfer on foreign investors. Treaty practice displays two main types of limitations concerning this right: one concerning the non-discriminatory and good-faith application of domestic law, and another relating to the adoption of temporary safeguard measures in situations of extreme economic and monetary difficulties.

The first type is applicable in at least three sets of situations: (1) bankruptcy, insolvency or protection of the rights of creditors; (2) criminal or penal offences; and (3) compliance with orders or judgments in legal or administrative proceedings relating to investment. In those situations notably, host States can by and large restrict transfers through the equitable, non-discriminatory, and good-faith application of their laws and regulations. The second type of limitations that entitles those States to adopt safeguard measures restricting transfer in situations of extreme economic and monetary difficulties encompasses usually two main types of situations: (1) serious difficulties with regard to balance of payments and external finance, or a threat thereof; and (2) exceptional circumstances in which movements of capital cause or threaten to cause serious difficulties for macroeconomic management, notably monetary and exchange rate policies. The main condition attached to this limitation is that such safeguard measures must be temporary.

d Performance Requirements

As explained above, IIAs prohibit performance requirements. However, this is often also subject to certain limitations in treaty practice. Again, the range of issues concerned is very broad and diverse, covering for instance intellectual property rights, agricultural lands or technology, depending on the IIA at hand.

3.2.2 Obligations to Respect and Protect Public Interests

Preliminary Remarks

Similar to the limitations introduced above, this second aspect of the evolution of treaty practice is to be seen in the general context of the criticism formulated against international investment law and arbitration as to the lack of consideration paid to public interests. More specifically, however, it can be said to derive from two societal trends. The first – which comes as a reaction to a traditional inner feature of IIAs – consists of criticism as regards the absence of obligations binding upon foreign investors and aiming at the protection of public interests from harmful investment operations. The second trend is not explained by the inner feature of international investment law; it relates more generally to the increasing importance given to sustainable development and human rights in public international law.

As a result of these two phenomena, one has witnessed, in particular in the 2010s, the development in IIA practice of a series of obligations intended to ensure the respect and protection of public interests. This development has been a progressive one, and the relevant IIA provisions are often characterised by their soft law language. Nonetheless, it remains that this constitutes a remarkable evolution as compared to the traditional features of IIAs. It is worth highlighting also that this development leads to the possibility of IIAs becoming tools to contribute to the better enforcement of international law, notably human rights law, and to the 'horizontalisation' of human rights. All this will be discussed in Chapter 8; however, as a first step, the present subsection introduces these obligations by distinguishing between the obligations that are binding upon States and those that are binding upon foreign investors.

3.2.2.1 Obligations upon States

Preliminary Remarks

Private persons, be they natural or legal persons, have traditionally had no obligations under public international law, in particular under international human rights law. This situation has been evolving slowly since the Second World War (WWII), especially in the field of international criminal law. This general feature of public international law, together with the reluctance displayed by developed States in the 1970s to impose binding obligations upon their enterprises, explains the traditional absence of investors' obligations in IIAs. As introduced below and examined in detail in Chapter 8, some IIAs concluded in the 2010s evidence a slow but undeniable evolution of treaty practice in this respect. In parallel to this evolution, another strategy to regulate foreign investors' conduct has been to impose obligations upon States as regards the conduct of these investors. These obligations can be distinguished from the States' obligations which pertain to the conduct of States themselves.

a   Obligations Pertaining to Investors' Conduct

For the purpose of this discussion, States' obligations pertaining to the conduct of foreign investors can be divided into two categories depending on whether they address investors' past or future conduct.

The first category, which has a 'forward-looking' dimension, relates typically to 'corporate social responsibility'; those obligations aim at leading investors to conduct their activities in a way that takes into account their societal and natural environment. As seen below, a few IIAs place those obligations directly upon investors themselves. However, mainstream treaty practice places the obligation on IIA States parties, the objective being that they encourage their enterprises to incorporate into their internal policies and practices internationally recognised standards, guidelines and principles of corporate social responsibility.

Those States' obligations that have a 'backward-looking' dimension aim mainly at imposing on States that they ensure that investors' conduct that is harmful to public interests is redressed or repressed. Such an approach, which is scarce in treaty practice, is well illustrated by the 2016 Morocco–Nigeria IIA, which is analysed in Chapter 8.

b   Obligations Pertaining to States' Conduct

With a view to making the examination clearer, the IIA obligations forming part of this category can be divided into two groups: one group that aims – 'positively'– at ensuring that States protect public interests and another that seeks – 'negatively' – to avoid the lowering of the protection afforded to those interests.

The first group of obligations typically aim at the protection of the environment, labour conditions and human rights. Rather than being set out in the abstract, this objective is typically attached to the international obligations binding upon States and/or their respective situations and capacities. This can be seen from Article 15.5 and 6 of the 2016 Morocco–Nigeria IIA, which is intended to ensure that States parties protect public interests and respect their obligations thereto. The relevant part provides:

> Each Party shall ensure that its laws and regulations provide for high levels of labour and human rights protection appropriate to its economic and social situation, and shall strive to continue to improve these law and regulations.
>
> All parties shall ensure that their laws, policies and actions are consistent with the international human rights agreements to which they are a party.

The second group of obligations prohibit host States from lowering the protection afforded to public interests in order to encourage the establishment, acquisition, expansion or retention of investments. These obligations aim usually at the protection of the environment and labour conditions. The rationale and objective of such a practice are illustrated by Article 10.1 of the 2016 Slovakia–Iran IIA:

The Contracting Parties recognize that it is inappropriate to encourage invest-ment by relaxing labor, public health, safety or environmental measures. They shall not waive or otherwise derogate from, or offer to waive or otherwise derogate from, such measures as an encouragement for the establishment, acquisition, expansion or retention in their territories, of an investment.

3.2.2.2 Obligations upon Foreign Investors

Preliminary Remarks

As examined in Chapter 14, a number of IIAs include within the definition of an investment a legality requirement that entails that assets shall be acquired in conformity with the law, typically with the domestic law of the host State. Such a requirement impacts notably on the jurisdiction of arbitration tribunals, the failure to comply with this requirement having the potential to lead tribunals to decline jurisdiction. In this respect, it is worth noting that mainstream arbitration practice considers that compliance with domestic law is inherent to the definition of an investment and shall be treated as such even when this is not expressly provided in the IIA at hand.

The requirement to comply with the law is provided in a few IIAs with regard also to the operation and management of investments. Treaty practice also displays the incorporation in some IIAs of obligations pertaining to corporate social responsibility. These two types of obligations constitute the main obligations placed on foreign investors in the IIAs that have been concluded mainly in the 2010s.

a   Compliance with the Law

The obligations placed upon foreign investors within a few IIAs to comply with the law in the management and operation of their investments can, for the purposes of this study, be distinguished based on whether they are attached to domestic law or international law.

The obligation to comply with domestic law is well illustrated by Article 11 of the 2016 Argentina–Qatar IIA, which provides: 'The Contracting Parties acknowledge that investors and their investments shall comply with the laws of the host Contracting Party with respect to the management and operation of an investment.' Such a reference to domestic law obliges foreign investors to comply in particular with all its prescriptions that are geared to the protection of public interests. In relation to the preliminary remarks made above as to the contribution of IIAs to the enforcement of international law, it is noteworthy that such a provision has, in general, a similar effect with regard to the domestic law of host States.

The obligation placed on foreign investors to comply with international law should be seen in the broader context of the traditional lack of interna-tional obligations binding upon private persons, in particular human rights obligations. In this respect, these obligations circumvent this void and can be seen as contributing to the 'horizontalisation' of human rights. More specifically, they bring within the ambit of IIAs international law instruments and obligations which are otherwise 'external' to these agreements, and which otherwise are not binding upon investors. This is exemplified by Articles 18.3 and 18.4 of the 2016 Nigeria–Morocco IIA, which provides: 'Investors and investments shall act in accordance with core labour standards as required by the ILO Declaration on Fundamental Principles and Rights at Work 1998. Investors and investments shall not manage or operate the investments in a manner that circumvents international environmental, labour and human rights obligations to which the host state and/or home state are Parties.'

Such obligations imposed by IIAs on foreign investors to comply with international law instruments and obligations can be contrasted with those IIA obligations binding upon them which set out themselves the conduct to be complied with. For instance, Article 11.ii of the 2018 Belarus–India IIA provides:

> Investors and their investments shall not, either prior to or after the establishment of an investment, offer, promise, or give any undue pecuniary advantage, gratification or gift whatsoever, whether directly or indirectly, to a public servant or official of a Party as an inducement or reward for doing or forbearing to do any official act or obtain or maintain other improper advantage nor shall be complicit in inciting, aiding, abetting, or conspiring to commit such acts.

b   Corporate Social Responsibility

Content-wise, foreign investors' obligations concerning corporate social responsibility are similar to the above-mentioned obligations placed upon States, the main and essential difference being in their addressees. By using typically a soft law language, they aim directly at leading foreign investors to incorporate into their internal policies and practices internationally recognised standards, guidelines and principles of corporate social responsibility. Article 15 of the IIA adopted by Brazil and the United Arab Emirates (UAE) in 2019 provides a detailed illustration of this practice:

> 1. Investors and their investment shall strive to achieve the highest possible level of contribution to the sustainable development of the Host State and the local community, through the adoption of a high degree of socially responsible practices, based on the voluntary principles, and standards set out in the OECD Guidelines for Multinational Enterprises.
> 2. The investors and their investment shall endeavor to comply with the following voluntary principle and standards for a responsible business conduct and consistent with the laws adopted by the Host State receiving the investment:

(a) Contribute to the economic, social and environmental progress, aiming at achieving sustainable development;

(b) Respect the internationally recognized human rights of those involved in the companies' activities;

(c) Encourage local capacity building through close cooperation with the local community;

(d) Encourage the creation of human capital, especially by creating employment opportunities and offering professional training to workers;

(e) Refrain from seeking or accepting exemptions that are not established in the legal or regulatory framework relating to human rights, environment, health, security, work, tax system, financial incentives, or other issues;

(f) Support and advocate for good corporate governance principles, and develop and apply good practices of corporate governance;

(g) Develop and implement effective self-regulatory practices and management systems that foster a relationship of mutual trust between the companies and the societies in which its operations are conducted;

(h) Promote the knowledge of and the adherence to, by workers, the corporate policy, through appropriate dissemination of this policy, including programs for professional training;

(i) Refrain from discriminatory or disciplinary action against employees who submit grave reports to the board or, whenever appropriate, to the competent public authorities, about practices that violate the law or corporate policy;

(j) Encourage, whenever possible, business associates, including service providers and outsources, to apply the principles of business conduct consistent with the principles provided for in this Article; and

(k) Refrain from any undue interference in local political activities.

4

Promotion, Facilitation, Admission and Establishment

Introduction

Under public international law, States enjoy full discretion in regulating the flows of persons, goods and capital across their borders. Likewise, they can decide if, how and where economic activities can be undertaken within their territory by private persons. This holds true in relation to foreign investors and their investments. All of these considerations form part of States' sovereignty.

The principle, extent and modalities pursuant to which States open their borders to foreign investors and allow them to undertake economic activities depends mainly on domestic economic and social considerations. Host States strike a balance between conflicting interests and objectives, namely their economic development, on the one hand, and the protection of a range of other domestic interests, on the other. Indeed, allowing for the influx of foreign investments has the potential to stimulate the economy and labour market. At the same time, it can, for instance, create fierce competition, which may be damaging for domestic enterprises.

Beyond the promotion and facilitation of foreign investments which constitutes a common teleological denominator of international investment agreements (IIAs), treaty practice displays some diversity in relation to admission and establishment. This diversity displays different balances struck by States parties between the above-mentioned interests and objectives and, more generally, between liberal and protectionist policies. This chapter examines briefly the promotion and facilitation of foreign investments before analysing in detail admission and establishment.

4.1 Promotion and Facilitation

Although the protection of foreign investments is the objective of international investment law that attracts the most attention because of its prevalence in the context of investor–State arbitration, it is worth recalling that promotion is also an important objective in this field of law. This can be seen from its history, as retraced in Chapter 1, in particular during the time of its emergence.

In this respect, it is notable that the title of most IIAs make reference to both 'protection' and 'promotion'. This is well illustrated by IIA adopted by Armenia and the United Arab Emirates (UAE) in 2016: 'Agreement between the Government of the Republic of Armenia and the Government of the United Arab Emirates for the Promotion and Reciprocal Protection of Investments'. This is further evidenced by the preamble of a great number of IIAs. For instance, the 2017 China–Hong Kong SAR China IIA provides that 'the two sides decided to sign ... the Investment Agreement between the Mainland and the Hong Kong Special Administrative Region' in particular '[t]o promote and protect investments' and '[t]o protect the right of investors and to promote achieving progressive liberalisation and facilitation of investments of the two sides'. As is clear from this Preamble, 'promotion' and 'facilitation' go hand-in-hand, something which is further evidenced by the title of the IIAs concluded by Brazil in the 2010s. Reference can be made in particular to the 2018 Brazil–Suriname IIA: 'Cooperation and Facilitation Investment Agreement between the Federative Republic of Brazil and the Republic of Surinam'. The same holds true with regard to the reference made in some IIAs to the encouragement of investment (e.g. 2003 Ethiopia–Netherlands IIA).

While there is a great consistency across the titles and preambles of IIAs, treaty practice displays some heterogeneity as to the concrete conduct which is expected or required from States parties in promoting foreign investment. In this respect, three main categories of IIAs can be identified.

Forming part of the first category, a minority of IIAs simply do not address the matter at all, such as the 2017 Colombia–UAE IIA.

The second category is composed of IIAs that provide for a vague obligation requiring States parties to promote or encourage investments. In some of those agreements, this obligation consists of an obligation of best efforts; in other words, States parties must do their utmost to promote foreign investment. For instance, the IIA adopted by Germany and Madagascar in 2006 provides: 'Each Contracting State will encourage as far as possible investments by investors of the other Contracting State in its territory and will admit these investments in conformity with its legislation' (Article 2.1; translation by the author). On the other hand, the obligation to promote investment incorporated in other IIAs requires States parties to actually achieve this result, making it insufficient to simply show that efforts were made to do so. Such obligations of result are illustrated by Article 3.1 of the 2017 Qatar–Singapore IIA: 'Each Contracting Party shall encourage and create favourable conditions for investors of the other Contracting Party to make investments in its territory.' In addition to not specifying the conduct that is required from States, it should be noted that limitations are sometimes attached to these obligations; in this respect, the IIA adopted by Uzbekistan and Turkey in 2017 provides that investments shall be promoted as far as possible '[s]ubject to its laws and regulations' (Article 3.1). Such a limitation further contributes to the uncertainty that those IIAs display as to the concrete conduct which States parties are required to adopt in order to promote investment.

In contrast, IIAs belonging to the third category provide clarification as to the concrete conduct expected from States, typically through the inclusion of a non-exhaustive list. For instance, the 2016 Argentina–Qatar IIA provides that the 'Contracting Parties will make their best efforts to implement investment promotion measures including, though not exclusively: a) the exchange of information related to their respective laws; b) the reciprocal sending of economic promotion missions; c) the facilitation of business contacts between the investor of the two Contracting Parties' (Article 2.8). It can be noted that such conduct can be prescribed, not only in the IIA Article on promotion, but also in specific provisions, for instance on the exchange of information (e.g. 2016 Morocco–Nigeria IIA, Article 5), or on transparency (e.g. 2016 Hong Kong SAR China–Chile IIA, Article 12). Likewise, in some IIAs the relevant conduct is to be found in a provision concerning the facilitation of investment. This practice can be seen in Article 16 of the 2017 Hong Kong SAR China–ASEAN IIA:

> Subject to their laws and regulations, the Parties shall cooperate to facilitate investments among the Parties through, among others:
>
> (a) creating the necessary environment for all forms of investment;
> (b) simplifying procedures for investment applications and approvals;
> (c) promoting dissemination of investment information, including investment rules, regulations, policies and procedures; and
> (d) establishing one-stop investment centres in the respective host Parties to provide assistance and advisory services to the business sectors including facilitation of operating licences and permits.

Interestingly, the facilitation of investment in this IIA is an objective to be reached through a joint obligation to cooperate. This sheds light on the implicit collective and cooperative dimension that largely characterises treaty practice even in the majority of IIAs that explicitly place the obligation to facilitate and promote investment on States parties individually. More generally, and as explained in Chapter 2, cooperation proves to be a key element and objective of all IIAs.

4.2 Admission and Establishment

Preliminary Remarks

In both treaty practice and the literature, reference is often made to the admission and establishment of foreign investors and their investments. More precisely, and as noted by Salacuse,[1] 'admission' is typically used by IIAs attaching the admission and establishment to host States' domestic law, while

---

[1] JW Salacuse, *The Law of Investment Treaties* (2nd ed, Oxford University Press 2015), at 223.

'establishment' is classically used when agreements articulate those matters by reference to the prohibition of negative differentiations, meaning to the national treatment and most-favoured-nation treatment (MFNT) standards. Yet, the terms 'admission' and 'establishment' are not defined in treaty practice, leaving uncertainty as to their exact meaning. Attempts have been made in the literature to distinguish them. Schreuer and Dolzer state, for instance, that 'admission' is generally understood as relating to the right of entry of investments and 'establishment' to the condition under which investors are authorised to carry out their activities in the course of the investment period.[2]

Regardless of their exact meaning, IIA provisions and more generally treaty practice on admission and establishment are often categorised into two groups: (1) IIAs that grant a right of establishment, corresponding to the practice of specific States, in particular the United States of America (USA) or Japan; and (2) those agreements conferring no such right, concluded in particular by European States. In practice, the picture is not as clear-cut as this for reasons pertaining to the respective practice of each State and, more fundamentally, to the nuances and differences displayed by IIA provisions on admission and establishment.

As to the respective practice of each State, there is no doubt that general trends can be seen in particular in bilateral investment treaty models. Yet, a close analysis of treaty practice shows that the practice of each State is more diverse than what is often assumed. For instance, the IIAs adopted by Japan with Iran in 2016 and with Israel in 2017 adopt two different approaches: the latter confers a right of establishment, while the former does not. A similar discrepancy can be witnessed in the practice of some States over time. This is well illustrated by the evolution evidenced by the 2016 Comprehensive Economic and Trade Agreement (CETA) as to the practice of European States. Indeed, that Agreement adopts a liberal approach to admission and establishment, while European States have traditionally not conferred any right in relation to those matters in the IIAs they have concluded.

The dichotomy that is established between those IIA provisions that grant a right of establishment and those that do not must also be put into perspective. Treaty practice cannot be summed up as an opposition between those IIAs that would open State borders and those that would leave full discretion to States in deciding on the admission and establishment of foreign investors and their investments. First of all, it should be noted that no IIA grants an absolute right of establishment as does, for instance, European Union (EU) law. Instead, the IIAs that confer a right of admission and establishment qualify this right by reference to the treatment granted to other investors.

---

[2] R Dolzer, C Schreuer, *Principles of International Investment Law* (2nd ed, Oxford University Press 2012), at 88.

Second, those IIAs differ as to the extent to which this right is attached to such treatment. Some limit it to the treatment conferred to other foreign investors through the MFNT standard, while others extend it also to the treatment enjoyed by domestic investors through the national treatment standard. Finally, the operation of those two standards as to admission and establishment is typically subject to an important limitation, i.e. the fact that the extension of more favourable treatment is conditioned by the similarity of the circumstances.

For these reasons, then, instead of there being a clear-cut dichotomy, treaty practice on admission and establishment can be better conceived of in terms of a 'sliding scale' through which States' discretionary power varies. Three main categories of provisions – which are examined in turn – form part of this scale: (1) those that leave admission and establishment to be governed by host States' domestic law; (2) those that confer a relative right of admission and establishment to foreign investors and their investments based on the MFNT standard; and (3) those that grant a relative right of admission and establishment based on both the MFNT standard and the national treatment standard.

4.2.1 Admission and Establishment Governed by Host States' Domestic Law

Regardless of the differences in terms of drafting as detailed below, IIAs that leave admission and establishment as matters to be governed by host States' domestic law confer complete discretionary power on States to decide on those matters. This means, of course, that they are free to set the principles and conditions applicable to the admission and establishment of foreign investors and their investments. In this respect, this rule also entails that States are being left with the possibility to grant a different treatment to different categories of investors and investments. More precisely, they can treat domestic investors or foreign investors originating from specific home States more favourably. All this holds true both synchronically and diachronically. Indeed, this rule that allows host States' domestic law to govern admission and establishment offers States the opportunity to modify the relevant policies and legislation on those matters in order to reflect changing opinions as to the correct balance to be struck between the interests and objectives at hand.

A variety of approaches towards drafting are adopted by the States parties to IIAs in assigning the regulation of admission and establishment as a matter of domestic law.

The first – mainstream – approach entails explicitly delegating admission as a matter for the host State's domestic law. This approach is illustrated by Article 2.1 of the IIA adopted by Austria and Kyrgyzstan in 2016: 'Each Contracting Party shall, according to its laws and regulations, promote and admit investments by investors of the other Contracting Party.' Under such provisions, the regulation of admission is assigned to the law of host States and is considered as a sovereign prerogative. This appears even more clearly in Article 3.1 of the 2016 Japan–Iran IIA: 'Either Contracting Party shall, subject to its rights to exercise powers in accordance with its applicable laws and regulations, including those with regard to foreign ownership and control, admit investment by investors of the other Contracting Party.'

Adopting a second approach, some IIAs refer to 'pre-establishment' – as opposed to 'post-establishment' – and exclude the application of the treaty to that phase. For instance, the 2016 Slovakia–Iran IIA provides: 'For greater certainty, this Agreement provides only post-establishment protection and does not cover the pre-establishment phase or matters of market access' (Article 2.5). As a result of this kind of provision, establishment is left to the discretion of host States as a matter to be regulated by their domestic law.

The same conclusion can be reached with regard to those IIAs that do not explicitly address in any way the issue of admission and establishment. This third approach is, for instance, adopted by Colombia and the UAE in their 2017 IIA. Under this approach also, it is left to host States to decide these matters as per their own laws and policies. This is all the more true given that, under public international law, the limitations of sovereignty cannot be presumed.

4.2.2 Relative Right of Admission and Establishment Based on the Most-Favoured-Nation Treatment Standard

Irrespective of the differences that they display in terms of drafting, the IIAs that set a relative right of admission and establishment based on the MFNT standard prohibit States parties' investors and their investments from being treated less favourably than other foreign investors. On the other hand, they do not contain a similar rule relating to domestic investors. In other words, those IIAs adopt a liberal stance without sacrificing the possibility for host States to favour their domestic investors.

The effectiveness of this liberal approach that aims at creating a level playing field between foreign investors can, however, be 'relativised'. Indeed, because the extension of more favourable treatments under the MFNT standard is often conditioned onto the likeness of the circumstances, host States may justify differences of treatment by different circumstances with regard to foreign investors and their investments.

Furthermore, it is worth emphasising that the obligation that those IIAs place on host States to extend the MFNT does not annihilate or restrict their sovereign prerogative to freely set in their domestic law the rules applicable to the admission and establishment of foreign investors and their investments. This means also that those IIAs offer to a large extent the opportunity to modify those domestic rules over time.

In this respect, one should note that many IIAs that make the MFNT standard applicable to admission and establishment explicitly link those matters to host States' domestic law. For instance, the 2016 Rwanda–Turkey IIA provides: 'Each Contracting Party shall admit in its territory investments on a basis no less favourable than that accorded in like circumstances to investments of investors of any third State, within the framework of its laws and regulations' (Article 4.1). In other IIAs that also make the MFNT standard applicable to admission and establishment, there is no explicit attachment of admission and establishment to host States' domestic law. Yet, a contextual interpretation of those IIAs leads to the conclusion that the principle and modalities governing those matters are to be set by their domestic law. Such a practice is well illustrated by the IIA adopted in 2016 by Hong Kong SAR China and Chile.

This Agreement also sheds light on the policy choice made by the States parties to those IIAs that base the relative right of admission and establishment only on the MFNT standard, to the exclusion of the national treatment standard. Indeed, not only did Hong Kong SAR China and Chile not include establishment in the scope of application of the national treatment standard (Article 4.2), but they also found it necessary to stress, with regard to the application of this standard to the expansion of investments, that this concept of expansion does not include the establishment or acquisition of investments (Article 4.3).

4.2.3 Relative Right of Admission and Establishment Based on the National Treatment and the Most-Favoured-Nation Treatment Standards

The IIAs that base the right of admission and establishment on both the national treatment standard and the MFNT standard reflect a strong liberal approach. They create a level playing field between the investors of the host State and foreign investors and between foreign investors, respectively.

Here again, one should note that the effect of this liberalisation can be watered down by the reference to 'like circumstances' that is typical of both treaty standards. It is worth stressing here as well that this broad relative right of admission and establishment does not entail that the principles and modalities governing admission and establishment are not to be set by host States' domestic law. All this right does is to require that the investors of States parties and their investments are not conferred a less favourable treatment under domestic law.

In terms of treaty drafting, a number of the IIAs that adopt this third approach make explicit in both the national treatment provision and the MFNT provision that those standards cover the admission and establishment of investors and their investments. This practice is illustrated by, respectively, Articles 9.3 and 9.4 of the 2018 Korea–Republics of Central America IIA. Alternatively, the national treatment provision and the MFNT provision of some IIAs do not refer directly to 'admission' and 'establishment', but they do to 'investment activities', which is conceived of in the definitions provided as covering those matters (e.g. 2017 Israel–Japan IIA, Articles 1 and 3).

5

Standards of Treatment

Introduction

Together with the prohibition of illegal expropriation analysed in Chapter 6, the standards of treatment examined in this chapter constitute the core of the protection conferred by international investment agreements (IIAs) to foreign investors and their investments. They protect these investors and investments against a broad range of conduct attributable to host States, sometimes in connection with the conduct of private persons.

The extent and modalities of the protection granted by these standards have traditionally suffered from a lack of clarity in treaty practice. This has been a source of legal uncertainty for both host States and foreign investors, the former in relation notably to the exercise of their right to regulate, the latter with regard to the planning and execution of their operations. This normative vagueness and the lack of answers offered by IIAs to the legal issues that arise in practice have led arbitration tribunals to elaborate on the content of the standards of treatment and thereby to better delineate the protection that these standards confer. Beyond the normative vagueness that has been a common denominator of IIAs, nuances and differences can be seen across the various agreements with regard to how these standards are drafted.

This explains to a certain extent why tribunals have adopted different solutions to the legal issues to which their application has given rise. That being said, it remains that the inconsistency that characterises arbitration practice results also fundamentally from disagreements between tribunals that cannot be explained by the differences among the provisions being applied. This also has constituted a source of legal uncertainty for both host States and foreign investors. As regards host States, solutions adopted by some arbitration tribunals have also contributed to the wave of criticism formulated against international investment law and arbitration, in particular in the 2010s. All of this has led to an evolution in treaty practice over that period geared towards the clarification of the extent and modalities of the protection granted by the standards of treatment.

In addition to their drafting, IIAs differ in the ways in which they incorporate those standards. Some agreements combine all the standards in a single Article, while others 'dispatch' them across a series of Articles. Radically, some standards are simply not provided for at all in some IIAs. This has traditionally been the case for the umbrella clause. This constitutes another reason to pay due attention to the text of IIAs and not to presume that the protection that they confer through the standards of treatment is identical.

Irrespective of these differences between IIAs, the present chapter focuses on the following main standards, which are analysed in turn: (1) the fair and equitable treatment (FET) standard; (2) the full protection and security (FPS) standard; (3) the national treatment standard; (4) the most-favoured-nation treatment (MFNT) standard; and (5) the umbrella clause.

5.1 The Fair and Equitable Treatment Standard

Preliminary Remarks

The fair and equitable treatment standard finds its origins in treaties of friendship, commerce and navigation concluded by the United States of America (USA). This standard was also included in the 1967 Draft Convention on the Protection of Foreign Property prepared at the Organisation for Economic Co-operation and Development (OECD) which, as explained in Chapter 1, served as a template for European States' bilateral investment treaty (BIT) practice. Since then, it has been found in almost all IIAs. That being said, it is worth emphasising that in a few treaties concluded in the 2010s, States parties have not merely clarified the content of that standard as done in many other IIAs, but they have radically declined to incorporate the FET standard. This practice, which comes as a reaction to the criticism formulated against that standard and its application by some tribunals, is exemplified by the 2016 Rwanda–Morocco IIA, which does not mention it, as well as by the practice adopted by Brazil in the 2010s which makes it explicit 'for greater certainty' that the FET standard is not covered (e.g. 2018 Brazil–Suriname IIA, Article 4.3).

From the perspective of foreign investors, the FET standard constitutes no doubt the most important standard of treatment provided for in IIAs. This is evidenced by the many arbitration proceedings they have initiated wherein the violation of the FET provision is often claimed. This has led arbitration tribunals to often enter into theoretical and casuistic discussions as to the meaning and content of this standard. In this respect, a specific discussion has arisen concerning the interplay between the FET standard and the customary law minimum standard of treatment. All these issues are examined successively in the following subsections.

5.1.1 The Interplay between the FET Standard and the Customary Law Minimum Standard of Treatment

Preliminary Remarks

The FET standard and the customary law minimum standard of treatment share a similar objective: to ensure that the treatment granted by host States to foreign investors and their investments does not fall below a certain level of protection. Beyond this teleological common denominator, the issue of their interplay, which is often raised by the disputing parties to arbitration proceedings, remains controversial. In particular, it is debated whether the FET is a standard autonomous from the minimum standard of treatment and whether it confers a greater protection than the latter. Obviously, this has important concrete consequences for both host States and foreign investors. Legally speaking, the interplay between these two standards and how it is dealt with in practice raise two main issues that relate mainly to the minimum standard of treatment: (1) what is the normative content of that standard; and (2) how shall this content be identified and ascertained? These two issues are analysed in turn, in light of the links established between the FET standard and the minimum standard of treatment in treaty practice.

5.1.1.1 The Links between the FET Standard and the Customary Law Minimum Standard of Treatment in Treaty Practice

Treaty practice has traditionally not linked the FET standard to the customary law minimum standard of treatment. Most FET provisions within IIAs did not make any mention of that latter standard. As in the 1965 Germany–Tanzania IIA, they provided *mutatis mutandis*: 'It [each Contracting Party] shall in any case accord such investments fair and equitable treatment' (Article 1). Some IIAs concluded in the 2010s retain this approach, for instance the 2016 Austria–Kyrgyzstan IIA (Article 3.1).

Despite the lack of any such connection in the text of such agreements, it should be noted that there remains the potential to link the FET standard to the customary law minimum standard of treatment through interpretation. This can be done using the interpretative means codified in Article 31.3.c. of the 1969 Vienna Convention on the Law of Treaties (VCLT). As explained in Chapter 12, this method enables one to take into account any relevant rule of international law that is applicable in the relations between the parties. Given that the customary law minimum standard is such a rule in the context of investor–State disputes, it can be taken into account to interpret the FET provision of those IIAs which do not refer to it. It is worth mentioning that a few tribunals establish such a link without providing any justification. For instance, in *Union Fenosa Gas, S.A. v. Egypt*, the Tribunal merely explained that it was 'content' to apply under Article 4.1 of the 1992 Egypt–Spain IIA 'the customary international law standard as prohibiting (inter alia) conduct by the host State "which is unjust, arbitrary, unfair, discriminatory or in violation of due process," including conduct that frustrates an investor's "legitimate expectations"' (2018, Award, para. 9.51).

On the other hand, some IIAs do link the FET standard and the customary law minimum standard of treatment. This approach, which was initiated in particular by the USA, has spread over treaty practice, most notably during the 2010s. Two distinctions can be made with regard to this category of IIAs, based respectively on the type of links that they establish and 'to what' precisely the FET is linked.

Starting with the latter issue, it should be noted that a number of IIAs do not link the FET standard to the minimum standard of treatment only, but, more generally, to the principles of international law, customary international law (CIL), the rules of international law, or international law. Article 4.1 of the 1998 France–Mexico IIA provides, for instance:

> Either Contracting Party shall extend and ensure fair and equitable treatment in accordance with the principles of International Law to investments made by investors of the other Contracting Party in its territory or in its maritime area, and ensure that the exercise of the right thus recognized shall not be hindered by law or in practice.

Those references encompass the customary law minimum standard of treatment, the FET standard being thereby linked to it. That being said, it is important to realise that they have a broader scope that covers other relevant principles of international law.

Among those IIAs that link the FET standard only to the minimum standard of treatment, some approach this connection in two steps: they first connect the FET standard to CIL and then specify that the reference made to 'customary international law' is to be understood as the 'customary international law minimum standard'. This is well illustrated by the 'successor' of the 1992 North American Free Trade Agreement (NAFTA), meaning the 2018 United States–Mexico–Canada Agreement (USMCA) (Article 14.6.1).

Turning to the second item, i.e. the type of links set out between the FET standard and the customary law minimum standard of treatment, various trends can be identified in treaty practice that confer differing roles on the minimum standard of treatment.

Some IIAs align the protection granted under the FET standard to that conferred by the CIL minimum standard of treatment. In other words, the FET standard is not to be conceived of as granting a greater protection than the minimum standard of treatment. International investment agreements approach this link by specifying *mutatis mutandis* that '[t]he concepts of "fair and equitable treatment" ... do not require treatment in addition to or beyond that which is required by the customary international law minimum standard of treatment of aliens' (e.g. 2016 Japan–Iran IIA, Article 5). Other IIAs that provide for a similar specification contain also a type of '"in accordance" provision'. This practice is exemplified by the 2019 Australia–Uruguay IIA, which provides in Article 4.1: 'Each Party shall accord to investments of investors of the other Party treatment in accordance with the customary international law minimum standard of treatment of aliens, including fair and equitable treatment and full protection and security.'

Some IIAs contain another type of '"in accordance" provision'. For instance, Article 2.2 of the 1995 United Kingdom–Venezuela IIA merely provides:

'Investments of nationals or companies of each Contracting Party shall at all times be accorded fair and equitable in accordance with international law.' In *Anglo American PLC* v. *Venezuela*, the Tribunal considered – contrary to the defendant – that this provision does not have the effect of aligning the FET standard to the minimum standard of treatment (2019, Award, para. 439), referring in particular to the case *Compañia de Aguas del Aconquija S.A.* v. *Argentina*, in which the Tribunal interpreted a similar provision stressing that it could 'as readily set a floor as a ceiling on the Treaty's fair and equitable treatment standard', thereby allowing this standard to be conceived of as conferring a greater protection than the minimum standard of treatment (2007, Award, para. 7.4.7).

Such an interpretation equates those '"in accordance" provisions' with the provisions that link the FET standard and the minimum standard of treatment by apparently making of the protection conferred by the latter a 'minimum benchmark' for the treatment to be granted under the FET standard. This is illustrated by the 1991 USA–Argentina IIA, which provides that '[i]nvestment shall at all times be accorded fair and equitable treatment ... and shall in no case be accorded treatment less than that required by international law' (Article 2.2.a). Interpreting this provision, the Tribunal appointed in *Azurix Corp.* v. *Argentina* opined in that sense:

> The paragraph consists of three full statements, each listing in sequence a standard of treatment to be accorded to investments: fair and equitable, full protection and security, not less than required by international law. Fair and equitable treatment is listed separately. The last sentence ensures that, whichever content is attributed to the other two standards, the treatment accorded to investment will be no less than required by international law. The clause, as drafted, permits to interpret fair and equitable treatment and full protection and security as higher standards than required by international law. The purpose of the third sentence is to set a floor, not a ceiling, in order to avoid a possible interpretation of these standards below what is required by international law. (2006, Award, para. 361)

What does the treaty practice discussed above teach us about the oft-discussed issue of the autonomy of the FET standard from the minimum standard of treatment?

First, it draws our attention to the fact that this question cannot be tackled in the abstract; due attention needs first to be paid to the terms of each IIA. Second, it evidences that IIAs vary as to the status given to the FET standard – some agreements conferring autonomy to it, others not. In this respect, one should recall that interpretation may impact on this issue, in that typically the autonomy given to the FET standard by the text of some IIAs may be erased through Article 31.3.c of the VCLT allowing one to take into account the minimum standard of treatment in the interpretation of the FET provision.

Furthermore, and more generally, it is worth highlighting that the autonomy that derives from the text of some IIAs does not prevent the two standards from conferring a similar protection, which would actually deprive this autonomy from being of any practical consequence. It can be noted that the same argument applies to those IIA provisions that align the FET standard to the minimum standard of treatment, as such an alignment is indeed without any practical consequence if both standards confer a similar protection. As it appears here, the key question boils down to the content of those standards, in particular that of the customary law minimum standard of treatment.

5.1.1.2 The Content of the Customary Law Minimum Standard of Treatment

As recalled in Chapter 1, the minimum standard of treatment has emerged and developed as a CIL rule over the nineteenth century and early twentieth century. The decision of the Mexico–United States Claims Commission in *Neer (USA)* v. *Mexico* is often considered as having played a key role in this process. In this respect, this statement made by the Commission is often viewed as a formulation of that standard:

> [T]he treatment of an alien, in order to constitute an international delinquency, should amount to an outrage, to bad faith, to wilful neglect of duty, or to an insufficiency of governmental action so far short of international standards that every reasonable and impartial man would readily recognize its insufficiency. (1926, Award, para. 4)

Such a view that this 'Neer formula' 'encapsulates' and reflects the customary law minimum standard of treatment has been controversial, notably with regard to the high threshold that it requires in order for a State to be held internationally responsible. More precisely, the controversy is twofold. It first relates to the question as to whether the 'Neer formula' has ever reflected this standard. Second, and primarily, it zeroes in on the question as to whether it still, if indeed it has ever, reflects the minimum standard of treatment in the twenty-first century.

a Has the 'Neer Formula' Ever Reflected the Customary Law Minimum Standard of Treatment?

Concerning the first aspect of this controversy, there exist two main types of criticisms addressed against the 'Neer formula': one pertains to the alleged 'duality' of the minimum standard of treatment, the other to the situations to which it is applied.

As explained in Chapter 1, the 'law of the protection of aliens abroad' arose and developed in the context of European expansionism and imperialism that led European citizens to settle abroad, wherein they embarked upon a wide array of activities. In other words, this body of law did not develop specifically to protect economic operators and activities, but private persons abroad more generally. An understanding of this context helps to shed some light as to why it has been argued that the law of the protection of aliens abroad was actually composed of two branches: the first applicable to foreign private persons in general, and the second to foreign economic operators in particular. In this respect, the 'Neer formula' has *sensu stricto* not been criticised as such, but it has been argued that it is wrong to consider it as reflecting the customary law minimum standard of treatment that was applicable to economic operators at the time, as it would instead 'embody' the standard that was applicable to foreign private persons in general. For the proponents of this thesis, the minimum standard of treatment applicable to foreign economic operators was in fact more protective. This thesis and its consequences in terms of investor protection were explained in detail by the Tribunal in *Merrill & Ring Forestry L.P.* v. *Canada*:

> As foreshadowed above, just as there was a first track concerning the evolution of the minimum standard of treatment of aliens in the limited context indicated, there was also a second track that concerned specifically the treatment of aliens in relation to business, trade and investments. This other standard, which was much more liberal, is evidenced by the tendency of states to support the claims of their citizens in the ambit of diplomatic protection with an open mind, and without requiring a showing of 'outrageous' treatment before doing so ... The trend towards liberalization of the standard applicable to the treatment of business, trade and investments continued unabated over several decades and has yet not stopped ... State practice with respect to the standard for the treatment of aliens in relation to business, trade and investments, while varied and sometimes erratic, has shown greater consistency than in respect of the first track, as it has generally endorsed an open and non-restricted approach to the applicable standard to the treatment of aliens under international law. At the same time it shows that the restrictive Neer standard has not been endorsed or has been much qualified. (2010, Award, paras. 205–209)

As to the minimum standard of treatment of aliens in general, it is worth noting that the Tribunal in that case opined that it has moved over time towards a greater protection except for personal safety, denial of justice and due process for which a high threshold still applies (para. 204).

Turning to the second criticism formulated against the 'Neer formula', it has been argued that it is mainly concerned with situations of denial of justice and that the high threshold that it sets, meaning aggravating circumstances such as bad faith or wilful neglect of duty, was not intended to apply to the conduct of the executive and legislative bodies. In this respect, the Tribunal appointed in *Rusoro Mining Limited* v. *Venezuela* made a link between the decision in *Neer* and the decision in *Harry Roberts (USA)* v. *Mexico*, also rendered by the Mexico–United States Claims Commission, which it regarded as a leading historic case for claims arising from the conduct of those two bodies and which does not require aggravating circumstances to be established (2016, Award, paras. 517–518).

b Does the 'Neer Formula' Reflect the Customary Law Minimum Standard of Treatment?

The second aspect of the controversy, namely whether the 'Neer formula' reflects the content of the customary law minimum standard of treatment, has attracted much attention, in particular during the aftermath of the 2001 NAFTA Free Trade Commission's interpretation of Article 1105 of the 1992 NAFTA. Two issues need to be distinguished in this regard: (1) whether the perception of the threshold contained in the 'Neer formula' has evolved; and (2) whether this threshold itself has evolved.

As to the first issue, there is no doubt that the perception of what is egregious has evolved with the passage of time and that situations that were not perceived as being egregious in the early twentieth century are regarded as such in the twenty-first century. By the same token, it goes without saying that new situations have flourished over the twentieth century – which by definition did not exist at the time the Neer case was decided – and which can be perceived as being egregious. This was well explained by the Tribunal in Cargill, Incorporated v. Mexico:

> As the world and, in particular, the international business community become ever more intertwined and interdependent with global trade, foreign investment, BITs and free trade agreements, the idea of what is the minimum treatment a country must afford to aliens is arising in new situations simply not present at the time of the Neer award which dealt with the alleged failure to properly investigate the murder of a foreigner. (2009, Award, para. 282)

On the other hand, the question as to whether the threshold itself has evolved in CIL is more controversial in practice. It is worth connecting this issue with that of the ascertainment of the content of the minimum standard of treatment examined below. Indeed, the answer given to that question depends partly on the methodology and materials used to ascertain this content.

At one side of the spectrum, it is considered that the threshold has remained the same and that 'aggravating circumstances' that form part of the 'Neer formula' still characterises CIL. For instance, in the above-mentioned Cargill case, the Tribunal endorsed this formulation of the threshold made by Mexico and Canada in ADF Group Inc. v. USA: '[T]he conduct of the government toward the investment must amount to gross misconduct, manifest injustice or, in the classic words of the Neer claim, bad faith or the wilful neglect of duty' (2009, Award, para. 284). One can see, however, that there exist nuances between the exact views of those who adopt this approach. Indeed, contrary, for instance, to the Tribunal in the Cargill case, some consider that bad faith is no longer a requirement (e.g. Glamis Gold, Ltd v. USA, 2009, Award, para. 616).

At the other side of the spectrum, the 'Neer formula' is regarded as being outdated due to the evolution of the minimum standard of treatment since the time of its conception by the Mexico–United States Claims Commission. In that sense, the Tribunal opined in ADF Group Inc. v. USA that 'what customary international law projects is not a static photograph of the minimum standard of treatment of aliens as it stood in 1927 when the Award in the *Neer* case was rendered' (2003, Award, para. 179).

This approach leads many of those tribunals adopting it to argue that there is a substantial similarity between the protection granted by the minimum standard of treatment and that conferred by the FET standard, be it because they consider that there is an alignment between the two standards (e.g. *Murphy Exploration & Production Company-International* v. *Ecuador*, 2016, Partial Final Award, para. 208) or because they see the minimum standard as having led to the establishment of the FET standard (e.g. *Merrill & Ring Forestry L.P.* v. *Canada*, 2010, Award, para. 209). Content-wise, those tribunals lower the applicable threshold by detaching it from the requirement of aggravating circumstances. In that sense, the Tribunal appointed in that former case stated: 'In the end, the name assigned to the standard does not really matter. What matters is that the standard protects against all such acts or behaviors that might infringe a sense of fairness, equity and reasonableness' (para. 210).

5.1.1.3 Ascertaining the Content of the Customary Law Minimum Standard of Treatment

As mentioned above, the debate as to whether the customary law minimum standard of treatment has evolved concerns, in part, how and by whom such an evolution is to be determined. These formal issues and the difficulties that they entail are typical in public international law when it comes to identifying CIL rules. In this instance, they impact greatly on the content that the minimum standard of treatment is said to have and on the question as to whether or not it has evolved since the time the *Neer* decision was rendered.

a Who Shall Determine the Content of the Customary Law Minimum Standard of Treatment?

This first issue boils down to the role that disputing parties and arbitration tribunals should play in determining the content of the minimum standard of treatment.

The role to be played by the disputing parties raises mainly the issue of the burden of proof. In this respect, it is worth recalling that it is a key principle in international litigation that the party who makes a claim, be it legal or factual, shall adduce the evidence to support it. This task is quite difficult when it comes to CIL; in relation to the explanation given in Chapter 2, it requires evidence of not only the objective element, i.e. State practice, but also of the subjective element, i.e. the *opinio juris*. The particular difficulty in evidencing the subjective element is often stressed when the content of the minimum standard of treatment is debated. The Tribunal did so for instance in *Glamis Gold, Ltd* v. *USA* when stating that it was up to the claimant to establish the change in custom – in this respect, it acknowledged that the difficulty of the task leads to the freezing of the protection enjoyed by foreign investors to the concept of egregiousness which prevailed at the time the *Neer* case was decided (2009, Award, paras. 602–604). While it endorsed the principle governing the burden of proof, the Tribunal in *Windstream Energy LLC* v. *Canada* nonetheless considered that it was for each party to evidence their position as to the content of the minimum standard of treatment. It reached this conclusion by distinguishing two issues: the existence of a rule of CIL and its content. In the view of this Tribunal, it is only as to the former that the claimant bears the burden of proof (2016, Award, para. 350).

In addition to the role played by the disputing parties, it is often debated which role arbitration tribunals should play as to the ascertainment of the content of the minimum standard of treatment. Here again, the debate relates largely to the issue of the burden of proof. However, beyond this issue, the discussion is also influenced by another principle in international litigation known in Latin as *iura novit curia*. As explained in Chapter 12, this principle entails that international courts and tribunals are not bound by the materials put forward by the disputing parties and that they are themselves empowered to proceed to the analysis of the content of the law, provided that the due process rights of the disputing parties are respected.

Without explicitly referring to this principle, the Tribunal appointed in *Windstream Energy LLC* v. *Canada* approached the determination of the content of the minimum standard of treatment using the substance of this principle. It explained in the award that it had played an active role going beyond the arguments of the parties with regard to the ascertainment of this content (2016, Award, para. 350). On the other hand, the Tribunal in *Cargill, Incorporated* v. *Mexico* did not endeavour to have such a role as it was guided by burden of proof considerations only, explaining:

> The burden of establishing any new elements of this custom is on Claimant. The Tribunal acknowledges that the proof of change in a custom is not an easy matter to establish. However, the burden of doing so falls clearly on Claimant. If Claimant does not provide the Tribunal with the proof of such evolution, it is not the place of the Tribunal to assume this task. Rather the Tribunal, in such an instance, should hold that Claimant fails to establish the particular standard asserted. (2009, Award, para. 273)

b How Shall the Content of the Customary Law Minimum Standard of Treatment Be Determined?

As a starting point for this discussion, it is worth recalling Article 38 of the Statute of the International Court of Justice (ICJ), which refers to 'international custom, as evidence of a general practice accepted as law'. Even though that formulation can be criticised inasmuch as this is in fact the 'general practice accepted as law' that evidences 'international custom', it attracts the attention to the two above-mentioned elements that must be proven: the objective element, i.e. State practice, and the subjective element, i.e. the *opinio juris*. According to the 'two elements' theory, developed in particular by the ICJ, the general practice consists in a constant and widespread State practice which, to meet the subjective element, shall be conducted out of a sense of legal obligation.

From this public international law standpoint, ascertaining the content of the CIL minimum standard of treatment therefore requires the focus to be placed on State practice and *opinio juris*. As mentioned above, inquiring into these two elements in order to evidence whether there is a constant and widespread State practice characterised by an *opinio juris* is a challenge for disputing parties. The same is true for arbitration tribunals in reaching and justifying their decisions. Beyond the issue of the burden of proof discussed above, this leads those parties and tribunals to approach this issue by focusing usually on the materials most readily accessible to them, meaning IIAs and arbitration awards.

The main issue concerning arbitration awards relates to their exact role in the ascertainment of the customary law minimum standard of treatment. In this respect, there is among some tribunals a tendency to ascertain the content of this standard not by focusing on State practice and *opinio juris*, but instead by relying on awards. More precisely, a 'self-referential' approach is visible in the reasoning of those tribunals which do not base their conclusions on the practice of States – or if they do, they do it quite superficially – but rather on their own views and the views expressed by past arbitration tribunals as to the content of the minimum standard of treatment. In relation to the theory of the sources of public international law, such a 'self-referential' approach tends to replace State practice with arbitration practice and, more fundamentally, to substitute *jurisprudence constante* for CIL.

Often the tribunals that adopt this approach do not really endeavour to argue it as they simply express their views or refer to the views of other tribunals (e.g. *Deutsche Telekom AG* v. *India*, 2017, Interim Award, para. 331, Footnote 354). The Tribunal appointed in *Windstream Energy LLC* v. *Canada* is an exception as it openly addressed the issue of the lack of direct evidence and grounded its reliance on past arbitration awards on the argument of *non liquet*. More precisely, it started by recalling – in terms foreshadowing its argumentation – that the content of a rule of CIL 'can best be determined on the basis of the evidence of actual State practice and *opinio juris*' (2016, Award, para. 351). Having concluded that the disputing parties had not produced any such evidence, it then considered that it had to rely on indirect evidence as it could not declare *non liquet*. As such indirect evidence, it referred to past awards decided under the NAFTA that had addressed this issue, as well as to legal scholarship. The Tribunal noted in this respect:

> The Tribunal notes that other NAFTA tribunals have adopted a similar approach when seeking to determine the contents of the minimum standard

of treatment in Article 1105(1) of NAFTA. Both Parties have also extensively cited to NAFTA awards and legal scholarship. Furthermore, while decisions of earlier international tribunals such as the *Neer* tribunal are often referred to as reflective of the content of the customary international law minimum standard of treatment, including by the Respondent in the present proceedings, the Tribunal notes that *Neer* is also an award (or more accurately, a decision of an international claims commission), not direct evidence of State practice, and that the *Neer* tribunal itself did not have any direct evidence relating to State practice before it. (para. 352)

This approach has been criticised by other arbitration tribunals, which affirmed that arbitration awards can neither create and prove CIL nor replace State practice (e.g. *Glamis Gold, Ltd* v. *USA*, 2009, Award, para. 605). In this respect, it is worth mentioning that a number of IIAs concluded in the 2010s contain a treaty paragraph or annex that recalls that CIL is grounded in the practice and *opinio juris* of States. For instance, Annex 14-A of the 2018 USMCA provides: 'The Parties confirm their shared understanding that "customary international law" generally and as specifically referenced in Article 14.6 [Minimum Standard of Treatment] results from a general and consistent practice of States that they follow from a sense of legal obligation.'

The role of IIAs, and more precisely the role of their FET provisions, in evidencing the content of the minimum standard of treatment raises also a particular issue of public international law that is examined in Chapter 2, which boils down to the interplay between treaties and CIL. More specifically here, it begs the question as to whether a network of – mainly – BITs is constitutive of a State practice that evidences the existence of a customary rule and its evolution and whether such a network can also be considered as evidencing the *opinio juris* of States.

This question is generally not tackled by tribunals. Given the extensive treaty practice in existence, some conclude that this has had an impact on the content of the minimum standard of treatment. For instance, the Tribunal appointed in *Mondev International Ltd* v. *USA* argued:

> Thirdly, the vast number of bilateral and regional investment treaties (more than 2000 [footnote omitted]) almost uniformly provide for fair and equitable treatment of foreign investments, and largely provide for full security and protection of investments. Investment treaties run between North and South, and East and West, and between States in these spheres inter se. On a remarkably widespread basis, States have repeatedly obliged themselves to accord foreign investment such treatment. In the Tribunal's view, such a body of concordant practice will necessarily have influenced the content of rules governing the treatment of foreign investment in current international law. It would be surprising if this practice and the vast number of provisions it reflects were to be interpreted as meaning no more than the *Neer* Tribunal (in a very different context) meant in 1927. (2002, Award, para. 117)

It is worth noting, as an aside, that this final sentence is reminiscent of the last sentence in the above-mentioned excerpt of the award rendered in *Windstream Energy LLC* v. *Canada* (2016, Award, para. 352). Indeed, the Tribunals in both cases seem to partly justify – in a 'negative manner' – their reasoning by implicitly suggesting than it is not less valid than the *Neer* decision or the use which is made of it.

Returning our focus to treaty practice, there is a tendency among some arbitration tribunals to display more cautiousness in how they view BIT practice. For instance, the Tribunal appointed in *Cargill, Incorporated* v. *Mexico* did acknowledge that identical treaty language may serve as evidence of CIL, but stressed that this similarity is in fact lacking with regard to the FET provision inasmuch as some refer to the minimum standard of treatment while others do not. Concerning the FET provisions that do not refer to the minimum standard of treatment, it opined also that they should not be afforded any significant evidentiary weight as it could be assumed that they were adopted precisely to set a standard other than that required by the customary law minimum standard of treatment. The Tribunal noted in this respect that widespread adoption of such provisions 'may in time raise international expectations as to what constitutes good governance, but such a consequence is different than such clauses evidencing directly an evolution of custom' (2009, Award, para. 276). Interestingly, the Tribunal appointed in that case also grounded this cautious approach in an argument that seems to touch upon the subjective element:

> The Tribunal notes second that the explosion in the number of BITs is a recent phenomenon and that responses of States to the questions presented in terms, for example, of calls for renegotiation or statements of approval is only now emerging. In such a fluid situation, the Tribunal does not believe it prudent to accord significant weight to even widespread adoption of clauses. (para. 276)

5.1.2 The Meaning and Content of the FET Standard

Preliminary Remarks

Normative indeterminacy has traditionally been a key feature of FET provisions. This indeterminacy results from the vague meaning of the terms 'fair' and 'equitable' in and of themselves, as well as from the lack of any specific content given by IIAs to the obligation to confer fair and equitable treatment to foreign investors. Again, this normative indeterminacy is an issue in terms of legal certainty for host States which do not know precisely from the text of such FET provisions the type of conduct that must or must not be adopted. The same holds true for foreign investors with regard to the protection they can expect under those provisions.

This helps to explain why a number of IIAs concluded in the 2010s provide some clarification as to the content of the FET provision, typically through the incorporation of an exhaustive or non-exhaustive list of subcategories. Such clarification also come as a reaction – be it 'positive' or 'negative' – to the interpretations of those vague FET provisions given in arbitration practice. Indeed, seized by foreign investors, arbitration tribunals have had to deal with these traditional drafting features as regards the FET provision and, in the absence of interpretative guidance, determine whether or not the respondent host States had breached this treaty obligation.

In practice, only a few tribunals have endeavoured to ascertain the meaning of 'fair' and 'equitable', typically by relying on dictionaries (e.g. *Antin* v. *Spain*, 2018, Award, para. 518), with many tribunals considering this to be a worthless exercise. For instance, in *Joseph Charles Lemire* v. *Ukraine*, the Tribunal stated that 'any effort to decipher the ordinary meaning of the words used only leads to analogous terms of almost equal vagueness' (2010, Decision on Jurisdiction and Liability, para. 258). The Tribunal appointed in *Windstream Energy LLC* v. *Canada* went one step further, by considering that this exercise is not only worthless, but also inappropriate as this would create the risk of replacing the standard set out in the applicable IIA with another standard that might not be in conformity with the customary law minimum standard of treatment (2016, Award, para. 357).

For the most part, arbitration tribunals have endeavoured to give some content to the FET standard, typically – regardless of some nuances – using three main approaches: (1) a casuistic approach; (2) a theoretical approach; and (3) a material approach. These approaches have been used singly or in combination by tribunals, in the latter case with the emphasis placed on each approach varying from one award to the other. Each of these approaches is analysed in turn with a specific focus on the latter, more mainstream approach, which has paved the way for the above-mentioned evolution of treaty practice.

5.1.2.1 Casuistic Approach

This first approach is encapsulated very well by the metaphor used by the Tribunal in *Windstream Energy LLC* v. *Canada*: '[J]ust as the proof of the pudding is in the eating (and not in its description), the ultimate test of correctness of an interpretation is not in its description in other words, but in its application on the facts' (2016, Award, para. 362). In other words, this approach leads us to focus on the specifics of each case and to favour their examination and appraisal in deciding *in concreto* whether or not a host State has acted in conformity with its obligation under the FET provision. This approach was promoted at an early stage by the Tribunal appointed in *Mondev International Ltd* v. *USA*, which argued that '[a] judgement of what is fair and equitable cannot be reached in the abstract' and that this judgement 'must depend on the facts of the particular case' (2002, Award, para. 118).

5.1.2.2 Theoretical Approach

The second approach is abstract in nature. It aims to specify the general objective and features of the FET standard. At the outset, it is worth stressing that the drafting of FET provisions, i.e. whether or not they link the FET standard to the minimum standard of treatment, impacts on the abstract views that one can have as to its objective and features. As seen below, the same holds true for the material approach. Attention is paid here to the various conceptions of the FET standard as expressed in arbitration practice.

In this regard, arbitration practice displays a sliding scale running from broad conceptions of the standard, which offer a wide protection to foreign investors, to narrow ones, which confer more limited protection. These opposing conceptions of the FET standard were stressed by the Tribunal in *El Paso Energy International Company* v. *Argentina* (2011, Award, paras. 341–347), which pointed to the award rendered in *Tecnicas Medioambientales Tecmed* v. *Mexico* as an illustration of the broad approaches, and to the award in *Alex Genin* v. *Estonia* as an illustration of the narrow approaches.

In the following well-known passage, the *Tecmed* Tribunal conceived of the FET standard as follows:

> The Arbitral Tribunal considers that this provision of the Agreement, in light of the good faith principle established by international law, requires the Contracting Parties to provide to international investments treatment that does not affect the basic expectations that were taken into account by the foreign investor to make the investment. The foreign investor expects the host State to act in a consistent manner, free from ambiguity and totally transparently in its relations with the foreign investor, so that it may know beforehand any and all rules and regulations that will govern its investments, as well as the goals of the relevant policies and administrative practices or directives, to be able to plan its investment and comply with such regulations. Any and all State actions conforming to such criteria should relate not only to the guidelines, directives or requirements issued, or the resolutions approved thereunder, but also to the goals underlying such regulations. The foreign investor also expects the host State to act consistently, i.e. without arbitrarily revoking any preexisting decisions or permits issued by the state that were relied upon by the investor to assume its commitments as well as to plan and launch its commercial and business activities. The investor also expects the state to use the legal instruments that govern the actions of the investor or the investment in conformity with the function usually assigned to such instruments, and not to deprive the investor of its investment without the required compensation. (2003, Award, para. 154)

This approach was viewed by the Tribunal in *El Paso Energy International Company* v. *Argentina* as 'a programme of good governance that no State in the world is capable of guaranteeing at all times' (2011, Award, para. 342). More generally, it reflects a strong trend among arbitration tribunals to build their conception of the FET standard on the notion of legitimate expectations, even though their understanding of that latter notion – as discussed below – varies.

This focus on legitimate expectations is well illustrated by the following statement made by the Tribunal in *Oxus Gold* v. *Uzbekistan*:

> Considering the lack of specific definition in the BIT, the FET standard as contemplated by Article 2(2) must be understood as a means to guarantee justice to foreign investors, and when doing so, for the States' actions to give due regard to an investor's legitimate expectations by refraining from taking measures which are not justified under the circumstances, i.e. unreasonable, disproportionate or discriminatory. (2015, Final award, para. 318)

As discussed below, it is apparent from such an approach that 'legitimate expectations' appears in the reasoning of some tribunals as an 'overarching' subcategory of the FET standard.

At the other end of the conceptual sliding scale, the Tribunal appointed in *Alex Genin* v. *Estonia*, after noting the lack of clarity as to the content of the FET standard, explained that it 'understands it to require an "international minimum standard" that is separate from domestic law, but that is, indeed, a *minimum* standard'. This conception led the Tribunal to incorporate within the FET standard, in reference to Brownlie,[1] acts showing a wilful neglect of duty, an insufficiency of action falling far below international standards and subjective bad faith (2001, Award, para. 367). Such an approach is reminiscent of the '*Neer* formula' discussed above. In this respect, it is worth noting that the Tribunal adopted this view in applying an FET provision which provides that 'investment shall at all times be accorded fair and equitable treatment . . . and shall in no case be accorded treatment less than required by international law'. Indeed, while – as discussed above – the Tribunal appointed in *Azurix Corp.* v. *Argentina* interpreted a similar provision as permitting the interpretation of the FET as a higher standard than that required by international law (2006, Award, para. 361), the Tribunal implicitly aligned the former to the latter.

Between these two extremes, some arbitration tribunals adopt a moderate approach stressing the need to take into account the rights of both host States and investors in light of the specifics of each case. In that sense, the Tribunal appointed in *Devas* v. *India* viewed the FET as follows: 'FET is an objective concept; it is the result of interests and rights of both the investor and the State and the result of such balancing may vary with the circumstances' (2016, Award on Jurisdiction and Merits, para. 464). Even more precisely, the Tribunal stated in *Rusoro Mining Limited* v. *Venezuela*:

> In evaluating the State's conduct, the Tribunal must balance the investor's right to be protected against improper State conduct, with other legally relevant interests and countervailing factors. First among these factors is the principle that legislation and regulation are dynamic, and that States enjoy a sovereign

---

[1] I Brownlie, *Principles of Public International Law* (5th ed, Oxford University Press 1999), at 527–531.

right to amend legislation and to adopt new regulation in the furtherance of public interest. The right to regulate, however, does not authorize States to act in an arbitrary or discriminatory manner, or to disguise measures targeted against a protected investor under the cloak of general legislation. Other countervailing factors affect the investor: it is the investor's duty to perform an appropriate pre-investment due diligence review and to show a proper conduct both before and during the investment. [footnote omitted] (2016, Award, para. 525)

In relation to this balanced approach, it is worth referring to the 2016 Nigeria–Singapore IIA, which calls for taking into account the specificities of the States parties to determine the standard applicable to each of them. Indeed, its Article 3.4 provides: 'In applying this article, Parties understand that they have different forms of administrative, legislative, and judicial systems and are at different levels of development and may not achieve the same standard at the same time.'

5.1.2.3 Material Approach

Preliminary Remarks
The third approach identifies subcategories that form part of the FET standard. Four preliminary remarks can be formulated in this respect.

First, it should be noted that the methodology used by arbitration tribunals to determine the existence of such subcategories varies. Some adopt a classical public international law approach – based on the VCLT – by interpreting the terms of the FET provision in their context and in light of the object and purpose of the IIA in question (e.g. *Joseph Charles Lemire* v. *Ukraine*, 2010, Decision on Jurisdiction and Liability, paras. 256–273). In this respect, it is interesting to note that some tribunals emphasise that the content to be given to this provision depends in particular on the context. For instance, the Tribunal appointed in *Antin* v. *Spain* stressed that the specificity of the Energy Charter Treaty (ECT), as compared to other IIAs, concerning the focus on the stability of the legal framework, justified its conclusion that the FET provision of this treaty includes the obligation to provide a stable and predictable legal framework for investments (2018, Award, para. 533).

Other tribunals refer merely to the findings in past arbitration awards to justify the content that they give to the FET standard. In the case of *Murphy Exploration & Production Company-International* v. *Ecuador*, for instance, the Tribunal stated:

It is clear from the repeated reference to 'fair and equitable' treatment in investment treaties and arbitral awards that the FET treaty standard is now generally accepted as reflecting recognisable components, such as: transparency, consistency, stability, predictability, conduct in good faith and the fulfilment of an investor's legitimate expectations. (2016, Partial Final Award, para. 206)

In contrast, a few tribunals refute the utility of justifying the content they give to the FET standard by reference to the findings of past tribunals; for instance, in *RREEF* v. *Spain*, the Tribunal explained:

The Tribunal is convinced that it is of no avail to cite the long litany of the case-law in which investment tribunals have tried to define the FET standard. Suffice it to say that there can be no doubt that (i) transparency, (ii) constant protection and security, (iii) non-impairment including (iv) non-discrimination and (v) proportionality and reasonableness, are elements of the FET – and certainly so under the ECT . . . Similarly, and while it is not expressly mentioned in Article 10(1), the Tribunal is of the opinion that respect for the legitimate expectations of the investor is implied by this provision and is part of the FET standard. (2018, Decision on Responsibility and on the Principles of Quantum, para. 260)

Second, and in relation to the remarks made above, the link established by some IIAs between the FET standard and the minimum standard of treatment as well as the content given to the latter by tribunals impact on the threshold applied in appraising States' conduct with regard to the FET subcategories. For instance, in *Crystallex International Corporation* v. *Venezuela*, the Tribunal considered that the public international law principles concerning the treatment of aliens have evolved since the *Neer* case and that the FET standard is broader than the treatment enjoyed by these aliens at the start of the nineteenth century. It concluded that the FET standard comprises in particular the protection of legitimate expectations, the protection against discriminatory and arbitrary treatment, transparency and consistency. The Tribunal then shared its belief that 'the state's conduct needs not be outrageous or amount to bad faith to breach the fair and equitable treatment standard', meaning in relation to each of its subcategories (2016, Award, paras. 534 and 543). This is to be contrasted, for instance, to the views expressed by the Tribunal in *Cargill, Incorporated* v. *Mexico*. As explained above, that Tribunal considered that the aggravating circumstances referred to in the '*Neer* formula' still characterise CIL in this respect. Having stated that the violation of the FET provision may arise in particular from the lack of due process, discrimination, or denial of justice, it argued that in all these forms, 'the "lack" or "denial" of a quality or rights [must be] sufficiently at the margin of acceptable conduct' and 'that the lack or denial must be "gross", "manifest", "complete", or such as to "offend judicial propriety"' (2009, Award, paras. 284–285).

This award also shows that the link between the FET standard and the minimum standard of treatment as well as the content given to the latter impacts on the subcategories the former is said to contain. Indeed, the Tribunal concluded that the claimant had not established that transparency was included in the CIL minimum standard of treatment owed to investors per the requirement of Article 1105 of the NAFTA to afford FET treatment, stressing that the principal authority relied on by the claimant involved the interpretation of a treaty-based autonomous standard for FET (para. 294).

The third remark concerns the scope of the FET standard's subcategories and the interplay between them. As evidenced by the fact that these subcategories are often discussed in combination – these combinations varying – some of these are in fact intertwined and the protection that they offer overlaps, as illustrated by the crossover between legitimate expectations and stability.

Furthermore, some of these subcategories have a cross-cutting dimension in the sense that they appear not only or mainly to be stand-alone subcategories, but also as constitutive elements of the other subcategories, in particular good faith. For instance, in *Devas* v. *India*, the Tribunal stressed that good faith is the source of legitimate expectations (2016, Award on Jurisdiction and Merits, para. 458). To some extent, this also applies to transparency, which is often associated with legitimate expectations and stability (e.g. *Novenergia II – Energy & Environment (SCA)* v. *Spain*, 2018, Final Arbitral Award, para. 659), due process (e.g. *Bayindir Insaat Turizm Ticaret Ve Sanayi A.S.* v. *Pakistan*, 2009, Award, para. 178) or arbitrariness (e.g. *Crystallex International Corporation* v. *Venezuela*, 2016, Award, para. 576). As illustrated by the above-mentioned excerpt of the award rendered in *Tecnicas Medioambientales Tecmed* v. *Mexico* (2003, Award, para. 154), this holds true as well for legitimate expectations. Finally, proportionality also seems to emerge as such a cross-cutting subcategory (e.g. *RREEF* v. *Spain*, 2018, Decision on Responsibility and on the Principles of Quantum, paras. 260 and 467).

Given these combinations and crossovers, it is difficult to offer a clear-cut classification of the FET subcategories as they emerge from arbitration practice. This is all the more true given the fact that the components given to the FET standard by arbitration tribunals vary. To make sense of all this, four broad categories are distinguished and analysed in what follows: (1) the respect for legitimate expectations and stability; (2) the prohibition of procedural impropriety; (3) the prohibition of arbitrariness and discrimination; and (4) the prohibition of duress, coercion and harassment. This analysis will pave the way for our examination of treaty practice, whose evolution in the 2010s has come partly as a reaction to the relevant arbitration practice.

As a final remark, it is worth noting that in those cases where the facts make various FET subcategories relevant, tribunals tend not to appraise the responsibility of host States and the legality of their conduct in relation to each of them separately. Instead, they appraise more globally whether their conduct constitutes a breach of the FET provision. This methodology was well explained by the Tribunal appointed in *Crystallex International Corporation* v. *Venezuela*:

> In any event, the Tribunal emphasizes that, while resort to the elements of which FET is composed may be a useful tool to assess the facts in concrete cases, including this one, it is the overall evaluation of the state's conduct as "fair and equitable" that is the ultimate object of the Tribunal's examination. Rather than to focus on a mass of details and direct the analysis to specific instances of alleged violations of the standard, the Tribunal will endeavor to establish whether an overall pattern of conduct has emerged from these instances and whether that overall pattern of conduct does indeed breach the standard. (2016, Award, para. 545)

It should also be mentioned that tribunals, when relevant, appraise whether there exists – as is known in public international law – a 'composite act' that violates the FET provision. As such, each act in the series of conduct that makes up the composite act does not in and of itself constitute a breach of the FET provision; rather, it is the series of such acts altogether that constitute the breach. This notion is further discussed in Chapter 6 in relation to creeping expropriations.

a The Respect of Legitimate Expectations and Stability

Preliminary Remarks

Legitimate expectations is one of the subcategories of the FET standard that has attracted most of the criticism in the early twenty-first century. This is due to the fact that it has been seen as freezing the legal framework applicable to investments at the time they are made and thereby as preventing the exercise by host States of their right to regulate. As examined below, this criticism has led States parties in a few IIAs concluded in the 2010s to limit its scope and its role in the appraisal of the breach of FET provisions. In fact, legitimate expectations has not traditionally been incorporated into IIAs; rather, it has emerged in international investment law through arbitration practice and is now largely considered as forming part and parcel of the FET standard. In this respect, three preliminary remarks can be made regarding the source of legitimate expectations, its exact status and role in arbitration practice, and methodological considerations.

As to the source of legitimate expectations, it is worth noting that arbitration tribunals often merely assert the existence of this subcategory, as is illustrated by the above-mentioned excerpt of the award rendered in *RREEF* v. *Spain* (2018, Decision on Responsibility and on the Principles of Quantum, para. 260). When they justify their existence, they usually do so on the basis of the findings of past tribunals (e.g. *Murphy Exploration & Production Company– International* v. *Ecuador*, 2016, Partial Final Award, para. 247). A few tribunals link legitimate expectations to a primary source of international investment law, be it to general principles of law recognised by civilised nations or to CIL. The award rendered by the Tribunal in *Gold Reserve Inc.* v. *Venezuela* illustrates the former linkage, wherein the Tribunal argued:

> With particular regard to the legal sources of one of the standards for respect of the fair and equitable treatment principle, *i.e.* the protection of 'legitimate expectations', these sources are to be found in the comparative analysis of many domestic legal systems … Based on converging considerations of good faith and legal security, the concept of legitimate expectations is found in different legal traditions according to which some expectations may be reasonably or legitimately created for a private person by the constant behavior and/or promises of its legal partner, in particular when this partner is the public administration on which this private person is dependent. (2014, Award, para. 576)

Tribunals link legitimate expectations to CIL in different ways. In *Charanne B.V.* v. *Spain*, the Tribunal connected legitimate expectations to the customary law principle of good faith (2016, Final Award, para. 486). The Tribunal appointed in *Peter A. Allard* v. *Barbados* grounded this subcategory in CIL directly by arguing that the minimum standard of treatment in particular 'includes the protection of an investor's legitimate expectations arising from a host State's representations, under certain conditions' (2016, Award, para. 193).

Concerning the exact status and role of legitimate expectations in arbitration practice, there exist discrepancies across the views expressed by tribunals. As exemplified by the above-mentioned excerpt of the award rendered in *Tecnicas Medioambientales Tecmed* v. *Mexico* (2003, Award, para. 154), legitimate expectations appear to constitute for some the conceptual cornerstone of the FET standard. This tends to make of legitimate expectations an 'overarching' subcategory covering all the factual situations subsumed in the other FET subcategories. More frequently, legitimate expectations is conceived of as a self-standing subcategory in and of itself, the violation of which establishes the violation of the FET standard (e.g. *Gavrilovic* v. *Croatia*, Award, 2018, para. 955). On the other hand, some tribunals deny any such predominance and even any autonomy to the legitimate expectations inasmuch as they consider that a breach of the investors' legitimate expectations does not constitute in itself a violation of the FET provision, but instead a mere element to be taken into consideration in the assessment of the breach of the FET subcategories (e.g. *MESA Power Group, LLC* v. *Canada*, Award, 2016, para. 502). In this respect, it can be noted that those few IIAs concluded in the 2010s which mention legitimate expectations follow this approach. For instance, Article 8.10.4 of the 2016 Comprehensive Economic and Trade Agreement (CETA) makes of a breach of legitimate expectations an element that may be taken into consideration when applying the FET provision.

The methodology used to appraise the existence of legitimate expectations does not raise major difficulties. This existence is to be appraised through an objective analysis. This entails mainly that the subjective belief on the side of foreign investors that they have legitimate expectations is insufficient to ground a finding that legitimate expectations exist indeed. Furthermore, the existence of legitimate expectations should be assessed at the time the investment is made. As explained by the Tribunal in *Antin* v. *Spain*, this means that tribunals should 'consider the information and conditions available at such time, and . . . refrain from appraising the investor's expectations with the benefit of hindsight' (2018, Award, para. 537). If an investment is composed of a series of decisive steps, for instance if it includes expansion and development, tribunals have been ready to examine the existence of legitimate expectations also at these stages (e.g. *Peter A. Allard* v. *Barbados*, 2016, Award, para. 218).

Beyond all these issues, the concrete appraisal of whether foreign investors have legitimate expectations raises complex and intertwined questions. These questions are by and large twofold: (1) what can be expected by foreign investors? And (2) from which conduct of host States can investors' expectations derive? Of course, the answers to these questions depend on the facts of each case. That being said, the answers are also largely conditioned by the legal views that tribunals have as regards these questions.

i What Can be Expected by Foreign Investors?   This first issue arises mainly in relation to stability. Tribunals often refer to 'the stability of the legal and business framework' as a whole. It is important to stress that a distinction has to be made here between the stability of the business framework and the stability of the legal framework. The way to deal with the former is not problematic: foreign investors cannot expect under the FET standard, and IIAs more generally, to obtain a stability of the business framework. This is often recalled by arbitration tribunals (e.g. *UAB E Energija (Lithuania)* v. *Latvia*, 2017, Award, para. 848); interestingly, in *El Paso Energy International Company* v. *Argentina* (2011, Award, para. 366), the Tribunal did so by relying on the *Oscar Chinn* case decided by the Permanent Court of International Justice:

> No enterprise – least of all a commercial or transport enterprise, the success of which is dependent on the fluctuating level of prices and rates – can escape from the changes and hazards resulting from general economic conditions. Some industries may be able to make large profits during a period of general prosperity, or else by taking advantage of a treaty of commerce or of an alteration in customs duties; but they are also exposed to the danger of ruin or extinction if circumstances change. (1934, Judgment, at 88)

Turning to the expectations that foreign investors may legitimately have with regard to the stability of the legal framework, one can identify different views expressed across arbitration practice on the matter. The above-mentioned award rendered in *Tecnicas Medioambientales Tecmed* v. *Mexico* is often considered as having recognised the right for investors to expect complete legal stability. In its most relevant part, the Tribunal stated:

> The foreign investor expects the host State to act in a consistent manner, free from ambiguity and totally transparently in its relations with the foreign investor, so that it may know beforehand any and all rules and regulations that will govern its investments, as well as the goals of the relevant policies and administrative practices or directives, to be able to plan its investment and comply with such regulations. (2003, Award, para. 154)

Such an approach tends to make of the FET standard a kind of 'stabilisation clause' *mutatis mutandis* comparable to those that can be found in the 'State contracts' discussed in Chapter 1. It is therefore not surprising that it was criticised for conferring a freezing effect to that standard and as constituting a threat against the right of host States to regulate. In this respect, it can be suggested that this award in particular has greatly contributed to convincing civil society members that international investment law and arbitration is harmful to public interests. Yet, it is worth emphasising that this approach promoted by the Tribunal in

Tecmed has been strongly criticised and rebutted among tribunals themselves. For instance, the Tribunal appointed in *EDF (Services) Limited* v. *Romania* stated:

> The idea that legitimate expectations, and therefore FET, imply the stability of the legal and business framework, may not be correct if stated in an overly-broad and unqualified formulation. The FET might then mean the virtual freezing of the legal regulation of economic activities, in contrast with the State's normal regulatory power and the evolutionary character of economic life . . . Such expectation would be neither legitimate nor reasonable. (2009, Award, para. 217)

Under this approach, foreign investors cannot legitimately expect to benefit from legal stability which would result in the annihilation of the right of host States to exercise their normative power after their investment has been made. That being said, the right of States to amend their laws is not considered as being safeguarded in any circumstances. This leads us to the discussion of those circumstances in which foreign investors may have legitimate expectations concerning the stability of the legal framework applicable to their investment.

ii From Which Host State Conduct Can Legitimate Expectations Derive?   At stake here is the issue of what can constitute the 'basis' of legitimate expectations or, to put it differently, from which host State conduct can legitimate expectations derive? Arbitration practice in this respect is confusing, in particular because tribunals give a different meaning to the notion of specificity on which they focus. Specificity is used to refer – singly or in combination depending on the awards – to the content, the form, the addressee or the object of State conduct. This statement of the Tribunal appointed in *Crystallex International Corporation* v. *Venezuela* illustrates in particular the first two items: 'To be able to give rise to such legitimate expectations, such promise or representation – addressed to the individual investor – must be sufficiently specific, i.e. it must be precise as to its content and clear as to its form' (2016, Award, para. 547). Secondarily here, it is worth noting that such an approach opposes the views expressed by some tribunals following which legitimate expectations can be based on implicit undertakings and insurances (e.g. *Novenergia II – Energy & Environment (SCA) (Grand Duchy of Luxembourg), SICAR* v. *Spain*, 2018, Final Arbitral Award, para. 650). The conception of specificity in relation to the addressee and object of State conduct was explained by the Tribunal appointed in *El Paso Energy International Company* v. *Argentina*: 'In the Tribunal's view, no general definition of what constitutes a specific commitment can be given, as all depends on the circumstances. However, it seems that two types of commitments might be considered "specific": those specific as to their addressee and those specific regarding their object and purpose' (2011, Award, para. 375).

Another source of confusion derives from the fact that the tribunals that focus on the object in fact pay attention to two different types of object; this is again well exemplified by the two above-mentioned cases. In *El Paso Energy International Company* v. *Argentina*, the Tribunal argued that the precise object of the commitment is to give a real guarantee of stability to the investor

(2011, Award, para. 377). Instead of focusing on the guarantee of stability, the Tribunal in *Crystallex International Corporation* v. *Venezuela* put the emphasis on the concrete benefit that the State conduct offers to investors, stating: 'A legitimate expectation may arise in cases where the Administration has made a promise or representation to an investor as to a substantive benefit, on which the investor has relied in making its investment, and which later was frustrated by the conduct of the Administration' (2016, Award, para. 547).

Despite these differences, it is possible to identify a number of key trends in arbitration practice.

First of all, it is undisputed that legitimate expectations may derive from State conduct towards individual investors, typically from contracts entered into between host States and investors. Whether or not legitimate expectations can derive from host State conduct as regards investors or a group of investors is a more delicate issue. Arbitration tribunals have been reluctant to view such conduct, typically general legislation, as grounding legitimate expectations on the part of foreign investors. This is due to the nature of legislation which by definition can evolve and also to the consequences of regarding such instruments as a basis for legitimate expectations; again, it is feared that this would be harmful to the right of host States to regulate and ultimately harmful to public interests. In *El Paso Energy International Company* v. *Argentina*, the Tribunal explained that '[u]sually general texts cannot contain such commitments, as there is no guarantee that they will not be modified in due course'. It merely acknowledged as an exception that 'a reiteration of the same type of commitment in different types of general statements could, considering the circumstances, amount to a specific behaviour of the State, the object and purpose of which is to give the investor a guarantee on which it can justifiably rely' (2011, Award, para. 377). More systematically, some tribunals consider that, even though foreign investors cannot expect general legislation to be frozen, some modification of this legislation may constitute a breach of their legitimate expectations when it is unreasonable and disproportionate. The award rendered in *Charanne B.V.* v. *Spain* illustrates this approach, even though it should be recalled that the ECT – which the Tribunal applied in this case – focuses very much on stability. It stated that 'an investor has a legitimate expectation that, when modifying the existing regulation based on which the investment was made, the State will not act unreasonably, disproportionately or contrary to the public interest'. As to proportionality, it 'consider[ed] that this criterion is satisfied as long as the changes are not capricious or unnecessary and do not amount to suddenly and unpredictably eliminate the essential characteristics of the existing regulatory framework' (2016, Final Award, paras. 514 and 517). As illustrated by that case, the potential for a modification of general legislation to be viewed as a breach of the investor's legitimate expectations has been argued in particular when the legislation was put in place to induce foreign investments and when the investor actually relied on it. It should also be mentioned that, while acknowledging that general legislation and the modification thereof are relevant in appraising the existence of legitimate expectations and whether or not there has been a breach of the same, tribunals have increasingly considered that foreign investors must act diligently and make every effort to educate themselves as to the general legislation in place at the time they invest (e.g. *Masdar Solar & Wind Cooperatief U.A.* v. *Spain*, 2018, Award, para. 494).

That latter remark illustrates a trend that has gained growing importance in arbitration practice, according to which one should take into account whether it was reasonable for investors to have particular expectations and whether they acted diligently to appraise them. This includes taking into account what they knew, or should have known at the time they made their investment, the circumstances that prevailed at that time, and whether they evaluated the risk inherent in their operations when they relied on host States' representations. Such due diligence relates to legal considerations and, more generally, to considerations pertaining to society and to foreign investors themselves.

Legal considerations pertain first and foremost to the legal framework in force at the time the investment is made. This has been seen as including all the domestic laws and also international law rules which are relevant to an investment operation. In that sense, the Tribunal appointed in *Urbaser S.A.* v. *Argentina* stated:

> In the instant case, this obligation relates to the Government's responsibilities under the Federal Constitution to ensure the population's health and access to water and to take all measures required to that effect. This was an important objective of the privatization of the water and sewage services, including the investment in this particular case. When measures had been taken that have as their purpose and effect to implement such fundamental rights protected under the Constitution, they cannot hurt the fair and equitable treatment standard because their occurrence must have been deemed to be accepted by the investor when entering into the investment and the Concession Contract. In short, they were expected to be part of the investment's legal framework. This does not mean that they are not subject to the fair and equitable treatment standard. The Government must exercise such responsibility in a manner that comports with the standard. The investor may not invoke the protection of its own interests as a prevailing objective, because these interests were part of a legal environment also covering core interests of the host State, as protected by sources of law prevailing over the Contract, based on international or on constitutional law. (2016, Award, para. 622)

In addition to the legal framework applicable to investments existing at the time they are made, foreign investors are expected to display a 'forward-looking' due diligence. Indeed, a number of arbitration tribunals have argued *mutatis mutandis* that, because host States enjoy a right to regulate, foreign investors shall enquire into the potential changes that may affect in the future the regulatory framework applicable to their investment 'in light of the then prevailing or reasonably to be expected changes in the economic and social conditions of the host State' (*Philip Morris* v. *Uruguay*, 2016, Award, para. 427).

Beyond the law, tribunals pay attention to considerations pertaining to society and foreign investors themselves. For example, in *Duke Energy Electroquil*

Partners v. *Ecuador*, the Tribunal stated that '[t]he assessment of the reasonableness or legitimacy must take into account all circumstances, including not only the facts surrounding the investment, but also the political, socioeconomic, cultural and historical conditions prevailing in the host State' (2008, Award, para. 340). Focusing on foreign investors, tribunals have also taken into consideration the experience that they have acquired in the host State. In *Bayindir Insaat Turizm Ticaret Ve Sanayi A.S.* v. *Pakistan*, for instance, the Tribunal opined that the investor, because he had already 'suffered severely from political changes in Pakistan during the preceding years', 'could not reasonably have ignored the volatility of the political conditions prevailing in Pakistan at the time it agreed to the revival of the Contract' (2009, Award, para. 193).

b The Prohibition of Procedural Impropriety

The protection enjoyed by foreign investors against procedural improprieties is based on two subcategories of the FET standard: the respect of due process and the prohibition of denial of justice.

Both subcategories are mentioned in the IIAs that specify the content of the FET standard, be it or not in relation to the minimum standard of treatment. It is worth stressing that they constitute the 'common substantive denominator' of those IIAs inasmuch as the mention of other subcategories is not as systematic in treaty practice. Beyond this, one can see that the scope of the protection they confer and their interplay vary from one IIA to the other.

The 2018 USMCA links both subcategories and places due process as the 'guiding principle' to be applied to denial of justice. Article 14.6.2.a thereof provides: '"[F]air and equitable treatment" includes the obligation not to deny justice in criminal, civil or administrative adjudicatory proceedings in accordance with the principle of due process embodied in the principal legal systems of the world.' On the other hand, other treaties do not establish any link between these two subcategories of the FET standard. For instance, the IIA adopted by Colombia and the United Arab Emirates (UAE) in 2017 provides: 'The concept of "fair and equitable treatment" means protection against measures or series of measures that constitute: a) denial of justice in criminal, civil or administrative proceedings; b) fundamental breach of due process, in judicial and administrative proceedings; or c) manifest arbitrariness' (Article 5.2).

Another divergence to be noted in treaty practice concerns denial of justice specifically. Some agreements, like the 2017 Colombia–UAE IIA, refer to 'denial of justice' in relation to 'criminal, civil or administrative proceedings'; others, as exemplified by the USMCA, refer to this subcategory in connection with 'criminal, civil or administrative *adjudicatory* proceedings' (emphasis added). In other words, the former category of agreements covers proceedings in general, while the latter encompasses only adjudicatory proceedings. When applying Article 10.5.2. of the 2004 Dominican Republic–Central America Free Trade Agreement (CAFTA–DR) which adopts the same narrower drafting, the Tribunal appointed in *Corona Materials, LLC* v. *Dominican Republic* stressed that this IIA is not drafted in broad terms and stated:

> The inclusion of the word "*adjudicatory*" assumes importance because it requires a tribunal to focus on the nature of the State's measure(s) at issue. That is, not all criminal, civil or administrative matters, acts or procedures fall within the scope of DR–CAFTA Article 10.5.1 such that they are capable of giving rise to an international claim for denial of justice. (2016, Award, para. 250)

On this basis, the Tribunal concluded that the Ministry's receipt of motion for reconsideration and its alleged inaction could not be considered as an administrative adjudicatory proceeding (paras. 250–251).

Arbitration practice in general displays a similar lack of consistency in the way due process and denial of justice are connected to one another. It should be mentioned that this inconsistency cannot be explained by drafting differences between the IIAs applied, inasmuch as those IIAs have traditionally not mentioned those subcategories at all. In some awards, due process seems to be conceived of as an aspect of denial of justice (e.g. *International Thunderbird Gaming Corporation* v. *Mexico*, 2006, Arbitral Award, para. 197), while, to the contrary, this is denial of justice which appears in other awards as being considered as an aspect of due process (e.g. *Spyridon Roussalis* v. *Romania*, 2011, Award, para. 315).

In any event, denial of justice is the main ground used by foreign investors and discussed by arbitration tribunals with regard to procedural impropriety. As a preliminary remark to this focus on denial of justice, it is worth stressing its procedural and systemic dimension.

This subcategory of the FET standard is usually conceived of as protecting foreign investors against the malfunction of the host States' court system and not against its 'substantive outcome'. Instead, egregiously wrong decisions are typically seen as the result or as evidence of such malfunction. This approach is illustrated by this statement made by the Tribunal in *Liman Caspian Oil BV* v. *Kazakhstan*:

> Taking into account the above authorities, the Tribunal concludes that Respondent can only be held liable for denial of justice if Claimants are able to prove that the court system fundamentally failed. Such failure is mainly to be held established in cases of major procedural errors such as lack of due process. The substantive outcome of a case can be relevant as an indication of lack of due process and thus can be considered as an element to prove denial of justice. (2010, Award, para. 279)

By the same token, this focus on the procedural failure of the court system leads to situations in which it may be concluded that there has been a denial of justice even though the same outcome could have been reached absent the commission of the denial of justice (*Philip Morris* v. *Uruguay*, 2016, Award, para. 575).

As put above, denial of justice entails a failure of the court system; in other words, it shall have a systemic dimension. This entails that denial of justice is closely tied to the exhaustion of local remedies. Indeed, such an exhaustion is the *conditio sine qua non* to concluding that there has been a systemic failure of the court system. In its seminal piece on denial of justice in international law, Paulsson explains this requirement as follows:

> For a foreigner's international grievance to proceed as a claim of denial of justice, the national system must have been tested. Its perceived failings cannot constitute an international wrong unless it has been given a chance to correct itself ... [I]t is in the very nature of the delict that a state is judged by the final product – or at least a sufficiently final product – of its administration of justice. A denial of justice is not consummated by the decision of a court of first instance. Having sought to rely on national justice, the foreigner cannot complain that its operations have been delictual until he has given it scope to operate, including by the agency of its ordinary corrective functions.[2]

This means that foreign investors shall proceed 'step by step' to the highest court before a denial of justice can potentially be characterised if that court, while being aware of the complaint of serious procedural impropriety, fails to address it. This requirement suffers exceptions, typically when there is no remedy available or no effective remedy available. As stressed by the Tribunal appointed in *Marfin Investment Group Holdings S.A.* v. *Cyprus*, in reference to *Apotex Inc.* v. *USA* (2013, Award on Jurisdiction and Admissibility, para. 284), such an unavailability 'requires more than one side simply proffering its best estimate or prediction as to its likely prospect of success, if available recourse had been pursued' (2018, Award, para. 1275).

Focusing on the extent and modalities of the protection conferred by this subcategory of the FET standard, it is worth insisting that the threshold for recognising a breach of that standard on the ground of denial of justice is very high. As noted by the Tribunal in *Chevron Corporation* v. *Ecuador*, what is required is that the situation causes shock and surprise amounting to discreditable improprieties and the failure of the whole national system (2018, Second Partial Award on Track II, para. 8.40). This comes from the fact that rendering justice is a key attribute of State sovereignty that will not easily be equated to a breach of international law. The analysis of the minimum standard of treatment conducted above reflects this high threshold. Indeed, even some of the opponents to the '*Neer* formula' and the high threshold that it contains have acknowledged that this threshold applies to denial of justice, which is telling as regards the high threshold attached to findings of denial of justice.

As regards instances of denial of justice, the Tribunal appointed in *Robert Azinian* v. *Mexico* referred for instance to situations in which the relevant courts refuse to entertain a suit, where they administer justice in a seriously inadequate way or in those situations where they make a clear and malicious misapplication of the law (1999, Award, paras. 102–103). Whether in relation to the FET standard as such or the minimum standard of treatment, it is often stressed to the contrary that mere misapplications of the law are not constitutive of a denial of justice and that the protection against such a denial does not

---

[2] J Paulsson, *Denial of Justice in International Law* (Cambridge University Press 2005), at 108.

turn arbitration tribunals into appellate bodies that have to correct errors of domestic procedural or substantive law (e.g. *Liman Caspian Oil BV* v. *Kazakhstan*, 2010, Award, para. 274). Likewise, delays in judicial proceedings are not easily regarded as denials of justice. In the case of *Jan de Nul N.V.* v. *Egypt*, for instance, the Tribunal explained:

> [T]here is no doubt that ten years to obtain a first instance judgment is a long period of time. However, the Tribunal is mindful that the issues were complex and highly technical, that two cases were involved, that the parties were especially productive in terms of submissions and filed extensive expert reports. For these reasons, it concludes that, while the duration of the proceedings leading to the Ismaïlia Judgment is certainly unsatisfactory in terms of efficient administration of justice, it does not rise to the level of a denial of justice. (2008, Award, para. 204)

The high threshold attached to findings of denial of justice is also well exemplified by the specific situation at stake in *Philip Morris* v. *Uruguay* and the conclusion of the Tribunal. Indeed, it decided that a situation in which the highest domestic courts of a State adopt two conflicting interpretations on the same case is not sufficiently shocking and serious to be characterised as a denial of justice (2016, Award, para. 528).

c The Prohibition of Arbitrariness and Discrimination

Preliminary Remarks
The prohibitions of arbitrary conduct and of discriminatory conduct have long been recognised as subcategories of the FET standard in arbitration practice. As part of the above-mentioned trend towards specifying the content of the FET standard in IIAs concluded in the 2010s, both arbitrariness and discrimination are referred to as subcategories of that standard in the text of the agreements, the former being more often mentioned. For instance, the 2016 CETA provides for both (Article 8.10.2), while the 2017 Colombia–UAE IIA refers only to 'manifest arbitrariness' (Article 5.2). In this respect, it should be stressed that those FET provisions refer to *manifest* arbitrariness, setting thereby a high threshold which is in line with CIL. At the outset, and as explained in Chapter 3, it is worth recalling that a specific prohibition of unreasonable and discriminatory treatments has traditionally been incorporated into a number of IIAs. Given that the FET provision has been conceived of as encompassing the prohibition of arbitrary and discriminatory conduct, this specific prohibition appears to be actually largely redundant.

i Deference and the Margin of Appreciation   Under public international law, States have as a matter of principle the sovereign prerogative to regulate and to make decisions within their scope of jurisdiction. It is up to them to balance the various objectives and interests at stake in any situation and to set their own priorities in this regard. In addition to being a legal principle, this prerogative is also justified by the fact that States are often best positioned to conduct this decision-making process as to the weight to be given to the various competing objectives and interests at hand.

This is the reason why the review of host States' decisions by international courts and tribunals, and arbitration tribunals in particular, is marked by two key principles: deference and the margin of appreciation.

Deference entails that tribunals shall refrain from discussing the correctness and the appropriateness of States' decisions. In that sense, the Tribunal appointed in *Crystallex International Corporation* v. *Venezuela* stated: 'It is not for an investor–state tribunal to second-guess the substantive correctness of the reasons which an administration were to put forward in its decisions, or to question the importance assigned by the administration to certain policy objectives over others' (2016, Award, para. 583).

At the core of the margin of appreciation is the idea that States should enjoy a degree of room for manoeuvre in the fulfilment of their international obligations. In this respect, it is worth noting that the Tribunal in *Chemtura Corporation* v. *Canada* considered that this notion does not come to lessen the protection conferred by the IIA at hand in that case, rather highlighting that the factual enquiry of which it consists forms part and parcel of the determination of whether a breach of that agreement has occurred (2010, Award, para. 123).

As suggested by the very notion of margin, the freedom enjoyed by States under public international law is subject to limitation; deference would otherwise constitute a 'gaping loophole' which would undermine States' international obligations. This holds true in particular in the context of international investment law and arbitration, as stated, for instance, by the Tribunal appointed in *Unglaube* v. *Costa Rica*, which explained that deference finds its limits in arbitrariness and discrimination (2012, Award, para. 247).

ii Arbitrariness   Precisely because arbitrariness poses a limitation on a fundamental attribute of State sovereignty, the threshold for a finding of arbitrariness is high in the practice of international courts and tribunals, notably arbitration tribunals. In this respect, it can be noted that those tribunals, for instance the one appointed in *Mercer International Inc.* v. *Canada* (2018, Award, para. 7.78), often refer to that statement made by the ICJ in the *Elettronica Sicula S.p.A. (ELSI)* case when dealing with the prohibition of arbitrariness under the FET standard: 'Arbitrariness is not so much something opposed to a rule of law, as something opposed to the rule of law . . . It is a wilful disregard of due process of law, an act which shocks, or at least surprises, a sense of juridical propriety' (1989, Judgment, para. 128).

Adopting this approach, the Tribunal explained in *Crystallex International Corporation* v. *Venezuela* – in reference to the award rendered in *EDF (Services) Limited* v. *Romania* – that a measure is arbitrary under the FET standard 'if it is not based on legal standards but on excess of discretion, prejudice or personal preference, and taken for reasons that are different from those put forward by the decision maker' (2016, Award, para. 578). In that *EDF* case, the Tribunal had considered – in relation to the specific IIA provision prohibiting unreasonable and discriminatory treatment and Schreuer's legal opinion – the following measures as being arbitrary: (1) measures that inflict damage on the investor without serving any apparent legitimate purpose; (2) measures that are not based on legal standards but on discretion, prejudice or personal preference; (3) measures taken for reasons that are different from those put forward by the decision-maker; and (4) measures taken in wilful disregard of due process and proper procedure (2009, Award, para. 303).

iii Discrimination   The prohibition of discrimination is key in the protection conferred by IIAs to foreign investors. As discussed below, it constitutes the core pillar of the national treatment and MFNT standards. This is also true with regard to the FET standard, which is largely conceived of as also conferring a protection against discrimination.

Yet, this protection is not absolute in the sense that host States are left with the ability to treat foreign investors differently when there exists a reasonable justification to do so. This constitutes another illustration of the leeway that is left to States in exercising their sovereign prerogatives to promote or protect specific public interests. Another limitation to the protection against differential treatments comes from the requirement that foreign and domestic investors be in a similar situation. In other words, the prohibition of differential treatments only applies where a foreign investor, on the one hand, and a domestic investor or a group thereof, on the other, are in such a similar situation, provided also that there is no reasonable justification.

This test, which is often endorsed by arbitration tribunals (e.g. *Marfin Investment Group Holdings S.A.* v. *Cyprus*, 2018, Award, para. 1237), is not easily satisfied in practice. For instance, in *Crystallex International Corporation* v. *Venezuela*, the Tribunal concluded that the respondent State did not commit a breach of the FET provision because it had considered that there was no adequate comparator which would justify a finding of illegal discrimination; it reached this conclusion despite noting the following:

> The Tribunal has of course not overlooked the repeated and rather derogatory references to 'transnationals' and 'transnational companies' in the President's and some Ministers' statements. [footnote omitted] While the Tribunal is not unsympathetic to Crystallex's complains that it was targeted based on its 'transnational' nature and cannot exclude that discrimination actually occurred under the circumstances, it is of the view that a showing of discrimination would require more conclusive evidence of facts which are not reflected in the record. (2016, Award, para. 616)

d The Prohibition of Duress, Coercion and Harassment

The prohibition of duress, coercion and harassment has long been considered to constitute a subcategory of the FET standard. It is explicitly incorporated in some IIAs concluded in the 2010s, such as the 2016 CETA, which mentions these three types of wrongful conduct as examples of the abusive treatment that is prohibited under Article 8.10.2. It is worth highlighting – in relation to the full protection and security standard analysed below – that this FET subcategory protects foreign investors from host States' conduct directly and not from their failure to protect foreign investors from the conduct of private persons. Likewise, it should be mentioned that this subcategory is conceived of as protecting those investors and their investments, not only against physical constraints, but also against financial constraints.

To assess whether a host State has treated a foreign investor abusively, attention must be paid to the specifics of each case. Crucial in this appraisal is whether the facts display hostility on the part of the host State. For instance, in *Olin Holdings Limited* v. *Libya*, the Tribunal considered that the conduct of the respondent State amounted to a violation of the FET provision, but it declined to characterise its conduct as being a harassment on the ground that hostility had not been demonstrated (2018, Final Award, paras. 344–345). On the other hand, in *Desert Line Projects LLC* v. *Yemen*, the Tribunal decided that the conclusion between Yemen and the foreign investor of a settlement agreement following the delivery of an arbitration award constituted a breach of the FET provision as it considered that the agreement had been entered into by the investor under financial and physical duress. As to financial duress, the Tribunal found that the investor did not have any realistic alternative other than concluding the agreement in question as it was in severe financial difficulties due to the respondent's rejection of his requests for payment. Concerning physical duress, the Tribunal concluded that the investor had suffered threats and attacks, in particular the arrest of three of his managers, including his son (2008, Award, para. 181).

5.2 The Full Protection and Security Standard

The full protection and security standard has long been part of the international law rules protecting foreign private persons abroad, and foreign investors in particular. It belongs to CIL and was included in treaties of friendship, commerce and navigation. Likewise, the FPS clause is a typical provision to be found in IIAs since the inception of this treaty practice in the 1960s, even though it has not been included in all IIAs (e.g. 1970 Netherlands–Kenya IIA). In this respect, and in a way similar to the FET provision, this practice has evolved in the 2010s in particular to provide greater specification as to the scope of the protection conferred by the FPS standard. Again, this evolution partly comes as a reaction to the conception of that standard adopted by some tribunals. The scope and the characteristics of States' obligations under the FPS standard are analysed in turn, following a more general examination of treaty practice.

5.2.1 The FPS Standard in Treaty Practice

Traditionally, the FPS provisions incorporated in international investment agreements have been quite terse. Most of those provisions have referred merely to the 'full protection and security' to be granted to foreign investors and their investments. For instance, the 1975 United Kingdom–Egypt IIA provides: 'Investments of nationals or companies of either Contracting Party ... shall enjoy full protection and security in the territory of the other Contracting Party' (Article 2.2). Instead of 'full protection and security', other IIAs have referred in particular to the 'most constant protection and security' (e.g. 1994 ECT, Article 10.1), to 'protection and constant security' (e.g. 1990 United Kingdom–Argentina IIA, Article 2.2), or to 'full and complete protection and safety' (e.g. 1998 France–Mexico IIA, Article 4.3).

In addition to those references, a few treaties have entered into greater detail, in particular by specifying the type of protection conferred by the FPS standard to foreign investors and their investments. For instance, the 1991 Germany–Argentina IIA refers to 'full protection and *legal* security' (Article 4.1; emphasis added, translation by the author). In the same vein, a few other treaties have detailed the measures from which foreign investments are protected, as illustrated by the 1989 IIA adopted on the one side by the Belgium–Luxembourg Economic Union (BLEU), and on the other side by Burundi: 'These investments and activities shall benefit from a constant security and protection, which excludes any unjustified or discriminatory measure which could impede, in law or in fact, their management, their maintenance, their use, their enjoyment or their liquidation' (Article 3.2; translation by the author).

Another set of specifications that can be seen in part of treaty practice concerns the 'linkage' of the FPS standard. Most of those IIAs have established a link between that standard and customary international law or international law more generally. This is illustrated by Article 1105.1 of the NAFTA: 'Each Party shall accord to investments of investors of another Party treatment in accordance with international law, including fair and equitable treatment and full protection and security.' A few of those treaties – for instance the IIA adopted by France and Argentina in 1991 – have linked the FPS standard to the FET standard; Article 5.1 reads as follows: 'The investments made by the investors of either Contracting Party benefit, over the territory and in the maritime area of the other Contracting Party, from a full and complete protection and security pursuant to the fair and equitable treatment principle mentioned in Article 3 of this Agreement' (translation by the author). Such an approach and drafting are to be distinguished from mainstream treaty practice which distinguishes the FPS standard and the FET standard and referred to them in sequence, be it in the same sentence, or in different sentences, paragraphs or Articles.

While it has traditionally been rare to provide for further detail concerning the FPS standard in treaty practice, the IIAs concluded in particular in the

2010s have displayed a stronger trend towards specifying the content of that standard and circumscribing the protection it confers on foreign investors and their investments. This has led Brazil to more radically exclude it from its treaty practice by specifying that 'full protection and security' is not covered by the agreements it concludes (e.g. 2018 Brazil–Surinam IIA, Article 4.3). Again, this trend has largely been triggered by the practice of some tribunals, as discussed below. Two main approaches, which depending on IIAs are used in combination or in isolation, can be identified in this respect.

The first of these consists of limiting the protection granted under that standard to *physical* protection and security, as opposed to *legal* protection and security. This is illustrated by Article 8.10.5 of the 2016 CETA, which provides: 'For greater certainty, "full protection and security" refers to the Party's obligations relating to the physical security of investors and covered investments.' Other agreements do not refer to 'physical security', but to the 'police protection' to be accorded to the investors of States parties and their investments. For instance, Article 2.2 of the 2016 Rwanda–Morocco IIA provides:

> Investments made by investors of one Contracting Party in the territory of the other Contracting Party shall enjoy full protection and security. For greater certainty, the full protection and security required by this paragraph means only the obligation of each Contracting Party to provide the level of police protection necessary for investors and their investments in its territory and without any further obligation.

Adopting a second approach, the States parties to some IIAs have linked the FPS standard to bodies of law or treatments granted by host States, mainly with a view to limiting the protection to be conferred to foreign investors under that standard. As such, this mainstream approach can be seen as providing a 'ceiling' to the level of protection afforded.

The first type of linkage consists of attaching the FPS standard to international law. Typically, those IIAs specify that the standard does not require treatment 'in addition to or beyond' that which is required under CIL (e.g. 2017 Hong Kong SAR China–ASEAN IIA, Article 5.1.c), or under the CIL minimum standard of treatment of aliens (e.g. 2019 Australia–Uruguay IIA, Article 4.2). This is reminiscent of some of the treaty practice concerning the FET standard.

Other agreements, typically those concluded by the UAE move the focus away from international law and treatment by referring to national law and/or treatment. For instance, the IIA adopted by Nigeria and the UAE in 2016 attaches the standard not only to international law rules, but also to the laws of the host State (Article 4.1). While providing for such a 'double linkage', the 2017 Colombia–UAE IIA goes one step further by aligning the protection due by the host State under the FPS standard to that granted to its residents. Its Article 5.4 provides: 'The "full protection and security" standard does not imply, in any case, a better protection to that accorded to residents of the

Contracting Party where the investment has been made in accordance with its laws and regulations.' It is worth noting that the 2017 Rwanda–UAE IIA which adopts a similar national treatment approach also aligns the protection under the FPS standard – through an MFNT rationale – to the protection conferred to other aliens (Article 4.3).

5.2.2 The Characteristics of States' Obligations under the FPS Standard

Two specific characteristics as regards States' obligations under the FPS standard merit some discussion – namely the nature of such obligations and their object thereof.

5.2.2.1 The Nature of the Obligations

Under that standard, States do not have a strict obligation to confer full protection and security to foreign investors and their investments. Instead, they have an obligation to do their utmost to reach this result in the context of the circumstances specific to each situation. To use a civil law concept, this is an obligation of best effort/obligation of means, as opposed to an obligation of result.

In relation to this, it should be stressed that the reference made in some IIAs to 'most constant protection and security' does not change the nature of the obligation. In *MNSS B.V.* v. *Montenegro*, the Tribunal noted in that sense: '[T] he expression "most constant" does not increase the level of protection and security as understood under international law. This standard has been understood not to impose on the Government a strict obligation but only an obligation of vigilance and due diligence taking into account the circumstances and resources of the host State' (2016, Award, para. 351).

As illustrated by that case, arbitration tribunals almost systematically describe the obligations under the FPS standard as being due diligence obligations, or less frequently obligations of reasonable care (e.g. *Peter A. Allard* v. *Barbados*, 2016, Award, para. 243). This due diligence was well explained by the Tribunal in *El Paso Energy International Company* v. *Argentina*:

> A well-established aspect of the international standard of treatment is that States must use 'due diligence' to prevent wrongful injuries to the person or property of aliens caused by third parties within their territory, and, if they did not succeed, exercise at least 'due diligence' to punish such injuries. If a State fails to exercise due diligence to prevent or punish such injuries, it is responsible for this omission and is liable for the ensuing damage. It should be emphasised that the obligation to show 'due diligence' does not mean that the State has to prevent each and every injury. Rather, the obligation is generally understood as requiring that the State take reasonable actions within its power to avoid injury when it is, or should be, aware that there is a risk of injury. The precise degree of care, of what is 'reasonable' or 'due,' depends in part on the circumstances. (2011, Award, para. 523)

The key question and challenge raised by the due diligence nature of the States' obligations under the FPS standard consists of the determination of whether or not they have been violated, an issue which is obviously not as clear-cut as with obligations of result. Some tribunals consider that reasonableness is key in this respect (e.g. *Monsieur Joseph Houben* v. *Burundi*, 2016, Award, para. 161). However, this is to some extent only shifting the question in so far as it begs in turn the question of how reasonableness is to be evaluated.

As mentioned above, the circumstances of the case play a very significant role in appraising the existence of due diligence or the lack thereof, and whether host States have violated their obligations under the FPS standard. This is very well illustrated by the facts in *Ampal-American Israel Corp.* v. *Egypt*, which led the Tribunal to both uphold and reject the FPS claim in relation to two different periods of time and situations. The Tribunal took into account the difficult circumstances in North Sinai in the aftermath of the Arab Spring Revolution to conclude that the first attack of the Trans-Sinai Pipeline could not have been prevented and did not amount to a breach of the FPS standard. On the other hand, because the Tribunal considered that the first attacks should have been viewed by Egypt as a warning that further attacks might take place if security measures were not implemented, it concluded that Egypt's failure to take any concrete steps to protect the investor's investments and thereby prevent the subsequent nine attacks constituted a breach of its due diligence obligation under that standard (2017, Decision on Liability and Heads of Loss, paras. 283–291).

Another question is whether the capacities of host States should be taken into account in appraising whether or not they acted diligently and, as such, whether they complied with their obligations under the FPS standard. In *Asian Agricultural Products Ltd (AAPL)* v. *Sri Lanka*, the Tribunal emphasised an evolution – in relation to an argument made by international law authorities – towards taking as an objective benchmark the 'well-administered government' in conducting the analysis, thereby excluding tribunals from taking States' capacities into account. It stated:

> A number of other contemporary international law authorities noticed the 'sliding scale', from the old 'subjective' criteria that takes into consideration the relatively limited existing possibilities of local authorities in a given context, towards an 'objective' standard of vigilance in assessing the required degree of protection and security with regard to what should be legitimately expected to be secured for foreign investors by a reasonably well organized modern State. As expressed by Professor FREEMAN, in his 1957 Lectures at the Hague Academy of International Law: The 'due diligence' is nothing more nor less than the reasonable measures of prevention which a well-administered government could be expected to exercise under similar circumstances. (1990, Final Award, para. 77)

Such an approach provides that the factual circumstances of a case can be taken into account, but not the circumstances or capabilities pertaining to each State, which could, however, be seen as an element forming part of the circumstances of a case. This approach tends to 'rigidify' the FPS standard and to water down the flexibility inherent to due diligence obligations. In that vein, the Sole Arbitrator in *Pantechniki S.A. Contractors & Engineers (Greece) v. Albania* considered – in reference to Newcombe and Paradell[3] – that the due diligence under the FPS is a 'modified objective standard' enabling tribunals to take into account the resources of States and their level of development; he adopted their views according to which '[a]n investor investing in an area with endemic civil strife and poor governance cannot have the same expectation of physical security as one investing in London, New York or Tokyo' (2009, Award, para. 81). In that sense, it is worth highlighting the 2016 Nigeria–Singapore IIA which states, with regard to the FPS provision in particular, that the 'Parties understand that they have different forms of administrative, legislative, and judicial systems and are at different levels of development and may not achieve the same standard at the same time' (Article 3.4).

5.2.2.2 The Object of the Obligations

The object of the FPS standard is mainly twofold: (1) preventing the occurrence of certain conduct harmful to foreign investors and their investments; and (2) repressing such conduct where that conduct has not been prevented. That latter object includes the requirement for host States to act diligently in apprehending and prosecuting those responsible.

The obligation to prevent is well illustrated by the above-mentioned *Ampal-American Israel Corp.* v. *Egypt* case in which the Tribunal concluded that Egypt's failure to take concrete steps to protect the investor's investments and thereby to prevent attacks subsequent to other attacks constituted a breach of its due diligence obligation under the FPS standard (2017, Decision on Liability and Heads of Loss, paras. 283–291).

Parkerings-Compagniet AS v. *Lithuania* can be used as an illustration of States' obligations to repress under the standard. In that case, the Tribunal enquired in particular into whether the failure of the Lithuanian police to find the authors of conduct harmful to the foreign investor constituted a breach of the FPS provision. It concluded that no breach had been committed on the ground that an investigation had been initiated by Lithuanian authorities and that there was no proof that the investigation process evidenced a lack of due diligence on the part of Lithuania (2007, Award, paras. 356–357). As regards the obligation to prosecute, the Tribunal seemed to have conceived of this duty as being composed of two separate obligations: the obligation to have a judicial system available and the obligation to ensure its effectiveness (para. 360).

---

[3] A Newcombe, L Paradell, *Law and Practice of Investment Treaties* (Kluwer Law International 2009), at 310.

5.2.3 The Scope of the Obligations

To use the words of the Tribunal in *Suez, AWG Group* v. *Argentina* (2010, Decision on Liability, para. 160), the scope of the obligations under the FPS standard raises two questions: (1) from whom are foreign investors and their investments protected under that standard? And (2) against what are they protected?

5.2.3.1 Protection from Whom?

This issue boils down to the question of from whose harmful conduct host States are obliged to protect investors under the FPS standard. We can say without any doubt that the FPS standard protects foreign investors and their investments against the conduct of private persons. In addition, it is argued by some that the protection that the FPS standard confers is actually broader than this and that it also covers the conduct of State organs. In other words, host States would be obliged under the FPS standard to prevent and repress the conduct of their own components. A few tribunals have not provided any justification for taking this approach (e.g. *Parkerings-Compagniet AS* v. *Lithuania*, 2007, Award, para. 355). In *Biwater Gauff (Tanzania) Ltd* v. *Tanzania*, the Tribunal justified it as follows:

> The Arbitral Tribunal also does not consider that the 'full security' standard is limited to a State's failure to prevent actions by third parties, but also extends to actions by organs and representatives of the State itself. That is also implied by the term '*full*' as well as the purposes of the BIT and the *Wena* and *AMT* awards (discussed above). (2008, Award, para. 730)

Put in relation to the FET provision, this conception of the FPS standard runs counter to an interpretation based on effectiveness. Indeed, foreign investors and their investments are 'already' protected from State organs by the FET provision; such a conception of the FPS standard then tends to confer an overlapping protection to investors and their investments. In that sense, the Tribunal appointed in *Oxus Gold* v. *Uzbekistan* pinpointed the complementarity – rather than the overlap – between the two standards as follows:

> [U]nless otherwise expressly defined in a specific BIT, the general FPS standard complements the FET standard by providing protection towards acts of third parties, i.e. non-state parties, which are not covered by the FET standard. Thus, where an incriminated act is done by a State-organ, the applicable standard is the FET standard, whereas where such act is done by a non-state entity, the applicable standard becomes the FPS standard. (2015, Final Award, para. 353)

5.2.3.2 Protection against What?

The discussion as to the scope of conduct against which foreign investors and their investments are protected under the FPS standard is broadly similar to the discussion above. As with the protection against the conduct of private persons, there is also no doubt that this standard protects investors against the conduct involving the use of force which affects the physical integrity of investors and their investments. Similar to the issue of the protection against the conduct of State organs, the issue here is whether the FPS standard also confers legal protection and security to investors and their investments.

Under a few IIAs, this issue does not arise simply because the text of the FPS provision refers in one way or another to legal protection and security. For instance, the above-mentioned Article 4.1 of the 1991 Germany–Argentina IIA refers to 'full protection and legal security'.

With regard to the majority of FPS provisions which merely refer *mutatis mutandis* to 'full protection and security', some tribunals have decided that these provisions also cover legal protection and security. In *Anglo American PLC* v. *Venezuela*, for instance, the Tribunal argued that when the applicable IIA does not provide for any explicit limit, this means that the obligation is not limited to physical security and that it covers a duty to afford legal security (2019, Award, para. 482). In *Azurix Corp.* v. *Argentina*, the Tribunal offered the following justification:

> The inter-relationship of the two standards [FET and FPS] indicates that full protection and security may be breached even if no physical violence or damage occurs as it was the case in *Occidental v. Ecuador* ... The Tribunal is persuaded of the interrelationship of fair and equitable treatment and the obligation to afford the investor full protection and security. The cases referred to above show that full protection and security was understood to go beyond protection and security ensured by the police. It is not only a matter of physical security; the stability afforded by a secure investment environment is as important from an investor's point of view. The Tribunal is aware that in recent free trade agreements signed by the United States, for instance, with Uruguay, full protection and security is understood to be limited to the level of police protection required under customary international law. However, when the terms 'protection and security' are qualified by 'full' and no other adjective or explanation, they extend, in their ordinary meaning, the content of this standard beyond physical security. (2006, Award, paras. 406 and 408)

As it appears, the argument in support of such an extension of the protection conferred by the FPS standard to legal protection and security is twofold.

The first aspect of this argument pertains to the term 'full', and is similar to the above-mentioned argument made by the Tribunal in *Biwater Gauff (Tanzania) Ltd* v. *Tanzania* with regard to the extension of the protection conferred by that standard to the conduct of State organs (2008, Award, para. 730). Beyond the fact that such a textually based argument lacks general support, it seems that the main argument relates to the interplay between the FPS standard and the FET standard.

The reasoning of the Tribunal in *Occidental Exploration and Production Company* v. *Ecuador* helps to illustrate this argument. In that case, the Tribunal considered that Ecuador had failed to provide legal stability to the investor as it found in particular that the tax law had been changed without any clarity being provided as to its meaning and scope. From this lack of legal stability, the Tribunal concluded that there had been a breach of the FET provision of the 1993 USA–Ecuador IIA. It then explained, as regards the interplay between the FET and the FPS provisions: 'In the context of this finding the question of whether in addition there has been a breach of full protection and security under this Article becomes moot as a treatment that is not fair and equitable automatically entails an absence of full protection and security of the investment' (2004, Final Award, paras. 184–187).

Putting together the reasoning of the Tribunals in the *Occidental* and *Azurix* cases, the line of argumentation leading to the conclusion that the FPS standard confers legal protection and security seems to be the following: because the FET standard confers protection against legal instability to investors, and because a breach of the FET provision automatically entails a breach of the FPS provision, the result is that the FPS standard confers legal protection to investors.

It is interesting to note that among those who consider that there exists a large overlap between the FET and FPS standards, some disagree that a breach of the FET provision automatically entails a breach of the FPS provision because they consider that the former has a broader scope than the latter (e.g. *Teinver S.A.* v. *Argentina*, 2017, Award, para. 905).

But more fundamentally, the reasoning explained above raises again – as in respect of the extension of the protection conferred by the FPS standard to the conduct of State organs – an issue in terms of effectiveness. This was well explained by the Tribunal in *Monsieur Joseph Houben* v. *Burundi*: 'If the BIT has paid attention to providing two standards of protection [FET and FPS], this means that each confers a different type of protection, in application of the general principle of effectiveness in the interpretation of international treaties' (2016, Award, para. 156; translation by the author).

In any case, it should be recalled that a number of IIAs concluded in the 2010s specify that the FPS standard relates only to States' obligations as regards the physical security of investors and their investments or their obligation to provide the level of police protection as is necessary.

5.3 The National Treatment Standard

Preliminary Remarks

The national treatment standard is a rule that prohibits differential treatments between, one the hand, foreign investors and their investments and, on the other hand, the investors of host States and their investments. This standard has formed a part of States' policies and discourses since the nineteenth century. In this respect, it is important to emphasise that both the political and legal conception of that standard and the objective assigned to it have evolved over time.

As explained in Chapter 1, national treatment was originally invoked by those – notably Calvo – who opposed the idea that foreigners and their properties shall benefit from a minimum standard of treatment that could confer on them better treatment than that enjoyed by the nationals of host States under their domestic law. In other words, national treatment was primarily invoked to avoid foreigners receiving better treatment than nationals. The same holds true in the context of the claim for a New International Economic Order put forward by developing States in the wave of decolonisation that followed the Second World War.

In the IIA treaty practice that emerged in the 1960s, the objective assigned to the national treatment standard is the reverse. Such IIAs aim to avoid a situation in which domestic investors and their investments are granted better treatment than that conferred to foreign investors and their investments, the underlying objective being to create a level playing field between them.

It is worth stressing that the criticism against international investment law and arbitration, in particular in the 2010s, has led to a revival of the original objective assigned to national treatment, notably in the views expressed by local populations and politicians. This revival has spread across all the regions of the world, thereby transcending the traditional opposition of views between developing and developed States.

In any event, the national treatment standard is still conceived of in IIA practice as a tool to ensure that foreign investors and their investments are not afforded a treatment that is less favourable than that conferred upon their domestic counterparts. As long as host States treat such investors alike, they comply with the national treatment provision. As noted by the Tribunal in *Corn Products International, Inc.* v. *Mexico*, IIA national treatment provisions embody a principal of fundamental importance in international trade law and international investment law: non-discrimination (2008, Decision on Responsibility, para. 109). This holds true as well for the MFNT standard analysed below. On the other hand, it can be noted that IIAs do not prevent host States from conferring better treatment on foreign investors and their investments; this may even constitute a requirement in the event the treatment afforded under domestic law falls below the treatment set out by other IIA provisions, typically the FET provision.

The protection conferred by the national treatment standard is not absolute. In particular, as examined in Chapter 7, it can suffer limitations in certain economic sectors or as to certain types of measures or matters. This evidences the dilemma States are faced with when designing their policies and concluding IIAs. On the one hand, the creation of a level playing field between domestic and foreign investors is key to attracting the latter with a view to stimulating the national economy and the job market; at the same time, the support given to their domestic investors or the promotion of other public interest considerations may lead to situations in which foreign investors and their investments are treated less favourably.

Obviously, the application of the national treatment standard is very much fact-sensitive. This raises a methodological issue and also issues pertaining to the identification of the basis of comparison and the determination of the differences of treatment prohibited under that standard. Each is examined in turn, in light of the relevant treaty practice.

5.3.1 The National Treatment Standard in Treaty Practice

Although it is widespread in IIA practice, it is worth noting at the outset, in relation to the above-mentioned dilemma faced by States, that the national treatment standard has traditionally not been incorporated in all IIAs; this also holds true in relation to IIAs concluded in the 2010s as illustrated by the 2016 Nigeria–Singapore IIA. In the same vein, a few IIAs condition the granting of national treatment by reference to their domestic law, which tends to water down the obligation not to treat foreign investors and their investments less favourably (e.g. 2017 Rwanda–UAE IIA, Article 5). As to those treaties which do not incorporate the national treatment standard, the FET provision can be seen as a substitute as it has been conceived of as covering non-discrimination; the same remark can be formulated in relation to those IIA provisions that specifically prohibit unreasonable and discriminatory measures.

Some of those IIAs that do include the national treatment standard set out this standard in a specific dedicated Article (e.g. 2019 Australia–Indonesia IIA, Article 14.4). In some treaties, it can be provided for in an Article together with the MFNT standard, be it in the same paragraph (e.g. 2016 Japan–Iran IIA, Article 4) or not (e.g. 2016 UAE–Mexico IIA, Article 3), or in an Article containing treatment standards more generally (e.g. 2016 Austria–Kyrgyzstan IIA, Article 3). As illustrated by the Japan–Iran IIA, when both the national treatment standard and the MFNT standard are included in the same paragraph, it is often specified that States shall accord either treatment to foreign investors and their investments, 'whichever is more favourable'.

Concerning the scope of application, treaty practice displays different approaches on the issue as to whether the national treatment standard applies to establishment. This scope also varies depending on the limitations set by IIA States parties with regard to specific sectors, measures or matters. These issues are covered in Chapters 4 and 7, respectively. This subsection examines the 'inner features' of the national treatment provisions.

As a starting point for the analysis, one can refer to Article 2 of the 2017 Israel–Japan IIA: 'Each Contracting Party shall in its Territory accord to investors of the other Contracting Party and to their investments treatment no less favorable than the treatment it accords in like circumstances to its own investors and to their investments with respect to investment activities.'

As with this Agreement, the great majority of IIAs grant the protection under the national treatment standard to both investors and covered investments. But contrary to the Israel–Japan IIA, some IIAs specify those 'investstment activities' with respect to which the standard operates usually by detailing the 'facets and stages' of those activities. This is illustrated by the 2018 Comprehensive and Progressive Agreement for Trans-Pacific Partnership (CPTPP):

1. Each Party shall accord to investors of another Party treatment no less favourable than that it accords, in like circumstances, to its own investors with respect to the establishment, acquisition, expansion, management, conduct, operation, and sale or other disposition of investments in its territory.
2. Each Party shall accord to covered investments treatment no less favourable than that it accords, in like circumstances, to investments in its territory of its own investors with respect to the establishment, acquisition, expansion, management, conduct, operation, and sale or other disposition of investments. (Article 9.4)

As evidenced by this Article, the scope of those facets and stages with respect to which the national treatment standard applies is broad; this holds true even though treaty practice is nuanced in this respect.

Very importantly, most IIAs set a 'like circumstances' qualification that limits the operation of the standard. As illustrated by the above-mentioned Articles, host States shall only grant to foreign investors and their investments a treatment that is no less favourable than the treatment that they accord *in like circumstances* to their own investors and their investments. Some IIAs refer to 'comparable situations' (e.g. 2016 Slovakia–Iran IIA, Article 4) or 'like situations' (e.g. 1993 USA–Armenia IIA, Article 2.1) instead of 'like circumstances', while a few make a reference to none of these (e.g. 2016 Argentina–Qatar IIA, Article 4).

Among the IIAs that refer to 'like circumstances', 'comparable situations' or 'like situations', a number of agreements concluded in the 2010s elaborate on the meaning and content of this qualification. As a common denominator, they all flag the need to take into account all the circumstances of the case at hand and the need to pay attention to the objective pursued by State measures. This is illustrated by Article 15.4.4 of the 2018 USMCA, which provides: 'For greater certainty, whether treatment is accorded in "like circumstances" under this Article depends on the totality of the circumstances, including whether the relevant treatment distinguishes between investors or investments on the basis of legitimate public welfare objectives.' A few of those IIAs offer greater detail and add a non-exhaustive list of circumstances to be taken into account. For instance, Article 6.3 of the 2016 Morocco–Nigeria IIA provides:

For greater certainty, references to 'like circumstances' in paragraph 2 requires an overall examination on a case-by-case basis of all the circumstances of an investment including, but not limited to:

(a) its effects on third person and the local community;
(b) its effect on the local, regional or national environment, including the cumulative effects of all investments within a jurisdiction on the environment;
(c) the sector in which the investor is in;
(d) the aim of the measure concerned;
(f) the regulatory process generally applied in relation to the measure concerned;

The examination referred to in this paragraph shall not be limited or be biased toward any one factor.

On a different note, IIAs concluded by at least one 'non-unitary entity' should be singled out as they typically include a specification concerning the obligations of 'component units'. The terms used to designate such units and entities vary from one agreement to the other, in particular depending on the exact institutional structure of the entity concerned. This can be illustrated by the 2016 CETA, which refers, with respect to Canada, to 'a government other than at the federal level' and, with respect to the EU, to 'a government of or in a Member State of the European Union' (Article 8.6).

For instance, Article 4.2 of the 2018 Belarus–India IIA provides that national treatment 'means, with respect to a Regional government, treatment no less favourable than the treatment accorded, in like circumstances, by that Regional government to investors, and to investments of investors, of the Party of which it forms a part'. By doing so, those IIAs specify that the treatment granted to investors originating from other component units is to be considered as forming part of the 'benchmark' for the application of the national treatment standard by a component unit, in addition to the treatment it grants to its own investors.

In this respect, it is worth noting that tribunals have specified with regard to Article 1102.3 of the 1992 NAFTA – which contains a similar provision – that to appraise the compliance with the national treatment obligation with respect to the conduct of the local authorities, the treatment afforded to foreign investors by one local authority must be compared to that afforded by the *same* authority to domestic investors (*Merrill & Ring Forestry L.P.* v. *Canada*, 2010, Award, para. 82). As agreed in *Resolute Forest Products Inc.* v. *Canada* with the former Tribunal, 'the proper comparison is between investors which are subject to the same regulatory measures under the same jurisdictional authority' (para. 89) and there is no requirement of uniformity of treatment between those local authorities (2018, Decision on Jurisdiction and Admissibility, para. 290).

5.3.2 The Application of the National Treatment Standard: Methodology and Reasoning

As mentioned above, the application of the national treatment standard is very much fact-sensitive. Of course, this also holds true with regard to other treatment standards, like that of fair and equitable treatment. Yet, this factual dimension is of particular importance here inasmuch as national treatment is a relative standard. This means that the protection it grants to foreign investors and their investments does not exist in the abstract; instead, its content depends on the treatment granted to the investors of host States and their investments, who must not enjoy a more favourable treatment. As discussed below, the same applies *mutatis mutandis* to the MFNT standard in relation to the treatment afforded to – other – foreign investors. In other words, facts do not only constitute the 'field' of application of those relative standards, but they kind of 'fill out' their content on a case-by-case basis. Those relative standards are to be distinguished from absolute standards which, like the FPS, set 'on their own' the treatment to be conferred on foreign investors and their investments.

To make sense of the facts and to appraise whether host States violate or not their national treatment obligations, attention needs to be paid to two key issues: (1) the identification of the basis of comparison; and (2) the determination of what differential treatment is prohibited. Both of these issues are discussed below. As we shall see, the notion of like circumstances plays an important role with regard to both. From a conceptual point of view, it is worth stressing at the outset the relativity and contingency that characterise this notion and its application; this was well explained by the Tribunal appointed in *Pope & Talbot Inc.* v. *Canada*:

> The Tribunal must resolve this dispute by defining the meaning of 'like circumstances.' It goes without saying that the meaning of the term will vary according to the facts of a given case. [footnote omitted] By their very nature, 'circumstances' are context dependent and have no unalterable meaning across the spectrum of fact situations. [footnote omitted] And the concept of 'like' can have a range of meanings, from 'similar' all the way to 'identical'. [footnote omitted] In other words, the application of the like circumstances standard will require evaluation of the entire fact setting surrounding, in this case, the genesis and application of the Regime. [footnote omitted] (2001, Award on the Merits of Phase 2, para. 75)

In relation to the critical need to evaluate the facts with regard to the application of the national treatment standard, it is worth noting that tribunals endeavour to rationalise and formalise their analyses by relying explicitly or implicitly on analytical models or tests. This proves to be a difficult exercise and an objective which is in practice not fully achieved. This holds true in many awards as the components of the tests they use are very much intertwined. Similarly, this is also the case at the level of arbitration practice more generally despite the similarities that it displays. This derives from the fact that there exist nuances and differences in the practice of tribunals as regards which components of the test they employ, the content they give to similar components and the ordering through which they examine these components.

5.3.3 The Basis of Comparison

The application of the national treatment standard requires the identification of a domestic investor or a group thereof whose treatment can be compared with that afforded to the foreign investor. Again, the way of undertaking this identification depends very much on the facts of each case. Be that as it may, the economic sector and economic activity can typically be looked to in order to determine the basis of comparison, as well as looking to the applicable legal regime. In this respect, it is worth noting that arbitration practice displays nuances and differences, which can partly be explained by the specifics of the facts submitted to tribunals.

Many tribunals inquire into whether the foreign investor and the domestic investor(s) are operating in the same sector. Among those tribunals, some adopt a broad approach; for instance, the Tribunal appointed in *Archer Daniels Midland Company* v. *Mexico* expressed the view that the word 'sector' is to be interpreted broadly to include the concepts of economic sector and business sector (2007, Award, para. 198). In *Olin Holdings Limited* v. *Libya*, the Tribunal adopted the same approach; it also found that the similarity of the location of the factories concerned reinforced its finding on the basis of comparison (2018, Final Award, para. 207). Others have a narrower approach in so far as they consider that the focus should be on the specific activities conducted by the foreign investor and the domestic investor(s) operating in the same sector. This is illustrated by *Renée Rose Levy de Levi* v. *Peru*. In that case, the Tribunal noted that the foreign investor was in the same sector as the banks that had been cited. However, it stressed that there are marked differences between the various banks operating in the banking sector, as this is a sensitive area for any country. The Tribunal then considered that the market segment in which banks are engaged, e.g. asset management and investment or corporate and consumer banking, is key in appraising whether or not they are in like circumstances (2014, Award, para. 396).

   At the other end of the spectrum, mention can be made of *Occidental Exploration and Production Company* v. *Ecuador* in which the Tribunal, in reference to the specifics of the case, argued that the sector-based approach is too narrow. It explained: 'In fact, "in like situations" cannot be interpreted in the narrow sense advanced by Ecuador as the purpose of national treatment is to protect investors as compared to local producers, and this cannot be done by addressing exclusively the sector in which that particular activity is undertaken' (2004, Final Award, para. 173).

As mentioned above, 'like circumstances', which is used in most IIAs, is a notion which both conceptually and *in concreto* involves some relativity. 'Like' entails a 'sliding scale' between identity and comparability; and the appraisal of likeness is everything but purely objective. This applies to the identification of the basis of comparison. In that sense, some tribunals have taken as a basis of comparison a domestic investor or a group thereof who were not in an identical situation. The Tribunal appointed in *Methanex Corporation* v. *USA* explained, for instance:

> Given the object of Article 1102 [national treatment] and the flexibility which the provision provides in its adoption of 'like circumstances', it would be as perverse to ignore identical comparators if they were available and to use comparators that were less 'like', as it would be perverse to refuse to find and to apply less 'like' comparators when no identical comparators existed. (2005, Final Award of the Tribunal on Jurisdiction and Merits, Part IV, Chapter B, para. 17)

5.3.4 The Prohibited Differences of Treatment

The national treatment standard prohibits differential treatments – in other words, less favourable treatment. This prohibition raises three intertwined questions: (1) When can a treatment be said to be less favourable? (2) Which features shall such a treatment have? And (3) can any justifications be put forward to prevent differential treatment from being considered a breach of the national treatment obligation? Each question is analysed in turn below.

5.3.4.1 The Appraisal of Less Favourable Treatments

At the risk of being repetitive, it is worth stressing that the determination of whether a treatment is less favourable is highly fact-sensitive; it depends heavily on the respective facts of each case. Going one step further, it depends on one's own evaluation of such facts. In this respect, it can be noted that cases can be seen in arbitration practice in which arbitrators actually disagreed on this issue (e.g. *Marvin Feldman* v. *Mexico*, 2002, Award, para. 187, and Dissenting Opinion, Part VI).

That being said, there is one legal question that is raised when the basis of comparison is actually made of a group of domestic investors and that, among them, one or some enjoy better treatment than the other(s). In such a case, in order to appraise whether or not the foreign investor received a less favourable treatment as prohibited under the national treatment obligation, should one take into account the more favourable treatment received by the domestic investor(s) *vis-à-vis* its/their domestic counterparts or should one take into consideration less favourable treatment? To put it differently, should a host State which grants a foreign investor the same treatment as the less favoured domestic investor(s) be considered in breach of its obligation?

As noted by the Tribunal appointed in that former case in relation to the 1992 NAFTA, the text of most IIAs is unclear on this issue. In this respect, it reflected on this issue, drawing an analogy with the MFNT provision – it explained:

> NAFTA is on its face unclear as to whether the foreign investor must be treated in the most favorable manner provided for any domestic investor, or only with

regard to the treatment generally accorded to domestic investors, or even the least favorably treated domestic investor. There is no 'most-favored investor' provision in Chapter 11, parallel to the most favored nation provision in Article 1103, that suggests that a foreign investor must be treated no less favorably than the most favorably treated national investor, if there are other national investors that are treated less favorably, that is, in the same manner as the foreign investor. At the same time, there is no language in Article 1102 that states that the foreign investor must receive treatment equal to that provided to the most favorably treated domestic investor, if there are multiple domestic investors receiving differing treatment by the respondent government. (para. 185)

No doubt the language of Article 1102.1 and 1102.2 of the NAFTA does not state so. In this respect, it can be noted that under Article 1102.3 of the 1992 NAFTA – and under Article 14.4.3 of the 2018 USMCA – it is made explicit with regard to the treatment granted by a state and province that shall be accorded a 'treatment no less favorable than the most favorable treatment accorded'. In *Pope & Talbot Inc.* v. *Canada*, the Tribunal relied precisely on this specification made in Article 1102.3 to conclude that the national treatment standard under Article 1102 of the NAFTA means 'the right to treatment equivalent to the "best" treatment accorded to domestic investors or investments in like circumstances' (2001, Award on the Merits of Phase 2, para. 42).

5.3.4.2 The Features of Differential Treatments

While it is a requirement that the treatment received by a foreign investor be actually not less favourable than that granted to the domestic investor(s), it is usually seen as being irrelevant that the treatment be de jure or de facto less favourable. Typically, this means that the difference of treatment can be made explicit in a State measure, or it can emerge with the application of a measure that does not set such a difference in its plain reading. As stated by the Tribunal in *Marvin Feldman* v. *Mexico*, it can also result from differences of treatment in the enforcement of the law (e.g. 2002, Award, para. 169).

By the same token, it is usually not required that the difference of treatment be based on nationality. In particular, it has been stressed that limiting the scope of the national treatment standard to nationality-based differences of treatment would be problematic for foreign investors in terms of burden of proof. In this respect, that former Tribunal explained: '[R]equiring a foreign investor to prove that discrimination is based on his nationality could be an insurmountable burden to the Claimant, as that information may only be available to the government. It would be virtually impossible for any claimant to meet the burden of demonstrating that a government's motivation for discrimination is nationality rather than some other reason' (2002, Award, para. 183).

Intertwined with the two above-mentioned issues is the issue of States' intent. On the one hand, the question is whether intent is a requirement for a differential treatment to fall within the scope of the national treatment standard. It is largely agreed that it can be concluded that a differential treatment falls within this scope absent any evidence of intent. However, in *Alex Genin* v. *Estonia*, the Tribunal – which relied on Brownlie, who explained that 'the test of discrimination is the intention of the government'[4] – seems to have adopted the opposite view:

> In the present case, of course, any such discriminatory treatment would not be permitted by Article II(1) of the BIT, which requires treatment of foreign investment on a basis no less favourable than treatment of nationals. In any event, in the opinion of the Tribunal, there is no indication that the Bank of Estonia specifically targeted EIB in a discriminatory way, or treated it less favourably than banks owned by Estonian nationals. Moreover, Claimants have failed to prove that the withdrawal of EIB's license was done with the intention to harm the Bank or any of the Claimants in this arbitration, or to treat them in a discriminatory way. (2001, Award, paras. 368–369)

On the other hand, there is the question as to whether the intention to treat foreign investors and their investments differently makes – in and of itself – the treatment fall within the scope of the standard. This issue is often tackled in relation to the impact of the treatment. No doubt, intent matters. All tribunals agree on this, yet they draw different consequences from this.

According to a first line of authority, intent is insufficient; a differential treatment must have an adverse impact on the foreign investor to have this effect. The Tribunal appointed in *S.D. Myers, Inc.* v. *Canada* adopted this approach, for instance, by stressing that '[t]he word "treatment" suggests that practical impact is required to produce a breach of Article 1102 [NAFTA's national treatment provision], not merely a motive or intent that is in violation of Chapter 11' (2000, Partial Award, para. 254).

In contrast, according to a second line of authority, intent is sufficient to make the treatment fall within the scope of the national treatment standard. In *Corn Products International, Inc.* v. *Mexico*, the Tribunal stated in that sense:

> While the existence of an intention to discriminate is not a requirement for a breach of Article 1102 [NAFTA's national treatment provision] (and both parties seemed to accept that it was not a requirement), where such an intention is shown, that is sufficient to satisfy the third requirement. But the Tribunal would add that, even if an intention to discriminate had not been shown, the fact that the adverse effects of the tax were felt exclusively by the HFCS producers and suppliers, all of them foreign-owned, to the benefit of the sugar producers, the majority of which were Mexican-owned, would be sufficient to establish that the third requirement of 'less favourable treatment' was satisfied. (2008, Decision on Responsibility, para. 138)

Regardless of these differences concerning intent, it appears clearly that the adverse impact of the treatment received by the foreign investor and its

---

[4] Brownlie (n 1), at 541.

investment is key in establishing the existence of a differential treatment that falls within the scope of the national treatment standard.

5.3.4.3 The Justifications for Differential Treatments

The question here is whether there are circumstances that can justify a difference of treatment that meets all of the above-mentioned requirements, such that the differential treatment shall not be seen as constituting a breach of the national treatment obligation. Again, there are different views on the matter.

Some refuse to take into account and to give any effect to any possible justifications. In *Corn Products International, Inc.* v. *Mexico*, for instance, the Tribunal pointed out that this would confuse the 'nature' of the measure with its 'motive'. It argued:

> The Tribunal does not doubt either that there was a crisis in the Mexican sugar industry, or that the motive for imposing the HFCS tax was to address that crisis. That does not alter the fact that the nature of the measure which Mexico took was one which treated producers of HFCS in a markedly less favourable way than Mexican producers of sugar. Discrimination does not cease to be discrimination, nor to attract the international liability stemming therefrom, because it is undertaken to achieve a laudable goal or because the achievement of that goal can be described as necessary. (2008, Decision on Responsibility, para. 142)

On the other hand, other tribunals have been ready to take justifications into consideration in appraising the legality of host States' conduct. For instance, in *Apotex* v. *USA*, the Tribunal applied this test formulated in *Pope & Talbot Inc.* v. *Canada* (2001, Award on the Merits of Phase 2, para. 78): 'Differences in treatment will presumptively violate Article 1102(2), unless they have a reasonable nexus to rational government policies that (1) do not distinguish, on their face or *de facto*, between foreign-owned and domestic companies, and (2) do not otherwise unduly undermine the investment liberalizing objectives of NAFTA' (2014, Award, para. 8.56).

Interestingly, in *S.D. Myers, Inc.* v. *Canada*, the Tribunal stressed the need to take into account the legal context of the NAFTA national treatment provision in its entirety and not only the objective of liberalising investment. It explained:

> The Tribunal considers that the legal context of Article 1102 includes the various provisions of the NAFTA, its companion agreement the NAAEC and principles that are affirmed by the NAAEC (including those of the Rio declaration). The principles that emerge from that context, to repeat, are as follows:
>
> – states have the right to establish high levels of environmental protection. They are not obliged to compromise their standards merely to satisfy the political or economic interests of other states;
> – states should avoid creating distortions to trade;

– environmental protection and economic development can and should be mutually supportive . . .

The Tribunal considers that the interpretation of the phrase 'like circumstances' in Article 1102 must take into account the general principles that emerge from the legal context of the NAFTA, including both its concern with the environment and the need to avoid trade distortions that are not justified by environmental concerns. The assessment of 'like circumstances' must also take into account circumstances that would justify governmental regulations that treat them differently in order to protect the public interest. (2000, Partial Award, paras. 247 and 250)

Such an approach that focuses on the legal context can be considered in relation to the treaty trend – analysed in Chapter 8 – towards enlarging the legal context of IIAs to public interest considerations and dedicated provisions. Mention should also be made of the trend mentioned above that consists of specifying that the question of whether a differential treatment is based on legitimate public welfare objectives should be considered as part of the circumstances to be taken into account. More fundamentally, it is worth singling out those few IIAs that do not merely require that such objectives be taken into account but rather, subject to a series of conditions, provide that measures pursuing a legitimate public purpose shall not be viewed as being incompatible with the national treatment obligation. For instance, the 2016 Slovakia–Iran IIA provides:

A measure of the Contracting Party that treats investors of the other Contracting Party or their investments less favorably than . . . its own investors or their investments is not inconsistent with paragraph 1 of this Article . . . if it is adopted and applied by the Contracting Party in pursuit of a legitimate public purpose that is not based on the nationality of the investor or of nationality of the owner of an investment, either explicitly or factually, including the protection of health, safety, the environment, and internationally and domestically recognized labor rights, or the elimination of bribery and corruption, and it bears a reasonable connection to the stated purpose. (Article 4.4.a)

It can be noted that this Article 4 contains a paragraph that makes the above also applicable to the MFNT obligation (Article 4.4.b).

5.4 The Most-Favoured-Nation Treatment Standard

Preliminary Remarks

Like the national treatment standard, the MFNT standard is a rule that aims at creating a level playing field and that prohibits differential treatments. It also constitutes an embodiment of non-discrimination.

Beyond this common teleological denominator, the 'benchmarks' and the functioning of these two standards differ. For example, with regard to BITs and the treatment to be granted to investors, the national treatment standard prohibits investors of one of the two States parties from being granted treatment less favourable than that afforded by the other State party to its domestic investors. The MFNT standard provides that the investors of one of the two States parties shall not be treated by the other State party less favourably than the investors of any third State non-party to that BIT.

To illustrate the functioning of the MFNT standard, one can refer to Article 4.1.a of the 2017 Qatar–Singapore BIT: 'With respect to the management, maintenance, conduct, operation, and sale or other disposition of investments, each Contracting Party shall in its territory accord to investors of the other Contracting Party and their investments treatment no less favourable than that it accords, in like circumstances, to . . . investors of any third State and their investments.' This Article entails that if, for instance, Qatar, in like circumstances, treats French investors more favourably than Singaporean investors with regard to the management of investments, Qatar has the obligation to confer this treatment to Singaporean investors, the result being that they are no longer being treated in a less favourable manner. As it appears, the MFNT standard, like the national treatment standard, is a relative standard: the treatment to be granted to the investors of an IIA State party and their investments depends on the treatment afforded to other foreign investors and to their investments. This is in contrast to absolute standards, like the FET, which 'on their own' set the treatment to be granted to foreign investors and their investments.

There have been only a limited number of cases wherein the MFNT clause was invoked in relation to an alleged factual difference of treatment between foreign investors in the context of their investment activities (e.g. *MNSS B.V.* v. *Montenegro*, 2016, Award, paras. 357–364). As discussed below, arbitration tribunals have actually most often been seized by the claims of investors alleging that the more favourable treatment was composed of a rule contained in an IIA concluded between the host State and another State or a group thereof. Such an agreement amounts to what is often called a 'third treaty' and is named in what follows a 'third IIA'. It is to be distinguished from the agreement that contains the MFNT clause and that amounts to what is often referred to as the 'basic treaty'; it is called in what follows the 'basic IIA'. In this respect, two remarks can be made relating to two fundamental public international law principles mainly known in Latin as *pacta tertiis nec nocent nec prosunt* and *ejusdem generis*.

The former principle is codified in Article 34 of the 1969 VCLT. It provides: 'A treaty does not create either obligations or rights for a third State without its consent.' It is worth stressing that the extension of more favourable treatments granted under third IIAs through the MFNT clause of the basic IIA is not incompatible with this principle. Third IIAs do not create any right for the investors of the States parties to the basic IIA. To use the words of the ICJ in the *Anglo-Iranian Oil Co. Case (United Kingdom* v. *Iran)*, this is the MFNT clause that establishes a 'juridical link' between third IIAs and the investors of the

States parties to the basic IIA. The Court explained in its 1952 Judgment: 'It is this treaty which establishes the juridical link between the United Kingdom and a third-party treaty and confers upon that State the rights enjoyed by the third party. A third-party treaty, independent of and isolated from the basic treaty, cannot produce any legal effect as between the United Kingdom and Iran: it is *res inter alios acta*' (1952, Judgment, at 109).

Turning to the second remark, it is important to note that the functioning of MFNT clauses is conditioned by the *ejusdem generis* principle. As explained by the International Law Commission in its Commentaries to the 1978 Draft Articles on most-favoured-nation clauses, '[t]he essence of the rule is that the beneficiary of a most-favoured-nation clause cannot claim from the granting State advantages of a kind other than that stipulated in the clause'; 'a clause conferring most-favoured-nation rights in respect of a certain matter, or class of matter, can attract the rights conferred by other treaties . . . only in regard of the same matter or class of matter'. To use the example given by the Commission, this principle entails, for instance, that if an MFNT clause promises MFNT solely in relation to fish, then such treatment cannot be claimed under the same clause for meat (at 30). As examined below, diverging conceptions of this *ejusdem generis* principle can be seen in arbitration practice.

Most-favoured-nation clauses are widespread in IIA practice; at the same time, their scope of application is not unlimited. As analysed in Chapter 7, there have traditionally been limitations placed upon it; however, the number and object of these limitations has broadened in particular during the 2010s, all of them relating *sensu largo* to public interest considerations. On a different note, one can witness an evolution of treaty practice that brings some clarification as to the applicability of the MFNT clause to the other provisions of IIAs.

After an analysis of treaty practice, this applicability is examined from a general perspective and, more closely, in relation to three categories of provisions: (1) the provisions delineating the scope of application of IIAs; (2) the substantive provisions conferring a protection to investors and their investments; and (3) the provisions pertaining to the settlement of investor–State disputes.

5.4.1 The MFNT Standard in Treaty Practice

Preliminary Remarks

As a starting point for the analysis, one can refer to Article 5.1 of the 2011 Canada–Kuwait IIA to illustrate the MFNT clause: 'Each Party shall accord to investors of the other Party treatment no less favourable than that it accords, in like circumstances, to investors of a non-Party with respect to the establishment, acquisition, expansion, management, conduct, operation and sale or other disposition of investments in its territory.' Article 5.2 of that Agreement, which grants the benefit of the MFNT standard to the investments of investors, is also very representative of treaty practice.

The MFNT standard can usually be found in a specific Article (e.g. 2018 CETA, Article 8.7), or in an Article together with the national treatment standard. In that latter case, both standards can be referred to in different paragraphs (e.g. 2016 UAE–Mexico IIA, Article 3.2), or in the same one that usually specifies that States shall afford either treatment 'whichever is more favourable to the investor' (e.g. 2016 Japan–Iran IIA, Article 4.1). In a few agreements, the MFNT standard is referred to in a general provision on treatment, together for instance with the fair and equitable treatment (e.g. 2016 Austria–Kyrgyzstan IIA, Article 3).

Concerning the scope of application of the MFNT standard, it is worth referring at the outset to the analyses conducted in other chapters which inform that scope. As examined in Chapter 4, treaty practice displays different approaches as to the application of the standard to 'establishment'. As just recalled, its scope of application depends also on the limitations placed by the States parties. Those specific issues are not examined here; rather, this subsection focuses on three key general issues: (1) the 'beneficiaries' of the MFNT standard; (2) the 'benchmark' of the MFNT standard; and (3) the applicability of the MFNT clause to other provisions contained in the IIAs.

5.4.1.1 The 'Beneficiaries' of the MFNT Standard

Whether set out in the same paragraph (e.g. 2017 Pacific Agreement on Closer Economic Relations Plus (PACER Plus), Article 7.1 (Chapter 9)) or in two different paragraphs (e.g. 2018 USMCA, Article 14.5), the MFNT standard is usually granted to both investors and their investments. A few IIAs mention also 'returns', together with 'investors' and 'investments' (e.g. 2016 Austria–Kyrgyzstan IIA, Article 3) or with 'investments' only (e.g. 2016 Nigeria–UAE IIA, Article 5). Instead of 'returns', a few IIAs make mention of 'income' (e.g. 1990 Argentina–Italy IIA, Article 3.1). More restrictively, a few agreements grant the MFNT standard only to 'investments' (e.g. 2012 Turkey–Pakistan IIA, Article 4.2). More radically, it should be noted that a few IIAs do not even contain an MFNT clause (e.g. 2018 Belarus–India IIA).

As exemplified by the 2011 Canada–Kuwait IIA quoted above, a number of IIAs specify the 'facets and stages' of the investment operations with respect to which the standard operates. Some IIAs do so only as regards investors (e.g. 2016 Rwanda–Morocco IIA, Article 3), while others make this specification for both investors and their investments (e.g. 2017 China–Hong Kong SAR China IIA, Article 6). In any case, the scope of these 'facets and stages' is very broad, although treaty practice is nuanced in this respect. It can be noted that some agreements do not mention this scope, but instead specify the 'matters' with respect to which investors and investments, or investments only, can be granted MFNT. For instance, the 1991 Spain–Argentina IIA provides: 'In all matters subject to this

Agreement, this treatment shall not be less favorable than that extended by each Party to the investments made in its territory by investors of a third country' (Article 4.2). As explained below, this type of MFNT clause has been extensively discussed in arbitration practice in relation to the issue of the applicability of the clause to the investor–State dispute settlement provisions within IIAs.

5.4.1.2 The 'Benchmark' of the MFNT Standard

a The 'Origin' of Investors and their Investments

While the national treatment standard takes the treatment afforded to domestic investors and their investments as a point of reference for the determination of the treatment to be granted thereto, the MFNT standard focuses on the treatment afforded to foreign investors and their investments originating from other home States.

The 'origin' of those foreign investors and investments that can serve as a point of reference depends largely on the number of States parties to the IIA. With regard to an IIA to which two States are parties, meaning a BIT, the point of reference is the treatment granted to the investors of third States and their investments, meaning of States that are not a party to that treaty. As to the IIAs to which more than two States are parties, the determination of the point of reference is more complex as the language used across treaty practice varies.

For instance, Article 9.5.1 of the 2018 CPTPP provides with regard to investors: 'Each Party shall accord to investors of another Party treatment no less favourable than that it accords, in like circumstances, to investors of any other Party or of any non-Party with respect to the establishment, acquisition, expansion, management, conduct, operation, and sale or other disposition of investments in its territory.' Under this provision, the foreign investors and investments whose treatment serves as a point of reference can originate from a third State which is not a party to the IIA and from any other State party to that agreement. For instance, with regard to the 2018 USMCA MFNT clause which is drafted similarly (Article 14.5.1), this entails that Mexico shall afford Canadian investors a treatment which is no less favourable than the treatment it affords, in like circumstances, to investors originating from States non-party to the USMCA, such as Germany, as well as to investors originating from the USA that are a party to that Agreement.

Such provisions can be contrasted with the provisions of other IIAs which are differently drafted. This is illustrated by Article 7.1 (Chapter 9) of the 2017 PACER Plus, which reads as follows: 'Each Party shall accord to investors and covered investments of investors of any other Party treatment no less favourable than that it accords, in like circumstances, to investors of a non-party or to their investments with respect to the acquisition, establishment, expansion, management, conduct, operation, and sale or other disposition of investments in its territory.' Such a provision focuses on the treatment afforded to investors and their investments originating from States which are not parties to the IIA, with no reference being made to investors and investments of other States parties. With regard to the PACER Plus, this drafting leads to the conclusion, for instance, that New Zealand does not have the obligation to afford Australian investors the more favourable treatment granted, in like circumstances, to investors from Tonga.

With respect to IIAs concluded by at least one 'non-unitary entity', it can be noted that these IIAs *mutatis mutandis* specify 'for greater certainty' that the more favourable treatment to be afforded through the MFNT clause by a 'component unit' is the treatment conferred to investors and their investments originating from a third State (e.g. 2016 CETA, Article 8.7.2). As such, they make clear that the treatment granted by a component unit to investors and their investments originating from another unit of the entity does not constitute a valid point of reference for the MFNT standard and that it is not a treatment that can be extended through the MFNT clause. For instance, taking the USMCA, which contains such a specification, as an example, this means that a Canadian investor cannot invoke the MFNT clause in order to receive a better treatment as conferred in like circumstances by California to an investor from Florida. This obviously make sense as, from the perspective of public international law, Florida is not a State *vis-à-vis* California.

In fact, the Canadian investor could seek to be granted this treatment through the national treatment provision. Indeed, as explained above, the USMCA (Article 14.4.3), and more generally all those IIAs, consistently provide that the component units shall afford to foreign investors and their investments a treatment which is no less favourable than that granted, in like circumstances, to the investors and investments of the entity to which they belong.

b 'Like Circumstances'

As also provided for in the national treatment provision, IIAs most often condition the benefit of the MFNT standard to a 'like circumstances' requirement. This is well illustrated by Article 7.1 (Chapter 9) of the PACER Plus quoted above. Instead of 'like circumstances', some IIAs refer to 'comparable situations' (e.g. 2016 Slovakia–Iran IIA, Article 4) or 'like situations' (e.g. 1993 USA–Kyrgyzstan IIA, Article 2.1), while a few do not incorporate any such qualification (e.g. 2016 Argentina–Qatar IIA, Article 4.1).

Among the IIAs that refer to either 'like circumstances', 'like situations' or 'comparable situations', numerous IIAs concluded in the 2010s further specify the meaning and content of this qualification. All such IIAs stress at least the need to take into consideration all the circumstances of the case at hand and to pay attention to the objective of the measures. This common denominator is well illustrated by Footnote 4 attached to Article 4 of the 2016 Hong Kong SAR China–Chile IIA: 'For greater certainty, whether treatment is accorded in "like circumstances" under … Article 5 (Non-Discriminatory Treatment as Compared with a Non-Party's Investors) depends on the totality of the circumstances, including whether the relevant treatment distinguishes between investors or investments on the basis of legitimate public welfare objectives.' Other IIAs offer greater detail in this respect and an indicative list of circumstances to be taken into account. For instance, Article 4.3 of the 2016 Slovakia–Iran IIA provides:

> For greater certainty, a determination of whether an investment or an investor is in comparable situations for the purposes of paragraphs 1. [national treatment] and 2. [MFNT] of this Article shall be made based on an assessment of the totality of circumstances related to the investor or the investment, including:
>
> (a) the effect of the investment on
>   i. the local community where investment is located;
>   ii. the environment, including effects that relate to the cumulative impact of all investments within a jurisdiction;
> (b) the character of the measure, including its nature, purpose, duration and rationale; and
> (c) the regulations that apply to investments or investors.

It is worth recalling that this IIA provides, subject to a series of conditions, that measures adopted by a Contracting State conferring a less favourable treatment to the investors of the other Contracting State and their investments than that granted to investors of third States and their investments, but which are adopted and applied in pursuance of a legitimate public purpose, shall not be considered as being inconsistent with the MFNT obligation (Article 4.4.b).

5.4.1.3 The Applicability of the MFNT Clause to Other IIA Provisions

As examined below, the MFNT clause has been mainly invoked by foreign investors with regard to the provisions contained in third IIAs which they considered as conferring a more favourable treatment than that they received under the basic IIAs. This holds true in particular as to investor–State dispute settlement provisions. This has led to fierce debates, in particular between arbitrators, who have adopted diverging views on the matter. In the context of such claims and diverging arbitration practices, States have incorporated into IIAs a provision specifying the applicability of the MFNT clause to the other provisions of the agreements.

Such specifications concern mainly investor–State dispute settlement provisions. A number of IIAs, in particular those concluded in the 2010s, set out that such provisions are excluded from the scope of the treatment covered by the MFNT standard. For instance, the 2018 Australia–Peru IIA provides: 'For greater certainty, the treatment referred to in this Article does not encompass international dispute resolution procedures or mechanisms, such as those included in Section B [Investor–State Dispute Settlement]' (Article 8.5.3). As also exemplified by that Article, these specifications can have a wider scope and be concerned with international dispute mechanisms more broadly, with a view to excluding them from the scope of the MFNT clause.

In addition to investor–State dispute settlement provisions, a few IIAs contain a specification concerning the applicability of the clause to other IIA provisions. This holds true with regard to provisions that determine the scope of application of IIAs – and thereby play a role in determining the jurisdiction of arbitration tribunals – as well as to substantive provisions that protect the investors of States parties and their investments.

As to the former, the 2017 Colombia–UAE IIA provides, for example: 'For greater clarity, to limit the scope of Most-Favoured-Nation Treatment in respect of treatment referred to in paragraphs 1 and 2 of this Article, it does not encompass definitions, nor dispute resolution mechanisms, such as those in Articles 2, Section D and Section E' (Article 4.3). Those definitions pertain in particular to the notion of investment and investor under the applicable IIA. As to substantive provisions, one can refer to Article 4.4 of the 2016 Argentina–Qatar IIA, which provides that the MFNT clause cannot be used to 'invoke the fair and equitable treatment and the dispute settlement provisions accorded to investors of any Third State under treaties signed by one of the Contracting Parties prior to the entry into force of this Treaty'. The 2016 CETA goes even further: its Article 8.7.4 provides that no substantive obligations in any other international investment treaties and trade agreement can give rise to a breach of the Agreement's MFNT clause absent measures adopted or maintained pursuant to those obligations. This results from the clear affirmation provided by the Parties that such substantive obligations do not constitute themselves a 'treatment' under this Article.

It is worth recalling than States have adopted in some IIAs a more radical approach by making the choice not to incorporate an MFNT clause in the agreements (e.g. 2018 Belarus–India IIA).

5.4.2 The Applicability of the MFNT Clause to Other IIA Provisions: General Perspective

Contrary to the above-mentioned agreements that address the issue of the applicability of the MFNT clause to other IIA provisions, the majority of them do not do so. It is with respect to those IIAs that the issue as to the applicability of the clause arises, and more precisely with respect to three categories of provisions: (1) the provisions delineating the scope of application of IIAs; (2) the substantive provisions conferring protection to investors and their investments; and (3) the provisions pertaining to the settlement of investor–State disputes.

The applicability of the MFNT clause intertwined key issues. The first of these boils down to the question as to whether the operation of the MFNT clause should be conceived of differently depending on the object of the IIA provision in question. The second issue is more general: it begs the question of whether the clause can be used to make applicable to an investor the provision of a third IIA which is absent from the basic IIA. Central to this question is the distinction between the creation of new rights under the basic IIA and the modification of existing rights that it contains. As will be seen, the solution given to those two issues in arbitration practice depends not only on the drafting of the MFNT clause at hand, but often also on legal and policy considerations pertaining to the operation of the clause and to the functioning of international investment law and arbitration more generally.

Beyond the issue of the object of the provision at hand, which is often put forward to deny the applicability of the MFNT clause, there is a more systemic claim that is sometimes made against its applicability to IIA provisions in general, including substantive provisions. This claim zeroes in on the argument according to which MFNT clauses, as most of them are drafted, are not intended to cover any legal right conferred by IIAs. This claim was made notably by the Tribunal appointed in *Ickale Inssat Limited Sirketi* v. *Turkmenistan*, which argued in particular that the expression 'treatment accorded in similar situations' requires a comparison of factual situations, which excludes the comparison of IIA obligations. It is worth quoting in full the relevant part of the award rendered by this Tribunal:

> The terms 'treatment accorded in similar situations' therefore suggest that the MFN treatment obligation requires a comparison of the factual situation of the investments of the investors of the home State and that of the investments of the investors of third States, for the purpose of determining whether the treatment accorded to investors of the home State can be said to be less favorable than that accorded to investments of the investors of any third State. It follows that, given the limitation of the scope of application of the MFN clause to 'similar situations,' it cannot be read, in good faith, to refer to standards of investment protection included in other investment treaties between a State party and a third State. The standards of protection included in other investment treaties create legal rights for the investors concerned, which may be more favorable in the sense of being additional to the standards included in the basic treaty, but such differences between applicable legal standards cannot be said to amount to 'treatment accorded in similar situations,' without effectively denying any meaning to the terms 'similar situations.' Investors cannot be said to be in a 'similar situation' merely because they have invested in a particular State; indeed, if the terms 'in similar situations' were to be read to coincide with the territorial scope of application of the treaty, they would not be given any meaning and would effectively become redundant as there would be no difference between the clause 'treatment no less favourable than that accorded in similar situations . . . to investments of investors of any third country' and 'treatment no less favourable than that accorded . . . to investments of investors of any third country.' Such a reading would not be consistent with the generally accepted rules of treaty interpretation, including the principle of effectiveness, or effet utile, which requires that each term of a treaty provision should be given a meaning and effect. (2016, Award, para. 329)

Obviously, this reasoning can be applied to those MFNT clauses which refer to 'like situations' and 'like circumstances'. As regards this reasoning, it is worth recalling also the above-mentioned specification made in the 2016 CETA according to which substantive obligations and investor–State dispute settlement procedures do not constitute a 'treatment' as such under the MFNT provision. Mention should also be made of *UAB E Energija (Lithuania)* v. *Latvia*, where the Tribunal suggested a similar conclusion with regard to Article 3.2 of the 1996 Latvia–Lithuania IIA on the ground that it makes the obligation upon each State party to accord the MFNT 'subject to its laws and international agreements'. It noted that 'this casts doubt whether it [the MFNT] can be relied upon to import standards contained in other treaties at all because it may be limited to *de facto* treatment under national law' (2017, Award, para. 1112).

5.4.3 The Applicability of the MFNT Clause to IIA Provisions Delineating the Scope of Application of the Agreements

There is little question that the MFNT clause is not applicable to those IIA provisions that delineate the scope of application of the agreements and that thereby play a role in determining the jurisdiction of arbitration tribunals. This holds true in particular for the provisions defining the meaning of investor and investment under the agreements.

The main argument in support of this relates to the issue of consent: those provisions delineate the scope with regard to which States consent to the limitation of their sovereignty with regard to the treatment to be granted to foreign investors. From the perspective of public international law, this consent cannot be modified by the operation of the MFNT clause. This argument underlies the following statement made by the Tribunal appointed in *Tecnicas Medioambientales Tecmed* v. *Mexico* with regard to temporal matters:

> The Arbitral Tribunal will not examine the provisions of such Treaty in detail in light of such principle, because it deems that matters relating to the application over time of the Agreement, which involve more the time dimension of application of its substantive provisions rather than matters of procedure or jurisdiction, due to their significance and importance, go to the core of matters that must be deemed to be specifically negotiated by the Contracting Parties. These are determining factors for their acceptance of the Agreement, as they are directly linked to the identification of the substantive protection regime applicable to the foreign investor and, particularly, to the general (national or international) legal context within which such regime operates, as well as to the access of the foreign investor to the substantive provisions of such regime. Their application cannot therefore be impaired by the principle contained in the most favored nation clause. (2003, Award, para. 69)

Closely related to consent, another argument is built on the distinction made between, on the one hand, the conditions for 'access to rights' and, on the other hand, the rights themselves, which is discussed further below in relation to investor–State dispute settlement provisions. Pursuant to this argument, an

MFNT clause can be used only with regard to rights, but not with regard to the conditions set by IIA States parties to be entitled to accessing such rights. This argument was used implicitly, for example, by the Tribunal in *Vannessa Ventures Ltd* v. *Venezuela* to deny that the clause could be used to expand the categories of investments to which the IIA at hand applies (2013, Award, para. 133).

5.4.4 The Applicability of the MFNT Clause to IIA Substantive Provisions

The MFNT clause is – as a matter of principle – largely considered as being applicable to IIA substantive provisions, meaning that it is considered that the clause can be used to extend the benefit of substantive provisions contained in third IIAs which are seen as being more favourable. This is so typically when both the basic IIA and the third IIA contain the same category of provisions, such as an umbrella clause.

On the other hand, those situations in which there is no such 'sameness', for instance when the third IIA contains an umbrella clause while there is no umbrella clause in the basic IIA, have proven to be more problematic and have led arbitration tribunals to adopt diverging approaches.

Of course, the language of the MFNT clause impacts on the solution adopted. That being said, the language does not appear to be decisive in making sense of the discrepancies in arbitration practice. Indeed, tribunals that were asked by the claimant to consider the application of an MFNT clause referring to 'all matters' – a formulation which is often seen as being broad – denied that the clause could operate in such situations (e.g. *Teinver S.A.* v. *Argentina*, 2017, Award, paras. 884–885). On the other hand, other tribunals adopted the opposite solution when envisaging the application of an MFNT clause referring classically to 'treatment no less favourable than that accorded to investors' (e.g. *EDF International S.A.* v. *Argentina*, 2012, Award, paras. 929–937), a formulation that is often regarded as narrower than the 'all matters' type of MFNT clause.

In fact, the key issue, be it implicitly or explicitly addressed as such, seems to relate to the *ejusdem generis* principle mentioned above and how tribunals conceive of it. The two main alternative and diverging approaches are the following: is the subject matter of the MFNT clause, which delineates the rights that can be extended through it, circumscribed by the rights already contained in the basic IIA, or does it correspond more generally to the subject matter of that IIA, i.e. the protection of investors and their investments?

That latter approach was adopted, for instance, in *EDF International S.A.* v. *Argentina*. In that case, the Tribunal accepted that the benefit of the umbrella clause contained in a third IIA could be extended. In support of its finding, it stated in particular: 'In giving effect to the MFN provisions, the Tribunal does not in any way accord investors anything other "than those rights which fall within the limits of the subject matter of the clause"' (2012, Award, para. 934). In the same vein, the Annulment Committee appointed in that case noted:

> That situation falls squarely within the terms of the MFN clause. Even if Argentina is right in arguing that MFN clauses should be subjected to an *ejusdem generis* limitation – as to which, it is unnecessary for the Committee to comment – the umbrella clause is part of the same *genus* of provisions on substantive protection of investments as the fair and equitable treatment clause and other similar provisions which feature in the Argentina–France BIT. (2016, Annulment Decision, para. 237)

The former approach was adopted, for instance, by the Tribunal in *Teinver S.A. v. Argentina*, also with regard to an umbrella clause. The Tribunal endorsed the view of the respondent State that extending the benefit of an umbrella clause contained in a third IIA, while the basic IIA does not contain any such clause, would result in the creation of a new right absent from that basic agreement. To justify its finding, it also argued in particular that to limit the application of the MFNT clause to the provisions already present in the basic IIA does not deprive the clause of its effect as it 'could clearly "improve" the standards of protection contained in the Treaty by incorporating more favourable standards from another treaty' (2017, Award, paras. 884–885).

It is worth noting that with regard to the MFNT claim concerning the extension of the full protection and security standard contained in a third IIA, that Tribunal concluded that this extension was possible, despite the fact that this standard is *sensu stricto* absent from the basic IIA at hand in that case. It reached this conclusion on the ground that this IIA contains an obligation to protect the investments made by investors and therefore that the 'protection of investments is a matter governed by the Treaty' (para. 896). In other words, the Tribunal considered that the operation of the MFNT clause did not lead to the creation of a new right.

This conclusion is in line with a series of awards wherein tribunals have accepted the extension of the benefit of a substantive provision of a third IIA – despite the same category of provision not being contained in the basic IIA – by linking it to either of the elements of this basic agreement. In *MTD v. Chile*, for instance, the Tribunal linked the third IIA's obligation to award permits subsequent to the approval of an investment and to fulfilment of contractual obligations to the FET standard contained in the basic IIA (2004, Award, para. 104). Likewise, in *Bayindir Insaat Turizm Ticaret Ve Sanayi A.S. v. Pakistan*, the Tribunal connected the third IIA's FET provision to the Preamble of the basic IIA, which stresses the desirability of the FET treatment to maintain a stable framework for investment and maximum effective utilisation of economic resources (2009, Award, paras. 153–160).

5.4.5 The Applicability of the MFNT Clause to IIA Investor–State Dispute Settlement Provisions

From a quantitative point of view, it can be noted that most MFNT claims have concerned investor–State dispute settlement provisions, typically provisions setting conditions to submit disputes to arbitration. Aside from these claims being the most numerous, they have also been the most controversial, as compared to the MFNT claims pertaining to substantive provisions and to provisions delineating the scope of application of IIAs. In this respect, it is worth mentioning that arbitration practice displays conflicting views not only between arbitration tribunals, but also – within tribunals – between arbitrators themselves. In fact, of all the legal issues addressed in arbitration practice, MFNT claims relating to investor–State dispute settlement provisions have led to the greatest number of dissenting opinions. This is well illustrated by the dissenting views expressed by Arbitrator Stern in *Impregilo S.p.A.* v. *Argentina* (2011), Arbitrator Brower in *Daimler Financial Services AG* v. *Argentina* (2012), Arbitrator Boisson de Chazournes in *Garanti Koza LLP* v. *Turkmenistan* (2013) and Arbitrator Kohen in *Venezuela US, S.R.L.* v. *Venezuela* (2016).

The drafting of the basic IIA at hand in those cases is sometimes seen as explaining why tribunals and arbitrators have adopted different approaches. In particular, those few MFNT clauses that refer to 'all matters' have often been contrasted to the great majority of clauses that refer classically to 'treatment no less favourable than that accorded to investors'. In *Emilio Agustin Maffezini* v. *Spain*, which initiated the debate, the Tribunal noted that the reference to 'treatment' in the second category of MFNT clauses is a 'narrower' formulation than the reference made in other clauses to 'all matters' (2000, Decision of the Tribunal on Objections to Jurisdiction, para. 60).

That being said, arbitration practice displays conflicting interpretations of the same MFNT clause. Article 3 of the 1991 Germany–Argentina IIA in particular has been interpreted differently by a series of Tribunals, for instance in *Daimler Financial Services AG* v. *Argentina* (2012, Award), on the one hand, and *Hochtief AG* v. *Argentina* (2011, Decision on Jurisdiction), on the other hand. As noted by the Tribunal in *ST-AD GmbH* v. *Bulgaria*, even tribunals that have reached the same conclusion as regards this issue have done so for different reasons (2013, Award on Jurisdiction, para. 387).

In reality, those opposing views boil down to fundamental differences of views among arbitrators. The object of this disagreement is twofold. The first of these relates to the applicability as such of the MFNT clause to investor–State dispute settlement provisions; it begs the question as to whether, as a matter of principle, the clause is applicable at all to those provisions. The second of these pertains to the implications of applying the MFNT clause to those provisions; at the core of the matter is largely the issue as to whether the application of the clause leads to the creation of a right to arbitration or whether it simply modifies an existing right.

Of course, both issues are closely intertwined and they are often mixed up in the reasoning of arbitration tribunals. Content-wise, they both zero in on the issue of consent, meaning the consent that must be given, under public international law, by all the disputing parties for their dispute to be submitted and settled by an international court and tribunal. However, it is worth distinguishing them in particular as a tribunal may consider the MFNT clause as being applicable to investor–State dispute settlement provisions, but express concerns and set limits to its application due to the implications that it entails. This is well illustrated by the reasoning of the Tribunal in *Emilio Agustin Maffezini* v. *Spain*. Indeed, while acknowledging that the MFNT clause is applicable to those provisions, it stressed that 'the beneficiary of the clause should not be able to override public policy considerations that the contracting parties might have envisaged as fundamental conditions for their acceptance of the agreement in question'. Among other examples, it cited by way of limitations to the application of the clause the situations in which it would be used to bypass a requirement to exhaust local remedies or a 'fork-in-the-road' – examined in Chapter 14 – contained in a basic IIA (2000, Decision of the Tribunal on Objections to Jurisdiction, paras. 62–63).

Starting with the applicability issue, some tribunals and arbitrators make clear that in their views the MFNT clause is – as a matter of principle – applicable to investor–State dispute settlement provisions (e.g. *A11Y Ltd* v. *Czech Republic*, 2017, Decision on Jurisdiction, para. 95). For them, there is no reason to exclude those provisions from the scope of the clause, even though they acknowledge that this impacts on their jurisdiction. This was explained by the Tribunal in *RosInvestCo UK Ltd* v. *Russia* in relation to the limitation of the tribunal's jurisdiction provided in the basic IIA at hand in that case to some expropriation claims:

> Does that conclusion have to be changed in view of the further conclusion reached above that Article 8 of the UK–Soviet BIT expressly limits the jurisdiction of the Tribunal and does not give jurisdiction in respect of other aspects of expropriation? In the Tribunal's view, that is not so. While indeed the application of the MFN clause of Article 3 widens the scope of Article 8 and thus is in conflict to its limitation, this is a normal result of the application of MFN clauses, the very character and intention of which is that protection not accepted in one treaty is widened by transferring the protection accorded in another treaty. (2007, Award on Jurisdiction, para. 131)

For those tribunals and arbitrators, investor–State dispute settlement provisions should be treated in the same way as substantive provisions. This is all the more true for them as they usually stress the close connection between substantive and dispute settlement provisions, in particular the fact that dispute settlement has traditionally formed part of the protection granted to foreign investors together with substantive provisions, as well as the effectiveness that dispute settlement provisions confer on substantive provisions (e.g. *Emilio Agustin Maffezini* v. *Spain*, 2000, Decision of the Tribunal on Objections to Jurisdiction, paras. 54–55).

On the contrary, other tribunals and arbitrators explicitly opine that – as a matter of principle – the MFNT clause is not applicable to investor–State dispute settlement provisions (e.g. *Plama Consortium Limited* v. *Bulgaria*, 2005, Decision on Jurisdiction, para. 223). They often adopt this view by opposing the latter type of provisions to substantive provisions (e.g. *Telenor Mobile Communications A.S.* v. *Hungary*, 2006, Award, para. 92).

While acknowledging that dispute settlement can be seen as part of 'treatment', like substantive provisions, Arbitrator Stern provided a detailed explanation of why, in her view, investors do not have access to these 'two aspects of the overall treatment' under the same conditions. This difference is based on the distinction she made between 'rights' and 'conditions for access to rights'. According to her, 'an MFNT clause can only concern the rights that an investor can enjoy, it cannot modify the fundamental conditions for the enjoyment of such rights, in other words, the insuperable conditions of access to the rights granted in the BIT' (*Impregilo S.p.A* v. *Argentina*, 2011, Award, Concurring and Dissenting Opinion, para. 47). With regard to the access to substantive provisions, she explained that this entails that an MFNT clause cannot change the material (*ratione materiae*), personal (*ratione personae*) and temporal (*ratione temporis*) conditions set for permitting this access (para. 60). As to the access to jurisdictional rights, she opined that not only must the same conditions be met, but so too must a condition *ratione voluntatis*, meaning consent to arbitration, with all four of those conditions being unable to be modified through an MFNT clause. She argued:

> Just as an MFN clause cannot change the conditions *ratione personae, ratione materiae*, and *ratione temporis*, as has just been demonstrated, it must be equally true that an MFN clause cannot change the condition *ratione voluntatis*, which is a qualifying condition for the enjoyment of the jurisdictional rights open for the protection of substantial rights. In other words, before a provision relating to the dispute settlement mechanism can be imported into the basic treaty, the right to international arbitration – here ICSID arbitration – has to be capable of coming into existence for the foreign investor under the basic treaty, in other words the existence of this right is conditioned on the fulfillment of all the necessary conditions for such jurisdiction, the conditions *ratione personae, ratione materiae*, and *ratione temporis* as well as a supplementary condition relating to the scope of the State's consent to such jurisdiction, the condition *ratione voluntatis*. As long as the qualifying conditions expressed by the State in order to give its consent are not fulfilled, there is no consent, in other words no access of the foreign investor to the jurisdictional treatment granted by ICSID arbitration. An MFN clause cannot enlarge the scope of the basic treaty's right to international arbitration, it cannot be used to grant access to international arbitration when this is not possible under the conditions provided for in the basic treaty. (paras. 78–80)

This brings us to the second dimension of the debate, namely whether the application of the MFNT clause to investor–State dispute settlement provisions leads to the creation of a jurisdictional right and thereby creates consent to arbitration or whether this application entails simply the modification of an existing jurisdictional right. This issue has mainly been discussed in relation to the conditions set out in IIAs to submit disputes to arbitration, in particular the local remedy requirement. The opinions adopted by the Arbitrators in *Hochtief AG* v. *Argentina* reflect very well the opposing views displayed in arbitration practice on the matter.

Noting that the basic IIA at hand in that case grants a right to investors to submit an investment dispute to arbitration and to do so without any further specific consent having to be given by the State party to the dispute, the majority of the Tribunal stressed that the MFNT clause merely enables investors to reach the same position and 'to do so more quickly and more cheaply' (2011, Decision on Jurisdiction, paras. 84–85). It concluded that the local remedy requirement is 'a condition relating to the manner in which the right to have recourse to arbitration must be exercised – as a provision going to the admissibility of the claim rather than the jurisdiction of the Tribunal' (para. 96).

On the other hand, Arbitrator Thomas argued that the local remedy requirement is jurisdictional and mandatory in nature and that investors have no unconditional right to proceed to arbitration. He explained: 'Absent the respondent's waiving prior recourse, it is only when prior recourse has occurred that there is, to revert to *RosInvestCo*, a binding consent to arbitration with the effect that a prospective party to the arbitration proceedings does not need the agreement of the other prospective party to start arbitration proceedings' (2011, Separate and Dissenting Opinion, paras. 31 and 43). In other words, for Arbitrator Thomas, the use of the MFNT clause to 'bypass' a local remedy requirement set out in the basic IIA leads to the creation of a jurisdictional right and thereby creates consent, a power that he stressed falls out of the scope of the *Kompetenz-Kompetenz* principle (para. 30).

Such concerns in relation to the *Kompetenz-Kompetenz* principle have been expressed a number of times in arbitration practice, which is very well illustrated in the Dissenting Opinion of Arbitrator Boisson de Chazournes in *Garanti Koza LLP* v. *Turkmenistan*:

> At the same time, the principle of *compétence de la compétence* requires an arbitral tribunal or any other international court to establish the extent and limits of its jurisdiction objectively, i.e., on the basis of the title of jurisdiction that is conferred to the said tribunal, and not to go beyond it. The trust and confidence in third-party adjudication is dependent on the respect by international courts and tribunals of the limits to the jurisdiction conferred upon them. Tribunals should not create a de facto system of compulsory jurisdiction, which in the present stage of positive international law remains the exception. The international legal order still rests largely on a system of facultative jurisdiction, and because of that essential characteristic, a tribunal should never attempt to impose its jurisdiction and adjudicate the merits of a dispute when the parties have not consented to its jurisdiction ... The interpretation of MFN clauses is mutatis mutandis subject to the principle of consent [footnote omitted] as

enshrined both in general international law as well as in treaty law (the ICSID Convention in the context of the present dispute). (2013, Decision on the Objection to Jurisdiction for Lack of Consent, Dissenting Opinion, paras. 5–7)

In the same vein, Arbitrator Kohen stressed in his Dissenting Opinion in *Venezuela US, S.R.L.* v. *Venezuela* that the respect of the *Kompetenz-Kompetenz* principle is all the more needed in the context of investor–State arbitration:

> International courts and tribunals must be extremely cautious in this regard: an exercise of jurisdiction in a dispute by which consent has not been given constitutes a serious infringement of the sovereignty of the State or States concerned. This requirement for such care in the exercise of the *Kompetenz-Kompetenz* principle is even more acute in the case of ad hoc tribunals in which arbitrators are appointed to deal with a given dispute and consequently not acting as members of a permanent pre-established judicial body. This is more acute still in investment arbitration, in which the potential number of claimants invoking any kind of formula to establish consent and thereby the creation of tribunals could be unlimited. (2016, Interim Award on Jurisdiction, Dissenting Opinion, paras. 2–3)

5.5 The Umbrella Clause

Preliminary Remarks

Umbrella clauses find their origin in a proposal formulated in the 1950s by Lauterpacht to the Anglo-Iranian Oil Company with respect to the settlement of the Iranian oil nationalisation disputes. An umbrella clause was then notably incorporated in the 1967 Draft Convention on the Protection of Foreign Property prepared at the OECD. As explained in Chapter 1, this Draft served as a template for the BIT practice of European States; it is not surprising, then, that an umbrella clause is to be found in a number of IIAs. Yet it is not as widespread as the other standards in IIAs, a trend which has not been reversed in contemporary treaty practice.

As evidenced in other chapters as well, the field of international investment law and arbitration is sprinkled with metaphors that reflect the rationale, functioning or effect of some of its rules. 'Umbrella clause' is one such metaphor; it is used to designate such clauses which *mutatis mutandis* provide: 'Each Contracting Party shall observe any obligation it may have entered into with regard to investments of nationals of the other Contracting Party' (1992 Netherlands–Paraguay IIA, Article 3.4). This metaphor conveys the idea that this standard offers the protection of the treaty, which makes it compulsory for host States under international law to respect the obligations into which they have entered.

In this respect, it is worth noting that the exact effect of umbrella clauses is a matter of controversy. With regard to contractual undertakings notably, some consider that those clauses transform breaches of those undertakings into breaches of IIAs (e.g. *L.E.S.I. S.p.A.* v. *Algeria*, 2006, Decision, para. 84). Others confer on umbrella clauses the virtue of transforming not the breach of contractual undertakings, but those undertakings in and of themselves. In *Noble Ventures, Inc.* v. *Romania*, the Tribunal stated: '[T]he question for the Tribunal is whether Art. II (2)(c) BIT is an "umbrella clause" that transforms contractual undertakings into international law obligations and accordingly makes it a breach of the BIT by the Respondent if it breaches a contractual obligation that it has entered into with the Claimant' (2005, Award, para. 46). Such an approach was criticised, for instance, by the Annulment Committee in *CMS Gas Transmission Company* v. *Argentina*, which argued that the umbrella clause does not have the effect of transforming the obligation that is relied on into something else and that the content of the obligation and its proper law remain unaffected (2007, Annulment Decision, para. 95).

Irrespective of the exact effect attributed to umbrella clauses, these clauses raise a number of legal issues. The most debated pertain, in general, to the types of obligations that they cover and to contractual undertakings, in particular. Each is discussed successively in light of the relevant treaty practice.

In this regard, it can be mentioned at the outset that tribunals diverge as regards the role conferred to treaty drafting in explaining the differences of views displayed by arbitration practice. In *Noble Ventures, Inc.* v. *Romania*, the Tribunal stressed that the differences in the language of these clauses go far in explaining the different positions adopted by tribunals (2005, Award, para. 56). The Tribunal appointed in *Pan American Energy LLC* v. *Argentina* expressed its doubt about this argument, explaining on the contrary that it was not convinced that the umbrella clauses analysed in past awards should have received different interpretations (2006, Decision on Preliminary Objections, para. 99). In fact, as for instance with respect to the applicability of the MFNT clause to investor–State dispute settlement provisions, the discrepancies across arbitration practice seem to result largely from diverging legal and policy views on the operation of umbrella clauses.

5.5.1 The Umbrella Clause in Treaty Practice

Preliminary Remarks

A number of nuances and differences can be seen across IIAs with regard mainly to the 'location' of the umbrella clause in the agreements, its scope of application and the possibility of initiating arbitration proceedings in relation to the clause. Each of these dimensions of treaty practice is examined in turn.

As a preliminary issue, it is worth highlighting IIA provisions whose drafting casts doubt as to their 'status' as umbrella clauses, despite them at times being asserted, in particular by claimants. Three main types of provisions can be mentioned in this respect.

The first type is illustrated by Article 11 of the 1995 Switzerland–Pakistan IIA, which provides: 'Either Contracting Party shall constantly guarantee the observance of the commitments it has entered into with respect to the investments of the investors of the other Contracting Party.' It can be noted that such a provision does not place upon States parties the obligation to observe their commitments, but rather to guarantee their observance. In that sense, the Tribunal suggested in *Noble Ventures, Inc.* v. *Romania* the following interpretation of that Article 11:

> [T]he provision could be interpreted as laying down a kind of general obligation for the host State as a public authority to facilitate foreign investment, namely an obligation to 'guarantee' the observance of the commitments that the host State has entered into towards investors of the other Party, being an obligation to be implemented by, in particular, the adoption of steps and measures under its own municipal law to safeguard the guarantee. In other words, the formulation of Art. 11 of the bilateral investment treaty in *SGS v. Pakistan, supra*, may be interpreted as implicitly setting an international obligation of result for each Party to be fulfilled through appropriate means at the municipal level but without necessarily elevating municipal law obligations to international ones. (2005, Award, para. 58)

In the same vein, the Tribunal appointed in *Salini Costruttori S.p.A.* v. *Jordan* adopted *mutatis mutandis* a similar approach with regard to Article 2.4 of the 1996 Jordan–Italy IIA, which exemplifies the second type of provisions examined here. It reads as follows: 'Each Contracting Party shall create and maintain in its territory a legal framework apt to guarantee to investors the continuity of legal treatment, including the compliance, in good faith, of all undertakings assumed with regard to each specific investor.' The Tribunal noted:

> Article 2(4) of the BIT between Italy and Jordan is couched in terms that are appreciably different from the provisions applied in the arbitral decisions and awards cited by the Parties. Under Article 2(4), each contracting Party committed itself to create and maintain in its territory a 'legal framework' favourable to investments. This legal framework must be apt to guarantee to investors the continuity of legal treatment. It must in particular be such as to ensure compliance of all undertakings assumed under relevant contracts with respect to each specific investor. But under Article 2(4), each Contracting Party did not commit itself to 'observe' any 'obligation' it had previously assumed with regard to specific investments of investors of the other contracting Party as did the Philippines. It did not even guarantee the observance of commitments it had entered into with respect to the investments of the investors of the other Contracting Parties as did Pakistan. It only committed itself to create and maintain a legal framework apt to guarantee the compliance of all undertakings assumed with regard to each specific investor. (2004, Decision on Jurisdiction, para. 126)

Similar in a way to the first type of provisions, it is worth stressing that such provisions are not intended to place upon States parties the obligation to observe their commitments, but instead to create the legal framework guaranteeing in particular the compliance with the commitments.

The third type of provisions does not even relate – in one way or the other – to the observance by States of their commitments. This type can be illustrated by Article 9 of the 1997 France–Moldova IIA: 'Investments having formed the subject of a special commitment of one Contracting Party with respect to the nationals and corporations of the other Contracting Party, shall be governed, without prejudice to the provisions of this Agreement, by the terms of the said commitment to the extent that the latter includes provisions more favourable than those of this Agreement.' In *Mr Franck Charles Arif* v. *Moldova*, the Tribunal denied that such a provision is an 'umbrella clause', explaining:

> Firstly, the ordinary meaning of these Articles within their context and in light of the BIT's object and purpose makes the Tribunal find that Article 9 . . . has its own specific meaning and purpose, separate from that of an 'umbrella' clause, and agrees with Respondent in this regard. According to the ordinary meaning of the text, the specific purpose of these clauses is not to guarantee the observation of obligations assumed by the host State vis-à-vis the investor, but rather to provide investors with the right to claim the application of any rule of law more favourable than the provisions of the BIT. The doctrine refers to such clauses as preservation of rights clauses. (2013, Award, para. 388)

5.5.1.1 The 'Location' of the Umbrella Clause in IIAs

Irrespective of their exact formulation, IIA provisions that can without any doubt be characterised as umbrella clauses are referred to, either in an Article containing for instance also the FET standard (e.g. 1994 USA–Mongolia IIA, Article 2.2.c) or in a separate Article. In this latter situation, this Article, often named 'Other Provisions' or 'Other Obligations', is 'located' in sequence with other Articles specifying the treatment to be offered to foreign investors (e.g. 2005 Germany–Afghanistan IIA, Article 8.2) or after the Articles on dispute settlement (e.g. 1997 Philippines–Switzerland IIA, Article 10.2).

It is worth noting these 'structural' differences inasmuch as the 'location' of the umbrella clause has been used as an argument for interpretation purposes. In *SGS* v. *Philippines*, the Tribunal acknowledged that this 'factor is entitled to some weight', yet it did stress that the 'location' of the umbrella clause was not a decisive factor in its interpretation (2004, Decision on Jurisdiction, para. 124).

5.5.1.2 The Scope of Application of the Umbrella Clause

Regardless of the exact verb used in relation to States' obligations under the umbrella clause (typically 'observe' or 'respect'), or the exact formulation used to outline what is protected (typically 'commitments entered into' or 'obligations entered into'), the language used in IIAs displays differences that pertain to the scope of the commitments or obligations covered by the umbrella clause.

In most IIAs, the scope of these obligations and commitments is left unspecified; this is illustrated by the above-mentioned Article 3.4 of the 1992 Netherlands–Paraguay IIA.

When the umbrella clause contains a specification, it is most often intended to narrow down its scope. However, in contrast, the specification in a few clauses aims at ensuring that the scope will not be conceived as excluding some obligations. For instance, Article 11.1 of the 2016 Austria–Kyrgyzstan IIA provides as to contracts: 'Each Contracting Party shall observe any obligation it may have entered into with regard to specific investments by investors of the other Contracting Party. This means, inter alia, that the breach of a contract between the investor and the host State will amount to a violation of this treaty.' Such a specification comes certainly as a reaction to the debate – discussed below – concerning the coverage of contracts by umbrella clauses.

As for the specifications that narrow down the scope of the clauses, different approaches are used in treaty practice, be it either singly or in combination.

Some umbrella clauses refer to the written – as opposed to the oral – nature of the obligations and commitments. They refer, for instance, to 'obligation in writing' (e.g. 1998 Mexico–Germany IIA, Article 8.2), 'obligation deriving from a written agreement' (e.g. 2006 Colombia–Switzerland, Article 10.2), or to 'written commitments in the form of agreement or contract' (e.g. 2013 China–Tanzania IIA, Article 14.2).

As illustrated by that latter Agreement, some treaties narrow down the scope of the umbrella clause with regard to the nature of the obligation, typically referring to 'contractual obligation' (e.g. 1997 Chile–Austria IIA, Article 2.4). This practice also has the effect of limiting their scope from a *ratione personae* point of view, an effect which is also achieved by those umbrella clauses which *mutatis mutandis* provide that States 'shall observe any obligation [they have] assumed with regard to specific investments (1997 Philippines–Switzerland IIA, Article 10.2), or 'shall observe any obligation arising from a particular commitment [they] may have entered into with regard to a specific investment' (1980 United Kingdom–Philippines IIA, Article 3.3).

Another approach seen in treaty practice that narrows down the scope of umbrella clauses consists of attaching the obligations or agreements covered to the involvement of specific State organs. For instance, Article 12.2 of the 2013 Korea–Cameroon IIA provides: 'Each Contracting Party shall observe the provisions of this Agreement as well as any specific investment agreement between an authority at the central level of government of a Contracting Party and investors of the other Contracting Party that may have entered into force.' It can be deduced from such drafting that this umbrella clause does not cover the agreements concluded by 'component units' of States parties.

5.5.1.3 The Initiation of Arbitration Proceedings in Relation to the Umbrella Clause

It is worth noting that a minority of IIAs, while they contain an umbrella clause, exclude umbrella clause claims from the jurisdiction of arbitration tribunals, be it in the Article containing the clause, in the investor–State dispute settlement provisions, or in an annex.

This can be seen in the IIA adopted by Colombia and Switzerland in 2006, Article 10.2 of which contains an umbrella clause that provides: 'Each Party shall observe any obligation deriving from a written agreement concluded between its central government or agencies thereof and an investor of the other Party with regard to a specific investment, which the investor could rely on in good faith when establishing, acquiring or expanding the investment.' However, Article 11.3 specifies that '[e]ach Party hereby gives its unconditional and irrevocable consent to the submission of an investment dispute to international arbitration … except for disputes with regard to Article 10 paragraph 2 of this Agreement'. By the same token, the 1994 ECT contains an Annex (Annex IA) that lists the States parties that do not allow an investor to submit a dispute concerning the umbrella clause incorporated in the last sentence of Article 10.1.

5.5.2 The Types of Obligations and Commitments Covered by the Umbrella Clause

The debate, as it has emerged with the *SGS* cases analysed below, has focused on the coverage of contractual undertakings by umbrella clauses. Yet, the issue of their scope of application also arises with regard to two types of obligations and commitments: international obligations and, mainly, obligations contained in domestic statutes and regulations. Each is examined in turn.

5.5.2.1 International Obligations and Commitments

This issue does not arise with regard to all umbrella clauses. Indeed, those clauses that for instance provide that each State party 'shall observe any contractual obligation it may have entered into towards an investor of the other Contracting Party with regard to investments approved by it in its territory' (1997 Chile–Austria IIA, Article 2.4) do not have the potential to encompass obligations and commitments undertaken under international law. On the other hand, this issue does arise in relation to umbrella clauses which do not specify the nature of the obligations and commitments that they cover, typically when they merely provide that States shall observe 'any obligation'. Some tribunals have been prepared to consider that international obligations are covered by such clauses. In *Bureau Veritas* v. *Paraguay*, the Tribunal stated:

> It [the text of the umbrella clause] provides that Paraguay 'shall observe any obligation it may have entered into with regard to investments of the other Contracting Party.' The words 'any obligation' are all encompassing. They are not limited to international obligations, or non-contractual obligations, so that they appear without apparent limitation with respect to commitments that impose legal obligations. (2009, Decision of the Tribunal on Objections to Jurisdiction, para. 141)

It is interesting to note that international obligations are the first type of obligations mentioned by the Tribunal; this suggests that there was no doubt for this Tribunal that they are covered by Article 3.4 of the 1992 Netherlands–Paraguay IIA, which was under discussion in that case. While also mentioning international obligations, the Annulment Committee in *CMS Gas Transmission Company* v. *Argentina* was more cautious; it considered that Article 2.2.c of the 1991 USA–Argentina IIA is 'concerned with consensual obligations arising independently of the BIT itself (*i.e.* under the law of the host State or possibly under international law' (2007, Annulment Decision, para. 95; emphasis added).

The Tribunal appointed in *Noble Ventures, Inc.* v. *Romania* expressly doubted that the obligations referred to in the umbrella clause of the 1992 USA–Romania IIA encompass international obligations. It did so by arguing that States do not usually conclude special agreements with reference to specific investments in addition to BITs. In terms of effectiveness, it also noted that such agreements would in any case be subject to the principle of *pacta sunt servanda* and would thereby not have any need for an umbrella clause (2005, Award, para. 51).

5.5.2.2 Obligations and Commitments under Domestic Statutes and Regulations

Again, this issue does not arise with respect to all IIAs; those that – in one way or the other – limit the scope of the umbrella clause to contractual obligations fall obviously outside the scope of this discussion. At stake here are again those provisions that *mutatis mutandis* provide that States parties shall observe 'any obligation'.

Arbitration practice displays nuances and differences as regards this matter. Underlying these nuances and differences as well as this discussion more generally is the distinction between specific commitments and general commitments as well as the question as to whether specific commitments can be contained in domestic statutes and regulations.

In *Noble Ventures, Inc.* v. *Romania*, the Tribunal concluded that legislative acts are not covered by the umbrella clause at hand in that case as they constitute general commitments. In support of this conclusion, it argued that the reference made to 'entered into' in Article 2.2.c of the 1992 USA–Romania IIA indicates that the clause covers only specific commitments (2005, Award, para. 51). Likewise, in *Oxus Gold* v. *Uzbekistan*, the Tribunal reached the conclusion that the umbrella clause of the 1993 United Kingdom–Uzbekistan IIA – which is similar to the clause at hand in the *Noble* case – does not cover general obligations and encompasses only specific commitments. To do so, it relied on the following effect-based argument:

> If the violation of any legal obligation contained in the national legal order would be transformed by an umbrella clause into a violation of the Treaty, whatever the internal source of the obligation or the seriousness of the breach, it

would be sufficient to include an umbrella clause in the Treaty and no other standard of protection. This would result in the fact that the whole national legal order would be automatically internationalized through an umbrella clause, which cannot be. (2015, Award, para. 371)

In *Continental Casualty Company* v. *Argentina* – which dealt with an umbrella clause similar to the ones at hand in the previous two cases – the Tribunal also expressed the view that umbrella clauses do not come into play for alleged breaches of 'general obligations arising from the law of the host State'. It stated that obligations 'must be specific obligations concerning investment' and that '[t]hey do not cover general requirements imposed by the law of the Host State'. But it then distinguished those 'general obligations arising from the law of the host State' from, in particular, 'unilateral commitments arising from provisions of the law of the host State regulating a particular business sector and addressed specifically to the foreign investors in relation to their investment therein'. Applying this distinction, it found that the provisions of the Convertibility Law and the Intangibility Laws adopted by Argentina could not be a source of obligations that Argentina had assumed specifically with regard to the claimant's investment company, and it concluded therefore that these obligations were not covered by the umbrella clause. Interestingly, it referred to the findings of the Tribunal in *LG&E* v. *Argentina* to illustrate the above-mentioned 'unilateral commitments arising from provisions of the law of the host State regulating a particular business sector and addressed specifically to the foreign investors in relation to their investment therein' (2008, Award, paras. 300–302).

In the *LG&E* case, the Tribunal concluded that the provisions of the Gas Law and other regulations were not 'legal obligations of a general nature', but that they were 'very specific in relation to LG&E's investment in Argentina' which were thereby covered by the applicable umbrella clause – which is similar to the clauses in the above-mentioned cases. It based this finding notably on the reasoning below:

> Argentina's abrogation of the guarantees under the statutory framework – calculation of the tariffs in dollars before conversion to pesos, semi-annual tariff adjustments by the PPI and no price controls without indemnification – violated its obligations to Claimants' investments. Argentina made these specific obligations to foreign investors, such as LG&E, by enacting the Gas Law and other regulations, and then advertising these guarantees in the Offering Memorandum to induce the entry of foreign capital to fund the privatization program in its public service sector. These laws and regulations became obligations within the meaning of Article II(2)(c), by virtue of targeting foreign investors and applying specifically to their investments, that gave rise to liability under the umbrella clause. (2006, Decision on Liability, paras. 174–175)

To further evidence this divergence of views in arbitration practice, it is worth referring to the conflicting interpretations that were given within a few weeks by two tribunals of the last sentence of Article 10.1 of the 1994 ECT, which provides in its relevant part: 'Each Contracting Party shall observe any obligations it has entered into with an Investor or an Investment of an Investor of any other Contracting Party.' In *RREEF* v. *Spain*, the Tribunal started by mentioning that the expression 'any obligations' calls for a broad interpretation. Despite being cautious in the formulation of its reasoning, as it noted that the phrase 'it has entered into' seems to refer exclusively to bilateral relationships to the exclusion of general rules, it concluded without expressing any qualification that the ECT umbrella clause applies only to contractual obligations (2018, Decision on Responsibility and on the Principles of Quantum, para. 284). On the contrary, in *Greentech Energy Systems A/S* v. *Italy*, the majority of the Tribunal accepted an interpretation of the clause which encompasses certain legislative and regulatory instruments that are sufficiently specific to qualify as commitments to identifiable investments or investors (2018, Final Award, para. 464).

5.5.3 Contractual Undertakings

The interplay between umbrella clauses and contracts has been a most complex and sensitive issue in arbitration practice. It entails a series of specific issues that pertain mainly to: (1) the coverage of contracts by umbrella clauses; and (2) the effect of contractual exclusive jurisdiction clauses on umbrella clause claims. Each is examined in turn.

5.5.3.1 The Coverage of Contractual Undertakings by the Umbrella Clause

The coverage of contractual undertakings by umbrella clauses has been the most controversial question in arbitration practice with regard to those clauses. Mainly in the past, the object of the controversy has been whether or not umbrella clauses that do not specify it cover contracts; conflicting principled approaches have been adopted by tribunals to address this issue. Nowadays, the issues that arise are not so much a matter of principle. Instead, disagreements pertain to the modalities of the coverage of contracts by umbrella clauses, be they referring explicitly to contracts or not. Those issues relate to (1) the capacity in which the host State acts, i.e. as a sovereign (*jure imperii*) or as a regular commercial partner (*jure gestionis*), and (2) the contracts to which either or both disputing parties to arbitration proceedings are not a party.

a Principled Approaches

The principled approaches that emerge from arbitration practice are very well reflected in the two 'foundational' cases on this issue: *SGS* v. *Pakistan* and *SGS* v. *Philippines*. As noted by the Tribunal in *Bureau Veritas* v. *Paraguay*, 'the two decisions cannot be reconciled [as they reflect] different approaches to this issue to the effect of an umbrella clause, in the framework of a BIT' (2009,

Decision on Jurisdiction, para. 138). More generally, they also evidence different ways of conceiving of the application and interpretation of IIA provisions.

In *SGS* v. *Pakistan,* the Tribunal dealt with Article 11 of the 1995 Switzerland–Pakistan IIA, whose drafting – as explained above – casts doubt on its characterisation as an umbrella clause; it remains that the arguments and findings of that Tribunal have subsequently been taken on board to discuss the interplay between umbrella clauses and contracts. The principles of public international law as well as the consequences which it considered would follow for States from the application of this Article to contracts were key in the reasoning of the Tribunal. It explained:

> Considering the widely accepted principle with which we started, namely, that under general international law, a violation of a contract entered into by a State with an investor of another State, is not, by itself, a violation of international law, and considering further that the legal consequences that the Claimant would have us attribute to Article 11 of the BIT are so far-reaching in scope, and so automatic and unqualified and sweeping in their operation, so burdensome in their potential impact upon a Contracting Party, we believe that clear and convincing evidence must be adduced by the Claimant that such was indeed the shared intent of the Contracting Parties to the Swiss–Pakistan Investment Protection Treaty in incorporating Article 11 in the BIT. (2003, Decision on Jurisdiction, para. 167)

This principled approach was explicitly endorsed by the Tribunal in *El Paso Energy International Company* v. *Argentina,* which considered in particular that it could not entertain purely contractual claims that did not amount to a violation of the standards of the 1991 USA–Argentina IIA (2006, Decision on Jurisdiction, para. 85).

On the contrary, and as reported in *Eureko B.V.* v. *Poland* (2005, Partial Award, para. 254), the approach of the *SGS* v. *Pakistan* was rejected by the Swiss Government in a letter addressed to the International Centre for Settlement of Investment Disputes (ICSID). That government stated therein that it was 'alarmed about the very narrow interpretation given to the meaning of [the umbrella clause] by the Tribunal, which not only runs counter to the intention of Switzerland when concluding the Treaty but is quite evidently neither supported by the meaning of similar articles in BITs concluded by other countries nor by academic comments on such provisions'.

The reasoning and findings of that Tribunal were also criticised in *SGS* v. *Philippines.* Among other grounds, the Tribunal appointed in that case addressed the consequences drawn by the *SGS* v. *Pakistan* Tribunal from the principle according to which a violation of a contract entered into by a State with an investor of another State is not, by itself, a violation of international law. While it agreed that this amounts to a well-accepted principle, it criticised the presumption that the *SGS* v. *Pakistan* Tribunal deduced from it and the way in which it was used. In substance, the Tribunal argued that this principle should not lead to the text of the treaty being overlooked, and that the issue should be determined through interpretation and not by any presumption. Interpreting Article 10.2 of the 1997 Philippines–Switzerland IIA, the Tribunal concluded that it covers contractual undertakings entered into by host States (2004, Decision on Jurisdiction, paras. 122 and 127).

The Tribunal appointed in *SGS* v. *Paraguay* sided with the *SGS* v. *Philippines* Tribunal and directly answered the *SGS* v. *Pakistan* Tribunal. To the above-mentioned assertion of that latter Tribunal following which 'clear and convincing evidence must be adduced by the Claimant', it argued:

> To the contrary, we believe that Article 11's ordinary meaning must be respected, as required by the Vienna Convention (Article 31(1)) ... Like the *BIVAC* tribunal, we conclude that the umbrella clause before us 'establishes an international obligation for the parties to the BIT to observe contractual obligation[s] with respect to investors' and that this interpretation is necessary to give the umbrella clause purpose and effect. (2010, Decision on Jurisdiction, paras. 169–170)

b The Distinction between *Jure Imperii* and *Jure Gestionis* State Conduct

As analysed in Chapter 6, it is well accepted that the capacity in which a State acts, whether as a sovereign (*jure imperii*) or as a regular commercial partner (*jure gestionis*), impacts on the determination of whether a breach of a contract can amount to an expropriation. There is no such consensus with respect to umbrella clauses. More precisely, arbitration tribunals are divided on two issues that relate respectively to the types of contracts and the types of contractual breaches that fall within the scope of umbrella clauses. Although these two issues are interconnected and often mixed up in arbitration practice, it is worth distinguishing them for the purpose of this analysis.

i The Types of Contracts   As to this first issue, some argue that umbrella clauses do not confer any protection on foreign investors in relation to contracts entered into by host States as a normal commercial partner, only those contractual undertakings agreed on by them in their capacity as a sovereign being in their view covered. In that sense, the Tribunal appointed in *El Paso Energy International Company* v. *Argentina* decided that the umbrella clause contained in the 1991 USA–Argentina IIA does 'not extend the Treaty protection to breaches of an ordinary commercial contract entered into by the State or a State-owned entity'. In support of this finding, it stated the following:

> In view of the necessity to distinguish the State as a merchant, especially when it acts through instrumentalities, from the State as a sovereign, the Tribunal considers that the 'umbrella clause' in the Argentine–US BIT, which prescribes that '[e]ach Party shall observe any obligation it may have entered into with regard to investments',

can be interpreted in the light of Article VII (1), which clearly includes among the investment disputes under the Treaty all disputes resulting from a violation of a commitment given by the State as a sovereign State, either through an agreement, an authorisation, or the BIT. (2006, Decision on Jurisdiction, para. 81)

It can be suggested that the decision of the Tribunal was to some extent geared by a principled approach. This is notably apparent from the conclusive remarks made by the Tribunal, which actually appear to have played a pre-eminent role in its decision:

> In conclusion . . . an umbrella clause cannot transform any contract claim into a treaty claim, as this would necessarily imply that any commitments of the State in respect to investments, even the most minor ones, would be transformed into treaty claims. These far-reaching consequences of a broad interpretation of the so-called umbrella clauses, quite destructive of the distinction between national legal orders and the international legal order, have been well understood and clearly explained by the first Tribunal which dealt with the issue of the so-called 'umbrella clause' in the *SGS v. Pakistan* case and which insisted on the theoretical problems faced. (para. 82)

In reference to Schreuer's hope that investors will invoke umbrella clauses with appropriate restraint,[5] the Tribunal concluded: 'It is the firm conviction of this Tribunal that the investors will not use appropriate restraint – and why should they? – if the ICSID tribunals offer them unexpected remedies. The responsibility for showing appropriate restraint rests rather in the hands of the ICSID tribunals' (para. 82).

Others, on the contrary, do not exclude contracts entered into by host States acting *jure gestionis* from the scope of umbrella clauses. This view was, for instance, adopted by the Tribunal in *SGS v. Paraguay* with regard to Article 11 of the 1992 Switzerland–Paraguay IIA, which was considered in that case as an umbrella clause. Despite the fact that such a characterisation can be discussed, it is interesting to note, in light of the above, that the Tribunal rejected the appeal of the respondent 'to the putative "true meaning" of umbrella clauses'; it argued that this could not take precedence over the plain language of this Article and that there was no reason to import into it a non-textual limitation (2010, Decision on Jurisdiction, para. 168).

ii The Types of Contractual Breaches   The other issue that arises with regard to the *jure imperii/jure gestionis* distinction is whether a breach of a contract by a State acting as a merchant is covered by umbrella clauses. Here again there exist diverging views on the matter.

For the same reasons as explained above, the Tribunal appointed in *SGS v. Paraguay* decided that Article 11 of the 1992 Switzerland–Paraguay IIA does not lead to the conclusion that 'commitments may be breached only through

---

[5] C Schreuer, 'Traveling the BIT Route: Of Waiting Periods, Umbrella Clauses and Forks in the Road' (2004) 5 *Journal of World Investment & Trade* 231, at 255.

actions that a commercial counterparty cannot take, through abuses of state power, or through exertions of undue government influence' (2010, Decision on Jurisdiction, para. 168). In this respect, it can be mentioned that the Tribunal in *Noble Ventures, Inc.* v. *Romania* noted in the context of the umbrella clause claim that there is no reason to refuse to attribute commercial acts to States and to limit attribution to sovereign acts (2005, Award, para. 82).

On the other hand, others stress that – to use the words of the Tribunal in *Pan American Energy LLC* v. *Argentina* – 'it is essentially from the State as a sovereign that the foreign investors have to be protected' (2006, Decision on Preliminary Objections, para. 108). For that reason, they limit the operation of umbrella clauses to the breaches of contracts committed by States acting in their capacity as a sovereign. It is worth noting that the Tribunal appointed in *Sempra Energy International* v. *Argentina*, while applying this approach, stressed the difficulty in many situations of drawing a distinction between the conduct of States when acting as a merchant and their conduct in their capacity as a sovereign, as it considered that not every kind of conduct can easily be ascribed to either category (2007, Award, para. 311). Also from a practical point of view, Crawford emphasised the difficulty of appraising the nature or motive of State acts at the jurisdictional stage and argued that 'it would be very odd indeed if a state could defend itself against a claim for repudiation of an investment agreement by arguing that it was acting for commercial reasons'.[6]

c Contracts Not Concluded by the Disputing Parties

Another issue boils down to the question of whether umbrella clauses cover contracts concluded by entities other than the disputing parties. More precisely, the situation can be threefold: (1) the contract can be signed by an entity distinct from the State with the investor; (2) it can be concluded by the State with an entity distinct from the investor, typically a locally incorporated subsidiary; and (3) the contract can be concluded between an entity distinct from the State and an entity distinct from the investor. Irrespective of the exact situation, similar issues arise as to the link between the State and the separate entity, on the one hand, and the link between the investor and the separate entity, on the other hand. The notions of attribution and privity are key in the discussion conducted by arbitration tribunals of the former and latter links, respectively.

As to the link between the State and the separate entity, it is worth noting that tribunals frequently combine two discussions: (1) whether a contract concluded by an entity distinct from the State can be considered as a contract concluded by the State; and (2) whether the conduct of a separate entity in breach of a contract can be attributed to the State. This helps to explain why it

---

[6] J Crawford, 'Treaty and Contract in Investment Arbitration' (2008) 24 *Arbitration International* 351, at 368.

is often focused on the international rules pertaining to State responsibility and attribution, which are analysed in Chapter 15. In *Noble Ventures, Inc.* v. *Romania*, for instance, the Tribunal applied the international law rules on State responsibility and specifically the rule regarding the conduct of entities entitled to exercise elements of governmental authority, as codified in Article 5 of the 2001 Articles on Responsibility of States for Internationally Wrongful Acts. It considered that the contracts had been concluded by entities that were exercising on this occasion such a governmental authority as conferred by Romanian law. As a result, it concluded that the contracts had been concluded on behalf of Romania and that they were attributable to that State for the purpose of the umbrella clause (2005, Award, paras. 70, 79, 86).

In *Gavrilovic* v. *Croatia*, the Tribunal did not enter into the discussion of attribution matters; instead, it focused on the text of the umbrella clause contained in Article 8.2 of the 1997 Austria–Croatia IIA, which classically provides: 'Each Contracting Party shall observe any contractual obligation it may have entered into towards an investor of the other Contracting Party with regard to investments approved by it in its territory.' In this respect, it stressed that the term 'it' refers to the State and not to entities distinct from it; as Croatia did not enter into the contractual relationship and it was not responsible for any contractual obligation, the Tribunal decided that there could be no breach of that Article (2018, Award, para. 1159).

Concerning the link between the investor and a separate entity, arbitration practice displays differences of views which are well reflected in *Burlington Resources Inc.* v. *Ecuador*. In that case, the majority of the Tribunal denied that the contract concluded by an entity distinct from the investor was covered by the umbrella clause. It provided this detailed discussion of the matter in support of this view:

> The word 'obligation' is thus the operative term of the umbrella clause. The Treaty does not define 'obligation'. The Parties agree – and rightly so – that the clause refers to legal obligations. This is of little assistance, however, to resolve the question of privity. To answer this question, the Tribunal relies primarily on two elements which in its view inform the ordinary meaning of 'obligation'. First, in its ordinary meaning, the obligation of one subject is generally seen in correlation with the right of another. Or, differently worded, someone's breach of an obligation corresponds to the breach of another's right. [footnote omitted] An obligation entails a party bound by it and another one benefiting from it, in other words, entails an obligor and an obligee. Second, an obligation does not exist in a vacuum. It is subject to a governing law. Although the notion of obligation is used in an international treaty, the court or tribunal interpreting the treaty may have to look to municipal law to give it content. This is not peculiar to 'obligation'; it applies to other notions found in investment treaties, *e.g.* nationality, property, exhaustion of local remedies to name just these. [footnote omitted] In this case, the PSCs are governed by Ecuadorian law. It is that law that defines the content of the obligation including the scope of and the

parties to the undertaking, *i.e.* the obligor and the obligee. (2012, Decision on Liability, para. 214)

Enquiring into whose rights were correlated to the contractual obligations, the majority of the Tribunal concluded that they were not covered by the umbrella clause as the claimant had not established that, under the law governing the obligation, the non-signatory parent of a contracting party could directly enforce its subsidiary right. Secondarily, it also argued that the expression 'entered into' could be regarded as reinforcing the idea of privity; as to the expression 'with regard to investments', it noted that the link that it establishes between the obligation and the investment does not replace but instead qualifies the notion of obligation (paras. 215–216). This approach of the majority of the Tribunal was, for instance, endorsed by the Tribunal in *WNC Factoring Ltd (United Kingdom)* v. *Czech Republic* (2017, Award, paras. 335–337).

On the contrary, it was criticised by Arbitrator Orrego Vicuna, who dissented from the majority. He stressed in particular that the majority's conclusion leads to the exclusion of indirect investments lacking the privity requirement from the scope of the umbrella clause, thereby establishing, according to him, a distinction – absent from the treaty – between provisions that protect both direct and indirect investments and those that protect only direct investments. Instead, he argued that the entity whose interest in the investment is protected under the IIA is also entitled to benefit from the umbrella clause protection. According to this approach, then, contracts concluded by, for example, a locally incorporated subsidiary of the investor and the State do not fall outside the scope of the clause. Arbitrator Orrego Vicuna also emphasised that his conclusion was imperative with regard to those situations in which the creation of a local company constitutes a requirement under the domestic law of the host State (2012, Dissenting Opinion, paras. 8–9). Such an approach found support in *Continental Casualty Company* v. *Argentina*. The Tribunal noted in this case that, provided contractual obligations are entered 'with regard to investments', they can be entered with persons or entities other than foreign investors themselves 'so that an undertaking by the host State with a subsidiary . . . is not in principle excluded' from the scope of an umbrella clause (2008, Award, para. 297).

5.5.3.2 The Effect of Contractual Exclusive Jurisdiction Clauses on Umbrella Clause Claims

Among the numerous tribunals that accept that umbrella clauses cover contracts, disagreements exist as to the question of whether the provision of a clause in a contract conferring an exclusive competence on a tribunal – typically the domestic courts of the host State – to settle the disputes arising from them affect umbrella clause claims. This boils down to the question of whether umbrella clause claims pertaining to contracts, despite falling within the jurisdiction of tribunals, should be declared inadmissible or not.

Some consider that an investor must comply with an exclusive jurisdiction clause contained in a contract (e.g. *Bosh International, Inc.* v. *Ukraine*, 2012, Award, para. 252) and that the mention of such a clause in a contract has the effect of making the umbrella clause claim inadmissible (e.g. *Bureau Veritas* v. *Paraguay*, 2009, Decision of the Tribunal on Objections to Jurisdiction, para. 159). In that case, instead of dismissing the claim, that Tribunal opted for staying the proceedings as it saw this as the most cost-effective and efficient way to treat the issue of admissibility in relation to the objective to ensure the sound administration of justice. Indeed, it considered that, in the case that the investor would pursue its claims before the domestic courts of Paraguay in application of the contractual exclusive jurisdiction clause, and in the event Paraguay would disregard their decision if they decided in favour of the investor, the umbrella clause claim could become admissible depending on the circumstances (2012, Further Decision on Objections to Jurisdiction, para. 290).

Against this view, others argue that a contractual exclusive jurisdiction clause does not lead an umbrella clause claim to be declared inadmissible. This was the case in particular of the Tribunal in *SGS* v. *Paraguay*, which largely developed its reasoning in reaction to the conclusion reached by the Tribunal in *Bureau Veritas* v. *Paraguay* because of – as it explained – the 'extensive factual commonalities' between the two cases (2010, Decision on Jurisdiction, para. 172). In *Gavrilovic* v. *Croatia*, the Tribunal stressed that it would not fulfil its mandate if it refused to decide on the violation of the umbrella clause (2018, Award, para. 422).

At the core of the divergences between these two approaches is notably the issue and the conception of the fundamental basis of umbrella clause claims that tribunals address in relation to the test formulated by the Annulment Committee in *Compania de Aguas del Aconquija S.A.* v. *Argentina* – itself being based on the 1903 decision of the United States–Venezuela Mixed Claims Commission in *Woodruff*. That Committee stated:

> [W]here the 'fundamental basis of the claim' is a treaty laying down an independent standard by which the conduct of the parties is to be judged, the existence of an exclusive jurisdiction clause in a contract between the claimant and the respondent state or one of its subdivisions cannot operate as a bar to the application of the treaty standard . . . In such a case, the inquiry which the ICSID tribunal is required to undertake is one governed by the ICSID Convention, by the BIT and by applicable international law. Such an inquiry is neither in principle determined, nor precluded, by any issue of municipal law, including any municipal law agreement of the parties. (2002, Decision on Annulment, paras. 101–102)

In this respect, the Tribunal in *Bureau Veritas* v. *Paraguay* stated that an umbrella clause does not constitute an independent standard; it argued:

'[E]verything turns on the meaning and effect of the Contract . . . In the present case, in relation to Article 3(4) we do not see how it could be concluded that "the fundamental basis of the claim" was the BIT rather than the Contract. Any other approach strikes us as being so artificial as to be unreasonable' (2009, Decision of the Tribunal on Objections to Jurisdiction, para. 149).

This argument was criticised in *SGS* v. *Paraguay* as the Tribunal considered that it constituted an argument for declining jurisdiction, not for inadmissibility. On that basis, it stated: '[I]t would be incongruous to find jurisdiction on this basis [the umbrella clause], but then to dismiss the greater part of all Article 11 claims on admissibility grounds – because the effect would be, once again, to divest the provision of its core purpose and effect, to the same extent as if we had denied jurisdiction outright.' (2010, Decision on Jurisdiction, paras. 174–176). In that sense, Gaillard noted that the solution adopted in *Bureau Veritas* v. *Paraguay* in reality resulted in tribunals having jurisdiction over an empty shell.[7]

---

[7] E Gaillard, 'Investment Treaty Arbitration and Jurisdiction over Contract Claims: The SGS Cases Considered' in T Weiler (ed), *International Investment Law and Arbitration: Leading Cases from the ICSID, NAFTA, Bilateral Treaties and Customary International Law* (Cameron May 2005) 325, at 334.

6

The Protection against Illegal Expropriation

Introduction

As explained in Chapter 1, the law of expropriation has a very long history, which is deeply rooted in public international law. As illustrated in the nineteenth century by the controversies on compensation and in the twenty-first century by the issue of the right of States to regulate, it has for a long time been the object of fierce tensions and disagreements. This likely stems from the fact that the law of expropriation stands at the crossroads of three fundamental rights: the right of States to expropriate, their right to regulate and the right to property of foreign investors. Underlying these rights and their interplay, one finds the protection of public and private interests and the conflict between them.

In establishing a balance between these, international investment agreements (IIAs) have traditionally subjected the legality of expropriation to conditions and failed to address explicitly the issue of the right of States to regulate. A great number of IIAs concluded in the 2010s tackle this issue, typically by distinguishing expropriatory measures from regulatory measures. Likewise, it is noteworthy that those agreements contain also Articles or Annexes that specify the scope and modalities of application of the expropriation provision with regard to specific matters pertaining in particular to intellectual property rights, lands, subsidies, or grants. Those specifications are analysed in Chapter 7.

This chapter focuses on the two main issues raised by the protection of foreign investors against illegal expropriation: (1) the types of expropriation covered; and (2) the conditions of legality of expropriation. Prior to this, we shall first examine the issue of the types of property protected, with a specific focus on contractual rights.

6.1 The Types of Property Protected against Illegal Expropriation

The expropriation provisions within IIAs provide *mutatis mutandis* in their relevant part that '[n]either Party may nationalize or expropriate covered investments' (2016 Canada–Mongolia IIA, Article 10.1). While they refer to 'investments', they have traditionally not specified the scope of the properties protected against illegal expropriation. That silence directs us to the definition of an investment as provided by IIAs to delineate their scope of application. In this respect, and as analysed in Chapter 14, it is worth stressing that the notion of investment is broadly defined in those agreements. Some IIAs concluded in the 2010s offer some specification as to those properties protected by the agreements. For instance, Annex 1.1 of the 2016 Hong Kong SAR China–Chile IIA provides: 'A measure or a series of measures by a Party does not constitute an expropriation unless it interferes with a tangible or intangible property right or property interest in a covered investment.'

Of course, while IIAs delineate – in one way or the other – the scope of the properties that are protected against illegal expropriation, they are irrelevant in determining the existence as such of property rights. This existence and the appraisal as to whether an investor holds a property is a matter of domestic law.

The existence of property rights under the domestic law of the host State and the types of property protected by IIAs are usually not the subject of debate in arbitration practice. However, whether or not matters such as goodwill, customers, or market shares can be characterised as an investment has been at stake in some cases in relation to expropriation claims (e.g. *Chemtura Corporation* v. *Canada*, 2010, Award, para. 243). In fact, the types of property protected against illegal expropriation has most often been debated in relation to contracts and contractual rights.

The interplay between contractual rights and expropriation has a long history before international courts and tribunals. It is well established that contractual rights are protected against illegal expropriation under public international law, something which, akin to a *jurisprudence constante*, has been acknowledged and applied by arbitration tribunals when discussing the matter (e.g. *Koch* v. *Venezuela*, 2017, Award, para. 7.50). Tribunals have also referred more specifically to the typical incorporation of contractual rights in the definition of an investment provided in IIAs (e.g. *Crystallex International Corporation* v. *Venezuela*, 2016, Award, para. 662).

However, in relation mainly to the divide between the acts carried out by States in their capacity as a sovereign (*jure imperii*) and those carried out as a regular commercial partner (*jure gestionis*), arbitration tribunals do not consider that all violations of a contract or its termination by a State can constitute a breach of the IIA expropriation provision. It is well agreed that only the conduct of States acting *jure imperii* can constitute such a breach. When they are acting *jure gestionis*, their illegal conduct is deemed to constitute a mere contractual violation against which investors are not protected by the IIA expropriation provision (e.g. *Parkerings-Compagniet AS* v. *Lithuania*, 2007, Award, para. 443).

This divide and its implications are illustrated in *Biwater Gauff (Tanzania) Ltd* v. *Tanzania*. In that case, the Tribunal decided that the termination of a lease contract that resulted from a series of alleged contractual failures by the foreign investor could not be characterised as an act *jure imperii* and therefore as a conduct prohibited under the IIA expropriation provision; instead, it considered the decision to terminate the contract as the 'ordinary behaviour of a contractual counterparty' (2008, Award, para. 492). On the other hand, it concluded that a series of actions undertaken before the expiration of the notice of termination, such as the occupation of facilities or the deportation of staff, deprived the investor of the benefit of the lease contract and cumulatively expropriated its contractual rights (paras. 516–518). Implicitly, the Tribunal considered that such conduct constituted an exercise by the respondent State of its sovereign prerogatives.

6.2 The Types of Expropriation

Preliminary Remarks

In line with public international law, there is a great consistency across IIAs as to the scope of the conduct prohibited under the expropriation provision. That being said, there exist nuances and differences across treaty practice that are worth emphasising at the outset.

As a preliminary remark, it should be noted that, while a few IIAs refer only to 'expropriation' (e.g. 2017 Hong Kong SAR China–ASEAN IIA, Article 10.1), most of them refer also to 'nationalisation'. The difference between these two notions is not provided in those IIAs. As explained, for instance, by the Tribunal in *OI European Group B.V.* v. *Venezuela* (2015, Award, para. 328), nationalisation is usually construed as being analogous to expropriation, the main difference between them being that nationalisation involves complete sectors of the economy. More importantly, whatever the exact situations that these notions cover, it is well established that the distinction made between expropriation and nationalisation does not bear any legal consequences as for the protection granted by IIAs to investors. In addition to 'nationalisation' and 'expropriation', a few IIAs refer to 'confiscation' (e.g. 2018 Kazakhstan–United Arab Emirates (UAE) IIA, Article 6.1) or 'dispossession' (e.g. 2016 Rwanda–Morocco IIA, Article 4.1). Again, these notions are not defined in treaty practice; they are in fact synonymous with expropriation and their mention does not make any difference in legal terms either.

As to expropriation, almost all IIAs refer to both 'direct expropriation' and 'indirect expropriation', which are analysed below. Among the exceptions to this trend, it is worth highlighting the practice adopted by Brazil in the 2010s in excluding indirect expropriation from the protection offered to foreign investors. For instance, Article 7, entitled 'Direct Expropriation', of the 2019 Brazil–UAE IIA provides: 'For greater certainty, this Article only provides for direct expropriation, where an investment is nationalized or otherwise directly expropriated through formal transfer of title or ownership rights, and does not cover indirect expropriation.'

Mainstream treaty practice can in general be illustrated by the expropriation provision of the 2017 Israel–Japan IIA: 'Neither Contracting Party shall expropriate or nationalize an investment in its Territory of an investor of the other Contracting Party or take any measure equivalent to expropriation or nationalization' (Article 11.1). The terminology used to name 'direct expropriation' and mainly 'indirect expropriation' varies across treaty practice, as does the combination of terms used to refer to these notions.

Also, it can be seen that a few IIAs are drafted in such a way as to make it unclear whether States parties intend to protect investors against other types of State conduct. This can be seen from Article 7.1 of the 2016 Austria-Kyrgyzstan IIA, which provides: 'A Contracting Party shall not expropriate or nationalise directly or indirectly an investment of an investor of the other Contracting Party or take any measures having equivalent effect.' One may wonder what the prohibition 'to take any measures having an equivalent effect' means in the context of this provision. As discussed below, arbitration tribunals that had to apply the 1992 North American Free Trade Agreement (NAFTA) addressed this matter in relation to Article 1110.

6.2.1 Direct Expropriation

As illustrated by State practice and the case law of international courts and tribunals – for instance that of the Permanent Court of International Justice (PCIJ) (e.g. *Case concerning certain German interests in Polish Upper Silesia (Germany* v. *Poland),* 1926, Judgment) – situations of direct expropriation have traditionally been the most mainstream. On the other hand, it is worth noting that investor–State arbitration tribunals have mainly been called to decide on instances of indirect expropriation. As explained by Dolzer and Schreuer,[1] this is mainly due to the fact that States have become more concerned not to attract negative publicity that might harm their reputations. That being said, political evolutions at the domestic and international levels have led to a revival of instances of direct expropriation since the 2010s, notably as a result of nationalisations initiated in South America (e.g. *Rusoro Mining Limited* v. *Venezuela,* 2016, Award, paras. 370–410).

Whatever these factual and societal evolutions, the notion of direct expropriation does not raise any major definitional, conceptual or legal issues. This is so even though IIAs have traditionally not provided any detail on this notion, which has evolved in IIAs concluded during the 2010s. Indeed, a number of these latter agreements specify in the expropriation provision or in an annex attached to it that – *mutatis mutandis* – '"direct expropriation" means the formal transfer of ownership of the investment or its direct seizure' (2016 Argentina–Qatar IIA, Article 5.2). Such a definition is in line with the approach adopted by arbitration tribunals. For instance, in *S.D. Myers, Inc.* v. *Canada,* the Tribunal stated: 'In general, the term "expropriation" carries

---

[1] R Dolzer, C Schreuer, *Principles of International Investment Law* (2nd ed, Oxford University Press 2012), at 101.

with it the connotation of a "taking" by a governmental-type authority of a person's "property" with a view to transferring ownership of that property to another person, usually the authority that exercised its *de jure* or *de facto* power to do the "taking"' (2000, Partial Award, para. 280).

Be it the State itself or a third person, the beneficiary of a direct expropriation usually benefits de jure from the transfer of the legal title and de facto from the control and possession over the property. However, it has been considered that a measure may be characterised as a direct expropriation where the legal title is transferred but the foreign investor retains control over part of the property. The Tribunal adopted such a view in *von Pezold* v. *Zimbabwe* with regard to Zimbabwe, which transferred the legal title of investors but left them with control over parts of the Zimbabwean properties (2015, Award, para. 494).

Although typically stressed in relation to indirect expropriation, it is also well accepted with regard to direct expropriation that the taking must be permanent (e.g. *Quiborax S.A.* v. *Bolivia*, 2015, Award, para. 200). It should be noted, in relation to the analysis of indirect expropriation below, that this Tribunal also mentioned that a taking 'must not qualify as the legitimate exercise of the State's police powers' (para. 200), suggesting thereby that a taking qualifying as such is not a direct expropriation that must notably be compensated in order to be legal. As will be seen, this notion of police power is heavily discussed with regard to indirect expropriation.

6.2.2 Indirect Expropriation

Treaty practice displays a variety of terminologies to name indirect expropriation. International investment agreements refer mainly to 'measures equivalent to expropriation' (e.g. 2015 New Zealand–Korea IIA, Article 10.9.1), 'measures having an effect equivalent to expropriation' (e.g. 2015 Canada–Guinea IIA, Article 10.1), 'measures tantamount to expropriation' (e.g. 2016 UAE–Mexico IIA, Article 6.1), or 'measures having the same effect [as expropriation]' (e.g. 2016 Argentina–Qatar IIA, Article 5.1).

Irrespective of the exact terminology used, the notion of indirect expropriation raises three main issues: (1) the types of State measures that can constitute an indirect expropriation; (2) the categories of indirect expropriation; and (3) the identification of instances of indirect expropriation. Each of these is examined in turn below.

6.2.2.1 The Types of State Measures

Most IIAs have traditionally failed to define those measures that may constitute an indirect expropriation. This raises two main issues pertaining to the nature and the author of those measures.

As to the nature, it is well established that both actions and omissions can constitute measures equivalent to expropriation (e.g. *Saint-Gobain*

Performance Plastics Europe v. *Venezuela*, 2016, Decision on Liability and the Principles of Quantum, para. 394). This is in line with the law of State responsibility under which an internationally wrongful act can consist of actions or omissions.

In this respect, it is noteworthy that some IIAs concluded in the 2010s that clarify the notion of indirect expropriation *mutatis mutandis* refer exclusively to 'an action or series of actions by a Party' that has an effect equivalent to direct expropriation (e.g. 2018 Korea–Republics of Central America IIA, Annex 9-C.4). Such language may be considered as evidencing the intent of the States parties to exclude omissions from the types of measures that can be deemed to constitute an indirect expropriation. In this regard, one should mention that the Tribunal in *Mr Eudoro Armando Olguin* v. *Paraguay* departed from mainstream arbitration practice by considering that omissions cannot constitute an indirect expropriation. In response to the claim of the investor that the host State had committed an indirect expropriation comprising omissions, the Tribunal answered: 'Expropriation therefore requires a teleologically driven action for it to occur; omissions, however egregious they may be, are not sufficient for it to take place' (2001, Award, paras. 83–84).

Likewise, some of those IIAs, while listing factors to be taken into account to guide the determination of whether 'an action or series of actions by a Party' constitutes an indirect expropriation, refer exclusively to 'governmental actions' (e.g. 2018 United States–Mexico–Canada Agreement (USMCA), Annex 14-B.3. a). It is questionable, then, whether such a drafting is intended to exclude the acts of State organs other than the government from the scope of the actions that can be deemed to be an indirect expropriation. In any case, this can be contrasted to, for instance, Annex 8-A.2.a of the 2016 Comprehensive Economic and Trade Agreement (CETA), which does not contain any such exclusive references.

In arbitration practice, the traditional reference made in IIAs to simply a 'measure' have been interpreted as covering legislative, administrative or other measures undertaken by the State (e.g. *UP and C.D Holding Internationale* v. *Hungary*, 2018, Award, para. 331).

In any case, one should stress that the conduct of private persons that deprive de facto investors of their properties, but which are not attributable to host States, do not qualify as an indirect expropriation. However, in relation to the full protection and security (FPS) standard analysed in Chapter 5, it should be noted that the failure of States to prevent or repress such conduct may be characterised as a breach of the FPS obligation contained in IIAs.

6.2.2.2 The Categories of Indirect Expropriation

International investment agreements have traditionally not defined what constitutes an indirect expropriation. The above-mentioned specifications contained in some IIAs concluded in the 2010s, typically in an annex, provide some clarification. *Mutatis mutandis*, almost all of them define this notion as 'a measure or a series of measures by a Party [which] has an effect equivalent to direct expropriation without formal transfer of title or outright seizure' (e.g. 2016 Hong Kong SAR China–Chile IIA, Annex 1.3). Remarkably, the CETA provides a more developed definition in that, in addition to the reference it makes to the lack of formal transfer of title or outright seizure, it also makes clear that the measure or series of measures will be considered to be equivalent in effect to expropriation if it 'substantially deprives the investor of the fundamental attributes of property in its investment, including the right to use, enjoy and dispose of its investment' (Annex 8-A.1.b).

As evidenced by the drafting of the CETA and that of the Hong Kong SAR China–Chile IIA, those IIAs make an explicit distinction between indirect expropriations consisting of a single measure or action, on the one hand, and those consisting of a series of measures or actions on the other. This reflects a distinction that has long existed in public international law and that has been made by arbitration tribunals. While the first category does not raise any conceptual difficulty, the second requires some further explanations.

This second category of indirect expropriation is usually referred to as 'creeping expropriation' and sometimes as 'constructive expropriation' (e.g. *Spyridon Roussalis* v. *Romania*, 2011, Award, para. 329). This notion is itself a subcategory of what is called a 'composite act' in public international law.

As explained by the International Law Commission (ILC) in its Commentaries to the 2001 Articles on Responsibility of States for Internationally Wrongful Acts, a 'composite act' is an aggregate of actions, omissions, or a combination of both which, taken together, violate the international obligation at hand. This composite act does not occur at the time the first action or omission of the series takes place; instead, it occurs at the time when the last action or omission, taken together with the previous ones, is sufficient to constitute the wrongful act. Subsequent actions or omissions may follow that then also form part of the composite act. However, the time when the composite act occurs differs from the time when the breach is said to occur. While a composite act does not occur until sufficient actions or/and omissions have taken place, the time of the breach is set to the date of the first action or omission of the series. This breach then lasts over the entire period until the last action or omission of the series.

These features of a composite act apply to creeping expropriation. This was well explained by the Tribunal in *Siemens A.G.* v. *Argentina*:

> By definition, creeping expropriation refers to a process, to steps that eventually have the effect of an expropriation. If the process stops before it reaches that point, then expropriation would not occur. This does not necessarily mean that no adverse effects would have occurred. Obviously, each step must have an adverse effect but by itself may not be significant or considered an illegal act. The last step in a creeping expropriation that tilts the balance is similar to the straw that breaks the camel's back. The preceding straws may not have had

a perceptible effect but are part of the process that led to the break. (2007, Award, para. 263)

As emphasised in *Teinver S.A.* v. *Argentina*, this entails that 'the entirety of the measures should be reviewed in the aggregate to determine their effect on the investment rather than each individual measure on its own' (2017, Award, para. 948).

Secondarily and in relation to those few IIAs that, like the above-mentioned 2016 Austria–Kyrgyzstan IIA, refer *mutatis mutandis* to 'measures having equivalent effect' in addition to 'indirect expropriation', it is worth mentioning briefly the diverging views adopted by some tribunals that had the task of applying Article 1110 of the 1992 NAFTA. The question was whether the reference in that article to 'measures tantamount to expropriation' in addition to 'indirect expropriation' is meant to refer to another type of expropriation. The Tribunal appointed in *Pope & Talbot Inc.* v. *Canada* refused to distinguish indirect expropriation and measures tantamount to expropriation. It argued: '"Tantamount" means nothing more than equivalent [footnote omitted]. Something that is equivalent to something else cannot logically encompass more' (2000, Interim Award, para. 104). On the other hand, in *Waste Management Inc.* v. *Mexico*, the Tribunal considered that the reference to 'measures tantamount to expropriation' in that Article is 'intended to add to the meaning of the prohibition, over and above the reference to indirect expropriation' (2004, Award, paras. 143–144). In the end, the interpretation of *Pope & Talbot* has prevailed and measures tantamount to expropriation have not been viewed as another type of expropriation.

6.2.2.3 The Identification of Instances of Indirect Expropriation

The determination of whether or not an instance of indirect expropriation has occurred is one of the issues that has been most debated in contemporary international investment law and arbitration, as well as across domestic societies. This is due to the fact that this issue relates directly to the exercise by host States of their right to regulate. In this respect, some awards rendered by arbitration tribunals have been fiercely criticised by public opinion and politicians for unduly limiting this exercise. Mainly in reaction to this criticism, a number of States have provided specifications in newly concluded IIAs, particularly in free trade agreements (FTAs) containing an investment chapter. This evolution is remarkable inasmuch as IIAs have traditionally not provided for any such specifications, leaving it to arbitration tribunals to decide how to determine whether State measures constitute an indirect expropriation. However, this arbitration practice that has developed remains highly relevant, notably with respect to the vague expropriation provisions which are still predominant in current treaty practice. Both treaty practice and arbitration practice in this regard are analysed below.

a   Treaty Practice

The 2004 Model BIT of the United States of America (USA) has been the first main instrument to provide specifications intended to guide the identification of instances of indirect expropriation. The drafters of that Model have been largely influenced by the case law of the US Supreme Court, in particular by the 1978 *Penn Central* v. *New York City* case. Since then, such specifications have spread across treaty practice. More precisely, those specifications are composed of two dimensions: 'intrinsic' and 'extrinsic'. Intrinsically, they provide a number of factors to be used in determining whether a State measure or action or a series thereof constitute an indirect expropriation. Extrinsically, these specifications aim at distinguishing indirect expropriation from regulatory measure.

i The Factors for Identifying Instances of Indirect Expropriation   Aside from some nuances, almost all relevant IIAs follow the approach adopted by the above-mentioned US Model BIT. It is, then, worth referring to it as a starting point for this examination. Annex B.4.a provides:

> The determination of whether an action or series of actions by a Party, in a specific fact situation, constitutes an indirect expropriation, requires a case-by-case, fact-based inquiry that considers, among other factors:
>
> (i) the economic impact of the government action, although the fact that an action or series of actions by a Party has an adverse effect on the economic value of an investment, standing alone, does not establish that an indirect expropriation has occurred;
> (ii) the extent to which the government action interferes with distinct, reasonable investment-backed expectations; and
> (iii) the character of the government action.

All IIAs that provide the specifications as mentioned above start by emphasising the factual dimension of the determination of whether an indirect expropriation has occurred; this entails both a case-by-case approach and a fact-based inquiry. To guide those inquiries, they typically provide for a non-exhaustive list of factors, which are mainly threefold.

The first factor consists of the economic impact of the measure(s) or action(s). Most IIAs refer to this factor in a way similar to the US Model BIT. They do not offer any detail as to the meaning of 'economic impact', but they specify that the adverse effect of the measure(s) or action(s) on the economic value of an investment, standing alone, is insufficient to conclude that there has been an occurrence of indirect expropriation (e.g. 2017 Pacific Agreement on Closer Economic Relations Plus (PACER Plus), Annex 9-C.3.a).

A few IIAs provide greater detail as to 'economic impact'. This is well illustrated by the IIA adopted by Japan and Kenya in 2016, which refers exclusively but in a non-exhaustive manner to economic factors:

(a) permanent and complete or near complete deprivation of the value of investment;

(b) permanent and complete or near complete deprivation of the investor's right of management and control over the investment; or

(c) an appropriation of the investment by the Contracting Party which results in transfer of the complete or near complete value of that investment to that Contracting Party, to an agency of that Contracting Party or to a third party. (Article 10.2)

The second factor listed to provide guidance as to whether an indirect expropriation has occurred consists of the distinct, reasonable investment-backed expectations. This notion first emerged and was further developed in the case law of the US Supreme Court. On its face, the exact meaning and content of this notion is not self-evident. In this respect, it can be noted that, while a few IIAs do not provide for any clarification as to the meaning of the concept (e.g. 2018 Sri Lanka–Singapore IIA, Annex 10-A.2.a.ii), most of those agreements that refer to it do provide some guidance. However, there exist some nuances across those IIAs.

A few IIAs offer an exhaustive definition. For instance, Article 6.4.b of the 2016 Slovakia–Iran IIA specifies that reasonable investment-backed expectations can arise out of the Contracting Party's prior binding explicit written commitment given directly and specifically to the investor. In a few IIAs the reference to the interference with such written commitments replace the mention of the interference with distinct, reasonable investment-backed expectations (e.g. 2017 Hong Kong SAR China–ASEAN IIA, Annex 2.3.b).

Contrary to the Slovakia–Iran IIA, most IIAs mention illustrative factors to be used to appraise whether there is an interference with distinct, reasonable investment-backed expectations. Some of those agreements mention only one example, be it the above-mentioned interference with written commitments or the nature and extent of government regulation in the sector concerned (e.g. 2018 Korea–Republics of Central America IIA, Annex 9-C.4.a, Footnote 15). Others contain an illustrative list of factors; this is well illustrated by Footnote 36, which is attached to Annex B-3.a.ii of the 2018 Comprehensive and Progressive Agreement for Trans-Pacific Partnership (CPTPP): 'For greater certainty, whether an investor's investment-backed expectations are reasonable depends, to the extent relevant, on factors such as whether the government provided the investor with binding written assurances and the nature and extent of governmental regulation or the potential for government regulation in the relevant sector.'

The third factor consists of the character of the government measure(s) or action(s). Again, the exact meaning and content of this notion is not self-evident at first glance. While some IIAs do not give any indication as to its meaning (e.g. 2018 Peru–Australia IIA, Annex 8-B.4.c), others provide for some clarifications, typically via a number of non-exhaustive items. They all refer to the 'objective, object or purpose' of the measure(s) or action(s). In addition, some mention, alternatively or in combination, their context (e.g. 2018 Korea–Republics of Central America IIA, Annex 9-C.4.a.iii), their rationale (e.g. 2017 PACER Plus, Annex 9-C.3.c), or their duration (e.g. 2016 Slovakia–Iran IIA, Article 6.4.c). In some IIAs, duration is not conceived of as forming part of that third factor, but instead is a factor on its own (e.g. 2016 CETA, Annex 8-A.2.b). Importantly, a few IIAs refer to 'proportionality', as exemplified by the 2015 China–Korea IIA, which refers to the character and objectives of the action or series of actions, including whether such action is proportionate to its objectives (Annex 12-B-3.a.iii).

ii The Distinction between Indirect Expropriation and Regulatory Measure   The second type of specifications provided in some IIAs concluded in the 2010s is intended to distinguish indirect expropriation from regulatory measure or action. This is done typically in an annex that provides *mutatis mutandis* that, subject to conditions, regulatory measures or actions shall not be characterised as indirect expropriations, which require compensation to be paid in order to be legal; this includes series of such measures or actions. Here again, this trend in treaty practice has been initiated by the 2004 US Model BIT whose Annex B.4.b provides: 'Except in rare circumstances, non-discriminatory regulatory actions by a Party that are designed and applied to protect legitimate public welfare objectives, such as public health, safety, and the environment, do not constitute indirect expropriations.'

As examined below, such a treaty practice 'codifies' mainstream arbitration practice, which has either referred to the notion of regulatory measure or adopted a reasoning akin to it. The incorporation of this distinction in IIAs comes mainly as a reaction to the criticism formulated against part of arbitration practice whose conception of indirect expropriation has been seen as a threat to the right of host States to regulate.

As a common denominator, all those IIAs provide *mutatis mutandis* that non-discriminatory measures or actions designed and applied to protect a public interest do not constitute an indirect expropriation. The terminology varies across treaty practice with respect to the types of acts and their object.

Some treaties refer only to 'measures' (e.g. 2016 CETA, Annex 8-A.3) or 'legal measures' (e.g. 2016 Rwanda–Turkey IIA, Article 6.2), others to 'regulatory actions' (e.g. 2018 USMCA, Annex 14-B.3.b). Some IIAs adopt a more comprehensive approach, such as the 2018 Belarus–India IIA that, on the basis of the 2015 India Model BIT, refers to 'regulatory measures by a Party or measures or awards by judicial bodies of a Party' (Article 5.5).

With respect to the object of these measures or actions, most IIAs make reference to 'legitimate public welfare objectives' (e.g. 2019 Australia–Uruguay IIA, Annex B.3.b), while a few mention 'legitimate public interest *or* public purpose objectives' (e.g. 2018 Belarus–India IIA, Article 5.5; emphasis added) or 'measures … designed and applied in pursuit of public policy to achieve legitimate public interest *or* public welfare objectives' (2014 ASEAN–India IIA, Article 8.9; emphasis added). It is unclear here which distinctions States parties intend to make by mentioning such alternatives, given the close substantive connection that seems to exist between all these notions.

This connection appears clearly when looking at the examples provided by those IIAs which, irrespective of the formula used to name the objectives to be pursued by the regulatory measures or actions, are in fact similar. All of these agreements mention as examples 'health' (or 'public health'), 'safety' and the 'environment'. A few add another objective, such as the 2017 China–Hong Kong SAR China IIA, which also mentions 'public morals' (Annex 3.3). In addition to listing those objectives, a few IIAs provide greater detail as to the content of these objectives. For instance, Footnote 37, which is attached to Annex 9-B of the 2018 CPTPP, offers this illustrative list of actions geared towards the protection of public health: 'For greater certainty and without limiting the scope of this subparagraph, regulatory actions to protect public health include, among others, such measures with respect to the regulation, pricing and supply of, and reimbursement for, pharmaceuticals (including biological products), diagnostics, vaccines, medical devices, gene therapies and technologies, health-related aids and appliances and blood and blood-related products.'

More fundamentally, treaty practice displays nuances and differences as to the exact interplay between regulatory measure or action and indirect expropriation. Two main approaches can be identified in this respect which diverge on the issue of whether a non-discriminatory measure or action designed and applied to protect a public interest may nonetheless be characterised as an indirect expropriation in specific circumstances.

In this regard, following a first approach, the text of a few treaties, in particular that of the 2018 Belarus–India IIA – on the basis of the 2015 India Model BIT – does not provide for any circumstance in which such a measure or action may be characterised as an indirect expropriation. Article 5 of this Agreement provides: 'Non-discriminatory regulatory measures by a Party or measures or awards by judicial bodies of a Party that are designed and applied to protect legitimate public interest or public purpose objectives such as public health, safety and the environment shall not constitute expropriation under this Article.'

On the other hand, the IIAs that follow a second, more mainstream approach do provide for that possibility in 'rare circumstances'. There are a number of nuances across these IIAs in this respect. First, some of these agreements only make mention of this possibility without providing any specification as to what those 'rare circumstances' are, such as the 2008 USA–Rwanda IIA (Annex B.4.b). Other IIAs indicate the circumstances in which a non-discriminatory measure or action designed and applied to protect a public interest may be deemed to constitute an indirect expropriation by reference to the severity or disproportionality of its impact viewed in light of its purpose. In this respect, it is worth noting that such a reference to the severity or disproportionality of the impact of the measure or action is indicated in some IIAs as an example of the circumstances in which such measures or actions may be deemed to constitute an indirect expropriation (e.g. 2016 Canada–Mongolia IIA, Annex B.10.3), while in others it is conceived of as the only circumstance recognised by States parties (e.g. 2016 CETA, Annex 8-A.3). One should stress that the threshold for such a measure or action being characterised as expropriatory is high, as all of these agreements provide that the impact shall be 'so severe' or, less frequently, 'extremely severe' (2018 Korea–Republics of Central America IIA, Annex 9-C.4.b). Irrespective of the threshold, two main formulations emerge from treaty practice. Some of these refer to the severity as the sign of the manifestly excessive nature of the measure or action. For instance, the above-mentioned Annex of the 2016 CETA provides:

> For greater certainty, except in the rare circumstance when the impact of a measure or series of measures is so severe in light of its purpose that it appears manifestly excessive, non-discriminatory measures of a Party that are designed and applied to protect legitimate public welfare objectives, such as health, safety and the environment, do not constitute indirect expropriations.

Others refer to that severity as evidencing the lack of good faith of the State in the adoption and application of the measure or action. For instance, Article 6.5 of the 2016 Slovakia–Iran IIA reads as follows:

> Except in rare circumstances, such as when a measure or series of measures are so severe in the light of their purpose that they cannot be reasonably viewed as having been adopted and applied in good faith, non-discriminatory measures of the Contracting Party that are designed and applied to protect legitimate public welfare objectives, such as health, safety and the environment, do not constitute measures having equivalent effect to expropriation or nationalization.

b   Arbitration Practice

Preliminary Remarks

The issue of the identification of instances of indirect expropriation which is now at the 'forefront' of the public debate and of the evolution of treaty practice has long been discussed by arbitration tribunals. This history has been marked by fierce debates and controversies at the conceptual level. Indeed, tribunals and arbitrators have relied on different doctrines, namely the police power doctrine and the sole effect doctrine, to discuss whether or not State measures were to be characterised as an indirect expropriation. However, as explained below, the clash which is said to exist between these two doctrines needs to be moderated in light of both their conceptual foundation and their application in practice. Instead, more attention needs to be paid to the criteria used to identify the instances of indirect expropriation. These doctrines and criteria are analysed in the following subsections.

i The Doctrines of Indirect Expropriation   This subsection sheds light on the doctrines of indirect expropriation through a comparative analysis. For that purpose, we shall begin by looking at the police power doctrine.

When relying on the police power doctrine, tribunals focus on the notion of regulatory measures by referring to 'regulation' or 'general regulation', while also placing the emphasis on the objective of such measures, meaning public interest or public welfare. Apart from this, it is worth stressing that arbitration practice is characterised by ambiguities and inconsistencies as to the meaning, scope and operation of the police power doctrine as well as the meaning and scope of regulatory measures.

Some tribunals express a radical conception of this doctrine whose rationale boils down to this principle: any regulatory measure that pursues a public purpose and is non-discriminatory and which is enacted in accordance with due process does not constitute an indirect expropriation, whatever its effect. This conception was notably formulated and argued by the Tribunal in *Methanex Corporation* v. *USA*: '[A]s a matter of general international law, a non-discriminatory regulation for a public purpose, which is enacted in accordance with due process and, which affects, inter alios, a foreign investor or investment is not deemed expropriatory and compensable' (2005, Final Award on Jurisdiction and Merits, Part IV – Chapter D, para. 7). As the only exception to this principle, this Tribunal recognised that such a regulation may be deemed expropriatory and compensable where 'specific commitments had been given by the regulating government to the then putative foreign investor contemplating investment that the government would refrain from such regulation'. Commenting on this conception, the Tribunal appointed in *Pope & Talbot Inc.* v. *Canada* opined that such 'a blanket exception for regulatory measures would create a gaping loophole in international protections against expropriation' (2000, Interim Award, para. 99).

Along the same lines, the Tribunal explained in *El Paso Energy International Company* v. *Argentina* that it concurred with 'the decisions which ha[d] refused to hold that a general regulation issued by a State and interfering with the rights of foreign investors can *never* be considered expropriatory because it should be analysed as an exercise of the State's sovereign power or of its police powers' (2011, Award, para. 234). The tribunals that adopt this view in fact have a more nuanced conception of the police power doctrine. This conception leaves open the possibility that a non-discriminatory regulatory measure that pursues a public purpose and is enacted in accordance with due process may be deemed expropriatory if its economic impact is sufficient – to use the words of the Tribunal in *Tecnicas Medioambientales Tecmed S.A.* v. *Mexico* – 'to neutralize in full the value, or economic or commercial use of its investment' (2003, Award, para. 121).

This leads to the formulation of the following question: to what extent is this nuanced conception of the police power doctrine different from the sole effect doctrine which, as its name clearly states, focuses on the effect of the measure? Obviously, to determine whether a regulatory measure is or is not an indirect expropriation, these two doctrines focus on the objective of the measure and on its effect, respectively. But when one looks beyond this focus, it appears that they both lead to the conclusion that a non-discriminatory regulatory measure enacted in accordance with due process and pursuing a public interest objective is not an indirect expropriation, unless it indirectly deprives the investor of its property.

In light of the above, the 'doctrinal label' does not seem to matter much in practice. What matters most is the factual appraisal of the situations that consists of a balancing of right and interests, namely, on the one hand, the right of States to regulate to protect public interests and, on the other hand, the foreign investors' property right and interests. In achieving that balance, it is usually the significance of the impact that tilts the scales and leads tribunals to characterise the measure as being constitutive of an indirect expropriation. The key question raised in this balancing act and in arbitration practice more generally is the exact nature and degree of the impact required to tilt the balance, an issue that is examined below.

This is perfectly in line with the test of proportionality as it was first expressed in arbitration practice by the Tribunal in *Tecnicas Medioambientales Tecmed S.A. v. Mexico*. It stated in reference to the case law of the European Court of Human Rights:

> After establishing that regulatory actions and measures will not be initially excluded from the definition of expropriatory acts, in addition to the negative financial impact of such actions or measures, the Arbitral Tribunal will consider, in order to determine if they are to be characterized as expropriatory, whether such actions or measures are proportional to the public interest presumably protected thereby and to the protection legally granted to investments, taking into account that the significance of such impact has a key role upon deciding the proportionality. [footnote omitted] Although the analysis starts at the due deference owing to the State when defining the issues that affect its public policy or the interests of society as a whole, as well as the actions that will be implemented to protect such values, such situation does not prevent the Arbitral Tribunal, without thereby questioning such due deference, from examining the actions of the State in light of Article 5(1) of the Agreement to determine whether such measures are reasonable with respect to their goals, the deprivation of economic rights and the legitimate expectations of [those] who suffered such deprivation. There must be a reasonable relationship of proportionality between the charge or weight imposed [on] the foreign investor and the aim sought to be realized by any expropriatory measure. [footnote omitted] To value

such charge or weight, it is very important to measure the size of the ownership deprivation caused by the actions of the state and whether such deprivation was compensated or not. [footnote omitted] On the basis of a number of legal and practical factors, it should be also considered that the foreign investor has a reduced or nil participation in the taking of the decisions that affect it, partly because the investors are not entitle to exercise political rights reserved to the nationals of the State, such as voting for the authorities that will issue the decisions that affect such investors. (2003, Award, para. 122)

Some commentators, such as Pellet,[2] regard this test as the embodiment of the 'nuanced' conception of the police power doctrine. In light of the above, it seems that this test of proportionality should not be encapsulated in this conceptual box as it is also akin to the above-mentioned conception of the sole effect doctrine. In any case, it is worth stressing that this test has been spreading across arbitration practice and treaty practice. Indeed, the above-mentioned IIAs concluded in the 2010s, like the 2016 CETA, also set a limit to the principle pursuant to which a non-discriminatory regulatory measure designed and applied to protect a public purpose objective does not constitute an indirect expropriation. This limit concerns the severity of the impact of the measure.

ii The Criteria of Indirect Expropriation   Aside from realising that the police power doctrine and the sole effect doctrine are, conceptually speaking, not alien from one another as it is often claimed, it should be noted that the determination of whether a State measure constitutes an indirect expropriation is a fact-based inquiry that requires account to be taken of the specifics of each case. In addition to the effect and the objective of State measures that constitute the main criteria of identification inquired into by tribunals, such tribunals sometimes look into other criteria aside from these. These main and subsidiary criteria are analysed in turn in the following subsections.

– **Main Criteria**   In addition to the question discussed above as to the interplay between the effect and the objective of State measures, specific attention needs to be paid to the criteria underpinning the assessment of the effect of the measures, which has proven to be much more problematic than the discussion of their objectives. For that reason, this subsection focuses on these criteria. More precisely, the criteria for assessing the effect raise four main issues which pertain to (1) the intensity of the effect, (2) the types of effect, (3) the duration of the effect, as well as (4) the 'basis' of the investment with respect to which the effect is to be appraised. Of course, these issues are to a large extent intertwined, but for the purpose of this textbook, we shall analyse them here successively.

---

[2] A Pellet, 'Police Powers or the State's Right to Regulate' in M Kinnear, G Fischer, JM Almeida, et al. (eds), *Building International Investment Law: The First 50 Years of ICSID* (Wolters Kluwer 2015) 447, at 454.

The Intensity of the Effect

It is well accepted by arbitration tribunals – despite a few exceptions (e.g. *Venezuela Holdings, B.V.* v. *Venezuela*, 2014, Award, para. 286) – that a deprivation does not need to be a complete deprivation in order for a State measure to be characterised as an indirect expropriation. Beyond this common denominator and as noted by the Tribunal in *Monsieur Joseph Houben* v. *Burundi* (2016, Award, para. 200), it is often said that arbitration practice displays two main views as to the applicable threshold.

According to a first – mainstream – approach, a State measure shall have a substantial effect, meaning that it shall result in a substantial deprivation in order to be considered as an indirect expropriation (e.g. *Quiborax S.A.* v. *Bolivia*, 2015 Award, para. 238). The high level of this threshold is illustrated by the words used by the Tribunal in *Enkev Beheer B.V.* v. *Poland*, which stated that the establishment of an indirect expropriation requires the investor 'to establish the substantial, radical, severe, devastating or fundamental deprivation of [investor's] right or their virtual annihilation and effective neutralisation' (2014, First Partial Award, para. 344).

On the other side of the spectrum, the second approach that is said to exist requires less than a substantial deprivation, meaning a partial deprivation. The award rendered in *Metalclad Corporation* v. *Mexico* is often cited by tribunals – for instance the *Houben* Tribunal (para. 200) – to illustrate this approach. In that case, the Tribunal stated:

> Thus, expropriation under NAFTA includes not only open, deliberate and acknowledged takings of property, such as outright seizure or formal or obligatory transfer of title in favour of the host State, but also covert or incidental interference with the use of property which has the effect of depriving the owner, in whole or in significant part, of the use or reasonably-to-be-expected economic benefit of property even if not necessarily to the obvious benefit of the host State. (2000, Award, para. 103)

This statement appears in fact ambiguous. It refers to 'incidental interference', while the Tribunal in *OI European Group B.V.* v. *Bolivia*, for instance, mentioned a 'significant interference' (2015, Award, para. 329), which may lead one to conclude that it entails a lower threshold. At the same time, however, this 'incidental interference' is linked to a full or significant deprivation that is akin to the substantial deprivation test.

Whether or not there exist real divergences in arbitration practice as to the test to be used, it is worth stressing, as did the Tribunal in *Chemtura Corporation* v. *Canada*, that the enquiry into whether a measure has a sufficient effect to amount to an expropriation 'cannot be conducted on the basis of rigid binary rules'. It continued: 'It would make little sense to state a percentage or a threshold that would have to be met for a deprivation to be "substantial" as such *modus operandi* may not always be appropriate . . . Given the diversity of situations that may arise in practice, it is preferable to examine each situation in the light of its own specific circumstances' (2010, Award, para. 249).

The Types of Effect
The key issue that has emerged concerning the types of effect is whether one should focus on the effect that State measures have on the economic value of investments ('value-based approach'), or on their effect on the attributes of the right to property. Central here is the question as to whether the effect on the value is sufficient on its own, without the property rights being affected, for such measures to be characterised as an indirect expropriation. More precisely, the question seems to be the interplay between the effect on the value and the effect on the control of their investments by foreign investors. Indeed, as illustrated by the excerpt of the award rendered in *Burlington Resources Inc. v. Ecuador* mentioned below, there is a tendency in arbitration practice to equate the impact on the economic value to the impact on the use of the investment, which is one of the attributes of the right to property.

It is worth stressing at the outset that the analysis of the relevant practice is made difficult by the confusing terminology and the overall reasoning of tribunals. This can be seen from the opinion expressed by the Tribunal in *El Paso Energy International Company v. Argentina*. It denied that the awards rendered in prior cases, which are said to support the value-based approach, actually defend the idea that a State measure having merely a substantial impact on the value of an investment may be viewed as an indirect expropriation (2011, Award, para. 249). Whether or not that Tribunal is correct, it still remains that those two approaches, or indeed arguments in support of each of these approaches, can be seen across arbitration practice.

The value-based approach and its rationale were well explained by the Tribunal in *Burlington Resources Inc. v. Ecuador*:

> When a measure affects the environment or conditions under which the investor carries on its business, what appears to be decisive, in assessing whether there is a substantial deprivation, is the loss of the economic value or economic viability of the investment. In this sense, some tribunals have focused on the use and enjoyment of property. [footnote omitted] The loss of viability does not necessarily imply a loss of management or control. What matters is the capacity to earn a commercial return. After all, investors make investments to earn a return. If they lose this possibility as a result of a State measure, then they have lost the economic use of their investment. (2012, Decision on Liability, para. 397)

Further in its reasoning, that Tribunal made it clear that a 'reduction or loss of profits as such is insufficient' and that 'it must be shown that the investment's continuing capacity to generate a return has been virtually extinguished' (para. 399).

Other tribunals reject the idea expressed by the Tribunal in *Burlington*, that what is decisive is the loss of the economic value or economic viability of the investment. In *Mamidoil Jetoil Greek Petroleum Products Societe S.A.* v. *Albania*, the Tribunal grounded this view on the specificity of expropriation as contrasted with other IIA provisions. It explained:

> The definition of expropriation has developed over time and gone beyond the formalistic concentration on title. It encompasses the substance of property and protects the property even if title is not taken. However, a further extension into the sphere of damages, loss of value and profitability, without regard to the substance and attributes of property, would deprive the claim of its distinct nature and amalgamate it with other claims … The contrary approach would not only contradict the literal meaning of the term 'ex-propriation', but would also be inconsistent with the clear intention of State parties when they entered into the BIT and the ECT and provided for separate standards of protection. (2015, Award, paras. 570–571)

That Tribunal then adopted the approach set by the Tribunal in *El Paso Energy International Company* v. *Argentina*: '[F]or an expropriation to exist, the investor should be substantially deprived not only of the benefits, but also of the use of his investment. A mere loss of value, which is not the result of an interference with the control or use of the investment, is not an indirect expropriation' (2011, Award, para. 256).

Along the same lines, the Tribunal appointed in *Deutsche Bank AG* v. *Sri Lanka* stressed that a distinction has to be made between an interference with rights and economic loss. It concluded: '[T]he fact that the effect of conduct must be considered in deciding whether an indirect expropriation has occurred, does not necessarily import an economic test. The Tribunal also notes that in this case, the Treaty does not include "economic damage" as a requirement for expropriation nor does the Tribunal consider that there is any basis for importing such a standard' (2012, Award, para. 504).

The Duration of the Effect

Obviously, measures that have the effect of permanently depriving investors of their investment may amount to an indirect expropriation. The question is whether measures which do not have such a permanent effect may also be so characterised. Arbitration practice displays nuances and differences in this respect, partly due to the specifics of each case.

A number of tribunals consider *mutatis mutandis* that such a characterisation requires the deprivation be permanent and irreversible without providing any qualification to this principle (e.g. *Busta* v. *Czech Republic*, 2017, Final Award, para. 389).

Others, while adopting the same approach, opine *mutatis mutandis*, in the words of the Tribunal in *S.D. Myers Inc.* v. *Canada*, that 'in some contexts and circumstances, it would be appropriate to view a deprivation as amounting to an expropriation, even if it were partial or temporary' (2000, Partial Award, para. 283). The Tribunal appointed in *LG&E* v. *Argentina* considered that those exceptional circumstances are those where 'the investment's successful development depends on the realization of certain activities at specific moments that may not endure variations' (2006, Decision on Liability, para. 193).

Some Tribunals do not consider that there is a requirement of permanency, instead placing on the same footing permanent deprivations and deprivations imposed for a 'substantial period of time' (*Valeri Belokon* v. *Kyrgyzstan*, 2014, Award, 206). In that sense the Tribunal appointed in *Les Laboratoires Servier S.A.S.* v. *Poland* found it necessary to 'stress' that the terms of the 1989 France–Poland IIA 'do not require that dispossession be permanent in the sense of continuing *ad infinitum*', although it noted that 'deprivation must possess a character more than transitory' (2012, Final Award, para. 577).

The Investment's 'Basis' in Appraising the Effect

At stake here is the question as to whether the effect of State measures shall be appraised in relation to the investment as a whole or whether it is possible to do so in relation to only part(s) of it. Here again, nuances and differences exist across arbitration practice as to the answer to be given to this question.

On one side of the spectrum, some tribunals argue that the effect should be assessed in relation to the investment as a whole. This approach has been based, for instance, on the drafting of the expropriation provision within the particular IIA. In *Burlington Resources Inc.* v. *Ecuador*, the Tribunal noted: 'The Treaty provides that "investments shall not be expropriated." The Tribunal understands from this formulation that the focus of the expropriation analysis must be on the investment as a whole, and not on discrete parts of the investment' (2012, Decision on Liability, para. 257). The Tribunal appointed in *Electrabel S.A.* v. *Hungary* justified this approach by stressing the consequences that would result from appraising the effect of State measures in relation to parts of the investment only:

> If it were possible so easily to parse an investment into several constituent parts each forming a separate investment (as Electrabel here contends), it would render meaningless that tribunal's approach to indirect expropriation based on 'radical deprivation' and 'deprivation of any real substance' as being similar in effect to a direct expropriation or nationalisation. It would also mean, absurdly, that an investor could always meet the test for indirect expropriation by slicing its investment as finely as the particular circumstances required, without that investment as a whole ever meeting that same test. (2012, Decision on Jurisdiction, Applicable Law and Liability, para. 6.57)

On the other hand, some tribunals have accepted considering only part(s) of the overall investment to assess whether a State measure constitutes an indirect expropriation. For instance, in *Ampal-American Israel Corp.* v. *Egypt*, the Tribunal sided with the claimant who argued that a licence that conferred a tax-free status was an investment in its own right, whose revocation constituted an indirect expropriation even though that revocation did not destroy the entire pipeline project (2017, Decision on Liability and Heads of Loss, paras. 179–180). To support its findings, this Tribunal referred to *Gami Investments, Inc.* v. *Mexico*, where the Tribunal explained that 'the taking of 50 acres of a farm is equally expropriatory whether that is the whole farm or just a fraction [of it]' (2004, Final Award, para. 126).

– Subsidiary Criteria   The subsidiary criteria that are most often discussed by arbitration tribunals for the purpose of identifying instances of indirect expropriation pertain to (1) investors' expectations, (2) States' intent, and (3) States' benefit.

Investors' Expectations
At the outset, a distinction can be drawn between the 'status' of investors' expectations as a criterion to determine whether a State measure constitutes an indirect expropriation and the 'status' assigned to it in a few IIAs as a condition of legality of expropriation – something which is discussed below.

As explained above, the concept of investors' expectations is gaining an increasing importance in treaty practice as a criterion used to identify instances of indirect expropriation. As such, the IIAs that incorporate it follow the precedent set out by the 2004 US Model BIT and fine-tune the approach adopted by some arbitration tribunals. Some nuances and differences can be seen in the findings of arbitration tribunals as to the role and relevance of investors' expectations in appraising whether State measures may be characterised as an indirect expropriation.

For some tribunals, investors' expectations, typically based on contracts or specific insurances and representations, do play a clear role. This can be seen from the views expressed by the Tribunal in *Methanex Corporation* v. *USA*:

> [A]s a matter of general international law, a non-discriminatory regulation for a public purpose, which is enacted in accordance with due process and, which affects, *inter alios*, a foreign investor or investment is not deemed expropriatory and compensable *unless specific commitments had been given by the regulating government to the then putative foreign investor contemplating investment that the government would refrain from such regulation.* (2005, Final Award on Jurisdiction and Merits, Part IV – Chapter D, para. 7; emphasis added)

The investors' expectations were also relied on in *Metalclad Corporation* v. *Mexico*. In that case, the hazardous waste landfill project of the investor had been approved and endorsed by the federal government, but the municipality subsequently refused to accord a local construction permit for environmental and geological reasons. In concluding that the investor's investment had been expropriated, the Tribunal noted that the municipality had acted outside its authority, relying on the investor's expectations created by the federal government. It stated: 'These measures, taken together with the representations of the Mexican federal government, on which Metalclad relied, and the absence of a timely, orderly or substantive basis for the denial by the Municipality of the local construction permit, amount to an indirect expropriation' (2000, Award, para. 107).

Other tribunals downplay the role played by investors' expectations in determining whether a measure amounts to an indirect expropriation. At the core of this approach is the interplay between expropriation and the fair and equitable treatment (FET) standard, of which legitimate expectations forms a key part. This approach was well explained by the Tribunal in *Mamidoil Jetoil Greek Petroleum Products Societe S.A. v. Albania*:

> Firstly, the Tribunal emphasizes that there are distinct standards of protection, with distinct requirements, under the BIT and the ECT. Damage caused by a violation of legitimate expectations, or by arbitrary measures, or by a destabilization of the legal framework, or by a lack of regulation and distortions of the fuel market may give rise to claims under either of the standards of fair and equitable treatment, or the prohibition of discriminatory measures, or the most constant protection and security. However, they are not at the same time *per se* indicative of an illegal expropriation. In order to be capable of being considered expropriatory – even indirectly – the consequences for the property must be substantiated in accordance with the specificities of the claim for expropriation. (2015, Award, paras. 560–561)

The Intent of States to Expropriate

The question here is not that of the objective and purpose of the measures taken by States, i.e. to protect public interests, as discussed above as well as below with regard to the conditions of legality of expropriation. The question concerns here whether the State had the intention to expropriate. Obviously, this is not an issue with regard to instances of direct expropriation. Formal transfers of property necessarily require such an intent, as well as constituting evidence thereof. On the other hand, the situation is different with regard to indirect expropriation. State measures can have the effect of expropriating investments from investors without that being the intention of the States' authorities. This has begged the question in practice as to whether, and if so how, intent is relevant to determine whether a measure amounts to an indirect expropriation.

It is largely agreed that there is no requirement for States' authorities to intend to expropriate investors for their measure to be characterised as an indirect expropriation. This has been based notably on the wording of the expropriation provision within the particular IIA. For instance, the Tribunal in *Siemens A.G. v. Argentina* stressed that the applicable IIA in that case, like all IIAs, refers to the requirement that measures have the effect of an expropriation, but not to the States' intent to expropriate (2007, Award, para. 270).

That being said, tribunals often note, as did the Tribunal in *UAE B Energija (Lithuania) v. Latvia*, that 'some relevance must be attached to *intention*' (2017, Award, para. 1079). In that sense, they often consider that the evidence of an intent to expropriate constitutes an argument in support of the conclusion that a State measure is constitutive of an indirect expropriation. The Tribunal appointed in *Compania de Aguas del Aconquija S.A.* v. *Argentina* stated, for instance: 'There is extensive authority for the proposition that the state's intent, or its subjective motives are at most a secondary consideration. [footnote omitted] While intent will weigh in favour of showing a measure to be expropriatory, it is not a requirement, because the *effect* of the measure on the investor, not the state's intent, is the critical factor' (2007, Award, para. 7.5.20).

The Benefit to Host States
It is widely accepted that there is no requirement that States benefit from their measures for them to be characterised as an indirect expropriation. For instance, in *Sistem Mühendislik Insaat Sanayi ve Ticaret A.S.* v. *Kyrgyzstan*, the Tribunal opined that '[i]f the claimant has been deprived of its property rights by an act of the State, it is irrelevant whether the State itself took possession of those rights or otherwise benefited from the taking' (2009, Award, para. 118).

As an exception, mention can be made of *Ronald S. Lauder* v. *Czech Republic*, where the Tribunal stressed that the State measures at hand, even assuming they had the effect of depriving the investor of his property, could not amount to an expropriation as they did not benefit the host State or any other entity (2001, Final Award, para. 203).

6.3 The Conditions of Legality of Expropriation

Preliminary Remarks
As mentioned above, expropriations, be they direct or indirect, are not prohibited as such under international investment law nor public international law more generally. This is due to the fact that expropriation falls within the sovereign prerogatives of States. At the same time, as they affect the property of foreigners, notably that of foreign investors, States set limits and attached conditions of legality on the expression of this sovereign prerogative. Those conditions of legality are mainly fourfold, pertaining to (1) public purpose, (2) due process of law, (3) non-discrimination, and (4) compensation. Each of these main conditions of legality is analysed in turn below.

At the outset, it is worth mentioning that other conditions are at times provided in IIAs that typically pertain to host States' undertakings as well as the treatment of investors.

The former 'subsidiary' condition of legality is well illustrated by Article 6.b of the 1992 Netherlands–Estonia IIA, which provides that expropriatory measures shall not be 'contrary to any undertaking which the Contracting Party which takes such measures may have given'. It is important to distinguish such a 'status' of undertakings as a condition of legality of State measures 'already' characterised as an expropriation, from the 'status' of investors' expectations – discussed above – as an element forming part of the identification of indirect expropriation's instances.

The second 'subsidiary' condition of legality provided in IIAs typically consists of the requirement that expropriatory measures be in conformity with the States' obligations under those agreements to accord a minimum standard of treatment to investors. For instance, Article 10.7.1.d of the 2004 Dominican Republic–Central America Free Trade Agreement (CAFTA–DR) provides in its relevant part that no State party may expropriate or nationalise a covered investment either directly or indirectly through measures equivalent to expropriation or nationalisation except in accordance with due process and the Article pertaining to the minimum standard of treatment. Likewise, the IIA adopted by Rwanda and Turkey in 2016 provides that expropriatory measures shall be in accordance with the 'general principles of treatment' that it provides for, in particular national treatment and the most-favoured-nation treatment (MFNT) (Article 6.1).

6.3.1 Public Purpose

The first condition of legality of expropriation listed in IIAs consists of the public purpose that State measures shall pursue. This first condition is named differently across treaty practice. In addition to 'public purpose' (e.g. 2017 Uzbekistan–Turkey IIA, Article 6.1), reference is notably made – singly or in combination – to 'public and state interest' (e.g. 2015 San Marino–Azerbaijan IIA, Article 6.1), 'public interest' (e.g. 2015 UAE–Mauritius IIA, Article 7.1), or 'public benefit' (e.g. 2003 China–Germany IIA, Article 4.2). Some link explicitly public interest or public purpose to the internal needs of the host State (e.g. 2001 Australia–Egypt IIA, Article 7.1.a).

With regard to this diversity, it is worth noting a trend in IIAs concluded in the 2010s which aim at explicating the meaning and content of that first condition of legality. Some of them provide an 'overarching meaning' by linking this condition to CIL. For instance, Footnote 17 attached to Article 9.8.1.a of the 2018 CPTPP provides: 'For greater certainty, for the purposes of this Article, the term "public purpose" refers to a concept in customary international law. Domestic law may express this or a similar concept by using different terms, such as "public necessity", "public interest" or "public use".' On the other hand, other agreements 'individualise' the meaning of that first condition by linking it to the respective understanding of the States parties. This is illustrated by Annex 9-B of the 2018 Korea–Republics of Central America IIA, which reads as follows:

> For the effects of Article 9.7.1 (a), 'public purpose' shall be understood as: (a) for Costa Rica: public utility or public interest; (b) for El Salvador: public utility or social interest; (c) for Honduras: public purpose or public interest; (d) for

Nicaragua: public utility or social interest; and (e) for Panama: the concept of public purpose includes public order or social interest.

It is doubtful that these differences of drafting, be it in the same IIA or across treaty practice, entail real legal differences. Yet, it is worth noting that in *UP and C.D Holding Internationale* v. *Hungary*, the Tribunal suggested that the reference made to '*cause d'utilité publique*' in the 1986 France–Hungary IIA, which it translated as 'for reasons of public necessity', provided a higher threshold than the one attached to 'public purpose' (2018, Award, para. 413). One should also note that it is unclear what the CIL concept of 'public purpose' is and what it covers. In this respect, the Iran–United States Claims Tribunal noted in *Amoco International Finance Corporation* v. *Iran*: 'A precise definition of the "public purpose" for which an expropriation may be lawfully decided has neither been agreed upon in international law nor even suggested. It is clear that, as a result of the modern acceptance of the right to nationalize, this term is broadly interpreted, and that States, in practice, are granted extensive discretion' (1987, Partial Award, para. 147).

Since the award was released in that latter case, the granting of such an extensive discretion has been confirmed by the practice of arbitration tribunals that display great caution when appraising the fulfilment of this condition. Key in this appraisal are the notions of deference (e.g. *Ioannis Kardassopoulos* v. *Georgia*, 2010, Award, para. 391) and of margin of appreciation (e.g. *Crystallex International Corporation* v. *Venezuela*, 2016, Award, para. 712), which are discussed in Chapter 5.

In addition to the fact that the public purpose condition of legality has been considered not to require States to spell out in detail what the specific public purpose is (e.g. *Devas* v. *India*, 2016, Award on Jurisdiction and Merits, para. 413), it is noteworthy that the object of deference and of the margin of appreciation has in fact two intertwined dimensions.

The first of these pertains to the margin of appreciation enjoyed by States and the deference they are granted with regard to the designation of a purpose as being a public purpose. In *Rusoro Mining Limited* v. *Venezuela*, for instance, the Tribunal argued with regard to the purpose of 'ensuring sustainable and socially responsible exploitation of natural resources' stated in the Nationalization Decree applying to the gold sector: 'States enjoy extensive discretion in establishing their public policy. It is not the role of investment tribunals to second-guess the appropriateness of the political or economic model adopted by the legitimate organs of a sovereign State. The Nationalization Decree clearly states its purpose, and such purpose is a legitimate aim of economic policy' (2016, Award, para. 385).

The second of these dimensions relates to the margin of appreciation enjoyed by States and the deference they are afforded to choose and design the measures they deem appropriate to pursue the purpose they have identified as being a public purpose. In that sense, the Tribunal appointed in *Teinver S.A.* v. *Argentina* stated that 'a State must be accorded a certain amount of deference in determining how to best advance its public interest once a public interest has been demonstrated as the reason for which an expropriation occurred' (2017, Award, para. 985).

However, the deference granted by tribunals is subject to limitations that are grounded in 'necessity'. Indeed, some tribunals inquire into whether there were other less harmful means available to States to pursue the public purpose.

They usually appraise necessity in the context of a test of proportionality. This test was explained by the Tribunal in *PL Holdings S.à.r.l.* v. *Poland* as follows:

> Application of the principle of proportionality inevitably entails an exercise in judgment on the part of a court or tribunal, and this case is no exception. Regardless of the law specifically applicable to the principle of proportionality in this case, the principle is understood in largely similar terms across jurisdictions. To satisfy the principle, a measure must (a) be one that is suitable by nature for achieving a legitimate public purpose, (b) be necessary for achieving that purpose in that no less burdensome measure would suffice, and (c) not be excessive in that its advantages are outweighed by its disadvantages. (2017, Partial Award, para. 355)

With regard to proportionality, it can also be seen that some tribunals, for instance the Tribunal appointed in *Devas* v. *India* (2016, Award on Jurisdiction and Merits, para. 414), refer to the above-mentioned proportionality approach adopted by the Tribunal in *Tecnicas Medioambientales Tecmed S.A.* v. *Mexico* and in a series of other cases. Three remarks can be formulated in this respect.

First, in doing so, those tribunals refer to cases where proportionality was not used with regard to the conditions of legality of expropriation, but instead to determine whether a State measure was or was not an indirect expropriation.

More fundamentally, it is worth stressing that this proportionality approach is quite different from the test set out in *PL Holdings S.à.r.l.* v. *Poland.* Indeed, this approach focuses on the balancing between the purpose and the effect of the measure, meaning the third step of the test set out by the *PL Holdings* Tribunal, but it does not address the suitability and necessity of the State measure which corresponds to the first and second steps of that test.

Irrespective of the exact approach adopted, one can notice, as did the Tribunal in *South American Silver Limited (Bermuda)* v. *Bolivia* (2018, Award, para. 570), that IIAs do not expressly refer to a proportionality requirement as an element required to determine the legality of an expropriation.

Whatever the relevance of proportionality and the exact proportionality approach adopted by tribunals, this practice illustrates that the public purpose condition of legality is not an 'empty shell'. Although tribunals defer to States' choices as a matter of principle, they still exercise a measure of control as to the ultimate decision regarding whether that condition has been fulfilled. In exceptional cases, this element of residual control can lead them to conclude that the condition has not been met when the expropriation fails the test of proportionality (e.g. *PL Holdings S.à.r.l.* v. *Poland*, 2017, Partial Award, para. 391) or, more radically, when they consider that the expropriation does not actually aim to fulfil any public purpose (e.g. *Valeri Belokon* v. *Kyrgyzstan*, 2014, Award, para. 212).

6.3.2 Due Process of Law

Due process of law plays an important role in international investment law and arbitration, constituting a key concept to ensure that foreign investors enjoy a level of treatment and protection in conformity with the standards of the rule of law. As discussed in Chapter 5, this is part of the FET standard.

Due process of law is examined here from the point of view of the role it plays in appraising the legality of expropriations under the expropriation provision. In this respect, the close connection that exists between the requirement of due process of law under these two treaty provisions is well evidenced by the reasoning of some tribunals that make cross-references in their award (e.g. *Crystallex International Corporation* v. *Venezuela*, 2016, Award, para. 714).

Although due process of law has traditionally not been mentioned in all IIAs as a condition of legality of expropriation (e.g. 1993 United Kingdom–Armenia IIA, Article 5.1), its incorporation has become more systematic over time. Those agreements that do provide for that condition of legality typically refer explicitly to 'due process of law' (e.g. 2014 Kenya–Turkey IIA, Article 5.1). A few IIAs do not make explicit reference to that concept, but instead refer in one way or the other to the respect of legal procedures; for instance, the 1998 Belgium–Luxembourg Economic Union–Venezuela IIA refers to 'in accordance with legal procedures' (Article 4.1.b). Among these IIAs, it is worth singling out the IIA adopted by Israel and Japan in 2017 which, in addition to mentioning the respect for the 'procedures established in the national legislation of either Contracting Party', also refers to the respect of 'fundamental internationally recognized rules' (Article 11.1.d).

Most IIAs do not provide any detail as to the scope and content of that condition of legality. Those that do typically specify that due process of law includes the right of review of investors against the expropriation they allege to have suffered; this is exemplified by the 2000 Austria–Bosnia and Herzegovina IIA, which provides: 'Due process of law includes the right of an investor of a Contracting Party which claims to be affected by expropriation by the other Contracting Party to prompt review of its case, including the valuation of its investment and the payment of compensation in accordance with the provisions of this Article, by a judicial authority or another competent and independent authority of the latter Contracting Party' (Article 5.3).

With regard to that right of review and its incorporation within the scope of due process of law in some IIAs, treaty practice calls for two additional remarks. First, in a few IIAs, the right of review is set out as an additional condition of legality and not as forming part of the due process of law condition; this practice is illustrated by Article 11.1.e of the 2017 Israel–Japan IIA. Second, in a few other IIAs, the right of review is not referred to as a condition of legality as such, but as a right on its own (e.g. 2016 CETA, Article 8.12.4). This difference appears clearly in Article 10.5 of the 2016 Japan–Kenya IIA, which provides for a 'no prejudice clause', meaning that it specifies that the investors' right to review by the domestic courts, tribunals and agencies of the host State is without prejudice to their right to arbitration under the investor–State dispute settlement provisions of the Agreement.

In addition to the *ex post* requirement that investors be offered the possibility to challenge expropriatory measures, due process of law is also conceived of in arbitration practice as requiring – *ex ante* – that those measures be properly decided.

Concerning these *ex ante* and *ex post* dimensions, a key issue that arises in practice regarding those IIAs that do not provide sufficient specification is the body of law serving as a reference point in appraising due process of law. Central here is the role to be played by international law. Some tribunals focus on the domestic law of the host State. For instance, in *Teinver S.A.* v. *Argentina*, the Tribunal found that '[a]n expropriation that is carried out in accordance with the local law will satisfy this branch of the test ["in accordance with the law"]'; it then seemed to have assigned a role to international law only with regard to the other conditions of legality of expropriation (2017, Award, para. 1001). On the other hand, the Tribunal appointed in *Rusoro Mining Limited* v. *Venezuela*, for instance, stressed the relevance of international law for due process purposes, arguing that the requirement that the nationalisation be effected 'under due process of law' 'does not specifically refer to the municipal expropriation law of Venezuela, but to due process in general, a generic concept to be construed in accordance with international law' (2016, Award, para. 389).

This view expressed by the Tribunal in *ADC* v. *Hungary* as to the content of this generic concept has been widely shared in arbitration practice:

> The Tribunal agrees with the Claimants that '*due process of law*', in the expropriation context, demands an actual and substantive legal procedure for a foreign investor to raise its claims against the depriving actions already taken or about to be taken against it. Some basic legal mechanisms, such as reasonable advance notice, a fair hearing and an unbiased and impartial adjudicator to assess the actions in dispute, are expected to be readily available and accessible to the investor to make such legal procedure meaningful. In general, the legal procedure must be of a nature to grant an affected investor a reasonable chance within a reasonable time to claim its legitimate rights and have its claims

heard. If no legal procedure of such nature exists at all, the argument that '*the actions are taken under due process of law*' rings hollow. (2006, Award, para. 435)

Even though the lack of compliance with this condition of legality rarely grounds on its own a finding of expropriation in practice, it remains that tribunals do not hesitate to conclude that there has been such a lack of compliance. In *Bear Creek Mining Corporation* v. *Peru*, for instance, the Tribunal opined that the investor was entitled to be heard before the expropriatory measure was considered and taken, despite the political pressure that resulted from demonstration and unrest in the country. It stressed in particular that the respondent State should have made an effort to contact and hear the investor, irrespective of the political pressure that existed to come to an expeditious solution (2017, Award, para. 446).

6.3.3 Non-Discrimination

Non-discrimination is to be found in all IIAs as a condition of legality of expropriation. In arbitration practice, this condition is treated by most tribunals *mutatis mutandis* in the same way as non-discrimination under other IIA provisions. This explains why, here as well, cross-references are made in awards with the analysis of the FET standard (e.g. *Crystallex International Corporation* v. *Venezuela*, 2016, Award, para. 715), or that of the national treatment standard (e.g. *Olin Holdings Limited* v. *Libya*, 2018, Final Award, para. 174). More fundamentally, this also explains why, when they examine the fulfilment of this condition of legality, tribunals apply a test which is largely similar to the one used in the context of the standards of treatment within IIAs.

For instance, when appraising this condition, the Tribunal appointed in *Teinver S.A.* v. *Argentina* stressed that 'discrimination requires differential treatment of Claimants' investment from other similar investments in like circumstances' (2017, Award, para. 1019).

In *Rusoro Mining Limited* v. *Venezuela*, the Tribunal considered in substance that the likeness of the circumstances was missing for a finding of discrimination. Indeed, it concluded that the difference of treatment between State-owned companies and privately owned companies did not amount to discrimination in so far as the former were not negatively affected by the Nationalization Decree which was a necessary consequence of the nationalisation of the gold sector in which both kind of companies coexisted (2016, Award, para. 397).

Likewise, in *Quiborax S.A.* v. *Bolivia* (2015, Award, para. 247), the Tribunal adopted and applied this test set out by the Tribunal in *Saluka Investments BV (The Netherlands)* v. *Czech Republic* in relation to the FET standard: 'State conduct is discriminatory, if (i) similar cases are (ii) treated differently (iii) and without reasonable justification' (2006, Partial Award, para. 313).

6.3.4 Compensation

Preliminary Remarks

At the outset, it is important to stress that this subsection focuses on compensation as a condition of legality of expropriation and not on the compensation which is due as a consequence of an internationally wrongful act constitutive of an illegal expropriation. This is a distinction to be kept in mind, even though, as discussed in particular in Chapter 15, the frontier between lawful and unlawful expropriation with regard to compensation matters is sometimes blurred in arbitration practice.

As explained in Chapter 1, the compensation of expropriation has historically been the most controversial issue in the law of expropriation. This was true in particular at the time of the development of the 'law of the protection of aliens abroad' and at the time when developing States required the establishment of a New International Economic Order. International investment agreements that refer to compensation as a condition of legality have greatly contributed to easing these controversies; compensation constitutes a well-accepted condition of legality that embodies the balance struck between the exercise by host States of their sovereign right to expropriate and the protection of the right to property of foreign investors.

This condition of legality raises four main issues that are analysed in turn. The first three of these, which each have a strong 'technical' dimension, pertain to (1) the standard of compensation, (2) the valuation methodology and factors, as well as (3) interest. The fourth boils down to the question as to whether the failure to pay compensation as such makes an expropriation illegal; as we shall see, this fourth issue has a fundamental theoretical dimension inasmuch as it pertains to the 'status' of compensation as compared to the other conditions of legality of expropriation.

The Standard of Compensation

Preliminary Remarks

Virtually all IIAs set out the standard applicable to the compensation which is due as a condition of legality of expropriation. Three preliminary remarks can be made in this regard.

First, it has been discussed whether that standard is applicable also to unlawful expropriations, that is in determining the compensation due as a consequence of an internationally wrongful act constitutive of an illegal expropriation. This issue is examined fully in Chapter 15.

Second, one can notice that States parties create a '*lex specialis*' in some IIAs concerning specific 'items'. This holds true typically with regard to the compensation for land expropriation, which is governed in some treaties by a specific provision. For instance, Article 6.3 of the 2018 Kazakhstan–Singapore IIA provides: 'Notwithstanding the obligations under paragraphs 1 and 2 of this Article, any measure of expropriation relating to land shall be for a purpose and upon payment of compensation in accordance with the applicable national legislation of the expropriating Party.'

Third, and irrespective of the provision of such a *lex specialis*, one can notice, as evidenced below, that there exists some diversity in the wording used in IIAs to set out the applicable standard of compensation and the details thereof. However, this semantic diversity does not in general entail practical differences. In fact, treaty practice embodies largely the 'Hull formula', which – as discussed in Chapter 1 – sets a requirement of prompt, adequate and effective compensation for expropriations to be legal.

A large number of IIAs provide explicitly that States must pay compensation which shall be 'prompt, adequate and effective' (e.g. 2018 CPTPP, Article 9.8.1.c), a minority replacing 'adequate' with 'appropriate' (e.g. 2016 Slovakia–Iran IIA, Article 6.1.d). A few IIAs do not refer to the three components of the standard, but typically to two of them, be it 'effective and adequate' (e.g. 2016 Argentina–Qatar IIA, Article 5.1), or 'prompt and effective' (e.g. 2016 Singapore–Iran IIA, Article 5.2).

Other IIAs refer to the payment of a 'just compensation' (e.g. 2008 Netherlands–Macao SAR China IIA, Article 6.1.c). Read by tribunals in conjunction with subsequent sentences or paragraphs of the expropriation provision in question, such a reference has been interpreted as linking the treaty standard of compensation to the 'Hull formula'. The Tribunal appointed in *Enkev Beheer B. V.* v. *Poland* did so in particular in relation to the reference made to 'real value' in the IIA at hand in that case (2014, First Partial Award, para. 355), as did the majority of the Tribunal in *CME Czech Republic B.V. (The Netherlands)* v. *Czech Republic* with regard to the mention made in the applicable agreement to 'genuine value' (2003, Final Award, para. 497). It is worth noting that Arbitrator Brownlie dissented on the matter, arguing that the standard of 'just compensation' could not be equated to the 'Hull formula' (2003, Separate Opinion, paras. 31–32).

International investment agreements that adopt a third approach simply state at the outset that compensation shall be paid in accordance with the subsequent paragraphs of the expropriation provision (e.g. 2016 Hong Kong SAR China–Chile IIA, Article 10.1.d).

Irrespective of the approach chosen by the drafters, IIAs then detail – with a degree of specification that varies across treaty practice – the standard of compensation. As evidenced by the three components of the 'Hull formula', most IIAs address three issues: (1) the timing of the payment of compensation; (2) the adequacy of its amount; and (3) its effectiveness. Each of these issues is analysed in turn.

a   The Timing of the Payment of Compensation

Various formulations and degrees of specification can be seen across treaty practice as regards the timing of the payment of compensation.

Some IIAs simply require that compensation be paid 'without delay' (e.g. 2017 Israel–Japan IIA, Article 11.3). The 2016 Austria–Kyrgyzstan IIA, for instance, also provides for a payment without any delay in Article 7.2.a, with Article 1.5 specifying what this entails: '"[W]ithout delay" means such period as is normally required for the completion of necessary formalities for the payments of compensation or for the transfer of payments. This period shall commence for payments of compensation on the day of expropriation and for transfers of payments on the day on which the request for transfer has been submitted. It shall in no case exceed one month.' Some IIAs that provide for a payment 'without undue delay' contain a similar specification. For example, Footnote 9 attached to Article 10.2.c of the 2017 Hong Kong SAR China–ASEAN IIA specifies that '[t]he Parties understand that there may be legal and administrative processes that need to be observed before payment can be made'. Other IIAs simply require that compensation be paid 'without undue delay' (e.g. 2017 PACER Plus, Article 13.3 (Chapter 9)), or 'without unjustified delay' (e.g. 2017 Colombia–UAE IIA, Article 7.4).

Irrespective of the formula used, IIAs typically provide – as discussed below – that interest must be paid in the event compensation is paid at a time that is not in compliance with the treaty requirement.

b The Adequacy of Compensation

Most IIAs provide that the compensation shall be equivalent to the fair market value of the expropriated investment. They do so directly, by referring to this notion (e.g. 2014 Korea–Kenya IIA, Article 4.2) or to 'market value' (e.g. 2006 Colombia–Switzerland IIA, Article 6), or indirectly. For instance, the 2018 Kazakhstan–UAE IIA provides that compensation shall amount to the 'actual value' of the expropriated investment, this actual value being determined on the basis of the 'fair market value' of the expropriated investment (Article 6.3). A similar approach is adopted in the 2017 China–Hong Kong SAR China IIA, which refers to the 'real value' of the expropriated investment in Article 11.2 and which then specifies in Footnote 5 that 'the real value shall be calculated on the basis of the market value of the expropriated investment'. In other agreements, reference is made to 'real value' without any reference to be found in the treaty to the 'fair market value' (e.g. 2016 Hong Kong SAR China–Chile IIA, Article 10.2.b); the same goes for some agreements that simply refer to 'genuine value' (e.g. 1991 Netherlands–Czech and Slovak Republic IIA, Article 5.c), or 'value' (e.g. 1997 Germany–Turkmenistan IIA, Article 4.2).

Such references have been considered by some tribunals as being equivalent to the 'fair market value', for instance the Tribunal appointed in *Rusoro Mining Limited* v. *Venezuela* with respect to 'genuine value' (2016, Award, paras. 404 and 647). On the other hand, in *Adem Dogan* v. *Turkmenistan*, the Annulment Committee denied that 'value' should be equated to 'fair market value', explaining that "'[v]alue" is a general term encompassing any valuation method to assess compensation due, including but not limited to "fair market value"' and that '[b]y referring to "value", the BIT permitted the Tribunal to choose a standard other than the FMV in light of the specific circumstances of the case' (2016, Decision on Annulment, para. 160).

It is noteworthy that there are discrepancies in treaty practice as to the interplay between 'fair market value' and the reference made in treaties to other notions, in particular 'real value'. Contrary to the above-mentioned China–Hong Kong SAR China IIA which assimilates real value and market value, other agreements contrast these two notions. This is apparent in the 2017 Hong Kong SAR China–ASEAN IIA, which addresses the matter differently with regard to ASEAN countries, on the one hand, and Hong Kong SAR China, on the other hand – the relevant part reads as follows:

> For the purpose of subparagraph 1 (d), compensation shall: (a) be equivalent to the fair market value (if the expropriating Party is an ASEAN Member State) or real value (if the expropriating Party is the Hong Kong Special Administrative Region) of the expropriated investment at the time when the expropriation was publicly announced [footnote omitted], or when the expropriation occurred, whichever is applicable. (Article 10.2.a)

All of this begs the question as to the meaning of these notions. In this respect, it is worth noting that virtually no IIAs provide any indication about the meaning of fair market value. In this context, arbitration tribunals often refer to the case law of the Iran–United States Claims Tribunal, in particular the 1987 *Starrett Housing Corp.* v. *Iran* case, or to the 1992 World Bank Guidelines on the Treatment of Foreign Direct Investment in order to shed light on this notion.[3] Both adopt a similar approach, the World Bank Guidelines being, however, more detailed. Those Guidelines that World Bank Group institutions can – according to Guideline 1 – apply as a complement to applicable international treaties and instruments, provided they are compatible, explain:

> In the absence of a determination agreed by, or based on the agreement of, the parties, the fair market value will be acceptable if determined by the State according to reasonable criteria related to the market value of the investment, i.e., in an amount that a willing buyer would normally pay to a willing seller after taking into account the nature of the investment, the circumstances in which it would operate in the future and its specific characteristics, including the period in which it has been in existence, the proportion of tangible assets in the total investment and other relevant factors pertinent to the specific circumstances of each case. (Guideline 4.5)

---

[3] 1992 World Bank Guidelines on the Treatment of Foreign Direct Investment, available at www .worldbank.org.

There is an obvious temporal dimension in the appraisal of fair market value in that the value of the investment shall be appraised *ex ante*, meaning before it is affected by the expropriation. This is made explicit in virtually all IIAs which – according to various combinations and formulations – provide that the value shall be appraised (1) before the expropriation occurs, (2) before it is publicly announced, or (3) before it is (publicly) known. The reference made to the last two dates aims at preventing the amount of the compensation from being unduly impacted by the fall of the value of the investment caused by the prior knowledge of the forthcoming expropriation. This treaty practice is well illustrated by Article 13.2 of the 2017 PACER Plus (Chapter 9), which provides that 'compensation shall be equivalent to the fair market value of the expropriated investment at the time when the expropriation was publicly announced or when the expropriation occurred, whichever is the earlier.' A few agreements are even more specific as they specify the exact time when the value of the investment shall be assessed. For instance, as to the Philippines, the 2017 Hong Kong SAR China–ASEAN IIA makes it clear that 'the time when or immediately before the expropriation was publicly announced' refers to 'the date of filing of the Petition for Expropriation' (Article 10.2.a, Footnote 8).

This *ex ante* valuation has been conceived of as not preventing future prospects from being taken into account in appraising the value of the expropriated investment, in order to substantiate or validate the value determined on the basis of the features of the investment before the expropriation takes place or is known. Relying in particular on the above-mentioned World Bank Guidelines which provide that the circumstances in which the investment would operate in the future should be taken into consideration in appraising its fair market value, the Tribunal in *Tidewater* v. *Venezuela* explained and justified as follows the use of *ex post* information:

> The purpose of referring to subsequent events is not to present a hypothetical business that never in fact occurred and would not reasonably have been taken into account by a willing buyer prior to expropriation. Rather, it is permitted in cases where such events shed more light in concrete terms on the value of the investment prior to expropriation. In assessing the value of the business at that date, the Tribunal disregards business prospects that it considers to be too remote or speculative to justify inclusion. (2015, Award, para. 161)

As discussed below, the issue then is the actual determination of the fair market value of the expropriated investment, an issue which boils down to valuation methodology and factors.

c   The Effectiveness of Compensation

Apart from a few exceptions (e.g. 2016 Singapore–Iran IIA, Article 5), treaty practice displays a series of specifications – according to various formulations and combinations – with regard to the effectiveness of compensation. As is made explicit in some agreements, like the 2016 Slovakia–Iran IIA (Article 6.3), the effectiveness of compensation is a matter of currency convertibility.

Depending on the exact formulation adopted by States parties, compensation is deemed to be effective if it is paid in a 'freely convertible currency' (e.g. 2016 Canada–Mongolia IIA, Article 10.3), or if compensation is in a 'freely usable currency' (e.g. 2017 PACER Plus, Article 13.3 (Chapter 9)).

In a few IIAs, specifications are given about the currency in which compensation shall be paid; for instance, the 2016 Austria–Kyrgyzstan IIA provides that compensation shall be paid in any freely convertible currency accepted by the claimant or in the currency of its home State (Article 7.2.c). This obligation of effectiveness is explicitly extended in a few IIAs with regard to the payment of interest (e.g. 2016 Japan–Iran IIA, Article 8.4).

It is worth noting that in addition to 'convertibility', IIAs typically provide that compensation shall be fully or effectively realisable as well as freely transferable (e.g. 2013 Guatemala–Trinidad and Tobago IIA, Article 8.2.d). Again, a few agreements provide for greater details. For instance, the above-mentioned Austria–Kyrgyzstan IIA specifies that compensation shall be freely transferred to the country designated by the claimant (Article 7.2.c). The above-mentioned Japan–Iran IIA also provides that interest shall be effectively realisable and freely transferable (Article 8.5).

6.3.4.2 Valuation Methodology and Factors

While virtually all IIAs are silent on the meaning of fair market value, a number of them provide some information as to how it should be determined. Those agreements typically provide for the body of rules and principles to be applied to reach such a determination. They usually refer – *mutatis mutandis* – to the domestic law of the host State (e.g. 2018 Kazakhstan–UAE IIA, Article 6.3) or to 'the generally recognized principles of valuation and equitable principles' (e.g. 2017 PACER Plus, Article 13.2 (Chapter 9)). That latter Agreement also provides for a non-exhaustive list of factors to be taken into account, namely the capital invested, depreciation, capital already repatriated and replacement value. Some agreements refer directly to such factors without any reference being made to bodies of rules or principles. For instance, the 2013 Canada–Benin IIA provides: 'Valuation criteria must include going concern value, asset value including declared tax value of tangible property, and other criteria, as appropriate, to determine fair market value' (Article 11.2).

Even though the above-mentioned IIAs provide for some guidance, they do not set out the method to be used to determine the fair market value of the expropriated investment. For those agreements as well as those which are completely silent on the matter (e.g. 2009 Canada–Latvia IIA, Article 8), guidance can be found again in the World Bank Guidelines on the Treatment of Foreign Direct Investment.

Guideline 4.6 distinguishes between three different categories: (1) going concern with a proven record of profitability; (2) enterprises that are not a proven going concern and demonstrate lack of profitability; and (3) other assets. The Guidelines recommend an appraisal to be made of the following values by way of illustration of a reasonable determination of the investment market value that should be arrived at with respect to each of these three categories.

As to the first category, going concern is defined as follows:

> [A]n enterprise consisting of income-producing assets which has been in oper-
> ation for a sufficient period of time to generate the data required for the
> calculation of future income and which could have been expected with reason-
> able certainty, if the taking had not occurred, to continue producing legitimate
> income over the course of its economic life in the general circumstances
> following the taking by the State.

For such going concern, the valuation method aims at determining the dis-
counted cash flow (DCF) value. As to this value, Guideline 4.6 provides:

> '[D]iscounted cash flow value' means the cash receipts realistically expected from
> the enterprise in each future year of its economic life as reasonably projected
> minus that year's expected cash expenditure, after discounting this net cash flow
> for each year by a factor which reflects the time value of money, expected
> inflation, and the risk associated with such cash flow under realistic circum-
> stances. Such discount rate may be measured by examining the rate of return
> available in the same market on alternative investments of comparable risk on
> the basis of their present value.

With regard to the second category, i.e. enterprises that are not a proven
going concern and demonstrate lack of profitability, Guideline 4.6 states
that the fair market value should be based on the liquidation value. This
is defined as 'the amounts at which individual assets comprising the
enterprise or the entire assets of the enterprise could be sold under
conditions of liquidation to a willing buyer less any liabilities which the
enterprise has to meet'.

Concerning the third category – other assets – it recommends that their fair
market value be based either on the replacement value or the book value in the
case that this value 'has been recently assessed or has been determined as of the
date of the taking and can therefore be deemed to represent a reasonable
replacement value'. Guideline 4.6 defines the replacement value as 'the cash
amount required to replace the individual assets of the enterprise in their
actual state as of the date of the taking' and the book value as follows: '[T]he
difference between the enterprise's assets and liabilities as recorded on its
financial statements or the amount at which the taken tangible assets appear
on the balance sheet of the enterprise, representing their cost after deducting
accumulated depreciation in accordance with generally accepted accounting
principles.'

Those valuation methods have largely been used by arbitration tribunals, in particular the DCF, to determine the fair market value of the expropriated investment and the compensation to be paid. In this respect, it is worth noting that the DCF is also used to reach such determinations with regard to unlawful expropriations. Instances in which the DCF has been used in relation to lawful expropriation can be illustrated by the award rendered in *Tidewater* v. *Venezuela* (2015, Award, paras. 151–202). Two elements are worth emphasising in the way that Tribunal applied the DCF.

First, the Tribunal considered that there was no other enterprise to which the company into which the investor had invested could be compared to determine the fair market value of this investment; it stressed in particular that the business of this company was limited to one country and one customer. As a result, it proceeded by focusing on the specific features of the business of this company for the purpose of this valuation. In this respect, it inquired into (1) the scope of the business, (2) the accounts receivable, (3) the historical cash flow, (4) the equity risk, (5) the country risk, and (6) the business risk.

From a legal point of view, the determination of the country risk is the most interesting item. The country risk premium is used to discount the value of the investment, for the reason that this is an element that a willing buyer would take into account in ascertaining the value of an investment. The issue that was debated by the parties in that case was whether the political risk should be included in the country risk. In particular, the expert on behalf of the claimant argued that it should not be included as its inclusion would lead to conferring an illegitimate benefit to the host State in that it would, according to him, benefit from its own wrong, meaning that it would have to pay less compensation because of the risks it generates itself. The Tribunal rejected this approach mainly by distinguishing the general political risk that exists in host States from the specific expropriatory measure. It argued that host States are not benefiting from their own wrong inasmuch as they are obliged to compensate such measures as a matter of liability. Furthermore, as a matter of valuation, it opined that the inclusion of the political risk does not confer an illegitimate benefit to host States, but instead is in line with a common practice – as evidenced by the above-mentioned Guideline 4.6 – and the due diligence displayed by a willing buyer.

6.3.4.3 Interest

To use the words of the Tribunal in *Tidewater* v. *Venezuela*, the payment of interest required in IIAs aims to compensate the investor 'from being kept out of its money' between the date on which it ought to have been compensated and the actual date of payment – as such it appears that the payment of interest does not have a punitive dimension (2015, Award, para. 205).

Apart from a few exceptions (e.g. 2003 Laos–Myanmar IIA, Article 4), IIAs provide that States shall pay such interest or less frequently, for instance that they shall bear the financial cost related to the delayed payment (e.g. 2016 Slovakia–Iran IIA, Article 6.2). More precisely, they typically provide for two series of specifications that pertain respectively to the temporal dimension of the calculation of interest and the rate thereof.

Beginning with the temporal dimension, it can be noted that a few IIAs merely provide that it shall be taken 'into account the length of time until the time of payment' (e.g. 2012 Japan–Iraq IIA, Article 11.3). Most IIAs specify dates in this regard. More precisely, while all of those agreements provide an end date for the calculation, that date being the date of payment, many do not specify the starting date (e.g. 2007 France–Seychelles IIA, Article 6.2). Those that do specify this date typically provide that interest accrues from the date of expropriation (e.g. 2000 Jordan–Sudan IIA, Article 4), or from the date at which the payment of compensation becomes due (e.g. 2016 Slovakia–Iran IIA, Article 6.2).

With regard to the rate, two main approaches are followed in treaty practice. The first of these, which is adopted by a minority of States parties, makes applicable a rate as set out in the domestic law of the host State (e.g. 2012 Macedonia–Kazakhstan IIA, Article 4.3). The other approach refers to a commercial rate. More precisely, depending on the IIA, reference can be made to the 'applicable commercial rate' (e.g. 2016 Singapore–Iran IIA, Article 5.2), the 'normal commercial rate' (2016 CETA, Article 8.12.3), or the 'commercially reasonable rate' (2017 PACER Plus, Article 13.3 (Chapter 9)). A few agreements provide greater specification in this regard, often in relation to the London InterBank Offered Rate (LIBOR), which is an average interest rate – calculated on a daily basis – at which global banks borrow from one another. For instance, the 2012 Armenia–Iraq IIA provides that the interest shall be 'at a commercial rate established on a market basis, however, in no event less than the prevailing LIBOR rate of interest or equivalent' (Article 5.1.b).

6.3.4.4 The Status of Compensation as a Condition of Legality

As examined above, compensation is set out in IIAs as a condition of legality in the same way as – mainly – public interest, non-discrimination and due process of law. It is uncontested that if an expropriation fails to meet any of these last three conditions, it is to be considered an illegal expropriation. On the other hand, it has been discussed whether the lack of compensation can on its own lead an expropriation to be characterised as being illegal.

Some tribunals do consider that the non-payment of compensation can on its own render an expropriation illegal, thereby making moot the analysis of the other conditions of legality (e.g. *UP and C.D Holding Internationale v. Hungary*, 2018, Award, para. 411). Those tribunals that enquire into these conditions and find that they are fulfilled reach the same conclusion when compensation is not paid (e.g. *Compania de Aguas del Aconquija S.A. v. Argentina*, Award, 2007, para. 7.5.21).

On the other hand, other tribunals consider that the failure to pay compensation does not *ipso facto* make the expropriation illegal.

Some tribunals adopt this approach with regard to situations in which there is no disagreement as to the existence of an expropriation, but instead as to the compensation as such. In that sense, the Tribunal appointed in *South American Silver Limited (Bermuda)* v. *Bolivia* noted: 'It is not a question of simply verifying whether payment was made or not. Rather, it is necessary, on the one hand, to take into account the substance of the international obligation of the State to compensate under the corresponding international instrument – the Treaty in this case – and, on the other hand, the circumstances that led to the non-payment' (2018, Award, para. 596). With regard to the circumstances, the Tribunal considered in *Venezuela Holdings, B.V.* v. *Venezuela* that if an offer of compensation has been made, the legality of the expropriation depends on the terms of that offer (2014, Award, para. 301). Likewise, it can be deduced – *a contrario* – from the reasoning of the Tribunal in *ConocoPhillips* v. *Venezuela* that the failure to pay compensation does not make the expropriation illegal if the parties have engaged in good faith negotiations to fix the compensation in line with the standard provided in the applicable IIA (2013, Decision on Jurisdiction and the Merits, para. 362).

In *Tidewater* v. *Venezuela*, the Tribunal addressed those situations in which the existence of the expropriation itself was in question, explaining:

> Most expropriation claims turn on the question whether a measure is expropriatory at all. In such cases, where the tribunal finds expropriation, compensation is almost always due. Cases where expropriation is acknowledged and the dispute revolves around the proper amount of compensation are rare; cases where no compensation has been paid because the label of expropriation itself is contested are the norm. That means that almost every decision finding expropriation would also find unlawful expropriation – and almost every tribunal would then set aside the 'fair market value at the time of expropriation' standard for compensation for expropriation. Such an approach thus would make a detailed and elaborate element of the expropriation provision in modern BITs, including the provisions of Article 5 of the Venezuela–Barbados BIT, effectively nugatory. The Tribunal's approach is also consistent with the World Bank Guidelines ... Determination of such fair market value is acceptable if conducted on a basis agreed between the State and the foreign investor '*or by a tribunal or another body designated by the Parties*'. The Guidelines thus reinforce the conclusion of the Tribunal that an expropriation wanting only a determination of compensation by an international tribunal is not to be treated as an illegal expropriation. (2015, Award, para. 138–140)

This line of argumentation is twofold, the first element of which pertains to effectiveness. In substance, this Tribunal argued that because most expropriation claims relate to the existence of an expropriation as such, if a finding of expropriation leads to its characterisation as an unlawful expropriation, then the standard of compensation for lawful expropriation is largely deprived of any effectiveness. The second argument relates to the role tribunals play in fixing the amount of compensation if the parties have not done so. It boils down to the following: because arbitration tribunals can fix this amount, an expropriation that only lacks compensation is not illegal.

This argument was articulated by Arbitrator Stern as follows:

> In other words, an expropriation, which only lacks fair compensation to be lawful has to be treated as a potentially lawful expropriation (or a provisionally unlawful expropriation until the tribunal has awarded the compensation due for the expropriation to be legal): this is so, because, as soon as the fair compensation needed for a lawful expropriation is granted, the situation has been reestablished and that condition for a lawful expropriation has been fulfilled. (*Quiborax S.A. v. Bolivia*, 2015, Award, Partially Dissenting Opinion, para. 17)

This approach seems to confer a specific 'status' to compensation as a condition of legality, and it could even be wondered whether it does not in some circumstances lead in practice to an exclusion of compensation from the conditions of legality of expropriation.

7

Public Interest Limitations on Foreign Investors' Protection

Introduction

Treaty-making is always a delicate exercise for States. Not only does it require them to negotiate with one another to strike a balance between their respective interests, but it also requires them to strike a balance between their own potentially conflicting interests, typically those they have as duty bearers and rights holders, respectively. This is all the more true when we consider that their interests may vary over time. Several techniques, such as incorporating 'limitations'/'exceptions' in the text of the treaties or making reservations, can help States in this respect as they offer a degree of flexibility that allows them to achieve those balances in the conclusion of the treaties. These techniques also reduce the need to subsequently revise treaties and mitigate the risk of termination and withdrawal by States parties who, in re-drawing the 'balance', may later find that the treaties they concluded are no longer compatible with their priorities in foreign and domestic policies.

At the time of the emergence of international investment law and arbitration, treaty-making appeared to be quite a simple exercise because of the specificities of the field and those of foreign direct investment (FDI) operations. As explained in Chapter 1, bilateral investment treaties (BITs) were concluded on the basis of the BIT models that European States developed and used in their relations with developing States. Those European States were concerned with the protection of their investors in developing States; this is due to the fact that the flow of FDI operations overwhelmingly travelled from developed States to developing States. This 'one-directional' dimension of the flow of FDI operations turned the de jure reciprocal nature of BITs into de facto non-reciprocal treaties that protected European investors in developing States. As a result of all of this, the parameters of treaty-making were clear: European States sought the greatest protection for their investors. They hardly had to take into consideration the de jure limitation that BITs placed on their sovereign prerogatives as – de facto – there were almost no foreign investors originating from the other State party who invested in their territory and who they had to treat in compliance with the provisions of these treaties. This partly explains why techniques intended to help States to strike a balance between the interests of one another, and between their own interests, have traditionally been rare in investment treaty-making.

As examined in Chapter 1, the situation has changed with the multilateralisation of FDI operations as well as the increase and evolution of treaty practice. Bilateral investment treaties have progressively acquired a de facto reciprocal dimension due to the growing presence of investors from developing States in developed States, who have had to be treated in conformity with those treaties, and also because of the conclusion of BITs between developing States themselves. Another relevant trend has consisted in the conclusion of free trade agreements (FTAs) containing an investment chapter involving developed States and/or developing States. This has led to more frequent situations in which developed States have been in the position of defendant in arbitration proceedings initiated by investors originating from developing or developed States.

The result of this evolution has been an alignment of the policies of developing and developed States in treaty-making: they have no longer been radically dictated by their traditional respective 'status' as host State and home State. At the same time, this evolution has placed these States in a contradictory situation: in their capacity as home State, they seek the greatest protection for their investors, while in their capacity as host State, they want the greatest protection for their sovereign prerogatives and public interest. Along with global criticism formulated against international investment law and arbitration, all of this has substantially contributed to the incorporation of new limitations impacting on the protection accorded by international investment agreements (IIAs) to foreign investors to the benefit of public interest *sensu largo*.

This chapter focuses on the limitations as contained in the IIAs concluded in the 2010s, as these IIAs incorporate both traditional limitations as well as those new limitations mentioned above. For didactic purposes, it provides an analysis of treaty limitations by distinguishing between them on the basis of their scope of application, meaning mainly whether they apply to the IIA as a whole or to specific provisions thereof. Of course, depending on the IIA at hand, a limitation – for instance pertaining to taxation – can apply either to the treaty as a whole or to one or several specific provisions.

7.1 Limitations Applying to IIAs

Treaty practice is not uniform with respect to the limitations that apply to IIAs as a whole – which limitations are included and the exact content thereof vary from one treaty to the other. Furthermore, the classification of these limitations also varies: for instance, security exceptions are incorporated in some IIAs in the Article on general exceptions (e.g. 2017 Colombia–United Arab Emirates (UAE) IIA, Article 11), while these two categories of exceptions are provided in two distinct articles in other agreements (e.g. 2016 Singapore–Iran IIA, Articles 13 and 14).

This subsection examines the main trends displayed by relevant treaty practice. It provides an analysis of the limitations pertaining to (1) the right to regulate, (2) general exceptions, (3) security exceptions, (4) taxation, (5) public debt as well as (6) financial and monetary matters.

7.1.1 The Right to Regulate

Under public international law, it is a fundamental prerogative of States to exercise freely their normative power over their territory. Of course, they can consent to limiting this power, as they do for instance with respect to the protection they consent to confer on foreign investors when they conclude IIAs. As a reaction to the criticism that this protection excessively hampers the exercise of their normative power, States have incorporated into a number of IIAs concluded in the 2010s provisions that aim at protecting the exercise of that power for the benefit of certain public interests, by specifying that the corresponding State measures shall not as a matter of principle be considered as being prohibited by the agreements. Nuances and differences can be seen across these treaties in the scope of such limitations and as to the conditions attached to them.

7.1.1.1 The Scope of the Limitation

Two series of considerations are relevant with regard to the scope of this limitation: (1) the circumstances under which State measures shall not be regarded as being prohibited by IIAs; and (2) the public interests protected by this limitation.

As to the first series of considerations, some IIAs adopt a broad approach. Such IIAs provide *mutatis mutandis* that their provisions do not restrict or shall not be considered as restricting the right of States to regulate and to adopt measures to protect public interests. For instance, Article 10 of the 2016 Argentina–Qatar IIA provides that '[n]one of the provisions of [the] Agreement shall affect the inherent right of the Contracting Parties to regulate within their territories through measures necessary to achieve legitimate policy objectives, such as the protection of public health, safety, the environment, public morals, social and consumer protection'. Other IIAs display a narrower approach in the sense that the entitlement to adopt such measures is conferred only to ensure that investors' conduct and activities are 'friendly' and 'respectful' of public interests. This is well illustrated by Article 9.1 of the 2017 Rwanda–UAE IIA, which reads as follows:

> Nothing in this Agreement shall be construed to prevent a Contracting Party from adopting, maintaining, or enforcing any measure that it considers appropriate to ensure that an investment activity in its territory is undertaken in

accordance with the applicable public health, security, environmental and labour law of the Contracting Party, such measures should not be applied in a manner that would constitute arbitrary or unjustifiable discrimination between investments or investors.

Instead of focusing on the conformity of investment operations with the domestic laws of the host State protecting public interests, other IIAs make a direct link between those operations and public interests. For instance, the 2018 Korea–Republics of Central America IIA provides: 'Nothing in this Chapter shall be construed to prevent a Party from adopting, maintaining or enforcing any measure otherwise consistent with this Chapter that it considers appropriate to ensure that investment activity in its territory is undertaken in a manner sensitive to environmental concerns' (Article 9.11).

Regardless of the solution opted for by States parties as to the circumstances under which State measures shall not be regarded as being prohibited by IIAs, their IIA practice displays also some diversity concerning which public interests are protected under the right to regulate limitation. As illustrated by the provisions mentioned above, the protection of the environment constitutes a common denominator in IIAs. Some agreements refer only to the environment (e.g. 2018 Korea–Republics of Central America IIA, Article 9.11), others to the environment and one or more additional public interests, typically labour conditions (e.g. 2017 Colombia–UAE IIA, Article 10). A few IIAs provide for a non-exhaustive list of public interests (e.g. 2014 Switzerland–Georgia IIA, Article 9.1).

7.1.1.2 Conditions Attached to the Limitation

In a few IIAs, there is no explicit condition attached to the right to regulate limitation; this approach can be seen in the Argentina–Qatar IIA quoted above. On the other hand, and as illustrated by the 2017 Rwanda–UAE IIA also mentioned above, most agreements require that the measures adopted, maintained or enforced should not be applied in a way that would constitute an arbitrary or an unjustifiable discrimination between investments or investors.

The first category of IIAs in particular raises the issue of the interaction between the right to regulate limitation and the other IIA provisions that confer rights and protection to foreign investors and their investments. At the core of this issue is the balance to be struck between the protection of public interests and that of foreign investors. In this regard, it is interesting to note that the 2016 Morocco–Nigeria IIA conceives of the exercise by States of their right to regulate in terms of a balance. After providing that host States have the right to take regulatory or other measures, in accordance with customary international law (CIL) and other general principles of international law, to ensure that development in their territories is consistent with the goals and principles of sustainable development, and with other legitimate social and economic policy objectives, the Agreement goes on to explain: 'Except where the rights of Host State are expressly stated as an exception to the obligation of this Agreement, a Host State's pursuit of its rights to regulate shall be understood as embodied within a balance of the rights and obligations of Investors and Investments and Host States, as set out in the Agreement' (Articles 23.1 and 23.2).

Another issue also relevant in this discussion is what the reference to 'otherwise consistent' means in those provisions that provide along the lines of Article 15 of the 2016 Hong Kong SAR China–Chile IIA: 'Nothing in this Agreement shall be construed to prevent a Party from adopting, maintaining, or enforcing any measure otherwise consistent with this Agreement that it considers appropriate to ensure that investment activity in its area is undertaken in a manner sensitive to environmental, health or other regulatory objectives.' It has been suggested that this formulation 'would seem to mean that the measures in question would be consistent but for the fact that they were taken to assure that investments will be conducted in an environmentally sensitive manner'.[1]

7.1.2 General Exceptions

Preliminary Remarks

General exceptions provisions are akin to the right to regulate limitation discussed above, in that they provide, as a matter of principle, that IIAs and their provisions shall not be considered as preventing States from adopting measures aimed at the protection of a set of public interests. It is worth noting at the outset that the text of most general exceptions provisions refers typically to 'measures which are necessary' to protect those public interests and not to 'measures that the States parties consider as being necessary'. This formulation indicates that such exceptions are not 'self-judging', meaning that the appraisal as to whether or not the measures are necessary is not reserved to States themselves and that it can therefore be subject to review, notably by arbitration tribunals.

Although other types of exceptions, usually those relating to security exceptions, can be found in the provisions that are most often called 'general exceptions', those provisions derive directly from Article XX of the 1947 General Agreement on Tariffs and Trade (GATT), which was incorporated in the 1994 GATT at the time of the creation of the World Trade Organization (WTO). Given this origin, it is worth quoting it in its entirety:

> Subject to the requirement that such measures are not applied in a manner which would constitute a means of arbitrary or unjustifiable discrimination between countries where the same conditions prevail, or a disguised restriction on international trade, nothing in this Agreement shall be construed to prevent the adoption or enforcement by any contracting party of measures:

---

[1] JW Salacuse, *The Law of Investment Treaties* (2nd ed, Oxford University Press 2015), at 385.

(a) necessary to protect public morals;

(b) necessary to protect human, animal or plant life or health;

(c) relating to the importations or exportations of gold or silver;

(d) necessary to secure compliance with laws or regulations which are not inconsistent with the provisions of this Agreement, including those relating to customs enforcement, the enforcement of monopolies operated under paragraph 4 of Article II and Article XVII, the protection of patents, trade marks and copyrights, and the prevention of deceptive practices;

(e) relating to the products of prison labour;

(f) imposed for the protection of national treasures of artistic, historic or archaeological value;

(g) relating to the conservation of exhaustible natural resources if such measures are made effective in conjunction with restrictions on domestic production or consumption;

(h) undertaken in pursuance of obligations under any intergovernmental commodity agreement which conforms to criteria submitted to the CONTRACTING PARTIES and not disapproved by them or which is itself so submitted and not so disapproved*;

(i) involving restrictions on exports of domestic materials necessary to ensure essential quantities of such materials to a domestic processing industry during periods when the domestic price of such materials is held below the world price as part of a governmental stabilization plan; *Provided* that such restrictions shall not operate to increase the exports of or the protection afforded to such domestic industry, and shall not depart from the provisions of this Agreement relating to non-discrimination;

(j) essential to the acquisition or distribution of products in general or local short supply; *Provided* that any such measures shall be consistent with the principle that all contracting parties are entitled to an equitable share of the international supply of such products, and that any such measures, which are inconsistent with the other provisions of the Agreement shall be discontinued as soon as the conditions giving rise to them have ceased to exist. The CONTRACTING PARTIES shall review the need for this subparagraph not later than 30 June 1960.

Despite the common origin of the general exceptions provisions contained within IIAs, nuances and differences can be seen across treaty practice with regard to two main issues: (1) the scope of the measures that they cover; and (2) the conditions attached to the exceptions.

7.1.2.1 The Scope of General Exceptions Provisions

In virtually all IIAs, general exceptions provisions cover those State measures relating to (1) the protection of human, animal or plant life or health, and (2) the conservation of exhaustible natural resources. A few treaties limit the scope of the measures covered by the general exceptions provision to these two series of public interest (e.g. 2016 Rwanda–Turkey IIA, Article 5.1). In addition to these two matters, many IIAs mention *mutatis mutandis* 'compliance with laws and regulations that are not inconsistent with the provisions of [the] Agreements' (e.g. 2016 Canada–Mongolia IIA, Article 17.1) and sometimes the protection of public morals or the maintenance of public order (e.g. 2017 Hong Kong SAR China–ASEAN IIA, Article 9.1).

The threshold for measures aiming at the protection of public morals or the maintenance of public order to be covered is high; the IIAs that refer to these measures usually specify that the 'public order exception may be invoked only where a genuine and sufficiently serious threat is posed to one of the fundamental interests of society' (e.g. 2016 Nigeria–Singapore IIA, Article 28, Footnote 7).

That IIA also illustrates the trend across treaty practice to provide a non-exhaustive list of those measures that are necessary to secure 'compliance with laws and regulations that are not inconsistent with the provisions of the agreement'. In this regard, it lists: (1) the measures relating to the prevention of deceptive and fraudulent practices or those dealing with the effects of a default on a contract; (2) the measures relating to the protection of the privacy of individuals in relation to the processing and dissemination of personal data and the protection of confidentiality of individual records and accounts; and (3) safety.

More exceptionally, treaty practice displays additional measures covered by this provision, notably those imposed for the protection of national treasures of artistic, historic or archaeological value (e.g. 2013 Japan–Mozambique IIA, Article 18).

7.1.2.2 Conditions Attached to General Exceptions

For State measures to fall within the scope of the general exceptions provisions, they must satisfy certain conditions, which are mainly twofold. 'Negatively', they must not be arbitrary or discriminatory and they shall not constitute disguised restrictions on investors and their investments; 'positively', such measures must be necessary. Nuances and differences can be seen across treaty practice as to the exact conditions that IIAs set out.

Non-arbitrariness and/or non-discrimination are systematically provided for in agreements. Some IIAs focus on non-arbitrariness; for instance, Article 18.1 of the 2016 Hong Kong SAR China–Chile IIA requires that State measures be 'not applied in an arbitrary or unjustifiable manner'. Other IIAs focus instead on non-discrimination, like the IIA adopted by Belarus and India in 2018, which provides that the measures shall be 'applied on a non-discriminatory basis in good faith' (Article 32.1). The 2017 Hong Kong SAR China–ASEAN IIA requires that State measures not be 'applied in a manner which would constitute a means of arbitrary or unjustifiable discrimination between the Parties or their investors where like conditions prevail' (Article 9.1). As illustrated by that latter provision, most IIAs usually make it explicit that non-discrimination is not an absolute requirement under such provisions as discrimination shall not be unjustifiable. Also a 'like circumstances' qualification applies as it does with regard to the national treatment and the most-favoured-nation treatment (MFNT) provisions analysed in Chapter 5. In that sense, the 2016 Nigeria–Singapore IIA, which is drafted similarly, specifies 'for greater certainty' that 'the application of the general exceptions to these provisions shall not be interpreted so as to diminish the ability of governments to take measures where investors are not in like circumstances due to the existence of legitimate regulatory objectives' (Article 28, Footnote 6).

Most general exceptions provisions mention that State measures shall be 'necessary' to protect the public interests identified, while some require instead for such measures to be, for instance, 'appropriate' (e.g. Colombia–UAE IIA, Article 11). Yet, those provisions typically do not specify what this entails. As an exception, the 2018 Belarus–India IIA provides that '[i]n considering whether a measure is necessary, the Tribunal shall take into account whether there was no less restrictive alternative measure reasonably available to a Party' (Article 32.1). Contrary to mainstream treaty practice, this specification also makes explicit that the general exceptions under that Agreement is not 'self-judging'. As discussed above, mainstream treaty practice does not address the matter; the lack of 'self-judging' character can only be deduced from the text of these agreements which refers to measures which 'are necessary' and not to measures that 'States parties consider as being necessary'.

7.1.3 Security Exceptions

Preliminary Remarks
IIA security exceptions provisions are akin to general exceptions provisions – they share a similar rationale by providing that IIAs and their provisions shall not be construed in particular as preventing States from adopting a set of measures geared towards the protection of public interests. It is then not surprising that, as mentioned above, they are provided for in the same Article in some IIAs and sometimes under the same title, be it 'security exceptions' or 'general exceptions'. Only, security exceptions have a specific focus; as their name indicates, the State measures covered by these exceptions concern State security.

Those IIA security exceptions provisions also originate from the 1947 GATT; given this origin, it is worth quoting the relevant Article in its entirety:

Nothing in this Agreement shall be construed

(a) to require any contracting party to furnish any information the disclosure of which it considers contrary to its essential security interests; or
(b) to prevent any contracting party from taking any action which it considers necessary for the protection of its essential security interests
    (i) relating to fissionable materials or the materials from which they are derived;

(ii) relating to the traffic in arms, ammunition and implements of war and to such traffic in other goods and materials as is carried on directly or indirectly for the purpose of supplying a military establishment;

(iii) taken in time of war or other emergency in international relations; or

(c) to prevent any contracting party from taking any action in pursuance of its obligations under the United Nations Charter for the maintenance of international peace and security. (Article XXI)

Despite this common origin, IIAs display again some nuances and differences in how the provision is drafted. In practice, one of the situations and types of measures covered by security exceptions provisions, i.e. 'the taking of actions necessary to protect essential security interests', has attracted most of the attention in the context of the series of cases that followed the 2000s Argentinian economic crisis. This is specifically discussed below after the examination of the relevant treaty practice.

7.1.3.1 Security Exceptions Provisions in Treaty Practice

Two main issues require examination in this respect: (1) the scope of the situations and measures covered by the security exceptions provisions; and (2) whether or not they are 'self-judging'.

a The Scope of Security Exceptions Provisions

Like Article XXI of the GATT, IIA security exceptions provisions typically cover three types of situations and measures: (1) no requirement to disclose information contrary to essential security interests; (2) no prevention from taking action necessary for the protection of essential security interests; and (3) no prevention from taking action pursuant to obligations with respect to the maintenance of international peace and security. Some IIAs do not refer to the situations and measures pertaining to the disclosure of information (e.g. 2017 Colombia–UAE IIA, Article 11) or to the maintenance of international peace and security (e.g. 2016 Slovakia–Iran IIA, Article 12).

The drafting of those provisions as to the first type of situations and measures is very consistent across treaty practice. *Mutatis mutandis*, it is provided that IIAs shall not be construed as 'requir[ing] a Party to furnish or allow access to any information the disclosure of which it determines to be contrary to its essential security interests' (2019 Australia–Uruguay IIA, Article 15.2).

Treaty practice also displays consistency with respect to the third type of situations and measures. As seen from the 2018 Turkey–Cambodia IIA, IIAs provide *mutatis mutandis* that '[n]othing in [the] Agreement shall be construed . . . to prevent any Contracting Party from taking action in pursuance of its obligations under the United Nations Charter for the maintenance of international peace and security' (Article 4.2.c).

With respect to the second type of situations and measures, more diversity can be seen across treaty drafting. First of all, although most agreements provide details about which situations and measures this type precisely covers, a few do not, such as Article 13 of the 2019 Brazil–UAE IIA. Second, among those agreements that set out details, some do so by reference to an exhaustive list (e.g. 2017 Hong Kong SAR China–ASEAN IIA, Article 8.b), while others simply provide an illustrative list (e.g. 2016 Argentina–Qatar IIA, Article 13). Be it exhaustive or merely illustrative, these lists vary as to the situations and measures that they encompass. Some are limited to a few sets of situations and measures. For instance, the 2018 Argentina–Japan IIA makes reference to (1) the measures 'taken in times of war, armed conflict, or other emergency situations in that Contracting Party or in international relations', and to (2) the measures 'related to the implementation of national policies or international agreements respecting the non-proliferation of weapons' (Article 16.a). Other lists are much more comprehensive and detailed, as is illustrated by Footnote 10 to Article 19.1.b of the 2019 Australia–Hong Kong SAR China IIA:

> For greater certainty, measures referred to in paragraph 1(b) include: (i) those relating to fissionable and fusionable materials or the materials from which they are derived; (ii) those relating to the traffic in arms, ammunition and implements of war and to such traffic in other goods and materials or relating to the supply of services as carried out directly or indirectly for the purpose of supplying or provisioning a military establishment; (iii) those taken so as to protect critical public infrastructure, whether publicly or privately owned, including communications, power, transport and water infrastructures from deliberate attempts intended to disable, degrade or otherwise interfere with such infrastructures (including measures taken to prevent such attempts); and (iv) those taken in time of national emergency, war or other emergency in international relations.

b The Character of the Security Exceptions

As evidenced below by the discussion of arbitration practice, a key issue pertaining to security exceptions boils down to the question as to whether they are 'self-judging' and 'non-justiciable', meaning respectively whether the host State concerned is the only authority entitled to appraise the situation involved and whether an arbitration tribunal is entitled to review such appraisal.

With regard to the disclosure of information, almost all IIAs refer to the disclosure of information that a State party 'considers' (e.g. 2018 Belarus–India IIA, Article 33.1) or 'determines' (e.g. 2016 Iran–Slovakia IIA, Article 12.a) to be contrary to its essential security interests. On the other hand, Article 13.1.a of the 2016 Argentina–Qatar IIA provides that '[n]othing in this Treaty shall be construed to require a Contracting Party to furnish any information the disclosure of which is deemed contrary to its essential security interests'.

Similar to the above, a number of IIAs refer to the measures that States 'consider necessary' to protect their essential security interests, as can be seen in the above-mentioned 2019 Australia–Hong Kong SAR China IIA. It is worth noting that the 2018 Belarus–India IIA specifies the 'non-justiciable' nature of such measures:

> Where the Party asserts as a defence that conduct alleged to be a breach of its obligations under this Treaty is for the protection of its essential security interests protected by Article 33, any decision of such Party taken on such security considerations and its decision to invoke Article 33 at any time, whether before or after the commencement of arbitral proceedings shall be non-justiciable. It shall not be open to any arbitral tribunal constituted under Chapter IV or Chapter V of this Treaty to review any such decision, even where the arbitral proceedings concern an assessment of any claim for damages and/or compensation, or an adjudication of any other issues referred to such arbitral tribunal. (Annex Security Exceptions)

On the other hand, some IIAs do not refer to measures that States 'consider necessary' to protect their essential security interests. For instance, Article 7.1 of the 2010 Israel–Ukraine IIA provides that '[e]ither Contracting Party may take measures strictly necessary for the maintenance or protection of its essential security interests'. It is noteworthy that such measures shall be 'strictly necessary' and not merely 'necessary', which can be interpreted as setting a higher threshold. Along the same lines, it should be mentioned that this provision – quite exceptionally – provides that those measures intended to protect States' essential security interests shall 'be taken and implemented in good faith, in a non-discriminatory fashion and so as to minimize the deviation from the provisions of this Agreement'.

As to the actions taken pursuant to obligations with respect to the maintenance of international peace and security, IIAs do not usually provide any such textual indication as to the 'self-judging' and 'non-justiciable' character of these actions. There are exceptions, for instance the 2016 Nigeria–Singapore IIA which refers to the 'measures that it [a Party] considers necessary for the fulfilment of its obligations with respect to the maintenance or restoration of international peace or security' (Article 29.b).

7.1.3.2 The Taking of Actions Necessary to Protect Essential Security Interests

As explained in detail in Chapter 15, the Argentinian economic crisis during the 2000s led to numerous arbitration proceedings filed by foreign investors, in particular on the basis of the 1991 United States of America (USA)–Argentina IIA. At the core of the debates between the parties and the awards of tribunals was Article 11, which provides: 'This Treaty shall not preclude the application by either Party of measures necessary for the maintenance of public order, the fulfilment of its obligations with respect to the maintenance or restoration of international peace or security, or the protection of its own essential security interests.'

Three main issues have arisen in respect of this Article: (1) whether economic crises are to be considered as affecting essential security interests; (2) whether that provision has a 'self-judging' character or not; and (3) the interplay between this exception and 'necessity' as a circumstance precluding wrongfulness under CIL.

a The Scope of the Exception

There is no doubt that a severe economic crisis can be seen as affecting States' essential security interests as conceived of under IIA security exception provisions. Such a finding can be supported by several arguments. In *Continental Casualty Company* v. *Argentina*, for instance, the Tribunal reached this conclusion by relying notably on the Preamble of both the UN Charter and the International Monetary Fund Article of Agreement, as well as, more specifically, US treaty practice (2008, Award, paras. 175–177). The Tribunal appointed in *CMS Gas Transmission Company* v. *Argentina* did so, noting that the object and purpose of the USA–Argentina IIA (as well as CIL) does not exclude major economic crises from the scope of Article 11 (2005, Award, para. 359). In fact, this consensus is largely based on the view that an economic crisis can have *mutatis mutandis* an effect as severe as a military action and invasion, as was explained by the Tribunal in *LG&E* v. *Argentina*:

> The Tribunal rejects the notion that Article XI is only applicable in circumstances amounting to military action and war. Certainly, the conditions in Argentina in December 2001 called for immediate, decisive action to restore civil order and stop the economic decline. To conclude that such a severe economic crisis could not constitute an essential security interest is to diminish the havoc that the economy can wreak on the lives of an entire population and the ability of the Government to lead. When a State's economic foundation is under siege, the severity of the problem can equal that of any military invasion. (2006, Decision on Liability, para. 238)

b The Character of the Exception

As discussed above, treaty practice displays diversity, with some IIAs referring to measures that 'States consider necessary' to protect essential security interests, while others to measures which 'are necessary' to reach this objective. Article 11 of the USA–Argentina IIA falls within that second category, which indicates a lack of 'self-judging' character. There was a consensus among those tribunals that had to determine the character of the exception under that

Article that it is not 'self-judging', even if it was considered that it involves a margin of appreciation for the host State which invokes it (*Continental Casualty Company* v. *Argentina*, 2008, Award, para. 187). This consensus was based on the wording of this provision and on the consequences attached to 'self-judging' provisions. This was well explained by the Tribunal appointed in that latter case:

> [C]aution must be exercised in allowing a party unilaterally to escape from its treaty obligations in the absence of clear textual or contextual indications. [footnote omitted] This is especially so if the party invoking the allegedly self-judging nature of the exemption can thereby remove the issue, and hence the claim of a treaty breach by the investor against the host state, from arbitral review. This would conflict in principle with the agreement of the parties to have disputes under the BIT settled compulsorily by arbitration, both between an investor and the host State or between the Contracting Parties, as the case may be. (para. 187)

Along the same lines, the Tribunal in *Sempra Energy International* v. *Argentina* considered, notably in reference to the case law of the International Court of Justice (ICJ), that the language of the provision must be very precise in order to conclude on its 'self-judging' nature (2007, Award, para. 383). Interestingly, in the *Case Concerning Military and Paramilitary Activities in and against Nicaragua (Nicaragua* v. *USA)*, the ICJ contrasted the language of the 1956 Nicaragua–USA Treaty of Friendship, Commerce and Navigation (FCN) – which also refers to 'measures necessary' – with Article XXI of the GATT – which refers to 'measures that the State considers as being necessary' – to reach the conclusion that the former does not contain a 'self-judging' 'security exception' (Judgment, 1986, para. 222). In *Enron Corporation Ponderosa Assets, L.P.* v. *Argentina*, the Tribunal found that to interpret Article 11 of the USA–Argentina IIA as being 'self-judging' would deprive the Agreement of any substantive meaning and would be inconsistent with its object and purpose (2007, Award, para. 332).

As a result of the lack of 'self-judging' character of the exception on which they concluded, tribunals have considered that it was justiciable and that State measures shall be substantially reviewed to appraise whether they were indeed necessary to protect essential security interests. In that sense, the Tribunal in *CMS Gas Transmission Company* v. *Argentina* concluded that the review is not limited to whether the measures are taken in good faith, but that it implies a substantive review (e.g. 2005, Award, para. 374). It is worth noting in this respect that the Tribunal appointed in *LG&E* v. *Argentina* stated, without further elaborating on this statement, that the good faith review that would be conducted, should the exception be considered as being 'self-judging', does not significantly differ from the substantive analysis that it conducted after having decided that the exception is not 'self-judging' (2006, Decision on Liability, para. 214).

c The Interplay between the Exception and 'Necessity' as a Circumstance Precluding Wrongfulness under Customary International Law

The substantive review of measures decided by States to protect their own essential security interests begs in fact the question of the condition of application of the exception. As a starting point, it can be noted that Article 11 of the USA–Argentina IIA, and more generally treaty practice, is silent on this issue. International investment agreements merely provide that State measures shall be necessary to protect essential security interests. In that context, the discussion has crystallised on the role and impact of 'necessity'; as explained in Chapter 15, necessity is a circumstance precluding wrongfulness under the law of State responsibility whose application is strictly subject to the fulfilment of a series of conditions. A number of tribunals have relied on this circumstance precluding wrongfulness.

Some of them have considered that the conditions of the security exception and those of necessity are all the same; in *Sempra Energy International* v. *Argentina*, the Tribunal expressed its belief that Article 11 of the USA–Argentina IIA is 'inseparable from the customary law standard insofar as the definition of necessity and the conditions for its operation are concerned, given that it is under customary law that such elements have been defined' (2007, Award, para. 376). By the same token, the Tribunal in *Enron Corporation Ponderosa Assets, L.P.* v. *Argentina* concluded from the silence of Article 11 that the agreement is inseparable from CIL as to the conditions for the operation of necessity (2007, Award, para. 334). As a result, some have simply deduced from their conclusion that the conditions of necessity were not met in the case, that they were not met either as to the security exception, or that it was unnecessary to undertake a substantial review under the security exception. This approach is well illustrated by the reasoning of the *Enron* Tribunal (para. 339).

Other tribunals have relied on interpretation to link the security exception provision and necessity, in particular on Article 31.3.c of the 1969 Vienna Convention on the Law of Treaties (VCLT) pursuant to which there shall be taken into account in the interpretation 'any relevant rules of international law applicable in the relations between the Parties' (e.g. *El Paso Energy International Company* v. *Argentina*, 2011, Award, paras. 613 and 616–617). On this basis in particular, that Tribunal concluded that the requirement that measures be 'necessary' under Article 11 of the USA–Argentina IIA presupposes that the State had not contributed to creating the situation that it then relied on when claiming the lawfulness of its measures.

In contrast, others have strongly opposed any reliance on necessity. For instance, in *Continental Casualty Company* v. *Argentina*, the Tribunal rejected the above-mentioned views of the *Enron* Tribunal concerning the inseparability of Article 11 of the USA–Argentina IIA and necessity as to the conditions for its operation, due to the specific role of necessity, discussed in Chapter 15. On the other hand, it stressed the 'filial link' between that Article and Article XX of the 1947 GATT, through the US FCN treaties, and therefore relied on the GATT and WTO case law instead. On this basis, it inquired whether the measures decided by Argentina were apt and did contribute materially and decisively to the protection of its essential security interests in the context of the economic and social crisis it was facing (2008, Award, paras. 192 and 196). In the same vein, the Annulment Committee in *Sempra Energy International* v. *Argentina*, after rejecting the idea that CIL establishes a peremptory definition of necessity and of the conditions of its operation, denied that it offered a guide to the interpretation of Article 11. It did so mainly by stressing their different roles, explaining:

> More importantly, Article 25 is concerned with the invocation by a State Party of necessity 'as a ground for precluding the wrongfulness of an act not in conformity with an international obligation of that State'. Article 25 presupposes that an act has been committed that is incompatible with the State's international obligations and is therefore 'wrongful'. Article XI, on the other hand, provides that 'This Treaty shall not preclude' certain measures so that, where Article XI applies, the taking of such measures is not incompatible with the State's international obligations and is not therefore 'wrongful'. Article 25 and Article XI therefore deal with quite different situations. Article 25 cannot therefore be assumed to 'define necessity and the conditions for its operation' for the purpose of interpreting Article XI, still less to do so as a mandatory norm of international law. (2010, Annulment Decision, para. 200)

7.1.4 Taxation

Taxation is at the core of States' sovereign prerogatives; it is crucial for the functioning and even for the very existence of States, providing them with the financial means to achieve their public interest goals. It then comes as no surprise that IIA States parties have aimed at limiting foreign investors' protection with regard to taxation by excluding it from the scope of application of IIAs. This limitation can be found in particular in specific provisions devoted to taxation (e.g. 2019 Australia–Uruguay IIA, Article 16), in provisions delineating the scope of application of the agreements (e.g. 2017 Hong Kong SAR China–ASEAN IIA, Article 2.2.c), or in general exceptions provisions (e.g. 2016 Slovakia–Iran IIA, Article 11.3).

Irrespective of where it is 'located' in IIAs, two main issues arise from this limitation: (1) the scope of the taxation limitation; and (2) the identification of the measures falling into its scope.

7.1.4.1 The Scope of the Limitation

The scope of the taxation limitation varies across treaty practice with regard to both the taxation measures and the IIA provisions concerned.

Adopting a radical approach, some agreements purely exclude all taxation measures from their entire scope of application, as does, for instance, the Slovakia–Iran IIA which provides that 'the provisions of this Agreement shall not apply to ... taxation measures' (Article 11.3).

Other treaties provide for a very large exclusion, except with regard to States' obligations under the expropriation provision (e.g. 2017 Hong Kong SAR China–Chile IIA, Article 14) and under the transfer provision (e.g. 2017 Hong Kong SAR China–ASEAN IIA, Article 2.2.c) typically. It can be noted that as part of the Work Programme set out in Article 22, this latter Agreement provides that the Parties shall enter into discussions on the application of the expropriation provision to taxation measures that constitute expropriation. As for the expropriation provision, it is worth stressing that IIAs typically provide for a 'filter mechanism' to decide whether a taxation measure can be considered as an expropriation justiciable before an arbitration tribunal. For instance, Article 16 of the 2019 Australia–Uruguay IIA provides:

1. Except as provided in this Article, nothing in this Agreement shall apply to taxation measures.
2. Article 7 (Expropriation) shall apply to taxation measures. However, no investor may invoke Article 7 as the basis for a claim if it has been determined pursuant to this paragraph that the measure is not an expropriation. An investor that seeks to invoke Article 7 with respect to a taxation measure must first refer to the competent authorities of the Party of the investor and the respondent Party, at the time that it gives its notice of arbitration under Article 14.9, the issue of whether that taxation measure is not an expropriation. If the competent authorities do not agree to consider the issue or, having agreed to consider it, fail to agree that the measure is not an expropriation within a period of six months of the referral, the investor may submit its claim to arbitration under Article 14.

In some IIAs, the scope of the taxation limitation is more limited. For instance, the 2016 Canada–Mongolia IIA excludes its application to taxation measures with regard to the provisions pertaining to the minimum standard of treatment, compensation for losses, senior management, board of directors and entry of personnel, as well as performance requirements and transfers (Article 16.7). As for the national treatment and the MFNT provisions, the exclusion pertains only to specific taxation measures detailed in Article 16.8:

Articles 4 (National Treatment) and 5 (Most-Favoured-Nation Treatment) shall not apply to:

1. taxation measures on income, capital gains, or the taxable capital of corporations; or
2. any new taxation measure that is aimed at ensuring the equitable and effective imposition or collection of taxes (including, for greater certainty, any measure that is taken by a Party to ensure compliance with the Party's

taxation system or to prevent the avoidance or evasion of taxes) providing that the measure does not arbitrarily discriminate between persons, goods or services of the Parties.

7.1.4.2 The Identification of Taxation Measures

As evidenced by various cases initiated against Ecuador in the 2010s, IIAs that provide for a taxation limitation may raise complex issues boiling down to the determination of the measures that fall into its scope. At stake in those cases was, for instance, the question of whether VAT (*EnCana Corporation v. Ecuador*) or custom duties (*Duke Energy Electroquil v. Ecuador)* can be characterised as taxation measures, or whether a measure that is not enacted as a tax or as a part of the national tax law regime can be so characterised (*Murphy Exploration & Production Company International v. Ecuador*).

In this context, it is worth highlighting the incorporation in some IIAs of provisions intended to provide clarification as to the measures to be considered as taxation measures.

Content-wise, some agreements specify the law applicable to the characterisation of State measures, or the types of measures covered. For instance, Article 1.8 of the 2016 Slovakia–Iran IIA provides that '[t]he term "taxation measures" refers to any tax measure under applicable law of the Host State'. In the same vein, the 2016 Hong Kong SAR China–Chile IIA defines taxation measures as 'any measure relating to direct or indirect taxes' and specifies that customs duties are not included in this definition (Article 1).

Alternatively, or in some cases cumulatively, some IIAs provide for a mechanism allocating the authority to decide on whether a measure is a taxation measure falling under the scope of the taxation limitation. Among those agreements, two approaches can be identified. Most agreements grant the main responsibility for making this determination to the States parties jointly, and in the case that it is not made within a specific time frame, this responsibility is transferred to the arbitration tribunal. This approach is illustrated by Article 14.6 of the 2016 Canada–Hong Kong SAR China IIA, which provides:

> If, in connection with a claim by an investor of a Party or a dispute between the Parties, an issue arises as to whether a measure of a Party is a taxation measure, a Party may refer the issue to the taxation authorities of the Parties. A joint determination of the taxation authorities shall bind a Tribunal formed pursuant to Section C (Settlement of Disputes between an Investor and the Host Party) or an arbitral panel formed pursuant to Section D (Settlement of Disputes between the Parties). A Tribunal or arbitral panel seized of a claim or a dispute in which the issue arises may not proceed until it receives the joint determination of the taxation authorities. If the taxation authorities have not determined the issue within six months from the date of the referral, the Tribunal or arbitral panel shall decide the issue.

On the other hand, the 2018 Belarus–India IIA grants a discretionary power to the host State to make the determination and makes this determination 'non-justiciable'. Article 2.4 clarifies 'for greater certainty' that 'where the State in which investment is made, decides that conduct alleged to be a breach of its obligations under this Treaty is a subject matter of taxation, such decision of that State, whether before or after the commencement of arbitral proceedings, shall be non-justiciable and it shall not be open to any arbitration tribunal to review such decision'.

7.1.5 Public Debts

In the aftermath of high-profile cases involving, in particular, Argentina, such as *Abaclat and Others* v. *Argentina*, and the criticism that they attracted, public debts have become a very sensitive issue in international investment law and arbitration. This has led some States to incorporate provisions in their IIAs aiming to protect States' prerogatives as regards these matters. In addition to the exclusion of public debts from the scope of the definition of an investment under the agreements (e.g. 2017 Israel–Japan IIA, Article 1.a) and specifications concerning the default and non-payment of debts (e.g. 2017 Colombia–UAE IIA, Protocol), those provisions tackle mainly the restructuring of debts with a view to limiting investors' protection in this respect. More precisely, they address and differentiate between negotiated restructuring and restructuring issued by host States, the former leading to a greater limitation of the protection granted to foreign investors by the agreements.

As set out by the 2016 Comprehensive and Economic Trade Agreement (CETA), 'negotiated restructuring' means *mutatis mutandis* 'the restructuring or rescheduling of debt of a Party that has been effected through (a) a modification or amendment of debt instruments, as provided for under their terms, including their governing law, or (b) a debt exchange or other similar process in which the holders of no less than 75 per cent of the aggregate principal amount of the outstanding debt subject to restructuring have consented to such debt exchange or other process' (Annex 8.B.1).

   With regard to such negotiated restructuring, IIAs consistently provide that no claim that an IIA obligation has been breached shall be made, or that it shall be discontinued if a restructuring is negotiated after it has been initiated. As an exception to this principle, they do not prevent such claims as to alleged breaches of the national treatment and MFNT obligations (e.g. 2018 Comprehensive and Progressive Agreement for Trans-Pacific Partnership (CPTPP), Annex 9-G.2). It is worth noting that even those claims concerning the national treatment and the MFNT obligations are prohibited with regard in particular to Singapore under that Agreement (Footnote 43). This exception concerning Singapore also applies to the restructuring issued by host States under that Agreement.

As to those restructurings issued by host States, IIAs provide classically for two rules applicable to different time periods in the dispute settlement process. This is well illustrated by Annex 8-B.3 of the 2016 CETA. It provides that an investor cannot submit a claim that a restructuring of debt is in breach of a Party's substantive obligations, except claims relating to the national treatment and the MFNT obligations, within 270 days from the date of submission of the request for consultation it has submitted. After the expiration of that period, there is no such limitation and claims can be made with regard to all substantive provisions.

It is noteworthy that this Agreement contains a specification that aims at limiting the scope of differential treatments that may be considered as a breach of the national treatment and the MFNT obligations. Footnote 7 provides 'for greater certainty' that 'mere differences in treatment accorded by a Party to certain investors or investments on the basis of legitimate policy objectives in the context of a debt crisis or a threat thereof, including those differences in treatment resulting from eligibility for debt restructuring, do not amount to a breach of Article 8.6 [national treatment] or 8.7 [most-favoured-nation treatment]'.

7.1.6 Financial and Monetary Matters

Specific State measures relating to financial and monetary matters are also largely excluded from the scope of application of IIAs, which thereby limits investors' protection in their respect.

As regards financial matters, IIAs provide *mutatis mutandis* that notwithstanding any other provisions of the agreements, a contracting party shall not be prevented from adopting measures for prudential reasons, including for the protection of investors, depositors, policy holders or persons to whom a fiduciary duty is owed by a financial service supplier, or to ensure the integrity and stability of the financial system (2018 Sri Lanka–Singapore IIA, Article 10.2.3). As in that Agreement, some IIAs make it clear that where such measures do not conform with the substantive provisions protecting investors, they shall not be used as a means of avoiding the Party's commitments or obligations. Instead of this good-faith specification, others provide that such measures shall be 'reasonable' (e.g. 2016 Canada–Mongolia IIA, Article 17.2). It is also worth noting that a few agreements provide for a mechanism aiming at the determination of the measures falling within the scope of this limitation; for instance, the 2017 China–Hong Kong SAR China IIA provides that resolution of such issues shall be sought through consultation by the financial services authorities of the two sides (Article 23.1, Footnote 12).

Provisions pertaining to monetary matters set out *mutatis mutandis* that the IIA does not apply to non-discriminatory measures of general application taken by a public entity in pursuit of monetary and related credit or exchange rate policies (2014 Canada–Serbia IIA, Article 18.3). In those agreements, this limitation applies typically to most, but not all, provisions. For instance, that Agreement specifies that it does not affect State parties' obligations with regard to performance requirements and transfers. In the same vein, the 2018 Belarus–India IIA provides that it is 'without prejudice' to States parties' obligations as regards transfers only (Article 32.2).

7.2 Limitations Applying to Specific IIA Provisions

The protection conferred to foreign investors by a number of specific provisions is typically curbed by limitations. Depending on the IIA, one and the same limitation can apply to more than one specific provision; this holds true in particular with regard to the national treatment and the MFNT provisions. Regardless of this exact number, those specific provisions that are mainly concerned with limitations pertain to (1) expropriation, (2) the national treatment and the MFNT, (3) transfers, and (4) performance requirements.

7.2.1 Expropriation

As discussed in Chapter 6, expropriation is a fundamental prerogative of States. For that reason, foreign investors have traditionally not been conferred an absolute protection against expropriation under public international law and IIAs, but instead a protection against those expropriations which do not fulfil conditions of legality.

In relation to the criticism pursuant to which the protection of foreign investors against indirect expropriation is a threat to the right of States to regulate, some States in their treaty practice during the 2010s have limited the protection traditionally conferred on investors by IIAs against the measures having an effect equivalent to expropriation, otherwise known as 'indirect expropriations'. Notably, Brazil has chosen to exclude those measures from the scope of the expropriation provision. This is well illustrated by the 2019 Brazil–UAE IIA, which provides: 'For greater certainty, this Article only provides for direct expropriation, where an investment is nationalized or otherwise directly expropriated through formal transfer of title or ownership rights, and does not cover indirect expropriation' (Article 7.5).

Less radically, India has decided to exclude in its 2015 Model BIT non-discriminatory regulatory measures as well as measures and awards by judicial bodies designed and applied to protect legitimate public interests from the scope of the prohibition of illegal expropriations by specifying that such measures do not constitute expropriation. This has been implemented in Article 5.5 of the 2018 Belarus–India IIA. Such a provision can be seen as a limitation inasmuch as it does not foresee any situation in which such measures may be characterised as an indirect expropriation, contrary to mainstream treaty practice on the matter.

As explained in Chapter 6, this mainstream practice has been modelled on the 2004 US Model BIT. It can be illustrated by Annex 8-A.3 of the 2016 CETA, which provides: 'For greater certainty, except in the rare circumstance when the impact of a measure or series of measures is so severe in light of its purpose that it appears manifestly excessive, non-discriminatory measures of a Party that are designed and applied to protect legitimate public welfare objectives, such as health, safety and the environment, do not constitute indirect expropriations.' Such a provision does not exist as a limitation to the protection accorded by IIAs to investors against indirect expropriation precisely because it does not radically exclude that such measures may constitute an indirect expropriation. More fundamentally, it can be construed as a 'reminder', 'for greater certainty', that under the law of expropriation such measures cannot be deemed to be an indirect expropriation unless they have a manifestly excessive impact.

7.2.2 Differential Treatment

Limitations exist in IIAs as to the protection afforded to investors against differential treatments, namely under the national treatment and the MFNT provisions. There is some diversity as to the types of limitations across IIA practice, which reflects the policy interests and priorities of IIA States parties. In this respect, it is worth noting at the outset that some of these limitations are drafted so as to apply either to only one or to a few States parties to those IIAs.

7.2.2.1 National Treatment

A typical limitation concerning the national treatment provision concerns cross-border capital transactions in situations of extreme economic and monetary difficulties, which are considered as justifying the adoption or maintenance by States of safeguard measures that are not in conformity with their obligations under that provision.

More precisely, this limitation is applicable *mutatis mutandis* in two situations: (1) in the event of serious balance of payments and external financial difficulties, or a threat thereof; and (2) in those exceptional circumstances where the movements of capital cause or threaten to cause serious difficulties for macroeconomic management, in particular monetary and exchange rate policies (2017 Hong Kong SAR China–ASEAN IIA, Article 13.1).

It is important to stress that this limitation on the protection conferred by the national treatment provision to investors has a temporary dimension; such safeguard measures shall stop as soon as the situation permits. In addition to this temporal condition, the measures decided in those situations of extreme economic and monetary difficulties shall meet *mutatis mutandis* four main conditions – which pertain to substance and procedure – in order to fall within the scope of the limitation: (1) they shall be consistent with the Articles of Agreement of the International Monetary Fund; (2) they shall not exceed what is necessary to deal with those situations; (3) they shall avoid unnecessary damage to the commercial, economic and financial interests of the other State party; and (4) they shall be promptly notified to it (2015 Japan–Oman IIA, Article 17.2).

In addition to this limitation, treaty practice displays other limitations that cover a broad range of measures or issues. The IIA adopted by France and Ethiopia in 2003 provides, for instance, that the protection of investors against differential treatment *vis-à-vis* nationals does not apply to tax matters (Article 4). In the same vein, Article 4.6 of the 2016 Iran–Slovakia IIA specifies that the national treatment provision does not apply to government procurement, subsidies or grants provided by States parties.

7.2.2.2 Most-Favoured-Nation Treatment

The main limitation that has traditionally been placed on the protection granted by the MFNT provision to foreign investors against differential treatment suffered *vis-à-vis* other foreign investors relates to preferential treatment accorded in the context of trade/economic cooperation. It aims in particular at avoiding the far-reaching economic and societal consequences that would result from the extension of such treatment through that provision. This limitation is *mutatis mutandis* illustrated by Article 4.4 of the 2010 Switzerland–Trinidad and Tobago IIA: 'If a Contracting Party accords special advantages to investors of any third State by virtue of an agreement establishing a free trade area, a customs union or a common market or by virtue of an international agreement regarding matters of taxation, it shall not be obliged to accord such advantages to investors of the other Contracting Party.'

In addition to that limitation, treaty practice displays a broad set of less frequent limitations on the protection conferred by the MFNT provision to foreign investors, some of which it shares with the national treatment provision, as illustrated by the above-mentioned limitations set by the Ethiopia–France IIA and the Iran–Slovakia IIA. For instance, the 2016 Hong Kong SAR China–Chile IIA provides that the MFNT provision shall not apply to treatment accorded by a State party under any bilateral or multilateral agreement or arrangement relating to aviation, fisheries and maritime matters (Annex 3.2.b).

Among those less frequent limitations, it is worth singling out the limitation incorporated in the Iran–Slovakia IIA – which is also applicable to the national treatment provision – relating to the right of States to regulate. Article 4.4 provides that a measure of the Contracting party that treats investors of the other State or their investments less favourably than investors of a third State or their investments is not inconsistent with the MFNT obligation 'if it is adopted and applied by the Contracting Party in pursuit of a legitimate public purpose that is not based on the nationality of the investor or of nationality of the owner of an investment, either explicitly or factually, including the protection of health, safety, the environment, and internationally and domestically recognized labor rights, or the elimination of bribery and corruption, and [if] it bears a reasonable connection to the stated purpose'.

7.2.3 Transfers

As explained in Chapter 3, the right of repatriation and transfer is a provision typically included in IIAs which protects investors against State measures that may restrict or prohibit notably the transfer of their profits, or the proceeds of the sale or liquidation of their investments. This protection can be subject to limitations in two sets of situations that pertain respectively to (1) the 'regulation of society' in general, and, more specifically, to (2) the situations – as discussed above – of extreme economic and monetary difficulties.

7.2.3.1 The Regulation of Society

The scope of the situations and matters covered by the limitation on the right of repatriation and transfer varies across IIA practice. As a common denominator, virtually all relevant IIA provisions refer *mutatis mutandis* to: (1) bankruptcy, insolvency or the protection of the rights of creditors; (2) criminal or penal offences; and (3) ensuring the compliance with orders or judgments in legal or administrative proceedings relating to investments. A minority of treaties refer only to these three items (e.g. 2016 Argentina–Qatar IIA, Article 7.4). Most agreements add other situations and matters; they usually refer *mutatis mutandis* to a combination of the following: 'issuing, trading, or dealing in securities, features, options or derivatives', 'financial reporting or record keeping of transfers when necessary to assist law enforcement or financial regulatory authorities' (e.g. 2005 Georgia–Latvia IIA, Article 7.4), 'social security, public retirement, or compulsory savings schemes (e.g. 2016 Nigeria–Singapore IIA, Article 7.3), or 'taxation' (e.g. 2017 Rwanda–UAE IIA, Article 10.3). A few IIAs contain an even longer list of situations – for instance, Article 12.3 of the 2017 Hong Kong SAR China–ASEAN IIA provides:

> Notwithstanding paragraphs 1 and 2, a Party may prevent or delay a transfer through the equitable, non-discriminatory, and good faith application of its laws and regulations relating to any of the following:
>
> (a) bankruptcy, insolvency, or the protection of the rights of creditors;
> (b) issuing, trading, or dealing in securities, futures, options, or derivatives;
> (c) criminal or penal offences and the recovery of the proceeds of crime;
> (d) financial reporting or record keeping of transfers when necessary to assist law enforcement or financial regulatory authorities;
> (e) ensuring compliance with orders or judgments in judicial or administrative proceedings;
> (f) taxation;

(g) social security, public retirement, or compulsory savings schemes;

(h) severance entitlements of employees; and

(i) requirement to register and satisfy other transfer formalities imposed by the Central Bank or other relevant authorities of a Party.

Like all the above-mentioned IIAs, most agreements refer to these situations and matters – irrespective of their number – in an exhaustive manner. On the contrary, the 2018 Belarus–India IIA, which makes reference to eleven situations and matters, contains merely an illustrative list (Article 6.3).

Whatever the list that they contain, all IIAs provide that they justify restrictions on transfer *mutatis mutandis* through the equitable, non-discriminatory and good-faith application of their laws and regulations by States, as illustrated by Article 12.3 of the Hong Kong SAR China–ASEAN IIA. At the same time, nuances and differences can be seen across treaty practice as to the type of restrictions permitted. Some agreements provide that States can prevent a transfer in such situations (e.g. 2009 Canada–Jordan IIA, Article 14.3); less radically, some authorise States only to delay a transfer (e.g. 2016 Argentina–Qatar IIA, Article 7.4). Others refer to both types of restriction (e.g. 2010 Congo–Mauritius IIA, Article 6.3). It is worth noting that the Belarus–India IIA provides for the possibility of conditioning a transfer (Article 6.3).

7.2.3.2 Situations of Extreme Economic and Monetary Difficulties

As with national treatment, a number of IIAs entitle States to adopt temporary safeguard measures that restrict transfers in situations of extreme economic and monetary difficulties. Most agreements cover *mutatis mutandis* those two types of situations: (1) serious balance of payments and external financial difficulties, or a threat thereof; and (2) exceptional circumstances in which movements of capital cause or threaten to cause serious difficulties for macroeconomic management, in particular monetary and exchange rate policies (e.g. 2016 Japan–Kenya IIA, Article 17.1). A few IIAs refer only to serious difficulties or threats pertaining to balance of payments (e.g. 2016 UAE–Mexico IIA, Article 7.3), while others make reference to additional situations, such as the 2016 Rwanda–Morocco IIA, which mentions the protection of the rights of creditors (Article 6.3.c).

It is interesting to note that some IIAs concluded in the 2010s by Nigeria contain a specific paragraph that stresses the specific problems and needs of developing States in this respect: 'It is recognized that particular pressures on the balance of payments of a Party in the process of economic development may necessitate the use of restrictions to ensure, inter alia, the maintenance of a level of financial reserves adequate for the implementation of its program of economic development' (2016 Morocco–Nigeria IIA, Article 12.1).

Many agreements do not specify the types of restrictions permitted, but a few treaties do so. For instance, Article 7.4 of the 2014 Pakistan–Bahrain IIA provides that transfers shall 'be subject to such reasonable regulatory procedures as shall, from time to time, be in force in the host State and shall likewise be subject to the right of the government of the host State to impose reasonable restrictions for temporary periods not exceeding three months to meet situations of fundamental economic disequilibrium provided that at least 50 percent of such transfers are allowed to be repatriated during such periods'.

As to the requirements attached to those restrictions on transfers in situations of extreme economic and monetary difficulties, the temporary nature of the restrictions is a common denominator of IIAs. In that sense, some treaties specify that the restrictions shall be eliminated as soon as the conditions permit (e.g. 2016 Rwanda–Morocco IIA, Article 6.4.b). As illustrated by the above-mentioned 2014 Pakistan–Bahrain IIA, a few set a time limit during which restrictions are permitted. A few agreements mention only the temporary nature of this limitation (e.g. 2018 Belarus–India IIA, Article 6.4), while most of them contain additional substantive and procedural requirements.

Substantive requirements consist notably of imposing that the restrictions be non-discriminatory and based on good faith (e.g. 2016 Rwanda–Turkey IIA, Article 8.3). International investment agreements also typically require that the restrictions be 'necessary' (e.g. 2016 UAE–Mexico IIA, Article 7.3), 'proportionate' (e.g. 2017 Rwanda–UAE IIA, Article 10.4) or 'reasonable' (2014 Pakistan–Bahrain IIA, Article 7.4). Some, like the Rwanda–UAE IIA, also provide that restrictions on transfer be consistent with the International Monetary Fund Articles of Agreement.

The procedural requirements classically consist of an obligation upon States to notify restrictions to the other State party or parties (e.g. 2016 Rwanda–Morocco IIA, Article 6.4.c). Nigerian practice is again interesting here as the treaties it concluded in the 2010s incorporate an obligation upon the restricting State to initiate consultations with the other State party in order to review the restrictions adopted (e.g. 2016 Nigeria–Singapore IIA, Article 8.4).

7.2.4 Performance Requirements

As explained in Chapter 3, host States can be tempted, for instance in order to stimulate the activity of their domestic enterprises or to modernise their industries, to take the best advantage of the presence of foreign investors in their territory by imposing on them performance requirements. This can consist of requiring them to achieve a given level of domestic content or transfer of technology, for example. Foreign investors are protected under IIAs against State measures imposing such performance requirements.

Nevertheless, such a protection is subject to some limitations. The matters, sectors or situations covered by the limitation across the various treaties are very diverse, with some being very specific. In the 2017 China–Hong Kong SAR China IIA, this limitation covers, for instance, traditional arts and crafts, Chinese medicines and lands (Table 2, Item 3). Other limitations are akin to the broad limitations analysed above concerning the right of States to regulate and those based on Article XX of the 1947 GATT.

As to the limitations on the prohibition of performance requirements relating to the right of States to regulate, Article 9.10.3.h of the 2018 CPTPP provides, for instance, that the prohibition placed upon States parties preventing them notably from requiring investors to purchase, use or accord a preference to their technology or the technology of one of their persons shall not be construed as preventing a Party from adopting or maintaining measures to protect legitimate public welfare objectives, provided that such measures are not applied in an arbitrary or unjustifiable manner, or in a manner that constitutes a disguised restriction on international trade or investment.

As regards those limitations relating to general exceptions, the 2018 Korea–Republics of Central America IIA provides, for example, that the prohibition against requiring the transfer of a particular technology, a production process or other proprietary knowledge to a person in its territory shall not be construed as preventing a State party from adopting or maintaining measures, including environmental measures, (1) necessary to secure compliance with laws and regulations that are not inconsistent with this Agreement; (2) necessary to protect human, animal or plant life or health; or (3) related to the conservation of living or non-living exhaustible natural resources (Article 9.9.3.c). Like general exceptions based on Article XX of the 1947 GATT, such measures, to fall within the scope of that limitation, shall not be applied in an arbitrary or unjustifiable manner and shall not constitute a disguised restriction on international trade or investment.

8

Obligations to Protect and Respect Public Interests

Introduction

Along with the increasing reference to public interest considerations in the pre-amble of many international investment agreements (IIAs), obligations geared at ensuring the respect and the protection of public interests have gained a progressive importance in treaty practice since the 1990s. Even though these obligations are not widespread, they constitute a noticeable evolution in international investment law. This evolution results from the combined effect of developments within this field and, more broadly, of systemic trends at play in public international law.

From 'within' international investment law, the incorporation of these obligations in IIAs is to a certain extent a response by States to the critics who denounce the imbalanced nature of international investment law. In this way, these States seek to re-equilibrate the traditional relationship between investors' rights and interests on the one hand, and their obligations towards societies, on the other. This approach is similar to the developments in public international law that aim to impose responsibility on non-State actors, in particular multinational corporations, *vis-à-vis* local societies. These developments intersect the broader concern of providing a greater protection to human rights *sensu largo* and sustainable development.

In this respect, it is noteworthy that the fulfilment of these objectives has traditionally been searched for in public international law through obligations placed upon States. This helps to explain why the relevant IIAs incorporate obligations placed primarily upon States and less frequently upon investors as a means of ensuring the protection and respect of the public interests attached to human rights and sustainable development. In line with this duality in terms of addressees, this chapter will in turn analyse the obligations placed upon States and those placed upon foreign investors.

Before doing so, it is worth stressing that those obligations and the evolution of which they form part have the potential to contribute towards enhancing the enforcement of human rights in particular. Likewise, they can be seen as contributing towards the 'horizontalisation' of human rights law, meaning the trend at play in public international law towards placing human rights obligations upon non-State actors, and in particular upon multinational corporations.

8.1 Obligations upon States

Among the obligations that are addressed de jure to States in relation to the protection and the respect of public interests, a distinction can be made between two series of obligations: those that pertain to their own conduct, and those that are connected to the conduct of investors. Each category of obligation is analysed in turn below.

8.1.1 Obligations Pertaining to States' Conduct

For the purpose of this analysis, two types of State obligations pertaining to their own conduct can be distinguished: (1) the obligations that aim at ensuring that States protect public interests; and (2) those that are intended to prevent them lowering the protection accorded to those interests. These obligations have the potential to contribute to the better enforcement by States of their obligations under international human rights law and international labour law in particular.

8.1.1.1 The Obligations to Protect Public Interests

The material scope of the public interests that these obligations seek to protect varies across IIA practice. From the various formulae found in IIAs, they appear to usually relate to the environment, labour and human rights.

This can be seen from the 2016 Morocco–Nigeria IIA, which is in many respects a 'pioneer' in treaty practice as regards the protection of public interests. Its Article 15.5 provides: 'Each Party shall ensure that its laws and regulations provide for high levels of labour and human rights protection appropriate to its economic and social situation, and shall strive to continue to improve these law and regulations.' It is worth noting that this IIA also places upon States parties the obligation 'to ensure that their laws, policies and actions are consistent with the international human rights agreements to which they are a Party' (Article 15.6). The object of the obligation found in Article 15.5, and in similarly drafted obligations in other IIAs, is to ensure that States' laws and regulations confer sufficient protection on labour and human rights. A similar objective is pursued in other treaties for the environment. For instance, Article 10.2 of the 2016 Slovakia–Iran IIA provides:

> Recognizing the right of each Contracting Party to establish its own level of environmental protection and its own sustainable development policies and priorities, and to adopt or modify its environmental laws and regulations, each Contracting Party shall ensure that its laws and regulations provide for

appropriate levels of environmental protection and shall strive to continue to improve those laws and regulations.

Notably, those obligations make no reference to investment considerations, which may be interpreted as conferring a broad outreach upon them.

At the same time, the drafting of most of them confers some flexibility on States in the realisation of their objective. For instance, they place upon States the obligation to provide an 'appropriate' protection, the Morocco–Nigeria IIA specifying that this appropriate protection depends on the economic and social situation of States parties. Furthermore, the obligation pertaining to the improvement of laws and regulations, which typically refers to the duty to 'strive' – as illustrated by the two treaties quoted above – are not obligations of result but rather obligations of best efforts. As explained in Chapter 5 with respect to the full protection and security standard, this means that States parties do not have a duty to improve their laws and regulations as such, but rather to do their utmost to realise this objective.

8.1.1.2 The Obligations Not to Lower the Protection of Public Interests

a   Treaty Practice

The IIA obligations analysed in this subsection are those that aim to avoid the lowering by host States of the protection afforded to public interests in order to encourage the establishment, acquisition, expansion or retention of investments. Article 10.1 of the 2016 Slovakia–Iran IIA provides a good illustration of this objective: 'The Contracting Parties recognize that it is inappropriate to encourage investment by relaxing labor, public health, safety or environmental measures. They shall not waive or otherwise derogate from, or offer to waive or otherwise derogate from, such measures as an encouragement for the establishment, acquisition, expansion or retention in their territories, of an investment.'

Beyond this common teleological denominator, IIAs display some differences as regards (1) the 'bindingness' of those provisions; (2) the settlement of disputes arising from their alleged violation; (3) the types of conduct they prohibit; and (4) their scope.

i Bindingness   Contrary, for instance, to the Slovakia–Iran IIA, which uses binding language, meaning 'shall' ('shall not waive or otherwise derogate from, or offer to waive or otherwise derogate from'), a number of IIAs use a 'soft law' language, typically by referring to 'should' (e.g. 2018 Japan–Jordan IIA, Article 20). This has the obvious effect of watering down the bindingness of such treaty provisions.

ii Dispute Settlement   A few of those provisions offer procedural indications as to dispute settlement. This is illustrated by Article 15 of the 2016 Canada–Mongolia IIA, which provides: 'If a Party considers that the other Party has offered such an encouragement, it may request consultations with the other Party and the two

Parties shall consult with a view to avoiding any such encouragement.' It is worth noting the political nature of such a dispute settlement mechanism as opposed to the use of a legal method, i.e. arbitration, to settle investor–State disputes in particular.

iii The Types of Conduct Prohibited   Concerning the types of conduct prohibited, all IIAs cover waivers and derogations as well as offers to waive and offers to derogate. For the sake of clarity, mention is only made to 'waivers' and 'derogations' in what follows. Some of the agreements cover only this conduct, as illustrated by the above-mentioned Slovakia–Iran IIA. Other agreements, in addition to waivers and derogations, cover also 'the failure to effectively enforce laws through a sustained or recurring course of action or inaction' (e.g. 2016 Morocco–Nigeria IIA, Article 15.2). One should stress the requirement that the failure must have a *sustained or recurring* dimension, a requirement that is not attached to the prohibition of waivers and derogations.

iv The Scope of the Conduct Prohibited   As for the scope of the conduct prohibited, a number of remarks can be made concerning the types of public interests protected and the origin of the investments concerned.

– **The Types of Public Interests Protected**   International investment agreements most often provide for an exhaustive list of those protected public interests. They pertain mainly to the protection of the environment and labour. In some agreements, they are the only interests protected, either alone (e.g. 2016 China–Hong Kong SAR China IIA, Article 25 – which mentions only the 'environment' – or the 2016 Morocco–Nigeria IIA, Article 15 – which mentions only 'labour') or in combination (e.g. 2017 Colombia–United Arab Emirates (UAE) IIA, Article 10.2). '(Domestic) health and safety' is also sometimes mentioned together with the 'environment' (e.g. 2016 Nigeria–Singapore IIA, Article 10), or with the 'environment' and 'labour' (e.g. 2016 Japan–Kenya IIA, Article 22). The 2017 Rwanda–UAE IIA refers also to 'security' (Article 9.2). Instead of an exhaustive list, a few IIAs provide a non-exhaustive list of the public interests protected. For instance, Article 15.2 of the 2016 Hong Kong SAR China–Chile IIA refers to 'other regulatory objectives':

> The Parties recognise that it is inappropriate to encourage investment by relaxing their measures related to environmental, health or other regulatory objectives. Accordingly, a Party should not waive or otherwise derogate from, or offer to waive or otherwise derogate from, those measures to encourage the establishment, acquisition, expansion or retention in its area of an investment of an investor of the other Party.

The prohibition against waiving and derogating is usually not provided in the abstract – such conduct is prohibited in relation to instruments and laws that protect the above-mentioned public interests. Their nature varies across treaty practice.

Most agreements provide that such conduct should not or shall not contravene State measures or standards protecting the public interests concerned (e.g. 2018 Argentina–Japan IIA, Article 22). Among those IIAs, a few provide a definition of those measures, such as the 2016 China–Hong Kong SAR China IIA, which specifies, for instance, that 'environmental measures are limited to environmental laws, regulations, procedures, requirements or practices' (Article 25, Footnote 15).

Other IIAs refer to the domestic laws and international law instruments binding upon States and protecting the public interests covered by the provision (e.g. 2016 Morocco–Nigeria IIA, Article 15.2). As exemplified by the 2016 Austria–Kyrgyzstan IIA, some IIAs, although they refer to 'domestic labour laws', link this to international law, with Article 5.2 of that Agreement specifying that 'labour laws' 'means a law or a normative legal act of the State of the Contracting Parties that are directly related to ... internationally recognised labour rights'. Interestingly, this IIA also provides an exhaustive list of those rights:

(a) the right of association;
(b) the right to organise and to bargain collectively;
(c) a prohibition on the use of any form of forced or compulsory labour;
(d) labour protections for children and young people, including a minimum age for the employment of children and the prohibition and elimination of the worst forms of child labour;
(e) acceptable conditions of work with respect to minimum wages, hours of work, and occupational safety and health;
(f) elimination of discrimination in employment and occupation.

So does the 2012 Bilateral Investment Treaty (BIT) Model of the United States of America (USA) with regard to the 'environment', although not in relation to international law:

> For purposes of this Article, 'environmental law' means each Party's statutes or regulations, [footnote omitted] or provisions thereof, the primary purpose of which is the protection of the environment, or the prevention of a danger to human, animal, or plant life or health, through the:
>
> (a) prevention, abatement, or control of the release, discharge, or emission of pollutants or environmental contaminants;
> (b) control of environmentally hazardous or toxic chemicals, substances, materials, and wastes, and the dissemination of information related thereto; or
> (c) protection or conservation of wild flora or fauna, including endangered species, their habitat, and specially protected natural areas,
>
> in the Party's territory, but does not include any statute or regulation, or provision thereof, directly related to worker safety or health. (Article 12.4)

As to those above-mentioned IIAs which – in one way or the other – link the duty not to waive and not to derogate to international law, it is worth emphasising that, while the Morocco–Nigeria IIA refers to international labour instruments to which both States are signatories, the Austria–Kyrgyzstan IIA mentions the 'internationally recognised labour rights'. Such a formulation and the list of rights provided is to be understood in reference to those fundamental rights that are deemed to be universally applicable to all States, irrespective of whether or not they are parties to the Convention of the International Labour Organization (ILO) protecting them. Indeed, the International Labour Conference adopted in 1998 the ILO Declaration on Fundamental Principles and Rights at Work, which stresses that all Member States of this organisation have the obligation to respect, irrespective of whether or not they have ratified the relevant convention, the following fundamental principles: (1) freedom of association and the effective recognition of the right to collective bargaining; (2) the elimination of all forms of forced or compulsory labour; (3) the effective abolition of child labour; and (4) the elimination of discrimination in respect of employment and occupation.

– The Origin of the Investments Concerned　As regards this issue, three different approaches emerge from treaty practice. Those IIAs that follow the first of these prohibit conduct that aims to encourage the investments of the investors of a State party (e.g. 2016 Hong Kong SAR China–Chile IIA, Article 15.2). Under the second, more mainstream approach, IIAs do not specify the origin of the investors and their investments (e.g. 2016 Slovakia–Iran IIA, Article 10.1). The third approach enlarges the scope of the prohibition by encompassing the investments of the investors of States non-parties to the agreements, in addition to those of States parties. For instance, Article 22 of the 2016 Japan–Kenya IIA provides:

> Each Contracting Party shall recognise the importance of encouraging investments by investors of the other Contracting Party or of a non-Contracting Party without relaxing its health, safety or environmental measures or by lowering its labour standards. To this effect each Contracting Party should not waive or otherwise derogate from such measures or standards as an encouragement for the establishment, acquisition or expansion of investments in its Area by investors of the other Contracting Party or of a non-Contracting Party.

This is quite an interesting approach as it tends *mutatis mutandis* to confer an *erga omnes* effect on those provisions, meaning an effect which relates not only to the encouragement of investments by the investors of States parties, but also by the investors of States non-parties to the IIAs in question.

b　The Key Features of Treaty Practice

There are a number of features that can be seen from obligations not to lower the protection of public interests that are worth highlighting.

The first of these is the limitation those obligations place upon States' normative power. No doubt, such limitations are inherent in international investment law in so far as the protection of foreign investors and their investments is concerned. But the limitation imposed by these obligations is remarkable when we consider its aim of protecting public interests. Indeed, as illustrated by the issue of the right of States to regulate discussed in Chapters 6 and 7, the protection of those interests in international investment law has traditionally been provided by the protection of States' normative power, not by its limitation.

The second specific feature concerns the ultimate 'beneficiaries' of the obligation not to lower the protection of public interests, meaning local populations in general and workers in particular. In this respect, one should note that those obligations protect populations and workers against the conduct of their own States. This is an outstanding feature given that IIAs and international investment law more generally have traditionally aimed at protecting *foreign* persons from host States.

The third feature relates to the complexity of the factual situations addressed by the obligation not to lower the protection of public interests. International investment law has traditionally addressed 'public–private' conflicts of interests, i.e. conflicts between the interests of host States and those of foreign investors. At first glance, it may appear that the conflicts of interests at stake in these situations are not any different: they would boil down only to the interests of investors to invest in the territory of host States as opposed, for instance, to the interests of workers entitled to good working conditions. However, there is at least one additional facet to the conflicts of interests arising in these situations. The lowering by host States of the protection of labour standards, for example, to attract investors can aim at stimulating their economic development, which is part of the notion of sustainable development, as are labour standards and conditions. This means that what is at stake here is not only a conflict between workers' interests and investors' interests, but also a conflict between workers' interests and societies' interests with regard to the stimulation of economic development. In that sense, the situations addressed by those obligations are not only characterised by a 'public–private' conflict of interests, but also by a conflict between various public interests.

8.1.2 Obligations Pertaining to Investors' Conduct

States' obligations pertaining to the conduct of investors have both a 'forward-looking' and a 'backward-looking' dimension: those pertaining to corporate social responsibility aim at guiding the conduct of investors in order to ensure that the protection of public interests becomes part of their operational policies and practices, while others are intended to ensure that investors' conduct which causes any harm to public interests can be repressed or redressed.

8.1.2.1 Corporate Social Responsibility

Obligations pertaining to corporate social responsibility seek to encourage investors to conduct their activities in a way that takes into account their societal and natural environment. As we will see below, some IIAs place those obligations directly upon them. However, most of these provisions place the obligation on States parties, requiring them to encourage enterprises to incorporate into their internal policies internationally recognised standards, guidelines and principles of corporate social responsibility.

Virtually all IIAs containing such a provision adopt extremely soft law language. For instance, Article 9.17 of the 2018 Comprehensive and Progressive Agreement for Trans-Pacific Partnership (CPTPP) provides: 'The Parties reaffirm the importance of each Party encouraging enterprises operating within its area or subject to its jurisdiction to voluntarily incorporate into their internal policies those internationally recognised standards, guidelines and principles of corporate social responsibility that have been endorsed or are supported by that Party.' As it appears, such provisions merely 'reaffirm the importance' of 'encourag[ing] enterprises' 'to voluntarily incorporate'.

With regard to the international standards, guidelines and principles of corporate social responsibility that enterprises should be encouraged to incorporate, it is worth noting that – as illustrated by the CPTPP – only those that 'have been endorsed or are supported' by the State party at hand are concerned. This may entail material differences from one party to the other. Content-wise, it is notable that the public interests protected by the standards, guidelines and principles to be incorporated by enterprises are most often not specified. However, a few IIAs do the contrary – for instance, the 2018 United States–Mexico–Canada Agreement (USMCA) provides for a non-exhaustive list that refers to labour, environment, gender equality, human rights, indigenous and aboriginal peoples' rights as well as corruption (Article 14.17).

8.1.2.2 Court Proceedings

Albeit not as frequently found in treaty practice as States' obligations to guide the conduct of investors, other IIA provisions aim at ensuring that investors' conduct that causes any harm to public interests can be repressed or redressed. Those obligations can relate to specific interests or they can have a broader scope. The IIA adopted in 2016 by Morocco and Nigeria incorporates both approaches.

As to the former, its Article 17.5, which tackles corruption matters, provides that '[t]he States Parties to this Agreement, consistent with their applicable law, shall prosecute and where convicted penalize persons that have breached the applicable law implementing this obligation'. This obligation is set out largely in Article 17.2:

Investors and their Investments shall not, prior to the establishment of an investment or afterwards, offer, promise or give any undue pecuniary or other advantage, whether directly or through intermediaries, to a public official of the Host State, or a member of an official's family or business associate or other person in close proximity to an official, for that official or for a third party, in order that the official or third party act or refrain from acting in relation to the performance of official duties, in order to achieve any favour in relation to a proposed investment or any licences, permits, contracts or other rights in relation to an investment.

Article 20 reflects the broader approach: 'Investors shall be subject to civil actions for liability in the judicial process of their home state for the acts or decisions made in relation to the investment where such acts or decisions lead to significant damage, personal injuries or loss of life in the host state.' As explained by the Commentary to Article 17 of the Model Bilateral Investment Treaty Template of the Southern African Development Community (SADC), which contains a similar provision, such a provision is intended to oblige home States to restrict the use of procedural or jurisdictional rules, such as *the forum non conveniens*, which can impede domestic legal proceedings relating to harmful conduct and situations occurring abroad.

8.2 Obligations upon Investors

Preliminary Remarks

As explained above and in Chapter 1, foreign investors have traditionally not been subject to any obligations under international investment law. This is due, in particular, to the reluctance displayed by developed States in imposing obligations upon their investors in IIAs. This has been changing slowly in reaction to the criticism formulated across civil societies, the result being the progressive incorporation of such obligations in IIAs concluded in the 2010s.

This section focuses on investors' obligations in relation to the operation of their investments. As examined in Chapter 14, a number of IIAs contain obligations pertaining to the time when the investments are made. As we will see, this can have an impact notably on the jurisdiction of arbitration tribunals. From this temporal standpoint, it is worth mentioning also that the 2016 Morocco–Nigeria IIA contains an obligation concerning pre-establishment, in particular the obligation to conduct environmental and social impact assessments. Article 14 provides:

Investors or the investment shall comply with environmental assessment screening and assessment processes applicable to their proposed investments prior to their establishment, as required by the laws of the host state for such an investment or the laws of the home state for such an investment, whichever is more rigorous in relation to the investment in question.

Investors or the investment shall conduct a social impact assessment of the potential investment. The parties shall adopt standards for this purpose at the meeting of the Joint Committee.

Investors, their investment and host state authorities shall apply the precautionary principle to their environmental impact assessment and to decisions taken in relation to a proposed investment, including any necessary mitigation or alternative approaches of the precautionary principle by investors and investments shall be described in the environmental impact assessment they undertake.

It is interesting to note that this article requires investors to apply the precautionary principle to their environmental impact assessment.

With regard to the conduct of investors in the operation of their investments, two main categories of obligations emerge from treaty practice: (1) obligations pertaining to corporate social responsibility; and (2) obligations to comply with the law.

8.2.1 Corporate Social Responsibility

Most of the obligations placed upon investors pertaining to corporate social responsibility are framed in a way analogous to States' corporate social responsibility obligations. This is illustrated by Article 12 of the 2018 Belarus–India IIA:

Investors and their enterprises operating within the territory of each Party shall endeavor to voluntarily incorporate internationally recognized standards of corporate social responsibility in their practices and internal policies, such as statements of principle that have been endorsed or are supported by the Parties. These principles may address issues such as labour, the environment, human rights, community relations and anti-corruption.

Within this frame, the main differences displayed by treaty practice relate to the nature of the obligation and what is required from investors.

Some IIAs, like the 2016 Argentina–Qatar IIA, adopt the language of soft law. They provide *mutatis mutandis* that '[i]nvestors operating in the territory of the host Contracting Party should make efforts to voluntarily incorporate internationally recognized standards of corporate social responsibility into their business policies and practices' (Article 12). Other IIAs place upon investors an obligation of best effort; this can be seen from the 2019 Brazil–UAE IIA, providing in particular that investors 'shall strive to achieve the highest possible level of contribution to the sustainable development of the Host State and the local community, through the adoption of a high degree of socially responsible practices' (Article 15.1).

This IIA also illustrates the high requirements explicitly set by some agreements. In this respect, the 2016 Morocco–Nigeria IIA, while it adopts soft law language, specifies that '[w]here standards of corporate social responsibility increase, investors should strive to apply and achieve the higher level standards' (Article 24.3). It is also worth noting that this Article provides that the requirement to make the maximum feasible contributions to the sustainable development of the host State and local community through high levels of socially responsible practice should be compatible with 'the size, capacities and nature' of investments (Article 24.1).

Content-wise, the above-mentioned Brazil–UAE IIA, and more generally the IIA practice adopted by Brazil in the 2010s, is worth highlighting. Indeed, in addition to grounding the socially responsible practices to be adopted by investors in the Guidelines for Multinational Enterprises of the Organisation for Economic Co-operation and Development (Article 15.1), this IIA provides an exhaustive list of the principles and standards for responsible business conduct. It is worth quoting this list in full to take stock of investors' obligations of corporate social responsibility:

(a) Contribute to the economic, social and environmental progress, aiming at achieving sustainable development;

(b) Respect the internationally recognized human rights of those involved in the companies' activities;

(c) Encourage local capacity building through close cooperation with the local community;

(d) Encourage the creation of human capital, especially by creating employment opportunities and offering professional training to workers;

(e) Refrain from seeking or accepting exemptions that are not established in the legal or regulatory framework relating to human rights, environment, health, security, work, tax system, financial incentives, or other issues;

(f) Support and advocate for good corporate governance principles, and develop and apply good practices of corporate governance;

(g) Develop and implement effective self-regulatory practices and management systems that foster a relationship of mutual trust between the companies and the societies in which its operations are conducted;

(h) Promote the knowledge of and the adherence to, by workers, the corporate policy, through appropriate dissemination of this policy, including programs for professional training;

(i) Refrain from discriminatory or disciplinary action against employees who submit grave reports to the board or, whenever appropriate, to the competent public authorities, about practices that violate the law or corporate policy;

(j) Encourage, whenever possible, business associates, including service providers and outsources, to apply the principles of business conduct consistent with the principles provided for in this Article; and

(k) Refrain from any undue interference in local political activities. (Article 15.2)

8.2.2 Compliance with the Law

For the purpose of this analysis, a distinction can be made between two main categories of obligations placed upon investors to comply with the law: the obligation to comply with domestic law and the obligation to comply with international law. This distinction is without prejudice to any link that may exist between these two categories, in particular from a domestic constitutional law perspective with regard to the incorporation of international law in national law. Alongside these two categories, a few IIA obligations are not attached to any of those bodies of law, but instead to transnational standards relating to corporate governance or to the protection of the environment. For instance, Article 18.1 of the 2016 Morocco–Nigeria IIA provides that '[c]ompanies in areas of resource exploitation and high-risk industrial enterprises shall maintain a current certification to ISO 14001 or an equivalent environmental management standard'.

By definition, foreign investors operating in the territory of host States have – as a matter of domestic law – the obligation to comply with their law. However, for various reasons pertaining in particular to the capacity of host States, it may not be possible to fully enforce domestic law in their domestic legal order. The States' obligations discussed above with regard to court proceedings have the potential to limit this lack of enforcement and thereby to increase the effectiveness and efficacy of domestic law.

Another strategy consists of the obligation placed upon investors to comply with domestic law: through its operation, it becomes a treaty obligation for investors to respect national law, its violation leading potentially to the violation of the IIA. Of course, there is then the question of the enforcement of this treaty obligation as such, an issue that is also relevant with regard to the obligations to comply with international law discussed below. As examined in Chapter 11, counterclaims – when they are possible – constitute a means of enforcing this obligation and, indirectly, of increasing the effectiveness and efficacy of domestic law. This obligation to comply with domestic law is well illustrated by Article 11 of the 2016 Argentina–Qatar IIA: 'The Contracting Parties acknowledge that investors and their investments shall comply with the laws of the host Contracting Party with respect to the management and operation of an investment.'

Among those IIAs that place an obligation upon investors to comply with international law, a distinction can be made on the basis of the field or instrument in which the conduct to be complied with is set out – this can be either in the IIA itself or in other instruments and fields of public international law.

Conduct directly set out in IIAs often relates to the prohibition of corruption. For instance, Article 11.ii of the 2018 Belarus–India IIA provides:

> Investors and their investments shall not, either prior to or after the establishment of an investment, offer, promise, or give any undue pecuniary advantage,

gratification or gift whatsoever, whether directly or indirectly, to a public servant or official of a Party as an inducement or reward for doing or forbearing to do any official act or obtain or maintain other improper advantage nor shall be complicit in inciting, aiding, abetting, or conspiring to commit such acts.

The failure to comply with that obligation as set out in the IIA is constitutive of a violation of the treaty. It can be noted that Article 17 of the 2016 Morocco–Nigeria IIA, which *mutatis mutandis* contains a similar prohibition, specifies that the breach of this Article is deemed to constitute a breach of the domestic law of the host State party concerning the establishment and operation of an investment.

Conduct set out in other fields of public international law typically pertains to international labour law and human rights law. This is well illustrated by the 2016 Morocco–Nigeria IIA, which provides: 'Investors and investments shall act in accordance with core labour standards as required by the ILO Declaration on Fundamental Principles and Rights of Work 1998. Investors shall not manage or operate the investments in a manner that circumvents international environmental, labour and human rights obligations to which the host state and/or home state are Parties' (Articles 18.3 and 18.4). It is noteworthy that this provision attaches investors' obligations in particular to the human rights obligations of States, be it the host or the home State. As explained above, this derives from the traditional lack of direct human rights obligations binding upon non-State actors under public international law. Such an approach to drafting constitutes a way of circumventing this void. At the same time, because it has de facto the effect of imposing human rights obligations upon investors, it can be seen as contributing to the above-mentioned horizontalisation of human rights.

9

Insurance against Political Risks

Introduction

Insurance granted to foreign investors against political risks – or non-commercial risks – in host States is often the forgotten component of international investment law and arbitration. Yet, as explained in Chapter 1 with regard to the emergence of this field of law, the improvement this insurance brings to the investment climate plays an important role in the promotion of foreign investments and in host States' economic development. This is evidenced in the Preamble of the 1985 Convention Establishing the Multilateral Investment Guarantee Agency (MIGA) which, after noting 'the need to strengthen international cooperation for economic development and to foster the contribution to such development of foreign investment in general and private foreign investment in particular', stresses 'that the flow of foreign investment to developing countries would be facilitated and further encouraged by alleviating concerns related to non-commercial risks'. This also holds true with regard to insurance granted by domestic agencies, even though their services are also conceived of as a tool to stimulate the domestic economies of home States. As to the development of host States, it is worth stressing at the outset that insured investment operations are intended to be socially and environmentally friendly and to respect human rights.

Domestic agencies have been the first to offer insurance services against political risks in the aftermath of the Second World War (WWII) and decolonisation; in this chapter, we shall refer as a case study to the Overseas Private Investment Corporation (OPIC), which is a government agency of the United States of America (USA) created in 1971, on the basis of the information made available by this entity.[1] Although such agencies were initially established by developed States, it is noteworthy that many developing States also created their own agencies later. For instance, Sudan established in 2005 the National Agency for Insurance and Finance of Exports. At the global level, it had been in the air since the 1950s to create an international agency, in particular at the International Bank for Reconstruction and Development (IBRD). This

---

[1] Since the completion of the book, OPIC has been replaced with the Development Finance Corporation. The relevant information is available at www.dfc.gov.

materialised with the adoption of the Seoul Convention in 1985, which established the above-mentioned MIGA, which is one of the five institutions that form the World Bank Group. At the regional level, mention can be made of the Inter-Arab Investment Guarantee Corporation, which also grants insurance against political risks. This insurance is also provided by private insurers.

The relationship between all these categories of insurance agencies and companies is largely characterised by cooperation and complementarity – as can be seen, for example, from the practices of co-insurance and re-insurance. Most of these insurers are part of the Berne Union, which is an international not-for-profit trade association representing the global export credit and investment insurance industry. In addition to the insurance that they provide, one can also mention that those agencies propose other services, typically loans.

This chapter focuses on insurance against political risks from two perspectives: (1) the protection that they bring to foreign investors and their investments against these risks; and (2) the protection of public interests against harmful investment projects and operations. As mentioned above, this analysis is illustrated by the services, policies and contracts of OPIC, as well as those of MIGA.

9.1 The Protection of Foreign Investors and Investments against Political Risks

Preliminary Remarks

Insurance agencies do not offer an absolute protection to foreign investors and their investments against political risks. Their insurance covers a set of eligible investments against specific risks; each of those eligible investments and specific risks are analysed successively in what follows, together with the settlement of disputes that can arise in relation to such insurance. In the same vein, it is worth noting at the outset that it is common practice among insurance agencies not to cover the total loss of insured investments. For instance, OPIC can insure as a matter of principle up to 90 per cent of the investment. As explained in the Commentaries to Article 16 of the MIGA Convention, which sets out this practice as to insurances accorded by the Agency, this is mainly intended to prevent moral hazard, meaning to discourage potential irresponsible conduct by foreign investors who may rely on total loss cover.

9.1.1 Eligible Investments

The eligibility of investment projects and operations depends on whether they meet conditions relating primarily to (1) investments, (2) investors, and (3) host States. Although the insurance policies of agencies display nuances and differences with regard to these conditions, they share common denominators that this subsection highlights.

9.1.1.1 Requirements Pertaining to Investments

Not all types of investments can benefit from an insurance against political risks. With regard to MIGA, the Seoul Convention provides notably that '[e]ligible investments shall include equity interests, including medium- or long-term loans made or guaranteed by holders of equity in the enterprise concerned, and such forms of direct investment as may be determined by the Board' (Article 12.a). As explained by the Commentaries to that Article, this provision aims to strike a balance between two considerations: the need to preserve MIGA's scarce capital to promote direct investment on the one hand, and the need to ensure future flexibility by allowing the Board of Directors of the Agency to extend coverage to other types of investments, on the other. To be eligible, the types of investments covered shall meet requirements pertaining primarily to their features and their impact.

Concerning their features, insurance agencies must be broadly satisfied with the solidity of the investments. In this respect, OPIC requires that the projects be within the demonstrated competence of the proposed management, which must have a proven record of success in the same or a closely related business. In the same vein, MIGA shall be convinced of the economic soundness of the investment (Seoul Convention, Article 12.e.i). Other features that investments shall display aim at ensuring they are in conformity with the 'rule of law' and that they promote development. The Seoul Convention provides, for instance, that investments shall comply with the host countries' laws and regulations and that they shall be consistent with the declared development objectives and priorities of these countries (Articles 12.e.ii and 12.e.iii).

Along the same lines, it is expected in terms of impact that investments promote sustainable development – including economic development – and respect human rights. As discussed further below, the assessment of this impact is conducted – 'upstream' – during the review of the investment projects, and – 'downstream' – in the course of the monitoring of insured investment operations. This requirement that investments contribute to the development of host States is provided in Article 12.e.i of the Seoul Convention. By the same token, OPIC shall be satisfied that the projects are environmentally and socially sustainable, that they respect human rights, including worker rights, and that they encourage positive host State development effects. It should be noted that, together with the impact on host States' public interests, OPIC's inquiries focus on the impact of investments on the US economy and US jobs.

9.1.1.2 Requirements Pertaining to Investors

The main condition pertaining to investors relates to 'nationality'. As regards domestic agencies, this nationality requirement is obviously attached to the State to which these agencies belong.

For instance, OPIC conditions the granting of insurance on the fulfilment of one or more of the following criteria: (1) to be a US citizen; (2) to be a corporation established in the USA and to be more than 50 per cent owned by US citizens or corporations; (3) to be a not-for-profit organisation established in the USA; or (4) to be an entity established outside the USA and to be at least 95 per cent owned by US citizens or corporations.

With respect to MIGA, the condition of nationality set out in Article 13 of the Seoul Convention is twofold. As a matter of principle, investors shall have (1) the nationality of a MIGA Member State, which (2) is not that of host States.

Concerning juridical persons, the eligibility may derive from two situations: they shall either (1) be incorporated and have their principal place of business in a Member State (other than the host State); or (2) the majority of their capital shall be owned by a Member or Member States (other than the host State) or by its/their national(s) thereof.

As an exception to the principle that investors shall not have the nationality of host States, the Board of Directors of the Agency may, by special majority, grant an insurance to a natural person who is a national of the host State or a juridical person that is incorporated in the host State or the majority of whose capital is owned by its nationals, provided that the assets invested are transferred from outside that State. As explained by the Commentaries to Article 13, the provision of this exception aims at taking into account the presence abroad of nationals of developing States who have significant off-shore funds and at allowing the repatriation of such capital into those States.

For the purpose of this nationality requirement and in the case of multiple nationalities, the nationality of a Member State shall prevail over the nationality of a non-Member State, and the nationality of the host State shall prevail over the nationality of any other Member State.

9.1.1.3 Requirements Pertaining to Host States

It is generally understood that only investments made in developing States can be insured. This is, for instance, made explicit in Article 14 of the Seoul Convention. Beyond this general requirement, conditions pertaining to host States have the effect of both conferring power and placing constraints upon them.

The main constraints are twofold: subrogation and legal security. Subrogation is a well-accepted principle of insurance law: it consists of the assignment of existing rights or claims from insured investors to insurance agencies. This mechanism avoids notably double recovery by investors and it ensures that agencies may recover the indemnification paid to them. Failing the acceptance by host States of this mechanism, investments in those States cannot usually benefit from insurance. With regard to MIGA, this acceptance is given when States ratify the Seoul Convention; its Article 18.b provides for the recognition by all Member States of the right of subrogation of the Agency set out in

Article 18.a. In the context of bilateral relations between States, the practice is twofold. As explained in Chapter 1 in relation to the emergence of international investment law and arbitration, a number of States parties incorporate a subrogation provision within international investment agreements (IIAs). This is, for instance, the practice adopted by the United Kingdom, as illustrated by Article 11 of the 2010 United Kingdom–Colombia IIA:

1. If one Contracting Party or its designated Agency ('the first Contracting Party') makes a payment under an indemnity given in respect of insurance against non commercial risk for an investment in the territory of the other Contracting Party ('the second Contracting Party'), the second Contracting Party shall recognise:
   (a) the assignment to the first Contracting Party by law or by legal transaction of all the rights and claims of the party indemnified; and
   (b) that the first Contracting Party is entitled to exercise such rights and enforce such claims by virtue of subrogation, to the same extent as the party indemnified.
2. The first Contracting Party shall be entitled in all circumstances to the same treatment in respect of:
   (a) the rights and claims acquired by it by virtue of the assignment; and
   (b) any payments received in pursuance of those rights and claims;

as the party indemnified was entitled to receive by virtue of this Agreement in respect of the investment concerned and its related returns.

Alternatively, other States conclude specific investment guarantee agreements that contain a subrogation clause, as exemplified by the practice of the USA.

The second constraint, which pertains to legal security as a condition of the granting of insurance, consists of the requirement that host States provide serious guarantees concerning the treatment granted to foreign investors and their investments over their territory. This is to be evidenced in particular by the conclusion of an IIA or by the treatment and protection granted under domestic law. For instance, the Seoul Convention provides that MIGA shall be satisfied with the investment conditions in host States, including the availability of fair and equitable treatment and legal protection for investments (Article 12.e.iv). As specified by the Commentaries to that Article, in case no such protection is conferred under domestic law or by an IIA, the Agency can provide insurance only under the condition that it concludes an agreement with the host State concerned regarding the treatment to be afforded to the investment covered by the Agency.

Turning to those requirements that have an empowering effect, one can refer in particular to the approval that may be needed from host States. Article 15 of the Seoul Convention provides, for instance, that the Agency shall not conclude any contract of guarantee before the host government has approved the issuance of the guarantee against the risks designated for cover. In this respect, the Commentaries to that Article explain that this enables the host State to evaluate a proposed investment before giving its consent. With regard to domestic agencies, the USA typically makes the granting of insurance subject to the approval of the investment by the host State, as can be seen in the investment guarantee agreements that it concluded, such as the 1960 USA–El-Salvador Agreeement: 'The Government of the United States of America or any official agencies it may designate to handle these matters will only authorize the guaranties mentioned in Article One for those projects which have had the prior written approval of the Government of El Salvador' (Article 2).

9.1.2 Risks Covered

As a common denominator, virtually all agencies propose insurance against political risks which cover: (1) currency inconvertibility and transfer; (2) expropriation; (3) contracts; and (4) war and civil disturbance.

9.1.2.1 Currency Inconvertibility and Transfer

The scope of the currency inconvertibility and transfer risk is broad. For instance, under OPIC policies, this risk includes: (1) new and more restrictive foreign exchange regulations; (2) the failure by an exchange control authority to approve of – or to act on – an application for hard currency; (3) unlawful efforts by the host State to block funds for repatriation; and (4) discriminatory host State's actions resulting in an inability to convert and transfer local earnings. The Seoul Convention also adopts a broad definition of this risk; in particular, it includes the failure of host States to act within a reasonable period of time on a transfer application (Article 11.a.i).

9.1.2.2 Expropriation

Insurance policies traditionally also cover expropriations, whether direct or indirect, as well as nationalisations. With regard to indirect expropriation, it is worth stressing that the Seoul Convention provides for a limitation in this regard, in that its Article 11.a.ii excludes 'non-discriminatory measures of general application which governments normally take for the purpose of regulating economic activity in their territories'. As explained by the Commentaries to that Article, this exception is deemed to encompass, for instance, taxation, environmental and labour legislation, as well as normal measures enacted for the maintenance of public safety. This is to be linked to the specification – examined in Chapter 6 – that has developed in IIAs concerning the distinction between expropriatory measure and regulatory measure. In this respect, one must note that the Seoul Convention, which was adopted in 1985, was a 'pioneer' in so far as such specification in IIA practice dates back to the 2000s only. This certainly helps to explain why the Commentaries make explicit that this limitation is not meant to prejudice the rights foreign investors have under bilateral investment treaties (BITs) in particular.

9.1.2.3 Contract

Contracts and contractual relationships have traditionally been protected by insurance agencies. The Seoul Convention protects foreign investors against the repudiation or breaches of contracts by host States in three specific situations: (1) when they do not have recourse to a judicial or arbitral forum to determine the claim of repudiation or breach; (2) when such a forum does not render a decision within a reasonable period of time, that period being set out in the insurance contract according to MIGA's regulations; and (3) when such a decision cannot be enforced (Article 11.a.iii). OPIC's insurance covers contracts under the ambit of 'expropriation and other forms of unlawful government interference'. More precisely, investors are insured against the abrogation, the repudiation and the impairment of contracts, which includes the forced renegotiation of contracts' terms.

9.1.2.4 War and Civil Disturbance

This risk covers a broad set of violent situations. For example, insurance provided by OPIC encompasses (1) declared and undeclared wars; (2) hostile actions by national and international forces; (3) revolutions, insurrections and civil strife; and (4) terrorism and sabotage. Insurance policies typically protect foreign investors against the damage and destruction of tangible assets as well as the interruption and abandonment of the investment operations that they may cause.

9.1.3 Disputes and Dispute Settlement

In order to illustrate the disputes that can arise in relation to insurance against political risks and how they are settled, the following focuses on MIGA and the Seoul Convention.

9.1.3.1 The Types of Disputes

It is worth noting at the outset that insurance agencies usually endeavour to mitigate the risks of disputes between foreign investors and their host States, for example arising from contracts, which may lead to a request for indemnification, as they endeavour to settle those disputes themselves. In that sense, MIGA expects from the investors it insures that they provide early notification of any problems that may give rise to a claim of loss under the insurance and it offers to use its good offices to help these investors and their host States to settle their disputes.

When a request for indemnification is made by an investor to the insurance agency, two main types of disputes can arise: (1) disputes between host States and insurance agencies seeking to recover the indemnification paid to insured investors; and (2) disputes between insurance agencies and insured investors when the former consider that those investors are not entitled to receive any indemnification. The settlement of those two types of disputes is examined in turn in what follows.

From this, one can distinguish those disputes that can arise in the context of insured investment operations and that pertain to the protection of public interests; their settlement is discussed in Section 9.2.

Mention can also be made of the disputes that can arise between States from the interpretation and application of the investment guarantee agreement that they conclude, or of the IIA provision relating to insurance, namely the subrogation clause. By the same token, disputes can arise between MIGA and its Member States or between Member States themselves concerning the interpretation and application of the Seoul Convention.

9.1.3.2 The Settlement of Disputes between Insurance Agencies and Host States

When a request for indemnification is made by insured investors and is accepted by insurance agencies, those agencies are subrogated in the rights and claims of these investors. As regards domestic agencies, such a subrogation is grounded either in an investment guarantee agreement concluded between States, or in the subrogation clause of an IIA they have concluded. For MIGA, it is provided in Article 18 of the Seoul Convention.

This subrogation means that agencies can seek to be reimbursed by host States for the indemnification they paid to the investors concerned, if necessary by initiating legal proceedings. Under that Convention, MIGA and the host State involved shall enter into negotiations to settle their dispute. In case negotiations fail, the dispute may be submitted to arbitration by either of these parties, or it may first be submitted to conciliation by mutual agreement between them.

As an exception to this procedure, MIGA and the host State may agree on an alternative dispute settlement method or methods (Article 57.b and Annex II). As explained by the Commentaries to Article 57.b, they may for instance agree on requiring the Agency to first seek available remedies under the host State's domestic law before initiating arbitration proceedings. Interestingly, the Commentaries also mention that an advisory opinion from the International Court of Justice (ICJ) may be sought as an alternative to arbitration.

9.1.3.3 The Settlement of Disputes between Insurance Agencies and Insured Investors

Upon a request for indemnification being made by an insured investor, an insurance agency may conclude that the situation at hand does not fall within the scope of the insurance contract concluded and, on that basis, reject the request. This can obviously lead to a dispute between this agency and the investor arising from the interpretation and application of the insurance contract. In such situations and in case the dispute cannot be settled amicably, the MIGA Convention provides, for instance, that those disputes arising under a contract of guarantee shall be submitted to arbitration in accordance with such rules as provided for or referred to in the contract (Article 58). That Article does not list those rules as it was considered that contracts would do so; however, as explained in the Convention's Commentaries, it was contemplated that use would be made of internationally recognised rules of arbitration, such as the arbitration rules of the International Centre for Settlement of Investment Disputes (ICSID), of the United Nations Commission on International Trade Law (UNCITRAL), or of the International Chamber of Commerce.

9.2 The Protection of Public Interests against Harmful Investment Projects and Operations

Insurance policies provided by agencies, be they domestic or international, are intended to display a degree of 'affinity' towards public interests. The investments insured must have a positive development outcome and must not be harmful to local communities and to the environment. To reach these objectives, insurance programmes place a 'shared responsibility' on the agencies and the foreign investors that is to be assumed at two stages: 'upstream', during the review of investment projects; and 'downstream', in the course of ongoing investment operations. These two stages are illustrated taking MIGA as a case study, on the basis of the information made available by this entity.[2]

9.2.1 The Review of Investment Projects

During the review of investment projects and prior to concluding the insurance contract with investors, insurance agencies endeavour to appraise the social, environmental and human rights risks and impact of these projects. This due diligence exercise aims at rejecting those projects that are too harmful and, for the projects that are not rejected, to provide a list of requirements to be included in the contract and to be complied with by investors in order to mitigate the risks. The performance standards that are required to be met by the investment operations act as a sort of template to be followed in reaching this objective.

At MIGA, the Policy on Environmental and Social Sustainability contains eight such standards: (1) assessment and management of environmental and social risks and impacts; (2) labour and working conditions; (3) resource

---

[2] Information available at www.miga.org.

efficiency and pollution prevention; (4) community health, safety and security; (5) land acquisition and involuntary resettlement; (6) biodiversity conservation and sustainable management of living natural resources; (7) indigenous peoples; and (8) cultural heritage.

Each of these standards set out the expected outcome and prescribed the corresponding requirements, taking into account in particular the level of environmental and social risk displayed by projects. In this respect, MIGA categorises as part of this review process the projects in light of their degree of risk and impact. There exist four main categories:

Category A: Business activities with potential significant adverse environmental or social risks and/or impacts that are diverse, irreversible, or unprecedented;
Category B: Business activities with potential limited adverse environmental or social risks and/or impacts that are few in number, generally site specific, largely reversible, and readily addressed through mitigation measures;
Category C: Business activities with minimal or no adverse environmental or social risks and/or impact;
Category FI: Business activities undertaken by financial intermediaries or through delivery mechanisms involving financial intermediation.

This categorisation also plays a role with regard to the public disclosure by MIGA of the Environmental and Social Review Summary of investment projects and of the Environmental and Social Action Plan, which contains the commitments to be undertaken by investors; it has a similar effect on the disclosure of the relevant documentation. For instance, the disclosure period lasts for sixty days for 'Category A' projects and thirty days for 'Category B' projects. The disclosure of the impact and of the mitigation measures required by MIGA entails, most importantly, that these are to be communicated to affected local communities. More generally, investors must consult with those communities with a view to establishing a constructive relationship between them.

At the end of this review and consultation process, insurance contracts submitted to the Board of Directors of the Agency for approval shall reflect the terms of the Environmental and Social Action Plan – except notably for 'Category C' projects which do not have such a plan – and any other environmental and social commitment to be made and complied with by investors.

9.2.2 The Review of Ongoing Investment Operations

Throughout the course of investment operations, their ongoing social, environmental and human rights 'friendliness' is appraised by agencies through two mechanisms: (1) the monitoring of operations by the insurance agency to ensure that investors comply with the mitigation requirements provided in the insurance contracts, or to update these requirements; and (2) independent grievance mechanisms available for affected communities.

At MIGA, there exist two monitoring tools: the visits by its environmental and social staff as well as the submission of reports by investors providing information concerning the fulfilment of the requirements set out in the insurance contracts. This monitoring can lead to the enhancement or to the revision of the mitigation requirements in the event of a change of circumstances, in particular with regard to the business activities.

In addition to supporting the development of grievance mechanisms by the insured investors themselves and to recognising the role that domestic tribunals may play, MIGA has established a Compliance Advisor/Ombudsman. This authority has the task of addressing the concerns expressed by local communities affected by insured investment operations with a view to enhancing the environmental and social outcomes of operations and to fostering the accountability of MIGA. This authority is independent from the Agency; however, it is worth emphasising that the reports it submits directly to the President of the World Bank Group are not binding.

Part III
The Settlement of Investor-State Disputes

10

Classification of Investment-Related Disputes and Dispute Settlement Mechanisms

Introduction

By way of context for the detailed analysis of investor–State arbitration conducted in Part III, this chapter examines in turn the types of investment-related disputes that can arise and the various dispute settlement mechanisms that can be availed of to settle such disputes.

10.1 Classification of Disputes

Various classifications can be used to introduce investment-related disputes. For this purpose, this section relies on a classification based on the 'nature' of the disputing parties. It introduces State–State disputes and investor–State disputes in turn, setting aside the disputes arising between an investor of the home State and an investor of the host State which are addressed in very few international investment agreements (IIAs) (e.g. 1992 Australia–Indonesia IIA, Article 13). Diplomatic protection is examined separately due to the hybridity of the situations it covers, although formally its exercise leads to a State–State dispute. Prior to these discussions, it is first necessary to clarify the notion of a dispute as such.

10.1.1 Definition of a 'Dispute'

Under public international law, a dispute is defined along the lines of the definition provided by the Permanent Court of International Justice (PCIJ) in the *Case of the Mavrommatis Palestine Concessions (Greece v. United Kingdom)*. Arbitration tribunals also rely on this 'canonical' definition according to which a dispute is 'a disagreement on a point of law or fact, a conflict of legal views or interests between two persons' (1924, Judgment, at 11). In this respect, it can be noted that the Annulment Committee in *Industria Nacional de Alimentos, S.A.* v. *Peru* suggested – without further elaborating – that '[t]he concept of "dispute" can clearly be defined in different ways depending on the context' after having noted the reliance of the Tribunal appointed in that case on the *Mavrommatis* definition (2007, Decision on Annulment, para. 91).

A dispute does not arise instantaneously – rather, there is a gradual process that leads to a dispute. In that sense, the Tribunal in *Emilio Agustin Maffezini* v. *Spain* described the emergence and crystallisation of a dispute as follows:

> [T]here tends to be a natural sequence of events that leads to a dispute. It begins with the expression of a disagreement and the statement of a difference of views. In time these events acquire a precise legal meaning through the formulation of legal claims, their discussion and eventual rejection or lack of response by the other party. The conflict of legal views and interests will only be present in the latter stage, even though the underlying facts predate them. (2000, Decision of the Tribunal on Objections to Jurisdiction, para. 96)

There must exist a positive opposition between the parties for a dispute to arise, meaning that the claims of one party must be positively opposed by the other party; as stated by the International Court of Justice (ICJ), '[a] mere assertion is not sufficient to prove the existence of a dispute any more than a mere denial of the existence of the dispute proves its non-existence' (*South West Africa Cases* (*Ethiopia* v. *South Africa, Liberia* v. *South Africa*, 1962, Judgment, at 328). It is noteworthy that the existence of a dispute may also be inferred from the failure of a party to respond to a claim.

10.1.2 State–State Disputes

State–State disputes are mainly twofold in nature: they can relate to a dispute that exists between a host State and a foreign investor who invested in its territory; or they can consist of a 'direct' dispute between States.

10.1.2.1 State–State Disputes Relating to Investor–State Disputes

This category of State–State disputes is itself composed of two subcategories: the disputes that relate to subrogation and those that relate to diplomatic protection.

The former are analysed in Chapter 9, which examines insurances against political risks. They pertain to those situations in which the home State directly or its domestic insurance agency indemnify an investor when such a risk has materialised. In such situations, subrogation is used as a mechanism through which the rights and claims of the investor against the host State are transferred to that home State or that domestic insurance agency, which can initiate legal proceedings to recover this indemnification from the host State.

As explained below, the exercise by States of diplomatic protection originates in disputes between their nationals and host States. Notably, because private persons have traditionally had no access to international courts and tribunals, diplomatic protection has developed as a mechanism through which States can endorse the claims of their nationals against the host States. Diplomatic protection entails a transformation of the original dispute into a State–State dispute. This was famously explained by the PCIJ in the *Case of the Mavrommatis Palestine Concessions (Greece v. United Kingdom)*:

> In the case of the Mavrommatis concessions it is true that the dispute was at first between a private person and a State – i.e. between M Mavrommatis and Great Britain. Subsequently, the Greek Government took up the case. The dispute then entered upon a new phase; it entered the domain of international law, and became a dispute between two States ... By taking up the case of one of its subjects and by resorting to diplomatic action or international judicial proceedings on this behalf, a State is in reality asserting its own rights – its right to ensure, in the person of its subjects, respect for the rules of international law. (1924, Judgment, at 12)

Such a mechanism has been used in the context of investment-related disputes, as evidenced by high-profile cases decided by the ICJ, such as the *Case of Barcelona Traction Light and Power Company, Limited (Belgium v. Spain)* and the *Case of Elettronica Sicula S.p.A (ELSI) (United States of America v. Italy)*.

10.1.2.2 'Direct' State–State Disputes

Investment-related disputes can arise directly between States typically in relation to the application and interpretation of IIAs. Virtually all agreements contain a dispute settlement mechanism that concerns specifically this type of disputes. That being said, such disputes prove to be rare in practice; mention can be made of *Italy v. Cuba* with regard to the application of the 1993 Italy–Cuba IIA (Final Award, 2008) and of *Ecuador v. United States of America* in relation to the interpretation of the 1993 United States of America (USA)–Ecuador IIA. In this latter case, it is noteworthy that the USA contested the existence of a dispute, an objection that was accepted by the Tribunal (2012, Award).

10.1.3 Investor–State Disputes

Contrary to State–State disputes, which are rare, the number of investor–State disputes has increased significantly in the late twentieth century and early twenty-first century. These disputes have mainly related to the application and interpretation of IIAs. This is well illustrated by the statistics of the International Centre for Settlement of Investment Disputes (ICSID) released in August 2019. In 1972, only one ICSID arbitration case was registered by the Centre, while fifty-five cases were registered in 2018, which constitutes an annual record. In total, 716 ICSID arbitration cases have been registered from 1972 to June 2019.[1] The reasons for this explosion are manyfold; however, three appear to have played a prominent role.

The first of these relates to the huge upsurge in foreign direct investment (FDI) operations over the course of the twentieth century onwards, and

---

[1] ICSID, 'The ICSID Caseload: Statistics', Issue 2019-2 (August 2019), available at https://icsid .worldbank.org/en.

thereby the multiplication of the factual situations in the context of which investor–State disputes can arise.

The second reason is the densification of the 'legal framework' aiming at the protection of foreign investors and their investments. Customary international law (CIL) has been complemented with IIAs whose number has dramatically increased since the adoption of the first bilateral investment treaty (BIT) between Germany and Pakistan in 1959, up until 2019. In that period, 2911 BITs have been adopted, among which 2353 were in force in 2019. To this figure, one should add the 388 treaties containing investment provisions that have also been adopted over the same period, 309 being in force in 2019.[2] This densification has automatically increased the situations in which foreign investors can avail of the protection of an IIA against the conduct of host States.

The third reason relates to the combined effect of the incorporation in treaty practice of investor–State arbitration with unqualified consent as of 1969 – something explained in Chapter 1 – and of the final award rendered in 1990 in *Asian Agricultural Products Ltd (AAPL)* v. *Sri Lanka*. As will be explained in Chapter 11, foreign investors have since then mainly initiated arbitration proceedings against host States – regardless of the existence of any contract concluded between them – by simply resorting to the offer to arbitrate contained in IIAs. Put in relation to the above-mentioned explosion of IIA practice, this also helps to explain the significant growth in the number of investor–State disputes.

10.2 Classification of Dispute Settlement Mechanisms

For the purpose of this examination, a distinction can be made between the dispute settlement mechanisms made available in IIAs to settle investment-related disputes and those that have been used prior to or in parallel to the development of IIA practice. As explained below, it is worth noting at the outset that the evolution of IIA practice in the 2010s with regard to the settlement of investor–State disputes has led to some extent to a revival of those mechanisms that have traditionally been relied on to settle such disputes.

10.2.1 'Traditional' Dispute Settlement Mechanisms

Investment-related disputes have traditionally arisen in two types of situations: (1) situations involving specific operations; and (2) situations concerning sets of operations. For the latter situations that have led to 'collective' disputes, tailor-made dispute settlement mechanisms have been created and utilised. These mechanisms will be examined following our analysis of the mechanisms typically used to settle 'single' investment-related disputes.

---

[2] UNCTAD, 'Investment Policy Hub', available at https://investmentpolicy.unctad.org/international-investment-agreements.

10.2.1.1 Mechanisms for 'Single Disputes'

Aside from 'State contracts' concluded between host States and foreign investors, which incorporate arbitration as a mechanism to settle disputes arising from their application, two main mechanisms have traditionally been available for the settlement of investment-related disputes: local courts and diplomatic protection.

a Local Courts

Domestic courts have for some time been the only dispute settlement mechanism foreign investors could resort to 'on their own' to settle their dispute with host States, without any need for the intervention of their home State. This advantage, in particular over the mechanism of diplomatic protection, as we shall see, was nonetheless insufficient to counterbalance the disadvantages, whether perceived or real, of dispute settlement by domestic courts.

Irrespective of the issue of the limitations that domestic law can place on domestic courts to decide on disputes relating to State conduct, three main criticisms have been formulated against the courts of host States in settling such disputes. The most prominent of these pertains to independence and impartiality: domestic courts have been criticised for being under the control of States, typically their executive organ, and for having a bias against foreign investors. Furthermore, domestic judges have been said to lack the legal expertise to decide on investment-related disputes. Finally, domestic proceedings have been denounced as being inadequate for the settlement of such disputes, particularly in terms of their length.

As investment-related disputes have traditionally involved developing States, those criticisms, notably those pertaining to independence and impartiality, have been directed against the domestic courts of these States. That being said, it is worth noting that such criticisms have recently also been formulated against the domestic courts of developed States. This was notably so against the Courts of Mississippi in the context of the *Loewen* v. *USA* case. Very tellingly, the Tribunal appointed in that case added this conclusion at the end of its award:

> We think it right to add one final word. A reader following our account of the injustices which were suffered by Loewen and Mr. Raymond Loewen in the Courts of Mississippi could well be troubled to find that they emerge from the present long and costly proceedings with no remedy at all. After all, we have held that judicial wrongs may in principle be brought home to the State Party under Chapter Eleven, and have criticised the Mississippi proceedings in the strongest terms. There was unfairness here towards the foreign investor. Why not use the weapons at hand to put it right? What clearer case than the present could there be for the ideals of NAFTA to be given some teeth?
>
> This human reaction has been present in our minds throughout but we must be on guard against allowing it to control our decision. Far from fulfilling the purposes of NAFTA, an intervention on our part would

compromise them by obscuring the crucial separation between the international obligations of the State under NAFTA, of which the fair treatment of foreign investors in the judicial sphere is but one aspect, and the much broader domestic responsibilities of every nation towards litigants of whatever origin who appear before its national courts. Subject to explicit international agreement permitting external control or review, these latter responsibilities are for each individual state to regulate according to its own chosen appreciation of the ends of justice. As we have sought to make clear, we find nothing in NAFTA to justify the exercise by this Tribunal of an appellate function parallel to that which belongs to the courts of the host nation. In the last resort, a failure by that nation to provide adequate means of remedy may amount to an international wrong but only in the last resort. The line may be hard to draw, but it is real. Too great a readiness to step from outside into the domestic arena, attributing the shape of an international wrong to what is really a local error (however serious), will damage both the integrity of the domestic judicial system and the viability of NAFTA itself. The natural instinct, when someone observes a miscarriage of justice, is to step in and try to put it right, but the interests of the international investing community demand that we must observe the principles which we have been appointed to apply, and stay our hands. (2003, Award, paras. 241–242)

Such criticisms have re-emerged, for instance, in the context of the negotiation of the Transatlantic Trade and Investment Partnership (TTIP) between the USA and the European Union (EU), against both US courts and the courts of some EU Member States.

b Diplomatic Protection

The means through which home States have brought their support to their nationals abroad, including investors, have varied over time.

At the time that the use of force was still legal under public international law, European States did not hesitate to use – or to threaten to use – force against host States. This was the case in particular in relation to disputes concerning the recovery of contractual debts owed by host States. This practice – known as 'gunboat diplomacy' – culminated in the intervention of Germany, Italy and Great Britain against Venezuela in 1902. Following these events, the Argentinian Minister for Foreign Affairs, Drago, sent a diplomatic note to his US counterpart, Porter, which constituted the basis of the Drago–Porter Convention, formally known as the 1907 Hague Convention Respecting the Limitation of the Employment of Force for Recovery of Contract Debts. In this note, Drago formulated what is known as the 'Drago doctrine', which provides that public debts do not justify any European military intervention or occupation.

When formulating his doctrine, Drago built in particular on the 'Calvo doctrine', which opposes the use of diplomatic protection, a mechanism that has a pacific nature, contrary to gunboat diplomacy. In opposition to the idea that States were entitled under public international law to endorse the claims of their nationals against host States, Calvo argued that domestic courts have exclusive jurisdiction to settle disputes between host States and foreigners, except claims relating to a denial of justice. This thesis is consistent with the other pillar of the 'Calvo doctrine' – discussed in Chapter 1 – following which foreigners could not pretend to receive any better treatment than the treatment received by nationals under the domestic law of the host State.

The 'Calvo doctrine' was incorporated in international instruments adopted by South American States. For instance, Article 7 of the 1948 American Treaty on Pacific Settlement – known as the 'Pact of Bogota' – provides: 'The High Contracting Parties bind themselves not to make diplomatic representations in order to protect their nationals, or to refer a controversy to a court of international jurisdiction for that purpose, when the said nationals have had available the means to place their case before competent domestic courts of the respective State.' Similarly, many South American States have incorporated the 'Calvo clause' in their domestic constitutions or legislation. For instance, as reported by Salacuse notably,[3] Article 35 of the Bolivarian Constitution reads as follows: 'Foreign subjects and enterprises are, in respect of property, in the same position as Bolivians, and can in no case plead an exceptional situation or appeal through diplomatic channels unless in case of denial of justice.' By the same token, similar clauses were included in contracts concluded with foreign investors, begging thereby the question of their effect on the exercise of diplomatic protection by home States. On the other hand, South American States did not manage to put forward their views worldwide, and the 'Calvo doctrine' did not become part of public international law, contrary to diplomatic protection which did.

It is worth noting at the outset that diplomatic protection is not a dispute settlement method as such. As explained above, it is a mechanism through which States can endorse the claim of their nationals against their host States, the State–State disputes deriving from this endorsement being then potentially settled through political or legal methods of dispute settlement. Furthermore, it should be emphasised that the exercise of diplomatic protection is subject to two types of conditions – objective and subjective.

Beginning with the former, there are two main objective conditions. The first of these pertains to nationality, and provides that the private person involved in a dispute with the host State shall have as a matter of principle the nationality of the State which endorses his claim. The determination of nationality raises a series of issues, notably the issue of its effectiveness as for natural persons, as evidenced by the *Nottebohm Case (Liechtenstein v. Guatemala)* decided by the ICJ (1955, Judgment). As discussed in Chapter 14, the determination of nationality proves to be particularly complex for corporations. Second, local remedies must have been exhausted

---

[3] JW Salacuse, *The Law of Investment Treaties* (2nd ed, Oxford University Press 2015), at 75.

before a State can endorse the claim of its national, to the extent of course that they are available and effective. Contrary to these two conditions which are well accepted in practice, the status of the 'clean hands' doctrine has been the subject of disagreements. As such, it has been debated whether the conduct of the private person in question, for example in violating the domestic law of the host State, has any bearing on the entitlement of his State of nationality to exercise diplomatic protection. In this respect, it is worth noting that the International Law Commission (ILC) did not incorporate this doctrine as a condition in its 2006 Draft Articles on Diplomatic Protection.

In addition to these objective conditions, there is an additional – subjective – condition: States have full discretion to choose whether or not to exercise diplomatic protection. This means that they are free to take into account the protection or promotion of interests other than those of the nationals in question in making their decisions. This was well explained by the ICJ in the *Case Concerning the Barcelona Traction Light and Power Company, Limited (Belgium v. Spain)*:

> [W]ithin the limits prescribed by international law, a State may exercise diplomatic protection by whatever means and to whatever extent it thinks fit, for it is its own right that the State is asserting. Should the natural or legal persons on whose behalf it is acting consider that their rights are not adequately protected, they have no remedy in international law ... The State must be viewed as the sole judge to decide whether its protection will be granted, to what extent it is granted, and when it will cease. It retains in this respect a discretionary power the exercise of which may be determined by considerations of a political or other nature, unrelated to the particular case. (1970, Judgment, paras. 78–79)

As pointed out by the Court in that case and as mentioned earlier in reference to the *Mavrommatis Case* decided by the PCIJ, this freedom derives formally from the fact that, when exercising its diplomatic protection, a State asserts a right of its own, namely its right 'to ensure, in the person of its subjects, respect for the rules of international law'. From this also stems the fact that private persons have no input in the course of the exchanges between States or in court proceedings, as well as the fact that States have no obligation to transfer any compensation that they may receive to these persons. In this respect, it can be noted that the ILC refers to such a transfer as a 'recommended practice' in its 2006 Draft Articles on Diplomatic Protection (Article 19).

The politicisation of the dispute settlement process that diplomatic protection entails as well as the uncertainty that it generates for private persons made it particularly inadequate for foreign investors in need of legal security. This largely explains why they have promoted the incorporation of compromissory clauses in State contracts, giving them access to arbitration.

As regards the above-mentioned freedom to choose whether or not to exercise diplomatic protection, it is noteworthy that this freedom can be limited in certain instances. The 1965 Washington Convention establishing ICSID has this effect with regard to its States parties once consent has been given by the disputing parties to ICSID arbitration. Indeed, Article 27 provides that '[n]o Contracting State shall give diplomatic protection, or bring an international claim, in respect of a dispute which one of its nationals and another Contracting State shall have consented to submit or shall have submitted to arbitration under [the] Convention'. As an exception, this Article authorises the exercise of diplomatic protection where the Contracting State to the ICSID Convention party to the dispute fails to abide by and comply with the award rendered. Some IIAs have also recently incorporated a similar rule and exception (e.g. 2019 Australia–Uruguay IIA, Article 14.12).

10.2.1.2 Mechanisms for 'Sets of Disputes'

Two mechanisms that have been made available to settle sets of investment-related disputes can be singled out for the purpose of our examination: claims commissions and tribunals; and lump-sum agreements.

a Claims Commissions and Tribunals

In order to settle disputes, particularly investment-related disputes, which arose in the context of some revolutions, civil wars or other public unrest during the course of the late eighteenth, nineteenth and twentieth centuries, claims commissions and tribunals were established by various treaties. These were composed of members of States parties and also frequently of members having the nationality of third States. Contrary typically to the Iran–United States Claims Tribunal, which is discussed below, not all of these commissions can be characterised as legal dispute settlement mechanisms. Indeed, many of them had a political dimension, notably in the sense that the outcome of their work constituted merely the basis of negotiated agreements.

Following the American Revolution, the first of these commissions was that established by the 1794 Treaty of Amity, Commerce and Navigation adopted by Great Britain and the USA, a treaty known as the 'Jay Treaty'. In fact, this Treaty established three commissions, one of which was in charge of settling disputes relating to the seizure of vessels and other properties (Article VII and VIII) and another being tasked with the charge of handling claims pertaining to debts contracted by Americans with British creditors (Article VI). As such, this Treaty constituted one of the first attempts to institutionalise the settlement of international disputes.

These commissions and tribunals are often seen as the 'ancestors' of investor-State arbitration. Irrespective of the institutional and procedural differences that exist between them, it is worth emphasising the substantive contribution made by these commissions to the protection granted by international law to foreign investors, notably with regard to the application and interpretation of IIA rules.

A landmark example is the 1926 decision of the Mexico–United States Claims Commission in *Neer (USA)* v. *Mexico*, which, as explained in Chapter 5, is central in the discussion of the content of the customary law minimum standard of treatment. Other examples are provided by the case law of the Iran–United States Claims Tribunal, such as those matters – analysed in Chapter 6 – relating to expropriation.

This Tribunal was created in the context of the crisis between Iran and the USA that resulted from the detention of US nationals at the US Embassy in Teheran and from the freezing of Iranian assets by the USA that followed. The creation of the Tribunal is actually one of the measures agreed by these two States in order to resolve this crisis. All these measures form part of the 'Algiers Declarations' made on 19 January 1981, for which Algeria played an important intermediary role. The Tribunal is made up of nine members, mainly appointed by the USA and Iran. Those members are divided between three Chambers. The Tribunal has jurisdiction especially to decide the approximately 3800 claims that were submitted by 19 January 1982, the deadline set to file the claims. Those claims oppose both US nationals to Iran and Iranian nationals to the USA. They concern debts, contracts, expropriations or other measures affecting property.[4] Deciding these claims is a long process that still keeps the Tribunal and its members busy, although it was created long ago.

b Lump-Sum Agreements

Lump-sum agreements have been mainly used after the Second World War (WWII) to settle disputes relating to nationalisations. Contrary to claims commissions and tribunals, they do not entail the intervention of a third body; rather, they involve only host States and home States. This is likely the reason why lump-sum agreements are viewed at times as a kind of diplomatic protection of a collective nature.

In any case, they consist of agreements negotiated between these States as to the amount of compensation to be paid for the damage suffered by a set of investors of the home States. In practice, this amount has not always corresponded to the full reparation of this damage, as prescribed by public international law – and discussed in Chapter 15 – but only to part of it. Regardless of the amount of compensation, it is paid entirely to home States, which are then responsible for allocating this compensation to their investors. In return, claims at both the domestic and international levels are precluded.

Lump-sum agreements have been a widespread practice to the extent that some States have established permanent bodies in charge of the allocation of compensation. Mention can be made, for instance, of the US Foreign Claims Settlement Commission, which was created in 1954.

---

[4] Information available at www.iusct.net.

10.2.2 IIA Dispute Settlement Mechanisms

International investment agreements typically contain provisions making available mechanisms for the settlement of both State–State disputes and investor–State disputes. Both are examined in turn.

10.2.2.1 Mechanisms Available for the Settlement of State–State Disputes

Irrespective of the settlement of those above-mentioned State–State disputes that relate to investor–State disputes through subrogation, a distinction must be made between two types of dispute settlement: (1) the settlement of disputes arising from the interpretation and application of IIA provisions; and (2) the settlement of disputes arising from the application of specific provisions that place obligations upon States to respect public interests.

a The Settlement of Disputes Arising from the Interpretation and Application of IIA Provisions

At the outset, mechanisms available to settle disputes arising from the interpretation and application of IIA provisions should be distinguished from the mechanism used to deal more generally with any treaty matter (e.g. 2015 Japan–Ukraine IIA, Article 24), known as, for instance, 'Joint Committees' or 'Commissions'. At the same time, it is worth noting that such bodies may be called upon to play a role in the settlement of those State–State disputes, as provided for under the terms of certain IIAs. This role varies across treaty practice. They can intervene at the consultation stage as notably provided for in Article 26 of the 2016 Morocco–Nigeria IIA; more substantially, these bodies can be assigned the function of settling the disputes arising from the interpretation and application of the agreements (e.g. 2006 Canada–Peru IIA, Article 50).

Virtually all IIAs provide that the parties shall or should attempt to settle their disputes concerning the interpretation and application of the agreements through diplomatic channels, typically through consultations/negotiations. If the dispute is not settled, almost all IIAs provide that either party can submit the dispute to arbitration. Some IIAs make recourse to arbitration possible only after the expiry of a certain period of time from the date of the notification, typically six months (e.g. 2003 Ethiopia–France IIA, Article 10.2), while others do not provide for any time restriction (e.g. 1982 United Kingdom–Belize IIA, Article 9.2). As for multilateral investment agreements, the States parties to the agreements but not to the dispute classically get the opportunity to participate in the settlement of the dispute if they consider that they have a substantial interest in it (e.g. 2012 Japan–Korea–China IIA, Article 17).

Arbitration tribunals tasked with the charge of settling those disputes are usually composed of three members. Two are appointed by each State disputing party and one, either by these two arbitrators (e.g. 2016 Armenia–United

Arab Emirates (UAE), Article 11.3) – in consultation or not with those parties – or by those parties directly (e.g. 2018 Kazakhstan–Singapore IIA, Article 15.3). That third arbitrator serves typically as the chairperson of the tribunal. Virtually all IIAs require that the third arbitrator be a national of a third State, while some agreements also require this arbitrator to have the nationality of a State having diplomatic relations with the States parties to the dispute (e.g. 2005 Turkey–Australia IIA, Article 12.3). In case of a failure by a party to appoint an arbitrator, or of the two State-appointed arbitrators to agree on the third arbitrator, IIAs usually provide that the President of the ICJ may be invited to proceed with the appointment or, if he has the nationality of a party or is otherwise excluded, the Vice-President of the Court. If the Vice-President cannot, for the same reason, perform this role, it is assigned to the Judge who is next in seniority and who is not excluded, to proceed with such an appointment (e.g. 2001 Mozambique–Netherlands IIA, Article 11). Alternatively, other IIAs instead confer this role on the Secretary-General of the Permanent Court of Arbitration (PCA) or, if he is excluded from performing this task, to the Deputy Secretary-General (e.g. 2017 Israel–Japan IIA, Article 23.4). As regards the rules applicable to the arbitration procedure and to the functioning of tribunals, IIAs typically leave the determination of these to the arbitrators, subject to any agreement between the parties and to some specifications provided in the agreements, most notably concerning the vote, the bearing of costs or the legal force of the award (e.g. 2002 Australia–Sri Lanka IIA, Annex A).

b The Settlement of Disputes Arising from the Application of Specific IIA Provisions Placing Obligations upon States to Respect Public Interests

In some IIAs that contain specific provisions placing obligations upon States to respect public interests, notably those discussed in Chapter 8 prohibiting the lowering of the protection of these interests in order to encourage investments, there exists a specific dispute settlement procedure to settle disputes that may arise from the application of such provisions. For instance, Article 13 of the 2008 USA–Rwanda IIA provides that '[i]f a Party considers that the other Party has offered such an encouragement, it may request consultations with the other Party and the two Parties shall consult with a view to avoiding any such encouragement'.

Such a dispute settlement procedure – which is a political mechanism – is clearly less developed than the procedure applicable to the settlement of the disputes arising from the interpretation and application of the other IIA provisions; in particular, it does not make available any mechanism in the event that the consultations between the parties do not lead to an agreement. This is also to be contrasted with the more developed and detailed dispute settlement procedure that is typically available under some free trade agreements (FTAs) to settle comparable disputes that arise from the application of similar provisions not contained in an investment chapter. For instance, in case the parties fail to reach an agreement through consultations, those agreements provide for the intervention of a Joint Committee or Commission and, if needed, for the establishment of a dispute settlement or arbitration panel. The panel's reports are non-binding and consist of a set of recommendations that serve as a basis for the parties to negotiate an agreement (e.g. 2000 USA–Jordan FTA, Article 17). Where no agreement can be reached, or where an agreement is reached but not implemented, FTAs typically entitle the complaining State party to take any appropriate and commensurate measure, or provide for a mechanism of annual monetary assessment (e.g. 2004 Dominican Republic–Central America Free Trade Agreement, Article 20.16).

10.2.2.2 Mechanisms Available for the Settlement of Investor-State Disputes

As explained in Chapter 11, the settlement of investor–State disputes, as it was designed at the origin of IIA practice, has been heavily criticised, in particular in the 2010s. This has triggered reform initiatives and new treaty practices. It is therefore necessary to distinguish the approach traditionally adopted in IIAs from those new practices and initiatives in order to review the mechanisms available under IIAs to settle investor–State disputes.

a 'Traditional' Practice

The settlement of investor–State disputes is often reduced to arbitration, as is illustrated by the – erroneous – use of the acronym 'ISDS' (for 'investor–State dispute settlement') to designate investor–State arbitration. Of course, arbitration has been the main mechanism provided for in IIAs to settle investor–State disputes; yet, other mechanisms are available to settle those disputes. In addition to arbitration, which is discussed in detail in Chapter 11, consultations/negotiations are utilised as a dispute settlement mechanism, as well as host States' domestic courts.

As is discussed in Chapters 11 and 14, the recourse to consultations/negotiations is often provided as a preliminary step before the recourse to arbitration. Irrespective of this early role in the dispute settlement procedure, it is important to realise that disputing parties still have the possibility of negotiating and consulting in parallel to the conduct of arbitration proceedings. This is well evidenced by the statistics made available by ICSID with regard to arbitration proceedings under the Washington Convention and the ICSID Additional Facility Rules.[5] Disputes have been settled by the disputing parties themselves or proceedings have been otherwise discontinued in 35 per cent of the 728 disputes registered by ICSID between 1972 and June 2019. Out of these, 48 per cent of the proceedings have been discontinued at the request of both parties, and 14 per cent have seen the award embodying a settlement agreement reached by the disputing parties.

---

[5] ICSID (n 1).

The recourse to host States' domestic courts is provided in some IIAs as a preliminary step before resorting to arbitration; this is analysed in Chapters 11 and 14. Irrespective of this early role in the dispute settlement procedure, some IIAs provide for the possibility to settle investor–State disputes through the local courts of the host State as an alternative to arbitration (e.g. 2017 Rwanda–UAE IIA, Article 14.1). As explained in Chapter 14, the choice made to initiate arbitration proceedings or domestic proceedings is final under the fork-in-the-road clause; in other words, once either of these has been initiated, it is not possible to have recourse to the other in order to settle the same dispute.

b 'New' Practices

Preliminary Remarks

At the core of the criticism – detailed in Chapter 11 – against investor–State arbitration has been, on the one hand, the alleged lack of legitimacy of arbitration tribunals as well as the lack of transparency of arbitration proceedings and, on the other hand, the possibility for investors to initiate arbitration proceedings 'directly' based on IIA offers to arbitrate and to participate in the constitution of arbitration tribunals. Also importantly, investor-State arbitration has been criticised for having a 'chilling effect', something also explained in Chapter 11. As examined in that chapter, this has led to reforms of arbitration proceedings intended to address some of these criticisms. But this has also led some States to change more radically their approach to the settlement of investor–State disputes as reflected in the IIAs they have concluded in the 2010s.

The most radical of these goes as far as not making available under the agreements any dispute settlement mechanism for the settlement of investor–State disputes. For instance, the 2017 Hong Kong SAR China–ASEAN IIA merely provides that States parties shall enter into discussions to agree on investor–State dispute settlement matters (Articles 20 and 22). With regard to the 2018 United States–Mexico–Canada IIA, a similar result derives *mutatis mutandis* from Canada's decision not to be bound by Annex 14-D, which contains the investor–State dispute settlement mechanism, an Annex which then applies only to the USA and Mexico.

In the context of the 2018 Comprehensive and Progressive Agreement for Trans-Pacific Partnership (CPTPP), New Zealand signed side letters with Australia and Peru in which they reciprocally exclude the resort to arbitration – provided in Article 9.19 – for their investors. It is noteworthy that New Zealand signed other side letters with Brunei Darussalam, Malaysia and Vietnam which do not radically exclude such resort, but instead require that those States give their consent to investor–State arbitration for each dispute. Through these side letters, they reject the 'classical' approach adopted under Article 9.19 that enables investors to initiate arbitration proceedings without States having each time to give a specific consent to arbitration.

Alternatively, some States have decided to replace or combine arbitration with other dispute settlement mechanisms in the settlement of investor–State disputes. Three main approaches can be identified in this respect: (1) the combination of investor–State arbitration with a strong local remedy requirement; (2) the combination of arbitration, be it investor–State arbitration or State–State arbitration, with a prevention mechanism; and (3) the creation of a standing court. It is striking that this trend leads to a certain revival of mechanisms – examined above – that have traditionally played a prominent role in the settlement of investor–State disputes and whose drawbacks led to the development of investor–State arbitration.

i Combination of a Strong Local Remedy Requirement and Arbitration   The local remedy requirement – which is analysed in Chapter 14 – is not new in IIA practice. Yet, the treaty practice that has developed in the 2010s displays a noticeable extension of the period of time during which local remedies are to be pursued. This period has traditionally ranged from three months (e.g. 1980 United Kingdom–Bangladesh IIA, Article 8) to eighteen months (e.g. 1991 Spain–Argentina IIA, Article 10).

No such limitation is provided for in the 2016 Morocco–Nigeria IIA; rather, Article 26.5 provides that the investor may resort to international arbitration mechanisms only after the exhaustion of local remedies. Less radically, the 2018 Belarus–India IIA, for instance, sets – on the basis of the 2015 Indian Model BIT – a time period that is still significantly longer than traditional treaty practice. According to Article 15.2, investors may initiate arbitration proceedings only if, after exhausting all relevant judicial or administrative remedies relating to the measure underlying the claim for at least a period of five years from the date on which the investor first acquired knowledge of the measure in question, no resolution satisfactory for the investor has been reached. Interestingly, this IIA – again on the basis of the Indian Model BIT – specifies that the requirement to exhaust local remedies shall not be applicable in those cases where the investor can demonstrate that 'there are no available domestic legal remedies capable of reasonably providing relief'.

ii Combination of a Prevention Mechanism and Arbitration   Prevention as such is not new in IIA practice; indeed, IIAs have traditionally foreseen an amicable settlement of disputes between investors and their home States intended to settle disputes at an early stage and to avoid the initiation of judicial proceedings, notably arbitration proceedings.

Yet, some IIAs concluded in the 2010s, in particular by Brazil, bring prevention into a new paradigm where investors are not parties, but mere participants. Indeed, prevention mechanisms are typically to be triggered by the home State of the investor concerned and a solution to be looked for by States with the assistance of a Joint Committee composed of representatives of the States parties to the agreement. Under the 2015 Brazil–Malawi IIA, investors' representatives shall participate whenever possible in meetings to facilitate the search for this solution (Article 13.3.c). Under the 2018 Brazil–Guyana IIA, investors do not even have this systematic role; Article 24.3.b provides merely that 'representative of the affected investor may be invited to appear before the Joint Committee'.

In the event that no solution can be reached, the relevant IIAs provide for the possibility to resort to arbitration. Here, a distinction must be made between those agreements depending on whether they refer to State–State arbitration or to investor–State arbitration. The latter option is well illustrated by the 2016 Morocco–Nigeria IIA, which entitles investors to initiate arbitration proceedings subject, as mentioned above, to the exhaustion of local remedies. The former approach is again typical of the practice adopted by Brazil. For instance, Article 13.6 of the Brazil–Malawi IIA provides that '[i]f the dispute cannot be resolved, the Parties to the exclusion of the investors may resort to arbitration mechanisms between States, which are to be agreed upon by the Joint Committee, whenever the Parties find it appropriate'. Two remarks can be made about this Article.

First of all, investors have no role to play in the decision on whether or not to initiate arbitration proceedings and they are not a party to those proceedings; this constitutes a fundamental departure from traditional IIA practice in that even though arbitration is maintained, it deprives investors from accessing arbitration. Instead, their home State is placed at the forefront, knowing that they have no obligation with regard to the initiation of arbitration proceedings. This is *mutatis mutandis* reminiscent of diplomatic protection as discussed above.

Second, the decision on whether or not to initiate State–State arbitration is to be made by the two States and not by the home State only. In other words, this means that provisions like Article 13.6 of the Brazil–Malawi IIA do not embody States' consent to arbitration; instead, for each such dispute, the consent of the host State is required. On the other hand, it is worth noting that the IIA adopted by Brazil and the UAE in 2019 confers on either party the power to submit the dispute to an arbitration tribunal (Article 25.1).

iii Establishment of a Standing Court   The establishment of a standing judicial body first made its way into IIA practice with respect to appeals, the objective being to provide for a mechanism that could review awards rendered by arbitration tribunals and ensure the consistent interpretation of treaties. The USA was a pioneer in this respect; it introduced in its 2004 Model BIT an Annex addressing the '[p]ossibility of a bilateral appellate mechanism'. Annex D states: 'Within three years after the date of entry into force of this Treaty, the Parties shall consider whether to establish a bilateral appellate body or similar mechanism to review awards rendered under Article 34 in arbitrations commenced after they establish the appellate body or similar mechanism.' This Annex was incorporated in the 2008 USA–Rwanda IIA, but no such appeal mechanism has ever been established.

In the 2010s, the EU in particular has gone one step further by promoting, not the combination of investor–State arbitration with a standing appeal mechanism, but the replacement of investor–State arbitration with an investment court system (ICS) composed of both a tribunal and an appeal tribunal. It can be noted that, even though this system is conceived of as a departure from arbitration, it is open to foreign investors, contrary to the above-mentioned mechanism incorporated in the IIAs concluded by Brazil. The incorporation of the ICS was first proposed by the EU in the context of the negotiation of the TTIP with the USA. Meanwhile, this system has been incorporated in the Comprehensive Economic and Trade Agreement (CETA) adopted in 2016.

In relation to the standing nature of the ICS, a key feature of this system that differs from investor–State arbitration relates to the appointment of its members. Contrary to arbitration tribunals whose members are as a matter of principle appointed by the parties to the dispute, ICS members are to be appointed by CETA's States parties. For instance, pursuant to Article 8.27, the fifteen members of the Tribunal are to be appointed by the CETA Joint Committee, five having the nationality of EU Member States, five being Canadian nationals, and five having the nationality of third States. Those members, as well as the members of the Appellate Tribunal, are required to comply with strict ethical and professional requirements. According to Article 8.30.1, they shall notably refrain from acting as counsel or as party-appointed experts or witnesses in any pending or new investment dispute under the CETA or any other international agreement.

It is worth noting that the promotors of the ICS see the establishment of standing courts in the context of bilateral agreements as a preliminary step, their ultimate goal being the creation of a multilateral standing court. In that sense, Article 8.29 of the CETA provides that '[t]he Parties shall pursue with other trading partners the establishment of a multilateral investment tribunal and appellate mechanism for the resolution of investment disputes'. Such efforts have notably contributed to the initiation of discussions at the United Nations Commission on International Trade Law in 2017, which may lead ultimately to the creation of a multilateral investment court.

Irrespective of the legal and political issues that the establishment of an ICS raises, be it at the bilateral or the multilateral level, one may wonder the extent to which such a court system can actually fix the legitimacy crisis faced by the settlement of investor–State disputes. As explained in Chapter 11, the lack of legitimacy of investor–State arbitration denounced across civil societies is grounded, not only in the procedural features of investor–State arbitration, but also its international dimension. Indeed, many reject radically the idea that State conduct be reviewed and disputes involving domestic public interest considerations be settled by tribunals that do not form part of the State apparatus. In this respect, an ICS appears to display the same defect and to open the door to the same criticism as investor–State arbitration does.

11

Investor–State Arbitration
Historical, Institutional and Procedural Dimensions

Introduction

As explained in Chapter 10, arbitration has traditionally been the main dispute settlement mechanism used to settle investor–State disputes. This chapter introduces the main features of this mechanism from a threefold perspective: historical, institutional and procedural.

11.1 The History of Investor–State Arbitration

Preliminary Remarks

Investor–State arbitration has since the 1990s been the most dynamic type of international arbitration. It is also the most familiar across civil society, in particular because of the negotiation and adoption of mega-regional free trade agreements (FTAs), such as the 2016 Comprehensive and Economic Trade Agreement (CETA). However, one should be aware that international arbitration has been used to settle other types of international disputes involving, in particular, States, international organisations and private entities. In the same vein, it is important to note that international arbitration has a long history that pre-dates by far the settlement of investor–State disputes. From this historical perspective, investor–State arbitration can be seen as having its roots both in State–State arbitration relating to public international law matters as well as in international commercial arbitration. Starting from this origin of international arbitration, this subsection then examines in succession the emergence and consolidation of investor–State arbitration as well as the growing criticism it has been facing since the turn of the last century.

11.1.1 The Emergence and Development of International Arbitration

11.1.1.1 State-State Arbitration

Arbitration has been resorted to for millennia in order to settle disputes between States or State-like entities. From as early as the time of Ancient Greece, for instance, arbitration was used to solve disputes between allied

States and city-States pertaining to their independence. In the Middle Ages, arbitration was also heavily relied upon, with, for example, the Pope acting as sole arbitrator. With the 1648 peace treaties of Westphalia, which followed the Thirty Years' War in Europe, arbitration declined in inter-State relations. During the eighteenth and nineteenth centuries, arbitration re-emerged, in particular to settle disputes originating in the claims of nationals engaged in economic operations abroad and endorsed by their home States, as seen in Chapter 10. This revival paved the way for the adoption of the landmark 1899 Convention for the Pacific Settlement of International Disputes, which established the Permanent Court of Arbitration (PCA), which is introduced below. The establishment of the PCA illustrates the process of institutionalisation and professionalisation that has accompanied this revival of State–State arbitration. Indeed, while, for instance, heads of States frequently acted as arbitrators, they were progressively replaced by professionals, be they jurists or experts in the subject matter of the disputes at hand. Since the end of the Cold War, arbitration has been increasingly popular among States as a means of settling all kind of disputes, such as territorial disputes. This is well illustrated by the growing number of cases settled under the auspices of the PCA. It is worth noting that arbitration has also been used, on the basis of the 2008 Abyei Arbitration Agreement, to settle an intra-State border dispute between the Government of Sudan and the Sudan People's Liberation Movement.

Various reasons together explain the important role played throughout history by arbitration in the settlement of State–State disputes. Among these, the control that it gives to States over the settlement of their disputes is certainly key. Of course, arbitration is a proper legal method of dispute settlement; it is characterised in particular by the binding nature of the decisions taken by tribunals. However, States retain a large degree of control over how the arbitration is conducted. In addition to the fact that the consent of the States disputing parties is necessary for arbitration tribunals to have jurisdiction to settle their disputes, they can decide issues as crucial as the individuals who will act as arbitrators, the applicable law and the procedural arrangements. While consent is a requirement that applies to all international courts and tribunals, including standing courts, the ability to decide on those last three issues is specific to State–State arbitration. Although the settlement is left to arbitrators, all these features of State–State arbitration make it for States in many situations a convenient method to settle their disputes.

11.1.1.2 International Commercial Arbitration

As with State–State disputes relating to public international law matters, the use of arbitration to settle disputes arising in the context of international commercial operations has a long history worldwide; this also holds true for domestic commercial operations. Three main steps have been identified in the development of commercial arbitration that has accompanied the globalisation of commercial operations.[1] Originally, commercial arbitration could be characterised as a 'self-contained regime' in the sense that it existed in parallel to public legal orders. Arbitration was organised and used by merchants; the compliance with arbitration awards did not result from those legal orders, but instead from the expectations and pressures of merchant communities. However, public authorities realised that arbitration was too important to be left in the hands of merchants. In a second stage, this led to the regulation of arbitration by domestic law; for instance, in the course of the sixteenth century, the recourse to arbitration was made compulsory in France for all disputes arising between merchants from their commercial activities. The internationalisation of commercial operations and their growth after the Second World War (WWII), on the one hand, as well as the need to ensure the enforcement of arbitration agreements and the recognition and enforcement of awards worldwide, on the other hand, resulted in the adoption of international instruments and in the creation of institutions aimed at facilitating commercial arbitration. 'Centres', like the Arbitration Institute of the Stockholm Chamber of Commerce (SCC) and the International Chamber of Commerce (ICC) International Court of Arbitration in Paris were established in the early twentieth century. By the same token, arbitration rules, notably the 1976 Arbitration Rules of the United Nations Commission on International Trade Law (UNCITRAL Arbitration Rules), were later adopted; also importantly, States adopted in 1958 the Convention on the Recognition and Enforcement of Foreign Arbitral Awards. These centres and instruments are discussed further below in relation to investor–State arbitration.

The reasons for the frequent use of arbitration to settle disputes arising in the context of international commercial operations are manyfold. Similar to State–State arbitration, the control that it confers to the disputing parties, in particular over the choice of the arbitrators, the applicable law and procedural arrangements, has been decisive in this regard. As to the latter, it is worth stressing that the confidentiality of international commercial arbitration proceedings is seen by corporations as an advantage over domestic courts proceedings in order to ensure that information that may be vital to their businesses does not become public. Likewise, the greater swiftness of arbitration proceedings constitutes another reason that helps to explain the success of international commercial arbitration. The conclusion of the Convention on the Recognition and Enforcement of Foreign Arbitral Awards and its widespread ratification comes as a worldwide guarantee of effectiveness and efficacy that contributes to this success.

---

[1] N Blackaby, M Hunter, C Partasides, A Redfern, *Redfern and Hunter on International Arbitration* (6th ed, Oxford University Press 2018), at 4–6.

11.1.2 The Emergence and Consolidation of Investor–State Arbitration

The emergence and consolidation of arbitration to settle investor–State disputes is mainly the result of two phenomena: (1) the rise of instruments, namely 'State contracts' and international investment agreements (IIAs), in which States consent to investor–State arbitration; and (2) the adoption of the 1965 Washington Convention, which established the International Centre for Settlement of Investment Disputes (ICSID) which, in many respects, has always been at the forefront of the evolution of investor–State arbitration.

11.1.2.1 State Contracts and International Investment Agreements

As explained in Chapter 10, investment-related disputes were originally settled by host States' domestic courts or led, through the exercise of diplomatic protection by home States, to State–State disputes. For the reasons detailed thereto, both were considered as being inadequate by foreigners and by foreign investors, in particular because of the politicisation that both – in their own way – entailed. The emergence of arbitration to settle investor–State disputes constituted precisely an attempt to depoliticise this settlement and to give foreign investors access to an international adjudicative body.

Historically, the first type of instruments to have conferred foreigners such an access to arbitration has been those contracts they concluded as of the late nineteenth century with home States, such as concession agreements. This contractual practice was notably characteristic of a type of contract – called in the French-speaking literature 'State contracts' – which were intended to internationalise the contractual relationship. Those contracts aimed at avoiding situations in which home States could use their sovereign prerogatives in a way detrimental to their foreign co-contractors, either through the modification of the applicable domestic law or through the settlement of disputes by their domestic courts. As to the former, stabilisation clauses in particular were incorporated into those contracts to protect foreign investors from the harmful modifications of the applicable law; those clauses had the effect of 'freezing' the applicable domestic law at the time of the conclusion of the contracts. Following the same rationale, compromissory clauses granting jurisdiction to arbitration tribunals to settle the disputes arising from the interpretation and application of those contracts were included to internationalise the settlement of disputes and to protect foreign investors from the potential partiality of domestic courts. Given the confidential nature of such State contracts, it is difficult to provide figures to measure the scope of this phenomenon. That being said, there is no doubt that they have paved the way for the development of investor–State arbitration and for its consolidation as the main method used to settle investor–State disputes.

This consolidation has resulted in particular from the conclusion – discussed in Chapter 10 – of IIAs, notably that of bilateral investment treaties (BITs), which incorporate investor–State arbitration. In fact, the first BITs to have been concluded did not incorporate this mechanism. As noted by Arbitrator Söderlund in *Blue Bank International & Trust (Barbados) Ltd v. Venezuela*, in reference to Newcombe and Paradell,[2] the 1969 Italy–Chad BIT was the first BIT to incorporate investor–State arbitration with an unqualified State consent (2017, Award, Separate Opinion, para. 21). It was first relied on in 1990 in *Asian Agricultural Products Ltd (AAPL) v. Sri Lanka*. Along the same line, it is also worth noting that such a mechanism has also been introduced in domestic investment codes; the first case in which it was relied on was *Southern Pacific Properties (Middle East) Limited v. Egypt* in 1988.

The possibility thereby conferred to investors to initiate arbitration proceedings 'directly' by relying on the offer to arbitrate contained in IIAs, coupled with the rise in the number of these agreements, has greatly contributed to placing arbitration at the core of investor–State dispute settlement. At the same time, it has also contributed to placing this mechanism under fire, as discussed below.

11.1.2.2 The ICSID Convention

The adoption of the Washington Convention, known as the 'ICSID Convention', and the establishment of ICSID which derives therefrom, has played a key role in building the predominant role played by arbitration in the settlement of investor–State disputes. Of course, the adoption and widespread participation in this Convention and the establishment of ICSID as such do not explain this position on their own; this is evidenced by the fact that the ICSID docket became significant only as of the 1990s. On the other hand, there is no doubt that the services offered by ICSID and the key features of the Convention have encouraged States to incorporate investor–State arbitration in their IIAs and, more generally, have changed the traditional views of States as to the possibility for private persons – for investment matters – to benefit from access to an international adjudicative body.

Among those features that are discussed across Part III, it is worth noting that once States have given their consent to ICSID arbitration – a consent that does not result from the ratification of the Convention, but which is given in writing for that purpose – they cannot withdraw it unilaterally; the same holds true with respect to investors (Article 25.1). Other features that are telling about the innovation brought about by the Convention at the time it was adopted pertain to local remedies and diplomatic protection. As for the former, and albeit States retain the right under Article 26 to require the prior exhaustion of local administrative or judicial remedies as a condition of consent, that Article sets out a presumption that, in the case of silence of the parties in this regard, their intention is that they agree to have recourse to

---

[2] A Newcombe, L Paradell, *Law and Practice of Investment Treaties: Standards of Treatment* (Kluwer 2009).

arbitration to the exclusion of any other remedy. Concerning diplomatic protection, Article 27.1 provides that the home States of investors, parties to the Convention, shall not exercise their diplomatic protection once host States parties to the Convention and these investors have consented to submitting their dispute to ICSID arbitration. They regain this right only if these host States fail to abide by and to comply with the awards rendered.

Furthermore, it is worth noting the leading role played by the Washington Convention and ICSID in the development of rules and mechanisms adapted to the specifics of investor–State disputes. Of course, the establishment of ICSID forms part of the process of institutionalisation of international arbitration mentioned above and, more generally, that of international adjudication, as illustrated by the establishment of the Permanent Court of International Justice (PCIJ) and of the International Court of Justice (ICJ). Yet, its establishment as the first specialised dispute settlement centre dedicated to the settlement of investment-related disputes as well as the drafting of a set of specialised rules of procedure have shed light on the need to develop tailor-made structures and rules. This specialisation is an ongoing process, as illustrated by the successive revisions of the ICSID Arbitration Rules, in particular that proposed in the 2019 ICSID Working Paper n°3 analysed below.

11.1.3 The Crisis of Investor–State Arbitration

As evidenced by the criticisms that have been formulated in the context of the negotiation of mega-regional FTAs, like the Comprehensive and Progressive Agreement for Trans-Pacific Partnership (CPTPP) adopted in 2018, investor–State arbitration is harshly criticised by local populations, politicians and non-governmental organisations (NGO), in particular since the 2010s. Those criticisms have reached such a scale that they have led States, both developing and developed, to contemplate and engage in reforms of investor–State dispute settlement. As explained in Chapter 10, this has resulted in the substitution or combination of arbitration with other dispute settlement mechanisms, while another approach discussed below has consisted, less radically, in adapting investor–State arbitration to address some of the States' and public opinion's expectations and requirements.

The reasons underlying those criticisms are manyfold; yet, they are all grounded in the conviction that investor–State arbitration is inadequate to deal with the public interest considerations that underlie and surround investor–State disputes. First of all, investor–State arbitration has been criticised for its lack of transparency regarding, in particular, the access of the public to hearings, documents or awards, as well as the participation of non-disputing parties to the settlement of disputes. Additional criticisms relate to the costs of arbitration proceedings and the burden it entails on public budgets, the inconsistency of arbitration practice as well as the appointment of arbitrators by the disputing parties and, more specifically, by investors. This method for appointing the members of tribunals is criticised as it would allegedly lead to the appointment of arbitrators lacking impartiality and independence as well as legitimacy to rule over disputes involving domestic public interest considerations. Lastly, investor–State arbitration is criticised for having a 'chilling effect' on host States' regulatory power. In fact, some of these criticisms seem to go far beyond investor–State arbitration and arbitrators themselves and reveal more systemic concerns among local populations; this holds true notably with regard to the 'chilling effect' and the lack of legitimacy.

This 'chilling effect' as it is put forward by the critics of investor–State arbitration has two intertwined dimensions. According to the first of these, States first of all restrain themselves from regulating as arbitration practice would allegedly evidence that host States are often held internationally responsible for the breach of their IIA obligations and therefore required to pay heavy compensation to fully repair the damage caused to foreign investors. Irrespective of whether or not this appraisal of arbitration practice is correct, it remains that this first dimension of the 'chilling effect' largely derives from the rules that form part of IIA practice themselves. In other words, except in the few cases where the interpretation and application of IIA provisions by arbitration tribunals may be said to have been erroneous, tribunals' decisions to hold States internationally responsible are due first and foremost to the IIA obligations that States have consented to placing upon themselves.

The second dimension of the 'chilling effect' zeroes in on the threat that 'arbitration without privity' – discussed in Chapter 1 – constitutes for host States: the possibility offered to investors to initiate arbitration proceedings 'directly' based on IIA offers to arbitrate causes States to refrain from regulating in order to avoid such proceedings. Again, this criticism goes beyond investor–State arbitration, notably as it applies to other dispute settlement mechanisms and adjudicative bodies, such as the investment court system (ICS) incorporated in the 2016 CETA.

By the same token, the legitimacy criticism transcends investor–State arbitration. This appears clearly from the public consultation organised by the EU Commission in the context of the negotiation of the Transatlantic Trade and Investment Partnership (TTIP), which evidences that a large part of local populations actually expect investor–State disputes – where *domestic* public interest considerations are crucial – to be settled by *domestic* courts and not by any *international* adjudicative body. In other words, investor–State arbitration, beyond its alleged 'private' nature, has been criticised also because of its international dimension. In that sense, the criticisms formulated against it go far beyond its inner features and evidence a more general trend across domestic societies which consider that international courts and tribunals as well as international organisations, are unduly interfering with domestic affairs.

11.2 Institutional and Procedural Features of Investor–State Arbitration

Preliminary Remarks

Like State–State arbitration and international commercial arbitration, investor–State arbitration is to be contrasted with standing international courts and tribunals. This comes notably from the choice that arbitration leaves as regards the determination of procedural arrangements and the applicable law, as well as the appointment of the adjudicators.

That being said, an important distinction can be seen between investor–State arbitration and these two other types of arbitration. In State–State arbitration and international commercial arbitration, both disputing parties have full control over the determination of procedural arrangements and that of the applicable law. While this holds true in particular for investor–State arbitration based on contracts concluded between host States and foreign investors, the situation is quite different for the overwhelming majority of investor–State arbitration cases which are based on IIAs and on which Part III focuses. In that latter case, the modalities of the arbitration pertaining to institutional and procedural matters as well as the applicable law are first and foremost chosen by the States parties to the agreements. Investors can 'only' accept and endorse the choices made – what they do when they rely on the IIA offer to arbitrate and initiate arbitration proceedings, thereby expressing their consent to arbitration. That being said, it is worth mentioning that IIA States parties often leave investors with a choice of various institutional and procedural alternatives, as seen below. As in State–State arbitration and international commercial arbitration, investors are also of course empowered to participate in the establishment of the tribunals.

As can be seen from treaty practice, different options are available for States parties to IIAs to design the institutional and procedural features of investor–State arbitration. It is noteworthy that the most recent IIAs concluded provide much greater details about these features. Yet, it is still common practice that they rely – according to various combinations – on available dispute settlement centres and existing arbitration rules, which guide the conduct of arbitration proceedings. This section introduces the main dispute settlement centres and rules prior to sketching the key procedural features and phases of investor–State arbitration.

11.2.1 Dispute Settlement Centres and Arbitration Rules

Preliminary Remarks

Although they often come hand-in-hand in practice, as in the ICSID context, it is necessary to distinguish as a matter of theory between dispute settlement centres and arbitration rules. Dispute settlement centres are not standing adjudicative bodies that – in and of themselves – settle disputes. They are institutions that provide dispute settlement services, mainly with regard to arbitration, which is the focus of this subsection. In doing so, they assist the disputing parties and the tribunals appointed by them throughout the course of arbitration proceedings. Arbitration rules provide, in particular, the procedural steps and modalities according to which arbitration proceedings are to be conducted.

There exist two main situations in which dispute settlement centres and arbitration rules may interact in arbitration practice, namely where a centre administers a case under its own rules, and where a centre administers a case under the rules established by another institution. The first of these situations is illustrated by ICSID, the great majority of the cases administered by which are governed by its own Rules. The PCA illustrates the second situation in relation to the Rules established by UNCITRAL.

In light of these preliminary remarks and on the basis of the information made available by the relevant centres and institutions themselves, the following aims at introducing in turn the main dispute settlement centres[3] and arbitration rules.

11.2.1.1 Dispute Settlement Centres

From a statistical point of view, ICSID distinguishes itself by the number of arbitration cases it has administered since its establishment. In addition to this, ICSID can be singled out as the only centre that is fully dedicated to the settlement of investment-related disputes. As we shall see shortly, many centres that provide services with regard to investment-related disputes are also available for the settlement of commercial disputes, while the PCA is also open for the settlement of a wide range of public international law disputes.

a 'Specialised' Centre: The International Centre for Settlement of Investment Disputes

The International Centre for Settlement of Investment Disputes was created by the Washington Convention, which was adopted in 1965 and entered into force in 1966; in August 2019, it counted 163 Signatory and Contracting States. This international organisation is one of the five institutions that form part of the World Bank Group. As part of this Group, which aims at putting an end to extreme poverty, ICSID was established with the intention of contributing to achieving this objective by offering services for the resolution of investment-related disputes, mainly investor–State disputes, through arbitration, conciliation, fact finding and mediation. With respect to conciliation that comes second in rank after arbitration in statistical terms, it is worth noting that only twelve cases out of the total number of ICSID cases registered by ICSID

---

[3] Information available on the websites of – respectively – ICSID (https://icsid.worldbank.org /en), the PCA (https://pca-cpa.org/en/home) and the SCC (https://sccinstitute.com).

between 1972 and June 2019 were conciliation cases; this is to be contrasted with the 716 ICSID arbitration cases registered over that period.[4]

The International Centre for Settlement of Investment Disputes is composed of two organs: the Administrative Council and the Secretariat.

The Council is composed of one representative of each Member State and is chaired by the President of the World Bank Group. The Council does not administer individual cases; rather, it is endorsed with 'systemic' tasks, such as electing the ICSID Secretary-General or adopting rules of procedure. Yet, it is worth noting that the Chairman of the Council can play a role with respect to individual cases; for instance, he may appoint arbitrator(s) or decide on disqualification proposals in certain circumstances. Furthermore, he is the appointing authority of *ad hoc* committees for annulment proceedings. The Chairman does not participate in the adoption of decisions within the Council. Each Member State has one vote, the required majority depending on the decision to be made. Although most of these decisions require a simple majority, some require a two-thirds majority, in particular the adoption of the procedural rules mentioned above. The amendment of the ICSID Convention requires the unanimous approval of the Member States.

The ICSID Secretariat is in charge of the day-to-day activities of the Centre. It is led by the Secretary-General and is made up of four case management teams, a general administration, a financial team and a front office. The tasks of the Secretariat are mainly twofold: (1) the provision of support by the management teams in the settlement of individual disputes; and (2) the provision of support by the front office to Member States and the public at large.

As regards the first mandate and arbitration proceedings, the role of the Secretariat depends on whether or not the proceedings are governed by the ICSID Convention Arbitration Rules. For those that are governed by the ICSID Convention Arbitration Rules, its functions include: (1) acting as registrar, notably reviewing and registering requests and authenticating awards; (2) assisting in the constitution of arbitral tribunals and *ad hoc* committees; (3) assisting parties, tribunals and committees with all aspects of the case procedure; (4) organising and assisting hearings; (5) administering the finances of each case; and (6) providing any other administrative support as requested by tribunals and committees. As to arbitration proceedings governed by another set of rules, such as the settlement of investor–State disputes governed by the UNCITRAL Arbitration Rules, the range of services varies depending on the choices of the parties, extending from the organisation of hearings to full secretariat.

Concerning the second mandate – the support to Member States and the public at large – the tasks of the Secretariat relate to institutional matters and

---

[4] ICSID, 'The ICSID Caseload: Statistics', Issue 2019-2 (August 2019), available at https://icsid .worldbank.org/en.

knowledge dissemination, notably through the publication of the *ICSID Review* or the organisation of training.

Among the institutional tasks with which it is endorsed, the Secretariat maintains, in particular, the Panel of arbitrators in ICSID cases. The Panel of arbitrators is composed of persons designated by each Member State (four maximum), who can have a different nationality and who serve for a renewable period of six years; the Chairman of the Administrative Council can also designate up to ten persons. These persons do not exercise automatically an arbitration function over their term; instead, they are available for selection in arbitration tribunals and *ad hoc* annulment committees. It is worth noting that persons who are not on the Panel's list can still be appointed as arbitrators in ICSID cases, but they cannot be committee members in annulment proceedings, which is only open to those who are on the list of the Panel of arbitrators.

b 'Generalist' Centres

In contrast to ICSID, the other dispute settlement centres active in the administration of investor–State cases do not administer only such cases. Almost all these centres were initially created to settle commercial disputes, having later opened themselves to investor–State disputes. The Arbitration Institute of the Stockholm Chamber of Commerce, the ICC International Court of Arbitration in Paris and the London Court of International Arbitration are well-known examples of this category of dispute settlement centres. In illustrating this category, special attention is paid here to the Arbitration Institute of the Stockholm Chamber of Commerce. Unlike these centres, the PCA was initially created to settle State–State disputes pertaining to public international law matters. Since then, it has broadened the scope of the services it offers to encompass notably investor–State cases.

i The Permanent Court of Arbitration   The PCA is an international organisation that was established – on the occasion of the first Hague Conference convened by Czar Nicolas II of Russia – by the 1899 Convention on the Pacific Settlement of International Disputes. This Convention and the 1907 Convention on the Pacific Settlement of International Disputes, which revised it, constitute the basic foundational documents of the PCA. It is worth stressing that the PCA is older than the ICJ and even older than the PCIJ; in fact, the PCA is the oldest universal institution established with regard to the settlement of State–State disputes. In June 2019, it counted 122 Member States.

The name given to this organisation is misleading on several grounds. First, the Permanent *Court* of Arbitration is not a Court, meaning not a standing adjudicative body, like the ICJ, for example; rather, it is a centre that administers the settlement of a broad range of international law disputes. Second, the function of the Permanent Court of *Arbitration* is not limited to arbitration services. It also provides support in mediation and conciliation proceedings as well as to fact-finding commissions.

The subject matter of the disputes that can be submitted for resolution under the auspices of the PCA are very diverse. As evidenced by past disputes and aside from investment-related disputes, they can relate, for instance, to maritime boundary delimitations. As regards the parties, the disputes settled at the PCA oppose in particular States against one another as well as States against foreign investors.

The PCA is made of three components: the Administrative Council, the International Bureau and the Members of the Court.

The Administrative Council provides general guidance on the work of the PCA: it supervises its administration, budget and expenditure. It is made up of the Contracting Parties' diplomatic representatives accredited to the Netherlands and it is chaired by the Dutch Minister for Foreign Affairs.

The International Bureau is the PCA secretariat; it is headed by the Secretary-General. With regard to arbitration proceedings, it provides administrative support to the parties and tribunals. Depending on the request, it can provide a wide range of services, notably communication services, logistical and technical support for meetings and hearings, travel arrangements as well as general secretarial and linguistic support. A member or members of the Bureau can also be appointed as administrative secretary for cases. The PCA often provides full administrative support in arbitrations under the UNCITRAL Arbitration Rules. Under those Rules and upon the request of a disputing party to an arbitration proceeding, the Secretary-General of the PCA is endorsed with the task of designating an appointing authority, i.e. a person who will then appoint an arbitrator. Those Rules also provide that the Secretary-General can, himself, act as an appointing authority if the disputing parties so agree.

The Members of the Court are individuals who are appointed by the PCA Member States. As with the ICSID Panel of arbitrators, each State can appoint up to four members for a renewable period of six years; also in the same way as at ICSID, to be appointed as a Member of the Court does not mean that one will actually be appointed in arbitration proceedings. This all depends on the choice made by the disputing parties in each case who can decide to appoint as arbitrators individuals who are not such Members.

ii The Arbitration Institute of the Stockholm Chamber of Commerce   The Institute – known under the acronym 'SCC' – was created in 1917. Despite it being independent from the Stockholm Chamber of Commerce, the Institute is formally part of this institution, which was created in 1902. In contrast to ICSID and the PCA, it is not an international organisation, but is instead a Swedish institution.

Although it was originally established to settle domestic commercial disputes, the Institute has become very active in the settlement of international commercial disputes, and also investor–State disputes, be it through mediation or arbitration. Half of the commercial arbitration cases that it administers are international cases. The political neutrality that characterises Swedish diplomacy has greatly contributed to the internationalisation of the Institute's activities. In this respect, the United States of America (USA) and the Union of Soviet Socialist Republics (USSR) recognised it – in the context of the Cold War – as a neutral institution for the resolution of East–West trade disputes. The Institute was also recognised by China in the 1970s. This certainly helps to explain why it administers today a great number of cases involving Eastern European States or Central Asian countries. The key role played by the Institute in the arbitration of investor–State disputes arising from the interpretation and application of the 1994 Energy Charter Treaty (ECT) explains also the prevalence of those cases in the Institute's docket.

The Institute is composed of a Secretariat and a Board. The Board is composed of a maximum of twelve members, in addition to a Chairperson and two or three Vice-Chairpersons. It includes Swedish and non-Swedish members. In compliance with the Institute's Rules of Arbitration, the Board makes decisions pertaining, in particular, to the appointment of arbitrators and challenges, to *prima facie* jurisdiction, or to the costs of arbitration. The Secretariat is in charge of the day-to-day activities of the Institute. Its main tasks consist of the administration of the proceedings and the dissemination of knowledge.

11.2.1.2 Arbitration Rules

As explained above, there exists a broad set of arbitration rules. Those most frequently employed in practice are the UNCITRAL Rules of Arbitration and the ICSID Rules of Arbitration. This subsection introduces both of these Rules.

a ICSID Arbitration Rules

ICSID Arbitration Rules are used for arbitration proceedings administered by ICSID. Two sets of Rules can actually be resorted to, depending on the type of proceedings at stake: ICSID Convention arbitration proceedings and ICSID additional facility arbitration proceedings. Each of these is discussed in turn here; the chapters of Part III focus on the Rules applicable in ICSID Convention arbitration proceedings, which are referred to as 'ICSID Convention Arbitration Rules'.

i ICSID Convention Arbitration Proceedings   ICSID Convention arbitration proceedings pertain to the settlement of those legal disputes that arise directly out of an investment between a Contracting State to the Convention and a national of another Contracting State, who have both expressed their consent to the jurisdiction of ICSID. As for States, it is worth recalling that the ratification of the ICSID Convention does not amount to such an expression of consent – rather, such consent is typically given in IIAs, domestic investment codes or contracts.

Those proceedings are governed by (1) the ICSID Convention; (2) the Rules of Procedure for the Institution of Conciliation and Arbitration Proceedings

(Institution Rules); (3) the Rules of Procedure for Arbitration Proceedings (Arbitration Rules); and (4) the Administrative and Financial Regulations.

The ICSID Convention provides the framework for the conduct of arbitration proceedings. Its provisions are mandatory except as regards the provisions that authorise the parties to agree otherwise. The Institution Rules detail how proceedings shall be instituted, from the filing of a request to the dispatch of registration. The next steps of the proceedings are governed by the Arbitration Rules in addition to the relevant provisions of the ICSID Convention; the Arbitration Rules are to be read as subject to those relevant provisions of the ICSID Convention. By 2019, the Rules in force dated back to 2006, while a revision was ongoing. In this respect, the following analysis makes mention of the most important changes contemplated in the context of that revision in reference to the last Working Paper released by ICSID at the time this book was completed.[5] This 2019 Working Paper n° 3 reflects, according to the words of the ICSID Secretary-General, a 'developing consensus on the amendments through the consultation process' which was planned – in August 2019 – to end in November 2019 after a final consultation based on that Working Paper.[6] The Arbitration Rules are not mandatory aside from those that reflect mandatory provisions of the Convention. This means that all or some of those Rules can be modified, set aside or replaced. In this respect, it is worth mentioning that – as evidenced below – IIA States parties increasingly address procedural issues in the text of the agreements they conclude. In the case that there is no such agreement among the parties to derogate from the Rules, they are to be considered as binding for the parties and the tribunals. All the procedural questions that may arise in the course of the proceedings and that are not settled by the ICSID Convention, the Arbitration Rules or any rules agreed on by the parties shall be decided by the arbitration tribunals faced with them (ICSID Convention, Article 44).

In what follows, and in the chapters of this book, 'ICSID Convention Arbitration Rules' is used to designate 'collectively' the relevant provisions of the ICSID Convention and those Arbitration Rules, while 'ICSID Arbitration Rules' refers to those Arbitration Rules as such.

As examined below and in Chapter 16, the Rules governing ICSID Convention arbitration proceedings make them in many respects independent from the domestic legal orders and laws of the ICSID Member States. This holds true notably with respect to awards that cannot be reviewed and annulled by domestic courts; only ICSID annulment committees can annul those awards on the basis of a limited number of grounds. In the same vein, ICSID Member States are obliged to recognise these awards as binding as if they were final

---

[5] ICSID, 'Proposals for Amendment of the ICSID Rules', Working Paper n° 3 (August 2019), available at https://icsid.worldbank.org/en.

[6] Ibid., at 1.

judgments of their own courts and to enforce the pecuniary obligations that they may contain.

ii ICSID Additional Facility Arbitration Proceedings

ICSID additional facility arbitration proceedings were created in 1978 for investor–State disputes falling outside the scope of the ICSID Convention. They pertain mainly to the settlement of investment disputes between a State and a foreign national, one of which is not an ICSID Member State or a national of an ICSID Member State. In other words, while the ICSID Convention arbitration proceedings discussed above involve *both* a State which is a Member State to the ICSID Convention *and* a national whose State of nationality is also a Member State, ICSID additional facility arbitration proceedings involve *alternatively* a State which is not a Member State *or* a national whose State of nationality is not a Member State.

Those proceedings are governed by (1) the ICSID Additional Facility Rules; (2) the ICSID Arbitration (Additional Facility) Rules; and (3) the Administrative and Financial Regulations. The Arbitration Additional Facility Rules govern the entire arbitration proceedings. An agreement between parties to have their dispute settled in ICSID additional facility arbitration proceedings must be approved by the Secretary-General before the request can be registered and the proceedings start.

In many respects, ICSID additional facility arbitration proceedings are not as independent from domestic legal orders and laws as ICSID Convention arbitration proceedings are. In addition to the Rules, the domestic law of the place of arbitration applies to the proceedings and, in case of conflict between the Rules and the mandatory provisions of that law, the latter prevails. By the same token, given that the ICSID Convention does not apply to ICSID additional facility arbitration proceedings, the awards delivered under those proceedings do not benefit from the privileged system described above with respect to annulment, recognition and enforcement.

b UNCITRAL Arbitration Rules

The first version of the UNCITRAL Arbitration Rules, prepared under the auspices of UNCITRAL, was adopted in 1976. Those Rules, which are not mandatory, govern all the aspects of arbitration proceedings and can be used notably to settle commercial disputes and investor–State disputes, in the context of proceedings administered by dispute settlement centres or outside them. Since then, the Rules have been revised twice, in 2010 and 2013. The 2010 version was notably intended to increase the procedural efficiency of arbitration, for instance with regard to the replacement of arbitrators. In 2013, the Rules were revised in relation to investor–State arbitration proceedings. This revision has consisted in incorporating the UNCITRAL Rules on Transparency in Treaty-Based Arbitration (UNCITRAL Rules on

Transparency) adopted in 2013 and discussed further below. In what follows, as well as in the chapters of the book, reference is mainly made to this 2013 version of the UNCITRAL Arbitration Rules.

11.2.2 Arbitration Procedure

Preliminary Remarks
As we have seen above, investor–State arbitration has historical roots in State–State arbitration as well as in international commercial arbitration. Even though the ICSID Convention Arbitration Rules have from the outset been tailor-made for the settlement of investor–State disputes, this helps to explain why investor–State arbitration proceedings share many common features with these other types of arbitration. This is well illustrated by the UNCITRAL Arbitration Rules, which can be applied to commercial disputes and investor–State disputes, with the exception of the Rules on Transparency that are applicable to investor–State treaty-based disputes only. The criticisms summarised above and formulated by public opinions, politicians and NGOs have, as of the 2000s, led to an evolution of investor–State arbitration proceedings and the development of distinct features of such proceedings. This evolution, which translates into the revision of arbitration rules and in changes made in the investor–State dispute settlement provisions of IIAs, constitutes an alternative path followed by some States and institutions to the more radical changes examined in Chapter 10. The progressive paradigmatic move from confidentiality to transparency in investor–State arbitration proceedings symbolises this evolution.

Against the backdrop of this evolution, this subsection aims to introduce the key features of the proceedings that lead to the deliberations and awards as well as those of post-award proceedings and enforcement, while the following chapters delve into salient aspects of these proceedings in more detail. In examining these key features, we shall focus in particular on the sets of arbitration rules that are most often used: the ICSID Convention Arbitration Rules primarily, as well as the UNCITRAL Arbitration Rules and the SCC Arbitration Rules. Attention is also paid to the main features of the relevant IIA practice pertaining to the settlement of investor–State disputes in general, to the exclusion of the specific procedures set by some IIAs concerning in particular disputes in financial services (e.g. 2016 Hong Kong China SAR–Chile IIA, Article 22).

11.2.2.1 Arbitration Proceedings

For didactic purposes, four main phases are distinguished here: (1) the initiation of arbitration proceedings; (2) the establishment of arbitration tribunals; (3) the course of the proceedings; and (4) the closure and discontinuance of the proceedings. Each is analysed in turn.

a The Initiation of Arbitration Proceedings

i Conditions for Initiating Arbitration Proceedings   International investment agreements set – according to various formula and combinations – various steps and conditions for submitting disputes to arbitration. As examined in Chapter 14 in relation to jurisdiction and admissibility matters, they are mainly fivefold. First, some IIAs require from investors that they initiate arbitration proceedings during a definite period of time that starts running once they first acquire knowledge, or should have acquired knowledge, of the alleged IIA breach and of the loss or damage incurred. Second, a number of IIAs require that disputing parties hold a consultation/negotiation during a certain period of time to attempt to settle the dispute amicably before arbitration proceedings can be initiated. Third, some IIAs provide that disputes be submitted to the domestic courts of the host States during a certain period of time before proceedings can be initiated. While the IIAs that set out this requirement attach arbitration to local remedies, those that contain a fork-in-the-road clause do the opposite; under such a clause, disputes cannot be submitted to arbitration if they have already been submitted to host States' domestic courts. The fork-in-the-road clause is not to be confused with the waiver clause incorporated in some IIAs; under such a clause, investors shall waive their right to continue (or initiate) proceedings in particular before host States' domestic courts in order to be entitled to initiate arbitration proceedings.

ii Submission of a Request for Arbitration   The request for arbitration is not to be confused with the notice of claim – also called 'notice of intent' or 'notice of dispute'. The latter usually constitutes the starting point of the period during which an amicable settlement is to be searched for by the disputing parties.

As for the request for arbitration, the exact content of the request and the modalities of its filing depend on the arbitration rules applicable and also on whether the proceedings are administered by a dispute settlement centre. As regards ICSID Convention arbitration proceedings, there are formal and substantive requirements (ICSID Convention, Article 36).

The request for arbitration must be written in one of the three official languages of the Centre (English, Spanish or French), and it must be dated and be signed by the requesting party and sent to the Secretary-General. It is worth noting that the drafting of the Convention gives both foreign investors and States the opportunity to file a request, a possibility which is – as discussed below and in Chapter 14 – not open to States in a great number of IIAs.

Content-wise, the request must notably contain the name of all the parties and their contact details, information pertaining to the expression of consent to the jurisdiction of the Centre, as well as basic information evidencing that there exists a legal dispute arising directly out of an investment between an ICSID Member State and a national of another Member State to the Convention.

The party filing the request, or both parties in case of a joint request, must pay a non-refundable fee of US$25,000. The information provided in the request is of the utmost importance as it constitutes the basis on which the Secretary-General appraises and notifies the parties of whether or not the request is manifestly outside the jurisdiction of the Centre. In the case that it is, this leads to its rejection; if it is not, the request is registered and published.

iii Emergency Arbitration   As will be analysed in Chapter 13, disputing parties can request arbitration tribunals to grant provisional measures before the issuance of the award. When the measures are urgently needed, it is possible under the ICSID Convention Arbitration Rules – since the 2006 revision of the Arbitration Rules – to file such a request and all the necessary observations prior to the constitution of the tribunal, so that it can promptly decide the matter upon its constitution (Arbitration Rule 39.5).

The SCC Arbitration Rules go one step further to deal with emergency situations. They offer the possibility to formulate *mutatis mutandis* such a request to an emergency arbitrator before the referral of a case to an arbitration tribunal. This procedure was introduced in Appendix II to the Rules on the occasion of their 2010 revision, and still forms part of the 2017 version.

According to this procedure, '[a] party may apply for the appointment of an Emergency Arbitrator until the case has been referred to an Arbitral Tribunal pursuant to Article 22 of the Arbitration Rules.' When such an application is made, the SCC Board shall seek to appoint an emergency arbitrator within twenty-four hours of the receipt of the application, after having checked that the SCC does not manifestly lack jurisdiction. A decision shall be made by that arbitrator within five days from the date she received the application, a period that may be extended by the SCC Board upon request of the emergency arbitrator or if otherwise deemed necessary. The decision of the emergency arbitrator is binding on the parties, but not on the arbitration tribunal once the case has been referred to it. That tribunal – like the emergency arbitrator – can decide at some point that the decision shall not be binding on the parties any longer, an effect that results also in particular from the final award made by the tribunal. As a concrete example of this procedure, one can refer to the decision of the Emergency Arbitrator in *Mohammed Munshi* v. *Mongolia* who – despite denying other reliefs sought for – ordered Mongolia to permit the investor to have reasonable access to his local Mongolian counsel as well as to international counsel (2018, Award on Emergency Measures, para. 63.1).

It is worth noting that this procedure has been (successfully) initiated in cases in which a simple notice of dispute had been sent to the host State a few days earlier, but no request for arbitration had been filed to the SCC (e.g. *TSIKInvest LLC* v. *Moldova*). This illustrates that emergency arbitration under the SCC Rules of Arbitration can cover not only those situations in which a tribunal is being established, but also those in which no request has been filed.

With regard to those situations, it can be noted that Article 9.4 of Appendix II provides that the emergency decision ceases to be binding when an arbitration is not commenced within thirty days from the date of the emergency decision.

b The Establishment of Arbitration Tribunals

While the establishment of arbitration tribunals is the prerogative of the disputing parties, it remains that this prerogative is to be exercised in compliance with both formal requirements and substantive requirements set by arbitration rules. It is notable that such matters have been increasingly addressed over time in IIA practice in a way *mutatis mutandis* similar to that adopted by arbitration rules.

i Formal Aspects   In practice, arbitration tribunals are almost always composed of three arbitrators, each party appointing one arbitrator and the presiding arbitrator being in most cases appointed either by these two party-appointed arbitrators or by the parties directly. Even though the choices made by the disputing parties constitute the cornerstone of this practice, arbitration rules play a key role in this regard. As to these rules, one should distinguish between those rules that deal with the methodology of the appointment and the number of arbitrators to be appointed, on the one hand, and the rules that govern the actual appointment of arbitrators, on the other hand (although admittedly there is some overlap between these two sets of rules).

– **Methodology of the Appointment and Number of Arbitrators**   Arbitration rules give broad discretion to the disputing parties as to the choice of methodology in the appointment of arbitrators and as to the number of arbitrators to be appointed. However, this discretion must still be exercised in compliance with timelines and in accordance with procedures that vary from one set of rules to the other.

As a default, most arbitration rules provide that there shall be three arbitrators appointed, the exception of this being where one arbitrator is appointed under the SCC Arbitration Rules (Article 16.2) and the UNCITRAL Rules (Article 7.2) if – respectively – the SCC Board and the appointing authority, upon one party's request, deem it appropriate. Under this mainstream default methodology, each party is to appoint one arbitrator. The appointment of the presiding arbitrator depends on the applicable arbitration rules: in particular, she is appointed by agreement between the parties under Article 37.2.b of the ICSID Convention, by agreement between the party-appointed arbitrators under Article 9.1 of the UNCITRAL Arbitration Rules and by the SCC Board under Article 17.4 of the SCC Rules.

– **Appointment of Arbitrators**   Arbitration rules also address the actual appointment of arbitrators as such, notably the timeline left for the appointment and, most importantly, those situations in which one or both disputing parties fail to appoint an arbitrator. In such situations, the rules offer – according to various procedures that depend on the applicable set of rules – a key role to a 'third' person/body: the Chairman of the ICSID Administrative Council under the ICSID Convention Arbitration Rules; an appointing authority under the UNCITRAL Rules; and the SCC Board under the SCC Arbitration Rules.

Concerning, for instance, the ICSID Convention Arbitration Rules, Article 38 of the Washington Convention provides that, if the tribunal has not been appointed within ninety days after the dispatch of the notice of registration of the request or any other period agreed between the parties, either party can request the Chairman to appoint the arbitrator or arbitrator(s) not appointed yet, an action to be taken by him afterwards having as far as possible consulted with both parties.

ii **Substantive Aspects**   The substantive requirements placed upon the identity of arbitrators are mainly threefold: nationality, moral integrity, i.e. independence and impartiality, and professional expertise. Even though these are formally distinguished, it is worth noting that the first requirement appears in fact as a subcategory of the second inasmuch as the requirement for arbitrators to have a nationality different from that of the disputing parties is conceived of and perceived as a guarantee of impartiality and independence.

– **Nationality Requirement**   The scope and 'strictness' of the nationality requirement varies from one set of arbitration rules to the other.

The UNCITRAL Arbitration Rules appear to be the more liberal in this respect. They only address this issue with regard to appointments made by the appointing authority; pursuant to Article 6.7, he 'shall have regard to such considerations as are likely to secure the appointment of an independent and impartial arbitrator and shall take into account the advisability of appointing an arbitrator of a nationality other than the nationalities of the parties'. Even though the taking into account of nationality is expressed only as for appointments by appointing authorities, it proves in fact to play a role in all the arbitration proceedings governed by those Rules.

In a way similar to the UNCITRAL Arbitration Rules, the SCC Rules provide that when arbitrators are appointed by the SCC Board, it shall consider the nationality of the parties (Article 17.7); but they also provide specific requirements as for disputes whose disputing parties have different nationalities, which is typical of investor–State disputes. According to Article 17.6, the Chairperson of the tribunal or the sole arbitrator – depending on the number of arbitrators – shall be of a different nationality than those parties; this rule can be departed from if the parties agree otherwise or if it is deemed appropriate by the Board.

The ICSID Convention Arbitration Rules are the strictest of all. The regulating principle is formulated in Article 39 of the Washington Convention, which provides that the majority of the arbitrators shall be nationals of States other than the Contracting State party to the dispute and the Contracting State whose national is a party to the dispute; it can only be different if each arbitrator, or a sole arbitrator, is appointed by agreement between the disputing parties. By the same token, when an arbitrator or arbitrators are appointed by the Chairman of the Administrative Council, he/they shall not have those nationalities either (Article 38).

– Moral Integrity Requirement   Moral integrity is a key requirement in the judiciary, which is incorporated in the statute of all international courts and tribunals. This holds true with respect to investor–State arbitration; for instance, Article 18.1 of the SCC Arbitration Rules provides that all arbitrators must be impartial and independent. In the same vein, the ICSID Convention provides that 'the persons designated to serve on the Panels shall be persons of high moral character ... who may be relied upon to exercise independent judgment' (Article 14.1); this applies more generally to all appointed arbitrators even though they do not form part of the Panel of arbitrators discussed above. It is worth noting that the English and French versions of that latter Article refer to 'independent judgment', while its Spanish version mentions 'impartiality of judgement'; irrespective of these differences, there is no doubt that the Convention sets a requirement that covers both independence and impartiality. Those qualities have the common objective of ensuring that arbitrators rule over disputes by taking into account only the facts and merits of the cases, without being influenced by any other consideration. Yet, these two elements can nonetheless be distinguished as follows:

> Independence is characterized by the absence of external control, in particular of relations between the arbitrator and a party which may influence the arbitrator's decision. [footnote omitted] Impartiality, on the other hand, means the absence of bias or predisposition towards one party and requires that the arbitrator hears the parties without any favor and bases his or her decision only on factors related to the merits of the case. [footnote omitted] (*Saint-Gobain Performance Plastics Europe* v. *Venezuela*, 2013, Decision on Disqualification, para. 56)

Although these qualities are closely connected, there are certain situations in which they may not both be fulfilled. As explained by the Tribunal in *Suez* v. *Argentina*, it is, for instance, possible in certain situations for a judge or arbitrator to be independent of both parties, but not impartial (2007, Decision on Disqualification, para. 29).

Under the UNCITRAL Arbitration Rules, for instance, the moral integrity requirement entails that before being appointed and during the course of the proceedings, the persons approached shall disclose any circumstance likely to give rise to justifiable doubts as to their impartiality and independence (Article 11). The written declaration that arbitrators have to sign – before or at the first session of the tribunal at the latest – under the ICSID Convention Arbitration Rules also illustrates how the morality requirement materialises:

> To the best of my knowledge there is no reason why I should not serve on the Arbitral Tribunal constituted by the International Centre for Settlement of Investment Disputes with respect to a dispute between _____ and _____.
>
> I shall keep confidential all information coming to my knowledge as a result of my participation in this proceeding, as well as the contents of any award made by the Tribunal.
>
> I shall judge fairly as between the parties, according to the applicable law, and shall not accept any instruction or compensation with regard to the proceeding from any source except as provided in the Convention on the Settlement of Investment Disputes between States and Nationals of Other States and in the Regulations and Rules made pursuant thereto.
>
> Attached is a statement of (a) my past and present professional, business and other relationships (if any) with the parties and (b) any other circumstance that might cause my reliability for independent judgment to be questioned by a party. I acknowledge that by signing this declaration, I assume a continuing obligation promptly to notify the Secretary-General of the Centre of any such relationship or circumstance that subsequently arises during this proceeding. (Arbitration Rule 6.2)

A failure to sign this declaration by the end of the first session of the tribunal is construed as amounting to a resignation by the arbitrator concerned.

Irrespective of the phase of the proceedings where an issue of impartiality and independence arises, it is worth noting that arbitration rules do not elaborate much on those situations that justify reasonable doubts as to the impartiality and independence of arbitrators. Such uncertainty has certainly contributed to the rise of requests in disqualification – discussed below – during the course of arbitration proceedings. More generally, this has likely contributed to the perception in the public opinion, generated by the party-appointing method inherent to arbitration, that arbitrators lack impartiality and independence. In this respect, it is worth noting that, as part of the reform of investor–State arbitration initiated in IIA practice, one has witnessed the incorporation in some IIAs of detailed obligations of disclosure and, more generally, provisions pertaining to the independence and impartiality of arbitrators. It is worth quoting in full the relevant provisions of Annex 9-A of the 2015 Australia–China IIA which – *mutatis mutandis* – illustrates this trend:

Responsibilities to the Process

1. Every arbitrator shall avoid impropriety and the appearance of impropriety, shall be independent and impartial, shall avoid direct and indirect conflicts of interests and shall observe high standards of conduct so that the integrity and impartiality of the dispute settlement process are preserved. Former

arbitrators shall comply with the obligations established in paragraphs 16, 17, 18 and 19.

Disclosure Obligations

2. Prior to confirmation of his or her selection as an arbitrator under this Agreement, a candidate shall disclose any interest, relationship or matter that is likely to affect his or her independence or impartiality or that might reasonably create an appearance of impropriety or bias in the proceeding. To this end, a candidate shall make all reasonable efforts to become aware of any such interests, relationships and matters.

3. Once selected, an arbitrator shall continue to make all reasonable efforts to become aware of any interests, relationships and matters referred to in paragraph 2 and shall disclose them by communicating them in writing to the disputing parties. The obligation to disclose is a continuing duty, which requires an arbitrator to disclose any such interests, relationships and matters that may arise during any stage of the proceeding . . .

Independence and Impartiality of Arbitrators

11. An arbitrator shall be independent and impartial. An arbitrator shall act in a fair manner and shall avoid creating an appearance of impropriety or bias.

12. An arbitrator shall not be influenced by self-interest, outside pressure, political considerations, public clamour, loyalty to a Party or a disputing party or fear of criticism.

13. An arbitrator shall not, directly or indirectly, incur any obligation or accept any benefit that would in any way interfere, or appear to interfere, with the proper performance of the arbitrator's duties.

14. An arbitrator shall not use his or her position on the arbitral tribunal to advance any personal or private interests. An arbitrator shall avoid actions that may create the impression that others are in a special position to influence the arbitrator. An arbitrator shall make every effort to prevent or discourage others from representing themselves as being in such a position.

15. An arbitrator shall not allow past or existing financial, business, professional, family or social relationships or responsibilities to influence the arbitrator's conduct or judgment.

16. An arbitrator shall avoid entering into any relationship, or acquiring any financial interest, that is likely to affect the arbitrator's impartiality or that might reasonably create an appearance of impropriety or bias.

Duties in Certain Situations

17. An arbitrator or former arbitrator shall avoid actions that may create the appearance that the arbitrator was biased in carrying out the arbitrator's duties or would benefit from the decision or award of the arbitral tribunal.

Maintenance of Confidentiality

18. An arbitrator or former arbitrator shall not at any time disclose or use any non-public information concerning the proceeding or acquired during the

proceeding except for the purposes of the proceeding and shall not, in any case, disclose or use any such information to gain personal advantage or advantage for others or to affect adversely the interest of others.

– Professional Expertise Requirement   It is noteworthy that only the ICSID Convention Arbitration Rules provide for express professional requirements to be met to be appointed as an arbitrator. The persons appointed shall have a recognised competence particularly in the field of law; the Convention also refers to the competence in the field of commerce, industry or finance. This holds true for arbitrators designated on the Panel of arbitrators (ICSID Convention, Article 14.1) or appointed from outside the Panel (ICSID Convention, Article 40.2).

As part of the trend displayed by treaty practice to incorporate detailed investor–State dispute settlement provisions, IIAs also address this matter. For instance, the 2016 Canada–Hong Kong China SAR IIA provides that the '[a]rbitrators shall have expertise and experience in public international law, international investment or international trade rules, or the resolution of disputes arising under international investment or international trade agreements' (Article 25.2).

c The Course of Arbitration Proceedings

Even though the ICSID Convention arbitration proceedings have from the outset been tailor-made for the settlement of investor–State disputes, investor–State arbitration proceedings have traditionally shared common principles with other types of arbitration proceedings, in particular international commercial arbitration. As a result of the criticism formulated by local populations, politicians and NGOs, they have developed new specific features as of the 2000s. This subsection aims at introducing the traditional and innovative features that characterise those proceedings. In doing so, attention is first paid to the basic features of investor–State arbitration proceedings before a focus is put on specific requests that may be made in the course of the proceedings, depending on the specifics of each case and the applicable rules of arbitration.

i Basic Features

– Organisation of the Proceedings   The organisation of investor–State arbitration proceedings takes place typically during the first session. This session can be held in person, by videoconference or telephone, the objective being to quickly decide on the issues that must be determined before proceedings may fully commence. The importance of taking action swiftly can be seen quite clearly from the requirement under the ICSID Arbitration Rule that this first session be held within sixty days after the constitution of the tribunal unless it is agreed otherwise by the parties (Rule 13.1). Among those issues to be decided are matters such as the language and the place of the proceedings/place of arbitration, or the procedural calendar as regards the written and oral phases, notably the deadline for the submission of written pleadings and the schedule of oral hearings. This calendar may be revised later on in the course of the proceedings.

Regarding the issue of the place of the proceedings/place of arbitration, a distinction needs to be made between ICSID Convention arbitration proceedings and the proceedings governed by other sets of rules.

With respect to the latter, the choice of the place of arbitration entails important legal consequences as it determines the applicable domestic law and the competent domestic courts to decide on important matters such as typically the challenges to awards. Under the UNCITRAL Arbitration Rules, for instance, the parties can decide the place of arbitration, and where this cannot be agreed, it is up to the tribunals to decide, taking into consideration the circumstances of the particular case (Article 18.1). The fact that hearings may take place outside the place of arbitration is a mere geographical and logistical matter; this does not change the place of arbitration and the legal consequences it entails.

As for ICSID Convention arbitration proceedings, the determination of the place of the proceedings is actually a mere geographical and logistical matter. This is due to the fact that the ICSID Convention establishes a kind of 'self-contained regime', ICSID Convention arbitration proceedings being 'independent' from the domestic legal order and laws of its Member States. As a default rule (Article 62), the place of the proceedings is the seat of the Centre, which is the principal office of the International Bank for Reconstruction and Development – the first institution created that forms part of the World Bank Group – located in Washington. The parties can agree that they will take place at the seat of the PCA or of any other appropriate institution with which the Centre may have an arrangement for that purpose, or at any other place approved by the tribunals after consultation with the Secretary-General (Article 63).

In addition to the above-mentioned issues, which are dealt with in all cases, it is worth noting that in some cases the first session is the occasion to address specific requests – examined below – for instance, a request for expedited procedure under ICSID Arbitration Rule 41.5.

Of course, other issues may arise during the course of arbitration proceedings that were not discussed at the outset; in such a case, these are to be decided under the responsibility of tribunals and in compliance with the applicable rules of procedure. In this respect, it is worth recalling that Article 44 of the ICSID Convention provides that any question of procedure that is not covered by the Convention and the Arbitration Rules or by any rules agreed on by the parties shall be decided by tribunals themselves.

– Oral and Written Phases
Preliminary Remarks

Written and oral phases are typical of arbitration proceedings, and more generally of international adjudicative proceedings. ICSID Arbitration Rule 29 characterises the succession of these two phases as the normal procedure, from which the parties are entitled to derogate. They are governed by key principles, such as the equality of arms between the parties.

The written phase consists typically of two rounds of submissions between the parties comprising, at the first round, the submission of a memorial and a counter-memorial and, at the second round, the submission of a reply and a rejoinder; documents are joined to these submissions. All these exchanges allow the disputing parties to explain and argue their views on the facts of the case and the law, as well as to present their prayer for relief. The hearings that constitute the oral phase give the opportunity, on the one hand, to tribunals to hear the parties, their witnesses and experts and, on the other hand, to either party to argue its own views as well as to challenge the views defended by the other party.

Object and Sequence

The object and sequence of the written and oral phases vary. In this respect, a specific situation may arise when the respondent formulates objections to the jurisdiction of the tribunal and requests a bifurcation, meaning that these objections are decided prior to the discussion of the merits of the case. As illustrated by Article 41.2 of the ICSID Convention, arbitration rules give discretion to tribunals to decide on the opportunity to bifurcate. The criteria usually taken into account by tribunals relate mainly to the merits of the request as well as to considerations of time and costs. This is well reflected in the Procedural Order n° 2 rendered by the Tribunal in *Glencore Finance (Bermuda) Limited* v. *Bolivia* under the UNCITRAL Arbitration Rules:

> a) Whether the request is substantial or is the objection *prima facie* serious and substantial? b) Whether the request, if granted, would lead to a material reduction in the proceedings at the next stage or could the objection, if successful, dispose of all or an essential part of the claims raised?; c) Whether bifurcation is impractical in the sense that the issues are too intertwined with the merit that it is very unlikely that there will be any savings in time or cost or can the objection be examined without prejudging or entering the merits? (2018, Decision on Bifurcation, para. 39).

If bifurcation is not decided by tribunals, jurisdictional issues are joined to the merits. If a bifurcation is ordered, there is a specific written and oral phase devoted to jurisdiction. Of course, if tribunals then decline jurisdiction, no written and oral phases on the merits follow. It is also worth noting that the merits can be split into a liability and a damage phase. By the same token, specific phases may be devoted to other issues, for instance – as will be discussed in Chapter 13 – provisional measures.

Evidence

The parties have the responsibility of producing evidence to support the claims they make with respect to both the facts and the law. They shall do so on their own initiative following the timetable usually decided during the first session or notably when requested by tribunals to produce any evidence. The evidence that can be produced consists typically of documents, witness statements and expert opinions. Under the ICSID Convention Arbitration Rules, tribunals may, if they deem it necessary, also visit any place connected to the dispute or conduct inquiries there (ICSID Convention, Article 43.b and ICSID Arbitration Rule 34.2.b).

The failure to assume this responsibility may have consequences for the party concerned; in this respect, arbitration rules address the issue of the lack of cooperation of the parties with regard to the production of evidence. For instance, ICSID Arbitration Rule 34.3 provides that the parties shall cooperate with tribunals in the production of evidence, tribunals being required to take formal note of a failure to cooperate or of any reasons given for such failure. More generally, and as explained below, the failure to cooperate is an element that can be taken into consideration by tribunals when apportioning costs. In this respect, it is worth noticing that the revision of the ICSID Arbitration Rules contemplated in the 2019 ICSID Working Paper n° 3 makes it explicit that the parties' conduct during the proceeding is a circumstance to be considered by tribunals in allocating the costs of the proceedings (proposed Arbitration Rule 51.1.b).

While the parties have the responsibility of producing evidence, the task of appraising the admissibility and probative value of such evidence rests naturally on the tribunals themselves (ICSID Arbitration Rule 34.1; UNCITRAL Arbitration Rules, Article 27.4; SCC Arbitration Rules, Article 31.1). Beyond the enunciation of this principle, it is true that arbitration rules provide few guidelines as to how to appraise the admissibility of evidence and other evidentiary issues. In this respect, practice shows that the parties and the tribunals often rely on the 2010 Rules of the Taking of Evidence in International Arbitration adopted by the International Bar Association.

Default

Aside from the issue of the lack of cooperation with regard to evidence, the parties may fail to actively participate during the arbitration proceedings. Two situations must be distinguished here: both parties may fail to act, or only one of them may do so.

The first situation is notably addressed by ICSID Arbitration Rule 45: the failure of the parties to act during six consecutive months or any other period that they may have agreed with the approval of the tribunals, is considered as a discontinuance of the proceedings. It is worth noting that the revision of the ICSID Arbitration Rules contemplated in the 2019 Working Paper n° 3 introduces a preliminary warning to the parties before such discontinuance. Indeed, the proposed Arbitration Rule 56 provides that if the parties fail to take any steps for more than 150 consecutive days, tribunals shall notify them of the time elapsed since the last step taken in the proceedings; it is only if they persist in their failure to act for thirty days after this notice that they are deemed to have discontinued the proceedings.

If only one party is in a default situation, the proceedings shall not be discontinued where the other party requests the tribunal to deal with the questions submitted to it and to render an award; in such a case, the tribunal shall notify the defaulting party and leave it a period of grace unless it is satisfied that this party does not intend to appear or to present its case (ICSID Convention, Article 45.2 and ICSID Arbitration Rule 42). It can be noted that the 2019 ICSID Working Paper n° 3 proposes to specify the conduct to be adopted by tribunals if requested to deal with the questions to them by the non-defaulting party depending on the procedural step where the default occurs (proposed Arbitration Rule 48.4 and 48.5). With regard to such situations where only one party defaults, the UNCITRAL Arbitration Rules provide for different solutions depending on which party is defaulting and of what the default consists (Article 30). If the claimant fails to communicate its statement of claim, the proceedings shall as a matter of principle be terminated; if the respondent fails to communicate notably its statement of defence, the proceedings shall continue. In the same vein, if a party – be it the claimant or the respondent – fails to appear at a hearing, without showing sufficient cause for such failure, the tribunal may proceed with the arbitration.

Irrespective of the difficulties that default creates in the work of arbitration tribunals and for the non-defaulting party, it is worth insisting that tribunals shall not draw any consequences from the default which would impact on the substance of their decision, be it on jurisdiction or on the merits; in that sense, Article 45.1 of the ICSID Convention makes it clear that the failure of a party to participate shall not be treated by the tribunal as an admission of the other party's allegations.

– Access of the Public to Information and Hearings   As part of the reform of investor–State arbitration in the 2000s, one has witnessed a progressive paradigmatic move from confidentiality to transparency. This trend, evidenced by the evolution of both arbitration rules and IIA practice, concerns the access of the public to information and hearings, the possibility for a non-disputing party to participate in the proceedings and the publication of awards. This subsection focuses on access to information and hearings; the participation of a non-disputing party in the proceedings and the publication of awards are discussed below.

Arbitration Rules

Beyond the obligation already existing for the Secretary-General to make available significant information pertaining to the institution, conduct and disposition of all the proceedings under the Administrative and Financial Regulation 23, ICSID has been the first institution to revise – in 2006 – its Arbitration Rules in order to make its proceedings more 'transparent'. In addition to new rules concerning non-disputing party submissions and the publication of awards – discussed below – this revision has modified the rules applicable to oral procedures with a view to facilitating the attendance of the public.

In this respect, Arbitration Rule 32 provides that tribunals may, after consultation with the Secretary-General and unless either party objects, allow other persons – besides the parties, agents, counsels and advocates, as well as the officers of the tribunals, the witnesses and the experts during their testimony – to attend or observe all or part of the hearings, subject to appropriate logistical arrangements. It is worth noting that in the previous version of the Rules, there was a requirement that both parties affirmatively give their consent, while in the 2006 version it is merely required that none of them objects (the revision of the ICSID Arbitration Rules contemplated in the 2019 ICSID Working Paper n° 3 goes one step further by proposing that the parties be only consulted and that the decision be made by tribunals – proposed Arbitration Rule 64.1). As to the logistical arrangements, tribunals shall in such cases establish procedures for the protection of proprietary and privileged information. As it appears, the intention of the 2006 revision has been to make the procedure more open without sacrificing the confidentiality that some categories of information necessarily require. In this respect, one can note that the ICSID Convention Arbitration Rules – contrary to the 2013 UNCITRAL Rules on Transparency in Treaty-Based Arbitration examined below – do not provide any indication as to the information that shall actually be considered as being proprietary or privileged information and as such protected.

Apart from the above, the ICSID Convention Arbitration Rules contain no rules on the access of the public to information. In this respect, the revision of the Arbitration Rules envisaged in the 2019 ICSID Working Paper n° 3 proposes to incorporate a rule providing that the Centre shall, upon request of either party, publish any document filed in the proceeding (proposed Arbitration Rule 63.1). As seen below, the UNCITRAL Rules on Transparency go further, providing that publication is not a matter for the wishes of the parties, but rather an obligation.

As it appears, those UNCITRAL Rules make arbitration proceedings more open to the public. In addition to the publication of information at the commencement of arbitration proceedings, they contain provisions pertaining to the publication of documents, the attendance at hearings, as well as submissions by third persons and by non-disputing parties to the treaty at hand. Those submissions are discussed below.

Pursuant to Article 3 of the UNCITRAL Rules on Transparency, the following shall be made available to the public, in addition to the notice of arbitration and the response to it : (1) the statement of claim, the statement of defence and any further written statements or written submissions by any disputing party; (2) a table listing all exhibits (but not the exhibits themselves) to the aforesaid documents and to expert reports and witness statements if this has been prepared; (3) any written submissions by the non-disputing treaty party (or parties) and by third persons; (4) the transcripts of hearings where available; and (5) the orders, decisions and awards of the tribunals. Furthermore, the expert reports and witness statements, exclusive of the exhibits thereto, shall be made available to the public upon request by any person to the tribunal. Finally, tribunals may decide, on their own initiative or upon request from any person, and after consultation with the disputing parties, whether and how to make available exhibits and any other documents – not listed above – provided to or issued by the tribunals.

As a matter of principle, hearings for the presentation of evidence or for oral arguments shall be public according to Article 6 of the Rules. However, where in particular it is needed to protect confidential information or the integrity of the arbitral process, the part of the hearings concerned shall be held in private.

More generally, it is worth noting that the UNCITRAL Rules on Transparency provide for limits on the publication of documents and the possibility for the public to attend hearings that pertain to the protection of confidential and protected information as well as to the integrity of the arbitral process. Article 7.2 provides an exhaustive list of the confidential or protected information that can limit the access of the public to information, namely: (1) confidential business information; (2) information that is protected against being made available to the public under the treaty; (3) in case of the information of the respondent State, information that is protected against being made available to the public under its domestic law; (4) any other information that is protected against being made available under any law or rules determined by the tribunal to be applicable to the disclosure of such information; and (5) information whose disclosure would impede law enforcement. For the avoidance of doubt, Article 7.5 specifies that respondent States shall not in any case be required to make available to the public any information if they consider that its disclosure is contrary to their essential security interests. This discretion granted to respondent States comes as an exception to the power given to tribunals, after consultation with the parties, to determine whether any information is to be considered as confidential or protected. When tribunals decide that information is confidential or protected, they shall, after consultation with the parties, make arrangements to prevent this information being made available to the public. In those cases where tribunals consider that certain information should not be prevented from being made available to the public, the disputing party, the non-disputing treaty party or the third person who voluntarily introduced the document is permitted to withdraw all or part of the document from the record of the arbitration proceedings. In order to ensure the protection of the integrity of the arbitral process, tribunals can under Article 7 decide, on their own initiative or upon request of a disputing party, and after consultation with the disputing parties when practicable, to restrain or delay the publication of information if it could for instance lead to the intimidation of witnesses, lawyers acting for disputing parties or members of the tribunals.

IIA Practice

To some extent, the evolution of arbitration rules seems to have both inspired and been inspired by IIA practice.

The practice of the States parties to the North American Free Trade Agreement (NAFTA) has been one of the first key moves to incorporate transparency into investor–State arbitration and ensure greater access of the public to information. To better understand this, it is worth quoting in full the relevant part of the Interpretative Note adopted by the NAFTA Free Trade Commission in 2001:

1. Nothing in the NAFTA imposes a general duty of confidentiality on the disputing parties to a Chapter Eleven arbitration, and, subject to the application of Article 1137(4), nothing in the NAFTA precludes the Parties from providing public access to documents submitted to, or issued by, a Chapter Eleven tribunal.
2. In the application of the foregoing:
   (a) In accordance with Article 1120(2), the NAFTA Parties agree that nothing in the relevant arbitral rules imposes a general duty of confidentiality or precludes the Parties from providing public access to documents submitted to, or issued by, Chapter Eleven tribunals, apart from the limited specific exceptions set forth expressly in those rules.
   (b) Each Party agrees to make available to the public in a timely manner all documents submitted to, or issued by, a Chapter Eleven tribunal, subject to redaction of:
       i. confidential business information;
       ii. information which is privileged or otherwise protected from disclosure under the Party's domestic law; and
       iii. information which the Party must withhold pursuant to the relevant arbitral rules, as applied.
   (c) The Parties reaffirm that disputing parties may disclose to other persons in connection with the arbitral proceedings such unredacted documents as they consider necessary for the preparation of their cases, but they shall ensure that those persons protect the confidential information in such documents.
   (d) The Parties further reaffirm that the Governments of Canada, the United Mexican States and the United States of America may share with officials of their respective federal, state or provincial governments all relevant documents in the course of dispute settlement under Chapter Eleven of NAFTA, including confidential information.
3. The Parties confirm that nothing in this interpretation shall be construed to require any Party to furnish or allow access to information that it may withhold in accordance with Articles 2102 or 2105.

Following the revision of the ICSID Arbitration Rules and the adoption of the UNCITRAL Rules on Transparency, one has witnessed a growing trend in IIA practice towards incorporating provisions on the transparency of arbitration proceedings. This practice is well illustrated by Article 9.24 of the 2018 CPTPP; again, it is worth quoting this in full in order to take stock of the contribution made by IIAs to the progressive paradigmatic shift from confidentiality to transparency in investor–State arbitration proceedings:

1. Subject to paragraphs 2 and 4, the respondent shall, after receiving the following documents, promptly transmit them to the non-disputing Parties and make them available to the public:
   (a) the notice of intent;
   (b) the notice of arbitration;
   (c) pleadings, memorials and briefs submitted to the tribunal by a disputing party and any written submissions submitted pursuant to Article 9.23.2 (Conduct of the Arbitration) and Article 9.23.3 and Article 9.28 (Consolidation);
   (d) minutes or transcripts of hearings of the tribunal, if available; and
   (e) orders, awards and decisions of the tribunal.
2. The tribunal shall conduct hearings open to the public and shall determine, in consultation with the disputing parties, the appropriate logistical arrangements. If a disputing party intends to use information in a hearing that is designated as protected information or otherwise subject to paragraph 3 it shall so advise the tribunal. The tribunal shall make appropriate arrangements to protect such information from disclosure which may include closing the hearing for the duration of the discussion of that information.
3. Nothing in this Section, including paragraph 4(d), requires a respondent to make available to the public or otherwise disclose during or after the arbitral proceedings, including the hearing, protected information, or to furnish or allow access to information that it may withhold in accordance with Article 29.2 (Security Exceptions) or Article 29.7 (Disclosure of Information). [footnote omitted]
4. Any protected information that is submitted to the tribunal shall be protected from disclosure in accordance with the following procedures:
   (a) subject to subparagraph (d), neither the disputing parties nor the tribunal shall disclose to any non-disputing Party or to the public any protected information if the disputing party that provided the information clearly designates it in accordance with subparagraph (b);
   (b) any disputing party claiming that certain information constitutes protected information shall clearly designate the information according to any schedule set by the tribunal;
   (c) a disputing party shall, according to any schedule set by the tribunal, submit a redacted version of the document that does not contain the protected information. Only the redacted version shall be disclosed in accordance with paragraph 1; and

(d) the tribunal, subject to paragraph 3, shall decide any objection regarding the designation of information claimed to be protected information. If the tribunal determines that the information was not properly designated, the disputing party that submitted the information may:

(i) withdraw all or part of its submission containing that information; or

(ii) agree to resubmit complete and redacted documents with corrected designations in accordance with the tribunal's determination and subparagraph (c).

In either case, the other disputing party shall, whenever necessary, resubmit complete and redacted documents which either remove the information withdrawn under subparagraph (d)(i) by the disputing party that first submitted the information or redesignate the information consistent with the designation under subparagraph (d)(ii) of the disputing party that first submitted the information.

5. Nothing in this Section requires a respondent to withhold from the public information required to be disclosed by its laws. The respondent should endeavour to apply those laws in a manner sensitive to protecting from disclosure information that has been designated as protected information.

ii Specific Requests   A large variety of specific requests can be made during the course of arbitration proceedings. Most of these originate from the disputing parties themselves, pertaining in particular to the facts and circumstances of the cases, to their merits or to procedural issues. Those requests can also emanate from non-disputing parties when they wish to act as *amicus curiae*. This subsection focuses on those specific requests that appear to be the most topical in light of contemporary arbitration practice and of the reform of investor–State arbitration proceedings: (1) manifest lack of legal merit; (2) recusation of arbitrators; (3) counterclaims; and (4) non-disputing party submissions. Provisional measures are dealt with specifically in Chapter 13.

– Manifest Lack of Legal Merit   To avoid 'frivolous' claims and meaningless proceedings, the 2006 revision of the ICSID Arbitration Rules has incorporated a mechanism aiming at the early dismissal of a claim which is manifestly without legal merit (Arbitration Rule 41.5).

This mechanism is not to be confused with the review made by the Secretary-General after receipt of the requests for arbitration; as explained above, this review is limited to an appraisal of whether the disputes are manifestly outside the jurisdiction of ICSID, only on the basis of the information contained in the requests. This procedure is also to be distinguished from the expedited arbitration governed by the 2017 SCC Arbitration Rules for

Expedited Arbitration, which are available to the parties to settle disputes that are simpler than those settled under the SCC Arbitration Rules. In relation to this expedited arbitration, it is worth noting that the revision of the ICSID Convention Arbitration Proceedings contemplated in the 2019 ICSID Working Paper n° 3 proposes the incorporation of such a mechanism in the Arbitration Rules (proposed Chapter XII).

On the other hand, ICSID Arbitration Rule 41.5 is akin to the summary procedure that can be requested under Article 39 of the SCC Arbitration Rules regarding jurisdictional and admissibility issues, as well as the merits of cases.

Unless the parties agree on another procedure, ICSID Arbitration Rule 41.5 prescribes that the objection that a claim is manifestly without legal merit shall be made by a party no later than thirty days after the constitution of the tribunal, and in any event before the first session of the tribunal; as stated by the Tribunal in *Transglobal* v. *Panama*, those two conditions are cumulative (2015, Decision on the Admissibility of the Respondent's Preliminary Objection to the Jurisdiction of the Tribunal under Rule 41(5) of the ICSID Arbitration Rules, para. 29). The party shall specify as precisely as possible the basis for its objection. After both parties have had the opportunity to present their observations, the tribunal shall at its first session or promptly thereafter notify the parties of its decision.

As can be seen, the timeline is quite short and the procedural indications quite terse as to how parties can be provided with this opportunity. This leaves tribunals with the difficult task of figuring out, in light of the specifics of each case, how to organise that part of the proceedings. In this respect, the Tribunal appointed in *Global Trading Resource Corp.* v. *Ukraine* stressed that the possibility that the request be upheld and the serious consequences that this entails raises an important question as to the opportunities that ought to be offered to the parties to present their arguments and counter-arguments. It noted in this respect:

> On that question, the Tribunal has come to the clear view that, in principle, it would be right to non-suit a claimant under the ICSID system without having allowed the claimant (and therefore the respondent as well) a proper opportunity to be heard, both in writing and orally. That may raise organizational problems, in the face of the requirement that the Tribunal is to rule on the objection 'at its first session or shortly thereafter' ... There may be cases in which a tribunal can come to a clear conclusion in a Rule 41(5) objection, simply on the written submissions, but they will be rare, and the assumption must be that, even then, the decision will be one not to uphold the objection, rather than the converse. That is because, if an objection is not upheld at the Rule 41(5) stage, the rights of the objecting party remain intact, as the last sentence of the Rule makes plain: the rejection of an objection under Rule 41(5) at the pre-preliminary stage does not stand in the way of its resurrection later in the normal way as if Rule 41(5) did not exist. (2010, Award, para. 33)

As evident from the above extract, the Tribunal was very reluctant to consider that tribunals may decide on an objection that a claim is manifestly without legal merit, on the sole basis of written observations.

In addition to this procedural issue, requests for the early dismissal of a claim as being manifestly without legal merit call – content-wise – for four remarks.

First, the respondent can object to all the claims made by the claimant or only some of them.

Second, despite reference being made to 'legal merit' and a limitation to the substance of the claim having been envisaged during the drafting,[7] objections relating to both jurisdictional issues and the merits can be made in the context of this expedited procedure. This is made explicit in the revision of the ICSID Arbitration Rules contemplated in the 2019 ICSID Working Paper n° 3 (proposed Arbitration Rule 41.1).

Third, the wording is intended – as evidenced by the substitution of 'without merit' with 'without legal merit' in the course of the drafting[8] – to exclude inadequate discussions on the facts of the case at that stage. Despite this evolution, it is worth noting that the appraisal of the merit of a case necessarily involves a certain examination of its facts.

Fourth, a mere lack of legal merit does not meet the threshold for the objection to be upheld by tribunals; the requirement that the lack of such merit be 'manifest' sets a high standard. The formulation of this standard as provided by the Tribunal in *Trans-Global Petroleum, Inc.* v. *Jordan* is often referred to in arbitration practice; it stated that the respondent shall 'establish its objection clearly and obviously, with relative ease and despatch' (2008, Decision on the Respondent's Objection under Rule 41(5) of the ICSID Arbitration Rules, para. 88). Such a standard excludes objections concerning unsettled, novel, complex or difficult legal issues – which cannot be easily established – from being upheld. On the other hand, such a requirement for 'ease' should not be construed as entailing that any objection that is substantively discussed by the parties be declined by tribunals.

If tribunals consider that all the claims are manifestly without legal merit, they shall issue an award that can then be the object of annulment proceedings, which are examined below. However, if they conclude that none of the claims manifestly lack legal merit, or that only one or some lack legal merit, the proceedings shall continue, with those claim(s) considered to be lacking legal merit being excluded from the proceedings. For the rest of those proceedings, ICSID Arbitration Rule 41.5 makes it explicit that the tribunal's decision is without prejudice to the right of a party to file an objection on jurisdiction or to object that a claim lacks legal merit.

---

[7] A Antonietti, 'The 2006 Amendments to the ICSID Rules and Regulations and the Additional Facility Rules' (2006) 21 *ICSID Review* 427, at 439–440.
[8] Ibid., at 440.

It is worth noting that some IIAs provide *mutatis mutandis* for such an expedited procedure. This is well illustrated by Article 9.21.5 of the 2018 Korea–Republics of Central Americas IIA, which provides:

> In the event that the respondent so requests within 45 days of the date the tribunal is constituted, the tribunal shall decide on an expedited basis an objection under paragraph 4 and any objection that the dispute is not within the tribunal's competence. The tribunal shall suspend any proceedings on the merits and issue a decision or award on the objection(s), stating the grounds therefor, no later than 150 days after the date of the request. However, if a disputing party requests a hearing, the tribunal may take an additional 30 days to issue the decision or award. Regardless of whether a hearing is requested, a tribunal may, on a showing of extraordinary cause, delay issuing its decision or award by an additional brief period, which may not exceed 30 days.

– Disqualification   Once a tribunal has been constituted and the proceedings have begun, its composition shall remain unchanged. Yet, there exist a few exceptions to this principle that can lead to the replacement of the arbitrator(s) concerned. One set of exceptions relate to the resignation and the incapacity of arbitrators. Another exception concerns the disqualification of arbitrators on the request of either disputing party. Such requests can be made under the ICSID Convention Arbitration Rules (Washington Convention, Articles 57 and 58, and Arbitration Rule 9), the UNCITRAL Arbitration Rules (Articles 12 and 13) and the SCC Arbitration Rules (Article 19). Arbitration practice has displayed an increasing use of this mechanism since the 2010s.

The main ground invoked to request such a disqualification is the lack of moral integrity of arbitrators. The UNCITRAL and SCC Arbitrations Rules incorporate this ground by referring to 'impartiality' and 'independence'. In this respect, Article 57 of the ICSID Convention refers to Article 14.1, which mentions 'independent judgement' in its English and French versions and 'impartiality of judgement' in its Spanish version; as explained above, the morality requirement set by that Article is to be construed as covering both independence and impartiality.

Under the UNCITRAL and SCC Rules, an arbitrator may be challenged if circumstances exist that give rise to justifiable doubts as to the arbitrator's impartiality and independence; the ICSID Convention refers instead to any fact indicating a manifest lack of impartiality and independence. 'Manifest' means 'evident' and 'obvious'; it is largely accepted that this threshold relates to the ease with which the alleged lack of these qualities can be perceived (e.g. *Elitech B.V.* v. *Croatia*, 2018, Decision on Disqualification, para. 40). Based on this requirement that the lack of impartiality and independence be manifest, the mere appearance of dependence and partiality has been considered as being insufficient to ground a disqualification (*Amco Asia Corp* v. *Indonesia*, 1982, Decision on Disqualification, as reported in *Suez* v. *Argentina*, 2008, Decision on Disqualification, para. 29). It is worth noting that in *BSG*

Resources v. *Guinea* it was considered, on the other hand, that 'Article 57 and 14.1 of the ICSID Convention do not require proof of actual dependence or bias' and therefore that 'it is sufficient to establish the appearance of dependence or bias' (2016, Decision on Disqualification, para. 57). In any case, the requirement of a manifest lack of impartiality and independence sets an objective standard that is to be based on a reasonable evaluation of the evidence by a third party; as stated in *KS Invest GMBH* v. *Spain*, this implies that the subjective belief of the requesting disputing party and the personal views of the challenged arbitrator are not decisive in determining the request for disqualification (2018, Decision on Disqualification, para. 44).

In practice, requests on disqualification have been based on the existence of professional relationships between the challenged arbitrator or one of his collaborator(s) and a disputing party or its counsel (e.g. *Raiffeisen Bank* v. *Croatia*, 2018, Decision on Disqualification), on the participation of an arbitrator in previous related disputes (e.g. *Suez* v. *Argentina*, 2007, Decision on Disqualification), or on the views expressed by arbitrators either in dissenting opinions attached to awards rendered in prior cases (e.g. *Mathias Kruck* v. *Spain*, 2018 Decision on Disqualification) or expressed in their capacity as academics (e.g. *Urbaser* v. *Argentina*, 2010, Decision on Disqualification).

From a procedural point of view, there are also conditions pertaining to the timing of the request and the procedure more generally, in particular in the revision of the ICSID Convention Arbitration Proceedings contemplated in the 2019 ICSID Working Paper n° 3. The incorporation of these conditions results from the severe consequences, both in terms of time and costs, that requests for disqualification entail: proceedings are suspended during the examination of the requests, and if they lead to a successful challenge, one or more arbitrators must be re-appointed depending on the situation. It is noteworthy that Arbitration Rule 22.2 proposed in that Working Paper envisages that the parties may agree to continue the proceedings in whole or in part.

The UNCITRAL and SCC Arbitration Rules provide for strict temporal conditions to formulate such requests. They shall be filed within fifteen days from the date when the circumstances giving rise to the challenge became known to the party. The SCC Rules make clear that a failure to do so is tantamount to a waiver of the party's right to make the challenge. The ICSID Convention Arbitration Rules only make mention that the request shall be made promptly and in any case prior to the closure of the proceedings. In *Suez* v. *Argentina*, it was considered – in reference to Schreuer[9] – that '[p]romptly means that the proposal to disqualify must be made as soon as the party concerned learns of the grounds for a possible disqualification' and that, in application of Arbitration Rule 27, a failure to do so entails a waiver of the right to challenge (2007, Decision on Disqualification, para. 23). Arbitration Rule

---

[9] CH Schreuer, *The ICSID Convention: A Commentary* (Oxford University Press 2001), at 1198.

22.1.a, as proposed in the 2019 ICSID Working Paper n° 3, follows *mutatis mutandis* this approach, providing that the proposal for disqualification should be filed within 21 days after the later of 'the date on which the party proposing the disqualification first knew or first should have known of the facts on which the proposal is based' or of the constitution of the tribunal. The UNCITRAL and SCC Rules specify that, as regards the arbitrator they appoint – and, in the case of the SCC Rules also the arbitrator in whose appointment they participate – only circumstances known after the appointment can ground a request.

From this starting point, the exact procedure to decide on the request varies from one set of rules to the other, and, within each set, from one circumstance to the other depending in particular on the reaction of the non-challenging party and that of the challenged arbitrator. Under the ICSID Convention Arbitration Rules, if the challenge concerns a sole arbitrator or a majority of the members of a tribunal, the decision is to be made by the Chairman of the Administrative Council. In other situations, notably when only one arbitrator out of the three is challenged, the decision is to be made by the other members of the tribunal, and where such members are divided, it is up to the Chairman to decide. Interestingly, the 2019 ICSID Working Paper n° 3 envisages situations in which successive requests for disqualification are filed, with the proposed Arbitration Rule 23.2.b providing in this respect that if a subsequent proposal is filed while the decision on a prior proposal is pending, both proposals shall be decided by the Chairman as if they were a proposal to disqualify a majority of the tribunal. Irrespective of the exact situation at hand, the Rules offer the possibility to the challenged arbitrator to furnish an explanation, which the Working Paper proposes should be limited to factual information (proposed Arbitration Rule 22.1.d). Under the UNCITRAL Arbitration Rules, it is primarily up to the parties to agree on the challenge; if they do not, or if the challenged arbitrator has not withdrawn, the challenging party may decide to continue the challenge and seek a decision by the appointing authority. It is worth noting that those Rules specify that the agreement of the parties on the challenge or the withdrawal of the challenged arbitrator are not to be construed as entailing an acceptance of the validity of the grounds for challenge. Likewise, the SCC Arbitration Rules provide that it is primarily up to the parties to agree on the challenge. Where they do not, or where the challenged arbitrator does not withdraw, the decision is to be made by the Board.

– Counterclaims   Investor–State arbitration based on IIA offers to arbitrate is often criticised for its asymmetry, i.e. the fact that, for reasons explained in Chapter 14, claims are initiated by foreign investors against host States. Yet, there exists a mechanism, in the form of counterclaims, that helps to correct this asymmetry by offering States the chance to file a claim against investors who have initiated proceedings, provided the States' claim is connected to that of the investors. It is noteworthy that such counterclaims have no bearing on the status of investors and States as claimants and respondents to the proceedings, respectively.

This possibility for States to file counterclaims is provided for in arbitration rules. This is so notably in the ICSID Convention Arbitration Rules and in the UNCITRAL Arbitration Rules. As to the latter, it is worth noting that the 2010 revision adapted the Rules regarding counterclaims made in the context of investor–State arbitration. Specifically, Article 19.3 of the 1976 version of the Rules limited the possibility for the respondent to 'make a counter-claim arising out of the same contract', while Article 21.3 of the 2010 and 2013 version refers instead more broadly to the possibility to make a counterclaim 'provided that the arbitral tribunal has jurisdiction over it'. This change has brought the UNCITRAL Rules more in line with Article 46 of the ICSID Convention and Rule 40 of the ICSID Arbitration Rules. Article 46 provides as follows: 'Except as the parties otherwise agree, the Tribunal shall, if requested by a party, determine any incidental or additional claims or counterclaims arising directly out of the subject matter of the dispute provided they are within the scope of the consent of the parties and are otherwise within the jurisdiction of the Centre.' Arbitration Rule 40.2 sets a temporal requirement to the filing of a counterclaim: it shall be submitted no later than in the counter-memorial, unless the tribunal authorises the presentation of the claim at a later stage upon justification by the submitting party and upon consideration of any objection made by the other party.

International investment agreements have traditionally not referred to the possibility of submitting counterclaims. Treaty practice began to change in the 2010s, the potential of which can be seen in relation to the trend towards incorporating obligations binding upon investors, as discussed in Chapter 8. The 2018 CPTPP illustrates this trend, Article 9.19.2 of which provides that 'the respondent may make a counterclaim in connection with the factual and legal basis of the claim'.

With regard to IIAs that have traditionally not made any explicit reference to counterclaims, the issue has arisen whether or not the disputing parties have given their consent for tribunals to decide on counterclaims.

Of course, this has been an issue in practice for foreign investors who have almost systematically denied that they had given such a consent when initiating arbitration proceedings. As an exception, mention can be made of *Burlington Resources Inc.* v. *Ecuador*, where the issue did not arise; this stems from the fact that the parties had concluded an agreement expressing their consent to the resolution of a set of potential counterclaims by the arbitration tribunal (2017, Decision on Counterclaims, para. 60).

It is also worth noting that – in the context of ICSID Convention arbitration proceedings – this has been an issue for the great majority of tribunals that have considered, in the context of arbitration based on IIA offers to arbitrate, that this consent to counterclaims is to be appraised with regard to such offers. In contrast, this has not been an issue for the few arbitrators who focused instead on Article 46 of the ICSID Convention, as set out above, as a source of consent to the submission of counterclaims. For instance, in *Antoine Goetz & Consorts* v. *Burundi*, the Tribunal concluded that it did not matter that the applicable IIA did not contain any provision giving jurisdiction to the tribunal to decide on counterclaims as it considered that the consent given to the jurisdiction of ICSID encompasses consent to all of the conditions and procedures set out by the Convention, including counterclaims (2012, Award, paras. 278–279). To sustain this reasoning, the Tribunal built on the declaration made by Arbitrator Reisman in *Spyridon Roussalis* v. *Romania*, in which he explained: '[W]hen the States Parties to a BIT contingently consent, *inter alia*, to ICSID jurisdiction, the consent component of Article 46 of the Washington Convention is *ipso facto* imported into any ICSID arbitration which an investor then elects to pursue' (2011, Declaration, at 1). Adopting this approach, he dissented from the majority of the Tribunal, which considered that consent to counterclaims as such shall be based directly on IIAs and that the agreement at hand in that case did not ground such a consent (2011, Award, para. 866).

Those tribunals that have, like the majority of the Tribunal in *Spyridon Roussalis* v. *Romania*, focused on the IIA offers to arbitrate to appraise consent to counterclaims have had to deal with various types of offers to arbitrate. This holds true as well for tribunals operating under arbitration rules other than the ICSID Convention arbitration rules.

Of these various types of offers, the type of offers at stake in that case, contained in the 1997 Greece–Romania IIA, reads in its most relevant part as follows:

> Disputes between an investor of a Contracting Party and the other Contracting Party concerning an obligation of the latter under this Agreement, in relation to an investment of the former, shall, if possible, be settled by the disputing parties in an amicable way.
>
> If such disputes cannot be settled within six months from the date either party requested amicable settlement, the investor concerned may submit the dispute either to the competent courts of the Contracting Party in the territory of which the investment has been made or to international arbitration. Each Contracting Party hereby consents to the submission of such dispute to international arbitration. (Articles 9.1 and 9.2)

From this provision, two particular features serve to make the submission of a counterclaim by host States impossible. First, the subject matter of the disputes that can be submitted to arbitration is limited to those disputes that concern host States' IIA obligations; and second, it only grants investors the power to submit a dispute to arbitration. It comes as no surprise therefore that the majority of the Tribunal, which decided to focus on the IIA offer to arbitrate contrary to the Dissenting Arbitrator, concluded that its jurisdiction was limited to claims brought by investors and that counterclaims could not be introduced by host States (2011, Award, para. 869).

A similar finding was made by the Tribunal in *Karkey Karadeniz Elektrik Uretim A.S.* v. *Pakistan* in relation to another type of IIA offer to arbitrate contained in the 2012 Turkey–Pakistan IIA (2017, Award, para. 1014). Articles 10.1 and 10.2 of this Agreement provide:

> Disputes between one of the Contracting Parties and an investor of the other Contracting Party, in connection with his or her investment, shall be notified in writing, including detailed information, by the investor to the recipient Contracting Party of the investment. As far as possible, the investor and the concerned Contracting Party shall endeavor to settle these disputes by consultations and negotiations in good faith.
>
> If these disputes cannot be settled in this way within six (6) months following the date of the written notification mentioned in paragraph 1, the disputes can be submitted, as the investor may choose, to: (a) the competent court of the Contracting Party in whose territory the investment has been made, or (b) except as provided under paragraph 4 (a) and (b) of this Article, to: (i) the International Center for Settlement of Investment Disputes (ICSID) set up by the 'Convention on Settlement of Investment Disputes between States and Nationals of Other States', or (ii) an ad hoc arbitral tribunal established under the Arbitration Rules of Procedure of the United Nations Commission for International Trade Law (UNCITRAL).

Such a provision does not limit the subject matter of the disputes that can be submitted to arbitration in the way that Article 9 of the Greece–Romania IIA does; however, it also allows only investors to submit disputes to arbitration.

The drafting of IIA offers to arbitrate like Article 10 of the 2012 Pakistan–Turkey IIA can be contrasted with another type of offers that, not only does not restrict the subject matter of the dispute that may be submitted to arbitration to that pertaining to host States' IIA obligations, but also does not reserve the submission of disputes to arbitration to investors. When interpreting such a provision, i.e. Article 10 of the 1991 Spain–Argentina IIA, the Tribunal appointed in *Urbaser S.A.* v. *Argentina* concluded 'from the dual possibility to initiate an arbitration that the BIT does include in the dispute resolution mechanisms retained in Article X the hypothesis of a counterclaim' (2016, Award, para. 1144).

– Non-Disputing Party Submissions   Irrespective of the exact terminology used – 'non-disputing party submissions', 'third-party submissions' or '*amicus (curiae)* briefs' – this mechanism offers the possibility to non-disputing parties to participate in the proceedings via briefing submissions. This mechanism should be distinguished from that provided in some IIAs (e.g. 2016 Hong Kong China SAR–Chile IIA, Article 27.2) and in the 2013 UNCITRAL Rules on

Transparency in Treaty-Based Arbitration (Article 5), which authorises IIA States parties that are not a party to a dispute to make submissions on issues pertaining to the interpretation and application of the agreements. It is worth noting in this respect that the 2019 ICSID Working Paper n° 3 contemplates the incorporation of non-disputing treaty party submissions in ICSID Convention arbitration proceedings along the same lines (proposed Arbitration Rule 67).

Although non-disputing party submissions are not specific to investor–State arbitration, as these can be seen in other international adjudicative settings, such as the European Court of Human Rights, this mechanism is gaining a particular importance before arbitration tribunals. This is notably due to the fact that it plays an important role in addressing the criticism concerning the traditional confidentiality of investor–State arbitration proceedings and in enabling civil society members to express their views on the public interest issues often at stake in these proceedings. As stated by the Tribunal in *Philip Morris* v. *Uruguay* when accepting the request of the World Health Organization (WHO) to file a submission, non-disputing party submissions support the transparency of the proceedings and its acceptability by users at large (2015, Procedural Order n° 3, para. 28).

The genesis of non-disputing party submissions lies in the practice of arbitration tribunals themselves which, in the silence of the applicable IIAs and arbitration rules, determined that they have the power to consider and potentially accept requests to submit *amicus curiae* briefs. This was particularly so in NAFTA cases, most notably in *Methanex Corporation* v. *USA* (2001, Decision on Petitions from Third Persons to Intervene as 'Amici Curiae'). Subsequent to these cases, the NAFTA Free Trade Commission issued in 2003 a statement on non-disputing party participation that was followed by the incorporation of this mechanism in arbitration rules, namely in the ICSID Arbitration Rules on the occasion of their 2006 revision and in the UNCITRAL Rules on Transparency in 2013, as well as in IIA practice. The 2018 Korea–Republics of Central Americas IIA provides a recent example of this treaty practice (Article 9.21.3 and Annex 9-G). In light of the foregoing, it is noteworthy that this early arbitration practice and the NAFTA Free Trade Commission statement have largely served as a template for the above evolutions. This subsection focuses mainly on the ICSID Convention Arbitration Rules (Arbitration Rule 37) and the UNCITRAL Rules on Transparency (Article 4) for the purpose of examining the conditions that must be met for tribunals to accept a written submission by a non-disputing party; as can be seen below, the conditions that these instruments set are very similar. It is worth stressing at the outset that the decision to authorise such submissions is to be made by tribunals and that disputing parties have a mere consultative role under those Arbitration Rules.

As a general comment, it is important to shed light on and emphasise a requirement that is implicit in these Arbitration Rules – but is explicit in the 2003 NAFTA Free Trade Commission statement – according to which there must be a public interest at stake in the subject matter of the dispute. This condition can be construed as follows: '[T]he subject-matter of an arbitration proceeding is to be considered of public interest when the decisions to be issued in that arbitration are likely to affect individuals or entities beyond the Disputing Parties' (*Apotex* v. *USA*, 2013, Procedural Order on the Participation of the Applicant, Mr Barry Appleton, as a Non-Disputing Party, para. 42). Such a definition entails that the mere participation of a State as a respondent in proceedings does not *ipso facto* mean that there is a public interest at stake in the subject matter of the dispute.

In relation and in addition to this implicit requirement, the ICSID Convention Arbitration Rules and the UNCITRAL Rules on Transparency set specific conditions that are intended to strike a balance between the importance for non-disputing parties to contribute to the proceedings where public interests are at stake, the interests of the disputing parties, and the integrity and efficiency of the proceedings. The non-exhaustive list of conditions that they mention pertain to the content of the submission itself as well as to the applicant who files it.

Starting with the former, the first requirement mandates that the subject matter of the submission must be within the scope of the dispute, both factually and legally. As noted by the Tribunal in *Apotex* v. *USA*, such a condition 'is intended to avoid the unnatural broadening of the scope of the dispute by non-disputing parties' (2013, Procedural Order on the Participation of the Applicant, Mr Barry Appleton, as a Non-Disputing Party, para. 35).

Under the second condition set by those Rules, the submissions shall assist tribunals in the determination of a factual or legal issue related to the proceedings by bringing a perspective, particular knowledge or insight that is different from that of the disputing parties. This condition is not easy to meet, notably with respect to legal issues. Arbitration practice shows indeed that tribunals often conclude that the experience of the counsels and the work they produce precludes applicants, irrespective of their experience and expertise, from being considered as bringing a particular legal perspective (e.g. *Resolute Forest Products Inc.* v. *Canada*, 2017, Procedural Order n° 6, para. 4.4). The case of *Philip Morris* v. *Uruguay* offers an interesting example of a tribunal finding that the applicant brought a particular perspective on the facts. In that case, the WHO, in its capacity as the directing and coordinating authority on international health work, offered to contribute a particular perspective on the evidentiary basis underlying tobacco control measures and bans on misleading tobacco packaging, as well as on information pertaining to tobacco control globally (2015, Procedural Order n° 3).

As a third condition, submissions must not disrupt the proceedings or unduly burden or unfairly prejudice either party. This requirement is complemented by the above-mentioned requirement that both parties be consulted by tribunals before they make their decision. Likewise, the ICSID Convention Arbitration Rules and the UNCITRAL Rules on Transparency provide that the disputing parties shall be given the opportunity to present their observations on the applicant's submission.

As is evident from these requirements, the status of *amicus curiae* should not be equated with that of a disputing party. In that sense, the Tribunal stressed in *Philip Morris* v. *Uruguay* that a 'submission shall confer to the petitioner neither the status of a party to the arbitration proceedings nor the right to access the file of the case or to attend hearings', the 'need to safeguard the integrity of the arbitral process requir[ing] in fact that no procedural rights or privileges of any kind be granted to the non-disputing parties' (2015, Procedural Order n° 3, para. 22). It is worth noting that other tribunals have adopted a different opinion as to the possibility for non-disputing parties to access the file of the case. For instance, the Tribunal appointed in *Infinito Gold Ltd.* v. *Costa Rica* authorised access to certain documents by the non-disputing party on the ground that this would enable it to effectively discharge its task, namely to provide the tribunal with a useful and particular insight on facts or legal questions relevant to its jurisdiction (2016, Procedural Order n° 2, para. 43). With regard to this issue, it is worth noting that the revision of the Arbitration Rules contemplated in the 2019 ICSID Working Paper n° 3 proposes that tribunals may give access to relevant documents filed in the proceedings, unless either party objects (proposed Arbitration Rule 66.6).

Turning to the requirements concerning applicants, the conditions set by the ICSID Convention Arbitration Rules and the UNCITRAL Rules on Transparency are twofold.

The first of these is that all applicants, both natural or legal persons, must have a significant interest in the proceedings. The requirement that the interest be 'significant' aims at preventing any person who has only a 'general' or 'vague' interest in the proceedings from submitting a non-disputing party submission. In *Resolute Forest Products Inc.* v. *Canada*, the Tribunal considered that this condition had not been met, explaining in support of its conclusion: 'While the Applicants have stated the admirable goal of "maintain[ing] respect [for] the rule of law, international public law and the application of the principle of *pacta sunt servanda* within dispute resolution under the NAFTA [footnote omitted]", this does not prove a "significant interest" in this arbitration beyond "having the Tribunal adopt legal interpretations of NAFTA" that the Applicants favour' (2017, Procedural Order n° 6, para. 4.6). On the other hand, the Tribunal considered in *Philip Morris* v. *Uruguay* that the applicants had a significant interest in the proceedings because of the status of the WHO as the world authority on public health matters and that of the Framework Convention on Tobacco Control (FCTC) Secretariat as the designated global authority concerning the FCTC and its Implementation Guidelines (2015, Procedural Order n° 3, para. 25).

The second set of conditions pertain to disclosure requirements. These conditions aim to ensure the independence of applicants from the disputing parties, and also at preventing 'shadow' entities from using applicants and the ability to brief *amicus curiae* in order to serve their own interests. Under the 2013 UNCITRAL Rules on Transparency, applicants shall in particular: (1) '[d]escribe the third person, including, where relevant, its membership and legal status ..., its general objectives, the nature of its activities and any parent organisation (including any organisation that directly or indirectly controls the third person)'; (2) '[d]isclose any connection, direct or indirect, which the third person has with any disputing party'; (3) '[p]rovide information on any government, person or organisation that has provided to the third person (i) any financial or other assistance in preparing the submission; or (ii) substantial assistance in either of the two years preceding the application'; and (4) '[d]escribe the nature of the interest that the third person has in the arbitration'. Although the ICSID Convention Arbitration Rules do not provide for such requirements, tribunals operating under those Rules have the power to adopt these, as the list of condition set in Arbitration Rule 37 is non-exhaustive. This is well illustrated in *Philip Morris* v. *Uruguay*, where the Tribunal denied a request to submit an *amicus curiae* brief in particular because of the close relationship between the applicant and the claimant in the arbitration proceedings (2016, Award, para. 55). In this respect, it can be noted that the 2019 ICSID Working Paper n° 3 proposes to incorporate requirements *mutatis mutandis* similar to those set by the UNCITRAL Rules on Transparency (proposed Arbitration Rule 66.2).

d Closing and Discontinuance of Arbitration Proceedings

As a matter of principle, the proceedings are closed when the parties have presented their case. It is worth noting that the UNCITRAL Arbitration Rules (Article 31) do not refer to the closing of proceedings, but rather to the closure of hearings – however, as noted by Caron and Caplan, the use of the term 'hearings' in Article 31 appears to have been 'a misnomer'.[10] The SCC Arbitration Rules provide that arbitration tribunals shall declare the proceedings closed when they are satisfied that the disputing parties have had a reasonable opportunity to present their cases (Article 40); in the same vein, the UNCITRAL Rules offer the possibility to tribunals to inquire with the disputing parties whether they have any further proof to bring, witnesses to be heard or submissions to be made before they declare the hearings closed.

Subject to exceptional circumstances, arbitration rules entitle tribunals to reopen the proceedings until the award is rendered. The SCC and UNCITRAL Arbitration Rules specify that the re-opening can be decided on the initiative of the tribunal or following a request by either party. Pursuant to the ICSID Convention Arbitration Rules, such exceptional circumstances shall consist in

---

[10] DD Caron, LM Caplan, *The UNCITRAL Arbitration Rules: A Commentary* (2nd ed, Oxford University Press 2013), at 625.

the revelation of new evidence that constitutes a decisive factor, or in the vital need to clarify some specific points (Arbitration Rule 38.2).

Irrespective of the suspension of the proceedings that may be decided by tribunals in the course thereof, proceedings can end at an earlier stage in certain circumstances. This results typically from the agreement of the parties to settle their disputes. Depending on the applicable arbitration rules and on the circumstances, this settlement agreement may be recorded in the form of an award or lead to the discontinuance of the proceedings.

   The discontinuance may have other grounds. Under the ICSID Convention Arbitration Rules, it can also derive, for instance – as discussed above – from the failure of the parties to act (Arbitration Rule 45). Under the UNCITRAL Rules, the termination of the proceedings may also be decided by tribunals themselves if they consider that it is unnecessary or impossible to continue the proceedings (Articles 36.2).

11.2.2.2 Deliberations and Awards

This subsection examines the key features of deliberations as well as awards, with a specific focus on the apportionment of costs.

Preliminary Remarks

As a preliminary matter, it is necessary to clarify the meaning of 'award'. In ICSID Convention arbitration proceedings, the last decision that disposes of the case is designated as the 'award', after which an annulment proceeding – analysed in Chapter 16 – can be initiated against it. This means, for instance, that if proceedings are bifurcated and a tribunal decides first on its jurisdiction, the decision on jurisdiction is considered as an award if the tribunal declines jurisdiction, as this decision disposes of the case. In contrast, if it upholds jurisdiction and the proceedings move on to the merits, this decision on jurisdiction is not considered as an award. It will subsequently form part of the award. The same reasoning applies if the decision on jurisdiction and liability – or two distinct decisions on those matters – are dissociated from the decision on damages which is then the last decision to dispose of the case. On the other hand, matters of jurisdiction, merits and damages can be dealt with in the same decision, which is then to be considered as the award. Under the UNCITRAL and SCC Arbitration Rules, any decision taken by the tribunals operating under them are called 'awards' (respectively, Articles 34.1 and 44); this common denomination does obviously not entail that all tribunals' decisions have the same legal consequences beyond all being final and binding on the parties.

a Deliberations

After the parties have presented their case, awards – as well as decisions – constitute the output of the tribunals' deliberations. As in any international adjudicative setting, deliberations are to be held confidentially between the members of the tribunals; in that sense, the ICSID Convention Arbitration Rules make it explicit that the deliberations shall take place in private between the members of the tribunals and remain secret. As an exception to this, deliberations can be opened to other persons if tribunals decide so (Arbitration Rule 15).

Except obviously where tribunals consist of one sole arbitrator, awards shall be made by a majority of the arbitrators – the ICSID Convention Arbitration Rules specify in this respect that abstention counts as a negative vote (Arbitration Rule 16.1).

Notably, deliberations are increasingly addressed in IIAs – for instance, the 2018 Argentina–Japan IIA provides that a tribunal 'shall within a reasonable period of time reach its decision by a majority of votes' (Article 25.21).

b Awards

Awards shall be made in writing, signed and contain specific information. Most importantly, they shall state the reasons upon which they are based, except under Article 34.3 of the UNCITRAL Arbitration Rules and Article 42.1 of the SCC Arbitration Rules when the parties agree otherwise. Such a possibility offered to the parties to agree that the tribunals do not state the reasons – which can be explained by the original orientation of those Rules towards commercial arbitration – is alien to the practice of investor–State arbitration tribunals, which has given rise over time to an increasing trend in providing reasons and justifications in support of the conclusions that they reach. In this respect, it is noteworthy that providing reasons and justifications is an obligation under a growing number of IIAs that require that awards be motivated with reasons, as discussed below. It can also be noted in relation to the criticism formulated against investor–State arbitration that the mention of reasons and justifications facilitates a greater transparency of arbitration and can thereby help in reinforcing the legitimacy of tribunals in the eyes of civil society members. Together with those reasons, the ICSID Convention Arbitration Rules specify that the award shall contain the decision of the tribunal on every question submitted to it (ICSID Convention, Article 48.3 and Arbitration Rule 47.1.i). Under those provisions, any member of an ICSID tribunal is authorised to attach an individual opinion, whether or not they dissent from the majority, or a statement of the dissent.

For awards rendered by tribunals operating under the UNCITRAL and SCC Arbitration Rules, the date of the award is the one indicated by tribunals in the award (respectively, Articles 34.4 and 42.2). For tribunals operating under the ICSID Convention Arbitration Rules, the award is deemed to be rendered on the date on which the certified copies of the award are dispatched by the Secretary-General (ICSID Convention, Article 49.1 and Arbitration Rule 48.2). The date is of utmost importance with regard to the post-award remedies examined below.

Awards are final and binding upon the parties. It is worth recalling here that, as discussed in Chapter 2 devoted to the sources of international investment law and arbitration, awards and individual opinions can have a larger systemic impact. In this respect, mention can be made of Regulation 22 of the ICSID Administrative and Financial Regulation, which stresses the role that the publication of awards plays to 'further the development of international law in relation to investments'.

As part of the criticism denouncing the confidentiality of investor–State arbitration, there has long been the fact that awards are not automatically made public. While the SCC Arbitration Rules do not address the matter at all, the publication of award is subject to the consent of the parties under the ICSID Convention Arbitration Rules. However, the above-mentioned calls for increased transparency of investor–State arbitration proceedings has led to an evolution of arbitration rules in this respect. ICSID has been a 'pioneer' in this respect. While the 1984 revision of the Arbitration Rules authorised ICSID to publish excerpts of the legal rules applied in the award, the 2006 revision has broadened the scope of the publication to the legal reasoning of the tribunal and made this publication an obligation that must be promptly fulfilled (Arbitration Rule 48.4). On the other hand, under this Rule, the ICSID shall not publish the award without the consent of the parties. It is worth noting in this respect that the revision contemplated in the 2019 ICSID Working Paper n ° 3 sets up a presumption of consent of the parties to publish the award, with the proposed Arbitration Rule 61.3 providing that the consent to publish the award shall be deemed to have been given if no party objects in writing to such publication within sixty days after its dispatch. Going one step further, the UNCITRAL Rules on Transparency count the award as part of the documents that shall be made available to the public (Article 3.1).

Forming part of the evolution of IIA practice mentioned above towards specifying and strengthening investor–State dispute settlement provisions, one can notice that a number of IIAs concluded in the 2010s provide greater information on the awards beyond the mere traditional specification that they shall be final and binding. They pertain in particular to the content of the awards and their finality.

As regards the content, similar to arbitration rules, some agreements provide *mutatis mutandis* that the final award shall set out its findings of law and fact, together with the reasons for its ruling (e.g. 2018 Korea–Republics of Central Americas IIA, Article 9.27.1). As an alternative, the 2017 Qatar–Singapore IIA provides that tribunals shall give reasons and the bases for its decision at the request of either party (Article 10.4.d). In relation to the content of awards, it is also worth noting that a few IIAs, i.e. FTAs containing an investment chapter, establish a 'commentary stage', akin to the proceedings at the World Trade Organization (WTO), in the course of the drafting of the award. This is well illustrated by the 2018 CPTPP, which provides:

In any arbitration conducted under this Section, at the request of a disputing party, a tribunal shall, before issuing a decision or award on liability, transmit its proposed decision or award to the disputing parties. Within 60 days after the tribunal transmits its proposed decision or award, the disputing parties may submit written comments to the tribunal concerning any aspect of its proposed decision or award. The tribunal shall consider any comments and issue its decision or award no later than 45 days after the expiration of the 60 days comment period. (Article 9.23.10)

With regard to the finality of the award, it is worth recalling that some IIAs envisage the establishment of an appellate system endorsed with the task of reviewing the substance of awards. This possibility, which – as explained in Chapter 10 – has been initiated in the US IIA practice, has taken on another dimension in the context of the reform of the settlement of investor–State disputes initiated in the 2010s. Indeed, while some treaties refer to the potential establishment of a bilateral appellate body (2008 USA–Rwanda IIA, Annex D), others refer to external and broader initiatives. For instance, Article 9.23.11 of the 2018 CPTPP provides that '[i]n the event that an appellate mechanism for reviewing awards rendered by investor–State dispute settlement tribunals is developed in the future under other institutional arrangements, the Parties shall consider whether awards rendered under Article 9.29 (Awards) should be subject to that appellate mechanism'. Although the investment court system first promoted by the European Union and implemented notably in the 2016 CETA departs from arbitration, the Appeal Tribunal that forms part of it further confirms this trend.

c Costs

The cost of arbitration proceedings is one of the key elements that grounds the criticism formulated against investor–State arbitration. Critics denounce the burden that it places on public budgets, notably those of developing States. This is said to contribute to the 'chilling effect' of international investment law and arbitration discussed above. But it is worth noting that the cost of arbitration is also seen as limiting the access to justice of natural persons as well as small or medium-sized companies that do not have financial resources comparable to those of larger companies, typically multinational corporations.

Costs in practice have a threefold dimension: the fees and expenses of arbitrators; the expenses and charges of dispute settlement centres; and the fees and expenses incurred by the parties for legal representation in the proceedings. Prior to examining how those costs are to be apportioned, it is first necessary to formulate some preliminary remarks pertaining to the duration of the proceedings and third-party funding.

i Preliminary Issues

– Duration of Proceedings   The costs of arbitration proceedings arise from various factors, in particular their length. Of course, an oft-mentioned feature of arbitration is the speed of proceedings as compared to domestic court proceedings. At the same time, investor–State arbitration often entails complex factual and legal issues that cannot be settled expeditiously. Irrespective of the litigation tactics that may be implemented by parties' counsels, it is inherent in an adversarial process that the debate between the parties takes quite some time; in the same vein, it is also one of the core features of justice that time is needed for collegial tribunals to form and argue their decisions. It remains that, as noted by the ICSID Secretariat in the context of the fifth round of amendment of the ICSID Convention Arbitration Rules, 'there appears to be consensus on reiterating the obligation to issue timely awards and to determine disputes in an economic fashion'.[11] As a result, the revision of the Arbitration Rules contemplated in the 2019 ICSID Working Paper n° 3 proposes to streamline the proceedings at various stages and also to incorporate an expedited arbitration procedure (Proposed Chapter 12).

Such an evolution is in line with the approach notably adopted in the CETA, which aims at limiting the length of the proceedings in the ICS that it sets up. For instance, its Article 8.39.7 targets the conduct of both disputing parties and that of the Tribunal. It provides that they shall make every effort to ensure that the dispute settlement process is carried out in a timely manner. It also requires the final award to be made within twenty-four months of the date on which the claim is submitted and it obliges the Tribunal to provide the disputing parties with the reasons for any delay where additional time is required to issue the award. It is also worth noting that this Agreement contemplates the adoption of supplemental rules aiming to reduce the financial burden of the proceedings for claimants who are natural persons and small or medium-sized companies (Article 8.39.6).

– Third-Party Funding   The 2010s have borne witness to a multiplication of the proceedings financed by entities often called 'third-party funders', mainly to the benefit of the claimant investors. There currently exists no universally accepted definition of third-party funding, which can take many forms and is a phenomenon that expands beyond the sphere of investor–State arbitration. In the field of international investment law, a definition of this mechanism can be found in the CETA, which provides: '[T]hird party funding means any funding provided by a natural or legal person who is not a disputing party but who enters into an agreement with a disputing party in order to finance part or all of the cost of the proceedings either through a donation or grant, or in return for remuneration dependent on the outcome of the dispute' (Article 8.1).

Irrespective of the exact definition and scope conferred to this notion, the fact that a third party may fund a disputing party has raised fierce debates that

---

[11] ICSID, 'The ICSID Rules Amendment Process' (2016), at 3, available at https://icsid
.worldbank.org/en.

fall more generally within and contribute to the debate about the reform of the settlement of investor–State disputes. On the one hand, third-party funding is notably considered as favouring and even making possible access to justice for investors lacking the resources to finance proceedings. On the other hand, it is criticised for favouring the submission of speculative cases and thereby for contributing to the increase in the number of cases filed that have a 'chilling effect' on host States.

In addition to these policy issues, third-party funding has raised legal issues in arbitration practice pertaining to jurisdiction (e.g. *Teinver S. A.* v. *Argentina*, 2012, Decision on Jurisdiction), potential conflicts of interests for arbitrators (e.g. *Muhammet Cap* v. *Turkmenistan*, 2015, Procedural Order n° 3), and costs. With respect to the latter, the main issue discussed is whether the recourse to third-party funding justifies on its own security for costs, a question which arbitration tribunals have consistently answered in the negative (e.g. 2016 *South American Silver Limited (Bermuda)* v. *Bolivia*, 2016, Procedural Order n° 10, para. 74).

Although IIA practice and arbitration rules have traditionally been silent on third-party funding, this has been changing throughout the 2010s.

As part of IIA practice, the first instrument to have addressed the matter is the CETA. Article 8.26 makes it an obligation for the disputing party benefiting from third-party funding to disclose the name and the address of the funder to the other party and to the tribunal at the time of the submission of the claim, or after and without delay if a financing agreement is concluded subsequently.

As regards arbitration rules, the first set of rules to have addressed the matter are the 2017 Investment Arbitration Rules of the Singapore International Arbitration Centre. More recently, this has also been proposed in the context of the revision of the ICSID Arbitration Rules envisaged in the 2019 ICSID Working Paper n° 3. Proposed Arbitration Rule 14 provides that the disputing party concerned shall file a written notice with the Secretary-General – upon the registration of the request or immediately upon the conclusion of the third-party funding arrangement after registration – that discloses the name of any non-party from which this party, its affiliate or its representative has received funds for the pursuit or defence of the proceedings through a donation or grant, or in return for remuneration dependent on the outcome of the dispute. The notice is then to be transmitted to the other party and to the arbitrators proposed for appointment or appointed. In relation to the above-mentioned conflicts of interests that third-party funding may generate for arbitrators, it is worth noticing that this proposed rule specifies that the transmission to arbitrators is for the purpose of the completion of the arbitrator's declaration discussed above in relation to the moral integrity requirement.

ii The Apportionment of Costs   The UNCITRAL Arbitration Rules provide that as a matter of principle the costs shall be borne by the unsuccessful party (Article 42.1). At the same time, Article 42.2 provides that tribunals may apportion the costs between the parties if they consider this to be reasonable in light of the circumstances of the case. Under Article 49 of the SCC Rules, the apportionment of the costs of the arbitration – which in these Rules do not include the fees and expenses incurred by the parties for legal representation – shall be made by tribunals – if the parties do not agree otherwise – at the request of a party, having regard to the outcome of the case and the relevant circumstances, in particular the respective contribution of the parties to the efficiency and expeditiousness of the arbitration. Likewise, with regard to the costs incurred by a party, the Rules provide that unless otherwise agreed by the parties, tribunals may at the request of a party order one party to pay in particular any reasonable costs for legal representation, having regard to the outcome of the case, each party's contribution to the efficiency and expeditiousness of the arbitration and any other relevant circumstances (Article 50). The ICSID Convention Arbitration Rules leave a greater discretion to tribunals as, except in cases of agreement between the parties, they provide simply that tribunals shall decide how and by whom costs shall be paid (ICSID Convention, Article 61.2).

This discretion left by the ICSID Convention Arbitration Rules has raised the question of the principles and factors to be used by tribunals to make their decisions on costs. In this respect, there has been a noticeable evolution in arbitration practice. Tribunals operating under those Rules have traditionally considered that the parties shall bear their respective costs while sharing the fees and expenses of arbitrators as well as the charges and expenses of ICSID. More recently, an increasing number of those tribunals have applied the costs-follow-the-event principle and have awarded costs, or a part of them, to the successful party. Yet, this is not a *jurisprudence constante*, as illustrated by the decision of the Tribunal in *Fabrica de Vidrios Los Andes, C.A. v. Venezuela* (2017, Award, para. 317). It is also worth noting that in practice a number of tribunals adopt a hybrid approach taking into account a number of factors (e.g. *Antin v. Spain*, 2018, Award, para. 744).

The factors taken into consideration vary depending on the circumstances of each case. Most fall into three main categories: (1) the overall findings of the tribunal on jurisdiction, admissibility, merits and quantum issues; (2) the conduct of the investor with regard to the initiation of the proceedings, notably any fraudulent or bad-faith behaviour; and (3) the conduct of the parties during the proceedings, in particular abusive or delaying litigation manoeuvres. The reasonableness of the parties' costs or the complexity of the issues raised in the course of the proceedings constitute other factors often taken into consideration. It is noteworthy that the good faith of the State when adopting the measure that is considered by the tribunal in breach of its IIA obligations has also been viewed as an element to be taken into account. In *Burlington Resources Inc. v. Ecuador*, the Tribunal stated:

> In the Tribunal's view, after a consideration of all the relevant circumstances, the principles above may be adjusted to take into account that the respondent is a sovereign State. In particular, it considers that, even if a tribunal finds that a State has breached its international obligations vis-à-vis an investor, consideration must be given to the State's motives and good faith. In particular, where the actions of a State have been guided by its good faith understanding of the public interest and the State could reasonably doubt that it was breaching its international obligations, the Tribunal may consider it appropriate to apportion costs in a manner that alleviates the burden on the respondent State. These considerations apply to situations in which the State is the respondent, not the claimant. (2017, Decision on Reconsideration and Award, para. 621)

The revision of the ICSID Convention Arbitration Rules contemplated in the 2019 ICSID Working Paper n° 3 fills the existing gap in the 2006 version of the Rules by providing a non-exhaustive list of circumstances that tribunals shall take into account. In line with the practice of ICSID arbitration tribunals, the proposed Arbitration Rule 51.1 refers to (1) the outcome of the proceeding or any part of it; (2) the conduct of the parties during the proceeding, including the extent to which they acted in an expeditious and cost-effective manner; (3) the complexity of the issues; and (4) the reasonableness of the costs claimed.

International investment agreements have also traditionally contained little information on the apportionment of costs apart from a few exceptions. Such exceptions are illustrated by the 1991 China–Mongolia IIA, which provides: 'Each party to the dispute shall bear the cost of its appointed member of the tribunal and of its representation in the proceedings. The cost of the appointed Chairman and the remaining costs shall be borne in equal parts by the parties to the dispute' (Article 8.8).

In contrast, a number of IIAs concluded in the 2010s contain a provision on costs. Most of these simply refer to the applicable arbitration rules that tribunals shall apply when they award costs (e.g. 2016 Canada–Mongolia IIA, Article 34.2). However, a few directly address the apportionment of costs. For instance, the 2018 CPTPP provides specific indications with respect in particular to the objection that a claim is manifestly without legal merit. Article 9.23.6 provides that tribunals may award to the prevailing disputing party reasonable costs and attorney's fees incurred in submitting or opposing such an objection. For that purpose, tribunals shall consider whether either the claimant's claim or the respondent's objection was frivolous and they shall provide the disputing parties a reasonable opportunity to comment.

11.2.2.3 Post-Award Proceedings

As mentioned above, awards are final; yet, certain proceedings may be initiated with regard to certain potential deficiencies in those awards. Among such proceedings, a distinction is to be made between those relating to the 'modification' or the 'clarification' of awards, and those that pertain to their annulment.

a Modification and Clarification of Awards

The proceedings that can be engaged with a view to modifying or clarifying awards varies depending on the features of awards and the circumstances. They pertain to the correction, the supplementation, the interpretation, or the revision of the awards.

i Correction   The correction of an award may be requested by a party, after giving notice to the other party, when there is a clerical, typographical, arithmetical or any similar error in the award. Contrary to the UNCITRAL and SCC Arbitration Rules (respectively, Articles 38.2 and 47.2), the ICSID Convention Arbitration Rules do not provide for the possibility for tribunals to make such corrections on their own initiative (ICSID Convention, Article 49 and Arbitration Rule 49).

Such requests can only be made within a limited time frame after the date on which the award is received (UNCITRAL and SCC Arbitration Rules) or rendered (ICSID Convention Arbitration Rules). In this respect, ICSID Arbitration Rule 49.5 specifies that the Secretary-General shall refuse to register a request for correction if she receives it more than forty-five days after the award is rendered.

The ICSID Convention Arbitration Rules do not confer any discretion to tribunals as to the rectification of the errors falling within the scope of Article 49 of the Convention, as the Rules provide that they 'shall' rectify any of them. On the other hand, the UNCITRAL and SCC Arbitration Rules place such an obligation upon tribunals only if they consider the request as being justified.

ii Supplementation   There can be two types of omissions in awards: 'technical' omissions (e.g. arithmetical omissions) and 'substantive' omissions.

Under the UNCITRAL Arbitration Rules, technical omissions shall be supplemented by tribunals following the same procedure as for technical errors as discussed above (Article 38.1). Concerning substantive omissions, Article 39 of those Rules as well as Article 48 of the SCC Arbitration Rules – which do not address technical omissions – provide that either party, upon notice to the other party, may request the tribunal within a limited time frame to supplement the award. If the tribunal considers the request to be justified, it shall make an additional award.

The ICSID Convention Arbitration Rules (ICSID Convention, Article 49 and Arbitration Rule 49) do not make any such distinction; they refer to the questions that the tribunal omitted to decide in the award. In such a case, the same procedure as to rectification applies, with the notable exception that the tribunal enjoys discretion, as the Rules provide that it 'may' decide any question which it omitted to decide – this is to be contrasted to the lack of discretion in relation to rectification.

iii Interpretation   Interpretation proceedings aim at clarifying awards; they shall not be used by parties to argue a new point, to re-argue the case, or to contest the tribunal's conclusions.

Under the UNCITRAL and SCC Arbitration Rules, interpretation shall be made by tribunals following the same procedure as for the correction of technical errors as well as – concerning UNCITRAL Rules – the supplementation of omissions of a similar nature (respectively, Articles 37.1 and 47.1). On the other hand, tribunals do not have the possibility to make interpretations on their own initiative.

Under the ICSID Convention Arbitration Rules (ICSID Convention, Article 50 and Arbitration Rules 50, 51, 53 and 54), interpretation can also result only from the request of a party, but with no time limit. It is worth stressing that under those Rules and – contrary to the UNCITRAL and SCC Arbitration Rules – such a request can be formulated only if a dispute has arisen between the parties as to the meaning or scope of the award. In other words, mere questions that the parties may have about the meaning or the scope of the award or general complaints that they may have, but which do not materialise in a dispute, fall outside the scope of the interpretation that can be requested from tribunals under the ICSID Convention Arbitration Rules. Another notable difference that those Rules display consists of the establishment of a new tribunal to deal with the request, in the event that such request cannot be submitted to the tribunal that rendered the award. In any case, the tribunal deciding on the request for interpretation may – pending its decision – stay the enforcement of the award if it considers that the circumstances so require, upon request of the applicant in its request for interpretation, or by either party at any time before the tribunal decides on the interpretation request. Tribunals cannot stay the enforcement of awards on their own initiative.

iv Revision   Among all the requests discussed in this subsection, requests for revision impact the most on the finality of awards. This certainly explains why this possibility is not provided for in the UNCITRAL and SCC Arbitration Rules, and why it is strictly regulated under the ICSID Convention Arbitration Rules (ICSID Convention, Article 51 and Arbitration Rules 50, 51, 53 and 54).

Content-wise, only the discovery of factual elements can ground such requests; furthermore, those facts must decisively affect the awards. From a temporal point of view, the facts must, at the time when awards were rendered, have been unknown to tribunals and to applicants and, as for the latter, their ignorance must not have been due to negligence.

The timeline for requesting the revision of awards is strictly set out – such requests must be made within ninety days after the discovery of the facts and in any case within three years after the date the award was rendered. As with the requests for interpretation, the Rules provide that the request shall be submitted to a new tribunal, in case it cannot be submitted to the tribunal that rendered the award.

A stay of enforcement of the award can be requested by the applicant in its request for revision; in such a case, the enforcement shall be stayed automatically. Once the tribunal has been reconstituted, a party that wants to have the stay continued must submit a request to that effect, otherwise the stay is automatically terminated. A stay of enforcement can also be requested by either party after the reconstitution of the tribunal and at any time before it decides on the request for revision. It is up to the tribunal to decide whether or not the circumstances require a stay. Tribunals cannot stay the enforcement of awards on their own initiative.

b Annulment of Awards

As mentioned above, arbitration awards are final. They have traditionally not been subject to any appeal, a situation which – as discussed above – is contested and has started to evolve in treaty practice. On the other hand, it is possible for either party to seek the annulment of the award. Here, a distinction is to be made between the awards rendered by tribunals operating under the ICSID Convention Arbitration Rules and those rendered under other sets of rules, including the ICSID Additional Facility Arbitration Rules referred to above. As examined in detail in Chapter 16, the ICSID Convention provides for a 'self-contained' annulment mechanism independent from domestic courts. Instead, 'non-ICSID Convention awards' are to be challenged before domestic courts, typically those of the seat of arbitration, in application of their domestic law.

There are of course differences between those domestic laws as regards the grounds that may justify the annulment of awards. That being said, they display similarities, notably as many of them have been influenced by Article 34.2 of the 1985 UNCITRAL Model Law on International Commercial Arbitration (last revised in 2006), which was itself based on the 1958 Convention on the Recognition and Enforcement of Foreign Arbitral Awards examined below.

Following Article 34.2, the grounds that can *mutatis mutandis* be relied upon to request an annulment are: (1) the incapacity of a party to the arbitration agreement; (2) the invalidity of the agreement to arbitrate; (3) the lack of proper notice of the appointment of an arbitrator or of the arbitration proceedings to the applicant; (4) the inability of the applicant to present its case; (5) the fact that the award deals with a dispute or contains decisions on matters falling outside the scope of the submission to arbitration; (6) the fact that the composition of the tribunal or the arbitration proceedings are not in conformity primarily with the agreement of the parties; (7) the non-arbitrability of the subject matter of the dispute; and (8) the conflict between the award and public policy. Of course, those grounds have been developed in relation to international commercial arbitration.

As seen below, it is worth noting that under the 1958 Convention on the Recognition and Enforcement of Foreign Arbitral Awards, the annulment of an award by the competent authority of the country where or under the law of which the award is made constitutes a ground for refusing the recognition and the enforcement of the award (Article V.1.e). By the same token, if a request for annulment is pending before such competent authority, the authority where enforcement is sought may, if it considers it appropriate, adjourn its decision (Article VI).

11.2.2.4 Recognition and Enforcement of Awards

In law, awards are binding upon disputing parties which must abide by them. When host States are held responsible, they must comply with their obligation to repair, as analysed in Chapter 15. In practice, States are not always willing to do so. In such cases, investors are faced with a deficiency that international arbitration – be it State–State, commercial or investor–State arbitration – as well as standing international courts and tribunals have *mutatis mutandis* in common: the lack of an enforcement mechanism. In this context, investors have no other choice than to rely on domestic courts by seeking the recognition and enforcement of the awards. Recognition is a requirement which derives fundamentally from State sovereignty and the necessity for States to control the compatibility of awards – and also of foreign judgments – with a set of legal and policy principles applicable under their jurisdiction.

As with annulment, a distinction must be made here between the recognition and enforcement of the awards rendered under the ICSID Convention Arbitration Rules and those rendered under other sets of rules, including the ICSID Additional Facility Arbitration Rules.

Under the former, it is an obligation for all Members States to recognise awards as binding as if they constituted a final judgment of their domestic courts as well as to enforce the pecuniary obligations imposed by those awards (ICSID Convention, Article 54). It is worth noting that this enforcement obligation is, however, limited to pecuniary obligations. Recognition and enforcement are 'automatic' in all the ICSID Member States, meaning that those awards shall not be subject to review by the competent courts or authorities of those Member States in which they are sought to be recognised and the pecuniary obligations enforced. All that is required from investors is that they furnish to those courts or authorities a copy of the awards certified by the ICSID Secretary-General for authentication purposes. If such recognition and enforcement can be sought simultaneously in several Member States, subject to the prohibition of multiple recovery, it goes without saying that investors do not benefit from this facilitation in States that are not party to the ICSID Convention. But even in ICSID Member States, this facilitation has its limits, deriving from the privileged position of States that enjoy immunity from execution. In other words, the obligation for States to recognise awards and to enforce pecuniary obligations does not necessarily entail that awards can be executed in practice. In this respect, Article 55 of the Washington Convention makes it clear that the obligation for ICSID Member States to recognise awards and to enforce pecuniary obligations is not to be construed as derogating from the law in force in any Member State relating to the immunity of States from execution. As regards the issue of States' immunities, awards rendered by tribunals operating under the ICSID Convention Arbitration Rules are treated in the same way as awards rendered by tribunals operating under other sets of arbitration rules.

The fact that this second category of awards does not benefit from a regime similar to that established by the ICSID Convention with regard to recognition and enforcement means that they can be reviewed by domestic courts or authorities. The nature and extent of this review is set by domestic laws and mainly by the 1958 Convention on the Recognition and Enforcement of Arbitral Awards for those numerous States that are parties to that Convention. The grounds on the basis of which recognition and enforcement may be rejected under Article V of that Convention correspond *mutatis mutandis* to those mentioned above in relation to the annulment of 'non-ICSID arbitration awards', in addition to the above-mentioned ground set out in Article V.1.e. As explained above, in addition to the fact that the annulment of an award by the competent authority of the country where or under the law of which the award is made constitutes a ground for refusing the recognition and enforcement of the award, the authority where enforcement is sought may, if it considers it appropriate, adjourn its decision in case a request for annulment is pending.

Turning to immunities, it is worth referring to the 2004 United Nations Convention on Jurisdictional Immunities of States and their Property (UN Convention) which – albeit not in force – reflects common trends in the practice of States on those matters. More specifically, attention is to be paid to Article 19 which addresses State immunity from 'post-judgment measures of constraint'. In addition to waivers, meaning situations in which a State has expressly consented to the taking of such measures, notably in an international agreement, an arbitration agreement or a written contract, this Article relies on the traditional distinction made between 'commercial-oriented properties' and 'non-commercial oriented-properties' by stating that the former may in certain situations be seized. It provides in this respect that it shall be 'established that the property is specifically in use or intended for use by the State for other than government non-commercial purposes and is in the territory of the State of the forum, provided that post-judgment measures of constraint may only be taken against property that has a connection with the entity against which the proceeding was directed'.

As evidenced by IIA practice, such waivers prove to be irrelevant in the context of investor–State arbitration based on IIA offers to arbitrate; more generally, and as explained above, the ICSID Convention makes it explicit that it is not to be construed as derogating from the law in force in any Member

State relating to the immunity of States from execution. The seizure of States' commercial properties seems to be more promising for investors. Yet, there remains the question – which can be difficult to answer in practice – of the delineation between 'commercial-oriented properties' and 'non-commercial-oriented properties'. Irrespective of this question, there is an additional hurdle with respect to the properties considered as being used for commercial purposes, which results from the requirement mentioned in Article 19 of the UN Convention that the 'post-judgment measures of constraint' be taken against properties that have a connection with the entity against which the proceeding was directed. This constitutes an issue inasmuch as the properties maintained by States abroad are often not owned by States themselves.[12]

In such situations where immunities may constitute an irreducible obstacle for investors and, more generally, where respondent States may not be willing to abide by and comply with the awards, it is worth noting that investors may rely on their home State. They can typically do so by asking them to exercise their diplomatic protection, knowing that – as discussed in Chapter 10 – the decision on whether or not to exercise this protection is at the discretion of home States and may in fact be geared by interests other than those of the investors.

This option to resort to diplomatic protection is possible even for ICSID awards. Indeed, as an exception to the prohibition against ICSID Member States exercising their diplomatic protection when their nationals and the home States have consented to submit their dispute to an ICSID tribunal, Article 27.1 provides that they can do so when host States have failed to abide by and comply with the awards rendered. Such an exception is also provided in those IIAs that prohibit the exercise of diplomatic protection in such circumstances (e.g. 2017 Colombia–United Arab Emirates, Article 14). Along the same lines, the 2018 CPTPP provides an interesting mechanism through which a panel shall be established at the request of the State of the claimant when the respondent State fails to abide by or comply with the award. Following this procedure, the investor may seek a determination that such failures are inconsistent with the obligations under the CPTPP and a recommendation that the respondent State eventually abide by and comply with the award (Article 9.29.11).

More classically, Article 9.29.12 provides that the investor may seek enforcement under the ICSID Convention, the Convention on the Recognition and Enforcement of Arbitral Awards and the 1975 Inter-American Convention on International Commercial Arbitration, regardless of whether or not the above-mentioned panel has been established. In this way, the CPTPP evidences the growing reference made in IIA practice to recognition and enforcement matters.

---

[12] CF Dugan, D Wallace, ND Rubins, B Sabahi, *Investor–State Arbitration* (Oxford University Press 2011), at 684.

12

Applicable Law and Interpretation

Introduction

At the core of the settlement of any legal dispute, there is a dialectic between the facts and the law. This holds true with regard to investor–State arbitration, in particular arbitration based on international investment agreement (IIA) offers to arbitrate pertaining to the alleged breach of IIA substantive provisions, on which this chapter focuses. The legal component of this dialectical exercise draws our attention to two issues in particular: the law to be applied in the settlement of disputes and the interpretation of IIAs. Each of these issues is analysed in turn in what follows.

12.1 Applicable Law

Preliminary Remarks

Chapter 11 examines the law that governs the procedural aspects of investor–State arbitration as set out in IIAs and arbitration rules. This section focuses on the determination and the content of substantive applicable law, meaning the law governing the merits of disputes. References made to 'applicable law' in this chapter are then to be construed as 'substantive applicable law'.

Substantive applicable law is also to be distinguished from the law governing jurisdiction. In this respect, it is worth noting that the provisions of arbitration rules that deal with the issue of applicable law only address substantive applicable law. Article 35 of the Rules of Arbitration of the United Nations Commission on International Trade Law (UNCITRAL) refers to the law 'as applicable to the substance of the dispute', and Article 27 of the Stockholm Chamber of Commerce (SCC) Rules refers to the law to be applied in order to 'decide the merits of the dispute'. Similarly, Article 42.1 of the 1965 Convention on the Settlement of Investment Disputes between States and Nationals of Other States (ICSID Convention) refers to the law to be applied in order to 'decide a dispute'. In that sense, the Tribunal appointed in *Noble Energy, Inc.* v. *Ecuador* stated:

> The Tribunal is of the opinion that Article 42(1) is irrelevant for purposes of jurisdiction. Article 42 of the ICSID Convention is a conflict rule which deals with the law governing the merits of the dispute. [footnote omitted] Jurisdiction

is a different matter. It is not subject to this conflict rule but is governed by Article 25 of the ICSID Convention or, as the tribunal in *CSOB* v. *Slovakia* held, '*[t]he question of whether the parties have effectively expressed their consent to ICSID arbitration is not to be answered by reference to national law. It is governed by international law as set out in Article 25(1) of the ICSID Convention.*' [footnote omitted] (2008, Decision on Jurisdiction, para. 57)

If Article 25.1 of the Convention is key in appraising the jurisdiction of ICSID as regards ICSID Convention arbitration proceedings, it is important to stress that – in the context of investor–State arbitration based on IIA offers to arbitrate – the jurisdiction of the tribunals appointed in those proceedings is also governed in particular by the IIA at hand. In relation to non-ICSID Convention arbitration proceedings, IIAs constitute the cornerstone of the law applicable in determining the jurisdiction of tribunals. Even though domestic law is not applicable as such to jurisdiction matters, it may none-theless be relevant in all types of proceedings, in particular in cases where the terms that the IIAs incorporate refer directly to national law or where they can only be construed in light of domestic law.

The above distinctions having been made, this subsection provides an analysis of the choice of substantive applicable law and content thereof.

12.1.1 Choice of Applicable Law

As discussed in Chapter 11, the choice of the applicable law by the disputing parties is one of the distinguishing traits of arbitration as compared to standing international courts and tribunals. It illustrates the control that those parties have over the modalities of the settlement of their disputes. When there is no applicable law chosen in investor–State arbitration proceedings, arbitration rules provide, as explained below, a default rule on the matter.

This freedom of choice applies as such in the context of investor–State arbitration based on contracts concluded between host States and foreign investors as the disputing parties are also the parties to the contracts wherein the applicable law may be chosen. With regard to investor–State arbitration based on IIA offers to arbitrate, the means of application of this principle requires further explanation.

Distinctions can be made depending on the subject matter of the disputes covered by the offers, something which is discussed in Chapter 15. With regard, for instance, to offers that cover disputes relating to the alleged breaches of IIA substantive provisions, investment authorisations or invest-ment agreements concluded between host States and investors, the means of application of this principle varies. This is illustrated by the 2018 Comprehensive and Progressive Agreement for Trans-Pacific Partnership (CPTPP). This IIA provides with regard to disputes relating to the alleged breaches of investment agreements that the law specified in the agreements or the law otherwise agreed by the disputing parties is applicable; in case no such specification or agreement exists, it provides as a default rule that the law of the host State party to the disputes as well as the rules of international law as they may be applicable shall be applied by the tribunals (Article 9.25.2.b). As for disputes relating to the alleged breaches of the substantive provisions of the Agreement, Article 9.25.1 sets out that these disputes shall be decided in accordance with the Agreement and the applicable rules of international law.

Concerning the settlement of disputes relating to the alleged breaches of investment agreements, the CPTPP merely 'acknowledges' the choice of applicable law made by the disputing parties – be it in the agreements or otherwise – providing only a default rule in case they have not made it. On the other hand, concerning the settlement of disputes relating to alleged breaches of its substantive provisions, this treaty sets out the applicable law. As it appears, the law applicable to the settlement of such disputes is in fact chosen by the States parties to the CPTPP.

It can be seen from arbitration practice that tribunals are mainly concerned with those disputes that relate to the alleged breaches of IIA substantive provisions. With regard to those disputes and when the applicable law is actually chosen by IIA States parties, the choice is subsequently deemed to be accepted by foreign investors when they file their request for arbitration, and thereby express their consent to arbitration as it is set out in the agreements.

This section focuses on the law applicable to the settlement of those disputes that relate to the alleged breaches of IIA substantive provisions. The remarks made herein are of course *mutatis mutandis* relevant for the law applicable to the settlement of other types of investor–State disputes where appropriate.

12.1.2 Content of Applicable Law

12.1.2.1 'Law', 'Rule of Law' and Amiable Composition

It is worth emphasising that the SCC (Article 27) and UNCITRAL Arbitration Rules (Article 35), as well as the ICSID Convention (Article 42), refer to 'law' and 'rule of law' with regard to the law applicable to the settlement of disputes in the context of the proceedings that they each govern.

More precisely, with regard to the choice that the parties can make, these rules provide *mutatis mutandis* that those parties can designate the 'rules of law' to be applied by tribunals. This means that the parties can choose for only some of the rules that form part of a legal order to be applied in settling their disputes. Following the same rationale, parties are also free to opt for a combination of rules belonging to different legal orders, be they domestic legal orders or the international legal order. In addition to 'rules of law', the SCC Rules refer to the 'law(s)' to be applied.

On the other hand, the possibility to apply 'rules of law' is not systematically provided in arbitration rules in default situations in which the applicable law has not been chosen by the parties. Notably, the UNCITRAL Rules provide for the application of the 'law' that the tribunals deem appropriate to apply. In contrast, the default rule contained in the SCC Rules refers to the 'rules of law' in addition to the 'law' that the tribunals consider most appropriate to apply; it is worth noting in this respect that reference is made to 'law' while those Rules refer to 'law(s)' as to the choice that the parties can make. The ICSID Convention adopts another approach by referring to the domestic law of the host State and the rules of international law as may be applicable. As to the latter, one point to note is that the French version of Article 42 of the ICSID Convention refers to the *principes de droit international* – however, it is evident from the preparatory works of the Convention that this disparity of the French version as compared to the English and Spanish versions has no legal bearing.[1]

In addition to these references to 'law' and 'rules of law', the UNCITRAL, SCC and ICSID Convention Arbitration Rules also allow tribunals to settle disputes *ex aequo et bono* or as *amiable compositeur*. In such cases, the settlement of the disputes is akin to an equitable settlement. The discretion that such a possibility confers to arbitration tribunals explains why disputes can be settled *ex aequo et bono* only if the parties consent to it.

12.1.2.2 Practice

Whether due to the choice of States parties or as a result of the default position provided in arbitration rules, practice evidences that both domestic law and international law are often applied by arbitration tribunals to settle disputes. It is worth noting that this distinction is without prejudice to the applicability of international law as part of domestic law. Aside from this possibility, this duality of applicable law in mainstream practice begs the question of the interplay between these two bodies of law, as well as the normative content thereof.

a IIAs and Arbitration Rules

As mentioned above, IIA States parties can set out the applicable law within their agreements, otherwise the default rule as set out in the relevant arbitration rules applies.

There has been a growing trend in IIA practice towards incorporating an applicable law provision. These provisions adopt two main approaches: the choice of international law only, or the choice of international law as well as domestic law. Within these two approaches, variations can be observed.

Starting with the former, all IIAs make reference to the agreement itself as a source of applicable law. In addition, they typically refer to the 'applicable rules of international law' (e.g. 2018 Agreement between the United States of America, the United Mexican States and Canada, Annex 14.D, Article 9.1), or

---

[1] CH Schreuer, L Malintoppi, A Reinisch, A Sinclair, *The ICSID Convention: A Commentary* (2nd ed, Oxford University Press 2009), at 603.

'the applicable rules and principles of international law' (e.g. 1994 Energy Charter Treaty, Article 26.6). Crucially, all these provisions make customary international law (CIL) applicable to the settlement of disputes. With regard to such IIAs, domestic law is no more than a fact that, as noted by the Tribunal in *Corona Materials, LLC* v. *Dominican Republic*, may inform tribunals in their application of international law (2016, Award on the Respondent's Expedited Preliminary Objections, para. 187). In the same vein, mention can be made of the 2018 CPTPP which specifies '[f]or greater certainty' that the application of the Agreement and the applicable rules of international law 'is without prejudice to any consideration of the domestic law of the respondent when it is relevant to the claim as a matter of fact' (Article 9.25.1, Footnote 34).

As regards the IIAs that adopt the second approach, each of these agreements refers *mutatis mutandis* to the applicable IIA, the domestic law of the State party to the dispute and the principles of international law. For instance, Article 11.6 of the 2011 Turkey–Azerbaijan IIA provides: 'The arbitral tribunal shall take its decisions in accordance with the provisions of this Agreement, the laws and regulations of the Contracting Party involved in the dispute on which territory the investment is made (including its rules on the conflict of law) and the relevant principles of international law as accepted by both Contracting Parties.' In addition, some treaties provide typically for the application of the terms of any specific agreement that may have been entered into regarding the investment (e.g. 2004 Belgo–Luxembourg Economic Union–Bosnia and Herzegovina IIA, Article 9.5), or of the terms of other international agreements concluded between the States parties (e.g. 1991 Spain–Argentina IIA, Article 10.5). It is noteworthy that this latter Article provides that the Agreement shall be systematically applied, but that domestic law, the other international agreements and the general principles of international law shall only be applied where appropriate.

The default solutions provided by arbitration rules are twofold. The SCC and UNCITRAL Arbitration Rules leave it up to the tribunals to determine the applicable law – and also, under the SCC Rules, the applicable rules of law – that they deem appropriate. Under Article 42.1 of the ICSID Convention, tribunals must apply the law of the Contracting State party to the dispute (including its rules on the conflict of laws) and such rules of international law as may be applicable.

As it appears in the language of Article 42.1, the text of the ICSID Convention does not specify the sources from which the rules of international law that are applicable may be derived. On the other hand, the preparatory works of the Convention evidence that arbitration tribunals governed by the ICSID Convention Arbitration Rules can rely on the international law sources as they are listed in Article 38 of the Statute of the International Court of Justice (ICJ). This is made explicit in the Report of the Executive Directors of the International Bank for Reconstruction and Development (IBRD) on the ICSID Convention, which states: 'The term "international law" as used in this context should be understood in the sense given to it by Article 38(1) of the Statute of the International Court of Justice, allowance being made for the fact that Article 38 was designed to apply to inter-State disputes. [footnote omitted]' (para. 40). Accordingly, such tribunals can resort to primary sources of law, meaning treaties, CIL and general principles of law recognised by civilised nations. They can also make use of subsidiary sources, meaning judicial decisions and 'the teachings of the most highly qualified publicists of the various nations' as 'subsidiary means for the determination of rules of law'. All of these sources are examined in relation to international investment law and arbitration more generally in Chapter 2.

Content-wise, the exact rules of international law to be applied depend on the specifics of each case. As noted by the Tribunal in *Urbaser S.A.* v. *Argentina*, 'they necessarily include all such rules which according to their self-determined scope of application cover the legal issue arising in the particular case' (2016, Award, para. 1202). This holds true as well when international law is applicable as a result of the choice made in the IIAs.

It is worth noting that tribunals diverge as regards the grounds for applying IIAs when those agreements do not contain an applicable law clause.

In *Burlington Resources Inc.* v. *Ecuador*, the Tribunal considered that IIAs, because they constitute the basis of investment treaty claims, are *ipso facto* part of the applicable law even where they do not incorporate an applicable law provision (2012, Decision on Liability, paras. 177–178). In other words, the Tribunal considered that in such situations, their application does not result from the default rule contained in Article 42.1 of the ICSID Convention; in the opinion of the Tribunal, this default rule is only to be applied in relation to those matters that are not regulated by the agreements. Notably, the Tribunal operating under the UNCITRAL Rules in *South American Silver Limited (Bermuda)* v. *Bolivia* adopted a similar approach, explaining:

> [T]he Tribunal observes that the Treaty does not contain an express provision by which the Contracting Parties have decided on an applicable law to the disputes that may arise between them and nationals or companies of the other State. However, the Tribunal notes that, as the Claimant noted, the Parties agree that the starting point for the Tribunal is the Treaty. [footnote omitted] The Parties gave their consent to submit to arbitration their differences 'concerning an obligation of the latter [Contracting Party] under this Agreement'. [footnote omitted] For the Tribunal, the absence of an express choice of applicable law in the Treaty does not imply that the Contracting Parties have left it to the adjudicator to determine such law to the extent that it may cease to apply the Treaty or to give it priority as a primary source in order to apply other sources of law. (2018, Award, para. 207)

On the other hand, a number of tribunals also operating under the ICSID Convention Arbitration Rules opined that, in the absence of a choice of law made by the States parties in the IIAs, the application of the agreements – as part of the rules of international law – derive from the default rule set out in Article 42.1. For instance, in *M.C.I. Power Group L.C.* v. *Ecuador*, the Tribunal stated in relation to the same IIA as in *Burlington Resources Inc.* v. *Ecuador*:

> [T]he tribunal finds no evidence of any agreement on the law applicable to this dispute. Therefore, the Tribunal considers that it must respect the provisions of the second part of Article 42(1) of the ICSID Convention, i.e., in the absence of an agreement, the Tribunal shall apply Ecuadorian law, including its rules of private international law and such rules of international law as may be applicable. With respect to the latter rules, the Tribunal finds that the rules contained in the BIT, as well as the other pertinent rules of general international law, are applicable in the present case. (2007, Award, para. 217)

In relation to the viewpoint expressed by the Tribunal in *South American Silver Limited (Bermuda)* v. *Bolivia*, mention can be made of *UAB E Energija (Lithuania)* v. *Latvia*, in which the Tribunal opined that the acceptance of the offer to arbitrate contained in the IIA at hand – which does not contain an applicable law provision – establishes an implicit agreement that the applicable law consists primarily of the standards of protection contained in the IIA, but also that recourse could be had to general international law as well as to the domestic law of the host State (2017, Award, para. 792). Implicitly, the Tribunal considered then that there was no need to apply the default rule set out in Article 42.1 of the ICSID Convention.

b The Interplay between Domestic Law and International Law

As highlighted by the title of a seminal piece by Gaillard and Banifatemi,[2] the use of 'and' in Article 42.1 of the ICSID Convention raises the issue of the interplay between domestic law and international law as they form part of the applicable law under the default rule set out in this Article. More generally, this issue arises *mutatis mutandis* whenever both bodies of law are applicable, irrespective of the source or authority determining their application.

As to the interplay in the context of ICSID Convention arbitration proceedings, arbitration practice displays two main approaches, although these can in practice lead to the same result depending on how precisely they are conceived of.

Following a first approach, the role of international law is construed as being to supplement or correct domestic law. As illustrated by the case *Amco Asia Corporation* v. *Indonesia*, the role of international law under this approach has been viewed from two different perspectives, a first one lessening the role of international law and a second one putting the emphasis on it. The former perspective was supported by the first Annulment Committee appointed in

---

[2] E Gaillard, Y Banifatemi, 'The Meaning of "and" in Article 42(1), Second Sentence, of the Washington Convention: The Role of International Law in the ICSID Choice of Law Process' (2003) 18 *ICSID Review* 376.

that case and the latter by the Tribunal in the resubmitted proceeding. This Tribunal thus explained:

> The Ad Hoc Committee then went on to state that Article 42(1) of the ICSID Convention 'authorises an ICSID tribunal to apply rules of international law only to fill up lacunae in the applicable domestic law and to ensure precedence to international law norms where the rules of the applicable law are in collision with such norm' [reference omitted]. The role of international law is thus 'supplemental and corrective' under Article 42(1) … This Tribunal notes that Article 42(1) refers to the application of host-state law and international law. If there are no relevant host-state laws on a particular matter, a search much [sic] be made for the relevant international laws. And, where there are applicable host-state laws, they must be checked against international laws, which will prevail in case of conflict. Thus international law is fully applicable and to classify its role as 'only' 'supplemental and corrective' seems a distinction without a difference. In any event, the Tribunal believes that its task is to test every claim of law in this case first against Indonesian law, and then against international law. (1990, Award, paras. 38 and 40)

Regardless of these nuances, a similar approach can be seen in arbitration practice when domestic law only is chosen as the applicable law by the parties, typically by way of a contract. For instance, in *Caratube International Oil Company LLP* v. *Kazakhstan*, the Tribunal stated that 'it cannot disregard, but must take into account international law, in particular mandatory rules of international law when deciding the present dispute'. It went on to explain: 'However, in doing so [applying Kazakh law], it will afford a supplemental and corrective function to international law, supplementing and informing the Parties' choice of law by application of relevant international law rules' (2017, Award, para. 290).

Pursuant to the second approach, there is no such *ipso facto* allocation of roles between domestic law and international law. Here again, two slightly different perspectives can be seen within this approach. Following the first of these, the choice between these two bodies of law depends on the issue at stake, some calling for the application of domestic law, while others are seen as more appropriate for the application of international law (e.g. *Vestey Group Limited* v. *Venezuela*, 2016, Award, para. 117). The second perspective envisages the application of domestic law and international law together, without referring to any allocation based on the specific issue at stake, which leads tribunals adopting it to address the potential conflict that may occur between these two bodies of law. For instance, in *M.C.I. Power Group L.C.* v. *Ecuador*, the Tribunal stated:

> [T]he Tribunal considers that it must respect the provisions of the second part of Article 42(1) of the ICSID Convention, i.e., in the absence of an agreement, the Tribunal shall apply Ecuadorian law, including its rules of private international law and such rules of international law as may be applicable … In the event of

possible contradictions between the rules of Ecuadorian law and the BIT and other applicable rules of general international law, the Tribunal will decide on their compatibility, bearing in mind the contents and purpose of those rules in light of the precedence that international rules take over the domestic legislation of a State. (2007, Award, paras. 217–218)

c *Iura Novit Curia*

Beyond the issue of the determination of which law is applicable to the settlement of investor–State disputes, it is worth setting out the role that arbitration tribunals play in the analysis of its content. In this respect, it is well accepted, notably by reference to the maxim *iura novit curia*, that they are not bound by the materials put forward by the disputing parties and that they are themselves empowered to proceed to this analysis. In *Casinos Austria* v. *Argentina*, the Tribunal considered this prerogative as corresponding to its 'public function as an adjudicatory body that is part of the administration of international justice' (2018, Decision on Jurisdiction, para. 172). It is worth noting that this prerogative exists with regard to the establishment of both domestic law and international law.

The only limit to this prerogative consists of the due process owed to the disputing parties and, in particular, their right to be heard. As stated by the Tribunal in *Churchill Mining PLC* v. *Indonesia*, this entails that arbitration tribunals shall 'not surprise the Parties with a legal theory that was not subject to debate and that the Parties could not anticipate' (2016, Award, para. 236).

12.2 Interpretation

Preliminary Remarks

The rules of IIAs, whatever their object, have *per essence* a public international law character. Two consequences derive from this nature in terms of their interpretation.

The first of these is that those rules, being the product of the law-making prerogative and consent of States, are authentically interpreted by the States in question. In this respect and following the example set out by the 1992 North American Free Trade Agreement (NAFTA), it is worth noting a growing trend in treaty practice towards incorporating an 'interpretative note' mechanism. This is well illustrated by the 2018 CPTPP, which endorses the Trans-Pacific Partnership Commission notably with the task of issuing interpretations of the provisions of the Agreement (Article 27.2.2.f), those interpretations being binding on tribunals whose decisions and awards must comply with them (Article 9.25.3).

Second, the tribunals that actually interpret those rules in the context of arbitration proceedings must do so using public international law rules of interpretation, in the same way as States themselves must do. In this respect, virtually all arbitration tribunals state that they shall apply Articles 31–33 of the 1969 Vienna Convention on the Law of Treaties (VCLT), or the customary rules that these provisions codify when typically the State party to the dispute is not bound by the Convention (e.g. *Crystallex International Corporation* v. *Venezuela*, 2016, Award, para. 537). Articles 31 and 32 of this Convention, which is based on the work of the International Law Commission (ILC), provide respectively for the general rule of interpretation and the supplementary means of interpretation. Article 33 pertains to the interpretation of treaties authenticated in two or more languages. At the outset of this analysis, it is worth quoting those Articles in full:

Article 31: General Rule of Interpretation

1. A treaty shall be interpreted in good faith in accordance with the ordinary meaning to be given to the terms of the treaty in their context and in the light of its object and purpose.
2. The context for the purpose of the interpretation of a treaty shall comprise, in addition to the text, including its preamble and annexes:
   (a) any agreement relating to the treaty which was made between all the parties in connection with the conclusion of the treaty;
   (b) any instrument which was made by one or more parties in connection with the conclusion of the treaty and accepted by the other parties as an instrument related to the treaty.
3. There shall be taken into account, together with the context:
   (a) any subsequent agreement between the parties regarding the interpretation of the treaty or the application of its provisions;
   (b) any subsequent practice in the application of the treaty which establishes the agreement of the parties regarding its interpretation;
   (c) any relevant rules of international law applicable in the relations between the parties.
4. A special meaning shall be given to a term if it is established that the parties so intended.

Article 32: Supplementary Means of Interpretation

Recourse may be had to supplementary means of interpretation, including the preparatory work of the treaty and the circumstances of its conclusion, in order to confirm the meaning resulting from the application of article 31, or to determine the meaning when the interpretation according to article 31:
   (a) leaves the meaning ambiguous or obscure; or
   (b) leads to a result which is manifestly absurd or unreasonable.

Article 33: Interpretation of Treaties Authenticated in Two or More Languages

1. When a treaty has been authenticated in two or more languages, the text is equally authoritative in each language, unless the treaty provides or the parties agree that, in case of divergence, a particular text shall prevail.
2. A version of the treaty in a language other than one of those in which the text was authenticated shall be considered an authentic text only if the treaty so provides or the parties so agree.
3. The terms of the treaty are presumed to have the same meaning in each authentic text.
4. Except where a particular text prevails in accordance with paragraph 1, when a comparison of the authentic texts discloses a difference of meaning which the application of articles 31 and 32 does not remove, the meaning which best reconciles the texts, having regard to the object and purpose of the treaty, shall be adopted.

As seen below, it is noteworthy that arbitration tribunals also resort to other means of interpretation, some of which can be linked to the VCLT.

Overall, the use and application of all these interpretative means by arbitration tribunals is not uniform. There are various reasons for this disparity, in particular the fact that the exact purpose of interpretation has always been a matter of controversy. To make sense of interpretation in international investment law and arbitration, it is therefore useful to first provide a general introduction to the purpose of interpretation in public international law.

12.2.1 The Purpose of Interpretation in Public International Law

There have been numerous debates as to the purpose of interpretation in public international law. Notably, voluntarists, who give prevalence to the contractual dimension of public international law, focus on the identification of the will of States parties, while objectivists, who emphasise its societal dimension, do not place as much importance on the question of the will of States. Among voluntarists themselves, there are disagreements between those who favour the will of States as it is declared by the parties (*Erklärungstheorie*) and those who promote the 'true will' of those parties (*Willenstheorie*).[3] This leads the former to focus on the text of the treaties and the latter to look beyond, for instance into their preparatory works.

These divergences as to the purpose of interpretation in public international law explain why various methods have been developed, these methods usually being used in combination, albeit with different weight given to each depending on the interpreter in question. Among these, the following methods are predominant: (1) the subjective method seeking to identify the true intention

---

[3] P-M Dupuy, Y Kerbrat, *Droit international public* (14th ed, Dalloz 2018), at 335.

of the drafters, notably by resorting to preparatory works; (2) the textual method focusing on the text viewed as 'the only and the most recent expression of the common will of the parties';[4] (3) the systemic method appreciating the meaning of the terms in their nearer and wider context; and (4) the functional method concentrating on the object and purpose, if necessary in the outer limits of the treaty text.[5]

The ILC Commentaries to Article 27 of the Draft Articles on the Law of Treaties (which corresponds to Article 31 of the VCLT) makes it clear that the approach retained by the Commission was based on the idea that the text of the treaty *sensu largo* must be presumed to be the authentic expression of the intention of States parties. Likewise, it also provides that the purpose of interpretation is the elucidation of the meaning of the text, rather than an investigation *ab initio* into the supposed intentions of the parties.

From this, the ILC formulated the general rule of interpretation to be guided by good faith, setting out the general criteria as being the ordinary meaning of terms, the context *sensu largo* of the treaty, its object and purpose, as well as the general rules of international law. Extrinsic evidence, notably preparatory works, were considered by the ILC only as subsidiary means to be used to confirm an interpretation based on the primary criteria, or in order to determine a meaning when these criteria leave an interpretation ambiguous and obscure, or when they lead to a result which is manifestly absurd or unreasonable.

As regards the components of the general rule of interpretation, the Commission conceived of their use as being a single operation intended to shed light on the intention of the parties; their arrangement in Article 31 is to be seen as being guided by considerations of logic and not by any legal hierarchy. That being said, Article 31 of the VCLT leaves open the question of the weight to be given to each of these components. Such an approach is understandable, given the difficulty attached to codifying the rules on interpretation due to the divergences explained above and given the need to accommodate the diversity of treaties to be interpreted through this general rule.

12.2.2 Interpretation in International Investment Law and Arbitration

The present subsection aims at shedding light on how arbitration tribunals interpret IIAs, specifically what means they employ and how these are used to interpret those agreements. It focuses successively on the means of interpretation explicitly mentioned in the VCLT and on additional means used in arbitration practice. Obviously, the features and trends that this subsection

---

[4] M Huber, reported in (1952) 44 *Yearbook of the Institute of International Law*, at 199 (translation by the author).
[5] M Villiger, *Commentary on the 1969 Vienna Convention on the Law of Treaties* (Brill 2008), at 422.

highlights are to be read in light of the interpretative practices of arbitration tribunals that are analysed across this book.

12.2.2.1 Interpretation under the VCLT

In relation to the above-mentioned Articles 31–33 of the VCLT, the present subsection analyses arbitration practice by focusing in turn on the (1) general rule of interpretation; (2) the supplementary means of interpretation; and (3) the interpretation of treaties authenticated in two or more languages.

a General Rule of Interpretation

Preliminary Remarks

Setting good faith as an overarching principle to guide treaty interpretation, Article 31 of the VCLT provides for a general rule of interpretation with three core dimensions: exegetic interpretation, teleological interpretation and contextual interpretation. These dimensions pertain respectively to the literal and ordinary meaning of the terms under interpretation, the object and purpose of the treaty that contains those terms, and their context. Arbitration tribunals and arbitrators often recall that Article 31 of the VCLT forms a 'whole process'; in that sense, the Tribunal appointed in *Antin* v. *Spain* reaffirmed that Article 31 provides for an 'integral single rule', meaning that tribunals 'should not analyse the text, context, object and purpose as separate elements of interpretation, but rather start with the ordinary meaning of the words ... in their context and considering the object and purpose of the Treaty' (2018, Award, para. 207).

While Article 31 of the VCLT sets out the process to be followed in order to reach an interpretation, it says nothing, on the other hand, as to the applicable 'standard of clarity' required, i.e. the 'threshold' that must be met for an interpretation to be considered as 'correct'. In this respect, a diversity of views have been adopted in arbitration practice in relation to the divide between restrictive interpretation and extensive interpretation.

A number of tribunals and arbitrators take an approach *mutatis mutandis* similar to the views expressed by Arbitrator Boisson de Chazournes in *Garanti Koza LLP* v. *Turkmenistan*, in which she argued that interpretation should be based on an *ex ante* neutral approach and that no doctrine of restrictive or extensive interpretation should prevail (2013, Decision on the Objection to Jurisdiction for Lack of Consent, Dissenting Opinion, para. 10). On the other hand, other tribunals have considered that interpretation should be restrictive in some circumstances, which implies that in such circumstances the 'standard of clarity' is set higher. This is well illustrated by the reasoning of the Tribunal appointed in *Noble Ventures, Inc.* v. *Romania* with regard to exceptions to rules of general international law. Referring to the *ELSI Case* in which the ICJ stated that 'it finds itself unable to accept that an important principle of customary international law should be held to have been tacitly dispensed with, in the absence of any words making clear an intention to do so' (*Elettronica Sicula S.p.A. (ELSI) (United States of America* v. *Italy)*, 1989, Judgment, at 42), the Tribunal stated:

> Thus, an umbrella clause, when included in a bilateral investment treaty, introduces an exception to the general separation of States obligations under municipal and under international law. In consequence, as with any other exception to established general rules of law, the identification of a provision as an 'umbrella clause' can as a consequence proceed only from a strict, if not indeed restrictive, interpretation of its terms and, more generally, in accordance with the well known customary rules codified under Article 31 of the Vienna Convention of the Law of Treaties (1969). (2005, Award, para. 55)

A similar approach was *mutatis mutandis* adopted by the Tribunal appointed in *SGS Société Générale de Surveillance S.A.* v. *Pakistan* (2003, Decision on Objections to Jurisdiction, para. 167). This approach was criticised by the Tribunal in *SGS Société Générale de Surveillance S.A.* v. *Philippines*, which considered that the Tribunal in that latter case had applied general principles of international law to generate a presumption against the broad interpretation of the umbrella clause and then stressed that the question put to the Tribunal was one of interpretation, which should not be determined by any presumption (2004, Decision on Objections to Jurisdiction, para. 122).

i Exegetic Interpretation As provided for in Article 31.1 of the VCLT, a treaty shall be interpreted in accordance with the ordinary meaning to be given to the terms of the treaty. This 'ordinary meaning' is to be opposed to the 'special meaning' that shall be given to a term under Article 31.4 of the Convention if it is established that States parties so intended.

To determine this ordinary meaning, it is a common practice among arbitration tribunals to make use of dictionaries (e.g. *Orascom TMT Investments S.à.r.l.* v. *Algeria*, 2017, Award, para. 283), be they legal dictionaries or 'general' dictionaries. At the same time, they often stress that the dictionary meaning of the terms is insufficient in light of Article 31 of the VCLT when considered as a whole. In that sense, the Tribunal appointed in *Cem Cenzig Uzan* v. *Turkey* noted: '[A] simple dictionary reading of the terms in a treaty is not what is called for. Rather, a treaty's language must be examined having regard also to the entirety of the text read together (to provide context), and having regard to what the objects and purposes were in enacting the treaty' (2016, Award on Respondent's Bifurcated Preliminary Objection, para. 137).

ii Teleological Interpretation According to Article 31.1 of the VCLT, a teleological interpretation requires tribunals to take into account the object and purpose of a treaty in order to shed light on the ordinary meaning of its terms.

When relying on this means of interpretation, arbitration tribunals typically turn to the preamble of IIAs in order to identify their object and purpose. However, they have adopted diverging conceptions as to the purpose of such treaties. Of course, some of these differences are explained by the exact language of the preambles, which can vary from one treaty to another, as analysed in Chapter 2. However, it is also the case that tribunals reached opposing conclusions even where the preambles in question are substantively equivalent, albeit drafted differently. To illustrate this point, one can compare the Preamble of the 1997 Philippines–Switzerland IIA and the Preamble of the 1994 United States of America (USA)–Ukraine IIA and how they have been read for interpretation purposes. For argument's sake, it is helpful to reproduce them in their entirety. The former provides:

> The Government of the Republic of the Philippines and the Swiss Federal Council, Desiring to intensify economic cooperation to the mutual benefit of both States, Intending to create and maintain favourable conditions for investments by investors of one Contracting Party in the territory of the other Contracting Party, Recognizing the need to promote and protect foreign investments with the aim to foster the economic prosperity of both States, Have agreed as follows . . .

The Preamble of the 1994 USA–Ukraine IIA provides:

> The United States of America and Ukraine (hereinafter the 'Parties'); Desiring to promote greater economic cooperation between them, with respect to investment by nationals and companies of one Party in the territory of the other Party; Recognizing that agreement upon the treatment to be accorded such investment will stimulate the flow of private capital and the economic development of the Parties; Agreeing that fair and equitable treatment of investment is desirable in order to maintain a stable framework for investment and maximum effective utilization of economic resources; Recognizing that the development of economic and business ties can contribute to the well-being of workers in both Parties and promote respect for internationally recognized worker rights; and Having resolved to conclude a Treaty concerning the encouragement and reciprocal protection of investment; Have agreed as follows . . .

Interpreting the latter, the Tribunal established in *Joseph Charles Lemire* v. *Ukraine* argued:

> The main purpose of the BIT is thus the stimulation of foreign investment and of the accompanying flow of capital. But this main purpose is not sought in the abstract; it is inserted in a wider context, the economic development for both signatory countries. Economic development is an objective which must benefit all, primarily national citizens and national companies, and secondarily foreign investors. Thus, the object and purpose of the Treaty is not to protect foreign investments *per se*, but as an aid to the development of the domestic economy. (2010, Decision on Jurisdiction and Liability, paras. 272–273)

Such a reading of the Preamble is akin to the last paragraph of the Preamble of the Philippines–Switzerland IIA, in which the States parties recognise 'the need to promote and protect foreign investments with the aim to foster the economic prosperity of both States'. However, in *SGS Société Générale de Surveillance S.A.* v. *Philippines*, the Tribunal opined as for this latter IIA:

> The BIT is a treaty for the promotion and reciprocal protection of investments. According to the preamble it is intended 'to create and maintain favourable conditions for investments by investors of one Contracting Party in the territory of the other'. It is legitimate to resolve uncertainties in its interpretation so as to favour the protection of covered investments. (2004, Decision on Objections to Jurisdiction, para. 116)

This opinion, beyond the fact that it can appear as being at odds with the letter of the Preamble of the Switzerland–Philippines IIA, helps to understand the denunciation made by the Tribunal in *Noble Ventures, Inc.* v. *Romania* of a trend in arbitration practice towards interpreting the clauses of IIAs exclusively in favour of investors (2005, Award, para. 52).

As a reaction, a growing number of tribunals express the view that a balanced interpretation is needed; in *Pan American Energy LLC* v. *Argentina*, the Tribunal explained that this requires 'taking into account both State's sovereignty and its responsibility to create an adapted and evolutionary framework for the development of economic activities, and the necessity to protect foreign investment and its continuing flow' (2006, Decision on Preliminary Objections, para. 99).

iii Contextual Interpretation

Preliminary Remarks

Article 31 of the VCLT distinguishes between the context of the terms under interpretation, subsequent agreements and practices, as well as rules of international law. For didactic purposes, all of these elements can be construed as forming part of contextual interpretation as they each shed light on specific aspects of the context *sensu largo*.

More precisely, two types of contexts can be identified: the context relating to the treaty as such ('internal context') and the context relating to international law more broadly ('external context').

The internal context can itself be subdivided between the context at the time of the conclusion of the treaty and its subsequent context. As to the former, in addition to the text of the treaty, its preamble and its annexes, the Convention refers to: (1) the agreements relating to the treaty which were made between all the States parties as regards the conclusion of that treaty; and (2) the instruments made by one or more parties in connection with the conclusion of the treaty and accepted by the other parties as an instrument related to the treaty. Concerning the subsequent context, the VCLT provides that the following can be taken into account in this regard: (1) any subsequent agreement between the States parties regarding the interpretation of the treaty or the application of its provisions; and (2) any subsequent practice in the application of the treaty which establishes the agreement of the parties regarding its interpretation.

The external context relates to the principle of systemic integration and is based on Article 31.3.c of the VCLT, which requires account to be taken of any relevant rules of international law applicable in the relations between the parties.

– Internal Context Concerning the internal context at the time of the conclusion of IIAs, arbitration tribunals have relied mainly on the text and preamble of the agreements. This is due to the fact that annexes, agreements and instruments as described above have in reality been scarce in IIA practice. On the other hand, evolutions in treaty practice as of the 2010s will likely change the contextual interpretation conducted by arbitration tribunals in the future. The increasing incorporation of annexes, such as those relating to indirect expropriation as discussed in Chapter 6, will result in a more frequent use of annexes as an internal contextual tool to interpret IIA provisions. The same holds true with regard to interpretative statements issued by IIA States parties at the time of the conclusion of IIAs, a practice that is well illustrated by the Joint Interpretative Declaration on the 2016 Comprehensive and Economic Trade Agreement (CETA).

Arbitration tribunals have also traditionally made little reference to subsequent agreements or practice, precisely because these have also been few and far between. It is worth noting that when tribunals have expressed their intent to inquire into the subsequent practice of States, they have often relied on the respective treaty practice of States parties with other States (e.g. *National Grid PLC* v. *Argentina*, 2006, Decision on Jurisdiction, paras. 84–85) and not on their practice pertaining to the IIAs at hand, as prescribed by Article 31.1 of the VCLT. When tribunals have referred to subsequent agreements or practice in the sense of the VCLT, they have mainly referred to interpretations issued by IIA States parties. In this respect, it has been stressed that tribunals have no obligation to follow such interpretations under the VCLT as Article 31.3.a provides only for an obligation to 'take into account' subsequent agreements and practice (*The Renco Group Inc.* v. *Peru*, 2016, Partial Award on Jurisdiction, para. 156). On the other hand, when such a subsequent interpretation was based on an IIA provision that makes it binding on tribunals – such as the above-mentioned Article 9.25.3 of the 2018 CPTPP – they have acknowledged that this is a different situation; in that sense, the Tribunal appointed in *Clayton* v. *Canada* noted:

> Article 31(3)(a) of the Vienna Convention on the Law of Treaties calls on treaty interpreters to take into account 'any subsequent agreement between the parties regarding the interpretation of the treaty or the application of its provisions'. Yet NAFTA Article 1131(2) contains a *lex specialis*, which goes further in providing that '[a]n interpretation by the Commission of a provision of this Agreement shall be binding on a Tribunal established under this Section'. Under the general rule on interpretation set out in the Vienna Convention, a NAFTA tribunal would only need to 'take into account' the subsequent agreement [footnote omitted]. However,

by virtue of NAFTA Article 1131(2), acts of authentic interpretation by the States parties to the Agreement, like the Notes just referred to, are binding and conclusive. (2015, Award on Jurisdiction and Liability, para. 430).

The proliferation of such 'interpretative note' mechanisms in the IIAs concluded as of the 2010s have the potential to reinforce the role of the internal context subsequent to the conclusion of IIAs in the interpretation of their provisions, to the extent of their actual use by States parties.

– External Context As to the external context, explicit references to Article 31.3.c of the VCLT and actual use of 'relevant rules of international law applicable in the relations between the parties' have again been scarce in arbitration practice. This is changing however, as illustrated by the award rendered in *Marfin Investment Group Holdings S.A. v. Cyprus* (2018, Award, para. 827). This is certainly due to the evolution of international investment law and arbitration examined in Chapter 1 and the strengthening of its belonging to the universe of public international law. At the same time, some have called for a careful use of Article 31.3.c; in *South American Silver Limited (Bermuda) v. Bolivia*, for instance, the Tribunal stressed that the principle of systemic integration must be applied in harmony with the rest of the provisions of Article 31 of the VCLT and cautiously, to prevent tribunals from exceeding their jurisdiction and applying rules to disputes upon which the parties have not agreed (2018, Award, para. 216).

Article 31.3.c. has the potential to attract in the interpretative process international law rules that shed light on and aim at protecting the public interests that are often at stake in investor–State arbitration. It does not come as a surprise, then, that it has been used, for instance, in relation to international human rights law. The Annulment Committee appointed in *Tulip Real Estate and Development Netherlands B.V. v. Turkey* noted in this respect that '[t]here is a widespread sentiment that the integration of the law of human rights into international investment law is an important concern' (2015, Decision on Annulment, para. 86). This Committee found this field of international law to be relevant to the interpretation of procedural provisions, in that case Article 52.1.d of the ICSID Convention pertaining to the 'serious departure from a fundamental rule of procedure' (para. 92), which is discussed in Chapter 16. Human rights law has also been resorted to in interpreting IIA provisions, as illustrated by the award rendered in *Hesham Talaat M. Al-Warraq v. Indonesia*, where the Tribunal took into account the 1966 International Covenant on Civil and Political Rights in interpreting the fair and equitable treatment provision (2014, Final Award, paras. 556–621).

b Supplementary Means of Interpretation

Pursuant to Article 32 of the VCLT, in order to confirm the meaning that results from the general rule of interpretation, or to determine this meaning in the case that this rule leaves it ambiguous or obscure on the one hand, or leads to a result which is manifestly absurd or unreasonable on the other, recourse may be made to the preparatory work of the treaty and the circumstances of its conclusion, among other supplementary means.

Although the VCLT does not define 'preparatory work', it is largely understood as covering all the documents produced by States during the entire preparation of a treaty. The 'circumstances of the conclusion of a treaty' refers mainly to the political, economic, social and cultural background against which treaties are negotiated, as well as the events that lead to their conclusion. Finally, it is worth emphasising that the preparatory work and the circumstances of the conclusion of a treaty are not the only supplementary means of interpretation, but mere examples of supplementary means that can be resorted to under Article 32 VCLT.

While all tribunals acknowledge that supplementary means can be used in the above-mentioned situations, it is worth noting at the outset that the use of these means is conceived of in two directly opposing ways in arbitration practice – one that reserves their use solely for exceptional circumstances, and another that envisages it as being always available for tribunals. The first approach was adopted, for instance, by the Tribunal appointed in *Orascom TMT Investments S.à.r.l.* v. *Algeria*, which noted that recourse to supplementary means is only allowed in limited circumstances due to the primacy that the VCLT gives to the text of treaties viewed in their context and in light of their object and purpose (2017, Award, para. 299). On the contrary, the Tribunal argued in *El Paso Energy International Company* v. *Argentina* that '[d]espite [the] opinions according to which the supplementary means of interpretation cannot normally be resorted to ... in practice it is always possible to have recourse to them' (2011, Award, para. 607).

In reality, tribunals have not frequently resorted to preparatory work in practice. Aside from the subsidiary nature of this means of interpretation, this may be due to the fact that IIAs have traditionally not been properly negotiated, notably due to the use of models, as discussed in Chapter 1. In that sense, and as quoted in the award, Schreuer made the following expert testimony before the Tribunal appointed in *Wintershall Aktiengesellschaft* v. *Argentina*:

> [M]any times, in fact in the majority of times, BITs are among clauses of treaties that are not properly negotiated. BITs are very often pulled out of a drawer, often on the basis of some sort of a model, and are put forward on the occasion of state visits when the heads of states need something to sign, and the typical two candidates in a situation like that are Bilateral Investment Treaties, and treaties for cultural co-operation. In other words, they are very often not negotiated at all, they are just being put on the table, and I have heard several representatives who have actually been active in this Treaty-making process, if you can call it that, say that, 'We had no idea that this would have real consequences in the real world.' (2008, Award, para. 85)

Tribunals will likely increasingly resort to preparatory work to interpret IIAs in the future as a result of the fact that a growing number of agreements are properly negotiated, in particular free trade agreements (FTAs) that contain an investment chapter.

On the other hand, arbitration tribunals have traditionally relied more frequently on the circumstances of the conclusion of treaties. In this respect, one can note that they refer in particular to circumstances that do not have a direct causal relationship with the IIAs at hand, but rather simply enlighten the general circumstances of their conclusion. For instance, in *Plama Consortium Limited* v. *Bulgaria*, the Tribunal took into account for the purpose of interpreting the 1987 Bulgaria–Cyprus IIA the fact that Bulgaria was, at the time of the conclusion of the Agreement, under a communist regime that favoured bilateral investment treaties (BITs) with limited protections for foreign investors and with very limited dispute resolution provisions (2005, Decision on Jurisdiction, para. 196).

Aside from the above, arbitration tribunals also rely on a broad range of instruments and documents in relation to Article 32 VCLT. They refer in particular to the respective treaty practice of IIA States parties at the time of the conclusion of the agreements in question, the idea being that they see this as potentially reflecting their policy as to the type of provision under interpretation (e.g. *Ickale Insaat Limited Sirketi* v. *Turkmenistan*, 2016, Award, paras. 216–218). Among other items, mention can also be made of the unofficial English translation of an IIA submitted to the United Nations (UN) for publication (e.g. *Orascom TMT Investments S.à.r.l.* v. *Algeria*, 2017, Award, paras. 301–302), or judicial decisions and awards (e.g. *Caratube International Oil Company LLP* v. *Kazakhstan*, 2009, Decision on Provisional Measures, paras. 71–73).

c Interpretation of Treaties Authenticated in Two or More Languages

According to Article 33 of the VCLT, when a treaty has been authenticated in two or more languages, the text is equally authoritative in each language unless provided otherwise by the treaty or agreed upon by the States parties in case of any divergence. The translation into another language can only be considered as authoritative if the treaty so provides or the parties so agree. The terms of the treaty are presumed to have the same meaning in each authentic text. In case there exists a difference of meaning between the authentic texts that cannot be removed through the application of Articles 31 and 32, a particular text prevails over the other if the treaty so provides or if the parties so agree; otherwise, the meaning that best reconciles the texts, having regard to the object and purpose of the treaty, shall be adopted.

A number of IIAs are authenticated in two or more languages, all of which are equally authoritative. In practice, these various versions do not often raise any particular issue. *Orascom TMT Investments S.à.r.l.* v. *Algeria* offers an interesting case where Article 33 of the VCLT was used. Despite the French, Dutch and Arabic versions of the applicable IIA being equally authentic and having been considered as such by the Tribunal, the fact that the disputing parties focused on the French version and that this IIA was negotiated in French led to a particular focus being put on this version of the Agreement (2017, Award, para. 282).

12.2.2.2 Other Means of Interpretation

In addition to the means of interpretation provided by the VCLT under Articles 31 and 32, arbitration practice shows that additional means are used by arbitration tribunals. It is worth noting in this respect that some of these can be linked to the general rule of interpretation, although they are not explicitly mentioned therein. This is so in particular because they are grounded in 'good faith', with principles such as effectiveness and reasonableness falling into this category. Likewise, some may be seen as falling within the scope of Article 32, as this Article refers to supplementary means of interpretation without specifying their scope.

In addition to effectiveness and reasonableness, the use of legal presumptions, rules of logic and past arbitration awards can also be highlighted in the practice of arbitration tribunals.

a Effectiveness

Effectiveness – also often referred to in French and Latin as *effet utile* and *ut res magit valeat quam pereat*, respectively – is a well-recognised principle of interpretation in public international law. In its Commentaries to the Draft Articles on the Law of Treaties, the ILC explained that it entails that 'when a treaty is open to two interpretations one of which does and the other does not enable the treaty to have appropriate effects, good faith and the objects and purposes of the treaty demand that the former interpretation should be adopted'.[6]

Actually, effectiveness seems to be construed in two different ways in public international law. On the basis that a treaty as a whole as well as each of its provisions must be taken to have been intended to achieve some end, effectiveness is first construed as requiring that an interpretation that leaves the text ineffective to achieve that end must be considered as incorrect and set aside; this approach is very close to teleological interpretation. Second, based on the premise that each provision of a treaty is intended to have some significance, effectiveness is also conceived of as leading to favouring an interpretation that gives a specific reason to a provision, notably as compared to the other treaty provisions.

Effectiveness is quite often relied upon by arbitration tribunals in interpreting IIAs. More precisely, tribunals mainly do this using the second conception

---

[6] ILC, Draft Articles on the Law of Treaties with Commentaries (1966) *Yearbook of the International Law Commission*, at 219.

of effectiveness. For instance, the Tribunal appointed in *Sanum Investments Limited* v. *Laos* explained:

> The task of the Tribunal is to interpret the Treaty in such a way that all the provisions of the Treaty have effect even if specific provisions do not refer to each other. The principle of *effet utile* requires international courts and tribunals to interpret international rules 'so as to give them their fullest weight and effect consistent with the normal sense of the words and with other parts of the text and in such a way that a reason and a meaning can be attributed to every part of the text.' [footnote omitted] (2013, Award on Jurisdiction, para. 333)

As discussed in Chapter 5, this principle of interpretation has notably been resorted to in order to interpret the full protection and security (FPS) standard in relation to the fair and equitable treatment (FET) standard.

b Reasonableness

There exist different ways to define 'reasonableness' and to conceive of its role in interpretation. As noted in the literature,[7] this ranges from the idea that reasonableness orients interpretation towards its consequences, to the narrower approach according to which an interpreter should not give to the text a meaning that the parties would not have been able to envisage. In public international law and in investor–State arbitration in particular, this principle of interpretation is closely connected to the principle of good faith.

In *Postova Banka, A.S.* v. *Greece*, the Tribunal referred to 'reasonableness' as follows:

> [A]n interpretation in good faith is not simply interpretation *bona fides*, as opposed to the absence of *mala fides*, or a principle providing for the rejection of an interpretation that is abusive or that may result in the abuse of rights. It also means that the interpretation requires elements of reasonableness that go beyond the mere verbal or purely literal analysis. (2015, Award, para. 284).

Reference was made to this principle of interpretation in that case in order to determine whether the term 'investment' in the IIA at hand should be interpreted as covering government securities.

c Legal Presumptions and Rules of Logic

Arbitration tribunals resort to legal presumptions that are specific to international law or shared with other legal systems.

Use is notably made of the *in dubio pars mitior est sequenda* presumption. As explained by Gardiner, this entails that 'if the meaning of a term is ambiguous, that meaning is to be preferred which is less onerous to the party assuming an obligation, or which interferes less with territorial and

---

[7] H Ascencio, 'Article 31 of the Vienna Conventions on the Law of Treaties and International Investment Law' (2016) 31 *ICSID Review* 366, at 374.

personal supremacy of a party, or involves less general restrictions upon the parties'.[8] This presumption was invoked for instance by the Tribunal in *SGS Société Générale de Surveillance S.A.* v. *Pakistan* in order to deny the application of Article 11 of the 1995 Switzerland–Pakistan IIA to contractual obligations. It argued:

> The consequences of accepting the Claimant's reading of Article 11 of the BIT should be spelled out in some detail. Firstly, Article 11 would amount to incorporating by reference an unlimited number of State contracts, as well as other municipal law instruments setting out State commitments including unilateral commitments to an investor of the other Contracting Party. Any alleged violation of those contracts and other instruments would be treated as a breach of the BIT ... We believe, for the foregoing considerations, that Article 11 of the BIT would have to be considerably more specifically worded before it can reasonably be read in the extraordinarily expansive manner submitted by the Claimant. [footnote omitted] The appropriate interpretive approach is the prudential one summed up in the literature as *in dubio pars mitior est sequenda*, or more tersely, *in dubio mitius*. (2003, Decision of the Tribunal on Objections to Jurisdiction, paras. 168 and 171)

Arbitration tribunals also refer to rules of logic such as *a contrario* arguments or the principle *unius est exclusio alterius*, typically in relation to the issue of the application of the most-favoured-nation treatment (MFNT) clause to the investor–State dispute settlement provisions within IIAs. For instance, the Tribunal appointed in *National Grid PLC* v. *Argentina* noted that 'dispute resolution' is not included among the exceptions to the application of the MFNT clause set out by the IIA at hand in that case. It stressed that '[a]s a matter of interpretation, specific mention of an item excludes others: *expressio unius est exclusio alterius*' (2006, Decision on Jurisdiction, para. 82).

d Past Awards and Decisions

Irrespective of whether they can be formally considered as 'supplementary means of interpretation' under Article 32 of the VCLT as argued by the Tribunal in *Caratube International Oil Company LLP* v. *Kazakhstan* (2009, Decision on Provisional Measures, para. 72), arbitration awards are very often – if not systematically – referred to in the process of interpreting IIA provisions. As discussed in Chapter 2, their role in ascertaining the meaning and content of IIA provisions has proven to be controversial.

---

[8] R Gardiner, *Treaty Interpretation* (2nd ed, Oxford University Press 2017), at 405.

13

Provisional Measures

Introduction

Subject to certain conditions, either party in investor–State arbitration proceedings can request that provisional measures be granted to protect specific
rights until the arbitration tribunal has decided on the dispute. In practice,
such requests are most frequently formulated by investors.

As explained below, arbitration tribunals enjoy a large degree of power in
deciding whether or not to grant such provisional measures, with respect to
both the appraisal of the circumstances in question and the determination of
the appropriate measures required to protect the rights at hand. Such power
derives from the need for tailor-made measures adapted to the specifics of each
case. This point is systematically recalled by tribunals, whether they are
operating, for instance, under the International Centre for Settlement of
Investment Disputes (ICSID) Convention Arbitration Rules (e.g. *United
Utilities (Talinn) B.V.* v. *Estonia*, 2016, Decision on Provisional Measures,
para. 74), or the United Nations Commission on International Trade Law
(UNCITRAL) Arbitration Rules (e.g. *Merck Sharp & Dohme (I.A.) LLC*
v. *Ecuador*, 7 March 2016, Decision on Interim Measures, para. 65). At the
same time, tribunals usually exercise caution in using this power, something that is explained by two intertwined key features of provisional
measures.

The first of these features relates to the timing of provisional measures and
the consequences of such measures for the party concerned – in most cases,
they are requested and granted at a time when disputing parties have not had
the full opportunity to defend their case and views. This feature led the
Tribunal appointed in *Rizzani de Eccher S.p.A.* v. *Kuwait* to argue that 'provisional measures are extraordinary measures which ought not to be granted
lightly [footnote omitted]' (2017, Decision on Provisional Measures, para. 99).

The second feature pertains to State sovereignty. Obviously, by agreeing on
the application of arbitration rules that give arbitration tribunals the power to
grant provisional measures, or by incorporating this mechanism into the IIAs
they conclude, States acknowledge that such measures may be granted that will
necessarily restrict their freedom to act as they would wish. That being said,

tribunals often stress the exceptional impact of provisional measures on sovereignty and as such call for cautiousness in their application. This is well-illustrated by this statement made by the Tribunal in *Nova Group Investments, B.V. v. Romania*: '[B]ecause this grant of authority is an exception to the general principal of State sovereignty, tribunals should exercise their jurisdiction only within the strict confines of the power thus granted, namely as an exceptional remedy, reserved for exceptional circumstances. [footnote omitted]' (2017, Decision on Provisional Measures, para. 227). In this respect, some arbitration tribunals have been criticised for applying low standards, such as by Arbitrator Kohen in *Fouad Alghanim* v. *Jordan*, who argued that they make it 'easier to obtain provisional measures in investment arbitration against a State, than a State itself would against its peers in any other tribunal or Court' (2014, Order on Application for the Grant of Provisional Measures, Statement of Dissent, para. 2).

Although one can witness a trend in IIA practice towards addressing provisional measures (e.g. 2018 Comprehensive and Progressive Agreement for Trans-Pacific Partnership (CPTPP), Article 9.23.9), the matter has traditionally been and is still largely governed by arbitration rules. In this respect, and as evidenced below, it is noteworthy that the ICSID Convention Arbitration Rules (ICSID Convention, Article 47 and ICSID Arbitration Rule 39) and the 2017 Stockholm Chamber of Commerce (SCC) Rules of Arbitration (Article 37) are much less detailed than the 2010 version of the UNCITRAL Arbitration Rules (Article 26). Contrary to the 1976 version of this latter set of Rules, which was also sparse in terms of details, the 2010 version does not only specify procedural aspects, but also provides a definition and examples of interim measures as well as the substantive conditions under which they shall be granted.

As a result of the brevity of the ICSID Convention Arbitration Rules, it has been up to arbitration tribunals to design the regime of provisional measures in the context of the proceedings governed by those Rules. In doing so, and in particular because Article 47 of the ICSID Convention was modelled on Article 41 of the Statute of the International Court of Justice (ICJ), they have notably relied on the case law of that Court for that purpose. That being said, it is worth noting that the revision of the ICSID Convention Arbitration Rules contemplated in the 2019 ICSID Working Paper n° 3 proposes that the Rules should enter into greater details, in particular by providing examples of provisional measures as well as the conditions under which they shall be granted (proposed Rule 46).[1]

In practice, provisional measures have mainly been requested and discussed in relation to the ICSID Convention Arbitration Rules and the UNCITRAL

---

[1] ICSID, 'Proposals for Amendment of the ICSID Rules', Working Paper n° 3 (August 2019), available at https://icsid.worldbank.org/en.

Rules. Both regimes are examined herein. Unless specified, the UNCITRAL Rules referred to are those of the 2013 version that are identical to the 2010 version on those matters. The ICSID Arbitration Rules discussed are those contained in the 2006 version; mention is also made of the relevant revisions proposed by ICSID, at the time of completion of this book, in the above-mentioned Working Paper. For the sake of clarity, reference is made to 'provisional measures' only, being synonymous with 'interim measures' as employed in the UNCITRAL Arbitration Rules. The chapter analyses successively: (1) the notion of provisional measures; (2) the rights and interests that can be preserved through them; (3) the substantive conditions that shall be met for those measures to be granted; and (4) the procedural aspects of provisional measures and their legal force.

13.1 The Notion of Provisional Measures

At the outset, it is important to highlight that the term 'provisional measures' carries two intertwined meanings – it refers to both the mechanism through which these specific measures can be requested and granted as well as the measures themselves. The procedural modalities of this mechanism are examined below. They are addressed here only instrumentally to distinguish between the different types of provisional measures that can be granted depending on the circumstances and to contrast them with emergency reliefs that can be sought via emergency arbitration.

13.1.1 The Types of Provisional Measures

According to Article 26.2 of the UNCITRAL Arbitration Rules, a provisional measure is any temporary measure by which, at any time prior to the issuance of the award by which the dispute is finally decided, the arbitral tribunal orders a party to, for example, maintain or restore the status quo pending the determination of the dispute. Importantly, one should bear in mind the temporary nature and effect of provisional measures. This temporal feature is made explicit in Article 26.2 of the UNCITRAL Arbitration Rules; more generally, it is reflected in the terms used to describe this type of measures, i.e. *interim* measures under the latter set of rules and the SCC Arbitration Rules and *provisional* measures under the ICSID Convention Arbitration Rules.

Irrespective of the possibility given to the parties by ICSID Arbitration Rule 39.5 to file a request for provisional measures prior to the constitution of tribunals so that those tribunals can promptly decide on them upon their constitution, provisional measures are typically requested during the course of the proceedings. In such situations, the urgency that is inherent in provisional measures leads tribunals to give priority to this request over and above any other issue, pertaining for instance to the merits. This is made explicit in ICSID Arbitration Rule 39.2.

In some situations, arbitration tribunals have been asked and have agreed to give priority to a request for provisional measures over another request for provisional measures that was filed earlier in the proceedings. This happened in situations in which the occurrence of a new factual event made it a matter of urgency for the tribunal to decide first on this second request for provisional measures. For instance, in *Gavrilovic* v. *Croatia*, the investors had first requested the Tribunal to recommend the suspension of criminal investigatory actions and criminal proceedings; three months later, the Tribunal was asked to recommend the suspension of the interrogation of one of the investors until it had decided on the suspension of the entire criminal prosecution, which the Tribunal did after having heard the observations of both parties (19 March 2015, Decision on the Claimants' Urgent Application for Provisional Measures, at 4).

Such situations are to be distinguished from other situations in which the urgency of the situation led applicants not only to file a request for provisional measures, but also to request preliminary measures in order to ensure that their rights were protected while tribunals examined the request for provisional measures. From a procedural point of view, such a mechanism can be singled out as it constitutes a preliminary procedure in the broader context of the procedure addressing the provisional measures as such. It can all the more be set apart in those cases where the other party is not heard during this preliminary procedure. In terms of effect, the key feature of such preliminary measures lies in the fact that they have a temporary effect until tribunals decide on whether to grant the corresponding provisional measures.

Such preliminary measures have, for instance, been requested from and granted by the Tribunal in *Igor Boyko* v. *Ukraine*. In that case, the investor formulated such a request on the ground that he had suffered extrajudicial injuries and that he apprehended imminent and greater injuries. The Tribunal accepted this request without having received the observations of the respondent State, ordering a temporary restraining measure to be reviewed after receipt of the respondent's comments in the course of the claimant's application for interim measures. In support of its decision, the Tribunal explained:

> Interim measures under Article 26 of the UNCITRAL Rules preserve the rights of the parties in the subject matter of the dispute which includes their rights as to the integrity of the agreed arbitral process. Interim measures preserve such rights pending the conclusion of the underlying proceedings. In rare cases, the urgency of the threat to such rights may outstrip even the speed with which interim measures may be granted. In such instances, the procedural rules or practice of a number of international courts and tribunals adopt the practice of issuing a form of temporary restraining measure. [footnote omitted] Practice under the 1976 UNCITRAL Rules recognizes that temporary restraining measures may be granted pending the resolution of a request for interim measures. Moreover, such practice indicates that temporary restraining measures may be granted pending the receipt of the views of the party against whom the measures

are sought ... The Tribunal further notes that there are indications that the existence of such authority under the UNCITRAL Rules was raised at the time of the drafting of the rules. [footnote omitted] (2017, Procedural No 3 on Claimant's Application for Emergency Relief, paras. 2.3–2.4)

Arbitration tribunals operating under the UNCITRAL Arbitration Rules have consistently considered that it is part of their prerogative to consider and order such preliminary measures when the circumstances so require. They have done so even while the Rules do not address the situation explicitly, and this issue was debated in the context of the revision that led to the adoption of the 2010 version of the Rules. Tribunals governed by ICSID Convention arbitration proceedings have adopted the same approach, as illustrated in *Perenco Ecuador Ltd* v. *Ecuador* (2009, Decision on Provisional Measures, paras. 28 and 35).

13.1.2 Provisional Measures *versus* Emergency Arbitration

All of the above-mentioned situations and measures that can be granted by tribunals can be procedurally contrasted to emergency arbitration. This is the case even though they are both intended to protect rights in urgent situations.

As examined in Chapter 11, the SCC Arbitration Rules offer parties the possibility under Appendix II to request the appointment of an emergency arbitrator with the SCC Board before the referral of a case to an arbitration tribunal. If the Board concludes that the SCC does not manifestly lack jurisdiction, it shall seek to appoint the emergency arbitrator within twenty-four hours of the receipt of the application. The arbitrator shall – as a matter of principle – make a decision within five days from the date of receipt of the application. The decision to grant the relief, which is binding upon the parties, can subsequently be declared as no longer binding by the emergency arbitrator herself, or at a later date by the tribunal once the case has been referred to it, or the decision can cease to be binding as a result of the final award made.

This mechanism was relied upon in particular in *Mohammed Munshi* v. *Mongolia*, where the Emergency Arbitrator – despite denying other reliefs sought for – ordered Mongolia to permit an investor to have reasonable access to his local Mongolian counsel as well as to international counsel (2018, Award on Emergency Measures, para. 63.1).

While such reliefs are temporary in nature and effect, similar to provisional measures, it is worth noting the key procedural differences between provisional measures and emergency arbitration. First, emergency reliefs are decided by an authority that is different to the one ultimately called upon to decide the dispute. Second, and more importantly, it should be recalled that emergency reliefs can be requested not only pending the establishment of a tribunal, but also in situations in which no request for arbitration has yet been filed. The significance of the power conferred to emergency arbitrators is even more acute in those latter situations, and distinguishes emergency arbitration even more from provisional measures.

13.2 The Rights and Interests Protected by Provisional Measures

Article 26 of the UNCITRAL Arbitration Rules provides for a non-exhaustive list of provisional measures that can be ordered, and as a corollary of the rights and interests that can be protected by them. It mentions the measures by which tribunals can order parties to (1) maintain or restore the status quo pending determination of the dispute; (2) take action that would prevent, or refrain from taking action that is likely to cause, (i) current or imminent harm or (ii) prejudice to the arbitral process itself; (3) provide a means of preserving assets out of which a subsequent award may be satisfied; and (4) preserve evidence that may be relevant and material to the resolution of the dispute. While the ICSID Arbitration Rules in their 2006 version do not provide such indications, it is worth noting that the 2019 Working Paper n° 3 proposes to incorporate them (proposed Rule 46.1); the list it contains is similar to that of the UNCITRAL Rules, except that it does not refer to the measures that provide a means of preserving assets out of which a subsequent award may be satisfied.

As evident from the above, the rights and interests that can be preserved in the course of UNCITRAL arbitration proceedings are not only substantive rights, i.e. the rights forming part of the main claim or the subject matter of the dispute, but also procedural rights relating to the settlement of the dispute, in particular the rights ensuring the integrity and fairness of arbitration proceedings. As for the ICSID Convention Arbitration Rules, there is a consensus among tribunals operating under these Rules that they cover procedural rights as well as substantive rights (e.g. *Valle Verde Sociedad Financiera S.L.* v. *Venezuela*, 2016, Decision on Provisional Measures, para. 88). In fact, the request of applicants often relates to the preservation of those procedural rights, typically with regards to the exclusivity of ICSID Convention arbitration proceedings.

The right to exclusivity of ICSID Convention arbitration proceedings is enshrined in Article 26 of the ICSID Convention, which reads as follows: 'Consent of the parties to arbitration under this Convention shall, unless otherwise stated, be deemed consent to such arbitration to the exclusion of any other remedy. A Contracting State may require the exhaustion of local administrative or judicial remedies as a condition of its consent to arbitration under this Convention.' According to that provision, the parties lose – as a matter of principle – the right to seek relief before any other court, be it national or international, once they have consented to ICSID arbitration.

There is a consensus among arbitration tribunals that this exclusivity conferred on the ICSID Convention arbitration proceedings can be preserved by way of provisional measures (e.g. *Rizzani de Eccher S.p.A.* v. *Kuwait*, 2017, Decision on Provisional Measures, para. 134). Yet, they consider that the mere existence of proceedings in another forum, typically before domestic courts, does not in and of itself evidence a threat to the right to the exclusivity of the proceedings in a given situation. This is due to the fact that tribunals usually make a distinction between related proceedings and parallel proceedings, with only the latter constituting such a threat. In making this distinction, tribunals rely on the triple identity test and on this basis appraise whether there exists – between the proceedings – identical parties, subject matter and relief sought. As illustrated by the Order and the Dissenting Opinion in *Fouad Alghanim v. Jordan*, there are divergences as to how to apply this test and its precise content. With regard to the subject matter, for instance, the Dissenting Arbitrator in that case stressed that the Tribunal did not affirm the existence of an 'identity' between the domestic and the arbitration proceedings, but instead of 'a very substantial overlap'. By the same token, contrary to the majority of the Tribunal, he denied the identity of the relief sought for in those proceedings, acknowledging only a relationship between them (2014, Order on Application for the Grant of Provisional Measures, Statement of Dissent, paras. 28–30).

In addition to the above-mentioned duality of rights covered, it is also largely recognised that only existing rights can be preserved; in that sense, the Tribunal appointed in *Nova Group Investments, B.V.* v. *Romania* stated that '[t]he nature of "rights", within the meaning of Article 47, is that these must be entitlements that exist at the time of the application' (2017, Decision on Provisional Measures, para. 232). Yet, it is worth noting that in *Interocean Oil* v. *Nigeria*, the Tribunal argued that provisional measures aim at the protection or preservation of rights that 'either actually exists, or will (or is at least likely to) materialize, and is susceptible of being harmed' (2017, Decision on Provisional Measures, para. 27).

13.3 The Substantive Conditions to Grant Provisional Measures

Preliminary Remarks

The UNCITRAL Arbitration Rules specify the substantive conditions to be met for provisional measures to be granted in the context of UNCITRAL arbitration proceedings. These conditions are threefold, requiring that: (1) a harm not adequately reparable by an award of damages shall be likely to result if the interim measure is not ordered; (2) that the harm shall substantially outweigh the harm that is likely to result to the party against whom the measure is directed if the interim measure is granted; and (3) there shall be a reasonable possibility that the requesting party will succeed on the merits of the claim. The first two conditions consist respectively in necessity and proportionality. It is noteworthy that they are not *ipso facto* applicable to the requests concerning the preservation of evidence that may be relevant and material to the resolution of disputes; they are applicable only to the extent tribunals deem it appropriate. Despite the wording that suggests that the *prima facie* test concerns the merits of cases, the third condition has been construed as covering also the *prima facie* jurisdiction of tribunals.[2] In any case, the UNCITRAL Arbitration Rules make it clear that this *prima facie* determination shall not affect the discretion of tribunals in making any subsequent determination.

Unlike the 2010 and 2013 version of the UNCITRAL Rules, the 1976 version of those Rules and the ICSID Convention Arbitration Rules do not provide for any such substantive conditions. Article 47 of that Convention only mentions that provisional measures may be recommended if the tribunal considers that the circumstances so require. On the other hand, the 2019 ICSID Working Paper n° 3 proposes to incorporate – in a non-exhaustive manner – into the Arbitration Rules three conditions: urgency, necessity and proportionality (proposed Rule 46.3). In the current context, it has been up to tribunals to design the applicable test. Five conditions arise from their practice: *prima facie* jurisdiction, *prima facie* case on the merits, necessity, urgency and proportionality. Each is analysed in turn in what follows – however, prior to this, two main remarks must first be made relating to the content of those substantive conditions and the standard used to evaluate them.

Starting with the former, two intertwined variations can be seen in arbitration practice pertaining to the content of the test as a whole and to the content of some of those conditions.

As to the content of the test, a common denominator can be seen across arbitration practice: *prima facie* jurisdiction, necessity and urgency. The fulfilment of the other conditions is not systemically looked into by tribunals. This is illustrated by the decision rendered in *Merck Sharp & Dohme (I.A.) LLC v. Ecuador* where the Tribunal, after having explained that it would focus on *prima facie* jurisdiction, necessity and urgency, argued: 'The Tribunal sees no need for present purposes to go into the question whether other elements, such as a balance of hardship or a *prima facie* case on the merits, are appropriate for consideration in all cases' (7 March 2016, Decision on Interim Measures, para. 69). Certainly, the specifics of each case contribute towards explaining the variations in the exact test used by arbitration tribunals; that being said, one may suggest that those variations result also partly from diverging views on the exact test to be applied.

It is also worth noting that these variations are sometimes no more than apparent. This comes from the fact that the content of some conditions, in particular that of necessity, varies across arbitration practice, notably in that it is seen by some tribunals as incorporating proportionality. This can be explained by the fact that necessity, urgency and proportionality are actually very much intertwined.

---

[2] DD Caron, LM Caplan, *The UNCITRAL Arbitration Rules: A Commentary* (2nd ed, Oxford University Press 2013), at 522.

Irrespective of this issue, it is also important to realise that there exist divergences among arbitration tribunals and arbitrators as to the standard to be used to appraise the fulfilment of these conditions. This is again well illustrated by *Fouad Alghanim* v. *Jordan*, in which the Dissenting Arbitrator denounced the 'extremely low standard employed by the majority in order to evaluate each of the conditions required for the recommendation of provisional measures' and the fact that the order decided by the majority was 'not the first one to apply such low standards in ICSID practice'. He also stressed that ICSID case law presents significantly divergent criteria in this regard (2014, Order on Application for the Grant of Provisional Measures, Statement of Dissent, para. 2).

In this respect, one can note that these divergences – notably the use of a higher standard – are sometimes justified by tribunals on the basis of the specifics of the case. This is typically so in those cases where the measures requested interfere with criminal investigations and prosecutions conducted by the host State. For instance, the Tribunal appointed in *Caratube International Oil Company LLP* v. *Kazakhstan* explained that it 'fe[lt] that a particularly high threshold must be overcome before an ICSID tribunal can indeed recommend provisional measures regarding criminal investigations conducted by a state' (2009, Decision on Provisional Measures, para. 137).

13.3.1 *Prima Facie* Jurisdiction and *Prima Facie* Case on the Merits

Preliminary Remarks
To use the words of the Tribunal appointed in *Victor Pey Casado* v. *Chile* (2001, Decision on Provisional Measures, para. 46), the conclusions reached as to jurisdiction and merits at the stage of provisional measures are not presumptions, but hypotheses. More precisely, they constitute the hypotheses on the basis of which it is deemed relevant to appraise whether or not there are rights to be preserved and whether the conditions required to grant provisional measures are met. The hypothetical nature of their conclusion explains why tribunals systematically recall that their findings as to their *prima facie* jurisdiction and the existence of a *prima facie* case on the merits do not pre-judge their future analyses and conclusions on those matters.

13.3.1.1 *Prima Facie* Jurisdiction

As mentioned above, provisional measures can be requested at any time before the issuance of an award. This entails that such measures may be requested by an investor even while the respondent State is in the course of objecting to the jurisdiction of the tribunal and where a tribunal has not yet decided on its own jurisdiction. The fact that an objection to jurisdiction has been raised and has not yet been decided cannot bar the exercise by tribunals of their power to grant provisional measures; as stated by the Tribunal in *Millicom International Operations B.V.* v. *Senegal*, it would otherwise be easy for a party to deprive tribunals from this power simply by objecting to their jurisdiction (2009, Decision on Provisional Measures, para. 42). On the other hand, a request for provisional measures cannot as such entitle tribunals to intervene in disputes with respect to which it is crystal clear that they have no jurisdiction. In that context, the requirement that the *prima facie* jurisdiction of tribunals be established acts as a compromise between these two unsatisfactory options. This explains why it constitutes a well-recognised condition in the practice of tribunals operating under both the ICSID Convention Arbitration Rules and the UNCITRAL Arbitration Rules (e.g. *Gavrilovic v. Croatia*, 30 April 2015, Decision on Provisional Measures, paras. 181–182), and more generally in the case law of international courts and tribunals, like the ICJ (e.g. *Armed Activities on the Territory of the Congo (New Application: 2002) (Democratic Republic of the Congo v. Rwanda)*, 2002, Order, para. 58).

In appraising this *prima facie* jurisdiction, most tribunals focus, in the context of arbitrations based on IIA offers to arbitrate, on the IIA provisions that ground and delineate their jurisdiction; with regard to ICSID Convention arbitration proceedings, they also rely on the ICSID Convention (e.g. *Quiborax S.A. v. Bolivia*, 2010, Decision on Provisional Measures, paras. 108–112). Other tribunals have adopted a different approach to evaluate their *prima facie* jurisdiction. For instance, in *Italba Corporation v. Uruguay*, the Tribunal deduced from the fact that the respondent State did not request a bifurcation while objecting to the jurisdiction *ratione materiae* of the Tribunal, that the respondent had vested it with the necessary adjudicative powers to conduct the arbitration, including the power to recommend provisional measures (2017, Decision on Provisional Measures and Temporary Relief, paras. 113–114).

With regard to the appraisal of ICSID *prima facie* jurisdiction more specifically, the assessment made by the Secretary-General that the dispute is not manifestly outside the jurisdiction of the Centre when considering the registration of a request for arbitration may not on its own be seen as sufficient to uphold *prima facie* jurisdiction; this is due to the summary nature of the control, which is explained in Chapter 11. In that sense, the Tribunal explained in *Millicom International Operations B.V. v. Senegal*:

> For the Arbitral Tribunal, the mere fact that the Request for Arbitration has been registered might certainly constitute a sign of *prima facie* jurisdiction, but under no circumstances may it constitute a sufficient condition. The registration process is summary in nature and is intended solely to perform an initial check in order to dismiss immediately any requests manifestly outside the jurisdiction of the Centre. The decision is taken solely on the basis of the Request for Arbitration and the additional information provided by the requesting party, without waiting for or formally requesting any comments from the other party. (2009, Decision on the Application for Provisional Measures, para. 43)

13.3.1.2 *Prima Facie* Case on the Merits

Somewhat comparable to the condition of *prima facie* jurisdiction, the requirement that a *prima facie* case on the merits be established constitutes a compromise between two alternatives. Requiring a deeper examination into the merits would require lengthy exchanges that would run counter to the urgency that characterises provisional measures. On the other hand, allowing tribunals to reach a decision without having analysed the merits would create the possibility for tribunals to intervene in claims that are clearly frivolous.

Requiring a *prima facie* case on the merits is a trade-off between these two inadequate options and is often set as a substantive condition to the grant of provisional measures by tribunals operating under the UNCITRAL Arbitration Rules and the ICSID Convention Arbitration Rules. As explained by the Tribunal in *Sergei Paushok* v. *Mongolia*, it means that tribunals should appraise 'whether a reasonable case has been made which, if the facts alleged are proven, might possibly lead the [t]ribunal to the conclusion that an award could be made in favor of Claimants' (2008, Order on Interim Measures, para. 55).

13.3.2 Necessity

ICSID Convention Arbitration Rules do not specify what 'necessity' entails, nor does the 1976 version of the UNCITRAL Arbitration Rules, which merely provides that tribunals may take the interim measures they deem 'necessary'. This has begged the question of the standard to be applied in determining whether provisional measures are necessary – in other words, in appraising necessity. It is worth noting that the revision of the Rules contemplated in the 2019 ICSID Working Paper n° 3 does not answer this question as it merely refers to the fact that tribunals shall notably consider whether the measures are 'necessary' in deciding whether to recommend provisional measures. On the other hand, the 2010 and 2013 versions of the UNCITRAL Rules are crystal clear on the matter as they provide that tribunals shall be satisfied that a 'harm not adequately reparable by an award of damages is likely to result if the measure is not ordered'.

It is worth noting at the outset that the answer given to this question by arbitration tribunals in general lack clarity. This is fundamentally due to the vagueness and the elliptical nature of the explanations provided by tribunals, in particular as to the exact standard that they adopt in order to appraise necessity. Secondarily, it can also be noted that the inconsistencies and ambiguities as regards the terminology used across their practice can only reinforce this lack of clarity.

Tribunals have traditionally considered that a provisional measure is deemed to be necessary, and the condition of necessity thus fulfilled, when the harm that would occur if the measure were not granted could not be compensated by an award of damages. For instance, the Tribunal appointed in *Quiborax S.A.* v. *Bolivia* emphasised that 'any harm caused to the integrity of the ICSID proceedings, particularly with respect to a party's access to evidence or the integrity of the evidence produced could not be remedied by an award of damages'; having also appraised proportionality, it then decided to grant part of the provisional measures requested (2010, Decision on Provisional Measures, para. 157). This standard – which is in line with the approach incorporated in the 2010 and 2013 versions of the UNCITRAL Arbitration Rules – is most often expressed in terms of 'irreparable harm' or 'irreparable loss' (e.g. *Occidental Petroleum Corporation* v. *Ecuador*, 2007, Decision on Provisional Measures, para. 92). It is notable that tribunals that have criticised this terminology have nonetheless adopted a standard whose content is similar (e.g. *Perenco Ecuador Ltd.* v. *Ecuador*, 2009, Decision on Provisional Measures, para. 43).

Using the term 'irreparable harm', the Tribunal appointed in *PNG Sustainable Development Program Ltd* v. *Papua New Guinea* made use of language which, as stated by the Tribunal in *Gavrilovic* v. *Croatia* (30 April 2015, Decision on Provisional Measures, para. 187), suggests a preference for a lower standard. It stated:

> [T]he term 'irreparable' harm is properly understood as requiring a showing of a material risk of serious or grave damage to the requesting party, and not harm that is literally 'irreparable' in what is sometimes regarded as the narrow common law sense of the term. The degree of 'gravity' or 'seriousness' of harm that is necessary for an order of provisional relief cannot be specified with precision, and depends in part on the circumstances of the case, the nature of the relief requested and the relative harm to be suffered by each party; suffice it to say that substantial, serious harm, even if not irreparable, is generally sufficient to satisfy this element of the standard for granting provisional measures. (2015, Decision on Provisional Measures, para. 109)

In addition to stressing that this language is suggestive of a lower standard, two remarks can be made in relation to this statement. First, it draws attention to the highly factual dimension of the appraisal of necessity. In this respect, it is noteworthy that the Tribunal appointed in the above-mentioned *Gavrilovic* case found it simply unnecessary to formulate a single test of necessity to be applied in all cases. Instead, it stressed the need to ascertain a test that could be adapted to the specifics of each case, in that case in particular the fact that the relief sought would interfere with the exercise of the sovereign State's rights and duties to investigate and prosecute crimes (para. 189). In relation to this first remark and the above-mentioned excerpt, it is also notable that the *PNG* Tribunal included the 'relative harm to be suffered by each of the parties if the provisional measure is granted or not' as a factor to be taken into account in appraising necessity. This in fact leads to the incorporation of the condition of proportionality into that of necessity.

By the same token, tribunals sometimes merge the analysis of necessity with the condition of urgency. For instance, the Tribunal appointed in *Rizzani de Eccher S.p.A.* v. *Kuwait* explained that 'in view of the twin requirements of urgency and necessity, it must follow that the harm alleged by the requesting party must be "imminent", and not "potential or hypothetical"' (2017, Decision on Provisional Measures, para. 104).

This requirement that the harm be 'imminent', and not 'potential' or 'hypothetical', requires the harm to be a matter of certainty. In this respect, it is noteworthy that some tribunals have stressed, on the contrary, that the existence of a 'sufficient risk' is enough for granting provisional measures. In that sense, the Tribunal argued in *PNG Sustainable Development Program Ltd* v. *Papua New Guinea*:

> The Tribunal is also of the view that the requesting party need not prove that 'serious' harm is certain to occur. Rather, it is generally sufficient to show that there is a material risk that it will occur. The requirement of showing material risk does not, however, imply a showing of any particular percentage of likelihood, or probability, that the risk will materialize. The proper requirement is that the requesting party must establish the existence of a sufficient risk or threat that grave or serious harm will occur if provisional measures are not granted. (2015, Decision on Provisional Measures, para. 111)

13.3.3 Urgency

The degree of urgency required in order to validate the granting of provisional measures, subject to the fulfilment of the other conditions, depends on the specifics of each case. This means that the appraisal of whether the condition of urgency is fulfilled requires focusing in particular on the rights to be protected, the nature of the threat to those rights and the measures requested. For instance, there is a consensus that in the case of a threat to specific rights, notably the integrity of the proceedings, measures are to be considered as being inherently urgent (e.g. *Teinver S.A.* v. *Argentina*, 2016, Decision on Provisional Measures, para. 235). The Tribunal in *Quiborax S.A.* v. *Bolivia* explained this as follows:

> [I]f measures are intended to protect the procedural integrity of the arbitration, in particular with respect to access to or integrity of the evidence, they are urgent by definition. Indeed, the question of whether a Party has the opportunity to present its case or rely on the integrity of specific evidence is essential to (and therefore cannot await) the rendering of an award on the merits. (2010, Decision on Provisional Measures, para. 153)

It is worth noting that in *PNG Sustainable Development Program Ltd* v. *Papua New Guinea*, similar to its appraisal of necessity, the Tribunal in appraising urgency took into account 'the balance of injuries that would be suffered by both parties if provisional measures are (or are not) ordered' (2015, Decision on Provisional Measures, para. 117). This in reality has the effect of incorporating the condition of proportionality into that of urgency.

13.3.4 Proportionality

As noted by the Tribunal appointed in *Merck Sharp & Dohme (I.A.) LLC v. Ecuador* (6 September 2016, Second Decision on Interim Measures, para. 32), the balance of hardship is inherent in any decision to order provisional measures, which helps to explain why – as seen above – some tribunals enquire into matters of proportionality in examining the conditions of necessity and urgency. Whether it is seen as forming part of those conditions or as existing as a stand-alone condition, proportionality requires that the harm to be prevented by the measure requested by a party is not outweighed by the hardships to which the other party would be subjected if that measure were granted. Again, the appraisal of this condition is very much fact-sensitive.

13.4 Procedural Aspects and Legal Force of Provisional Measures

13.4.1 Procedural Aspects of Provisional Measures

Requests for provisional measures can be made by either party. Although requests are most of the time filed by the claimant investors, this nonetheless means that the possibility is also offered to the respondent States. It is worth noting that the ICSID Arbitration Rules, contrary to the UNCITRAL Rules, also entitle tribunals to recommend provisional measures on their own initiative. It should also be stressed that the parties can under the ICSID Rules exclude or limit the possibility of provisional measures.

While the UNCITRAL Rules do not provide any indication as to the content of the requests, one can safely assume that they must be similar to those mentioned in the ICSID Rules. According to these Rules, the requests must indicate the rights to be preserved, the measures which are sought and the circumstances that require such measures.

It is inherent to this mechanism that requests for provisional measures be dealt with urgently. As a result, the ICSID Convention Arbitration Rules provide that tribunals shall give priority to the consideration of these requests. Following that rationale, the 2019 ICSID Working Paper n° 3 proposes that a strict deadline for the issuance of the decisions be incorporated into the Rules, with a cut-off point of thirty days after the latest of (1) the constitution of the tribunal; (2) the last written submission on the request; or (3) the last oral submission on the request (proposed Rule 46.2.d).

The ICSID Convention Arbitration Rules also make it compulsory for tribunals to give the opportunity to each party to present its observations before making their decision.

Tribunals may decide to grant all, some or none of the provisional measures sought by the applicants, or alternatively, to grant measures other than those requested.

As explained above, the provisional measures granted are by definition temporary, being effective only until the tribunal has decided the dispute or until the proceedings have been discontinued. A change in circumstances may require that the measures granted be revoked earlier or at least be modified or suspended. This is why the UNCITRAL Arbitration Rules specify that tribunals may require from any party that it promptly disclose any material change in the circumstances on the basis of which the interim measures were granted. Under the revision proposed by ICSID in the 2019 ICSID Working Paper n° 3, such a disclosure shall be made by the parties on their own initiative.

Those modifications or revocations under the UNCITRAL Arbitration Rules shall be granted following the application of any party or, in exceptional circumstances and upon prior notice to them, from the tribunal's own initiative. The ICSID Arbitration Rules make no such distinction – contrary to the revision proposed by ICSID in the above-mentioned Working Paper – but rather simply provide that tribunals may do so at any time. On the other hand, the Rules reiterate the requirement that each party shall first be given the opportunity to present its observations as regards modifications and revocations.

13.4.2 Legal Force of Provisional Measures

The issue of the legal force of provisional measures has arisen in the context of ICSID Convention arbitration proceedings. Since the decision rendered by the Tribunal in *Emilio Agustin Mafezzini* v. *Spain*, almost all ICSID tribunals and arbitrators have agreed that provisional measures are binding. This is so despite the fact that the English and French version of the ICSID Convention and of the ICSID Arbitration Rules refer respectively to 'recommend' and 'recommander'. To justify its finding, that Tribunal emphasised that the Spanish version refers to 'dictar' and it argued that the parties to the ICSID Convention did not mean to create a substantial difference in effect between the word 'recommend' and the word 'order' that is used elsewhere in the Rules to describe the ability of tribunals to require a certain action from a party (1999, Procedural Order n° 2, para. 9). In other cases, tribunals referred to the Statute of the ICJ on which Article 47 of the ICSID Convention is based and the relevant practice of that Court to justify this approach (e.g. *United Utilities (Tallinn) B.V.* v. *Estonia*, 2016, Decision on Provisional Measures, para. 109).

Against this consensus, it is worth mentioning the opinion expressed by Arbitrator Kohen in his Dissenting Opinion delivered in *Fouad Alghanim* v. *Jordan* (2014, Order on Application for the Grant of Provisional

Measures, Statement of Dissent, paras. 52–57). In arguing that provisional measures are non-binding, he set out a series of justifications.

As a matter of literal interpretation, he stated that Article 47 of the ICSID Convention repeats almost every word of Article 41 of the ICJ Statute except for 'indicate'; the term 'recommend' chosen instead of this term is, according to him, 'explicit and cannot be interpreted in any other way than to suggest something without binding effect'.

In relation to the preparatory works, Arbitrator Kohen also argued that provisional measures were not intended to be binding. He recalled in particular that it was decided to refer to 'recommend' instead of 'prescribe', which was used in the first draft of the relevant Article.

From a policy point of view, he explained the departure that the non-binding nature of provisional measures in ICSID Convention arbitration proceedings constitutes, as compared to the binding nature of those measures in other international adjudicative systems, by reference to the specificities of ICSID arbitration:

> We are dealing here with disputes between States on the one hand, and individuals or private corporations engaged in investment on the other. This is a completely different relationship to a State–State one. The questions at issue here do not relate to the protection of fundamental human rights either. In the context of interests of a commercial nature, which by definition may be protected by way of compensation, a given conduct cannot be imposed on a State without having previously obtained a final determination in the specific case. (para. 56)

It is worth noting that while Arbitrator Kohen denied that provisional measures are binding in the context of ICSID Convention arbitration proceedings, he acknowledged – in reference to Lauterpacht[3] – that States are bound to give them due consideration in good faith.

---

[3] *Voting Procedure on Questions Relating to Reports and Petitions Concerning the Territory of South-West Africa* (1955, ICJ Advisory Opinion, Separate Opinion of Judge Lauterpacht, at 118–119).

14

Jurisdiction and Admissibility

Introduction

Before arbitration tribunals can decide on the merits of a case, they must first appraise whether they have jurisdiction to hear it. As seen in Chapter 11, such an appraisal can be the object of a specific procedural stage when a bifurcation is requested by the respondent and granted by the tribunal. Regardless of these procedural considerations, if a tribunal considers that it does not have jurisdiction, it then does not decide on the merits of the case. A finding of inadmissibility also impacts on the ruling of the tribunal on the merits.

The establishment of jurisdiction is a complex exercise that raises numerous issues. To make sense of this, this chapter examines how jurisdiction is formally appraised. From a substantive point of view, the remainder of the chapter then delves into the key aspects and issues of jurisdiction and admissibility. First, however, it begins with an explanation of the relevant fundamental notions and principles in order to shed light on these analyses.

14.1 Fundamental Notions and Principles

14.1.1 Consent

Consent is one of the most fundamental principles in public international law, deriving from the preeminence of State sovereignty. It concerns both substantive obligations and the settlement of disputes arising from the alleged breach of such obligations. In other words, only States can place obligations upon themselves to regulate and govern their conduct; likewise, only they can confer the power on international courts and tribunals to decide on the disputes to which they are a party. It is worth stressing in this respect that the giving of consent to be bound by a substantive obligation does not entail that consent is given for adjudicative purposes – these are two different issues that require two different expressions of consent. This results from the decentralised nature of the international legal order, as explained by Arbitrator Abi-Saab:

[I]n the absence of a centralized power on the international level that exercises the judicial function through a judicial system empowered from above (or rather incarnating the judicial power as part of the centralized power), all international adjudicatory bodies are empowered from below, being based on the consent and agreement of the subjects (i.e. the litigants, *les justiciables)* themselves. (*Abaclat* v. *Argentina*, 2011, Decision on Jurisdiction and Admissibility, Dissenting Opinion, para. 7)

This principle and the consequences thereof also apply *mutatis mutandis* to investor–State arbitration. This is well illustrated by the Report of the Executive Directors of the International Bank for Reconstruction and Development (IBRD) on the 1965 Convention on the Settlement of Investment Disputes between States and Nationals of Other States, which established the International Centre for Settlement of Investment Disputes (ICSID). It stresses indeed that the consent of the parties is the cornerstone of the jurisdiction of the Centre (para. 23).

Of course, in investor–State disputes – as contrasted with State–State disputes discussed in Chapter 10 – consent is required from two different types of entities, i.e. States and foreign investors. As regards foreign investors, apart from counterclaims which are analysed in Chapter 11, consent does not raise any major issue – in the context mainly of arbitrations based on the offer to arbitrate contained within international investment agreements (IIAs), the filing of the request for arbitration is deemed to evidence their acceptance of the offer and their consent. Consent is actually at the 'forefront' of arbitration practice with regard to States. Tribunals often recall that State consent is the exception and not the principle (e.g. *Menzies Middle East and Africa S.A.* v. *Senegal,* 2016, Award, para. 130) and insist that the existence of consent must be established (e.g. *Daimler Financial Services AG* v. *Argentina*, 2012, Award, para. 175).

In this respect, a number of tribunals and arbitrators have expressed the view that consent cannot be presumed and that tribunals must be cautious in determining the existence and the scope of consent. For instance, Arbitrator Boisson de Chazournes explained in *Garanti Koza LLP* v. *Turkmenistan* that international courts and tribunals should respect the limits of the jurisdiction conferred upon them, as acting otherwise would weaken the trust and confidence in third-party adjudication (2013, Decision on the Objection to Jurisdiction for Lack of Consent, Dissenting Opinion, para. 6). By the same token, Arbitrator Kohen stressed that the need for care in the exercise of the *Kompetenz-Kompetenz* principle – which is explained below – is particularly acute in the context of investor–State arbitration as the potential number of claimants invoking State consent could be unlimited (*Venezuela US, S.R.L.* v. *Venezuela*, 2016, Interim Award on Jurisdiction, Dissenting Opinion, para. 3).

In line with such approaches, some Tribunals have insisted that consent and the scope thereof must be established with certainty. For instance, in *Fireman's*

Fund Insurance Company v. *Mexico*, the Tribunal opined that 'under contemporary international law a foreign investor is [not] entitled to the benefit of the doubt with respect to the existence and scope of an arbitration agreement' (2003, Decision on the Preliminary Question, para. 64). In the same vein, the majority of the Tribunal in *Daimler Financial Services AG* v. *Argentina* argued that the establishment of consent requires affirmative evidence (2012, Award, para. 175). This 'affirmative evidence' requirement was equated by Arbitrator Brower in that latter case to a restrictive interpretation (Dissenting Opinion, para. 3), which was denied by the majority (Award, para. 175).

14.1.2 Jurisdiction and Admissibility

Jurisdiction is closely connected to the notion of consent. As explained above, the power of arbitration tribunals to decide on disputes derives from the disputing parties' consent. Tribunals must therefore respect and be the 'guardian' of this consent which grounds and delineates their jurisdiction. This explains why arbitration tribunals must consider issues of jurisdiction *proprio motu* when they are not raised by the parties themselves. As stressed by the Tribunal appointed in *Spence International Investments, LLC* v. *Costa Rica*, the effective administration of international justice requires that tribunals do not adjudicate on matters over which they do not have jurisdiction, whether the parties would wish this to be the case or not (2016, Interim Award, para. 225).

The notion of jurisdiction has several dimensions that are covered by two conceptual 'pairs', which were both well explained by Arbitrator Abi-Saab in *Abaclat* v. *Argentina*. Under the first pair, jurisdiction is used to designate (1) a power and (2) its ambit. The notion refers respectively to the legal power that the parties consent to give to an adjudicative body to exercise the judicial function and to the ambit within which this power must be exercised. The second pair, namely special jurisdiction/general jurisdiction, pertains to the jurisdiction conceived of as an ambit. As explained by Arbitrator Abi-Saab, general jurisdiction is relevant for all the situations in which adjudication takes place within an institutional setting, either a framework within which *ad hoc* tribunals are established, like ICSID, or a standing court, like the International Court of Justice (ICJ). It defines the 'outer limits' of the special jurisdiction, meaning the limits set by the constitutive instrument of the framework or the court to the specific jurisdictional title bearing the consent of the parties in each case (2011, Decision on Jurisdiction and Admissibility, Dissenting Opinion, paras. 7 and 12–13). This combination of general jurisdiction and special jurisdiction as regards ICSID Convention arbitration proceedings explains why the jurisdiction of ICSID arbitration tribunals is subject to a 'double-barrelled test' under both the Convention and, with regard to arbitrations based on IIA offers to arbitrate, the IIA at hand.

Arbitration tribunals are in charge of appraising their own jurisdiction. This is well illustrated by Article 41.1 of the ICSID Convention, which provides that 'the Tribunal shall be the judge of its own competence'. This reflects the *Kompetenz-Kompetenz* principle which is, as stressed by the Tribunal in *Blue Bank International & Trust (Barbados) Ltd* v. *Venezuela*, universally accepted, including in investor–State arbitration (2017, Award, para. 102).

Admissibility is often distinguished from jurisdiction in investor–State arbitration (e.g. *Gavrilovic* v. *Croatia*, 2018, Award, paras. 411–413), despite the divide between the two not being clear-cut in the practice of tribunals. The basis for this distinction is often said to lie in the 'object' of the objection, i.e. whether it pertains to the tribunal or to the claim – in that sense, the Tribunal appointed in *Hochtief AG* v. *Argentina* stated: 'Jurisdiction is an attribute of a tribunal and not of a claim, whereas admissibility is an attribute of a claim but not of a tribunal' (2011, Decision on Jurisdiction, para. 90). Put differently, this distinction entails that jurisdictional objections go to the ability of tribunals to decide on cases, while admissibility objections focus on the features of the claims formulated by the claimants. As seen below in relation to the conditions set out in IIAs for the submission of disputes to arbitration, the determination as to whether an objection pertains to jurisdiction or admissibility is often controversial in investor–State arbitration.

Finally, it is worth noting that jurisdiction and admissibility are sometimes distinguished from the notion of receivability. In reality, receivability is rarely discussed in investor–State arbitration. In *Hochtief AG* v. *Argentina*, the Tribunal contrasted receivability with admissibility, explaining:

> A distinction may also be drawn between questions of admissibility and questions of receivability. A tribunal might decide that a claim of which it is seised and which is within its jurisdiction is inadmissible (for example, on the ground of *lis alibi pendens* or *forum non conveniens*); or it might refuse even to receive and become seised of a claim that is within its jurisdiction because of some fundamental defect in the manner in which the claim is put forward. (2011, Decision on Jurisdiction, para. 90)

In *Monsieur Joseph Houben* v. *Burundi*, the Tribunal opposed receivability to jurisdiction. It considered that the alleged lack of detail in the notification of the dispute – and the attached *aide-memoire* – was not a matter of jurisdiction, but instead a matter of receivability as it viewed this as relating to the question as to whether the dispute is sufficiently ripe to be submitted to arbitration (2016, Award, para. 140).

In relation to the controversies referred to above concerning the characterisation of issues as pertaining to jurisdiction or admissibility, it is worth noting that arbitration practice shows that divergences on classification exist as for receivability as well. Indeed, while 'ripeness' was conceived of by the *Houben* Tribunal in terms of receivability, the Tribunal considered it in *Gavrilovic* v. *Croatia* as pertaining to admissibility (2018, Award, para. 412).

14.2 Formal Considerations on Jurisdiction

The establishment of jurisdiction raises two main issues: (1) the methodology to be employed in appraising jurisdiction; and (2) the standard and burden of proof on the matter. Each issue is analysed in turn below.

14.2.1 The Methodology for Appraising Jurisdiction

As explained above, the jurisdiction of international courts and tribunals derives from the consent of the disputing parties to have their dispute settled in international adjudicative proceedings. In investor–State arbitration, this consent can derive mainly from an investment contract concluded between a host State and a foreign investor, a domestic investment code, or an IIA, i.e. the offer to arbitrate contained within the IIA. As explained earlier, the latter option is by far the most widespread. The present chapter focuses on this option, and as such, mentions made to 'investor–State arbitration' in the following sections refer to arbitrations based on IIA offers to arbitrate.

Investor–State arbitrations based on IIA offers to arbitrate – as with arbitrations based on offers contained within domestic investment codes – are peculiar in that the disputing parties do not express their consent at the same time. Rather, the States parties to the IIAs express their consent to arbitrate disputes with the investors of the other States parties in the offer to arbitrate when concluding the agreements, an offer which is subsequently deemed to be accepted by each claimant when it files the request for arbitration, this request amounting to the expression of consent. As such, the offer to arbitrate formulated by States parties in IIAs is the cornerstone of the arbitration agreements between the disputing parties and thereby of the tribunals' jurisdiction. Two remarks can be made in this respect.

First, it is worth noting that when the offer to arbitrate refers to ICSID Convention arbitration proceedings, this offer – and its acceptance – express not only the consent to the special jurisdiction of arbitration tribunals as defined above, but also the consent to their general jurisdiction in relation to the ICSID Convention. The expression of this consent in writing to the jurisdiction of the Centre is a requirement under Article 25 of the Convention. It should be recalled here that the ratification of the ICSID Convention by States does not amount to such an expression of consent.

Second, it is important to realise that to be in the position to validly accept an offer to arbitrate, a claimant must be entitled to access this offer. This means that the IIA that contains the offer to arbitrate must apply to that claimant.

From a methodological point of view, the result of the above is that the establishment of jurisdiction is a two-step process. First, it must be determined whether the IIA applies to the claimant in order to know whether it can access the offer to arbitrate. If it does apply, it is necessary to then appraise whether the dispute that it brings meets the characteristics of the offer as they are set out by the IIA States parties and – as for ICSID Convention arbitration proceedings – the characteristics set out in the ICSID Convention.

Concerning the issue of the application of the IIA, it is required to examine the application (1) *ratione materiae* and (2) *ratione personae* of the IIA, meaning respectively whether the claimant (1) has a covered investment under the terms of the particular IIA, including from a temporal and geographical point of view; and (2) is an investor of another State party, as defined in this IIA.

The appraisal as to whether the dispute meets the characteristics of the offer entails an inquiry into (1) whether it was submitted in accordance with the conditions attached to that offer; and (2) whether the dispute falls within its scope. Specific remarks are warranted at this preliminary stage as for each of these characteristics.

As to the first characteristic, it is worth mentioning that it is debated whether all of the conditions that can be found in IIA practice should be considered as constitutive of consent, or whether some of these should be construed as pertaining to the implementation of consent. This is discussed further below.

Concerning the second characteristic, one should note that, irrespective of the appraisal of the existence of a dispute (as discussed in Chapter 10), the determination of whether a dispute falls within the scope of the offer to arbitrate requires an examination into (1) the subject matter and (2) the personal scope of the offer, as well as (3) the temporal ambit of the disputes covered by the offer.

This determination overlaps in practice with the examination of the application of the IIA to the claimant. This is, for instance, illustrated by those offers that cover disputes between a State party and the investors of the other States parties in relation to an investment – under this formulation, the determination as to whether a dispute falls within the scope of such an offer to arbitrate requires in particular a determination of whether the claimant is an investor of another State party and whether the dispute relates to an investment, as defined in the IIAs. This explains why, for those overlapping elements, arbitration tribunals usually do not formally distinguish between the examination of the application of the IIA to the claimant and the determination as to whether the dispute falls within the scope of the offer to arbitrate. On the other hand, tribunals do distinguish – when warranted – between the examination of their jurisdiction under the applicable IIA and under the ICSID Convention.

14.2.2 Standard and Burden of Proof

As recalled above, jurisdictional issues can be decided at a specific stage of arbitration proceedings when a bifurcation is requested by the respondent and upheld by the tribunal. At that stage, the merits are not yet pled, and ultimately may not be examined at all if the tribunal declines jurisdiction. Under such a procedural sequence, tribunals inquire into their jurisdiction by focusing in particular on whether the claimant qualifies as an investor and has an investment under the applicable IIA and, when relevant, under Article 25 of the ICSID Convention. But they also look into the merits of the case to ensure the claim is not irrelevant. A distinction is warranted as regards merits and jurisdictional matters regarding the standard of proof.

Concerning the merits, all that needs to be established is a *prima facie* case. In that respect, arbitration tribunals (e.g. *Blue Bank International & Trust (Barbados) Ltd* v. *Venezuela*, 2017, Award, para. 68) often refer to and endorse the following test as famously articulated by Judge Higgins in the *Case Concerning Oil Platforms (Islamic Republic of Iran* v. *United States of America)* decided by the ICJ:

> The only way in which, in the present case, it can be determined whether the claims of Iran are sufficiently plausibly based upon the 1955 Treaty is to accept *pro tem* the facts as alleged by Iran to be true and in that light to interpret Articles I, IV and X for jurisdictional purposes – that is to say, to see if on the basis of Iran's claims of fact there could occur a violation of one or more of them. (1996, Judgment, Separate Opinion, para. 32)

In other words, a *prima facie* case is shown if a tribunal is satisfied that the facts as alleged may constitute a breach of the respondent State's obligations. This *prima facie* test does not require the veracity of the facts to be established. From a legal perspective, it is sufficient that the tribunal be convinced of the potential merits of a claim under a plausible interpretation and application of the law. The Tribunal appointed in *Casinos Austria* v. *Argentina* explained the essence and purpose of this test and the cautious balancing of which it consists as follows:

> This raises the question as to what the *prima facie* test implies for the Tribunal's task in dealing with competing propositions of the Parties as to the proper interpretation of the applicable law and its application to the alleged facts. This issue is particularly salient in the face of legal indeterminacies and competing legal theories or lines of jurisprudence relating to the applicable law, a phenomenon regularly occurring in investment arbitration. In such a situation, an investment tribunal must steer a careful course. On the one hand, it should take into account the right of both parties to fully present their case and their legal arguments to the Tribunal, including arguments that are novel or go against the predominant views and would hence contribute to the further development of the law. On the other hand, the Tribunal should prevent frivolous, spurious, and legally clearly unfounded cases, which would impose an illegitimate burden on the time and resources of both Respondent and the Tribunal, from going forward to the merits.
>
> In finding the right balance, an investment tribunal should not simply rubberstamp Claimants' legal qualification of their case on the merits, but make an independent determination on the interpretation of the applicable law, here the Argentina–Austria BIT. [footnote omitted] At the same time, the Tribunal's

independent determination should not, as suggested in *SGS v. Philippines* 'require the definitive interpretation of the treaty provision which is relied on' [footnote omitted] as this may cut short the Parties' possibility of making a full presentation of their case. Instead, the Tribunal's determination of whether a *prima facie* claim exists should be limited to ascertaining whether Claimants' case relies on a plausible interpretation of the applicable law. (2018, Decision on Jurisdiction, paras. 209–210)

In contrast, plausibility is not sufficient for jurisdictional matters, including when there is no bifurcation. Factual and legal claims that are decisive in the appraisal of jurisdiction must be proven; this is so, for instance, as regards the characterisation of the claimant as an investor or of the asset as a covered investment under the applicable IIA and the ICSID Convention when relevant. As to the investment, it is worth noting that tribunals make a distinction between the proof of its existence and the proof of its scope – they consider that the precise scope of the investment needs not necessarily be established for jurisdictional purposes as this may require them to enter into a substantive examination of the merits of the case (e.g. *Vladislav Kim v. Uzbekistan*, 2017, Decision on Jurisdiction, para. 244).

As stated by the Tribunal in *Philip Morris Asia Limited* v. *Australia*, all of this entails in particular that claimants must prove the facts establishing the conditions for the jurisdiction of the tribunals, and that respondent States must do the same with regard to their objection to jurisdiction (2015, Award on Jurisdiction and Admissibility, para. 495). It is worth stressing that the burden of proof does not operate in a linear and 'clear-cut' manner; as noted by the Tribunal appointed in *Caratube International Oil Company LLP v. Kazakhstan*, the allocation of the burden varies throughout the course of the proceedings and may shift depending on the nature and strength of the evidence presented by each party in support of its arguments (2017, Award, para. 314).

14.3 Substantive Aspects and Issues of Jurisdiction and Admissibility

What follows examines the salient substantive aspects and issues of jurisdiction and admissibility. Attention is paid to (1) the offer to arbitrate; (2) the notion and definition of 'investment'; (3) the notion and definition of 'investor'; and (4) the impact of investors' conduct on jurisdiction and admissibility. While they are distinguished here for didactic purposes, it is worth stressing at the outset, as can be seen below, that the definitions of investment and investor are very much intertwined.

14.3.1 The Offer to Arbitrate

The offer to arbitrate contained in IIAs usually provides for various conditions attached to the submission of disputes to arbitration. They also specify the subject matter of the disputes that States parties have consented to submit to arbitration. These two aspects are analysed in succession below. The issue of the temporal ambit of the disputes that are covered by the offer to arbitrate is also examined.

14.3.1.1 The Conditions for Submitting a Dispute to Arbitration

According to various formulae and combinations, IIAs set out conditions for the submission of disputes to arbitration. Each of these conditions raises specific issues worthy of analysis, each of which is dealt with in turn. On the other hand, most of these conditions raise a common issue pertaining to the characterisation of their nature in relation to consent.

a The Types of Conditions

Preliminary Remarks
Most of the conditions provided in IIAs for submitting disputes to arbitration are intended or have the effect of limiting the resort to arbitration and/or avoiding multiple proceedings. Six main such conditions can be singled out in this regard.

The first of these, contained in limitation period clauses, limits the time period during which disputes can be submitted to arbitration.

The second condition is found in a great number of IIAs and consists of a requirement to consult/negotiate for a certain period of time with a view to attempting to reach an amicable settlement before disputes can be submitted to arbitration.

The third condition pertains to adjudicative settlement, requiring investors to resort to local remedies during a certain period of time before the disputes can be submitted to arbitration.

The second and third conditions make clear that the purpose of the passage of time is for the parties to engage in negotiation or to allow for domestic adjudication, respectively. As a preliminary remark, one can contrast these two conditions with another condition contained in a number of IIAs that requires a certain period of time to pass before disputes can be submitted to arbitration, but which often does not specify any purpose for this passage of time. This is often referred to as a 'waiting period' or a 'cooling-off period'. In addition to often having an indeterminate purpose, this requirement is characterised by another source of complexity that pertains to the 'timing' thereof. Indeed, there are differences among IIAs as to when and how the period of time it sets is inserted in the sequence that pre-dates the submission of disputes to arbitration. For instance, in some IIAs, this period encompasses the period of the negotiation (e.g. 2016 Canada–Mongolia, Article 21.2), while in other agreements the waiting period can be construed as matching with the time period of the negotiation (e.g. 1994 United States of America (USA)–Ukraine IIA, Article 6). Likewise, there are differences as to the exact starting point of that period, with some agreements setting it at the date of the events giving rise to the claim (e.g.

2016 Canada–Mongolia, Article 21.2) and others at the date when the dispute arises (e.g. 1993 USA–Croatia IIA, Article 10.3). This issue of timing – and the language used in IIAs more generally – impacts on the purpose that one may assign to this cooling-off requirement or, more precisely, it may lead to assigning a different purpose to this requirement, depending on the drafting of the IIA at hand.

The fourth and fifth conditions share the common objective of avoiding multiple proceedings. Under the former, which derives from fork-in-the-road clauses, disputes can be submitted to arbitration only if they have not first been submitted to the host State domestic courts. The fifth condition makes it necessary for investors to waive their right to continue or to initiate domestic court proceedings in order to access arbitration.

Under the sixth condition, foreign investors can access arbitration only if they submit their dispute to an arbitration setting listed in the IIA at hand and in accordance with the modalities set out therein.

i Limitation Period
Preliminary Remarks

Limitation period clauses are specifically intended to confer some finality and certainty to host States as regards the measures they take by barring foreign investors from invoking their international responsibility at any remote point in time in the future. Article 12.3.d of the 1996 Canada–Venezuela IIA provides a good illustration of such clauses: 'An investor may submit a dispute ... to arbitration ... only if ... not more than three years have elapsed from the date on which the investor first acquired, or should have first acquired, knowledge of the alleged breach and knowledge that the investor has incurred loss or damage.'

Limitation period clauses within IIAs are to be distinguished from 'prescriptive extinction' that exists under public international law, which pertains also to the passage of time and the submission of claims. Under prescriptive extinction, there is no definite time period set, contrary to limitation period clauses which typically provide for a cut-off point of three years. More fundamentally, while the passage of time as such is sufficient to bar access to arbitration under those clauses, it is not so under prescriptive extinction. This was recalled by the Tribunal in *Salini Impregilo S.p.A.* v. *Argentina* (2018, Decision on Jurisdiction and Admissibility, paras. 85–88) in reference to the work of the International Law Commission (ILC) on State Responsibility; in particular, the last ILC Special Rapporteur on the matter – Judge Crawford – explained:

> [A] case will not be held inadmissible on grounds of delay unless the respondent state has been clearly disadvantaged and tribunals have engaged in a flexible weighing of relevant circumstances, including, for example, the conduct of the respondent state and the importance of the right involved. The decisive factor is not the length of elapsed time in itself, but whether the respondent has suffered

prejudice because it could reasonably have expected that the claim would no longer be pursued.[1]

Arbitration tribunals often emphasise that the time period set by limitation period clauses is 'clear and rigid'. In *Grand River Enterprises Six Nations, Ltd* v. *USA*, for example, the Tribunal insisted that it does not suffer any suspension, prolongation or qualification (2006, Decision on Objections to Jurisdiction, para. 29). In *Marvin Feldman* v. *Mexico*, the Tribunal did not construe limitation period clauses as being that 'rigid'. It expressed the view that a formal acknowledgement of a claim made by the competent State organ 'would probably interrupt the running of the period of limitation'. Short of such an acknowledgement, it opined also that other States' behaviours can amount to an interruption or stop States from presenting a regular limitation defence in exceptional circumstances, in particular 'a long, uniform, consistent and effective behavior of the competent State organs which would recognize the existence, and possibly also the amount, of the claim' (2002, Award, para. 63).

Limitation period clauses raise two main issues: (1) what is the *dies a quo*, meaning the date from which the limitation period starts to run; and (2) what is the *dies ad quem*, meaning the date when the limitation period ends. Both are discussed in turn.

– Dies a Quo International investment agreements provide typically that the limitation period starts to run from the date of the first knowledge of the alleged breach and that of the loss or damage incurred. Two sets of remarks can be formulated here that are concerned, first, with the nature of the knowledge and, second, with its object.

The Nature of the Knowledge
IIAs refer to the date on which the investors first acquired knowledge, or the date on which they should have first acquired knowledge. Thereby, they refer not only to 'actual knowledge', but also to 'constructive knowledge', which is characterised by the due diligence expected from investors. This was well explained by the Tribunal in *Grand River Enterprises Six Nations, Ltd* v. *USA*:

> 'Constructive knowledge' of a fact is imputed to a person if by exercise of reasonable care or diligence, the person would have known of that fact. [footnote omitted] Closely associated is the concept of 'constructive notice.' This entails notice that is imputed to a person, either from knowing something that ought to have put the person to further enquiry, or from willfully abstaining from inquiry in order to avoid actual knowledge. (2006, Decision on Objections to Jurisdiction, para. 59)

The Object of the Knowledge
The object of the knowledge under limitation period clauses is typically twofold: (1) the knowledge of the alleged breach; and (2) the knowledge of

[1] J Crawford, *State Responsibility: The General Part* (Cambridge University Press 2013), at 563.

the loss or damage. Three sets of remarks are warranted here, pertaining to each of these objects and to their interplay.

Starting with the latter, it is worth stressing that the knowledge of the alleged breach and the knowledge of the damage or loss are cumulative; in other words, the limitation period starts running when the investor has knowledge of both. This means that in situations in which the dates of knowledge of each of these elements do not coincide, meaning when the date of the first knowledge of the damage is posterior, the period starts running as of this date. For instance, in *Resolute Forest Products Inc. v. Canada*, the Tribunal found that the date of the knowledge of the alleged breach of the IIA national treatment provision and the minimum standard of treatment provision was September 2012 at the latest, but that the investor did not know or could not reasonably have known by December 2012 that it had suffered damage as a result of those alleged breaches. It concluded then that the limitation period started running as of that time and therefore that the investor, which submitted the claim on 30 December 2015, did so on time and was not time-barred (2018, Decision on Jurisdiction and Admissibility, paras. 89, 158, 178–179).

As for the knowledge of the alleged breach, the main issue that has arisen in proceedings pertains to continuing State conduct that amounts to alleged continuing wrongful acts. Under the law of State responsibility, such acts are to be distinguished from instantaneous wrongful acts that have continuing effects. As provided in Article 14 of the 2001 Articles on Responsibility of States for Internationally Wrongful Acts (ARSIWA), the 'breach of an international obligation by an act of a State not having a continuing character occurs at the moment when the act is performed, even if its effects continue', while the 'breach of an international obligation by an act of a State having a continuing character extends over the entire period during which the act continues and remains not in conformity with the international obligation'. A number of investors have argued that the continuing nature of State conduct and of the corresponding alleged wrongful acts had renewed the limitation period, the argument being in substance that each new day during which the wrongful act continues constitutes a new starting point for the limitation period. This line of reasoning was adopted by the Tribunal in *United Parcel Service of America Inc. v. Canada*; it stated: 'The generally applicable ground for our decision is that . . . continuing courses of conduct constitute continuing breaches of legal obligations and renew the limitation period accordingly' (2007, Award on the Merits, para. 28). Since then, this solution has been opposed by arbitration tribunals mainly on the ground of effectiveness. The Tribunal appointed in *Spence International Investments, LLC v. Costa Rica* explained this argument as follows:

> While it may be that a continuing course of conduct constitutes a continuing breach, the Tribunal considers that such conduct cannot without more renew

the limitation period as this would effectively denude the limitation clause of its essential purpose, namely, to draw a line under the prosecution of historic claims. Such an approach would also encourage attempts at the endless parsing up of a claim into ever finer sub-components of breach over time in an attempt to come within the limitation period. This does not comport with the policy choice of the parties to the treaty. While, from a given claimant's perspective, a limitation clause may be perceived as an arbitrary cut off point for the prosecution of a claim, such clauses are a legitimate legal mechanism to limit the proliferation of historic claims, with all the attendant legal and policy challenges and uncertainties that they bring. (2016, Interim Award, para. 208)

Concerning the knowledge of the loss or damage, the relevant date is the one when the investors know or should have known the fact of the loss or damage, not when they know their extent and quantum. As stated by the latter Tribunal, it is neither required nor permitted that claimants wait and see the full extent of the loss or damage before briefing a claim (para. 213). It is well recognised that the reference made in limitation period clauses to the knowledge of the loss or damage 'incurred' covers not only the damage that has actually occurred, but also the damage that the investors know, or should have known, will occur with a reasonable degree of certainty (e.g. *Mobil Investments Canada Inc. v. Canada*, 2018, Decision on Jurisdiction and Admissibility, para. 155).

– **Dies Ad Quem** Turning to the *dies ad quem* of the limitation period, it can be said that its determination does not raise any major issues. Whether directly in the text of the limitation period clause or by reference to other investor–State dispute settlement clauses, IIAs express clearly that the *dies ad quem* is the date of the submission of the dispute to arbitration. Contrary to what is at times argued by the disputing parties, this is neither the date when the notice of intent is submitted to the respondent State, nor the date when the request for arbitration is registered. Regardless of the textual clarity of IIAs on the matter, it would, as noted by the Tribunal in *Ansung Housing Co., Ltd* v. *China*, be unreasonable to make the end date of the limitation period dependent on the uncertain date of registration, which may itself depend on various extraneous factors (2017, Award, para. 119).

ii Consultation Requirement The holding of consultations and negotiations between host States and investors is the most widespread condition provided in IIA practice for the submission of disputes to arbitration. This condition is to be distinguished from the requirement set out in a few IIAs that the States parties enter into conciliation before the dispute can be submitted to arbitration, in case of the failure of the negotiation between the host State and the investor. For instance, Article 10.1 of the 1980 Belgo–Luxembourg Economic Union (BLEU)–Cameroon IIA provides that investment disputes 'shall preferably be resolved amicably, by direct agreement between the parties to the dispute and, failing this, by conciliation between the Contracting Parties through the diplomatic channel'. More fundamentally, it is to be contrasted

with the inter-State prevention mechanism incorporated in some IIAs concluded in the 2010s, in particular by Brazil, which either exclude investors or
leave them only a minor role in the search for an amicable settlement. This
prevention mechanism is examined in Chapter 10.

The holding of consultations and negotiations is an obligation of best efforts
and not of result; this means that the disputing parties are required to do their
utmost to settle the dispute amicably, but that they do not have an obligation to
reach this result as such. This appears clearly in the language used by IIAs that
refer, for instance, to 'an attempt' (e.g. 2016 Canada–Mongolia IIA, Article
21.1) or 'as far as possible' (e.g. 2019 Hong Kong SAR China–United Arab
Emirates (UAE) IIA, Article 8.1). This obligation of best efforts is not an
'empty shell' – as stated by the Tribunal in *Teinver S.A.* v. *Argentina*, disputing
parties are not simply required to wait before the dispute can be submitted to
arbitration (2012, Decision on Jurisdiction, para. 108). Furthermore, disputing
parties shall be guided in this process by good faith. Even if 'good faith' is
expressly mentioned in only some IIAs (e.g. 1986 Netherlands–Turkey IIA,
Article 8.2), this is a requirement that applies to all investor–State negotiations
as it is inherent to the conduct of negotiations under international law in
particular.

In mainstream IIA practice, the time period for consultations and negotiations is six months and starts running typically when the investor notifies the
host State of the dispute. Some IIAs elaborate on the information that
the notice must contain. For instance, the 2013 Mexico–Kuwait IIA lists:
(1) the name and address of the disputing investor; (2) the provisions of the
IIAs conferring protection to investments that have allegedly been breached;
(3) the factual and legal basis of the claim; (4) the kind of investment involved
pursuant to the IIA definition of an investment; and (5) the relief sought and
the approximate amount of damages claimed (Article 10.2). Other IIAs specify
merely that the notice should include detailed information (e.g. 2012 Turkey–
Pakistan IIA, Article 10.1).

Those latter IIAs beg a question that is similar to that raised by the majority
of IIAs that are completely silent on the matter: how detailed must the notice
be? There is no doubt a balance to be struck when answering this question.
Indeed, for negotiations to have any chance of being successful, host States
should be well informed of the subject matter of the disputes and of investors'
claims and requests; at the same time, at this early stage, it cannot be expected
from investors that they provide detailed and soundly articulated claims.
Arbitration tribunals do adopt a balanced approach in answering this question.
For instance, in *Tulip Real Estate Investment and Development Netherlands B.
V.* v. *Turkey*, the Tribunal argued – in agreement with the Tribunal appointed
in *Burlington Resources Inc.* v. *Ecuador* (2010, Decision on Jurisdiction, para.
338) – that it is not required that investors invoke the breach of specific IIA
provisions. It considered as being sufficient that investors inform host States
that they face allegations of treaty breach that may later be invoked to engage

their international responsibility (2013, Decision on Bifurcated Jurisdictional Issue, para. 83). In *Supervisión y Control, S.A.* v. *Costa Rica*, the Tribunal emphasised the importance of proper notice as it viewed it as allowing host States to examine and possibly to resolve the dispute through negotiation (2017, Award, para. 339).

iii Local Remedy Requirement In public international law, there has traditionally been a requirement – as a matter of principle – that private persons exhaust local remedies before their dispute with States can be settled on the international plane. This holds true as regards diplomatic protection analysed in Chapter 10 as well as in international law regimes that give access to private persons to an international court, such as the European Court of Human Rights.

In investor–State arbitration, the logic is the opposite in that the requirement to exhaust local remedies before disputes can be submitted to arbitration is the exception to the norm. This is illustrated by Article 26 of the ICSID Convention, which provides: 'Consent of the parties to arbitration under this Convention shall, unless otherwise stated, be deemed consent to such arbitration to the exclusion of any other remedy. A Contracting State may require the exhaustion of local administrative or judicial remedies as a condition of its consent to arbitration under this Convention.' Only a few agreements, concluded in particular in the early years and decades of IIA practice, have actually set such a condition (e.g. 1981 Romania–Sri Lanka IIA, Article 7.2). In contrast, some IIAs make it explicit that their consent to ICSID jurisdiction implies the renunciation of the requirement to exhaust domestic administrative or juridical remedies (e.g. 1997 Austria–Croatia IIA, Article 9.2.a).

That being said, one finds in a number of IIAs a requirement to pursue local remedies in the host State during a limited period of time before disputes can be submitted to arbitration. This requirement is to be distinguished from the option mentioned in many IIAs for investors to initiate domestic court proceedings as an alternative to arbitration proceedings, as discussed below. This period of time has traditionally ranged from three months (e.g. 1980 United Kingdom–Bangladesh IIA, Article 8.1) to eighteen months (e.g. 1991 Spain–Argentina IIA, Article 10.3.a). As seen in Chapter 10, Indian practice notably – based on the 2015 Indian Model bilateral investment treaty (BIT) – extends this period significantly (2018 Belarus–India IIA, Article 15.2). Interestingly, this latter IIA specifies that this requirement shall not be applicable in cases where the investor can demonstrate that 'there are no available domestic legal remedies capable of reasonably providing relief', something that holds true *mutatis mutandis* for local remedy requirements in general.

This requirement to pursue local remedies during a limited period of time constitutes a middle ground between the two available options laid down in Article 26 of the ICSID Convention quoted above, i.e. exclusion of any remedy other than arbitration and exhaustion of local remedies. By the same token, it can be seen as striking a balance between States' interests and investors' interests. With regard to States, the Tribunal appointed in *Ambiente Ufficio S.p.A.* v. *Argentina* opined that the requirement to pursue local remedies 'serve[s] the purpose of honoring the host State's sovereignty by providing the latter the opportunity to settle a dispute in its own fora before moving on to the international level'. That Tribunal also argued that it offers the opportunity to host States 'to address the allegedly wrongful act within the framework of its own domestic legal system, thus avoiding potential responsibility therefore' (2013, Decision on Jurisdiction and Admissibility, para. 602). Concerning investors' interests, this requirement to pursue local remedies during a limited period of time can be seen, as noted by Arbitrator Thomas in *Hochtief AG* v. *Argentina*, as being preferable to a requirement of exhaustion of local remedies (2011, Decision on Jurisdiction, Separate and Dissenting Opinion, para. 7). Although a limited period of time is preferable from the standpoint of foreign investors, some of them have tried to bypass this requirement by invoking the IIA most-favoured-nation treatment (MFNT) clause, analysed in Chapter 5. Likewise, and as discussed below, some have stressed the limited time period of the local remedy requirement to argue its pointlessness.

iv Fork-in-the-Road While the previous requirement makes arbitration contingent upon the submission of the disputes to local remedies, fork-in-the-road clauses, which are the embodiment of the Latin maxim *una via electa non datur recursus ad alteram*, do the opposite. Under such clauses, the submission of the disputes to the domestic courts of the host States excludes those disputes from later being submitted to arbitration. The IIAs that incorporate such a clause thereby make of the non-submission of the disputes to those domestic courts a condition for submitting those disputes to arbitration. This is formulated as such in those IIAs that provide *mutatis mutandis* that the investor may choose to submit the dispute to arbitration if it 'has not brought the dispute before the courts of justice or administrative tribunal of competent jurisdiction of the Party that is a Party to the dispute' (1986 USA–Egypt IIA, Article 7.3). It is worth noticing that this article also excludes arbitration if the disputes have been submitted to a dispute settlement procedure previously agreed on by the disputing parties. In other IIAs, this condition can be deduced from the possibility of submitting the disputes *either* to the host State domestic court *or* to arbitration (e.g. 1991 Greece–Albania IIA, Article 10.2).

The key issue that arises in practice as regards those fork-in-the-road clauses is the need to determine whether the dispute submitted to an arbitration tribunal is the same dispute as the one previously submitted to the domestic courts of the host State. This issue has been at stake in particular with regard to alleged IIA breaches relating to breaches of contracts, in circumstances where such contractual breaches had already been submitted to domestic courts. To determine this issue, arbitration tribunals have referred mainly to two tests: the triple identity test and the fundamental basis of the claim test.

Traditionally, arbitration tribunals have relied – explicitly or implicitly – on the triple identity test to assess whether the disputes submitted to domestic courts and to arbitration are one and the same. Borrowed from the *res judicata* doctrine, this test concerns the identity of the parties, of the objects and of the causes of action. For instance, in *Ronald S. Lauder* v. *Czech Republic*, the Tribunal explained that the purpose of the fork-in-the-road clause contained in the IIA at hand in that case is to avoid a situation in which the same investment dispute is brought by the same claimant against the same respondent for resolution before, in particular, the domestic courts of the host State and an arbitration tribunal. It stressed that in that case, neither the claimant investor in the arbitration proceedings nor the respondent State was a party to the domestic court proceedings that had been initiated; it also insisted that the domestic courts seised had not been called to decide disputes on the basis of the IIA at stake in the arbitration proceedings (2001, Final Award, paras. 161–163).

The use of the triple identity test to assess whether the disputes are the same has been criticised, notably on the ground of excessive formalism in particular with regard to the identity of the disputing parties. In *H&H Enterprises Investment, Inc.* v. *Egypt*, the Tribunal stressed – in reference to Ole Vosses[2] – that the test defeats the purpose of IIAs and allows form to prevail over substance as proceedings before domestic courts are often brought against State instrumentalities having a separate legal personality and not the States themselves (2014, Award, para. 367). In the same vein, while acknowledging the relevance of the fundamental basis of the claim test in appraising whether the disputes are one and the same, the Sole Arbitrator in *Pantechniki S.A. Contractors & Engineers (Greece)* v. *Albania* insisted that the matter should be approached *in casu* and that general approaches hardly enable tribunals to make a decision on the matter (2009, Award, para. 61).

v Waiver Under the fork-in-the-road clause, the submission of the dispute to the domestic courts of the host State has the radical consequence of depriving investors of accessing arbitration. Under the waiver clause contained in some IIAs, the submission to domestic courts does not have such a consequence – rather it requires investors to waive their right to continue these domestic court proceedings and to initiate any in the future. It is the failure to waive such a right that deprives investors of access to arbitration.

This waiver requirement is illustrated by Article 11.3 of the 1997 Costa Rica–Spain IIA:

> Once an investor has submitted the dispute to an arbitral tribunal, the award shall be final. If the investor has submitted the dispute to a competent court of the Party

---

[2] J Ole Vosse, *The Impact of Investment Treaties on Contracts between Host States and Foreign Investors* (Martinus Nijhoff 2011), at 291.

in whose territory the investment was made, it may, in addition, resort to the arbitral tribunals referred to in this article, if such national court has not issued a judgment. In the latter case, the investor shall adopt any measures that are required for the purpose of permanently desisting from the court case then underway.

Contrary to this IIA, a number of agreements do not refer to the requirement to waive the right to continue proceedings before the domestic courts to which the *dispute* has been submitted or to submit the *dispute* to domestic courts in the future, but instead contain a waiver requirement with respect to the *measures* which allegedly constitute a breach and which ground the dispute. For instance, the 2018 United States–Mexico–Canada Agreement (USMCA) provides:

> No claim shall be submitted to arbitration under this Annex unless . . . the notice of arbitration is accompanied (i) for claims submitted to arbitration under Article 3.1(a) (Submission of a Claim to Arbitration), by the claimant's written waiver; and (ii) for claims submitted to arbitration under Article 3.1(b) (Submission of a Claim to Arbitration), by the claimant's and the enterprise's written waivers, of any right to initiate or continue before any court or administrative tribunal under the law of an Annex Party, or any other dispute settlement procedures, any proceeding with respect to any *measure* alleged to constitute a breach referred to in Article 3 (Submission of a Claim to Arbitration). (Annex 14-D, Article 5.1.e.ii; emphasis added)

One can note that the USMCA specifies that the waiver does not concern domestic court proceedings only, but, more generally, any dispute settlement procedures.

It is also worth stressing that, as an exception to this principle, the IIAs that contain a waiver clause usually authorise investors to initiate or continue proceedings before domestic courts – which do not involve the payment of monetary damages – *mutatis mutandis* in order to seek interim injunctive relief intended to preserve their rights and interests during the arbitration proceedings (e.g. 2018 Comprehensive and Progressive Agreement for Trans-Pacific Partnership (CPTPP), Article 9.21.3).

As illustrated by the award rendered in *Supervision y Control, S.A.* v. *Costa Rica*, those waiver clauses that refer to 'dispute' – and not to 'measure' – raise the same issue as that discussed in relation to fork-in-the-road clauses – namely the determination of whether the dispute submitted to domestic courts is the same as that submitted to arbitration tribunals (2017, Award, paras. 293–335).

But waiver clauses also raise specific issues, in particular with regard to the appraisal of whether investors have indeed waived their rights. As illustrated by the USMCA quoted above, this issue derives from the fact that the obligation to waive has often both a formal dimension and a substantive dimension. The latter consists of the abstention from initiating proceedings and the active withdrawal from ongoing proceedings. The former refers to the written waiver to be submitted together with the notice of arbitration. As regards this formal requirement, tribunals have considered that the written waiver must be clear, explicit, categorical and comprehensive. This led the Tribunal appointed in *The Renco Group Inc.* v. *Peru* to consider that the investor had failed to meet this formal requirement because it had included a reservation of rights in its waiver concerning the submission to another forum in case the tribunal would have declined to hear any claims on jurisdictional or admissibility grounds (2016, Partial Award on Jurisdiction, paras. 78–83). This Tribunal stressed in this respect that 'formal invalidity is as critical as material invalidity' (para. 136).

vi Access to Specific Arbitration Settings International investment agreements do not confer general access to arbitration – investors must submit their disputes to the specific arbitration fora listed, according to various formulae and combinations, in the IIAs. As explained in Chapter 11, there exist various such fora, such as ICSID or the Arbitration Institute of the Stockholm Chamber of Commerce (SCC). International investment agreement practice also displays the possibility of submitting disputes to arbitration tribunals operating 'autonomously' outside such fora.

It is important to stress that when IIAs provide for a variety of arbitration settings, the determination of the setting may not be left to the discretion of the investors, but rather may be dependent on a series of factors. Typically, it may be subject to an agreement between the disputing parties. In case no agreement can be reached, the IIAs that require such an agreement typically specify the arbitration setting in which the dispute shall be settled (e.g. 1995 United Kingdom–Turkmenistan IIA, Article 8.2). The determination of the arbitration setting may also be dependent on the ratification of the ICSID Convention by IIA States parties. For instance, Article 8.2 of the 1994 Barbados–Venezuela IIA provides that disputes shall be submitted to ICSID under the Additional Facility mechanism as long as Venezuela has not become a Party to the ICSID Convention. It is interesting to note that after having become a Party to that Convention, Venezuela denounced it with effect from 25 July 2012. In *Venezuela US, S.R.L.* v. *Venezuela*, the Tribunal considered that this sequence – ratification and denunciation – is not contemplated by this Article 8.2, which focuses on the pre-ratification period, and therefore that the access to ICSID under the Additional Facility mechanism is not possible after the denunciation (2016, Interim Award on Jurisdiction, paras. 85–86).

b The Object and Nature of the Conditions

With regard to some of the above-mentioned conditions, in particular the resort to local remedies, there have been fierce debates in investor–State arbitration as to the consequences deriving from the failure of foreign investors to comply with them. At the core of these debates, one finds two main – intertwined but distinct – issues. The first is whether these conditions are a matter of jurisdiction or admissibility. At stake in this characterisation is the question as to whether – as a matter of principle – they shall be conceived of as being constitutive of States' consent or as being merely conditions pertaining to the implementation of consent. The second of these issues concerns whether, and under what circumstances, these conditions can be bypassed, with or without reliance on the IIA MFNT clause.

In public international law, it is well recognised that such conditions are constitutive of the consent of the disputing parties to the jurisdiction of international courts and tribunals. The ICJ stressed, for instance, that the negotiation requirement that can be found in compromissory clauses conferring jurisdiction to the Court and to other international courts and tribunals plays an important function in that it indicates the limit of consent given by States (*Case Concerning Application of the International Convention on the Elimination of All Forms of Racial Discrimination (Georgia v. Russia)*, 2011, Judgment, para. 131). More generally, the Court has argued:

> The Court recalls in this regard that its jurisdiction is based on the consent of the parties and is confined to the extent accepted by them ... When that consent is expressed in a compromissory clause in an international agreement, any conditions to which such consent is subject must be regarded as constituting the limits thereon. The Court accordingly considers that the examination of such conditions relates to its jurisdiction and not to the admissibility of the application. (*Case Concerning Armed Activities on the Territory of the Congo (New Application: 2002) (Democratic Republic of the Congo v. Rwanda)*, 2006, Judgment, para. 88)

Some IIAs address this issue. For instance, the 2016 Canada–Mongolia IIA provides that States parties consent to the submission of claims to arbitration in accordance with the terms of the Agreement, and it specifies that the failure to meet any of the conditions precedent to this submission nullifies consent (Article 24.1). Arbitration practice displays diverging approaches and views on the matter – as noted by the Tribunal in *Tulip Real Estate Investment and Development Netherlands B.V.* v. *Turkey* with regard to negotiation, the *jurisprudence* is in fact very much *non constante* (2013, Decision on Bifurcated Jurisdictional Issue, para. 57). Three cases and the views adopted by the majority of the Tribunals therein illustrate this *jurisprudence non constante*.

In *Daimler Financial Services AG* v. *Argentina*, the majority of the Tribunal aligned with the public international law approach and regarded those conditions as jurisdictional requirements. It stated:

> All BIT-based dispute resolution provisions, on the other hand, are by their very nature jurisdictional. The mere fact of their inclusion in a bilateral treaty indicates that they are reflections of the sovereign agreement of two States – not the mere administrative creation of arbitrators. They set forth the conditions under which an investor–State tribunal may exercise jurisdiction with the

contracting state parties' consent, much in the same way in which legislative acts confer jurisdiction upon domestic courts. (2012, Award, para. 193)

While acknowledging the public international law roots of the conditions, the majority of the Tribunal appointed in *Casinos Austria* v. *Argentina* claimed that they shall be approached in a less 'formalistic manner' in the context of investor–State arbitration, as compared to inter-State dispute settlement. It grounded that claim mainly by stressing the object and purpose of IIAs, meaning the promotion and protection of foreign investment for the development of economic cooperation between States, and also the view following which investors 'cannot be expected [– contrary to States –] to be accustomed to the formalities of inter-State communication and inter-State dispute settlement'. As a result, while stating that the conditions are in principle mandatory, it argued that arbitration tribunals shall construe them less formalistically and accord greater flexibility to the disputing parties than the ICJ does, unless the conditions are formulated clearly and unmistakably to require the same formalistic approach (Decision on Jurisdiction, 2018, paras. 271–276).

In *Ickale Insaat Limited Sirketi* v. *Turkmenistan*, the majority of the Tribunal – when characterising the local remedy requirement – considered that the conditions pertain to the implementation of consent, not to its existence; it explained:

> The provision does not concern the issue of whether the State parties have given their consent to arbitrate – they have – but rather the issue of *how* that consent is to be invoked by a foreign investor; as an issue of 'how' rather than 'whether', it must be considered a matter of procedure and not as an element of the State parties' consent. Consequently, any objection raised on the basis of alleged non-compliance by an investor with any of the required procedural steps must be characterized as an objection to the admissibility of the claim rather than as an objection to the tribunal's jurisdiction. (2016, Award, para. 242)

In connection to this issue, it has been debated whether, and if so, under what circumstances, those conditions can be bypassed, particularly in relation to the local remedy requirement. The reasoning of tribunals on this issue is obviously impacted by the specifics of each case. However, in some cases, they seem also to have been influenced by the views of the tribunals and arbitrators on the rationale and usefulness of these conditions.

For instance, in *Hochtief AG* v. *Argentina*, the majority of the Tribunal considered the obligation to resort to domestic remedies for a period of eighteen months under the applicable IIA as being potentially 'pointless' (2011, Decision on Jurisdiction, para. 51). Likewise, when discussing the MFNT clause in relation to the *Emilio Agustin Maffezini* v. *Spain* case, the Tribunal appointed in *Plama Consortium Limited* v. *Bulgaria* stated: 'The case concerned a curious requirement that during the first eighteen months the dispute be tried in the local courts. The present Tribunal sympathizes with a tribunal that attempts to neutralize such a provision that is nonsensical from a practical point of view' (2005, Decision on Jurisdiction, para. 224).

Such views were denounced, from a 'deontological' point of view, by Arbitrator Thomas in *Hochtief AG* v. *Argentina*, who considered that it 'is not the place of international tribunals to second-guess the choices of the States Parties even when one can envisage instances where such choices might lead to inefficiency and additional cost to a would-be claimant' (2011, Decision on Jurisdiction, Separate and Dissenting Opinion, para. 10). From a legal point of view, the Tribunal appointed in *Daimler Financial Services AG* v. *Argentina* criticised those views as follows:

> [T]he requirement for waiving treaty-based jurisdictional pre-requisites in international law is not nonsensicality but futility. Sovereign States are free to agree to any treaty provisions they so choose – whether concerning substantive commitments or dispute resolution provisions or otherwise – provided these provisions are not futile and are not otherwise contrary to peremptory norms of international law. (2012, Award, para. 198)

Futility and also ineffectiveness are usually not addressed in IIAs; only a few agreements deal with these matters, such as the 2018 USMCA, which provides in particular that the requirement under that Agreement to resort to the competent court or administrative tribunal is not applicable to the extent that such resort is 'obviously futile or manifestly ineffective' (Annex 14-D, Articles 5.1.a and 5.1.b, Footnote 24). The failure of most IIAs to address the matter has not prevented disputing parties and tribunals from discussing and relying on futility. This reliance has been justified in particular by an analogy with the law of diplomatic protection, and futility has been introduced in their reasoning on the basis notably of Article 31.3.c of the 1969 Vienna Convention on the Law of Treaties (VCLT), which is analysed in Chapter 12. In this respect, it is worth referring to Article 15.a of the 2006 Draft Articles on Diplomatic Protection, prepared by the ILC, which codifies this exception as follows: 'Local remedies do not need to be exhausted where … there are no reasonably available local remedies to provide effective redress, or the local remedies provide no reasonable possibility of such redress.' The Commentaries attached to these Draft Articles specify the threshold to be applied to the futility exception as follows:

> [I]t is not sufficient for the injured person to show that the possibility of success is low or that further appeals are difficult or costly. The test is not whether a successful outcome is likely or possible, but whether the municipal system of the respondent State is reasonably capable of providing effective relief. This

must be determined in the context of the local law and the prevailing circumstances. (at 48)

Relying on these Draft Articles on Diplomatic Protection, the majority of the Tribunal in *Ambiente Ufficio S.p.A.* v. *Argentina* reached the conclusion that having recourse to the Argentinian courts would have been futile. It considered indeed, in light of the jurisprudence of the Supreme Court of Argentina and the circumstances of the case, that this would not have offered a reasonable possibility to obtain effective redress for the claimants (2013, Decision on Jurisdiction and Admissibility, para. 620).

14.3.1.2 The Subject Matter of the Disputes Covered by the Offer

The subject matter of disputes that can be submitted to arbitration varies across IIAs. Three main categories of offers to arbitrate can be singled out in this respect: (1) offer to arbitrate the disputes relating to an investment; (2) offer to arbitrate the disputes relating to investment agreements, authorisations and IIA substantive provisions; and (3) offer to arbitrate the disputes relating to IIA substantive provisions.

a Disputes in Relation to an Investment

The first category of IIAs contain an offer to arbitrate concerning the disputes arising between an investor of one State party and another State party in connection with an investment. Such an offer can be seen as having a broad scope going beyond the disputes arising from the alleged violation of IIA substantive obligations. For instance, in *SGS Société Générale de Surveillance S. A.* v. *Paraguay*, the Tribunal opined that the ordinary meaning of Article 9.1 of the 1992 Switzerland–Paraguay IIA – referring to 'disputes relating to investments' – gives jurisdiction to hear alleged breaches of contracts (2010, Decision on Jurisdiction, para. 129). On the other hand, the Tribunal appointed in *SGS Société Générale de Surveillance S.A.* v. *Pakistan* adopted the opposite approach as it considered that the offer made in the 1995 Switzerland–Pakistan IIA – which also refers to 'disputes relating to investments' (Article. 9.1) – could not 'be read as vesting this Tribunal with jurisdiction over claims resting *ex hypothesi* exclusively on contract' (2003, Decision on Jurisdiction, para. 161).

Such offers to arbitrate vary with regard to who can initiate arbitration. Some agreements limit this possibility to investors (e.g. 2015 Macedonia–Denmark IIA, Article 9.2). Other agreements do not provide for such a limitation, but instead offer the opportunity to either disputing party to refer the dispute to an arbitration tribunal (e.g. 1995 Peru–Norway IIA, Article 9.2). Thereby, such provisions leave open the possibility for host States not only to submit counterclaims – which are analysed in Chapter 11 – in their capacity as respondents, but also to act as claimants against foreign investors.

b Disputes Relating to Investment Agreements, Authorisations and IIA Substantive Provisions

Like the 1998 USA–Lithuania IIA, some agreements provide *mutatis mutandis* that the disputes that may be submitted to arbitration tribunals can relate to (1) an investment agreement concluded between either State party and a national or company of the other State party; (2) an investment authorisation granted by either State party's foreign investment authority to a national or company of the other State party; or (3) an alleged breach of any right conferred or created by the IIA with respect to an investment (Article 6.1). In other agreements, the offer covers disputes relating only to items (2) and (3) (e.g. 1986 Netherlands–Turkey IIA, Article 8.1).

c Disputes Relating to IIA Substantive Provisions

As regards those IIAs that limit the scope of the offer to arbitrate to disputes arising out of the alleged breach of the substantive obligations in the agreements, distinctions can be made between various formulae that impact on the exact scope of the offer. In order to appraise this scope, attention must be paid not only to the investor–State dispute settlement provisions as such, but also, depending on the IIA at hand, to other provisions therein.

Starting with the broadest scope conferred to the offer to arbitrate, most of the IIAs that form part of that third category, such as the 2015 Japan–Ukraine IIA, provide *mutatis mutandis* that the following can be submitted to arbitration:

> [A] dispute between a Contracting Party and an investor of the other Contracting Party that has incurred loss or damage by reason of, or arising out of, an alleged breach of any obligation of the former Contracting Party under this Agreement with respect to the investor of that other Contracting Party or its investments in the Area of the former Contracting Party. (Article 18.1)

As it appears, the scope of the offer to arbitrate contained in those IIAs extends to alleged breaches of all IIA substantive obligations binding upon States. It is worth noticing that the mention made of 'loss' and 'damage' suggests that these elements must exist for a dispute to fall within the scope of the offer and thereby for a tribunal to have jurisdiction.

Another group of IIAs limit the scope of the host States' obligations, the alleged violation of which can generate an investor–State dispute that may be submitted to arbitration. Typically, they list the obligations that are excluded from the scope of the offer to arbitrate. For instance, Article 20.1 of the 2016 Canada–Mongolia IIA provides:

> An investor of a Party may submit to arbitration under this Section a claim that: (1) the other Party has breached an obligation under Section B (Substantive Obligations), other than an obligation under paragraph 3 of Article 8 (Senior Management, Boards of Directors and Entry of Personnel), Article 12 (Transparency), 14 (Corporate Social Responsibility) or 15 (Health, Safety and

Environmental Measures); and (2) the investor has incurred loss or damage by reason of, or arising out of, that breach.

The IIAs that form part of another subcategory do not limit the scope of the offer to arbitrate by excluding some obligations, but instead by excluding specific sectors, measures or situations. For instance, Article 10.2 of the 2014 Burkina Faso–Singapore IIA expressly states that arbitration is not open to 'any dispute concerning any measure adopted or maintained or any treatment accorded to investors or investments by a Party in respect of tobacco or tobacco-related products [footnote omitted] that is aimed at protecting or promoting human health'.

Other IIAs combine the two above-mentioned approaches, adopting a restrictive approach as regards specific sectors, measures or situations by limiting the scope of the offer to arbitrate with respect to disputes arising out of the alleged violation of specific obligations within the agreements. This is well illustrated in relation to financial services by the IIA adopted by Canada and Hong Kong SAR China, Article 22 of which limits the offer to arbitrate to disputes arising from the alleged violation of the provisions on expropriation, transfers and denial of benefits. Such an approach is also typical of taxation measures (e.g. 1990 USA–Poland IIA, Article 6.2).

Finally and more radically, a few IIAs limit the scope of the offer to arbitrate to disputes relating to one treaty provision, typically expropriation. This has traditionally been the case in the IIA practice of China and that of the Union of Soviet Socialist Republics (USSR). More precisely, those agreements provide *mutatis mutandis* that it is open to either party to initiate arbitration proceedings with regard to disputes 'involving the amount of compensation for expropriation' (e.g. 1994 Peru–China IIA, Article 8.3).

As for disputes arising from the alleged violations of the other provisions of those IIAs, some agreements provide that those disputes can be submitted only to the domestic courts of the host States – as is also open to disputes involving the amount of compensation for expropriation (e.g. 1993 China–Laos IIA, Article 8.2). In other agreements, those disputes can be submitted to arbitration if the disputing parties (e.g. 1994 Peru–China IIA, Article 8.3) or the IIA States parties (e.g. 1998 China–Yemen IIA, Article 10.2 (as translated in *Beijing Urban Construction Group Co. Ltd* v. *Yemen*, 2017, Decision on Jurisdiction, para. 50)) so agree; they can also be submitted to the domestic courts of the host States – something that is again also possible as regards disputes involving the amount of compensation for expropriation.

Many of all these IIAs include a fork-in-the-road clause, as examined above. As a result of the operation of this clause, disputes involving the amount of compensation for expropriation first submitted to host States' domestic courts cannot be submitted to arbitration tribunals.

In a number of cases, arbitration tribunals have had to decide on the meaning of 'dispute involving the amount of compensation for expropriation' or 'dispute relating to the amount of compensation for expropriation'. At stake in these proceedings has been the question as to whether the jurisdiction of tribunals is limited to the issue of compensation, or whether it covers expropriation more generally. Actually, arbitration practice is split on the matter, although a majority of tribunals have favoured an interpretation under which expropriation is covered.

Those tribunals in the majority have based their findings on the text of the offer to arbitrate, stressing notably that 'involving' is inclusive rather than exclusive – contrary to 'limited to' – (e.g. *Sanum Investments Limited* v. *Laos*, 2013, Award on Jurisdiction, para. 329), or on the object and purpose of the applicable IIA (e.g. *Beijing Urban Construction Group Co. Ltd* v. *Yemen*, 2017, Decision on Jurisdiction, para. 92). But at the core of their reasoning is mainly the notion of effectiveness – which is discussed in Chapter 12 – in connection with the IIA fork-in-the-road clause. The line of reasoning adopted is, *mutatis mutandis*, as follows. Restricting arbitration to claims relating to the amount of compensation implies that foreign investors must seek a finding of expropriation before the domestic courts of host States, which requires them to address the issue of compensation; because of the fork-in-the-road clause, this means that investors are then barred from resorting to arbitration with respect to the amount of compensation. This is seen as depriving the offer to arbitrate of its effectiveness. In that sense, the Tribunal appointed in *Beijing Urban Construction Group Co. Ltd* v. *Yemen* stressed that such reasoning leads to the conclusion that investors never have access to arbitration, unless host States agree to it by conceding their liability (para. 84). Such a view was also expressed by the Singapore Court of Appeal in *Sanum Investments Limited* v. *Laos* (2016, Judgment, para. 133).

The incorporation or non-incorporation of a fork-in-the-road clause in the IIAs applicable in the relevant cases has been seen, in particular by the Tribunal in *Sanum Investments Limited* v. *Laos*, as the explanation for the diverging interpretations made by arbitration tribunals up until 2013 (2013, Award on Jurisdiction, para. 340). But it is worth noting in this respect that the Tribunal appointed in *China Heilongjiang International Economic & Technical Cooperative Corp.* v. *Mongolia* concluded that its jurisdiction was limited to the compensation issue under the applicable IIA, while that agreement in fact contains a fork-in-the-road clause. It argued in particular that in the course of prior domestic judicial proceedings where investors seek to protect their investment against measures having an effect equivalent to expropriation, they can reserve the issue of compensation for an out-of-court procedure, thereby neutralising the fork-in-the-road clause. By the same token, this Tribunal opined that to limit the scope of arbitration to the amount of compensation does not deprive the arbitration clause of legal effect in so far as arbitration is available where the dispute is limited to the amount of compensation for a proclaimed expropriation (2017, Award, paras. 448–449).

14.3.1.3 The Temporal Scope of the Disputes Covered by the Offer

Three main categories of IIAs can be identified with regard to the issue of the temporal scope of the disputes covered by the offer to arbitrate.

The IIAs that form part of the first category inform the temporal scope of the disputes covered by the offer to arbitrate by making it explicit that they do not apply to the disputes arising prior to their entry into force (e.g. 2001 BLEU–Zambia IIA, Article 12). The IIAs belonging to the second and third categories do not provide for this.

With regard to the second category of agreements, the subject matter of the disputes encompassed by the offer to arbitrate helps to some extent to determine the temporal scope of the disputes covered. The offer contained in those IIAs links the disputes that may be submitted to arbitration to specific instruments and obligations.

As discussed above, some link them to IIA substantive provisions only, like the 2015 Japan–Ukraine IIA, which provides that the following may be submitted to arbitration:

> [A] dispute between a Contracting Party and an investor of the other Contracting Party that has incurred loss or damage by reason of, or arising out of, an alleged breach of any obligation of the former Contracting Party under this Agreement with respect to the investor of that other Contracting Party or its investments in the Area of the former Contracting Party. (Article 18.1)

Because, as seen in Chapter 2, investors and their investments are protected by IIA substantive provisions against host States' conduct only as of the entry into force of the agreements, this entry into force constitutes the starting point of the temporal scope of the disputes covered by those offers to arbitrate, as do the termination and more precisely the end of the sunset clause period – also discussed in that chapter – with regard to its endpoint. Arbitration tribunals have no jurisdiction *ratione temporis* over disputes arising from the host States' conduct occurring prior to the entry into force of the agreements; this is so even if the disputes relating to conduct prior to the entry into force arise after the entry into force of the agreements. As noted by the Tribunal in *Chevron Corporation (USA)* v. *Ecuador*, such conduct can constitute merely a factual background that provides information about the conduct that post-dates the entry into force (2008, Interim Award, para. 283). The only exception is where that conduct, typically comprising continuing acts as opposed to instantaneous acts, extends beyond the entry into force of the agreements. It is important to distinguish such continuing acts from instantaneous acts occurring prior to the entry into force which have simply continuing effects or consequences that extend after the entry into force.

These considerations also apply in relation to the disputes relating to the alleged violation of IIA substantive provisions that are covered by the offer to arbitrate contained in those agreements that adopt a broader approach in the sense that, as exemplified by the above-mentioned 1998 USA–Lithuania IIA, they cover not only such disputes, but also those relating to investment authorisations and agreements. That being said, these do not apply to those two latter subject matter categories of disputes, nor to some of the disputes that are content-wise covered by the offer to arbitrate contained within the IIAs that form part of the third category of IIAs discussed in this subsection.

Italian treaty practice is very representative of the IIAs that form part of this category of agreements. For instance, Article 9 of the 2001 Italy–Ecuador IIA refers merely to '[a]ny dispute which may arise between one of the Contracting Parties and the investors of the other Contracting Party on investments'. No doubt, with regard to the disputes arising from the alleged breach of the IIA substantive provisions, the object of such disputes delineates the temporal scope of the disputes that are covered by the offer to arbitrate along the same lines as explained above. On the other hand, the object of the disputes does not have such an effect when it concerns, for instance, the alleged breach of customary international law (CIL). As for such breaches by State conduct committed prior to the entry into force of the agreements, it is a matter for discussion whether the disputes fall within the temporal scope of the disputes covered by the offer and therefore within the jurisdiction of arbitration tribunals.

14.3.2 Investment

Preliminary Remarks

Regardless of the issue – discussed below – as to whether the notion of investment has objective characteristics under IIAs and the ICSID Convention, it proves to be difficult to grasp from a conceptual point of view. This is notably due to the fact that, as noted by Salacuse,[3] this notion refers both to the process by which an investment is made and to the asset acquired as a result of that process. It is also worth noting, from a terminological point of view, that the expression 'foreign property' was originally preferred to the term 'investment'; this is well illustrated by the title given to the Draft Convention prepared at the Organisation for Economic Co-operation and Development in the 1960s: the Draft Convention on the Protection of Foreign Property. This derives in particular from the fact that foreigners owned mainly tangible properties or bonds issued by developing States in the nineteenth and the early twentieth centuries. Since then, one has witnessed a diversification of the forms of foreign investment – as seen in the following subsection, IIA States parties have as a result adopted broad definitions of 'investment' in keeping with these economic realities. From a legal

---

[3] JW Salacuse, *The Law of Investment Treaties* (2nd ed, Oxford University Press 2015), at 26.

point of view, the way 'investment' is construed in IIAs is, as explained above, relevant to the appraisal of the special jurisdiction of tribunals and, more generally, the application of the agreements. The meaning of 'investment' under Article 25 of the ICSID Convention is also relevant here in relation to the appraisal of the general jurisdiction of tribunals operating under the ICSID Convention Arbitration Rules. 'Investment' is therefore analysed below in relation to IIAs and the ICSID Convention.

14.3.2.1 'Investment' under International Investment Agreements

The concept of *asset* constitutes the cornerstone of the definition of 'investment' in IIA practice. Yet, to be considered an investment covered by an IIA, an asset must meet a series of conditions, the exact combination of which varies across treaty practice. This requires us to focus in turn on the types of assets and the various conditions listed in IIAs. For didactic purposes, the following subsections shall inquire into the definition and notion of investment by focusing on assets individually considered. It goes without saying that economic realities and the cases submitted to arbitration demonstrate that what is at stake is usually investment operations that comprise a plurality of assets.

a The Types of Assets

Almost all IIAs specify the types of assets that are to be considered as investments covered by the agreements, subject to the fulfilment of the conditions that they set out. More precisely, they adopt either of these two main approaches: (1) an asset-based approach providing an exhaustive list; (2) an asset-based approach providing a non-exhaustive list.

The first approach provides two kinds of exhaustive list: one that details the assets that may qualify as covered investments, and another that details the assets excluded as a matter of principle from the coverage of the agreements. This approach is well illustrated by the 2013 Canada–Benin IIA, Article 1 of which provides that 'investment' means:

    (a) an enterprise;
    (b) a share, stock or other form of equity participation in an enterprise;
    (c) a bond, debenture or other debt instrument of an enterprise;
    (d) a loan to an enterprise;
    (e) notwithstanding subparagraphs (c) and (d) above, a loan to or debt security issued by a financial institution is an investment only where the loan or debt security is treated as regulatory capital by the Contracting Party in whose territory the financial institution is located;
    (f) an interest in an enterprise that entitles the owner to share in income or profits of the enterprise;
    (g) an interest in an enterprise that entitles the owner to share in the assets of that enterprise on dissolution;

(h) an interest arising from the commitment of capital or other resources in the territory of a Contracting Party to economic activity in that territory, such as under: (i) a contract involving the presence of an investor's property in the territory of the Contracting Party, including a turnkey or construction contract, or a concession, or (ii) a contract where remuneration depends substantially on the production, revenues or profits of an enterprise;

(i) intellectual property rights; and

(j) any other tangible or intangible, movable or immovable, property and related property rights acquired in the expectation of or used for the purpose of economic benefit or other business purpose;

Article 1 of this Agreement goes on by providing that 'investment' does not mean:

(k) a claim to money that arises solely from: (i) a commercial contract for the sale of a good or service by a national or enterprise in the territory of a Contracting Party to an enterprise in the territory of the other Contracting Party, or (ii) the extension of credit in connection with a commercial transaction, such as trade financing; or

(l) any other claim to money, that does not involve the kinds of interests set out in subparagraphs (a) to (j).

The IIAs that adopt the second approach begin typically by specifying that an investment is 'any kind of asset' and then provide a non-exhaustive list of assets that usually fall – subject to variations – within at least one these five categories: (1) movable and immovable property; (2) interests in companies; (3) claims to money and claims under a contract having a financial value; (4) intellectual property rights; and (5) business concessions under public law.[4] This approach is well illustrated by Article 1.1 of the 2003 Ethiopia-France IIA:

The term 'investment' means every kind of assets, such as property, rights and interests of whatever nature and in particular though not exclusively:

(a) movable and immovable property as well as any other right in rem such as mortgages, liens, usufructs, pledges and similar rights;

(b) shares, stocks, premium on share and other forms of participation, including minority or indirect forms, in a company, and rights derived there from;

(c) bonds, debentures, loans and other forms of debt, and rights derived there from;

(d) claims to money and claims to performance having an economic value;

(e) intellectual, commercial and industrial property rights such as copyrights, patents, licenses, trademarks, industrial models, technical processes, know-how, trade names and goodwill;

---

[4] OECD, 'Definition of Investor and Investment in International Investment Agreement' (2008), available at www.oecd.org.

(f) concessions conferred by law or under contract, including concessions to search for, cultivate, extract or exploit natural resources.

Any alteration of the form in which assets are invested shall not affect their qualifications as investments provided that such alteration is not in conflict with the legislation of the Contracting Party in the territory or in the maritime area of which the investment is made.

Some IIAs, while adopting this approach, borrow from the first approach the provision of a list that excludes specific assets from the scope of the agreements. This practice can be linked to the debates that have arisen in arbitration practice with respect in particular to portfolio investments and sovereign debts; it reflects the will of States to avoid specific assets from being considered as investments covered by the agreements they conclude. For instance, the 2017 Israel–Japan IIA provides that, 'for the avoidance of doubt', an investment does not include 'public debt' (Article 1.a). By the same token, the 2016 Morocco–Nigeria IIA excludes as a matter of principle 'debt securities issued by a government', 'loans to a government' and 'portfolio investments' from the scope of the covered investments (Article 1). Among those exclusions, IIAs have also traditionally listed the claims to money arising solely from commercial contracts for the sale of goods or services (e.g. 2015 UAE–Mauritius IIA, Article 1.2.d.i). A few additional remarks are warranted here.

First, it is worth noting that some IIAs specify that both 'direct investments' and 'indirect investments' are covered by the agreements. For instance, Article 1.1 of the 2016 Japan–Iran IIA provides that the 'term "investment" refers to every kind of asset, invested directly or indirectly by an investor of a Contracting Party'. A few of those agreements specify what an indirect investment is – for instance, the 2003 China–Germany IIA provides that '"[i]nvested indirectly" means invested by an investor of one Contracting Party through a company which is fully or partially owned by the investor and having its seat in the territory of the other Contracting Party' (Protocol, Ad Article 1.b).

Second, one can notice some diversity as to the language used by those IIAs, which refer, for instance, to 'any kind of asset *invested*' (e.g. 2016 Japan–Iran IIA, Article 1.1; emphasis added), 'every kind of asset *owned* or *controlled*' (e.g. 1996 Canada–Venezuela IIA, Article 1.f; emphasis added), or 'every kind of asset *invested, established* or *acquired*' (e.g. 2011 India–Lithuania IIA, Article 1.1; emphasis added). These terminological variations should not be overlooked – indeed, they can play a role in the determination of the scope of the assets that may qualify as covered investments subject to the fulfilment of the conditions set out in the agreements. For instance, in *Flemingo DutyFree Shop Private Limited* v. *Poland*, the Tribunal relied notably on the reference made to 'acquired' in the investment's definition of the IIA at hand to confirm its interpretation that the acquisition of shares falls within that scope (2016, Award, para. 306). Likewise, it stressed that the inclusion of the term 'acquired' in the definition leads to the conclusion that the IIA covers those investments that had been made in the territory of an IIA State party and subsequently been acquired by investors of the other State party (para. 324).

The two remarks mentioned above are relevant – to a lesser or greater extent – for the IIAs that adopt the first approach (i.e. the asset-based approach providing an exhaustive list). This appears when one links the definition of 'investment' to other definitions provided for by the agreements. For instance, the Canada–Benin IIA defines 'covered investment' 'with respect to a Contracting Party' as 'an investment in its territory of an investor of the other Contracting Party existing on the date of coming into force of this Agreement, as well as an investment *made* or *acquired* subsequently' (emphasis added); likewise, it defines 'investment of an investor of a Contracting Party' as 'an investment owned or controlled *directly* or *indirectly* by an investor of that Contracting Party' (emphasis added (Article 1)).

Finally, one can single out the last paragraph of Article 1.1 of the 2003 Ethiopia–France IIA quoted above, which illustrates those IIAs that provide that changes in the form in which the investment has been made, or alterations of the form in which assets are invested, do not exclude them from the scope of the agreements. That being said, it is worth noting that many of those IIAs require that this alteration does not conflict with the host States' domestic law (e.g. 2003 Ethiopia–France IIA, Article 1.1) and/or the provisions of the agreements (e.g. 2016 Argentina–Qatar IIA, Article 1.6).

By the same token, some IIAs specify that any change in the form in which assets are reinvested does not affect their character as an investment (e.g. 2008 Finland–Kenya IIA, Article 1.1). Likewise, 'returns' are typically covered under those IIAs (e.g. 2009 Hong Kong SAR China–Finland, Article 1.c).

b The Types of Conditions

Preliminary Remarks
To be characterised as covered investments, assets listed in IIAs, or in any case not excluded, must meet certain conditions. Those conditions are fourfold in treaty practice – these pertain to: (1) the characteristics of an investment; (2) a legality requirement as well as (3) geographical and (4) temporal requirements. Each of these is analysed in turn. It is worth noting at the outset that the first and second of these conditions are not provided in all IIAs.

Depending on the IIA at hand, these conditions, or some of them, are to be found in the definition of 'investment', or in a specific provision pertaining to the IIA's scope of application. Regardless of their exact 'location' within IIAs, it is worth stressing that variations exist in treaty practice as to the role of these conditions in the characterisation of the assets. In particular, if all have the effect of ultimately leading to the inclusion or the exclusion of assets from the coverage of IIAs, some are construed in IIA practice as pertaining essentially to the characterisation of assets as *investments*, typically investment's characteristics, while others are conceived of as playing mainly a role in the characterisation of assets, considered as investments, as being *covered* investments, typically temporal and geographical requirements. But what is more, from one IIA to the other, the same condition can be construed as playing either role – for example, the geographical requirement. All of this explains the variations in the approach and terminology adopted across the discussion.

i The Characteristics of an Investment Some IIAs provide that assets must have the characteristics of an investment to be covered by the agreements, some making it explicit – like the 2016 Nigeria–Singapore IIA – that if they lack these characteristics then they are not an investment (Article 1, Footnote 1). Among these IIAs, some agreements provide for a non-exhaustive list of characteristics. For instance, the 2012 Japan–Iraq IIA provides: 'The term "investments" means every kind of asset owned or controlled, directly or indirectly, by an investor, which has the characteristics of an investment, such as the commitment of capital or other resources, the expectation of gain or profit, or the assumption of risk' (Article 1.1). Other agreements provide for a closed list of characteristics. This is exemplified by the 2016 Slovakia–Iran IIA, which lists (1) the commitment of capital or other resources; (2) the expectation of regularity of profit; (3) the assumption of risk; (4) a reasonable duration; and (5) an effective contribution to the host State's economy (Article 1.2).

It is worth insisting that an asset that is 'positively' listed in an IIA, or in any case not excluded, but which fails to meet the characteristics of an investment as provided in the agreement, is not covered by that agreement.

As discussed below, the question as to whether the notion of investment entails objective characteristics, and if so, what these are, has tinged arbitration practice in relation to Article 25 of the ICSID Convention and the term 'investment' therein. However, a similar debate has also flourished with regard to the interpretation of IIAs that do not incorporate such characteristics in their definition of the term 'investment'.

One line of authority argues that interpretation does not result in construing 'investment' as being made of objective characteristics. For instance, with regard to the 1994 Energy Charter Treaty (ECT), the Tribunal appointed in *RREEF* v. *Spain* declared:

> The definition of investment must be interpreted according to article 31 of the Vienna Convention on the Law of Treaties and not in accordance with tests, criteria or guidelines beyond the terms, the context or the object and purpose of the ECT. There is no test, set of criteria or guidelines that can or should be relied upon in international law to restrict or replace the definition that exists in the ECT. (2016, Decision on Jurisdiction, para. 157)

On the other hand, other Tribunals that sustain a second line of authority have adopted the opposite view. For instance, the Tribunal opined in *Capital Financial Holdings Luxembourg SA* v. *Cameroon*:

> The arbitration Tribunal must interpret Article 1(3) of the Treaty in accordance with international law, by attributing to its terms their ordinary meaning in their context but always in light of the object and purpose of the Treaty (article 31(1) of the Vienna Convention). In this respect, the arbitration Tribunal agrees with the Respondent who considers that the interpretation of article 1(3) of the Treaty must be conducted taking into account the purpose of the Treaty, which is to encourage foreign investments in Cameroon. The only acquisition of shares without any contribution and without any risk being taken by the Claimant ... does not correspond to this interpretation of article 1(3) in accordance with international law. (2017, Award, paras. 461–462; translation by the author)

In a way similar to the IIAs that incorporate 'investment's characteristics' in their definition of the term 'investment', these tribunals have identified contribution, duration and risk as constituting the characteristics of an investment (e.g. *Romak S.A. (Switzerland)* v. *Uzbekistan*, 2009, Award, para. 207). Arbitration practice displays a consensus, on the other hand, towards excluding the contribution to the economic development of the States from the characteristics of an investment (e.g. *Ickale Insaat Limited Sirketi* v. *Turkmenistan*, 2016, Award, para. 291). This is so notably because of the difficulty in appraising the contribution to economic development. As seen below, this is in line with the approach tribunals adopt as regards Article 25 of the ICSID Convention, as it is with most IIAs that set out characteristics of an investment. The Iran–Slovakia IIA quoted above constitutes one of the exceptions in this respect. On the other hand, arbitration tribunals sometimes include as part of the characteristics of an investment the expectation of a commercial return, while others view it as forming part of the risk element (e.g. *KT Asia Investment Group B. V.* v. *Kazakhstan*, 2013 Award, paras. 170–171).

It is worth stressing that this line of authority that considers that an investment has objective characteristics under IIAs leads to the same conclusion as the IIAs that provide for investment's characteristics: an asset that is 'positively' listed in an IIA, or in any case not excluded, but that fails to meet the characteristics of an investment as set by the tribunal is not considered as being covered by that agreement.

ii **Legality Requirement** The second condition displayed by treaty practice that must be met for assets listed, or in any case not excluded, to be considered as a covered investment pertains to the conformity with the law. It is, for instance, incorporated in Article 1.1 of the 2006 Morocco–Gambia IIA, which provides: '"Investments" means every kind of assets invested by investors of one Contracting Party in the territory of the other Contracting Party *in accordance* *with the laws and regulations of the latter Contracting Party*' (emphasis added). This condition is widespread in IIA practice – it has been regarded as the product of 'international public policies designed to sanction illegal acts and their resulting effects' (*Inceysa Vallisoletana, S.L. v. El Salvador*, 2006, Award, para. 247).

As illustrated by the 2014 Colombia–Turkey IIA, which provides in its relevant part that '"investment" means every kind of asset ... acquired ... in conformity with its [a Contracting Party] laws and regulations' (Article 1.1), the great majority of IIAs which contain a legality requirement provide *mutatis mutandis* that the condition of conformity applies to the time when the asset is acquired. The formulations adopted in a few IIAs lead to an extension of the application of this condition to the lifetime of the investment; this is illustrated by the 2016 Slovakia–Iran IIA, which refers to investment 'maintained' (Article 1.2). As for the majority of IIAs, tribunals do acknowledge that the temporal restriction placed on the legality requirement makes it inoperative for jurisdictional and admissibility purposes with regard to illegalities committed during the investment operation; however, they stress that this is an element to be taken into account in relation to the merits in particular (e.g. *ECE Projektmanagement International GmbH v. Czech Republic*, 2013, Award, para. 3.166).

A series of comments can be made with regard to these IIAs which pertain to (1) the scope of application of the requirement; (2) its 'normative yardstick'; and (3) the breaches that can amount to a failure to comply with the requirement.

First, it is worth stressing that the obligation to comply with the domestic law of host States pertains to the assets that can constitute an investment. This means that the breaches of domestic law that do not relate to those assets fall outside the scope of the legality requirement and have no consequence for their coverage by IIAs.

Second, it is necessary to clarify the 'content' of the legal framework to be complied with under the legality requirement. Treaty practice displays some diversity in the formulations used to delineate this legal framework. For instance, treaties refer to the 'law of the Party in whose territory the investment is made' (2016 Morocco–Nigeria IIA, Article 1.3), the 'national legislation' of the host State (2015 San Marino–Azerbaijan IIA, Article 1.1.a), or 'applicable laws and regulations' (2017 Israel–Japan IIA, Article 1.a). A number of remarks can be made as regards these formulations. First, while it is obvious that the legal framework includes host States' domestic law *sensu stricto*, international law appears also to be relevant. Depending on the status of international law in the host States' domestic legal order, international law can indeed come into play as part of domestic law; this holds true regardless of the exact formulation of the legality requirement within the IIAs. More fundamentally, the formulation used in some IIAs, for instance 'laws and regulations', may be interpreted as 'directly' encompassing international law.

Second, as for host States' domestic law *sensu stricto*, it must be determined which sources are encompassed by this. Obviously, the variations in the language of IIAs, illustrated above, are informative in this regard. It is to be noted that some tribunals have adopted broad conceptions, such as the Tribunal appointed in *Vladislav Kim* v. *Uzbekistan* with regard to Article 12 of the 1997 Kazakhstan–Uzbekistan IIA that refers to the 'legislation' of the host State. It concluded that this term 'encompasses those normative actions regarded as "law" by the Host State's legal system', although it acknowledged that it could be argued that 'the term "legislation" is a narrower form of "law" pointing only to statutory law' (2017, Decision on Jurisdiction, para. 378).

A third remark is that not all the breaches of the relevant legal framework are considered as amounting to a failure to comply with the legality requirement – in this respect, minor or trivial breaches are not seen as establishing such a failure. This is due to the severe consequences of a finding of illegality as it deprives the private person concerned of the protection of the IIA. In *Vladislav Kim* v. *Uzbekistan*, the Tribunal approached this issue in terms of 'proportionality', expressing the view that '[t]he denial of the protections of the BIT is a harsh consequence that is a proportional response only when its application is triggered by *noncompliance with a law that results in a compromise of a correspondingly significant interest of the Host State*'. In appraising proportionality, that Tribunal argued that it is necessary to focus 'on the seriousness of the law viewed in concert with the seriousness of the violation' (2017, Decision on Jurisdiction, paras. 396–398). A typical violation of the legal framework that amounts to a failure to comply with the legality requirement is corruption (e.g. *Metal-Tech Ltd* v. *Uzbekistan*, 2013, Award, para. 165).

Moving outside IIA practice, it is notable that a great number of arbitration tribunals have considered that the legality requirement is applicable even when it is not provided for in the text of the IIA. They have justified this approach by referring in particular to respect for the international public order (*Blusun S.A.* v. *Italy*, 2016, Award, para. 264), the principle *nemo auditur propriam turpitudinem allegans* (*Plama Consortium Limited* v. *Bulgaria*, 2008, Award, para. 143), or the principle of good faith (*Gustav F W Hamester GmbH & Co. KG* v. *Ghana*, 2010, Award, paras. 123–124). Arbitration tribunals consider that this requirement does not apply to the performance of the investment (e.g. *David Aven et al.* v. *Costa Rica*, 2018, Final Award, para. 342).

iii Geographical Requirement All IIAs add a geographical requirement that must be met for investments to be covered by the agreements, i.e. their 'location' in the territory of a host State party to those agreements. Two sets of remarks can be formulated in this respect.

Even though this geographical requirement displays similarities across IIA practice, there are notable differences from one treaty to the other. Likewise, one can notice that there are, in some IIAs, differences with regard to the States parties themselves. This is illustrated by Article 1.12 of the 2018 Kazakhstan–Singapore IIA, which provides two definitions of 'territory' for each State party:

(a) In respect of the Republic of Kazakhstan: the territory within its land, sea and air borders, including the land, internal waters, subsoils, air space, and any area outside the state border, where the Republic of Kazakhstan exercises or may hereafter exercise its sovereign rights and jurisdiction with respect to the sea-bed, subsoil and their natural resources in accordance with its national legislation and international law;

(b) In respect of the Republic of Singapore: its land territory, internal waters and territorial sea, as well as any maritime area situated beyond the territorial sea, which has been or might in the future be designated under its national law, in accordance with international law, as an area within which Singapore may exercise sovereign rights or jurisdiction with regard to the sea, the sea-bed, the subsoil and the natural resources...

As illustrated by this example also, this geographical element, as set in some IIAs, has a prospective and hypothetical dimension.

Second, it is worth stressing that the determination as to whether specific investments meet this geographical requirement can raise difficulties in practice. Contrary to movable properties for which the appraisal of the geographical nexus with the host States' territory does not usually raise any major issue, this has proven to be a controversial issue in particular in relation to financial instruments. This is well illustrated by the disagreement between the majority of the Tribunal and the Dissenting Arbitrator in *Abaclat* v. *Argentina* as to security entitlements in Argentinian bonds (2011, Decision on Jurisdiction and Admissibility and Dissenting Opinion). This has led to calls for a flexible approach to be taken in the matter, meaning that the geographical nexus set out by IIAs between investment and territory should be construed taking into account the type of asset at hand (*Renta 4 S.V.S.A.* v. *Russia*, 2009, Award on Preliminary Objections, para. 144).

iv Temporal Requirement The temporal requirement to be met for investments to be covered by IIAs is usually easily satisfied. This results from the fact that, in addition to the investments made after the entry into force of the agreements that are obviously covered, mainstream treaty practice provides that investments made prior to this entry into force are also covered by the IIAs. This is illustrated by Article 2.1 of the 2018 Brazil–Guyana IIA, which provides in its relevant part: 'This Agreement shall apply to all investments made before or after its entry into force by investors of either Party in accordance with laws and regulations of the other Party in the territory of the latter.'

14.3.2.2 'Investment' under the ICSID Convention

Preliminary Remarks

The notion of investment is key in the determination of the jurisdiction of ICSID arbitration tribunals, with Article 25.1 of the Convention providing that the 'jurisdiction of the Centre shall extend to any legal dispute arising directly out of an investment'. The main issues that have arisen in this respect are twofold: (1) what is the meaning of 'investment' under the Convention? And (2) how does it interact with the definition of the term 'investment' in IIAs? Each is analysed in turn below. The notion of dispute is examined in Chapter 10; as for the condition of 'directness', it is to be construed as referring to the close link that must exist between the investment and the dispute, and not the investment as such (*Fedax N.V.* v. *Venezuela*, 1997, Decision on Jurisdiction, para. 24).

a The Definition of 'Investment' in Article 25

'Investment' is not defined in Article 25 of the ICSID Convention, nor in any other of its provisions. According to the Report of the Executive Directors of the IBRD on the Convention, no attempt was in fact made to reach a definition of the term, first because the Convention sets a requirement of consent by the parties, and, second because it provides a mechanism under Article 25.4 through which Contracting States can notify in advance the classes of disputes they would or would not consider submitting to the Centre (para. 27).

As noted by the Tribunal in *Ambiente Ufficio S.p.A.* v. *Argentina*, this statement that no attempt was made to define the term 'investment' can be qualified – indeed, even though they were unsuccessful, various attempts were made to define that term. That being said, the Report has the potential to draw attention to the fact that Article 25 constitutes a compromise reached by capital-exporting States, which wanted the term to be left undefined, and capital-importing States, which desired a narrowing-down of the definition of an investment by incorporating a list of covered investments. In fact, no definition was included (as capital-exporting States wished), precisely because States can circumscribe the investments covered (as capital-importing States intended) when consenting to the jurisdiction of the Centre or through the above-mentioned notification mechanism (2013, Decision on Jurisdiction and Admissibility, para. 449).

Different consequences are drawn by arbitration tribunals from this lack of definition in terms of interpretation. One line of authority stresses that the interpretation of 'investment' under Article 31 of the VCLT does not lead to the adding of any test, criteria or guidelines to the language of Article 25 (e.g. *RREFF* v. *Spain*, 2016, Decision on Jurisdiction, para. 157). Another line adopts the opposite viewpoint, as is well illustrated by the reasoning of the Tribunal in *Orascom TMT S.à.r.l.* v. *Algeria*, which considered that the lack of a definition implies that the term 'investment' shall be given its ordinary meaning under Article 31.1 of the VCLT – as opposed to a special meaning under Article 31.4. It concluded that the ordinary meaning of the term is an objective one and comprises specific elements (2017, Award, para. 370).

The second line of authority is the mainstream approach adopted in the practice of arbitration tribunals. In this regard, the award rendered by the Tribunal in *Salini Costruttori S.p.A.* v. *Morocco* is often viewed as having first set a list of criteria – known as the *Salini* test – to be used to determine whether or not an asset qualifies as an investment under the ICSID Convention. It listed four criteria: contributions, a certain duration of performance of the contract, a participation in the risks of the transaction, and the contribution to the economic development of the host State. Importantly, the Tribunal noted that these criteria should be assessed globally as it saw them as being interdependent (2001, Decision on Jurisdiction, para. 52).

The *Salini* test is often taken as a point of reference by the tribunals that consider that 'investment' has an objective meaning and content under Article 25 of the ICSID Convention. Yet, these tribunals most of the time stress that the test is only a 'point of departure' (e.g. *Ickale Insaat Limited Sirketi* v. *Turkmenistan*, 2016, Award, para. 289), or that it is an element they may take into account in their reasoning (e.g. *Capital Financial Holdings Luxembourg SA* v. *Cameroon*, 2017, Award, para. 420), while some specify that the criteria it contains shall not be considered as jurisdictional criteria (*Vincent J. Ryan* v. *Poland*, Award, 2015, para. 197). In that sense, the Tribunal argued in *Philip Morris* v. *Uruguay*:

> [T]he four constitutive elements of the *Salini* list do not constitute jurisdictional requirements to the effect that the absence of one or the other of these elements would imply a lack of jurisdiction. They are typical features of investments under the ICSID Convention, not 'a set of mandatory legal requirements' [footnote omitted]. As such, they may assist in identifying or excluding in extreme cases the presence of an investment but they cannot defeat the broad and flexible concept of investment under the ICSID Convention to the extent it is not limited by the relevant treaty, as in the present case. (2013, Decision on Jurisdiction, para. 206)

Of these criteria, most arbitration tribunals rely on contribution, duration and risk. Some add the expectation of a commercial return as a criterion, be it conceived of as an independent one (e.g. *Joy Mining Machinery Limited* v. *Egypt*, 2004, Award on Jurisdiction, para. 53), or as forming part of the element of risk (e.g. *Orascom TMT S.à.r.l.* v. *Algeria*, 2017, Award, para. 370). It is worth noting that the Tribunal added in *Phoenix Action, Ltd* v. *Czech Republic* both a legality requirement and a good-faith requirement (2009, Award, para. 114), additions that were later rejected by the Tribunal appointed in *Mr Saba Fakes* v. *Turkey* (2010, Award, para. 112).

As to the contribution to host States' economic development, there is a consensus that it shall not be regarded as a characteristic of an investment under Article 25. Various arguments are used to justify this exclusion. In *Capital Financial Holdings Luxembourg SA* v. *Cameroon*, the Tribunal argued that such a contribution is an objective, but not a characteristic of an investment; it also stressed its subjectivity and thereby the difficulty in appraising it (2017, Award, para. 422). Other tribunals have noted that the ICSID Convention Preamble referred to by the *Salini* Tribunal to justify the inclusion of this criterion does not in fact support this claim (e.g. *Mr Saba Fakes* v. *Turkey*, 2010, Award, para. 111). Without completely excluding it from the test, some tribunals consider the 'contribution to the economic development of the host State' as being implicitly covered by the other criteria forming part of the *Salini* test (e.g. *Monsieur Joseph Houben* v. *Burundi*, 2016, Award, para. 112, Footnote 43).

As already explained by the *Salini* Tribunal, a number of tribunals make it clear that the criteria are to be considered as a whole and flexibly, taking into account the specifics of each situation (e.g. *MNSS B.V.* v. *Montenegro*, 2016, Award, para. 189).

The award rendered in that latter case also illustrates that for the purpose of testing the fulfilment of these criteria, it is important as regards investments made of several components to consider the investments as a whole, rather than each of their components individually. The Tribunal noted in this respect that a loan in itself is not an investment for the purpose of the Convention – to be considered as such, the Tribunal opined that it must contribute to an economic venture that consists of an investment (para. 196). Such a holistic approach – which is also used in determining the existence of a covered investment under IIAs (e.g. *Tenaris S.A.* v. *Venezuela*, 2016, Award, paras. 284–285) – focuses on the unity of the investment. As explained by the Tribunal in *Koch* v. *Venezuela*: 'It is thus not permissible to slice up an overall investment into its constituent parts, like a sausage, so as to contend that one part, isolated by itself alone, is not an "investment" whereas as an integrated part of the whole investment, it is' (2017, Award, para. 6.59).

b The Interplay between the ICSID Convention and IIAs

As discussed above, arbitration tribunals adopt different approaches as to how to construe 'investment' under Article 25 of the ICSID Convention. This is reflected to some extent in the way they conceive of the interplay between the Convention and IIAs for the purpose of appraising their jurisdiction in relation to 'investment'. Although they start from different premises, it is worth noting that the reasoning of tribunals often leads in practice to the same result.

There is a consensus in arbitration practice that IIA States parties enjoy some latitude in defining 'investment' as they see fit, but that they cannot make an investment dispute out of something that lacks this nature under the ICSID Convention (e.g. *OI European Group B.V.* v. *Venezuela*, 2015, Award, para. 216). As put by the Tribunal in *Vladislav Kim* v. *Uzbekistan*, this entails *mutatis mutandis* that 'for jurisdiction to be established, the claim must pass both through the institutional jurisdictional keyhole set forth in Article 25 as well as the specific jurisdictional keyhole defined in the BIT' (2017, Decision on Jurisdiction, para. 242). Underlying this consensus, there exist two approaches that diverge as to the exact strictness of the limit set by Article 25 and the degree of latitude to be left to IIA States parties.

Under the first approach, some tribunals consider that the parties cannot as a matter of principle define as an investment, for the purpose of ICSID jurisdiction, something that does not satisfy the criteria of an investment under Article 25 of the Convention (e.g. *Joy Mining Machinery Limited v. Egypt*, 2004, Award on Jurisdiction, para. 50) as set out notably in *Salini Costruttori S.p.A. v. Morocco*.

On the other hand, other tribunals criticise this approach of the 'double-barrelled test' as it leads *mutatis mutandis* in their view to restrict the broad range of economic assets that they consider Article 25 is susceptible to cover, in particular atypical investments, and to limit the possibility to adapt it to the evolving nature of economic activities (*Ambiente Ufficio S.p.A. v. Argentina*, 2013, Decision on Jurisdiction and Admissibility, para. 481). Instead, those tribunals adopt a different approach to the 'double-barrelled test' and a different conception of the 'ICSID keyhole'. They opine *mutatis mutandis* that it is appropriate to defer to the States parties' articulation provided in IIAs of what constitutes an investment – notably as it is indicative of what these parties consider to be constitutive of an 'investment' within the meaning of the ICSID Convention – and to conceive of Article 25 as setting jurisdictional limits that arise only at the outer margins of economic activity (e.g. *Inmaris Perestroika Sailing Maritime Services GmbH v. Ukraine*, 2010, Decision on Jurisdiction, para. 130). The Tribunal stressed in that latter case that there should be compelling reasons to disregard the definition contained in an IIA on the grounds of Article 25, such reasons being, for instance, according to the Tribunal appointed in *Enron Corporation and Ponderosa Assets, L.P. v. Argentina*, the absurdity of this definition or the impossibility of reconciling it with the object and purpose of the ICSID Convention (2004, Decision on Jurisdiction, para. 42).

14.3.3 Investor

Preliminary Remarks

Various terminologies and approaches are used in IIAs to specify the categories of persons covered by the agreements – among these, three in particular can be isolated. Under the first, mainstream approach, IIAs define the term 'investor' by drawing a distinction between *mutatis mutandis* 'natural persons', on the one hand, and 'legal entities', on the other (e.g. 2014 Switzerland–Georgia IIA, Article 1). The IIAs that adopt the second approach define 'investor' by distinguishing *mutatis mutandis* between 'nationals' and 'companies', these terms referring themselves *mutatis mutandis* to 'physical persons' and 'legal entities', respectively (e.g. 1985 China–Italy IIA, Articles 2.3–2.5). Under a third approach that is used in some agreements, there is no definition of the term 'investor' provided as such, but instead definitions of 'nationals' and 'companies' (e.g. 1994 USA–Ukraine IIA, Articles 1.1.b and 1.1.c). For didactic purposes, use is made in this section of the divide between 'natural persons' and 'legal persons'; other terminologies and distinctions are made in the following when appropriate.

Two key elements are used by States parties to delineate the scope of the natural and legal persons covered by the IIAs. First, they shall be connected to one of the States parties through a 'link' specified in the agreements. Second, they shall have a link with an asset qualifying as a covered investment, the characterisation of this link varying from one agreement to another, as seen above – for instance, requiring them to 'acquire' an asset or to 'control' it. This close link between 'investor' and 'investment' has already been stressed, and should be contemplated in light of the analyses of 'investment' provided above.

This section focuses on the links that establish the connection between IIA States parties and natural persons, on the one hand, and IIA States parties and legal persons, on the other. The links that must exist between States and both natural persons and legal persons for the purpose of ICSID tribunals' jurisdiction are also examined in relation to the ICSID Convention. A final subsection analyses the specific situation as investors of States themselves, public legal persons and mixed legal persons.

14.3.3.1 Natural Persons

Preliminary Remarks

At the outset, it is worth noting the semantic diversity that characterises the designation of this category – instead of 'natural person', use is made in some IIAs of the terms 'physical person' (e.g. 1985 China–Italy IIA, Article 2.4) or 'individual' (e.g. 1980 BLEU–Cameroon IIA, Article 1.a and 1.b). This diversity has no legal bearing; all these terms are functionally equivalent. Reference is made only to 'natural person' in this subsection.

International investment agreement practice displays three types of links that natural persons shall have with an IIA State party in order to be 'eligible' to be considered as an investor under the agreement: nationality, citizenship and permanent resident.

While some agreements refer either to 'nationality' or to 'citizenship', others refer to both (e.g. 1994 ECT, Article 1.7.a.i). 'Nationality' and 'citizenship' are equivalent in the context of international investment law and arbitration; they do not constitute two different types of links. For that reason, reference is made in what follows mainly to 'nationality'. On the other hand, they are to be distinguished from 'permanent resident'.

Most IIAs refer only to 'nationality/citizenship' (e.g. 2016 Rwanda–Turkey IIA, Article 1.2.a). Some agreements refer to both 'nationality/citizenship' and 'permanent resident' as alternative links – in other words, a natural person shall either have the nationality/citizenship of an IIA State party, or be a permanent resident on its territory (e.g. 2016 Morocco–Nigeria IIA, Article 1.1). Other IIAs do not refer to natural persons who are a 'permanent resident' in an IIA State party, but rather to those who are 'permanently residing' in an IIA State party (e.g. 1994 ECT, Article 1.7. a.i); as discussed below, this semantic variation has been interpreted as having legal consequences.

Interestingly, a few IIAs provide for different applicable types of links depending on the State party concerned – for instance, the IIA adopted by Israel and Japan in 2017 provides that, with respect to Japan, a natural person shall be a national of the State, while providing for Israel that a natural person shall be a national or a permanent resident of the State (Article 1.c). Irrespective of the various formulae opted for by IIA States parties, both types of links are analysed in turn.

a Nationality and Citizenship

Nationality goes to the core of sovereignty. The determination of the conditions to be met for a natural person to be considered as a national of a State is fundamentally a sovereign prerogative. This applies to both the acquisition of nationality and its loss, and, as for the former, in particular to naturalisation. In other words, this is a matter governed by the domestic law of the State concerned. International law is merely called to play a role in a few specific situations, typically where the effectiveness of nationality is at hand. This is well recognised in the practice of international courts and tribunals, as famously illustrated by the Judgment rendered in the *Nottebohm Case (Liechtenstein* v. *Guatemala)* by the International Court of Justice (ICJ) (1955, Judgment, at 23).

As for international investment law and arbitration, this entails that the incorporation of the nationality link within IIAs and in the ICSID Convention constitutes an implicit referral to the domestic law of States parties. In that sense, it is worth noting that the 2003 China–Germany IIA, for instance, does not even mention nationality, but provides directly that '"investors" means ... in respect of the Federal Republic of Germany ... Germans within the meaning of the Basic Law for the Federal Republic of Germany' (Article 1.2.a).

This also explains why arbitration tribunals are very cautious when appraising the fulfilment of the nationality requirement. They acknowledge not only the predominance of domestic law, but also the great weight to be given to the interpretation and application of that law by States' authorities, in particular as they translate into nationality conferments. They all agree that passports and certificates of nationality constitute *prima facie* evidence, and that States' decisions pertaining to nationality can only be disregarded in exceptional circumstances, typically when there is decisive evidence that the granting of nationality was based on fraud or a material error (e.g. *Mr Franck Charles Arif* v. *Moldova*, 2013, Award, para. 357). That being said, some nuances and differences can be identified across the reasoning of tribunals.

This pertains, for instance, to the *prima facie* evidence that passports and nationality certificates constitute. In the above-mentioned case, the Tribunal considered that the failure of the respondent State to show that the granting of nationality was obtained fraudulently or was based on a material error was sufficient as such to satisfy the fulfilment of the nationality requirement (para. 357). On the other hand, the Tribunal appointed in *Waguih Elie George Siag* v. *Egypt*, while noting that passports in particular are *prima facie* evidence, argued that tribunals must nevertheless apply the domestic law as it considered it as the 'only means' to determine nationality (2007, Decision on Jurisdiction, para. 153).

Furthermore, some tribunals stress that the appraisal of nationality conferments is not simply a matter of probative value, but that it also begs the question as to the conditions under which tribunals should overcome the sovereign decision made by a State to grant nationality (e.g. *Micula* v. *Romania*, 2008, Decision on Jurisdiction and Admissibility, para. 94). The Tribunal appointed in that latter case stressed in this respect that 'the State conferring nationality must be given a "margin of appreciation" in deciding upon the factors that it considers necessary for the granting of nationality. [footnote omitted]'.

The nationality link raises a series of issues in investor–State arbitration, mainly in situations in which two nationalities are in question in relation to the claimant, in particular the nationalities of both the home State and the host State party to the dispute. In practice, those situations may be manyfold; for instance, the natural person may have the nationality of those two States, or may have the nationality of the home State but have closer ties with the host State – whose nationality she used to have – than with the home State. In those situations, the question is whether such persons are covered by the IIAs at hand and whether tribunals have jurisdiction over them in relation to these agreements and, when required, the ICSID Convention.

Article 25.2.a of the ICSID Convention is relevant in relation to the first sub-situation, i.e. natural persons having the nationality of both the home State and the host State party to the dispute, with regard to the Contracting parties to the Convention. It provides that disputes involving any natural person who has the nationality of an ICSID Contracting State and the nationality of the ICSID Contracting State party to the dispute falls outside the scope of the Convention. As stated in the Report of the Executive Directors of the IBRD on the Convention, this ineligibility is absolute and cannot be cured even if the State party to the dispute has given its consent (para. 29). As it appears, this Article sets a 'negative' nationality requirement, in that natural persons who have the nationality of an ICSID Contracting State *shall not* have the nationality of the ICSID Contracting State party to the dispute. Four remarks can be made in relation to this 'negative' nationality requirement.

First, one should stress that the applicability of this requirement and its effects is limited to those dual nationals who have the nationality of the ICSID Contracting State party *to the dispute* – it does not concern those who have also the nationality of another Contracting State to the Convention. In other words, it does not exclude from the scope of the Convention disputes involving natural persons having the nationality of different ICSID Contracting States, other than that of the Contracting State party to the dispute.

Second, it is worth noting that this 'negative' nationality requirement is as a matter of principle not ruled out by any consideration of effectiveness, a consideration that can be traced back to the above-mentioned *Nottebohm* case in which the ICJ set and used a 'genuine and effective nationality' test in relation to the diplomatic protection case with which it was seized. Disputes involving a natural person who has formally both the nationality of an ICSID Contracting State and the nationality of the ICSID Contracting State party to the dispute, but whose latter nationality is not effective or merely less effective than the former, still falls outside the scope of the ICSID Convention. This is confirmed by the preparatory works to the Convention[5] and acknowledged by arbitration tribunals (e.g. *Champion Trading Company* v. *Egypt*, 2003, Decision on Jurisdiction, at 15–17). Interestingly, the Tribunal appointed in that latter case contemplated the possibility that, in a situation in which a country continues to apply the *jus sanguinis* over many generations, the third or fourth foreign-born generation, which has no ties with the country of its forefathers, may be considered not to have, for the purpose of Article 25.2.a, the nationality of this State.

Third, and in relation to Article 25.2.b of the ICSID Convention discussed below, it is noteworthy that it has been specified that the requirement not to have the nationality of the Contracting State party to a dispute cannot be bypassed by a dual national which would establish a company in that State and invoke foreign control over it by relying on its second (foreign) nationality (*Burimi SRL* v. *Albania*, 2013, Award, para. 121).

Fourth, one should mention that the 'negative' nationality requirement and the inability to waive this by consent entails that an offer to arbitrate disputes under the ICSID Convention contained in an IIA that would be construed as covering such dual nationals would actually be inoperative for ICSID jurisdiction purposes.

---

[5] CH Schreuer, L Malintoppi, A Reinisch, A Sinclair, *The ICSID Convention: A Commentary* (2nd ed, Oxford University Press 2009), at 271–272.

No such problem arises in relation to the IIAs that on their face follow *mutatis mutandis* the approach of the ICSID Convention, such as the 2017 Israel–Japan IIA. Article 1.c.i of that Agreement provides indeed in its relevant part that an 'investor of a Contracting party' means a natural person who is a national of one State and who is not also a national of the other State. In other words, the text indicates that natural persons having the nationality of both Japan and Israel are not covered at all by the Agreement.

The 2016 Comprehensive Economic and Trade Agreement (CETA) adopts a different approach. According to Article 8.1, '[a] natural person who is a citizen of Canada and has the nationality of one of the Member States of the European Union is deemed to be exclusively a natural person of the Party of his or her dominant and effective nationality'. As it appears, those dual nationals are not excluded from the coverage of the Agreement; for the purpose of its application, they shall be considered as investors having the nationality of the State with respect to which they have a dominant and effective nationality. If they are not excluded as they are under the text of the Israel–Japan IIA, this entails, however, that an investor having, say, French and Canadian nationality, the latter being the dominant and effective nationality, is not covered by the CETA for its operations in Canada and cannot in particular initiate proceedings against that State. It can do so only against France if that investor owns an asset in France qualifying as an investment and has a dispute with this country that falls within the scope of the offer to settle disputes as set in Section F of the Agreement. A remark is warranted here as to this possibility enjoyed by such dual nationals. While Section F provides for the resolution of disputes by a standing court and not by an arbitration tribunal, it foresees that claims may be submitted in particular following the ICSID Convention Arbitration Rules (Article 8.23.2.a). In relation to the remark made above, it is noteworthy that disputes involving such dual nationals cannot be submitted under those Arbitration Rules.

Cases in which a claimant has the nationality of both the home State and the host State are rare in practice. Arbitration tribunals have mainly been faced with situations in which the claimant had the nationality of the home State, but closer ties with the host State, though no longer having its nationality. In such cases, mainstream arbitration practice opposes the idea that considerations of effectiveness, predominance or genuine link should lead to the setting aside of the nationality of the home State. This holds true in relation to both IIAs and the ICSID Convention (e.g. *Micula v. Romania*, 2008, Decision on Jurisdiction and Admissibility, paras. 100–102). In support of its reasoning and finding, the Tribunal appointed in that latter case referred to the work of the International Law Commission on Diplomatic Protection (para. 99), stressing in particular that the Special Rapporteur on the matter had noted in his first report that '[t]he suggestion that the Nottebohm principle of an effective and genuine link be seen as a rule of customary international law in cases not involving dual or plural nationality enjoys little support'.[6]

b Permanent Resident

Under public international law, nationality/citizenship is the main and primary link that connects States to natural persons and that delineates the scope of the natural persons connected to a State. Yet, States can decide for specific purposes or matters to extend this scope, typically by recognising that the permanent residence of natural persons within their territory suffices to establish a connection between them. Some States make such a decision in the IIAs, incorporating 'permanent resident' as an alternative link to nationality/citizenship.

As it appears, the recognition of 'permanent resident' as a valid link is an expression of State sovereignty that grounds the principle of this validity and its modalities in domestic law. This means that the determination as to whether a natural person shall be considered as a permanent resident or as permanently residing in an IIA State party depends on the domestic law of that State. It is well recognised in that sense that the incorporation of this link within IIAs entails a reference to this domestic law (e.g. *Cem Cenzig Uzan v. Turkey*, 2016, Award on Respondent's Bifurcated Preliminary Objection, para. 156). Yet, the Tribunal appointed in that case considered that arbitration tribunals have the power to examine the facts of the case to determine if a natural person has been permanently residing in a State according to its domestic law, the evaluation of the domestic authorities being for it highly persuasive, but not absolutely determinative (para. 156).

It is worth noting that this Tribunal considered that it was also called upon to appraise whether the natural person in that case was actually living permanently in the territory of the State concerned. It justified this factual inquiry on the basis of the text of the IIA at hand, which refers to 'permanently residing' instead of 'permanent resident'. In this regard, it stressed that if the intention behind the IIA had been to refer solely to the legal status of the natural person as defined by domestic law, the text would have used the term 'permanent resident'. More generally, it argued that such an interpretation 'avoids a situation whereby a natural person could obtain resident permits from multiple jurisdictions (e.g. by becoming an investor in that state) in order to avail of such state's protections, without actually having to reside within any of those states' (para. 156).

As regards the ICSID Convention, it is worth noting that Article 25 does not set 'permanent resident' as a valid link between the State Contracting parties to the Convention and natural persons. This means that an offer to arbitrate disputes under the ICSID Convention contained in an IIA that covers permanent residents is actually inoperative as for these residents.

[6] 'Diplomatic Protection', Document A/CN.4/506 and Add. 1, First Report on Diplomatic Protection, by Mr John R. Dugard, Special Rapporteur (2000), para. 111.

14.3.3.2 Legal Persons

Preliminary Remarks

Contrary to 'natural person', which constitutes a homogeneous category composed of individuals having a nationality or a 'permanent resident' link with States, the category of legal person is very much heterogeneous. It encompasses various types of persons, which may each have varying features; likewise, the same type of persons can, like corporations typically, display several types of links with States. International investment agreements reflect this diversity in the definition of 'legal person' provided therein, both in terms of the types of legal persons covered by the agreements and the link(s) that they must display in order to be within scope, subject – as explained above – to the existence of a link with an investment. Each dimension is analysed in turn below, in relation also when appropriate to the ICSID Convention, which governs the general jurisdiction of tribunals operating under the ICSID Convention Arbitration Rules.

a The Types of Legal Persons

The ICSID Convention refers to the category of juridical person in Article 25.2.b without defining it or detailing the types of persons it covers. International investment agreements contain a broad range of formulations used to refer to legal persons; in addition to 'legal persons', they refer notably – singly or in combination – to 'legal entities', 'entities' or 'companies'. Whatever the formulation used by States parties, the IIAs provide specifications as to the exact types of persons they cover, those agreements adopting different approaches in this respect. Most of these provide for a non-exhaustive list. For instance, the IIA adopted by the Czech and Slovak Federal Republic and Switzerland in 1990 provides that 'legal entities' include 'companies, corporations, business associations and other organizations' (Article 1.1.b); by the same token, the 1998 USA–Lithuania IIA defines 'company' as 'any kind of corporation, company, association, partnership or other organization' (Article 1.1.b). In contrast, a few provide for an exhaustive list referring to one type; this is well illustrated by the 1980 BLEU–Cameroon IIA, which, for the BLEU, provides that '[t]he term "companies" shall mean ... any corporation' (Article 1.2.a).

Irrespective of the exact approach displayed by each IIA, specific issues arise from treaty and arbitration practices as to the coverage of, in particular: (1) entities that do not have a legal personality under the home State's domestic law; (2) non-profit entities; and (3) government-owned and -controlled entities. This third issue is discussed in Section 14.3.3.3.

Starting with the first issue, a great majority of IIAs simply do not address the matter – only a minority provide that entities that do not have a legal personality fall within the definition (e.g. 2005 Egypt–Germany IIA, Article 1.2.b). With regard to the IIAs that form part of that great majority, some arbitration tribunals have had to determine whether they cover entities lacking legal personality. In *Abaclat* v. *Argentina* and *Wirtgen* v. *Czech Republic*, the claimants did not have legal personality under Italian law and German law, respectively. The respondent States argued in both cases that they did not qualify, therefore, as legal persons under the IIAs in question. The Tribunals appointed in these cases reached the conclusion that they did qualify as such, in particular as they considered it sufficient that these entities enjoy the attributes specific to legal personality even if they do not formally have this legal personality. In *Wirtgen* v. *Czech Republic*, the Tribunal noted that the inter-pretation of 'juridical person' leads to the conclusion that this term covers entities that have the legal capacity to invest, conclude contracts, acquire property and sue and be sued (2017, Final Award, para. 229). The Tribunal appointed in *Abaclat* v. *Argentina* considered also that the entities having those capacities are to be regarded as a 'juridical person' under Article 25.2.b of the ICSID Convention (2011, Decision on Jurisdiction and Admissibility, para. 417).

Concerning non-profit entities, answers or elements of answers can be found by focusing closely on the language used in IIAs; four main categories of agreements can be identified in this respect. A first category of IIAs makes it explicit that non-profit entities are covered, as illustrated by those agreements that specify that they cover *mutatis mutandis* both entities whose activities are directed at profit and entities whose activities are not so directed (e.g. 2015 Macedonia–Denmark IIA, Article 1.3.b). The IIAs that form part of the second category do not directly address the matter, but instead refer to 'association'. More precisely, these IIAs refer to 'foundation' and/or 'association' (e.g. 2014 Korea–Kenya IIA, Article 1.3.b); this is to be contrasted with those IIAs that refer to 'business association' (e.g. 2014 Switzerland–Georgia IIA, Article 1.1.b). A third category of IIAs do not provide any information, be it direct or indirect, but refer broadly, for instance, to 'any entity', which leaves the possibility open to consider that non-profit entities are covered (e.g. 1994 Lithuania–Ukraine IIA, Article 1.2). Finally, the few IIAs that belong to the fourth category exclude non-profit entities as they, for instance, limit the scope of the legal persons covered to corporations (e.g. 1980 BLEU–Cameroon, Article 1.2.a).

b The Types of Links

The types of links set out in treaty practice to connect legal persons, in particular enterprises, to an IIA State party are numerous; what is more, the combination of links that may be required to establish this connection also vary from one agreement to the other. The following will examine the various formulae and combinations found in investment treaty practice before focus-ing on the main types of links and the specific issues they raise.

i **Salient Features of Treaty Practice** As noted by Arbitrator Orrego Vicuna, while the nationality of natural persons entails allegiance with the nation and the State, the connection existing between a State and a legal person is more a question of convenience (*Waguih Elie George Siag* v. *Egypt*, 2007, Decision on Jurisdiction, Partial Dissenting Opinion, at 62). This helps to explain two key features of investment treaty practice in this respect: the diversity of IIA practice and the flexibility displayed by the ICSID Convention on the matter. Each is analysed in turn.

– **The Diversity of IIA Practice** In public international law, the issue of the existence of a link connecting legal persons to States has arisen mainly in the context of the exercise of diplomatic protection by States with regard to corporations, as famously illustrated by the *Case Concerning the Barcelona Traction, Light and Power Company, Limited (Belgium* v. *Spain)*, decided by the ICJ. In that case, the Court stated that a long practice supports the 'rule [that] attributes the rights of diplomatic protection of a corporate entity to the State under the laws of which it is incorporated and in whose territory it has a registered office'. At the same time, it noted that although an absolute 'genuine link' has not found a general acceptance, a relative approach of this test has been adopted by some States that have required additional links, such as the presence of the corporation's seat or centre of control in their territory (1970, Judgment, para. 70).

Incorporation is also a key link in IIA practice, mentioned in almost all agreements. In some agreements, incorporation is provided as the only link required to connect a legal person to a State party. For instance, the 1998 Finland–South Africa IIA provides that '"investors" means . . . any legal person, corporation, firm or association incorporated or constituted under the laws of that Contracting Party' (Article 1.3.b). It is worth stressing that among those IIAs that refer to only one link, just a few opt for a link other than incorporation; for instance, the 1999 Italy–Eritrea IIA refers only to the 'head of office' (Article 1.4).

In a number of IIAs, incorporation is articulated with at least another link; this is intended in particular to avoid fictitious connections that the sole reference to 'incorporation' may allow. Among IIAs that refer to one additional link, it is typical that they require *mutatis mutandis* that the legal person also has its seat in the State of incorporation (e.g. 1985 China–Italy IIA, Article 2.5), or that it conducts 'effective economic activities' in that State (e.g. 2014 UAE–Greece IIA, Article 1.3.b). Some IIAs add those two links cumulatively to 'incorporation'. For instance, the 2010 Switzerland–Egypt IIA provides that legal entities shall be constituted or organised under the law of a State party and have their statutory seat together with real business activities in the territory of that State (Article 1.2.b.i).

In some IIAs, control is provided as an alternative link to incorporation and the other additional links mentioned above. As a matter of principle, this entails that, in addition to the legal persons that display the above-mentioned links and have therefore the required connection with an IIA State party, those legal entities that do not display such links, but which are controlled by a legal person that does display them and therefore has the required connection with an IIA State party, are considered as investors of that State party. This also applies as regards those legal entities that are controlled by a natural person having the nationality of an IIA State party. This is illustrated by the 2005 Netherlands–Suriname IIA, which provides: '[T]he term "nationals" shall comprise with regard to either Contracting Party ... legal persons not constituted under the law of that Contracting Party but controlled, directly or indirectly, by natural persons as defined in (i) [having the nationality of that Contracting Party] or by legal persons as defined in (ii) [constituted under the law of that Contracting Party]' (Article 1.b.iii).

Beyond this principle, IIAs that incorporate 'control' display some diversity in relation to which States the controlled legal person must be connected to in order to be covered by the agreement. Some IIAs limit the scope of those States to third States to the agreements. For instance, the 1991 Australia–Poland IIA provides that the legal person shall be incorporated under the law of a third country and be controlled by a legal person incorporated under the law of a Contracting Party or a natural person who is a national of a Contracting Party under its law (Article 1.1.e.ii). This means that if an Australian national controls a company incorporated in New Zealand, that company can be considered as an Australian investor for the purpose of this agreement. In contrast, this formulation excludes a company that is incorporated in Poland and controlled by an Australian national from being considered as an Australian investor for that very same purpose. Some agreements provide specifically for this possibility that a legal person connected to an IIA State party may be considered as an investor of another State party when controlled by a legal or natural person of that latter State. This is well illustrated by the 2001 Austria–Egypt IIA, following which 'investor' means, in particular: '[A]ny juridical person, or partnership, constituted in accordance with the legislation of a Contracting Party or of a third Party in which the investor referred to in a [any natural person who is a citizen of one of the Contracting Parties and makes an investment in the other Contracting Party's territory] or b [any juridical person, or partnership constituted in accordance with the legislation of one of the Contracting Parties having its seat in the territory of one of the Contracting Parties and making an investment in the other Contracting Party's territory] exercises a dominant influence' (Article 1.2.c). It is worth noting that some IIAs foresee, for the purpose of Article 25.2.b of the ICSID Convention analysed below, that a company incorporated in the territory of one State party, but controlled by a national or a company of another State party, shall be considered to be a company of that latter State (e.g. 1995, United Kingdom–Georgia IIA, Article 8.3).

On a different point, it is notable that the Austria–Egypt IIA quoted above illustrates the explicit requirement which is set in most IIAs that the control must be significant. Other equivalent formulations are used in IIA practice – for instance, 'effective control' (e.g. 2014 Switzerland–Georgia IIA, Article 1.1.c). As exemplified by the 2005 Netherlands–Suriname IIA also quoted above, it is worth noting that some IIAs specify that the control can be 'direct' or 'indirect'.

– The Flexibility of the ICSID Convention The ICSID Convention is very flexible as regards the connection that a legal person must possess with a Contracting State to the Convention for its dispute to fall within the jurisdiction of the Centre. This is evidenced by the two grounds on the basis of which this connection – meaning 'nationality' under the term of Article 25.2.b – can be established under the Convention.

The first ground consists of the nationality of an ICSID Contracting State other than the Contracting State party to the dispute. The Convention does not specify the link that must exist for a legal person to be considered as a national of such a Contracting State – rather, it is intended to leave a broad discretion to the Contracting States in the determination of what they consider to be a valid link. As stated by the Tribunal in *Orascom TMT Investments S.à.r.l* v. *Algeria* – in reference to Broches[7] – Article 25.2.b merely sets objective outer limits that prevent the use of unreasonable criteria (2017, Award, para. 266). This Tribunal considered that a criterion is reasonable as long as the jurisdictional requirements of Article 25 are not deprived of their objective significance (para. 267). The above-mentioned links displayed by IIA practice are reasonable links that stay within the limits set out by Article 25.2.b.

The second ground was incorporated into the ICSID Convention, taking into account the obligation often imposed by host States on foreign investors to create a local subsidiary to develop and conduct their operations. Based on an agreement between the parties to a dispute in that sense, this ground enables a juridical person having the nationality of the ICSID Contracting State party to the dispute to be treated as a national of another ICSID Contracting State for the purpose of the Convention on the basis of 'foreign control'. Here again, 'foreign control' is not defined in the Convention. As recalled by the Tribunal in *Autopista Concesionada de Venezuela, C.A.* v. *Venezuela*, it was decided, after initial attempts, to give a wide discretion to the parties to determine the circumstances and criteria under which the legal person shall be considered as a national of another Contracting State on the basis of foreign control, subject again to

---

[7] A Broches, 'The Convention on the Settlement of Investment Disputes between States and Nationals of Other States' (1972) 136 *Recueil des Cours de l'Académie de Droit International de la Haye* 331, at 360–361.

reasonableness and the conformity with the purposes of the ICSID Convention (2001, Decision on Jurisdiction, paras. 110–116).

As regards investor–State arbitrations based on IIA offers to arbitrate, the basis of this specific agreement is typically to be found in a specific provision of IIAs, as illustrated by the above-mentioned United Kingdom–Georgia IIA. This specific agreement is perfected when the investor files the request for arbitration and thereby accepts the terms of the offer, including those pertaining to foreign control for ICSID jurisdiction purposes.

ii Specific Issues Arising in Practice These specific issues pertain to the seat, the control and incorporation.

– Issues Relating to the Seat under IIAs The seat, as a link to connect a legal person to a State, raises two main intertwined issues: (1) which law is to be applied in order to define the notion – the domestic law of the State concerned or international law? And (2) what is the meaning of this notion in international law, and in IIAs more specifically – is it 'statutory seat' or 'effective seat'?

With regard to the first issue, a number of arbitration tribunals concur in the sense that they address it by relating seat to incorporation, a combination that is often provided in IIAs; on the other hand, they diverge in so far as they draw opposite conclusions from this.

This is well illustrated by the diverging interpretations of the similarly drafted Article 1 of the IIAs adopted by the BLEU with Cameroon, on the one hand, and with Algeria, on the other, by the Tribunals in *Capital Financial Holdings Luxembourg SA* v. *Cameroon* and *Orascom TMT Investments S.à.r.l* v. *Algeria*, respectively. In the former case, the Tribunal derived from the combination of 'incorporation' and 'seat' that the reference to domestic law with regard to 'incorporation' leads to the conclusion that the 'seat' is to be defined in accordance with domestic law. It found that it would be incoherent to define these two cumulative conditions in relation to two different bodies of law (2017, Award, para. 210). Taking the opposite approach, the *Orascom* Tribunal concluded from the lack of reference to domestic law in relation to the 'seat', in contrast to the reference made to it for 'incorporation', that the States parties to the IIA did not intend to define the 'seat' according to domestic law, but instead that they conceived of it as an autonomous notion for the purposes of the Agreement (2017, Award, paras. 278–279).

It is worth noting that some tribunals that consider that the seat is an autonomous notion still confer some role to domestic law. For instance, in *Tenaris S. A.* v. *Venezuela*, while the Tribunal opined that the interpretation of the term 'seat' is a matter of international law alone and not of domestic law, it nonetheless found it appropriate to consider domestic law 'by way of background to its interpretation' (29 January 2016, Award, paras. 165 and 169). Taking a different perspective, the Tribunal appointed in the second *Tenaris S.A.* v. *Venezuela* case relied not on the domestic law of the State concerned, but instead, in relation to the general principles of law recognised by civilised nations, on the different domestic legal systems as it saw them as being collectively relevant to give content to the notion of seat (12 December 2016, Award, para. 181).

General principals of law recognised by civilised nations have been conceived of by the drafters of the PCIJ's Statute as a way to avoid *non liquet*, meaning situations in which a dispute cannot be settled because of a gap in the law. In that sense, the referral made by the Tribunal in this second *Tenaris* case to such principles evidences the difficulty in identifying a clear definition of seat under international law. In this respect, one can only agree with the Tribunal appointed in the first *Tenaris* case, which stressed that this notion has not been used in international law as a consistent '"legal term of art" having only one meaning' (29 January 2016, Award, para. 144). Actually, it has been conceived of as having either a formal meaning, i.e. 'statutory seat', amounting to the seat referred to in official documentation, or a substantive meaning, i.e. 'effective seat', corresponding in particular to the place where the entity is effectively managed and administered.

The notion is not clearer in IIA practice. Given the vagueness of most IIAs, tribunals have mainly interpreted this notion in light of the context and/or effectiveness, both means of interpretation being analysed in Chapter 12. But here again, arbitration practice displays nuances and differences in this regard.

A first approach is illustrated by the first *Tenaris S.A. v. Venezuela* case. In that case, the Tribunal noted that the IIA at hand referred to both 'incorporation' and 'seat' and that for a company to be incorporated in either State party it must have its statutory seat in that State. It concluded that for the reference to 'seat' not to be entirely superfluous, it 'must connote something different to, or over and above, the purely formal matter of the address of a registered office or statutory seat'; this led it to construe 'seat' as 'effective seat' (29 January 2016, Award, para. 147 and 150). The Tribunal appointed in *Alps Finance and Trade AG v. Slovak Republic* adopted a similar reasoning when interpreting the 1990 Czech and Slovak Republic–Switzerland IIA, which refers to 'real economic activities', in addition to 'incorporation' and 'seat' (2011, Award, para. 216). On the other hand, the Tribunal adopted the opposite approach in *Orascom TMT Investments S.à.r.l v. Algeria*. Applying the 1991 BLEU–Algeria IIA, which mentions 'incorporation' and 'seat', it concluded that the Agreement 'simply spells out the place of incorporation test by specifying the two elements generally associated with it (constitution in accordance with local law and registered office)' (2017, Award, para. 298).

– Issues Relating to 'Foreign Control' under Article 25.2.b of the ICSID Convention As discussed above, Article 25.2.b of the ICSID Convention provides that a juridical person that has the nationality of the Contracting State party to the dispute should be considered as a national of another Contracting State for the purpose of the Convention if, due to 'foreign control', the parties have agreed it should be considered as such. This sets out two requirements: (1) a subjective requirement, namely the existence of an agreement; and (2) an objective requirement, meaning the actual existence of foreign control.

As explained above in relation to investor–State arbitrations based on IIA offers to arbitrate, the agreement can derive from a specific investor–State arbitration provision. In relation to arbitrations based on contracts concluded between host States and locally incorporated companies, it is well recognised that, even in the absence of an explicit agreement, the incorporation of an ICSID arbitration clause presupposes and implies the agreement – notably of the host State – to treat the contracting locally incorporated company as being under foreign control for the purpose of the ICSID Convention.

As for the objective requirement, there is a consensus that an agreement – whether explicit or not – in a contract constitutes a rebuttable presumption and, for some, a strong presumption that the locally incorporated company is under foreign control (e.g. *Vacuum Salt Products Limited* v. *Ghana*, 1994, Award, para. 38). On the other hand, and as stated by the Tribunal in *Caratube International Oil Company LLP* v. *Kazakhstan*, this idea that has developed as regards contracts 'cannot be applied to circumstances when the host State is clearly not aware of the foreign control of the locally incorporated company at the time when that State agrees to treat a juridical person as a foreign national, i.e. when it signs an investment treaty in question' (2012, Award, para. 366).

Whether it be in order to rebut or confirm a presumption, or more fundamentally to appraise the existence of a foreign control, the issue arises as to how to establish foreign control. In this respect, a discussion has emerged as to whether 'control' should be construed as 'legal control' or 'effective control' for the purpose of Article 25.2.b. In *Autopista Concesionada de Venezuela, C.A.* v. *Venezuela*, for instance, the Tribunal stressed that nothing in the text of the ICSID Convention nor in its *travaux préparatoires* supports the view that Article 25.2.b sets a requirement for effective control (2001, Decision on Jurisdiction, paras. 113–116). On the other hand, in *TSA Spectrum de Argentina S.A.* v. *Argentina*, the Tribunal considered that it would not be consistent with the text of the ICSID Convention to adopt the legal control test, explaining:

> It would not be consistent with the text, if the tribunal, when establishing whether there is foreign control, would be directed to pierce the veil of the corporate entity national of the host State and to stop short at the second corporate layer it meets, rather than pursuing its objective identification of foreign control up to its real source, using the same criterion with which it started. (2008, Award, para. 147)

– Issues Relating to Incorporation As seen above, incorporation is often combined in IIAs with other links in order to avoid legal persons that have no economic connection with the State of incorporation (often called 'mailbox' legal entities) from being protected by the agreements for the real and ultimate benefit of another – controlling – person connected to another State. Those IIAs that, on the other hand, do not provide for any such additional link leave the possibility open for such situations. Those situations are tackled by the denial of benefits clause incorporated into a number of IIAs. In addition to such clauses, it is also worth examining those situations in relation to the requirement under the ICSID Convention that the juridical person must have the nationality of a Contracting State other than the State party to the dispute.

Denial of Benefits Clauses
Preliminary remarks

It is worth noting at the outset that arbitration practice displays a consensus as to how to apply IIAs that only refer to incorporation and do not contain a denial of benefits clause in those cases in which the connection between a legal person and the home State is only formal. They consider *mutatis mutandis* that they should not impose limits on the scope of IIAs that are not found in their text (*Tokios Tokelés* v. *Ukraine*, 2004, Decision on Jurisdiction, paras. 35–36).

Article 14.2 of the IIA adopted by Korea and Kenya in 2014 provides an example of the denial of benefits clauses examined here; it reads as follows:

> Subject to prior notification and consultation, a Contracting Party may deny the benefits of this Agreement to an investor of the other Contracting Party that is a juridical person of such other Contracting Party and to investments of such investor if the juridical person has no substantial business activities in the territory of the other Contracting Party and persons of a non-Contracting Party, or of the denying Contracting Party, own or control the juridical person.

Comments can be made on such clauses that pertain to (1) the scope of the persons that can be denied the benefits of the IIAs as well as (2) the substantial and (3) formal conditions under which these benefits can be denied. These issues are examined successively below.

The Scope of the Persons that Can Be Denied Benefits

A denial of benefits clause is incorporated into an IIA to avoid a legal or natural person that is not considered per se entitled to the protection of that agreement from benefiting from it through a 'mailbox' legal entity incorporated in a State party to that agreement. The relevant factual situations may be twofold: (1) where that person is connected to the host State party to the IIA in which the incorporated legal person has an investment; and (2) where it is connected to a State that is not a party to the IIA. In the first situation, there is no entitlement on the basis that that legal or natural person is connected to the host State; in the second, the lack of entitlement derives from the fact that, as a person connected to a non-State party, it has no right under the IIA at hand.

Some IIAs tackle both situations. For instance, the 1991 USA–Argentina IIA provides in its relevant part: 'Each Party reserves the right to deny to any company of the other Party the advantages of this Treaty if . . . nationals of any third country, or nationals of such Party, control such company and the company has no substantial business activities in the territory of the other Party' (Article 1.2).

On the other hand, other IIAs tackle only the second situation. They entitle an IIA State party to deny benefits only to the legal persons incorporated in another State party which are controlled by persons connected to a State which is not a party to the agreement. Under such denial of benefits clauses, an IIA State party cannot thereby deny benefits to legal persons incorporated in another State party that are controlled by its own natural or legal persons. Such practice is illustrated by Article 17.1 of the 1994 ECT, which provides: 'Each Contracting Party reserves the right to deny the advantages of this Part [Part III] to . . . a legal entity if citizens or nationals of a third state own or control such entity and if that entity has no substantial business activities in the Area of the Contracting Party in which it is organised.'

The Substantive Conditions to Deny Benefits

The substantive conditions are twofold in those denial of benefits clauses. As seen above, one of these is control; in most agreements, ownership comes as an alternative condition to control, as illustrated by the above-mentioned Article 17.1 of the ECT. Control is combined with the criterion pertaining to the lack of conduct of substantial economic activities, those criteria being cumulative. With regard to, for instance, the 1991 USA–Argentina IIA referred to above, those conditions entail that for an IIA State party to be entitled to deny benefits to a legal person incorporated in the other State party, that person shall be controlled by a person connected to a State non-party to the agreement or to that denying State party and it shall also not conduct substantial economic activities in the territory of that State of incorporation. If the latter condition is not fulfilled, meaning if that legal person conducts substantial economic activities in the territory of the State where it is incorporated, it cannot be denied benefits; in such a situation, it is simply not a 'mailbox' entity and the link between them is not merely formal.

The Formal Conditions to Deny Benefits

From IIA practice, it can be seen that – according to formulations and combinations that can vary – some agreements set formal conditions to be met before States can deny benefits. These conditions pertain to notification and consultation. This is illustrated *mutatis mutandis* by the Korea–Kenya IIA quoted above. On the other hand, other IIAs are simply silent on the matter and do not provide for any such formal conditions (e.g. 2014 Canada–Côte d'Ivoire IIA, Article 18).

From a temporal point of view, one issue that has arisen relates to the 'timing' of the denial in a dispute settlement context, meaning whether there is a requirement that it be formulated prior the initiation of arbitration proceedings.

Some tribunals analyse the formulation of a denial of benefits as an objection to jurisdiction that can be raised until the time set out by the applicable arbitration rules for the filing of such objections. For instance, the Tribunal appointed in *Guaracachi America, Inc.* v. *Bolivia* concluded, in relation to Article 23.2 of the 2010 UNCITRAL Arbitration Rules, that the denial can be formulated until the submission of the respondent's statement of defence (2014, Award, paras. 381–382). So too did the Tribunal in *Pac Rim Cayman LLC* v. *El Salvador* under the ICSID Arbitration Rule 41, concluding that the denial can be expressed until the filing of the respondent's counter-memorial. It noted in this respect that any earlier time limit would not be justified by the wording of the IIA at hand in that case and that it would be contrary to its object and purpose as it would create practical difficulties for IIA States parties (2012, Decision on Jurisdiction, para. 4.85).

The Tribunal appointed in *Ampal-American Israel Corp.* v. *Egypt* disagreed with this approach. It considered that jurisdiction under the ICSID Convention being appraised at the time of the request for arbitration, and the IIA in question in that case having to be read in light of the Convention, 'there cannot be an embedded conditionality in the Treaty which could be triggered after the submission of the dispute to arbitration'. It concluded that States must deny benefits prior to this submission for it to be effective and to ground an objection to jurisdiction. Implicitly, it equated a denial of benefits formulated after the submission of the dispute to arbitration to a unilateral withdrawal of consent, which is prohibited under Article 25.1 of the ICSID Convention (2016, Decision on Jurisdiction, paras. 167–173).

ICSID Convention

At the outset, it is worth recalling the two types of situations involving legal persons that are addressed by Article 25.2.b with respect to the definition of a '[n]ational of another Contracting State'. For a dispute to fall within the jurisdiction of the Centre, this national must be either a national of a Contracting State other than the Contracting State party to the dispute, or a national of the Contracting State party to the dispute who the parties agree to consider as a national of another Contracting State because of foreign control. This second type of situation is examined specifically above – the focus here is on the first type.

In relation to this particular situation, it has been the subject of discussion whether a legal entity that does not have the nationality of the Contracting State party to the dispute, but that is controlled by nationals of that State, meet the personal requirement under Article 25.2.b. This begs the question as to whether a control test should be relied on for this first situation.

In *Tokios Tokelés* v. *Ukraine*, the majority of the Tribunal, which rejected the control test, stressed that the incorporation of this test in Article 25.2.b – as regards the second type of situations – was intended to expand the scope of the jurisdiction of the Centre. It considered therefore that to rely on this test as regards the first type of situations to appraise whether a legal person has the nationality of the Contracting State party to the dispute would be inconsistent with the object and purpose of this Article as it would restrict this scope (2004, Decision on Jurisdiction, para. 46). The Presiding Arbitrator disagreed with the majority as he favoured the use of the control test, explaining notably that this was 'not a question of extending the control test at the expense of the rule of the *siège social*', but 'simply giving effect to a provision the rationale of which is to grant the protection of the ICSID procedures to *all* genuinely international investments but, by the same token, *only* to genuinely international investments (2004, Dissenting Opinion, para. 24). Considering that the 'double-barrelled test' starts with the appraisal of jurisdiction under the ICSID Convention, which sets the outer limit of ICSID tribunals' jurisdiction, he concluded that the Tribunal did not have jurisdiction without it being then necessary to appraise jurisdiction under the IIA at hand in that case (paras. 14–15 and 29). The Tribunal appointed in *Rompetrol Group N.V.* v. *Romania* disagreed with this methodology; it saw it as being necessary to start the examination of jurisdiction with the IIA, given the wide discretion left by the ICSID Convention as regards the determination of the valid link to establish nationality. More fundamentally, it rejected the use of the control test, as it argued that it is open to IIA States parties to adopt incorporation as the only link to establish nationality for the purpose of the ICSID Convention (2008, Decision on Jurisdiction and Admissibility, paras. 82–83).

14.3.3.3 States, Public Legal Persons, and Mixed Legal Persons

When one examines the legal category of investor, the history of international investment law and arbitration, as well as the identity of the claimants in arbitration proceedings, lead us to focus on private persons. Yet, it is important not to exclude from the picture 'mixed' legal persons partially owned or controlled by States, public legal persons fully owned or controlled by them, and even States themselves. Indeed, one or several of these legal persons are considered under some investment treaties as investors. This holds true in IIA practice as well as under the ICSID Convention.

While some IIAs do not refer in any way to those legal persons, a number of them do so according to a variety of different formulations and combinations. Many of those IIAs provide that privately owned or controlled legal persons as well as those that are owned or controlled by the government can qualify as investors (e.g. 2018 Japan–Armenia IIA, Article 1.d). Those IIAs usually provide for an illustrative list referring in particular to 'corporations'. Some agreements list also specifically public legal persons that can be considered as investors, such as 'official agencies' (e.g. 2016 Argentina–Qatar IIA, Article

1.1.c). A few IIAs do not characterise government-owned or -controlled legal persons as such as investors, but instead define the government of the State party that owns or controls those persons as being an investor (e.g. 2014 UAE–Greece IIA, Article 1.3.c). Other IIAs do not even refer to 'government owned or controlled legal persons', but directly to State organs, like the 2015 Kyrgyzstan–Kuwait IIA, which mentions the 'government' of a State party (Article 1.2), or the 2016 Nigeria–UAE IIA, which lists the 'government', its 'subdivisions' and 'local governments' (Article 1.b.3). The 2014 Burkina Faso–Singapore IIA refers directly to a 'Party', meaning to States (Article 1).

Turning to the ICSID Convention, it is worth remembering that Article 25.1 provides that the jurisdiction of the Centre extends to disputes between a Contracting State and a national of another Contracting State. This begs the question as to whether the Convention sets an outer limit to the jurisdiction of ICSID arbitration tribunals with regard to the disputes involving public or mixed legal persons qualifying as investors under IIAs.

This issue has arisen in relation to disputes involving government-owned corporations or mixed-economy companies. Following the approach adopted by the Tribunal in *CSOB A.S.* v. *Slovak Republic*, which considered that the extent of the government's ownership is irrelevant (1999, Decision on Jurisdiction, para. 17), arbitration tribunals rely usually in this respect on the test formulated by Broches, the first Secretary-General of ICSID and one of the principal drafters of the Convention. He explained: '[F]or purposes of the Convention a mixed economy company or government-owned corporation should not be disqualified as a "national of another Contracting State" unless it is acting as an agent for the government or is discharging an essentially governmental function.'[8]

As it appears in this statement, which has since been followed in arbitration practice, there are two alternative situations in which such legal persons shall not be considered as a 'national of another Contracting State' under Article 25.1 of the ICSID Convention: when they are an agent of the State or when they are discharging an essentially governmental function. In this respect, it is worth noting that in order to appraise whether a mixed-economy company or a government-owned company is exercising governmental functions, the *CSOB A.S.* Tribunal stressed that it is important to focus, not on the purpose of the legal person's activities, but on their nature, meaning their commercial rather than governmental nature (para. 20). In *Beijing Urban Construction Group Co. Ltd* v. *Yemen*, the Tribunal insisted that the application of the 'Broches test' must consist of a 'context-specific analysis' that aims to determine the commercial or governmental function of the investment at hand (2017, Decision on Jurisdiction, para. 35).

---

[8] Ibid., at 354–355.

14.3.4 Investors' Conduct Impacting on Jurisdiction and Admissibility

Preliminary Remarks

To fully understand the conduct focused on in this subsection, it is worth drawing two distinctions at this preliminary stage.

The first distinction that can be made is between conduct that is intrinsically tinged with illegality ('illegal conduct') and conduct that, although intrinsically constituting the exercise of an existing right, may be characterised as an 'abusive conduct' due to the circumstances in which the right is exercised. Second, one can distinguish between different types of conduct depending on whether they relate to the acquisition of assets or are concerned with the initiation of arbitration proceedings. As examined below, 'illegal conduct' typically relates to the acquisition of assets, while 'abusive conduct' pertains to the initiation of arbitration proceedings.

As a final preliminary remark, the discrepancies displayed by arbitration practice concerning the classification of such conduct as relating to jurisdiction or to admissibility should be noted. These discrepancies do not seem to be fully explained by the fact that, as noted by the Tribunal in *Churchill Mining PLC* v. *Indonesia* with respect to fraudulent conduct, the legal consequences of such conduct depend to a large extent on the circumstances of each case (2016, Award, para. 494). The objective here is not to discuss this classification, but more generally to analyse the different types of investors' conduct that impact on jurisdiction and admissibility. To facilitate this analysis, it is worth first introducing the key notions used by arbitration tribunals to address illegal and abusive conduct.

14.3.4.1 Key Notions

a Good Faith

Good faith is a principle common to all legal systems, both domestic and international. In international investment law and arbitration, good faith or its counterpart, meaning bad faith, is relied on and discussed in relation to the conduct of both host States (e.g. *Jan Oostergetel and Theodora Laurentius* v. *Slovak Republic*, 2012, Final Award, paras. 300–303) and investors as evidenced in this subsection. In that sense, the Tribunal appointed in *Phoenix Action, Ltd* v. *Czech Republic* defined 'the principle of good faith', in reference to D'Amato,[9] as follows: '[It] requires parties "to deal honestly and fairly with each other, to represent their motives and purposes truthfully, and to refrain from taking unfair advantages" [footnote omitted] ... [It] governs the relations between States, but also the legal rights and duties of those seeking to assert an international claim under a treaty' (2009, Award, para. 107).

It comes as no surprise, then, that good faith constitutes the conceptual and legal cornerstone of the reasoning developed by arbitration tribunals to discuss

---

[9] A D'Amato, 'Good Faith' in R Bernhardt (ed), *Encyclopedia of Public International Law* (Vol. 7) (Oxford University Press 1984), at 107.

illegal and abusive conduct. Concerning the conduct of investors specifically, the Tribunal in *Abaclat* v. *Argentina* drew a distinction between 'material good faith' and 'procedural good faith'. It defined the former as referring to the context and the way in which the investment is made and for which the investor seeks protection, and the latter as relating to the context and way in which the investor initiates its treaty claim seeking protection for its investment (2011, Decision on Jurisdiction and Admissibility, para. 647).

b Abuse of Rights and Abuse of Process

Whether explicitly in connection with good faith or not, arbitration tribunals also rely on the theory of abuse of rights and/or the theory of abuse of process, which are common to numerous domestic legal systems and to international law.

'Abuse of rights' was explained as follows by Lauterpacht:[10] 'There is no right, however well established, which could not, in some circumstances, be refused recognition on the ground that it has been abused' (quoted in *Phoenix Action, Ltd* v. *Czech Republic*, 2009, Award, para. 107).

Abuse of process is a subcategory of abuse of rights, as applied to procedural rights. More precisely, as explained by De Brabandere in relation to *Chevron Corporation USA* v. *Ecuador* (2008, Interim Award, para. 137), it 'implies that although a claimant has a valid procedural right, the claimant cannot exercise that right because the exercise of the right amounts to an abuse of that procedural right'.[11] Conduct that amounts to such an abuse of process is also sometimes referred to as 'abuse of the law' (*Malicorp Limited* v. *Egypt*, 2011, Award, para. 116), '*détournement de procédure*' or, as for ICSID proceedings, 'abuse of the system of international ICSID investment arbitration' (*Phoenix Action, Ltd* v. *Czech Republic*, 2009, Award, paras. 143–144).

14.3.4.2 Acquisition of Assets

As discussed above, for assets to be considered a covered investment, a number of IIAs provide that they must have been acquired legally. In *Inceysa Vallisoletana, S.L.* v. *El Salvador*, the Tribunal considered that such a legality requirement is a manifestation of 'international public policy', which it defined – in reference to Cabra and Gerardo[12] and Goldschmidt[13] – as a series of fundamental principles which constitute the very essence of the State and which aims primarily at preserving the values of the international legal system against actions contrary to it (2006, Award, paras. 245–247). In line with the mainstream view expressed in arbitration practice following

---

[10] H Lauterpacht, *Development of International Law by the International Court* (Stevens 1958), at 164.

[11] E De Brabandere, '"Good Faith", "Abuse of Process" and the Initiation of Investment Treaty Claims' (2012) 3 *Journal of International Dispute Settlement* 609, at 619–620.

[12] M Cabra, M Gerardo, *Tratado De Derecho Internacional Privado* (5th ed, Temis 1999), at 249.

[13] W Goldschmidt, *Derecho Internacional Privado* (8th ed, Depalma 1999), at 163.

which the legality requirement is inherent to the notion of investment and is to be tested as such even in the absence of any reference to it in the text of the IIA at hand, this notion of 'international public policy' is also conceived of by some arbitration tribunals as being implicitly present in IIAs, typically in relation to corruption (*Vladislav Kim* v. *Uzbekistan*, 2017, Decision on Jurisdiction, para. 593). In *World Duty Free Company Limited* v. *Kenya*, the Tribunal considered corruption as being contrary to 'international public policy', without linking this finding in any way to the IIA at hand in that case, but by referring instead to domestic laws and international conventions (2006, Award, para. 157). It is worth noting that the existence and the role of the clean hands doctrine as a legal justification to bar claims relating to illegal conduct is more controversial (e.g. *South American Silver Limited (Bermuda)* v. *Bolivia*, 2018, Award, para. 443).

The types of illegal conduct of investors that may impact on jurisdiction and admissibility are manifold. Arbitration tribunals have typically dealt with concealments (e.g. *Plama Consortium Limited* v. *Bulgaria*), forgery (e.g. *Malicorp Limited* v. *Egypt*) and corruption (e.g. *Metal-Tech Ltd* v. *Uzbekistan*), whether allegedly committed by the claimant directly, or by a third party in connection with the asset at hand (e.g. *Alasdair Ross Anderson* v. *Costa Rica*). As illustrated by that latter case, those situations involving a third party have raised the issue as to whether the claimant lacked due diligence or whether it deliberately ignored the conduct of that party (2010, Award, para. 58).

Among such conduct, corruption has been a key issue in recent years. The legality of conduct allegedly constitutive of corruption has been appraised against both the domestic law of the host State and international public policy. As to the latter, arbitration tribunals have entered into detailed discussion of international instruments in appraising the exact scope and content of the prohibition of corruption. In this respect, and as noted by the Tribunal in *Vladislav Kim* v. *Uzbekistan*, there seems to be no consensus on this exact scope and content, beyond the consensus on the prohibition of the corruption of government officials (2017, Decision on Jurisdiction, para. 598).

14.3.4.3 Initiation of Proceedings

The circumstances of the initiation of arbitration proceedings that may impact on jurisdiction and admissibility are mainly twofold. They pertain to the restructuring of an investment and to multiple proceedings.

a Investment Restructuring

As noted by the Tribunal in *Aguas del Tunari, S.A.* v. *Bolivia*, 'it is not uncommon in practice and – absent a particular limitation – not illegal to locate one's operation in a jurisdiction perceived to provide a beneficial regulatory and legal environment in terms, for examples, of taxation or the substantive law of the jurisdiction, including the availability of a BIT' (2005, Decision on Jurisdiction, para. 330). The structuring and the restructuring of an investment with a view to accessing the substantive protection of an IIA and securing access to arbitration for potential future disputes is indeed not prohibited.

On the other hand, it is well agreed that a restructuring is constitutive of an abuse of process when it pursues such objectives at a time when a dispute has arisen or is foreseeable. In *Pac Rim Cayman LLC* v. *El Salvador*, the Tribunal articulated the test of foreseeability as follows, while acknowledging that its implementation is very much fact-sensitive: '[T]he dividing-line occurs when the relevant party can see an actual dispute or can foresee a specific future dispute as a very high probability and not merely as a possible controversy . . . before that dividing-line is reached, there will be ordinarily no abuse of process; but after that dividing-line is passed, there ordinarily will be' (2012, Decision on Jurisdiction, para. 2.99). In that sense, the Tribunal stated in *Philip Morris Asia Limited* v. *Australia* that '[a] dispute is foreseeable when there is a reasonable prospect that a measure that may give rise to a treaty claim will materialise' (2015, Award on Jurisdiction and Admissibility, para. 585).

Different types of investment restructurings have been considered as constitutive of an abuse of process: for instance, the creation of a foreign society (*Phoenix Action, Ltd* v. *Czech Republic*), the use of an existing 'fictitious' society which is 'awaken' – to use the term of the Tribunal in *Capital Financial Holdings Luxembourg SA* v. *Cameroon* – precisely at the time when the initiation of a proceeding is contemplated (2017, Award, para. 365), or the transfer of shares to a natural person (*Renée Rose Levy and Gremcitel S.A.* v. *Peru*).

b Multiple Proceedings

Preliminary Remarks

For any given asset and operation, various different persons may potentially qualify as an investor under the same or different IIAs and initiate arbitration proceedings in this respect. From a corporate point of view, this is due to the fact that investments are often structured through various layers of corporate entities. From a legal point of view, this results in particular from the approaches retained in IIA practice as regards the definition of an 'investment' and of an 'investor'. This can lead to various situations in which multiple proceedings are initiated, such as by legal persons and their shareholders. These situations fall into two categories: successive proceedings and parallel proceedings.

It is worth noting that IIAs have traditionally rarely addressed those latter situations, nor have the ICSID Convention Arbitration Rules, contrary to the SCC Arbitration Rules (Article 15). This practice is changing. The possibility to consolidate and coordinate proceedings is explicitly contemplated in the 2019 ICSID Working Paper n° 3 under proposed Arbitration Rule 45.[14] Likewise,

---

[14] ICSID, 'Proposals for Amendment of the ICSID Rules', Working Paper n°3 (August 2019), available at https://icsid.worldbank.org/en.

a greater number of IIAs concluded recently incorporate a consolidation clause as illustrated by Article 9.28 of the 2018 CPTPP.

Regardless of the fact that proceedings have been joined according to different modalities and scope, even in the ICSID context as illustrated by *BSG Resources Limited, BSG Resources (Guinea) Limited and BSG Resources (Guinea) SARL v. Republic of Guinea* (2016, Procedural Order n° 5), arbitration tribunals have dealt with the impact of parallel proceedings and also successive proceedings on jurisdiction and admissibility. It is worth noting in this respect that arbitration practice displays nuances and differences mainly in relation to the appraisal of the identity of the parties in the respective proceedings as well as the identity of the causes of action and reliefs sought for, something that is only partly explained by the specifics of the cases.

i Successive Proceedings There is a consensus that successive proceedings are not abusive as such. This was recognised for instance by the Tribunal in *Eskosol S.p.A. in Liquidazione* v. *Italy*. At the same time, this Tribunal stressed that, for instance, 'there may be certain circumstances in which a foreign shareholder and the local company in which it holds shares have such identical interests that it would be abusive to permit arbitration of a given dispute by one after the other already has concluded an arbitration over the same dispute' (2017, Decision on Application under Rule 41(5), paras. 167 and 170). Irrespective of the different views of arbitration tribunals on the circumstances in which successive proceedings are considered as being acceptable or not acceptable, it is worth mentioning that tribunals discuss the matter not only in relation to abuse of process, but also in relation to the notions of *res judicata* and estoppel (e.g. *Apotex* v. *USA*, 2014, Award, paras. 7.41–7.61)

ii Parallel Proceedings Likewise, there is a consensus that parallel proceedings are not abusive as such. For instance, in *Ampal-American Israel Corp.* v. *Egypt*, the Tribunal noted that, absent an agreement for consolidation between the parties, two treaty tribunals may each consider claims of separate investors, each of which holds distinct tranches of the same investment (2016, Decision on Jurisdiction, para. 329). But here again, as illustrated in that case, arbitration tribunals set limits to the acceptability of such parallel proceedings. The claimant in those proceedings advanced a claim in respect of the same interest in a company for which its 100 per cent subsidiary made a claim in another arbitration proceeding. The Tribunal found this as amounting to double pursuit of the same claim in respect of the same interest. It noted that 'while the same party in interest might reasonably seek to protect its claim in two fora where the jurisdiction of each tribunal is unclear, once jurisdiction is otherwise confirmed, it would crystallize in an abuse of process for in substance the same claim is to be pursued on the merits before two tribunals'. As a result, it invited the claimant to elect to pursue that portion of the claim in the ICSID proceedings, stating that it would otherwise revisit the question of abuse of process in this regard (paras. 330–339). Regardless of the different views of arbitration tribunals on the situations in which parallel proceedings are deemed acceptable or not, it is noteworthy that tribunals examine the matter not only in relation to abuse of process, but also on that of *lis pendens* (e.g. *Busta* v. *Czech Republic*, 2017, Final Award, paras. 211–215).

15

Investor–State Arbitration and the Law of State Responsibility
Attribution, Circumstances Precluding Wrongfulness and Reparation

Introduction

Parts I and II of this textbook aim to provide a detailed analysis of the obligations that international investment agreements (IIAs) place on States parties in their relations with foreign investors. As also explained, the substance of many of those obligations can also be found in customary international law (CIL). Under general public international law, the breach of such obligations is not the only element that grounds the international responsibility of States. The elements of an internationally wrongful act are in fact twofold: there must be a conduct that is attributable to the State under international law and that also constitutes a breach of its international obligation(s). Even where those two elements are met, there may be circumstances that preclude the wrongfulness of that conduct. To use the words of the International Law Commission (ILC), they constitute a shield against an otherwise well-founded claim for the breach of an international obligation attributable to the State.[1] Overall, the existence of an internationally wrongful act requires that three cumulative conditions be fulfilled: (1) attribution of the conduct to the State; (2) breach of the State's international obligation(s) by that conduct; and (3) lack of circumstances precluding the wrongfulness of that conduct. A finding that such an internationally wrongful act occurred entails certain legal consequences; it gives rise to a new legal relationship, often called a 'secondary obligation', which requires notably the State to provide full reparation for the damage caused. It is worth stressing in this respect that damage, as well as intent, are not elements of the wrongful acts under the international law of State responsibility.

The present chapter analyses how these rules apply in the context of investor–State arbitration. More precisely, it focuses on attribution, circumstances precluding wrongfulness and reparation, with Part II having set out a discussion of the relevant breaches of IIA obligations. It is worth noting that arbitration tribunals deal almost systematically with these issues in reference to the

---

[1] ILC, Draft Articles on Responsibility of States for Internationally Wrongful Acts with Commentaries (2001) (Vol. II, Part 2) *Yearbook of the International Law Commission*, at 71.

2001 Articles on Responsibility of States for Internationally Wrongful Acts (ARSIWA)[2] and their Commentaries,[3] which were prepared by the ILC. To provide a comprehensive analysis of attribution, circumstances precluding wrongfulness and reparation in international investment law and arbitration and to make sense of arbitration practice, it is therefore useful to recall in what follows the public international law background of these elements, by referring to the ARSIWA and summarising its Commentaries.

At the outset, some general remarks can first be formulated with respect to the ARSIWA and the CIL rules governing State responsibility.

Content-wise, the ARSIWA consists largely of a codification of those customary rules that are per se legally binding. But one should stress that the instrument containing the Articles, i.e. an annex to UNGA Resolution 56/83, is itself non-binding. For didactic purposes, this chapter sometimes refers to the relevant provisions of the ARSIWA directly as they codify CIL rules – however, this must not be understood as meaning that this annex to Resolution 56/83 is binding.

On a different note, it should be mentioned that the rules of CIL governing State responsibility constitute a *lex generalis*, States having the possibility to create a *lex specialis* specifying the rules on the matter, or some of them, in a treaty that they conclude. As discussed in relation to reparation, for instance, it is noteworthy in this respect that some IIAs concluded in the 2010s establish such a *lex specialis* on certain issues.

Finally, it should be said that those customary rules have developed in the context of inter-State relations and not of the relations between States and foreign private persons. This point has been noted by a few arbitration tribunals (e.g. 2016, *Masdar Solar & Wind Cooperatief U.A.* v. *Spain*, 2018, Award, para. 167).

15.1 Attribution

Preliminary Remarks

As explained above, attribution is an element of the internationally wrongful act – as such, issues of attribution pertain to the merits of investor–State disputes. It is noteworthy that similar issues are debated for jurisdictional purposes, with a number of tribunals relying on the rules on attribution to decide whether the host State can be considered as being a party to the dispute (e.g. *Flemingo DutyFree Shop Private Limited* v. *Poland*, 2016, Award, para. 418). Irrespective of this practice and what it may indirectly teach us about

---

[2] Articles on Responsibility of States for Internationally Wrongful Acts, Annex to the United Nations General Assembly Resolution (2001) 56/83 (Vol. II Part 2) *Yearbook of the International Law Commission*.

[3] ILC (n 1).

attribution in investor–State arbitration, it is worth stressing that the customary international law rules on attribution, as codified in the ARSIWA, have developed and pertain *sensu stricto* to State responsibility.

Attribution in investor–State disputes pertains to a broad range of entities, such as municipalities, regulators, enterprises and universities. In addition to this diversity, the nature of the link between the same type of entity, typically enterprises, and the host State may vary from one case to the other; likewise, in a given case, there may be various links that connect a given entity to the host State.

This helps to explain why, although one ground may be sufficient to establish attribution, arbitration tribunals often test and establish this element of State responsibility on several grounds. This trend is notably illustrated in *Emilio Agustin Maffezini* v. *Spain*, and was well explained by the Tribunal appointed in that case with reference to Brownlie:[4]

> Since neither the Convention nor the Argentine–Spanish BIT establish guiding principles for deciding the here relevant issues, the Tribunal may look to the applicable rules of international law in deciding whether a particular entity is a state body. These standards have evolved and been applied in the context of the law of State responsibility. Here, the test that has been developed looks to various factors, such as ownership, control, the nature, purposes and objectives of the entity whose actions are under scrutiny, and to the character of the actions taken. [footnote omitted] ... The question whether or not SODIGA is a State entity must be examined first from a formal or structural point of view. Here a finding that the entity is owned by the State, directly or indirectly, gives rise to a rebuttable presumption that it is a State entity. The same result will obtain if an entity is controlled by the State, directly or indirectly. A similar presumption arises if an entity's purpose or objectives is the carrying out of functions which are governmental in nature or which are otherwise normally reserved to the State, or which by their nature are not usually carried out by private businesses or individuals. [footnote omitted] ... Because of the many forms that State enterprises may take and thus shape the manners of State action, the structural test by itself may not always be a conclusive determination whether an entity is an organ of the State or whether its acts may be attributed to the State. An additional test has been developed, a functional test, which looks to the functions of or role to be performed by the entity [footnote omitted] ... It is difficult to determine, *a priori*, whether these various tests and standards need necessarily be cumulative. It is likely that there are circumstances when they need not be. Of course, when all or most of the tests result in a finding of State action, the result, while still merely a presumption, comes closer to being conclusive. (2000, Decision of the Tribunal on Objections to Jurisdiction, paras. 76–81)

---

[4] I Brownlie, *System of the Law of Nations: State Responsibility (Part I)* (Oxford University Press 1983), at 132 et seq.

This statement and the structural and functional tests it refers to have often been endorsed and used in arbitration practice (e.g. 2016, *Flemingo DutyFree Shop Private Limited* v. *Poland*, Award, para. 426).

From the point of view of CIL, as mentioned by the *Maffezini* Tribunal, one can only but notice that the essence of these tests and their use by arbitration tribunals tend to blur the distinction between the various grounds of attribution that it distinguishes. In that sense, it seems that these tests, although they are linked to CIL, constitute in fact a distinct and alternative way to appraise attribution. This was implicitly acknowledged by the Tribunal appointed in *Ioannis Kardassopoulos* v. *Georgia*, which noted that the issue of attribution shall be decided in the same way, regardless of 'whether one applies the principles of attribution set forth in the ILC Articles on State Responsibility or the tests developed in arbitral jurisprudence to ascertain whether the acts or omissions of a particular entity are attributable to a State' (2010, Award, para. 280).

Regardless of this body of arbitration jurisprudence and the extent to which it departs from the customary rules on attribution, it remains that these rules constitute the law to be applied to attribution matters in the absence of IIA provisions regulating it. For that reason, the following analyses attribution by distinguishing between the CIL grounds that are the most relevant in the context of investor–State disputes, namely: (1) the conduct of State organs; (2) the conduct of entities exercising elements of governmental authority; (3) the conduct directed or controlled by a State; and, secondarily, (4) the conduct acknowledged and adopted by a State as its own.

Before entering into these analyses, it is necessary to clarify at the outset the issue of due diligence that is encountered in Chapter 6 in relation to the full protection and security (FPS) standard. Due diligence is not a ground upon which to attribute the conduct of private persons to States – rather, it is an obligation placed upon those States to prevent and repress such conduct. The violation of the obligation of due diligence results typically from the conduct – more specifically the omission – of State organs leading to a failure to prevent and repress the conduct of those private persons, the conduct of those organs itself being attributable to States.

15.1.1 Conduct of State Organs

15.1.1.1 Public International Law Background: ARSIWA and its Commentaries

This ground of attribution is addressed in Article 4 of the ARSIWA and its Commentaries. With regard to the objective and the methodology explained in the introduction, this subsection summarises the Commentaries on this Article.

This ground of attribution derives from the unitary essence of the State, according to which all persons and entities that form part of the State apparatus and act on its behalf shall all have their conduct attributed to the State (para. 5). Those persons and entities, i.e. the 'organs', are primarily those designated as such by the State's domestic law – however, because such laws may not be exhaustive, it is acknowledged for the purpose of this ground that tribunals may look to practice in order to ascertain whether a given person or entity is to be considered as a State organ. This extension beyond domestic law's classification is also explained by the fact that domestic law's categories may not correspond to the scope of State organs as it is construed in CIL (para. 11).

The exact function, position and (de)centralised nature of the organ has no bearing on attribution. This ground covers the three classical functions – i.e. legislative, executive and judicial – as well as any other function consisting in a mix of them (para. 6). The situation of the organ in the hierarchy is also irrelevant: the conduct of subordinates is attributable to States, as is the conduct of superiors (para. 7). By the same token, it does not matter whether the organ is part of the central government or if it forms part of a territorial unit of the State (para. 8).

This ground of attribution covers the conduct of those persons acting in their official capacity. In other words, the purely private conduct of persons who happen to be a State organ is not attributable to States. Such private conduct is to be distinguished from *ultra vires* conduct – that is, conduct that amounts to an excess of authority or a contravention of instructions (para. 13). Under CIL, the conduct of State organs is attributable to States even if they exceed their authority or contravene instructions received (Article 7).

15.1.1.2 Investor-State Arbitration

Arbitration tribunals have characterised as State organs a broad range of persons and entities, in particular: local governments (e.g. *Metalclad Corporation* v. *Mexico*, 2000, Award, para. 73), domestic courts and custom authorities (e.g. *Flemingo DutyFree Shop Private Limited* v. *Poland*, 2016, Award, para. 424), regulators (e.g. *UAB E Energija (Lithuania)* v. *Latvia*, 2017, Award, para. 804), or enterprises (e.g. *Ampal-American Israel Corp.* v. *Egypt*, 2017, Decision on Liability and Heads of Loss, para. 138).

In order to reach such a characterisation, tribunals have either relied on or found confirmation in the key public international law principles mentioned above.

For instance, in *UAB E Energija (Lithuania)* v. *Latvia*, the Tribunal stressed in reference to the ARSIWA Commentaries that Article 4 'extends to organs of government of whatever kind or classification, exercising whatever functions, and at whatever level in the hierarchy, including those at provincial or even local level'. This Tribunal also noted that acts should be performed in an official capacity to be attributable to States (paras. 799–800).

Tribunals have also recalled the *ultra vires* rule. For instance, the Tribunal appointed in *Southern Pacific Properties (Middle East) Limited* v. *Egypt* stated:

> The principle of international law which the Tribunal is bound to apply is that which establishes the international responsibility of States when unauthorized or *ultra vires* acts of officials have been performed by State agents under cover of their official character. If such unauthorized or *ultra vires* acts could not be

ascribed to the State, all State responsibility would be rendered illusory. (1992, Award on the Merits, para. 85)

It is also worth mentioning that tribunals have acknowledged that the classification of organs provided by the host States' domestic law is not determinative as to whether a person or an entity will be characterised as a State organ (e.g. *Almas* v. *Poland*, 2016, Award, para. 207). While acknowledging this principle, the Tribunal appointed in *Union Fenosa Gas, S.A.* v. *Egypt* nonetheless warned – in reference to the case law of the International Court of Justice (ICJ) – that a finding that transcends a domestic law classification should remain extraordinary.[5] The Tribunal argued that the 'circumstances sufficient to connote the status of an organ of the State to a separate legal person must be extraordinary, involving functions and powers considered to be as quintessentially powers of Statehood, such as those exercised by police authorities' (2018, Award, para. 9.96).

In this respect, one can witness divergences in arbitration practice – partly explained by the specifics of each case – as to when a tribunal may 'pierce the veil' of legal personality in order to consider that the distinct legal personality of a legal person does not prevent it from being considered as a State organ.

In *Ampal-American Israel Corp.* v. *Egypt*, the Tribunal considered that the Egyptian General Petroleum Corporation (EGPC) was an Egyptian State organ, despite it being endowed with an 'independent juristic personality'. It reached this conclusion taking into account a number of factors, in particular the fact that: (1) it was overseen by the Minister of Petroleum; (2) its capital consisted of State funds; (3) the Chairman of the Board of Directors was appointed by the Egyptian President; (4) the Board members were appointed by the Prime Minister; and (5) the resolutions of the Board needed to be ratified by the Minister of Petroleum, who was empowered to amend or cancel them (2017, Decision on Liability and Heads of Loss, para.138). While it noted the differences between that case and the case before it, the Tribunal appointed in *Union Fenosa Gas, S.A.* v. *Egypt* commented on this decision reached by the *Ampal* Tribunal, arguing that it failed to explain the reason why the abovementioned factors show that EGPC is part of the structure of the State so as to deny its autonomous existence (2018, Award, para. 9.109).

Along the same lines, other tribunals have reached the opposite conclusion – for instance, in *Noble Ventures, Inc.* v. *Romania*, the Tribunal considered that the State Ownership Fund (SOF) and its 'successor' the Authority for the Privatisation and Management of the State Ownership (APAPS) could not be characterised as a 'State organ' under Article 4 of the ARSIWA precisely because they were legal entities separate from the State (2005, Award, para. 69). The Tribunal reached this conclusion despite the fact that these entities displayed features *mutatis mutandis* similar to those of EGPC in *Ampal-American*

---

[5] *Case Concerning Application of the Convention on the Prevention and Punishment of the Crime of Genocide (Bosnia and Herzegovina* v. *Serbia and Montenegro)*, 2007, Judgment, para. 393.

Israel Corp. v. *Egypt*, notably the fact that: (1) SOF was owned by the government; (2) the Prime Minister was an appointing authority of the Board of Directors; and (3) the Chairman of SOF/APAPS was the Minister of Privatisation. The rationale underlying this approach was well explained by the Tribunal in *Bayindir Insaat Turizm Ticaret Ve Sanayi AS* v. *Pakistan*:

> The fact that there may be links between NHA [a public corporation] and some sections of the Government of Pakistan does not mean that the two are not distinct. State entities and agencies do not operate in an institutional or regulatory vacuum. They normally have links with other authorities as well as with the government. Because of its separate legal status, the Tribunal discards the possibility of treating NHA as a State organ under Article 4 of the ILC Articles. (2009, Award, para. 119)

This refusal to 'pierce the veil' of legal personality did not prevent the *Nobel* and *Bayindir* Tribunals from considering the status of those entities under Article 5 of the ARSIWA, which led the former to conclude that the conduct of SOF and APAPS were attributable to Romania on the ground that they were exercising elements of governmental authority (paras. 70 and 80).

15.1.2 Conduct of Persons or Entities Exercising a Governmental Authority

15.1.2.1 Public International Law Background: ARSIWA and its Commentaries

This ground of attribution is addressed in Article 5 of the ARSIWA and its Commentaries. With regard to the objective and methodology explained in the introduction, this subsection summarises the Commentaries on this Article.

Under this ground of attribution, the conduct of persons and entities that are not an organ of the State but are empowered by the law of that State to exercise elements of governmental authority can be attributed to this State. In order to have this effect, the empowerment must be specific; it will not suffice for the empowerment to simply authorise a person or an entity to participate in general in the regulation of society (para. 7). More generally, the mere public interest dimension that a certain conduct may have does not make it attributable to States.

This ground applies to a broad range of entities, such as public corporations, public agencies and even, in special circumstances, private companies. In fact, the characterisation of such entities as being a public or a private entity is not decisive for the purpose of attribution. Likewise, factors such as the degree of participation of the State in the capital of an enterprise, or the fact that it is not subject to State control, are not decisive. What matters is the specific empowerment to exercise elements of governmental authority as such, even if the empowerment is of a limited extent (paras. 2–3).

Those persons that benefit from such an empowerment may contemporaneously be conducting other activities of a private or commercial nature. It is worth stressing that these contemporaneous activities will not be attributable to the State (para. 5). On the other hand, the conduct adopted *ultra vires* in the exercise of governmental authority does fall within the scope of this ground (ARSIWA, Article 7).

15.1.2.2 Investor–State Arbitration

Arbitration tribunals have attributed to States the conduct of a wide range of entities considered as exercising elements of governmental authority. This was, for instance, the case of a state-owned company in *Saint-Gobain Performance Plastics Europe* v. *Venezuela* (2016, Decision on Liability and the Principles of Quantum, paras. 457–460) and of a university in *Bosh International, Inc.* v. *Ukraine* (2012, Award, paras. 173–178).

When appraising whether the conduct of entities could be attributed to States based on this ground, tribunals have focused on the three key criteria mentioned above: (1) the exercise of a governmental authority; (2) the specific empowerment to do so under domestic law; and (3) the requirement that the conduct at hand be performed in the exercise of this authority.

At the outset, it is noteworthy that tribunals insist that entities must be specifically empowered to and must actually exercise elements of governmental authority, as opposed to conduct that merely has a general public interest dimension or purpose. In that sense, the Tribunal appointed in *Jan de Nul N.V.* v. *Egypt* distinguished the '"service public" element' of a conduct from the use of '"prérogatives de puissance publique" or governmental authority' (2008, Award, para. 170). In the same vein, the Tribunal argued in *Gustav F W Hamester GmbH & Co KG* v. *Ghana* that it was 'not enough for an act of a public entity to have been performed in the general fulfilment of some general interest, mission or purpose to qualify as an attributable act' under Article 5 of the ARSIWA (2010, Award, para. 202).

To ascertain whether entities exercise a governmental authority, tribunals have used a variety of factors. In *UAB E Energija (Lithuania)* v. *Latvia*, the Tribunal focused on the function of the regulator (2017, Award, para. 809). The Tribunal appointed in *Flemingo DutyFree Shop Private Limited* v. *Poland* appraised the conduct by reference to all of the non-exhaustive factors listed in the Commentaries to Article 5 of the ARSIWA, namely: the content of the powers, the way in which they are conferred, the purpose for which they are to be exercised and the accountability with the government (2016, Award, paras. 438–439). In both cases, the Tribunals concluded that the conduct at hand constituted an exercise of governmental authority. On the contrary, in *Tenaris* v. *Venezuela*, the Tribunal considered that CVG Ferrominera del Orinoco was not exercising any element of governmental authority (29 January 2016, Award, *Tenaris S.A.* v. *Venezuela*, para. 416).

As for the third criterion, some tribunals have concluded that only part of the conduct in question constituted an exercise of governmental authority, the other part being a commercial activity that could therefore not be attributed to States. For instance, in *Bosh International, Inc.* v. *Ukraine*, the Tribunal considered that the provision by the Taras Shevchenko National University of Kiev of higher education services and the management of State-owned property constituted a form of governmental authority, while on the other hand, it decided that the conclusion (and the termination) of a contract regarding the renovation and redevelopment of a property was a private, commercial activity that fell outside the scope of Article 5 of the ARSIWA (2012, Award, paras. 173 and 177). It reached this conclusion on the grounds that the university was an autonomous institution entitled to engage in joint activities without having to receive any particular authorisation from the State. These features contribute to the explanation of why the conclusion of this Tribunal differs from that reached in *Flemingo* v. *Poland*. In that case, the Tribunal considered that the conclusion and termination of a lease agreement by the Polish Airports State Enterprise was an exercise of governmental authority as it did not act autonomously. The Tribunal deduced this in particular from the requirement that the conclusion of the Agreement be approved by the State Treasury (2016, Award, paras. 443–447).

It is also worth mentioning that arbitration tribunals have referred to the *ultra vires* principle when examining this ground of attribution as well. This happened, for instance, in *Noble Ventures, Inc.* v. *Romania*, where the Tribunal contemplated the hypothesis that the acts of SOF and APAPS were *ultra vires*; it stated that because they had always acted in their capacity as persons specifically empowered by the domestic law to exercise elements of governmental authority, 'their acts would still have to be attributed to the Respondent, even if an excess of competence had been shown' (2005, Award, para. 81).

15.1.3 Conduct of Persons or a Group of Persons Acting under the Instruction, Direction or Control of the State

15.1.3.1 Public International Law Background: ARSIWA and its Commentaries

This ground of attribution is addressed in Article 8 of the ARSIWA and the Commentaries thereto. With regard to the objective and the methodology explained in the introduction, this subsection summarises the Commentaries on this Article.

This ground of attribution builds on the public international law principle according to which the conduct of private persons is – as a matter of principle – not attributable to States. As an exception, there can be attribution when there exists a real link between the conduct of such persons and the State. This link can be established, and the conduct thereby attributed, when private persons are in fact acting on the instructions of, or under the direction or control of, the State (para. 1). Any of these three situations can, on its own, ground attribution (para. 7).

The need for a real link helps to explain why, with regard to direction and control, the ICJ requires that the State directs or controls the specific operation in the context of which the conduct at hand is being performed. This requirement is known as the effective control test; it was first set out and applied by the Court in the *Case Concerning Military and Paramilitary Activities in and against Nicaragua*

(Nicaragua v. *United States of America)* (1986, Judgment, para. 115). Under this test, a general situation of dependence is not sufficient to ground attribution. In *Prosecutor* v. *Dusko Tadic*, the International Criminal Tribunal for the Former Yugoslavia (ICTY) relied on another test, namely the overall control test, stressing that 'international rules do not require that such control should extend to the issuance of specific orders or instructions relating to single military actions, whether or not such actions were contrary to international humanitarian law' (1999, Judgment, para. 145). Irrespective of whether or not the different approaches adopted by the ICJ and the ICTY can be explained by the subject matter and features of these cases, they nonetheless shed light on the requirement to take into account the specifics of each case in order to appraise whether there is indeed control or direction exercised by States over private persons (paras. 4–5).

As regards corporations, it is well established that the mere fact that these are created and controlled by States is insufficient to ground attribution. For that purpose, it must be shown that the State used control over the corporation in order to specifically achieve a particular result (para. 6).

15.1.3.2 Investor–State Arbitration

As examined above, in appraising attribution under Article 4 of the ARSIWA, arbitration tribunals have taken into account elements such as the State's appointing power and its decision-making authority. However, as stressed by the Tribunal in *Marfin Investment Group Holdings S.A.* v. *Cyprus*, tribunals have considered that such general control is not on its own enough to meet the test set out in Article 8 of the ARSIWA (2018, Award, para. 674). Rather, tribunals have required that the particular conduct at hand results from the State's instructions or is carried out under the State's direction or control. For instance, the Tribunal appointed in *Tulip Real Estate Investment and Development Netherlands B.V.* v. *Turkey* explained that 'the relevant enquiry remains whether Emlak was being directed, instructed or controlled by TOKI with respect to the specific activity of administering the Contract with Tulip JV in the sense of sovereign direction, instruction or control rather than the ordinary control exercised by a majority shareholder acting in the company's perceived commercial best interests' (2014, Award, para. 309). Commenting on this paragraph, the Annulment Committee appointed in that case stressed that it 'ha[d] no doubt that the Tribunal correctly interpreted Article 8 of the ILC Articles and applied the relevant test, that of effective control' (2015, Decision on Annulment, para. 189).

In the end, the Tribunal in that latter case reached the conclusion that the situation fell outside the scope of Article 8 of the ARSIWA. So, too, did the Tribunal in *Saint-Gobain Performance Plastics Europe* v. *Venezuela*, where it considered that the plant takeover by union members and 'sympathisers' of President Chavez could not be attributed to Venezuela. Although the Tribunal acknowledged that there existed a certain causal link between President Chavez's declaration and the takeover, it concluded that they did not act under his instructions, nor under his direction or control within the meaning of Article 8 of the ARSIWA. It stated: 'Plain causality, however, does not establish State responsibility under international law. Conduct of private persons can be attributed to the State only if there exists "*a specific factual relationship between the person or entity engaging in the conduct and the State*"' (2016, Decision on Liability and the Principles of Quantum, para. 450).

On the other hand, the Tribunal appointed in *Ampal-American Israel Corp.* v. *Egypt* concluded that the particular conduct in question, namely the decisions of the Egyptian General Petroleum Corporation and the Egyptian Natural Gas Holding Company to conclude and terminate the Gas Supply and Purchase Agreement, had been instructed by or made under the direction or control of Egypt (2017, Decision on Liability and Heads of Loss, para. 140).

15.1.4 Conduct Acknowledged and Adopted by a State as its Own

15.1.4.1 Public International Law Background: ARSIWA and its Commentaries

This ground of attribution is addressed in Article 11 of the ARSIWA and its Commentaries. With regard to the objective and methodology explained in the introduction, this subsection summarises the Commentaries on this Article.

Under this ground of attribution, the conduct of private persons that was not attributable to States at the time it was performed can be attributed to them as a result of their subsequent acknowledgement and adoption by those States as their own. It also builds upon the public international law principle pursuant to which the conduct of private persons is – as a matter of principle – not attributable to States (para. 3).

Acknowledgement and adoption are cumulative conditions (para. 9). Both conditions must be clear and unequivocal — yet, they can also be deduced from the conduct of States (para. 8). The conditions of acknowledgement and adoption are cumulative. Both must be clear and unequivocal – however, this does not prevent them from being inferred from the conduct of States. Such an acknowledgement and adoption of conduct should be distinguished from the general acknowledgement of a situation by States as well as from mere support and endorsement, which are all insufficient to ground attribution (para. 6).

15.1.4.2 Investor–State Arbitration

A few instances can be seen in arbitration practice where the conduct of private persons has been attributed as a result of their acknowledgement and adoption by States as their own. In *Ampal-American Israel Corp.* v. *Egypt*, for instance, the Tribunal inferred the acknowledgement and adoption from the fact that Egypt subsequently ratified the termination of the Gas Supply and Purchase Agreement made by the Egyptian General Petroleum Corporation and the Egyptian Natural Gas Holding Company (2017, Decision on Liability and Heads of Loss, para. 146). In *Saint-Gobain Performance Plastics Europe* v. *Venezuela*, the acknowledgement and adoption by Petróleos de Venezuela, S.A. (PDVSA) was deduced from internal notes and reports that made clear for the Tribunal that the union's plant takeover was subsequently made an integral part of a nationalisation process (2016, Decision on Liability and the Principles of Quantum, paras. 461–466).

15.2 Circumstances Precluding Wrongfulness

15.2.1 Introduction to Circumstances Precluding Wrongfulness

Circumstances precluding wrongfulness provide a shield against an otherwise well-founded claim for the breach of an international obligation attributable to the State, with the exception of the breach of *jus cogens* obligation (ARSIWA, Article 26). As seen in the analysis of arbitration practice and as provided in Article 27 of the ARSIWA, those circumstances, while they preclude wrongfulness, do not necessarily exclude the possibility that the States that rely on them may make good any material loss suffered by any State or entity directly affected. This is a form of compensation that is to be distinguished from the secondary obligation to repair stemming from internationally wrongful acts, as analysed below. In any case, if and to the extent that the circumstances no longer exist, compliance with the obligations shall be resumed (ARSIWA, Article 27).

Circumstances precluding wrongfulness form part of general international law. With regard to the objective and the methodology explained in the introduction, this public international law background is recalled here by referring to the ARSIWA and summarising its Commentaries. These circumstances are dealt with in Chapter V, Part 1 of the ARSIWA.

The notion of circumstances precluding wrongfulness can be traced back to the work of the Preparatory Committee of the 1930 Hague Conference, which focused in particular on self-defence and reprisals. It was then developed by the ILC, in particular in its work on international responsibility for injuries to aliens (Chapter V, Introduction, paras. 5–6). The ARSIWA lists six circumstances precluding wrongfulness: consent, self-defence, countermeasures, *force majeure*, distress and necessity.

Consent relates to those situations in which one State has consented to the act of another State, thereby making that act not wrongful in relation to this consenting State (ARSIWA, Article 20). As for self-defence, Article 21 of the ARSIWA provides that 'the wrongfulness of an act of a State is precluded if the act constitutes a lawful measure of self-defence taken in conformity with the Charter of the United Nations'. This provision does not address the use of force in self-defence as such; indeed, the use of force in self-defence is not a breach of the United Nations Charter as long as it conforms to the conditions therein. Instead, this circumstance precludes the wrongfulness of the conduct of a State acting in self-defence in certain situations and regarding certain of its obligations other than its obligation not to use or to threaten to use force (paras. 1–3). Countermeasures refers to conduct that aims at stopping prior internationally wrongful acts committed by other States and at achieving reparation (ARSIWA,

Article 22; para. 1). Article 23 of the ARSIWA defines *force majeure* as a situation in which States, involuntarily or at least with no other choice, are compelled to act in a manner contrary to one of their international obligations (para. 1). The circumstance of distress precludes the wrongfulness of acts that are decided in situations of peril, where there is no other reasonable way to save life; the peril can relate to the person committing the act or to a group of persons (ARSIWA, Article 24; para. 1).

Necessity, which is explained below, has been by far the most discussed circumstance precluding wrongfulness in investor–State arbitration. This is due to the numerous cases that have followed the Argentinian economic crisis during the 2000s. Among the other circumstances, one can single out counter-measures, which have been at stake in the context of three cases in particular: *Corn Products International, Inc.* v. *Mexico* (2008, Decision on Responsibility, paras. 153–192), *Archer Daniels Midland Company* v. *Mexico* (2007, Award, paras. 110–180) and *Cargill, Incorporated* v. *Mexico* (2009, Award, paras. 379–430). Due to this primacy of necessity, this subsection focuses on this circumstance precluding wrongfulness; this focus is without prejudice to the relevance of the other circumstances in investor–State disputes.

15.2.2 Necessity

15.2.2.1 Public International Law Background: ARSIWA and its Commentaries

'Necessity' is addressed in Article 25 of the ARSIWA and its Commentaries. With regard to the objective and the methodology explained in the introduction, this subsection summarises the Commentaries on this Article.

Necessity precludes the wrongfulness of a conduct when there is an irreconcilable conflict between an obligation of the State invoking this ground and one of its essential interests (para. 2). To avoid potential abuse, the recognition of a state of necessity is subject to very strict conditions and limitations. More precisely, two situations are completely excluded from the scope of necessity, while for the other remaining situations, two cumulative conditions must be fulfilled.

As to the former, necessity is first of all precluded in those situations where international obligations explicitly or implicitly exclude the possibility of invoking this ground. Implicit exclusions are to be read typically in those obligations intended *per essence* to apply to unusual situations of peril (para. 19). Second, when States contribute to the situation with respect to which necessity is alleged, this also falls short of the scope of this circumstance precluding wrongfulness. To have this effect, the contribution must be sufficiently important and not merely incidental or peripheral (para. 20).

In relation to those situations where necessity is not excluded, the first branch of the first condition to be met pertains to the requirement that necessity be invoked to safeguard an essential interest, be it of the State, its population or the international community as a whole, from a grave and imminent peril (para. 15). This peril must be clearly established based on the evidence that was reasonably available at the time (para. 16). The second branch of this first condition relates to the requirement that the conduct concerned be the only way available to safeguard the essential interest at stake, otherwise the shield of 'necessity' is set aside. By the same token, any conduct overstepping what is strictly necessary to safeguard the essential interest at hand will not be covered by necessity (para. 15). The second condition requires that the conduct at stake must not seriously impair an essential interest of the State(s) concerned or of the international community as a whole (para. 17).

15.2.2.2 Investor–State Arbitration

At the outset, it is worth recalling that necessity has often been discussed in arbitration practice in relation to security exceptions clauses. Those clauses and their interplay with necessity are examined in Chapter 7 – reference is only made here to the cases in which arguments concerning necessity were put forward for the purpose of applying and interpreting those clauses. This subsection focuses on necessity as such and more specifically on (1) the conditions and limits attached to necessity; (2) its temporary dimension; and (3) the issue of compensation.

a Conditions and Exclusions

Preliminary Remarks
In line with public international law, the threshold for a finding of necessity in investor–State arbitration is very high. Tribunals often insist on this threshold and on the need for necessity to remain an exceptional shield against illegality. For instance, the Tribunal appointed in *Enron Corporation Ponderosa Assets, L.P.* v. *Argentina* stressed that Article 25 of the ARSIWA begins by cautioning that the state of necessity 'may not be invoked' unless the conditions set out are met, and went on to explain that 'necessity is a most exceptional remedy subject to very strict conditions because otherwise it would open the door to elude any international obligation' (2007, Award, para. 304).

The conditions attached to necessity and the situations of exclusions are analysed here in light of the Argentinian cases that have attracted most of the discussion on necessity in investor–State arbitration. Apart from these cases, necessity has been examined in only a few cases (e.g. *Union Fenosa S.A.* v. *Egypt*, 2018, Award, Part 8). For this reason, before delving into these analyses, it is worth setting out a brief outline of the facts of the Argentinian economic crisis in the aftermath of which these cases arose.

In the early twentieth century, Argentina was hit by a major economic crisis, which led the government to default on its debt, as well as causing the collapse of the peso with respect to the US dollar to which it was fixed. The government reacted to this situation by deciding a series of measures, in particular the 'pesification' of all obligations and the freezing of the gas distribution tariffs. This latter measure was in particular challenged by numerous US foreign investors as being incompatible with the 1991 United States of America (USA)–Argentina

IIA. The arbitration proceedings that were initiated led to different outcomes, which can to a large extent be explained by the diverging views of tribunals, from a factual perspective, regarding the situation in Argentina, and from a legal perspective, regarding how they construed necessity. As such, these views provide a wealth of information on this circumstance precluding wrongfulness in investor–State arbitration more generally.

i The Conditions Attached to Necessity Along the lines of the public international law background provided above, the following subsections will discuss in turn the two conditions that must be fulfilled in order for the wrongfulness of a State conduct in breach of an IIA to be precluded, namely: (1) the act must be the only way for the host State to safeguard an essential interest against a grave and imminent peril; and (2) it must not seriously impair an essential interest.

– The Only Way to Safeguard an Essential Interest against a Grave and Imminent Peril This condition is threefold: (1) the act must be the only way to safeguard an interest; (2) this interest must be essential; and (3) the peril against which this interest must be safeguarded has to be grave and imminent. For each of these elements, arbitration practice displays varying and conflicting approaches and findings.

As for the second and third elements, those conflicting approaches are well illustrated by *LG&E* v. *Argentina* (2006, Decision on Liability) and *Sempra Energy International* v. *Argentina* (2007, Award).

Concerning the second element, the *LG&E* Tribunal concluded that Argentina 'faced an extremely serious threat to its existence, its political and economic survival, to the possibility of maintaining its essential services in operation, and to the preservation of its internal peace' (para. 257). In contrast, the Tribunal in *Sempra Energy International* v. *Argentina*, while acknowledging the severity of the crisis, opined that the situation did not compromise the very existence of the State and its independence, and therefore denied that the situation involved an essential State interest (para. 348).

Concerning the third condition, and as stated above, the Tribunal in *LG&E* v. *Argentina* considered that Argentina faced an 'extremely serious threat'. The *Sempra* Tribunal acknowledged that Argentina could not have let events continue, but it argued that there was 'no convincing evidence that events were actually out of control or had become unmanageable' (para. 349).

The appraisal of the first condition is also characterised by disagreement among tribunals. In *Enron Corporation Ponderosa Assets, L.P.* v. *Argentina*, the Tribunal concluded that the condition was not met simply on the ground that past economic crises had shown that there are always other approaches to fix such crises; it stated:

> It is thus quite evident that measures had to be adopted to offset the unfolding crisis. Whether the measures taken under the Emergency Law were the 'only

way' to achieve this result and no other alternative was available, is also a question on which the parties and their experts are profoundly divided, as noted above. A rather sad world comparative experience in the handling of economic crises, shows that there are always many approaches to address and correct such critical events, and it is difficult to justify that none of them were available in the Argentine case. While one or other party would like the Tribunal to point out which alternative was recommendable, it is not the task of the Tribunal to substitute for the governmental determination of economic choices, only to determine whether the choice made was the only way available, and this does not appear to be the case. (2007, Award, paras. 308–309)

This literal interpretation of the condition by the Tribunal was considered by the Annulment Committee appointed in that case as de facto greatly limiting and even excluding the possibility that any economic crisis could be considered as falling within the scope of necessity as there are almost inevitably various ways to fight such crises (2010, Decision on Annulment, para. 369). The Committee pointed towards an alternative interpretation of that condition, i.e. one following which necessity is to be precluded only if there is an alternative that would not involve a breach of international law or that would involve a less grave breach of international law (para. 370).

In *LG&E* v. *Argentina*, the Tribunal acknowledged that there may have been various ways to draft the economic recovery plan, but it decided that the evidence showed that 'an across-the-board response' was necessary, and that the tariffs on public utilities had to be addressed (2006, Decision on Liability, para. 257). The Tribunal appointed in *Urbaser S.A.* v. *Argentina* reached the same conclusion, stressing that two perspectives needed to be taken into account: 'the wide one, taking into account the needs of Argentina and its population nation-wide, and the narrower one of the situation of investors engaged in performing contracts protected by the international obligations arising out of one of the many BITs [footnote omitted]' (2016, Award, para. 716).

– No Impairment of an Essential Interest All tribunals agreed that the acts decided by Argentina did not affect an essential interest of the international community as a whole (e.g. *Sempra Energy International* v. *Argentina*, 2007, Award, para. 352). By the same token, they all concluded that they did not impair an essential interest of the other IIA State party (e.g. *Enron Corporation Ponderosa Assets, L.P.* v. *Argentina*, 2007, Award, para. 341).

On the other hand, arbitration practice displays inconsistency in relation to foreign investors. At the core of the debate is the relevance of their interest for the purpose of appraising this condition. Some tribunals addressed the issue by focusing on the State only, suggesting thereby the lack of relevance of the investor's interest (e.g. *LG&E* v. *Argentina*, 2006, Decision on Liability, para. 257). In *CMS Gas Transmission Company* v. *Argentina*, the Tribunal deduced from the fact that investors are specific beneficiaries of IIAs that those agreements are of interest to them and that the matter at stake is essential to them; however, it concluded merely that for the purpose of the case and looking at the treaty in the context of the States parties, no essential interest had been impaired. In this respect, it is noteworthy that it reached this conclusion after having contemplated that the applicable IIA was made to protect investors and therefore that their protection as such constituted an important interest for States parties (2005, Award, paras. 357–358). The Tribunal appointed in *Sempra Energy International* v. *Argentina* adopted the same approach, though it seemed to have gone one step further by drawing consequences from it. In doing so, it provided that, in the context of international investment agreements, there was a need to take into consideration the interest of the private entities who are the ultimate beneficiaries of obligations, and that the 'essential interest of the Claimant would certainly be seriously impaired by … a state of necessity in that case' (2007, Award, para. 391).

ii **The Situations Excluded from Necessity** As explained above in relation to public international law, the situations excluded from the scope of necessity are twofold: (1) the explicit or implicit exclusion of the possibility to invoke necessity by the international obligation itself; and (2) the substantial contribution of the State to the situation of necessity.

– Substantial Contribution of the State to the Situation of Necessity In our globalised world, the causes of an economic crisis are inevitably numerous and diverse. This is why arbitration tribunals usually considered that the Argentinian economic crisis had both endogenous and exogenous roots. They expressed this view on the basis of the inner features of the Argentinian crisis (e.g. *Sempra Energy International* v. *Argentina*, 2007, Award, para. 353) or, more generally, on that of the functioning of the global economy. In that sense, the Tribunal stated in *CMS Gas Transmission Company* v. *Argentina*: '[T]he Tribunal is again persuaded that similar to what is the case in most crises of this kind the roots extend both ways and include a number of domestic as well as international dimensions. This is the unavoidable consequence of the operation of a global economy where domestic and international factors interact' (2005, Award, para. 328).

Yet, tribunals did not reach the same conclusion as to whether or not Argentina's contribution to the economic crisis was substantial. Some tribunals considered that governmental policies over the past ten years had contributed significantly to the crisis (e.g. *CMS Gas Transmission Company* v. *Argentina*, 2005, Award, para. 329). The Tribunal in *Enron Corporation Ponderosa Assets, L.P.* v. *Argentina* reached the same conclusion after having stated that necessity is 'the expression of a general principle of law devised to prevent a party taking legal advantage of its own fault' (2007, Award, para. 311). As noted by the Annulment Committee in that case, this reference leaves two questions unanswered: (1) what amounts to a 'fault' – is it a deliberate course of conduct or a negligence? And (2) which degree of fault is required in order to conclude that there has been a substantial contribution? (2010, Decision on Annulment, para. 389). While not coining it in terms of 'fault', the Tribunal appointed in *Urbaser S.A.* v. *Argentina* explained that in order to conclude that there has been a substantial contribution by the State, the following would need to be demonstrated:

> For such a demonstration to be successful, it should be shown that the Government's acts were such that they either were directed towards a crisis resulting in the emergency situation that the country experienced in early 2002, or at least of such a nature that the Government must have known that such crisis and emergency must have been the outcome of its economic and financial policy. (2016, Award, para. 711)

Even though it acknowledged that part of the difficulties resulted from Argentina's own economic policies, this Tribunal concluded in that case that no causal link between these polices and the outbreak of the crisis could be established that showed that Argentina contributed substantially to the economic crisis (paras. 714–715).

– Exclusion by the International Obligation Regarding this second ground of exclusion, most arbitration tribunals have focused on the object and purpose of IIAs in discussing the matter. However, despite this common focus, arbitrators have nonetheless adopted diverging views on the matter.

In *CMS Gas Transmission Company* v. *Argentina*, the Tribunal noted that IIAs are designed to protect investments, in particular during times of economic difficulties. From there, it made a distinction between severe crises and situations of total collapse in appraising whether necessity is excluded. It stated:

> The Treaty in this case is clearly designed to protect investments at a time of economic difficulties or other circumstances leading to the adoption of adverse measures by the Government. The question is, however, how grave these economic difficulties might be. A severe crisis cannot necessarily be equated with a situation of total collapse. And in the absence of such profoundly serious conditions it is plainly clear that the Treaty will prevail over any plea of necessity. However, if such difficulties, without being catastrophic in and of themselves, nevertheless invite catastrophic conditions in terms of disruption and disintegration of society, or are likely to lead to a total breakdown of the economy, emergency and necessity might acquire a different meaning. (2005, Award, para. 354)

Implicitly, the Tribunal seemed to have considered that the object and purpose of IIAs do not exclude necessity from being invoked in those situations in which an economic crisis amounts to a grave peril.

The Tribunal appointed in *BG Group Plc* v. *Argentina* adopted a more radical stance. It argued that such an exclusion was implied in the 1990 United Kingdom–Argentina IIA on the grounds that the object and purpose of the Agreement is, in its view, precisely to protect foreign investors in situations of economic difficulty and to induce them to invest despite such risks. The Tribunal concluded therefore that compensation had to be paid as a result of the measures enacted. As an exception, it mentioned in Footnote 327 that compensation is not payable when the IIA contains an exculpatory provision which exonerates the party from liability (2007, Final Award, para. 409). In fact, the 1990 United Kingdom–Argentina IIA does not contain a security exceptions clause, contrary to the USA–Argentina IIA, which was in question in most of the Argentinian cases.

In this respect, this exception provided by the *BG* Tribunal can be linked to the argument developed by the Tribunal in *LG&E* v. *Argentina*. Focusing on the text of this Agreement – and not its object and purpose like most tribunals – this Tribunal argued: 'The international obligation at issue must allow invocation of the state of necessity. The inclusion of an article authorizing the state of necessity in a Bilateral Investment Treaty constitutes the acceptance, in the relations between States, of the possibility that one of them may invoke the state of necessity' (2006, Decision on Liability, para. 255). In this respect, it concluded that the security exceptions clause of the USA–Argentina IIA exempted Argentina from responsibility for measures enacted during the state of necessity (para. 257). It is worth stressing that the Tribunal thereby adopted an approach that is alien to Article 25 of the ARSIWA. Indeed, while it considered that an international obligation must allow the invocation of necessity, this Article provides that the possibility to invoke necessity must not be excluded by the international obligation in question, or to put it differently, that necessity can be invoked unless it is excluded.

b Temporary Nature of 'Necessity' and Compensation

In line with the public international law background recalled above, there has been a consensus in arbitration practice that compliance shall resume if and to the extent that the situation of necessity no longer exists. For instance, in *Urbaser S.A.* v. *Argentina*, where it was concluded that there was indeed necessity, the Tribunal explained that 'when the emergency measures were justified by the fact that no other reasonably available remedy did exist, such argument supporting the state of necessity defense disappears as soon as alternative measures become available and are no longer in breach of the State's international obligations' (2016, Award, para. 719).

By the same token, tribunals agree that compensation may be paid as a matter of principle; that being said, they differ on the exact circumstances as to when and upon what grounds this may be so.

In *CMS* v. *Argentina*, the Tribunal argued that international law does not require the foreign investor to bear the entire cost of the plea of the essential interest of the other party. It went on to say that in the absence of an agreement between the parties, the determination of compensation is a matter for the tribunal. It is worth stressing that this Tribunal seems to have considered that necessity has the effect of suspending temporarily the right to compensation and not of setting aside any obligation to compensate for the period with regard to which necessity is declared (2005, Award, paras. 390–394).

The Tribunal appointed in *LG&E* v. *Argentina* stated that Article 27 of the ARSIWA does not specify whether any compensation is payable to the party affected by losses during the state of necessity. Without really explaining this, the Tribunal considered that the IIA's security exceptions clause provides the answer as it saw this clause as establishing necessity as a ground for the exclusion of wrongfulness and thereby as exempting the State from liability. It concluded that the damage suffered during the state of necessity must be borne by the investor (2006, Decision on Liability, paras. 260–261 and 264).

15.3 Reparation

As mentioned above, (1) when a conduct is attributable to a host State party to an IIA, and (2) this conduct is in breach of its IIA obligation(s), (3) without any circumstance precluding the wrongfulness of that conduct, this conduct amounts to an internationally wrongful act, which entails the international responsibility of that State. A finding of international responsibility has particular legal consequences, creating certain types of legal obligations known as 'secondary obligations'. Customary international law, as codified in the ARSIWA, provides for the *lex generalis* governing those legal consequences. International investment agreements can, as a *lex specialis*, contain specific provisions that govern the matter or part(s) thereof. As discussed below, there is a clear trend in recent IIA practice to incorporate such provisions. This contrasts with traditional practice which has remained silent on this matter, which explains why arbitration tribunals have systematically applied CIL and referred to the ARSIWA and its Commentaries in order to decide on the consequences of host States' international responsibility – and more precisely, in determining how to deal with the key consequence of international responsibility in the context of investor–State arbitration, i.e. reparation.

As explained in the introduction, in order to provide a comprehensive analysis of reparation in international investment law and arbitration and to make sense of it, it is first necessary to recall its public international law background, by referring to the ARSIWA and summarising its Commentaries. On that basis, the following subsection then provides an in-depth analysis of reparation in IIA practice and in investor–State arbitration.

15.3.1 Public International Law Background: ARSIWA and its Commentaries

Preliminary Remarks

As mentioned above, the key legal consequence arising from the international responsibility of a host State in investor–State arbitration is that of reparation. However, from a public international law perspective, the scope of the legal consequences deriving from a finding of international responsibility is wider. Before focusing on the forms of reparation, as well as interest and the contribution to damage, it is worth detailing those legal consequences and explaining their specific purpose.

15.3.1.1 The Types of Legal Consequences of Internationally Wrongful Acts

Preliminary Remarks

It should be stressed at the outset that the secondary obligations that derive from an internationally wrongful act do not interfere with the continuing obligation of States to abide by the primary obligation breached if it still exists (ARSIWA, Article 29).

The nature and exact content of the secondary obligations owed by the responsible State vary depending on the specifics of each case, in particular on the primary obligation breached. As a matter of law, it can consist of: cessation, non-repetition and reparation. States can in no way rely on their domestic law to justify a failure to comply with those obligations (ARSIWA, Article 32).

a Cessation and Non-Repetition

These consequences are dealt with in Article 30 of the ARSIWA and its Commentaries. They have a common teleological denominator, namely the objective of restoring and safeguarding the legal relationship established by the primary obligation breached, provided that this obligation still exists (para. 1). Cessation is mainly relevant with regard to acts that have a continuing character, and consists of an obligation to put a stop to a continuing violation of the primary obligation, which thereby allows the restoration of its effectiveness (paras. 4 and 5). While cessation has a backward-looking dimension, non-repetition has a forward-looking one. It places the obligation upon the responsible State to provide assurances and guarantees that it will not violate the primary obligation at hand again. Non-repetition is intended to safeguard the effectiveness of this primary obligation for the future (para. 1).

b Reparation

Reparation is dealt with in Articles 31 and 34–39 of the ARSIWA and their Commentaries. The content and function of this obligation was famously articulated by the Permanent Court of International Justice (PCIJ) in the *Case Concerning the Factory at Chorzow (Germany v. Poland)*:

> The essential principle contained in the actual notion of an illegal act – a principle which seems to be established by international practice and in particular by the decisions of arbitral tribunals – is that reparation must, as far as possible, wipe out all the consequences of the illegal act and reestablish the situation which would, in all probability, have existed if that act had not been committed. Restitution in kind, or, if this is not possible, payment of a sum corresponding to the value which a restitution in kind would bear; the award, if need be, of damages for loss sustained which would not be covered by restitution in kind or payment in place of it – such are the principles which should serve to

determine the amount of compensation due for an act contrary to international law. (1928, Judgment, at 47)

It is worth stressing that 'damage' is key with regard to reparation. While the law of State responsibility does not set as a requirement for a finding of international responsibility that damage must have been caused, damage is a condition for the existence of an obligation to repair. More precisely, there must be a causal link, which must not be too remote, between the internationally wrongful act and the damage in order for this obligation to exist (ARSIWA, Article 31; para. 10). Even when causation is established, it is also worth noting that the obligation to repair may be affected in the event of the failure of the injured party to mitigate the damage (ARSIWA, Article 31; para. 11).

Regardless of this specific situation, the damage suffered, be it material and/or moral, must be fully repaired. To use the words of the PCIJ in the above-mentioned statement, this means that reparation shall 'wipe out all the consequences of the illegal act and reestablish the situation which would, in all probability, have existed if that act had not been committed'. To perform this function, reparation can consist of restitution, compensation or satisfaction, which can be relied on either singly or in combination depending on the nature and extent of the damage suffered.

15.3.1.2 The Forms of Reparation

a Restitution

Restitution is dealt with in Article 35 of the ARSIWA and its Commentaries. Under the approach chosen by the ILC, this form of reparation consists of the reestablishment of the situation that existed prior to the occurrence of the internationally wrongful act. It is important to stress that, under this definition, restitution does not provide the reparation of the losses suffered as it is not concerned with the appraisal of the situation that would have been if the act had not been committed. Where such losses result from the internationally wrongful act, the principle of full reparation requires that the restitution be completed with compensation (para. 2).

As a matter of law, restitution is the primary form of reparation contemplated; however, it can be excluded – in whole or in part – on two grounds: material impossibility and lack of proportionality.

Restitution is typically considered as being materially impossible when the object at hand was permanently destroyed or has been so deteriorated that it has become worthless. In some cases, the restitution may be impossible due to the acts of a third party, such as where a third party acquires the object in good faith without having been informed of the restitution claim (paras. 8 and 10).

Restitution is excluded for lack of proportionality when there is a grave disproportionality between the burden restitution would impose on the responsible State and the benefit that would be gained by the State that suffered from the internationally wrongful act (para. 10).

The forms of restitution depend on the specifics of each case, in particular on the primary obligation breached. It may notably consist of a material restitution, e.g. a return of property, and/or it may involve a change in the domestic law of the responsible State. This can be, for instance, a revocation of a statute or some of the provisions thereof which are in breach of the State's international obligations. It is worth noting that with regard to the reparation of damage caused by continuing breaches, restitution appears to be akin to cessation, which is discussed above (paras. 5–6 – ARSIWA, Article 30; para. 7).

b Compensation

Compensation, which is covered in Article 36 of the ARSIWA and the Commentaries thereto, can replace or complement restitution. As regards the latter option, it 'fills the gap' to ensure that the damage suffered is fully repaired. It usually consists of a monetary payment that covers the damage that can be assessed financially; this includes the loss of profits that can be proven and is not speculative (para. 27). It is worth stressing that this form of reparation does not encompass punitive damages (para. 4).

c Satisfaction

Satisfaction is dealt with in Article 37 of the ARSIWA and the Commentaries thereto. It is an exceptional form of reparation, coming into play only when restitution and/or compensation fail to provide full reparation. In fact, it is used to repair the damage that is not financially assessable and that has a symbolic dimension (para. 3). Depending on the circumstances of each case, it can for instance consist of an acknowledgement of the breach, an expression of regret or a formal apology. It is noteworthy that the formulation of assurances and guarantees of non-repetition can also amount to satisfaction (para. 5). In no case can satisfaction consist of punitive damages and, more generally, have a punitive, exemplary or disproportionate character (para. 8).

15.3.1.3 Interest

Interest is covered in Article 38 of the ARSIWA and the Commentaries to that Article. It is not an independent form of reparation, nor is it systematically awarded (para. 1). Interest on any principal sum due is awarded only when this is necessary to make reparation full. Interest starts to accumulate from the date when the sum is to be paid to the date when the obligation to pay is eventually fulfilled.

15.3.1.4 Contribution to the Injury

The issue of the contribution of the injured State to the damage suffered is dealt with in Article 39 of the ARSIWA and its Commentaries. They cover those situations in which the injured State, whether voluntarily or negligently, materially contributes to the damage (para. 1). Such wilful or negligent conduct mainly has an impact on the amount of compensation due, when compensation is considered as the adequate form of reparation (para. 4).

15.3.2 Reparation in IIA Practice

Preliminary Remarks

As explained above, the legal consequences of an internationally wrongful act, as set out in CIL, constitute a *lex generalis*. States can decide to establish their own *lex specialis* on the matter or part(s) thereof, which will then prevail over that *lex generalis*. States parties to IIAs have traditionally failed to establish such *lex specialis*, declining to include provisions addressing the legal consequences of an internationally wrongful act.

They have usually only addressed issues of reparation and/or compensation with regard to specific circumstances, such as situations of armed conflicts and internal disorders as explained in Chapter 3, as well as lawful expropriations, which are analysed in Chapter 6. It is worth stressing that the reparation and compensation foreseen in the relevant IIA obligations do not derive from the international responsibility of the host State. Instead, they form part of the obligations as such. That being said, and as examined below, it is discussed whether the compensation requirement set out for lawful expropriations plays any role with regard to the legal consequences resulting from the breach of the expropriation provision.

In contrast, recent IIA practice displays a clear trend towards incorporating provisions that address the consequences deriving from a breach of these agreements. The following subsections focus on the types of damage that they cover as well as the forms of reparation that they provide.

15.3.2.1 The Types of Damage Covered

Some IIAs exclude moral damage (2018 Belarus–India IIA, Article 26.4); implicitly, material damage is covered by the obligation to repair in all of those agreements.

The 2016 Slovakia–Iran IIA makes it clear that losses that are not actually incurred or are not probable shall not be compensated, and neither shall 'unreal' profits (Article 21.2). With a view to ensuring that there is a causal link between the breach and the damage as to 'attempts to make an investment', the 2018 Comprehensive and Progressive Agreement for Trans-Pacific Partnership (CPTPP) specifies that only the damage investors can prove to have been sustained in the context of this attempt can be awarded, provided that they also can prove that the breach was the proximate cause of this damage (Article 9.29.4).

15.3.2.2 The Forms of Reparation Provided

As a common minimum denominator, all the IIAs in question here specify the forms of reparation that arbitration tribunals may award. But for a few exceptions, such as the 2018 Belarus–India IIA, which provides only for the award of monetary compensation (Article 26.3), the great majority of those agreements foresee that tribunals may award monetary damages and any applicable interest or restitution of property. In line with CIL, some specify that these forms of reparation may be awarded singly or in combination (e.g. 2019 Australia–Uruguay IIA, Article 14.23). In addition to restitution and compensation, the 2017 Israel–Japan IIA provides that tribunals may award a judgment as to whether or not there has been a breach of the IIA by the host State with respect to the investor (Article 24.13.a). Such an award is akin to satisfaction, as discussed above. It is worth noting also that many IIAs prohibit the award of punitive damages (e.g. 2018, Canada— Moldova IIA, Article 34.4).

As regards restitution, it is worth noting that some agreements provide that if restitution is awarded, the award shall provide that the party may pay monetary damages and any applicable interest in lieu of restitution (e.g. 2014 Mauritius–Egypt IIA, Article 10.11.b).

Concerning compensation, some IIAs specify the elements that shall be taken into account in determining the amount of monetary damages to be awarded. In addition to specifying that it shall not be greater than the loss suffered, the 2018 Belarus–India IIA makes clear – based on the 2015 Indian Model BIT (Article 26.3, Footnote 4) – that it shall be reduced by the amount of any prior damages or compensation already provided, and also to take into consideration mitigating factors, notably 'any unremedied harm or damage that the investor has caused to the environment or local community or other relevant considerations regarding the need to balance public interest and the interests of the investor' (Article 26.3). Focusing also on public interest considerations, the 2016 Slovakia–Iran IIA provides more generally that account shall be taken notably of the 'equitable balance between the public interest and interest of those affected' and 'the purpose of the measure'; it also specifies that compensation may be adjusted to reflect any aggravating conduct by an investor or conduct that does not seek to mitigate the damage (Article 21.2).

That latter Agreement not only sets out the factors to be taken into consideration in calculating compensation, but also addresses the valuation thereof. It provides that damages shall be determined in accordance with generally recognised principles of valuation and that tribunals shall, when establishing the 'just quantum' of damages, base their decisions on a comparison of multiple valuation methods when appropriate (Article 21.2).

15.3.3 Reparation in Investor–State Arbitration

Reparation is almost always the only consequence of the international responsibility of host States that is invoked before and examined by arbitration tribunals. Cessation is rarely at hand in investor–State arbitration (e.g. *The AES Corporation* v. *Kazakhstan*, 2013, Award, para. 465), while non-repetition appears irrelevant in this context. Concerning reparation, the main form through which reparation is sought and awarded is compensation.

In analysing reparation, the following will examine in succession (1) damage; (2) the standard of reparation and the secondary forms of reparation in investor–State arbitration, i.e. restitution and satisfaction; and (3) the main form, namely compensation.

15.3.3.1 Damage

a Causation and Evidence

As explained above, the law of State responsibility does not require damage to have been caused for a finding of international responsibility. In investor–State arbitration, whether or not the existence of damage is necessary to conclude that host States committed an internationally wrongful act is rarely discussed – rather, tribunals focus primarily on issues of causation and quantum. That being said, this issue has arisen in a few cases, notably in *Merrill & Ring Forestry L.P.* v. *Canada*. In that case, the Tribunal discussed the matter by analogy with Article 31 of the ARSIWA and its Commentaries which, while recalling that damage is not in general an element of international responsibility, explains that the primary rule at hand may make of damage such an element. The Tribunal argued:

> Valid as that conclusion may be as far as state responsibility is concerned, in the case of conduct that is said to constitute a breach of the standards applicable to investment protection, the primary obligation is quite clearly inseparable from the existence of damage. Indeed, a finding of liability without a finding of damage would be difficult to explain in the context of investment law arbitration and would indeed be contrary to some of its fundamental tenets. (2010, Award, para. 245)

In this respect, and even though this is not a matter of State responsibility but of jurisdiction, it is worth noting here that the language used in some IIAs indicates that damage is a condition of the tribunals' jurisdiction. This results *mutatis mutandis* from provisions such as Article 12 of the 2016 Nigeria–Singapore IIA, which provides that '[t]his Section [Settlement of Disputes between a Party and an Investor of the Other Party] shall apply to disputes between a Party and an investor of the other Party concerning an alleged breach of an obligation of the former under this Agreement which causes loss or damage to the investor or its investment'.

In any case, damage is in all circumstances a condition of reparation. In addition to the fact that the existence of damage as such must be proven, this requires there to be a sufficient causal link between the wrongful act and the damage at hand. This causation requirement is made up of two intertwined elements. First, there must be a factual link between the wrongful act and the damage at hand. The lack of such a link led the Tribunal in *Garanti Koza LLP* v. *Turkmenistan*, for instance, to reject the damages claim formulated by the investor for the losses of its factory and equipment, concluding that there was no causal connection between the umbrella clause and fair and equitable treatment (FET) claims and those losses (2016, Award, paras. 423–424). As a second element, the damage must not be too indirect or remote. Both elements may give rise to difficulties in practice, in particular when the situation in which the foreign investor stands results from different causes. Faced with this difficulty, the Tribunal appointed in *Biwater Gauff (Tanzania) Ltd* v. *Tanzania* (2008, Award, para. 786) relied on the 'dominant cause analysis' used by the ICJ in the *Case Concerning Elettronica Sicula S.p.A. (ELSI) (United States of America* v. *Italy)* (1989, Judgment, paras. 100–101) in order to appraise the proximate cause of the damage in that case.

The burden of proving the existence of the damage and causation lies on the investor. As regards the standard of proof, a distinction should be made between the existence of the damage as such and its quantification; this results mainly from the technical difficulties attached to the quantification of the damage. As for the former, the threshold is high, requiring the damage to be proven with certainty. In contrast, the standard is lower with regard to quantification. In *Joseph Charles Lemire* v. *Ukraine*, the Tribunal explained:

> [T]he level of certainty is unlikely . . . to be the same with respect to the conclusion that damages have been caused, and the precise quantification of such damages [*sic*]. Once causation has been established, and it has been proven that the *in bonis* party has indeed suffered a loss, less certainty is required in proof of the actual amount of damages [*sic*]; for this latter determination Claimant only needs to provide a basis upon which the Tribunal can, with reasonable confidence, estimate the extent of the loss. [footnote omitted] (2011, Award, para. 246)

This standard of proof entails that the fact that it is impossible to prove the amount of damage with certainty shall not be considered a bar to the award of damages.

b Categories of Damage

Investor–State disputes are almost systematically concerned with material damage. Such damage and the compensation that host States are almost exclusively required to pay in the event of a finding of international responsibility can amount to the full value of the investment, typically in the case of (indirect) expropriation, or can be limited to the harm caused by the internationally wrongful acts.

Moral damage, in contrast, is rarely at stake and moral damages even less frequently awarded. This scarcity is not due to the features of international investment law and arbitration. For instance, as noted by the Tribunal in *Desert Line Projects LLC* v. *Yemen*, the fact that IIAs aim to protect property and economic value is no bar in this respect (2008, Award, para. 289); nor is the juridical nature that often characterises the person of the investor, as it is recognised that both natural and legal persons can be awarded moral damages, notably for loss of reputation (e.g. *Oxus Gold* v. *Uzbekistan*, 2015, Final Award, para. 895). Ultimately, this lack of instances in which moral damages are awarded results from the very high threshold set in arbitration practice in this regard, there being a consensus that moral damages can only be granted in exceptionally grave situations.

On the other hand, arbitration tribunals diverge on the test to be used in appraising whether investors have suffered moral damage. On the basis of past case law, the Tribunal appointed in *Joseph Charles Lemire* v. *Ukraine* set the strictest test by requiring the fulfilment of three conditions, stating:

> [A]s a general rule, moral damages are not available to a party injured by the wrongful acts of a State, but that moral damages can be awarded in exceptional cases, provided that the State's actions imply physical threat, illegal detention or other analogous situations in which the ill-treatment contravenes the norms according to which civilized nations are expected to act; the State's actions cause a deterioration of health, stress, anxiety, other mental suffering such as humiliation, shame and degradation, or loss of reputation, credit and social position; and both cause and effect are grave or substantial. (2011, Award, para. 333)

In *Mr Franck Charles Arif* v. *Moldova*, the Tribunal argued that it was inappropriate to require that the three conditions listed above be met cumulatively. It criticised the first condition in particular, which in its view reflects the circumstances in only one case, namely *Desert Line Projects LLC* v. *Yemen*. In this respect, it argued that the second condition set out in *Joseph Charles Lemire* v. *Ukraine* constitutes the right criteria as it leaves some discretion to tribunals without negating the exceptional nature of the award of moral damages (2013, Award, paras. 590–591).

Although they adopted two different tests, it is worth noting that both Tribunals considered that the compensation of material damage constitutes an element to be taken into account and actually goes against the award of moral damages. In *Mr Franck Charles Arif* v. *Moldova*, the Tribunal – drawing an analogy between investor–State arbitration and contractual/tortious relations – opined that the cumulation of a pecuniary premium for compensation for a sentiment of frustration and affront and the compensation of economic damage would 'systematically create financial advantages for the victim which go beyond the traditional concept of compensation' (para. 592). The Tribunal in *Joseph Charles Lemire* v. *Ukraine* considered that the payment of economic compensation constitutes an element of redress that can significantly repair the loss of reputation (2011, Award, para. 339). Interestingly, the Tribunal also stated that its acknowledgement of the breach of the IIA had a similar effect, an argument which is akin to satisfaction, as discussed below.

15.3.3.2 The Standard and Forms of Reparation

a Full Reparation

As explained above, the standard of full reparation was articulated by the PCIJ in the 1928 *Case Concerning the Factory at Chorzow*, which provides in its most relevant part that 'reparation must, as far as possible, wipe out all the consequences of the illegal act and reestablish the situation which would, in all probability, have existed if that act had not been committed' (at 47). Arbitration tribunals have systematically referred to this articulation of the full reparation standard.

As explained above, three forms of reparation can be resorted to in order to reestablish the situation: restitution, compensation and satisfaction. As noted by the Tribunal in *Occidental* v. *Ecuador* with respect to the language used by the parties in that case (2007, Decision on Provisional Measures, paras. 69–74), it is worth stressing that arbitration practice displays some inconsistency and lack of clarity in the use of these notions, in particular in relation to restitution and satisfaction. The reasons for this are manyfold, resulting in particular from the existence of such deficiencies in public international law practice more generally as well as the fact that these forms of reparation have developed in an inter-State context. The use of notions proper to investor–State arbitration, such as 'specific performance' that is related to 'restitution', reinforces this feature.

In practice, restitution and satisfaction are secondary in investor–State arbitration. This is due to the relief sought by the claimants and, more generally, to the characteristics of the investment operations and wrongful acts at hand in investor–State disputes. In contrast, compensation is almost systematically requested and, when required, awarded to fully repair the damage. Because of this prevalence and the complex legal and financial issues that this form of reparation raises, it is dealt with in more detail below. The key features of restitution and satisfaction in investor–State arbitration are discussed in turn here.

b Restitution

While restitution is rarely at stake in investor–State arbitration, the factual situations in which it has been discussed by arbitration tribunals are very diverse. They were concerned, for instance, with the restitution of a right to arbitration following the illegal extinguishment of an arbitration agreement (*ATA Construction, Industrial and Trading Company* v. *Jordan*) or the restitution of acquired rights over an oil concession following the termination of a concession agreement (*Occidental* v. *Ecuador*). From a legal point of view, restitution raises two main issues in investor–State arbitration. The first of these pertains in general to the power of arbitration tribunals to order restitutions. The second relates more specifically to the conditions set out in CIL pursuant to which restitution shall not be disproportionate.

It is beyond doubt that arbitration tribunals have the power to order restitutions. In this respect, it is worth stressing that Article 54 of the ICSID Convention is not to be construed as affecting this prerogative for tribunals operating under the ICSID Convention Arbitration Rules. As explained in Chapter 11, this Article limits the enforcement obligation of

ICSID Member States to pecuniary obligations. Yet, as recalled by the Tribunal in *Micula* v. *Romania* – in reference to Schreuer[6] – the preparatory works of the Convention make it clear that the limitation of the enforcement obligation to pecuniary obligations was not intended to exclude the possibility for those tribunals to award non-pecuniary remedies; instead, it was motivated by the uncertainties concerning the enforcement of some non-pecuniary remedies in domestic legal orders (2013, Award, para. 1310).

The issue of disproportionality arises in particular in those situations in which the wrongful act ends or changes a legal situation existing under a contract concluded between the host State and the investor or under domestic legislation. At the core of this issue is State sovereignty. As such, restitution has been considered as involving a burden out of all proportion to the benefit deriving from the grant of restitution instead of compensation, inasmuch as it is deemed to constitute an interference with States' normative prerogatives. For instance, in *LG&E* v. *Argentina*, the Tribunal explained:

> The judicial restitution required in this case would imply modification of the current legal situation by annulling or enacting legislative and administrative measures that make over the effect of the legislation in breach. The Tribunal cannot compel Argentina to do so without a sentiment of undue interference with its sovereignty. Consequently, the Tribunal arrives at the same conclusion: the need to order and quantify compensation. (2007, Award, para. 87)

The Tribunal appointed in *Occidental* v. *Ecuador* adopted a similar approach when discussing the opportunity to provide restitution in respect of contractually acquired rights. It argued:

> In order to decide whether specific performance is possible, the Tribunal must consider both the Claimants' and the Respondent's rights. To impose on a sovereign State reinstatement of a foreign investor in its concession, after a nationalization or termination of a concession license or contract by the State, would constitute a reparation disproportional to its interference with the sovereignty of the State when compared to monetary compensation. (2007, Decision on Provisional Measures, para. 84)

c Satisfaction

Satisfaction as such is rarely referred to or relied upon in investor–State arbitration. This is mainly due to the fact that this form of reparation is fundamentally tailor-made to repair very specific harms suffered by States.

When tribunals do refer to satisfaction, they tend to stress this inadequacy – for instance, the Tribunal appointed in *CMS Gas Transmission*

---

[6] C Schreuer, 'Non-Pecuniary Remedies in ICSID Arbitration' (2004) 20 *Arbitration International* 325, at 325–326.

Company v. *Argentina*, after having recalled the three forms of reparation existing under international law, set satisfaction aside from the outset as the case was not concerned with the reparation due to an injured State (2005, Award, para. 399). The Tribunal in *Quiborax S.A.* v. *Bolivia* adopted a similar approach; however, it conceded that '[t]he fact that some types of satisfaction are not available does not mean that [it] cannot make declaratory judgment as a means of satisfaction under Article 37 of the ILC Articles, if appropriate' (2015, Award, para. 560). In practice, some tribunals have deemed it appropriate to declare that their findings shall be considered as a remedy. In this respect, arbitration practice displays two key features.

First of all, such declaratory judgments are most often conceived of as a form of reparation for the damage which does not meet the threshold to be characterised as moral damage. For instance, the Tribunal appointed in *Joseph Charles Lemire* v. *Ukraine*, after having concluded that the injury did not amount to moral damage and as such could not justify the award of moral damages, stated that the acknowledgement of the IIA breach in particular was an element that may significantly repair the investor's loss of reputation (2011, Award, para. 339). In *Biwater Gauff (Tanzania) Ltd* v. *Tanzania*, the Tribunal adopted such a reasoning, but with the notable difference that it had previously concluded that there was no causal link between the damage to the investor and the breaches of the provisions of the IIA (2008, Award, para. 807).

From a different perspective, it should be mentioned that declaratory judgments have been made also for the benefit of respondent States. This was the case for instance in *Europe Cement Investment & Trade S.A.* v. *Turkey*, where the claimant had acted fraudulently. Again, after having considered that the circumstances of the case would not justify an award of moral damages, it argued that the potential reputational damage suffered by the respondent State was remedied by the award as such, this providing for the Tribunal 'a form of "satisfaction" for the respondent' (2009, Award, para. 181).

15.3.3.3 Compensation

Preliminary Remarks

As explained above, compensation is the main form of reparation used in investor–State arbitration. It raises four main issues: (1) the standard of compensation; (2) the nature of valuation and approaches thereto; (3) the impact of mitigating circumstances on the amount of compensation; and (4) the interest due in those situations in which the obligation to pay compensation is not complied with 'on time'. Each of these issues is analysed in turn. Prior to that, it is worth noting that in the case of multiple heads of loss that include unlawful expropriation, tribunals typically base the appraisal of compensation on the expropriation claim as it gives rise to the highest level of compensation (e.g. *UP and C.D Holding Internationale v. Hungary*, 2018, Award, para. 515).

a The Standard of Compensation

i Compensation for Unlawful Expropriations Two key issues arise in investor–State arbitration concerning the standard of compensation for unlawful expropriations: (1) the applicability of the standard of compensation for lawful expropriations to unlawful expropriations; and (2) temporal considerations pertaining to the date of valuation and the *data* to be taken into account.

– The Applicability of the Standard of Compensation for Lawful Expropriations to Unlawful Expropriations Lawful and unlawful expropriations are examined in Chapter 6; the latter amount to an internationally wrongful act. As such, the compensation that can be ordered to fully repair the damage they cause constitutes a secondary obligation under the law of State responsibility. As a matter of public international law, this is to be distinguished from the compensation due which forms part of the primary obligation setting the conditions of legality of expropriation.

This distinction is retained by some arbitration tribunals, such as by the Tribunal appointed in *Quiborax S.A. v. Bolivia*. That Tribunal stressed that the standard of compensation for lawful expropriations set out in the applicable IIA is not intended to create a *lex specialis* for unlawful expropriations that would depart from the customary law standard of full reparation articulated in the above-mentioned *Case Concerning the Factory at Chorzow* (2015, Award, para. 326).

On the other hand, other tribunals do not make this distinction. Among them, a few do so without providing any justification for this; this is illustrated by the award rendered in *Rusoro Mining Limited v. Venezuela*. The Tribunal, after having concluded that Bolivia committed a breach of the applicable IIA by unlawfully expropriating Rusoro, relied on the standard set out in the expropriation provision of that agreement with regard to lawful expropriations (2016, Award, para. 646). Other tribunals that adopt this approach provide justifications for doing so; for instance, in *Tenaris S.A. v. Venezuela*, the Tribunal stressed that the language of the IIA expropriation provision pertaining to compensation for lawful expropriations is very similar to that contained in the ARSIWA, which it considered to be the most accurate reflection of CIL (2016, Award, para. 515).

– Temporal Considerations Attached to the Standard of Compensation To start with, it is worth recalling the key excerpt of the Judgment rendered by the PCIJ in the *Case Concerning the Factory at Chorzow*, which articulates the standard of full reparation. The Court stated: '[R]eparation must, as far as possible, wipe out all the consequences of the illegal act and reestablish the situation which would, in all probability, have existed if that act had not been committed' (at 47). This requires tribunals to determine the compensation to be paid in a 'but for' scenario. Two main intertwined questions have arisen in arbitration practice in this respect: (1) what is the valuation date – is it the date of the expropriation or the date of the award? And (2) can *data* posterior to the date of the expropriation, i.e. *ex post data*, be taken into account?

Diverging views have been expressed by arbitration tribunals as evidenced in *Quiborax S.A.* v. *Bolivia*. These divergences were explained by Arbitrator Stern as follows:

> It could therefore be said that the Tribunal is unanimous in considering that 'full reparation' is due in case of an illegal expropriation. The main difference between my analysis and that of my two co-arbitrators is that I consider that this full reparation is the one foreseen in all probability at the time of the expropriation, while the majority considers that it is the full reparation as reconstructed in the world existing at the time of the award, which might be a completely different world than the one existing at the time of the expropriation, as will be explained in more details now. (2015, Award, Partially Dissenting Opinion, para. 24)

Beyond disagreements as to the interpretation of that judgment rendered by the PCIJ, there are two key issues at the core of these divergences: (1) the relation between restitution and compensation; and (2) causation.

Starting with the former, it is worth recalling that compensation comes into play when restitution is materially impossible or disproportionate, or when it is insufficient on its own to repair fully the damage suffered. Based on this relation between these two forms of reparation, the majority of the Tribunal in that case stated:

> The Tribunal thus concludes by majority that, dealing with an expropriation that is unlawful not merely because compensation is lacking, its task is to quantify the losses suffered by the claimant on the date of the award (or on a proxy for that date). This is easily explained by a reference to restitution: damages stand in lieu of restitution which would take place just following the award or judgment. (2015, Award, para. 377)

Also because of this connection, and because it considered that the 'obligation of restitution applies as of the date when a decision is rendered', the Tribunal appointed in *Yukos Universal Limited (Isle of Man)* v. *Russia* took the date of the award as the point of reference in assessing compensation (2014, Final Award, para. 1766). As a result, it concluded that unanticipated events that increase the value of the expropriated asset occurring between the date of the expropriation and the date of the award must be taken into consideration. In the case that unanticipated events decrease the value of the asset during that period, the Tribunal opined that such events should not be taken into account, not because of a disconnection in that case between the restitution date and the compensation date, but because it argued that the investor should not bear the risk of such events (paras. 1767–1768).

Irrespective of any consideration of fairness that this distinction may raise (a point stressed by Arbitrator Stern (*Quiborax S.A.* v. *Bolivia* 2015, Award, Partially Dissenting Opinion, paras. 55–60)), the taking into account of unanticipated events begs the question of causation. As explained above, there is a requirement under the law of State responsibility that a causal link must be established between the damage suffered and the internationally wrongful act. This causal link must not be too remote. International courts and tribunals have resorted in particular to the notion of foreseeability in appraising remoteness.

In that latter case, the majority of the Tribunal argued that – as a matter of principle – the loss of future profits determined by the fluctuations of the market is objectively foreseeable, concluding that it was 'satisfied that the test of foreseeability … [was] met in the circumstances before it'. It is worth stressing that this majority doubted that foreseeability is a part of causation (Award, para. 383). Arbitrator Stern disagreed with this finding as she considered that foreseeability is 'a test to determine the consequences that can be considered as resulting from an illegal act and thus attributable to the author of this illegal act', but that it is irrelevant as regards the role played by external causes as it 'is always "foreseeable" that other causes than the illegal act can happen and enhance or diminish the damage' (Partially Dissenting Opinion, paras. 93–95). As to the fluctuations of the economy and the market, she concluded therefore that they constitute simply external events, but not the foreseeable consequences of the unlawful expropriation (para. 99). More generally, she argued that all *ex post data* introduce an externality that might cause a diminution or an increase in the damage suffered, but which should not be taken into account as they are not caused by the illegal act (paras. 99–101).

ii Compensation for the Breach of Other IIA Provisions The standard of compensation set out by IIAs for lawful expropriations is not formally applicable to the breach of other IIA provisions, such as FET or FPS provisions. This is well accepted in arbitration practice (e.g. 2018 *Novenergia II* v. *Spain*, 2018, Final Arbitral Award, paras. 804–805). Instead, they rely, as did the Tribunal in *Antin* v. *Spain*, on the standard of compensation applicable under CIL, that is, the standard of full reparation (2018, Award, para. 664).

However, arbitration practice evidences a clear trend towards making reparation full by applying the standard of fair market value which, as discussed in Chapter 6, is typical of the standard of compensation for lawful expropriations (e.g. *Gold Reserve Inc.* v. *Venezuela*, 2014, Award, para. 681). Its application often results from the pragmatic approach adopted by tribunals that consider this standard as being adapted to the specifics of the cases. For instance, after having stated that the IIA applicable in the case offered no guidance as regards the compensation of the damage caused by the breach of the FET provision in particular, the Tribunal appointed in *CMS Gas Transmission Company* v. *Argentina* concluded that resort to the standard of fair market value was warranted because of the cumulative nature of the breaches (2005, Award, paras. 409–410). Along the same lines, arbitration tribunals typically deem it appropriate to use the fair market value when the breach of the IIA provision at stake, typically the FET provision, has an effect similar to that of an expropriation. For instance, in *Murphy Exploration '& Production Company – International* v. *Ecuador*, the Tribunal noted:

> Under customary international law, if an investor loses ownership or control of its primary investment due to the breach by a host state of its international law obligations, the commonly accepted standard for calculating damages is to appraise the fair market value of the lost investment at the time it was lost, without taking into account subsequent events. [footnote omitted] Although the Tribunal has found that Ecuador breached the FET provision of the Treaty, the result for Claimant was the loss of ownership of its investment. In this way, the outcome was akin to an unlawful expropriation, for which the fair market value of the asset represents the 'lower limit of the award'. [footnote omitted] (2016, Partial Final Award, para. 482)

b The Nature of Valuation and the Approaches Thereto

The existence of the damage must be established with certainty; on the other hand, no such certainty is required as to its valuation and thereby the determination of the amount of compensation. As noted by the Tribunal in *Gold Reserve Inc.* v. *Venezuela*, this is due in particular to the fact that this determination involves 'the weighing of competing (but equally legitimate) facts, valuation methods and opinions' (2014, Award, para. 686). With regard to the opinions expressed by the parties and their experts, arbitration tribunals at times stress that they lack legitimacy and that they add to the complexity inherent to quantification. For instance, the Tribunal noted in *Koch* v. *Venezuela*:

> The difficulties in this case arise from the quantification of the monetary damages required from the Respondent to compensate each of the two Claimants. As already indicated, international tribunals have traditionally resolved such difficulties applying a rule of reason, rather than a rule requiring certainty in calculating compensation based upon precisely calculated figures. Almost invariably, this approach now requires tribunals to reject the full extent of the parties' primary cases on quantum and the often wildly differing results of their respective expert witnesses' methodologies, assumptions and instructions. For tactical reasons, a claimant may not wish to discount downwards the full amount of its pleaded claim; and a respondent denying loss similarly may not wish to offer a methodology resulting in any significant damages being awarded in a claimant's favour. A tribunal must then work by itself in the rational no man's land left vacant by the parties and their expert witnesses, as best it can. In the present case, the Tribunal has faced grave difficulties in understanding how the Parties and their respective expert witnesses on quantum can have presented such very different figures. (2017, Award, para. 9.8)

To use the words of the Tribunal appointed in *Sistem Mühendislik Insaat Sanayi ve Ticaret A.S.* v. *Kyrgyzstan*, valuation does not amount to the 'search for the chimera of a sum that is a uniquely and indisputably correct determination of the value of what the Claimant lost', but instead it aims 'to arrive at a rational and fair estimate' (2009, Award, para. 155). In this respect, while they all acknowledge *mutatis mutandis* that valuation is rarely an exercise of arithmetical precision (*Union Fenosa Gas, S.A.* v. *Egypt*, 2018, Award, para. 10.101) and that they enjoy a margin of appreciation (e.g. *Gold Reserve Inc.* v. *Venezuela*, 2014, Award, para. 686), most tribunals strive to rationalise their findings on quantum.

This rationalisation consists mainly of the use of approaches and methods that are both well suited to the facts of the case and well accepted in international legal practice and in the financial community. Still with a view to objectivising their findings, tribunals do not hesitate to rely on several methods or in any case to subject a chosen method to 'a "sanity check" against other valuation methods' (*Rusoro Mining Limited* v. *Venezuela*, 2016, Award, para. 760).

There exists a plurality of valuation methods, all of which fall within three main approaches: (1) market approach, (2) income approach and (3) cost approach. For the sake of clarity and to help to make sense of arbitration practice, it is worth introducing these approaches by referring in full to the standards set out by the International Valuation Standards Council (IVSC) – a not-for-profit organisation recognised as a valuation standard setter – as they are set in the 2017 version of the International Valuation Standards.[7]

The market approach provides an indication of value by comparing the asset with identical or comparable assets for which price information is available (para. 20.1, at 30). According to the IVSC, this approach is relevant in three main situations: (1) where the asset at hand has recently been sold in a transaction appropriate for consideration under the basis value; (2) where the asset at hand or substantially similar assets are actively publicly traded; and (3) where there are frequent and/or recent observable transactions in substantially similar assets (para. 20.2, at 30).

The income approach offers an indication of value by converting future cash flow to a single current value (para. 40.1, at 36). For the IVSC, this approach proves to be adequate in two situations: (1) where the income-producing ability of the asset is the critical element affecting value from a participant's perspective; and (2) where reasonable projections of the amount and timing of future income are available for the asset at hand, but there are few, if any, relevant comparable markets (para. 40.2, at 36).

The cost approach offers an indication of value by calculating the current replacement or reproduction cost of an asset and making deductions for physical deterioration and all other relevant forms of obsolescence (para.

---

[7] IVSC, *International Valuation Standards* (2017), available at www.ivsc.org.

60.1, at 43). According to the IVSC, this approach is relevant in three main situations: (1) where the participants would be able to recreate an asset with substantially the same utility as the asset at hand, without regulatory or legal restrictions, and the asset could be recreated quickly enough that a participant would not be willing to pay a significant premium for the ability to use the subject asset immediately; (2) where the asset is not directly income-generating and the unique nature of the asset makes using an income approach or market approach unfeasible; and (3) where the basis of value being used is fundamentally based on replacement cost, such as replacement value (para. 60.2, at 43).

c Mitigating Circumstances

Two categories of mitigating circumstances are mainly relied on in arbitration practice: (1) the contribution of the investor to the realisation of the damage; and (2) its failure to mitigate the existing damage.

Each of these is now analysed in turn. It is worth recalling that some IIAs concluded in the 2010s that address this matter include mitigating circumstances that pertain to the protection of public interests. For instance, the 2018 Belarus–India IIA refers to the unremedied damage that the investor may have caused, notably to the environment or local communities, as well as to the need to balance public interest and the interests of the investor (Article 26.3).

i The Contribution to the Realisation of the Damage As evidenced below, findings that the investor contributed to the realisation of the damage are very much fact-specific; yet, such findings are to be based on legal criteria. Of course, there must first be a causal link between the investor's conduct and the damage. Second, not all investors' conduct that contributes to damage can lead to a reduction of the amount of compensation, as under public international law the conduct of the investor must display wilfulness or negligence. As noted by the ILC in its Commentaries to Article 39 of the ARSIWA, the relevance of any such wilful or negligent conduct depends in particular on the degree to which it has contributed to the damage.

Arbitration tribunals have concluded that investors contributed to the damage typically in situations where their conduct played a role in the host State's decision to adopt the conduct that was considered as being in breach of their IIA obligations. This is well illustrated by the award rendered in *Occidental* v. *Ecuador*. In that case, the Tribunal found that Ecuador had violated its obligation under the indirect expropriation provision by issuing the *Caducidad* decree. At the same time, it considered that the investors had acted negligently and in breach of their contractual obligation by failing to obtain a ministerial authorisation to transfer their right under the Participation contract to Alberta Energy Corporation. The Tribunal noted in particular that this conduct prevented Ecuador 'from exercising, in a formal way, its sovereign right to vet and approve AEC as the transferee of those rights'. It concluded: 'In the view of the Tribunal, the Claimants should pay a price for having committed an unlawful act which contributed in a material way to the prejudice which they subsequently suffered when the *Caducidad* Decree was issued' (2012, Award, paras. 679–680).

The appraisal of such complex factual situations can lead arbitrators to disagree on whether or not there has been a contribution. For instance, in *Bear Creek Mining Corporation* v. *Peru*, only Arbitrator Sands considered – as explained in his Partial Dissenting Opinion – that the investor contributed to the host State measure that was considered by all the members of the Tribunal as an indirect expropriation of its right to operate the Santa Ana concessions. He argued that the failure of the investor in particular to consult the local communities led to social unrest, which in turn forced the Peruvian authorities to take action in breach of its IIA obligations (2017, Award, Partial Dissenting Opinion, paras. 4–6).

Apart from those above-mentioned situations in which arbitration tribunals found that the investors' conduct had played a role in the host States' decision to adopt the conduct in breach of the applicable IIAs and thereby concluded that they had contributed to the realisation of the damage, it is worth noting that they also reached this conclusion as to situations in which the investors' behaviour was unrelated to the host States' unlawful conduct. For instance, in *MTD* v. *Chile*, the Tribunal considered that the investors had made decisions that had increased their risks by agreeing to pay a price for the land without appropriate legal protection. It stressed: 'A wise investor would not have paid full price up-front for land valued on the assumption of the realization of the Project; he would at least have staged future payments to project progress, including the issuance of the required development permits' (2004, Award, para. 242).

ii The Failure to Mitigate the Damage It is well recognised in investor–State arbitration that the failure on the side of the investor to mitigate the damage it suffers impacts on the amount of compensation to be paid (e.g. *Yukos Universal Limited (Isle of Man)* v. *Russia*, 2014, Final Award, para. 1603).

If it is true that this mitigating circumstance is often coined as a 'duty to mitigate losses', it should not be equated to a legal obligation yet, as noted by the ILC in its Commentaries on Article 31 of the ARSIWA. As reflected by the term 'duty', this mitigating circumstance is tinged with fairness. This is well reflected in *EDF International S.A.* v. *Argentina*, where the Tribunal explained that '[i]t would be patently unfair to allow Claimants to recover damages for loss that could have been avoided by taking reasonable steps' (2012, Award, para. 1301).

Whether or not an investor has failed to mitigate the damage is then a matter of fact and requires tribunals to take into account all the circumstances of the case. For instance, in *Middle East Cement Shipping and Handling Co. S. A.* v. *Egypt*, the Tribunal concluded that the fact that the investor had not resumed its activities after the revocation of the cement import prohibition decree in 1992 did not fall within the ambit of the duty to mitigate. It noted that '[a]n investor who has been subjected to a revocation of the essential license for its investment activity, three years earlier, has good reason to decide that, after that experience, it shall not continue with the investment activity, after the activity is again permitted' (2002, Award, para. 169).

d Interest

Preliminary Remarks

Most IIAs are silent about the interest payable in the case of a breach of the agreements. Some IIAs that have been recently concluded do provide for the possibility that interest be awarded, but they do not offer any further indication in this respect. For both categories of IIAs, it is necessary to look further for applicable rules.

The IIA rule on interest for lawful expropriations is not applicable; this is largely acknowledged in arbitration practice, be it for unlawful expropriations (e.g. *Vestey Group Limited* v. *Venezuela*, 2016, Award, para. 437) or the breach of the other IIA provisions, such as the FET (e.g. *Murphy Exploration & Production Company – International* v. *Ecuador*, 2016, Partial Final Award, para. 511). On the other hand, the Tribunal appointed in *Novenergia II* v. *Spain*, for instance, made an analogy between the interest due in relation to the breach of the FET provision and the interest rule provided by the 1994 Energy Charter Treaty (ECT) for lawful expropriations, i.e. market interest rate (2018, Final Arbitral Award, para. 844).

In fact, absent the provision of any relevant *lex specialis* in IIAs, one should turn to the *lex generalis*. This is why most arbitration tribunals apply the customary law standard of full reparation and look for guidance into Article 38 of the ARSIWA (and its Commentaries), which provide: 'Interest on any principal sum due under this chapter shall be payable when necessary in order to ensure full reparation. The interest rate and mode of calculation shall be set so as to achieve that result. Interest runs from the date when the principal sum should have been paid until the date the obligation to pay is fulfilled.' It is worth stressing that the purpose of awarding interest is to make reparation full. More precisely and as noted by the Tribunal in *Crystallex International Corporation* v. *Venezuela*, 'an award of interest is an integral component of the full reparation principle under international law, because, in addition to losing its property and other rights, an investor loses the opportunity to invest funds or to pay debts using the money to which that investor was rightfully entitled [footnote omitted]' (2016, Award, para. 932).

Apart from setting the objective of full reparation and addressing temporal considerations, one can only note that this Article and CIL more generally leave fundamental practical questions unanswered. It comes as no surprise, then, that tribunals usually stress that they enjoy a wide discretion to decide on interest matters (e.g. *Monsieur Joseph Houben* v. *Burundi*, 2016, Award, para. 256); this is all the more true for those tribunals that consider that arbitration practice is itself varied and inconsistent and that it fails to provide any clear guidance (e.g. *Murphy Exploration & Production Company – International* v. *Ecuador*, 2016, Partial Final Award, para. 514).

The calculation and award of interest raise three main issues: (1) the time period during which interest runs; (2) the applicable interest rate; and (3) the basis on which interest is calculated. Each is discussed in turn.

i *Dies a Quo* and *Dies ad Quem* The determination of the time period during which interest runs begs two questions: the determination of the *dies a quo*, i.e. the date from which it starts running, and that of the *dies ad quem*, i.e. the date the period ceases to run.

For the *dies a quo*, it is important to stress that the date on which the request for arbitration is filed or the date of the award are both irrelevant. Rather, the starting point from which interest begins to run is the occurrence of the internationally wrongful act that causes the damage.

Concerning the *dies ad quem*, interest runs until the compensation is actually paid. This is why tribunals accord pre-award interest, which runs from the *dies a quo* until the date of the award as well as – when needed – post-award interest, which runs from the date of the award until the date when the payment is made. As explained by the Tribunal appointed in *Autopista Concesionada de Venezuela, C.A. ('Aucoven')* v. *Venezuela*, 'post-award interest is intended to compensate the additional loss incurred from the date of the award to the date of final payment' (2003, Award, para. 380).

ii **Interest Rate** To set the interest rate, arbitration tribunals often rely on the LIBOR (London InterBank Offered Rate), which is an average interest rate – calculated on a daily basis – at which global banks borrow from one another. They often make this choice on casuistic grounds, as they argue that the specifics of each case make this rate the most reasonable and appropriate. They also sometimes find a systemic justification in the fact that it is widely used in arbitration practice (e.g. *Caratube International Oil Company LLP* v. *Kazakhstan*, 2017, Award, para. 1225).

It is also common practice among arbitration tribunals to increase this rate at which global banks borrow from one another, i.e. the prime rate; they do so typically by 1 per cent (e.g. *Crystallex International Corporation* v. *Venezuela*, 2016, Award, para. 938), 2 per cent (e.g. *Monsieur Joseph Houben* v. *Burundi*, 2016, Award, para. 258), or 4 per cent (e.g. *Murphy Exploration & Production Company – International* v. *Ecuador*, 2016, Partial Final Award, para. 517). As explained by the Tribunal in *Rusoro Mining Limited* v. *Venezuela*, this is due to the fact that loans to customers invariably include a surcharge as compared to the rate at which banks lend money to each other (2016, Award, para. 838).

iii **Simple Interest and Compound Interest** The determination of the amount of interest to be paid also depends on the basis on which it is calculated. There are two options available in this respect: simple interest or compound interest. 'Simple interest' is interest that is calculated on the principal sum due only. 'Compound interest' has a broader basis – it is calculated on this principal sum and the interest accumulated according to a certain periodicity.

Arbitration practice has evolved as to the choice made between these two options. While simple interest was originally most prevalent, compound interest has spread across arbitration practice in the past twenty years to the extent that it is equated to a *jurisprudence constante* (e.g. *Oko Pankki Oyj v. Estonia*, 2007, Award, para. 349). The award rendered in *Compania del Desarrollo de Santa Elena, S.A. v. Costa Rica* has been considered by the Tribunal in *Murphy Exploration & Production Company – International v. Ecuador* (2016, Partial Final Award, para. 519) – in reference to Ripinsky and Williams[8] – as a 'turning point in jurisprudence'. In that 'foundational' case, the Tribunal explained the merits of compound interest as follows:

> [T]he determination of interest is a product of the exercise of judgment, taking into account all of the circumstances of the case at hand and especially considerations of fairness which must form part of the law to be applied by this Tribunal. In particular, where an owner of property has at some earlier time lost the value of his asset but has not received the monetary equivalent that then became due to him, the amount of compensation should reflect, at least in part, the additional sum that his money would have earned, had it, and the income generated by it, been reinvested each year at generally prevailing rates of interest. It is not the purpose of compound interest to attribute blame to, or to punish, anybody for the delay in the payment made to the expropriated owner; it is a mechanism to ensure that the compensation awarded the Claimant is appropriate in the circumstances. (2000, Final Award, paras. 103–104)

In this respect, the Tribunal appointed in *Crystallex International Corporation v. Venezuela* seems to have explained this move from simple interest to compound interest in investor–State arbitration by reference to an evolution of financial activities, stating:

> With regard to the issue of whether such interest should be simple or compound, the Tribunal decides that such interest should be compound. The Tribunal acknowledges that traditionally there was an inclination on the part of international tribunals to award only simple interest. [footnote omitted] However, more recently, it has become increasingly recognized that simple interest may not adequately ensure full reparation for the loss suffered and the award of interest on a compound basis is therefore not excluded. This is because modern financial activity normally involves compound interest. Thus, a judgment creditor promptly placed in the possession of the funds due would be able to lend them out or invest them at compound interest rates or, if forced to borrow as a result of the respondent's wrongful act, will do so at compound rates. [footnote omitted] Indeed, while arbitral case law on this issue is not unanimous, the

---

[8] S Ripinsky, K Williams, *Damages in International Investment Law* (BIICL 2008), at 385.

Tribunal is able to discern a clear trend in recent decisions in favor of the award of compound interest. [footnote omitted] (2016, Award, para. 935)

In *Oxus Gold* v. *Uzbekistan*, the Tribunal found that the length and the complexity of arbitration proceedings constitute also appropriate justifications to award compound interest instead of simple interest (2015, Final Award, para. 989).

Whatever the justification provided, the choice of compound interest raises as such another issue – that is the periodicity according to which interest should be added to the principal sum to determine the basis of calculation of future interest. As noted by the Tribunal in *Murphy Exploration & Production Company* v. *Ecuador*, there is no general rule in this respect (2016, Partial Final Award, para. 521); it remains that tribunals have most often used semi-annual compounding periods (e.g. *Caratube International Oil Company LLP* v. *Kazakhstan*, 2017, Award, para. 1226) and yearly periods (e.g. *Crystallex International Corporation* v. *Venezuela*, 2016, Award, para. 937).

Finally, it is worth stressing that tribunals usually apply the same interest rate and the same terms to both pre-award interest and post-award interest. For the Tribunal appointed in *Vestey Group Limited* v. *Venezuela*, '[t]his is the consequence of the fact that the . . . obligation to pay damages does not arise on the date of the award but rather at the time when the internationally wrongful act caused harm' (2016, Award, para. 448). On the other hand, in *Yukos Universal Limited (Isle of Man)* v. *Russia*, the Tribunal made a distinction by awarding simple pre-award interest and compound post-award interest (2014, Final Award, para. 1689).

16

ICSID Convention Annulment Proceedings

Introduction

The Convention on the Settlement of Investment Disputes between States and Nationals of Other States (ICSID Convention) provides for a 'self-contained' annulment mechanism independent from domestic courts and laws. It is worth recalling that this mechanism is available to challenge the awards rendered by arbitration tribunals operating only under the ICSID Convention Arbitration Rules; it is not for those rendered by tribunals operating under the ICSID Additional Facility Arbitration Rules. Those awards and, more generally, 'non-ICSID Convention awards' can only be challenged before domestic courts, as discussed in Chapter 11.

The present chapter focuses on the annulment mechanism applicable to 'ICSID Convention awards' as is set out in Article 52 of the ICSID Convention and in ICSID Arbitration Rules 50, 52, 53 and 54. More specifically, it first sheds light on the main features of that mechanism before analysing in turn the main grounds for annulment relied upon before annulment committees as set out in the Convention – namely, manifest excess of powers, serious departure from a fundamental rule of procedure and failure to state the reasons on which the award is based. It then reviews the two additional grounds mentioned in Article 52, i.e. improper constitution of a tribunal and corruption on the part of a member of the tribunal. It should be stressed at the outset the key role played by annulment committees in giving substance to these grounds, the content of which are otherwise left largely unspecified by the ICSID Convention Arbitration Rules.

16.1 Salient Features of Annulment

16.1.1 Purpose of Annulment

The aim of annulment is to guarantee procedural justice – more specifically, to ensure the integrity, propriety and fairness of the settlement of disputes by the arbitration tribunals operating under the ICSID Convention Arbitration Rules. Annulment is not to be confused with appeal, which is a mechanism concerned with the substantive justice and correctness of adjudicative decisions.

A series of consequences flow from this specific purpose of annulment. Annulment committees cannot review the substantive correctness of awards, either in fact or in law. They are not entitled either to revisit the merits of the cases nor, as stressed by the Committee in *Total S.A.* v. *Argentina*, are they permitted to comment on what they would have decided had they acted in place of the arbitration tribunals in that matter (2016, Decision on Annulment, para. 165). This also entails that annulment committees cannot review arguments already decided by tribunals even if they are developed by the parties before them and they cannot examine new arguments. By the same token, it is not part of their mandate to re-evaluate the record as arbitration tribunals are the judge of the admissibility and of the probative value of evidence, as explained in Chapter 11. Neither can they consider any new evidence on the merits – however, as noted by the Annulment Committee in *Sempra Energy International* v. *Argentina*, new evidence, particularly expert evidence, may exceptionally be accepted in so far as it is specifically relevant for the purposes of the annulment (2010, Decision on Annulment, para. 74).

The guarantee of integrity that annulment brings to ICSID Convention arbitration proceedings and awards comes as a limit to another fundamental feature of ICSID Arbitration: the finality of awards. This helps to explain why annulment committees often stress that annulment is an extraordinary remedy to which a high threshold is to be applied (e.g. *Postova Banka, A.S.* v. *Greece*, 2016, Decision on Annulment, para. 127). Likewise, this also explains why an annulment can only be requested and decided on a limited number of grounds under Article 52 of the ICSID Convention. At the same time, committees often insist that those grounds shall not be interpreted restrictively, no more than extensively. For instance, the Committee appointed in *Klöckner Industrie-Anlagen GmbH* v. *Cameroon and Société Camerounaise des Engrais* explained: '[A]pplication of the paragraph [paragraph 1 of Article 52] demands neither a narrow interpretation, nor a broad interpretation, but an appropriate interpretation, taking into account the legitimate concern to surround the exercise of the remedy to the maximum extent possible with guarantees in order to achieve a harmonious balance between the various objectives of the Convention' (1985, Decision on Annulment, para. 3). In the same vein, tribunals sometimes emphasise that there shall be no presumption in favour of the validity of the awards (e.g. *Hussein Nuaman Soufraki* v. *United Arab Emirates*, 2007, Decision on Annulment, para. 22).

16.1.2 Scope of Annulment

Annulment can only be sought against an award, but not directly against a decision (if any) that may be rendered earlier, in particular a decision upholding the jurisdiction of the tribunal. Parties can, of course, subsequently argue that an award should be annulled on the basis of a deficiency of the decision on jurisdiction which forms part of the award. The situation is different when a tribunal declines jurisdiction – it renders an award in that sense that can then be challenged.

A party can request the annulment of all or part of an award. Where a party requests an award to be partially annulled, committees are bound by the scope of the request, meaning that they cannot annul any part of the award that has not been challenged. On the other hand, tribunals have the prerogative, depending on the merits of the request, to uphold the request in full or in part only, whether it be a request for partial annulment or for annulment of the entire award. In any case, it is worth making clear that a partial annulment of an award does not – as a matter of principle – affect the remainder of the award. That being said, it has been considered that, in some circumstances, the annulment of part of the award necessarily entails the annulment of other portion(s) (*Maritime International Nominees Establishment (MINE)* v. *Guinea*, 1989, Decision on Annulment, para. 4.08). Less radically, the Committee appointed in *Enron Creditors Recovery Corp.* v. *Argentina* could only but conclude that the annulment of the arbitration tribunal's decisions on liability and damages rendered the remaining portions of the award incapable of enforcement (2010, Decision on Annulment, para. 427).

16.1.3 Power of Annulment Committees

Annulment committees can conclude that one or more of the five grounds listed in Article 52 of the ICSID Convention have been successfully made out. When they do so, this gives them the power to annul the award partially or fully. That being said, based on the wording of that Article, which provides that they 'shall have the authority to annul the award' and not that they 'shall annul the award', committees consider that they enjoy some discretion to decide otherwise depending on the overall circumstances. In *CEAC Holdings Limited* v. *Montenegro*, the Committee listed as part of the relevant circumstances the gravity of the circumstances constituting the ground for annulment, their material effect upon the outcome of the case as well as the finality of the award and the fairness due to the parties (2018, Decision on Annulment, para. 84).

If they do decide to fully or partially annul the award, annulment committees are not empowered to amend or replace the part(s) annulled. Rather, this function is given to a new arbitration tribunal, at the request of either party, bearing in mind that this tribunal is not entitled to reconsider any part that has not been annulled (ICSID Arbitration Rule 55). That being said, it has been argued that committees can substitute the arbitration tribunal's figure of damages with the correct one if this task consists simply of an arithmetic exercise and does not require further submissions from the parties and any additional marshalling of evidence (*Occidental* v. *Ecuador*, 2015, Decision on Annulment, para. 299). The Committee considered in that case that this substitution – which in its view was not an amendment or a replacement – was required by 'basic reasons of procedural economy' to avoid the additional costs and delay that a second arbitration would involve.

If a stay of enforcement of the award is requested by the applicant in its application, enforcement is stayed provisionally. Once the committee has been constituted, a party that wants to have the stay continued must submit a request to that effect, otherwise the stay is automatically terminated. A stay can also be requested by either party after the constitution of the committee and at any time before it decides on the annulment's request. Annulment committees may stay the enforcement of the award pending their decision if they consider that the circumstances so require. They cannot stay the enforcement of the award on their own initiative.

16.1.4 Procedural Aspects

Annulment requests shall be made in writing to the ICSID Secretary-General within 120 days after the date on which the award is rendered. However, the ground of corruption is an exception to this rule, in which case the period of 120 days runs after the discovery of the fact of corruption, subject to a cut-off point of three years after the date on which the award was rendered, within which time the request must be made.

In contrast to the appointment of members of arbitration tribunals, the members of annulment committees are *ipso facto* appointed by the Chairman of the Administrative Council, from the Panel of Arbitrators. The methodology of this appointment derives from the specific purpose of annulment as explained above – i.e., annulment committees are entrusted with the task of protecting the integrity of dispute settlement at ICSID and are not empowered to re-settle disputes between the parties. All annulment committees are composed of three members.

In order to be appointed to a given committee, individuals listed on the Panel must meet a series of criteria pertaining in particular to nationality. They shall not have been nominated to the Panel by the State, or by the State whose investor is involved in the proceedings; by the same token, they must not be nationals of those two States. In addition, they shall not have the same nationality as that of the arbitrators who decided the dispute. Obviously, those individuals shall not have acted as arbitrator in the case at hand, nor shall they have acted as conciliator. As noted with respect to arbitrators in Chapter 11, these nationality-based requirements can be linked in one way or the other to the requirements of independence and impartiality. In that sense, committee members are also required, as are arbitrators, to sign the declaration provided in Arbitration Rule 6.2 – reproduced in Chapter 11 – pertaining to confidentiality and independence.

It is worth noting that substantive parts of the ICSID Convention applicable to the ICSID Convention arbitration proceedings and awards are *mutatis mutandis* applicable to annulment proceedings and decisions: Articles 41–45 of Section 3 ('Powers and Functions of the Tribunal'), Articles 48 and 49 of Section 4 ('The Award'), Articles 53 and 54 of Section 6 ('Recognition and Enforcement of the Award'), as well as Chapters VI ('Cost of Proceedings) and VII ('Place of Proceedings').

16.2 Manifest Excess of Powers

This ground for annulment raises two issues: (1) what is an excess of powers? And (2) when can such an excess be said to be manifest? These two issues often lead annulment committees to conduct a two-step analysis focusing first on the determination of an excess of powers, and second (if needed) on the determination of its manifest nature or not. According to another approach, a summary examination is first to be conducted with the view to appraise whether any of the alleged excesses of powers could be considered as being manifest (e.g. *Venezuela* v. *Tenaris S.A. & Talta*, 2018, Decision on Annulment, para. 72). Irrespective of the exact methodology used by committees, it is worth examining these two issues successively for didactic purposes.

16.2.1 What Is an *Excess of Powers*?

This ground for annulment is deeply rooted in disputing parties' consent. As explained in Chapter 11, consent grounds the tribunal's jurisdiction, like it does *mutatis mutandis* in any international adjudicative setting – however, as with *mutatis mutandis* any type of international arbitration, it is also the primary basis of the applicable law.

This explains why excess of powers pertains to both jurisdiction and applicable law. Although these matters are addressed separately by parties and committees, jurisdiction and applicable law may be viewed as being interconnected in certain circumstances. In that sense, the Committee in *Venezuela* v. *Tenaris S.A. & Talta* argued that an excess of powers as regards jurisdiction results from the non-application of the law applicable to jurisdictional matters, namely Article 25 of the ICSID Convention and any other agreement between the parties (2018, Decision on Annulment, para. 68).

Concerning jurisdiction, this ground for annulment relates to the requirements set out in Article 25 of the ICSID Convention as well as those provided in international investment agreements (IIAs) with regard to arbitrations based on IIA offers to arbitrate. As noted by the Committee in *Micula* v. *Romania*, an excess of powers can consist, *infra petita*, in a failure to exercise jurisdiction or, *ultra petita*, in an excess of jurisdiction (2016, Decision on Annulment, para. 126).

Regardless of the means of choosing and determining what law is applicable, as discussed in Chapter 12, where a tribunal fails to apply the law applicable and/or when it applies a law that is not applicable, an excess of powers results. Those situations in which the proper law is not applied are – as a matter of principle – distinguished from errors committed in the application or the interpretation of the law applicable. It is generally agreed that those errors do not qualify as an excess of powers (e.g. *Hussein Nuaman Soufraki* v. *United Arab Emirates*, 2007, Decision on Annulment, para. 85). Yet, as illustrated in that case, it is also considered that an erroneous application that is highly egregious may amount to a non-application of the proper law giving rise to an annulment; the Committee explained in this respect:

> Misinterpretation or misapplication of the proper law may, in particular cases, be so gross or egregious as substantially to amount to failure to apply the proper law. Such gross and consequential misinterpretation or misapplication of the proper law which no reasonable person (*'bon père de famille'*) could accept needs to be distinguished from simple error – even a serious error – in the interpretation of the law which in many national jurisdictions may be the subject of ordinary appeal as distinguished from, *e.g.*, an extraordinary writ of *certiorari*. (2007, Decision on Annulment, para. 86)

It is important to stress that the threshold for a finding of annulment based on misinterpretation or misapplication of the proper law can only be very high, as the contrary would otherwise turn annulment into an appeal.

While the review of errors committed in the application and interpretation of the proper applicable law can constitute a complex exercise for committees, there have been a number of other situations that annulment committees have easily found fell short of amounting to an excess of powers. For instance, with regard to situations in which the text of an IIA provides for several applicable laws without providing any hierarchy or any allocation, it has been considered that it is not for committees to review the correctness of the approach chosen by tribunals (e.g. *Total S.A.* v. *Argentina*, 2016, Decision on Annulment, paras. 196–197).

16.2.2 What Is a *Manifest* Excess of Powers?

The standard adopted in assessing the manifest nature of an excess of powers is similar for excesses relating to both jurisdiction and applicable law, something which is uncontroversial in the practice of annulment committees (e.g. *Duke Energy International Peru Investments No 1, Limited* v. *Peru*, 2011, Decision on Annulment, paras. 98–99). On the other hand, nuances and differences can be seen throughout the different cases as to how the standard is conceived of.

A first stream of jurisprudence focuses on whether the excess of powers can be readily discerned. Committees adopt a wide array of terms in order to express this standard – for example the excess must be 'plain on its face', 'evident', 'obvious', 'clear' or 'easily recognisable'. Within this stream, there seem to be nuances as to how to apply this standard in practice. In *CDC Group plc* v. *Seychelles*, the Committee considered that any excess apparent in a tribunal's conduct is not manifest if it is susceptible to argument "'one way or the other'" and added – in reference to Feldman[1] – that "'[i]f the issue is debatable or requires examination of the materials on which the tribunal's decision is based, the tribunal's determination is conclusive'" (2005, Decision on Annulment, para. 41). On the other hand, in *EDF International S.A.* v. *Argentina*, the Committee explained that some examination of the materials on which a tribunal's decision is made may be necessary and it argued that the need for inquiries and analyses as to complex reasoning does not prevent an excess of powers from being manifest; at the same time, it agreed – making reference to *Duke Energy International Peru Investments No 1, Limited* v. *Peru* (2011, Decision on Annulment, para. 99) – that a debatable solution is not amenable to annulment since the excess of powers is then not manifest (2016, Decision on Annulment, para. 193).

A second stream of jurisprudence appraises the manifest nature of the excess of powers by focusing on its effect and inquiring into whether or not it has serious consequences. For instance, in *Compania de Aguas del Aconquija S.A.* v. *Argentina*, the Committee suggested that this 'is only where the failure to exercise a jurisdiction is clearly capable of making a difference to the result that it can be considered a manifest excess of power' (2002, Decision on Annulment, para. 86).

A third stream of jurisprudence combines these two approaches. Again, this stream displays some nuances. In *Malicorp Limited* v. *Egypt*, the Committee opined simply that what has serious and substantial implications is also clear and obvious (2013, Decision on Annulment, para. 56). The Committee in *Hussein Nuaman Soufraki* v. *United Arab Emirates* went further by suggesting that the two requirements must be cumulatively met in order to consider an excess of powers as being manifest; it noted: '[A] strict opposition between two different meanings of "manifest" – either "obvious" or "serious" – is an unnecessary debate. It seems to this Committee that a manifest excess of power implies that the excess of power should at once be textually obvious and substantively serious' (2007, Decision on Annulment, para. 40).

16.3 Serious Departure from a Fundamental Rule of Procedure

Preliminary Remarks

Not every procedural deficiency can provide a ground for annulment under the ICSID Convention. There must first be a fundamental rule of procedure at stake and, second, the departure from such rule must be serious. It is worth noting that the English and French versions of Article 52.1.d of the Convention mention the first of these two requirements, while the Spanish version does

---

[1]   MB Feldman, 'The Annulment Proceedings and the Finality of ICSID Arbitral Awards' (1987) 2 *ICSID Review* 85, at 101.

not. In reference to Article 33 of the 1969 Vienna Convention on the Law of Treaties (VCLT) pertaining to the interpretation of treaties authenticated in two or more languages – examined in Chapter 12 – committees have consistently concluded that the English and French versions shall prevail as they best reconcile the texts, having regard to the object and purpose of the Convention (e.g. *EDF International S.A.* v. *Argentina*, 2016, Annulment Decision, para. 199). These two conditions must be met cumulatively; this means that a serious departure from a rule that is not fundamental does not give rise to annulment, while a 'basic' departure from a fundamental rule of procedure does not have this effect either.

Both requirements as they are set out in the ICSID Convention beg the question of their exact meaning and content: which rules of procedure can be said to be fundamental, and which departures can be deemed to be serious?

16.3.1 What Is a *Fundamental* Rule of Procedure?

The threshold for finding that a rule of procedure is fundamental is very high. Only those rules that form part of the 'minimum standard of procedural treatment' that parties shall receive are constitutive of fundamental rules of procedure. As noted by the Committee in *CDC Group plc* v. *Seychelles*, not all the ICSID Convention Arbitration Rules are fundamental in this respect (2005, Decision on Annulment, para. 49).

More precisely, committees have identified in particular the following as fundamental rules of procedure: the equal treatment of the parties, the right to be heard, the independence and impartiality of the tribunal, the treatment of evidence and burden of proof as well as the deliberations among members of the tribunal (*Joseph C Lemire* v. *Ukraine*, 2013, Decision on Annulment, para. 263).

16.3.2 What Is a *Serious* Departure from a Fundamental Rule of Procedure?

Contrary to the appraisal of the first condition that can be made in the abstract, the ascertainment of the seriousness of the departure requires an examination into the specifics of each award. When undertaking this task, committees build on the following test set out by the Annulment Committee in *Maritime International Nominees Establishment (MINE)* v. *Guinea*: 'In order to constitute a ground for annulment the departure from a "fundamental rule of procedure" must be serious. The Committee considers that this establishes both quantitative and qualitative criteria: the departure must be substantial and be such as to deprive a party of the benefit or protection which the rule was intended to provide' (1989, Decision on Annulment, para. 5.05).

This test has often been interpreted as requiring that the departure from the fundamental rule of procedure caused tribunals to reach a result substantially different from that which they would have reached had such a rule been observed (e.g. *Wena Hotels Ltd* v. *Egypt*, 2002, Decision on Annulment, para. 58).

Annulment committees diverge as to whether the fulfilment of the test depends on the demonstration of a potential material effect on the award, or of an actual one. The latter conception was adopted by the Committee appointed in *Venezuela v. OI European Group B.V.*; it argued that annulling an award based on a lesser showing would amount in particular to speculation and the second-guessing of decisions taken in the original arbitration in a manner that is improper for annulment proceedings (2018, Decision on Annulment, para. 248). Ironically enough, the rejection of speculation also grounds the adoption of the former approach by a number of committees. In particular, the Committee appointed in *TECO Guatemala Holdings LLC v. Guatemala* argued:

> Requiring an applicant to show that it would have won the case or that the result of the case would have been different if the rule of procedure had been respected is a highly speculative exercise. An annulment committee cannot determine with any degree of certainty whether any of these results would have occurred without placing itself in the shoes of a tribunal, something which is not within its powers to do. What a committee can determine however is whether the tribunal's compliance with a rule of procedure could potentially have affected the award. (2016, Decision on Annulment, para. 85)

16.4 Failure to State the Reasons on Which the Award Is Based

Preliminary Remarks

There is a close connection between this ground for annulment and Article 48.3 of the ICSID Convention, which provides that awards shall deal with every question submitted to the tribunals and that awards shall state the reasons upon which they are based. In this respect, it is noteworthy that the possibility of allowing the parties to waive the requirement to state reasons was contemplated during the preparatory works, but was ultimately not retained. This is telling as regards the importance of stating reasons in investor–State arbitration and the difference that exists in this respect from commercial arbitration, as illustrated by the fact that such waivers are possible under the United Nations Commission on International Trade Law (UNCITRAL) and Stockholm Chamber of Commerce (SCC) Rules of Arbitration. This importance was explained by the Committee appointed in *Venezuela v. Tidewater* as follows:

> The Committee recalls that the statement of reasons is one of the central duties of arbitral tribunals. An award is not a discretionary *fiat* but the result of the process of weighing evidence and applying and interpreting the law and subsuming the facts thus established under the law as interpreted by the Tribunal. The legitimacy of the process depends on its intelligibility and transparency. The statement of reasons allows the Parties to understand the process through which the tribunal makes its findings. Therefore, it is '*the Tribunal's duty to identify,*

and to let the parties know, the factual and legal premises leading the Tribunal to its decision' [footnote omitted]. (2016, Decision on Annulment, para. 163)

In order to make sense of this ground for annulment, it is necessary to focus first on the overall applicable test, and then on the main specific situations that have been discussed by committees, which are (1) contradictory reasons; (2) frivolous, inadequate and insufficient reasons; and (3) implicit reasons.

16.4.1 Applicable Test

This ground for annulment is not concerned with the substantive quality or persuasiveness of the reasoning of the award. As noted by the Committee in *Postova Banka, a.s. v. Greece*, it does not pertain to the validity of reasons, but to their existence (2016, Decision on Annulment, para. 136).

The test relied on by committees in appraising the existence of such reasons was first formulated by the Committee appointed in *Maritime International Nominees Establishment* v. *Guinea*. It provided that 'the requirement to state reasons is satisfied as long as the award enables one to follow how the tribunal proceeded from Point A to Point B and eventually to its conclusion, even if it made an error of fact or of law' (1989, Decision on Annulment, para. 5.09). A number of tribunals refine this test as they consider that the absence of reasons, in order to amount to a failure to state reasons under Article 52.1 of the ICSID Convention, must not relate to just any point, but to a point which is 'outcome-determinative' (e.g. *Postova Banka, a.s. v. Greece*, 2016, Decision on Annulment, para. 143).

The appraisal of whether or not this test is satisfied is not conducted in the abstract; it is attached to the readership of awards and the audience that is assigned to arbitration tribunals.

Disputing parties constitute the primary audience of such tribunals. In this respect, the Committee appointed in *Tulip Real Estate and Development Netherlands B.V.* v. *Turkey* considered that it is not necessary for tribunals to restate all the arguments and evidence in the awards as those parties are – obviously – familiar with the main issues, with the evidence and with the main legal arguments presented (2015, Decision on Annulment, para. 98).

Some committees have adopted a broad approach, focusing not only on the disputing parties, but also *mutatis mutandis* on the understanding of 'an informed reader' (*Impregilo S.p.A.* v. *Argentina*, 2014, Decision on Annulment, para. 181). This is in line with the views explained by the Committee appointed in *Venezuela* v. *Tidewater*:

> The documentation of the process that leads an arbitral tribunal to its award is of particular importance in investor–state arbitration. In agreeing to arbitration, States surrender part of their sovereign prerogatives and allow arbitral tribunals to scrutinize the legality of acts of *puissance publique*. It is a matter of public policy that the parties to the dispute but also other States' organs and the public

be enabled to understand, if a tribunal rules against the State, why the tribunal believes that a sovereign act violated the law and what would be – in the eyes of the tribunal – a lawful sovereign act under the circumstances. A similar reasoning applies, *mutatis mutandis*, to rulings against an investor. (2016, Decision on Annulment, para. 164)

Under such approaches, it is worth noting that the above-mentioned views expressed by the Committee in *Tulip Real Estate and Development Netherlands B.V.* v. *Turkey* may need to be adjusted. 'Informed readers' and *a fortiori* 'the public' do not have the same command of the cases as disputing parties have and certainly need extra information to be able to make sense of the reasoning of the tribunals.

16.4.2 Specific Grounds

16.4.2.1 Contradictory Reasons

Contradictory reasons is the main basis on which a failure to state reasons is upheld by annulment committees. However, the threshold for such a finding is very high. All committees agree *mutatis mutandis* that the reasons must be genuinely contradictory in that they cancel each other out so as to amount to a total absence of reasons (e.g. *Standard Chartered Bank (Hong Kong) Limited* v. *Tanzania Electric Supply Company Limited (Tanesco)*, 2018, Decision on Annulment, para. 610).

In addition to setting a high threshold, it is worth noting that committees pay great attention to ensure that they do not conclude too easily that there has been a genuine contradiction. This is due in particular to their awareness that the tribunal's reasoning most of the time reflects a compromise between conflicting considerations, which in their view should not be seen as amounting to a contradiction. In that sense, the Committee appointed in *Compania de Aguas del Aconquija S.A.* v. *Argentina* explained:

> It is frequently said that contradictory reasons cancel each other out, and indeed, if reasons are genuinely contradictory so they might. However, tribunals must often struggle to balance conflicting considerations, and an *ad hoc* committee should be careful not to discern contradiction when what is actually expressed in a tribunal's reasons could more truly be said to be but a reflection of such conflicting considerations. (2002, Decision on Annulment, para. 65)

More generally, annulment committees consider *mutatis mutandis* that they should go beyond apparent contradiction and try to follow the reasoning of the tribunals (*Lahoud* v. *Democratic Republic of* Congo, 2016, Decision on Annulment, para. 135) and that 'if possible, an annulment committee should prefer an interpretation which confirms an award's consistency as opposed to its inner contradictions' (*TECO Guatemala Holdings LLC* v. *Guatemala*, 2016, Decision on Annulment, para. 102).

16.4.2.2 Frivolous, Inadequate and Insufficient Reasons

In contrast to contradictory reasons, the practice of annulment committees displays nuances and differences as regards the possibility that frivolous, inadequate and insufficient reasons constitute a failure to state reasons. This is well illustrated by a comparison of the views adopted by the Committees appointed in *Adem Dogan* v. *Turkmenistan* and *TECO Guatemala Holdings LLC* v. *Guatemala*.

In the former case, the Committee radically rejected that inadequate and insufficient reasons could ground annulment under Article 52.1.e of the ICSID Convention; it stressed that annulment under this provision derives from the 'failure to state reasons' and not from the inadequacy or insufficiency of the reasons provided (para. 263).

On the other hand, the Committee adopted a more nuanced approach in *TECO*. It considered that the insufficiency and inadequacy of reasons can lead to annulment in specific circumstances, namely where a tribunal did provide some reasons in support of its decision, but these reasons are respectively insufficient from a logical point of view to justify the decision and incapable of providing a logical explanation of that decision (paras. 249–250).

In any case, grounding annulment in the inadequacy or insufficiency of reasons requires some caution. As regards inadequacy, this results from the fact that the lack of persuasiveness as such of the tribunal's reasoning is irrelevant for annulment purposes. Concerning insufficiency, this is mainly due to the fact that arbitration tribunals are only under the obligation to deal with every *question* submitted by the disputing parties, and not to address every argument or piece of evidence put forward by the disputing parties. This was well explained by the Committee appointed in *Enron Creditors Recovery Corp.* v. *Argentina*:

> [A] tribunal has a duty to deal with each of the *questions* ('*pretensiones*') submitted to it, but is not required to comment on all arguments of the parties in relation to each of those questions. Similarly, the Committee considers that the tribunal is required only to give reasons for its decision in respect of each of the *questions*. This requires the tribunal to state its pertinent findings of fact, its pertinent findings as to the applicable legal principles, and its conclusions in respect of the application of the law to the facts. If the tribunal has done this, the award will not be annulled on the basis that the tribunal could have given more detailed reasons and analysis for its findings of fact or law, or that the tribunal did not expressly state its evaluation in respect to each individual item of evidence or each individual legal authority or legal provision relied upon by the parties, or did not expressly state a view on every single legal and factual issue raised by the parties in the course of the proceedings. The tribunal is required to state reasons for its *decision*, but not necessarily reasons for its *reasons*. (2010, Decision on Annulment, para. 222)

16.4.2.3 Implicit Reasons

Arbitration tribunals enjoy some discretion as to how they state their reasoning. As a result, annulment committees accept that reasons may be implicit in the considerations and conclusions contained in the awards, provided that such reasons could reasonably be inferred by the readers (e.g. *Postova Banka, a.s.* v. *Greece*, 2016, Decision on Annulment, para. 142). In *Kazakhstan* v. *Rumeli*, the Committee explained this as follows:

> [I]f reasons are not stated but are evident and a logical consequence of what is stated in an award, an ad hoc committee should be able to so hold. Conversely, if such reasons do not necessarily follow or flow from the award's reasoning, an *ad hoc* committee should not construct reasons in order to justify the decision of the tribunal. (2010, Decision on Annulment, para. 83)

16.5 Improper Constitution of the Tribunal and Corruption on the Part of a Member of the Tribunal

'Corruption on the part of a member of the tribunal' has never been advanced in practice as a ground for annulment before any committee. As a matter of law, it can be linked to the declaration that arbitrators are required to fill out under ICSID Arbitration Rule 6.2, and, more precisely, to their commitment not to 'accept any instruction or compensation with regard to the proceeding from any source'.

Article 52 of the ICSID Convention does not specify what an 'improper constitution' is. It has been interpreted as referring to those parts of the ICSID Convention and of the ICSID Arbitration Rules dealing with the constitution of tribunals (*Azurix Corp* v. *Argentina*, 2009, Decision on Annulment, para. 276). 'Improper constitution of the tribunal' has been advanced in a few annulment proceedings, each time unsuccessfully. These proceedings have notably raised the issue of the interplay between this ground and disqualification, in relation to the alleged failure of arbitrators to meet in particular the moral integrity requirement, discussed in Chapter 11 (e.g. *Venezuela* v. *OI European Group B.V.*, 2018, Decision on Annulment, paras. 94–109). As explained in Chapter 11, disqualification is a mechanism that enables either disputing party to promptly challenge an arbitrator in the course of the arbitration proceedings on account of any fact indicating that she manifestly fails to meet in particular the moral integrity requirement.

Index

Introductory Note

References such as '178–179' indicate (not necessarily continuous) discussion of a topic across a range of pages. Wherever possible in the case of topics with many references, these have either been divided into sub-topics or only the most significant discussions of the topic are listed. Because the entire work is about 'international investment law' and 'arbitration', the use of these terms (and certain others which occur constantly throughout the book) as entry points has been minimised. Information will be found under the corresponding detailed topics.

www.ingramcontent.com/pod-product-compliance
Ingram Content Group UK Ltd.
Pitfield, Milton Keynes, MK11 3LW, UK
UKHW030807060825
461487UK00019B/1693